Retrieving Catholicity
in American Protestantism

The Mercersburg Theology Study Series
Volume 12

The Mercersburg Theology Study Series presents attractive, readable, scholarly modern editions of the key writings of the nineteenth-century theological movement led by Philip Schaff and John Nevin. It aims to introduce the academic community and the broader public more fully to Mercersburg's unique blend of American and European, and Reformed and Catholic theology.

Founding Editor
W. Bradford Littlejohn

Series Editors
Lee C. Barrett
David W. Layman

Published Volumes

1. *The Mystical Presence and the Doctrine of the Reformed Church on the Lord's Supper*
Edited by Linden J. DeBie

2. *Coena Mystica: Debating Reformed Eucharistic Theology*
Edited by Linden J. DeBie

3. *The Development of the Church*
Edited by David R. Bains and Theodore Louis Trost

4. *The Incarnate Word: Selected Writings on Christology*
Edited by William B. Evans

5. *One, Holy, Catholic, and Apostolic: John Nevin's Writings on Ecclesiology (1844–1849): Tome One*
Edited by Sam Hamstra Jr.

6. *Born of Water and the Spirit: Essays on the Sacraments and Christian Formation*
Edited by David W. Layman

7. *One, Holy, Catholic, and Apostolic: John Nevin's Writings on Ecclesiology (1851–1858): Tome Two*
Edited by Sam Hamstra Jr.

8. *The Early Creeds: The Mercersburg Theologians Appropriate the Creedal Heritage*
Edited by Charles Yrigoyen and Lee C. Barrett

9. *Christocentric Reformed Theology in Nineteenth-Century America: Key Writings of Emanuel Gerhart*
Edited by Annette G. Aubert

10. *The Heidelberg Catechism: The Mercersburg Understanding of the German Reformed Tradition*
Edited by Lee C. Barrett

11. *Philosophy and the Contemporary World: Mercersburg, Culture, and the Church*
Edited by Adam S. Borneman and Patrick Carey

Retrieving Catholicity in American Protestantism

Essays in Church History

By
JOHN WILLIAMSON NEVIN

Edited by
Michael J. Stell

General Editor
David W. Layman

Foreword by
Michael Root

WIPF & STOCK · Eugene, Oregon

RETRIEVING CATHOLICITY IN AMERICAN PROTESTANTISM
Essays in Church History

Copyright © 2024 Wipf and Stock Publishers. All rights reserved. Except for brief quotations in critical publications or reviews, no part of this book may be reproduced in any manner without prior written permission from the publisher. Write: Permissions, Wipf and Stock Publishers, 199 W. 8th Ave., Suite 3, Eugene, OR 97401.

Wipf & Stock
An Imprint of Wipf and Stock Publishers
199 W. 8th Ave., Suite 3
Eugene, OR 97401

www.wipfandstock.com

PAPERBACK ISBN: 978-1-5326-9928-3
HARDCOVER ISBN: 978-1-5326-9929-0
EBOOK ISBN: 978-1-5326-9930-6

04/23/24

Contents

Foreword by Michael Root | vii

Editorial Approach and Acknowledgments | ix

Contributors | xiii

Abbreviations | xv

General Introduction | 1
    Michael J. Stell

Document 1: "Historical Development" | 31
    Historical Development. | 33

Document 2: "Early Christianity" | 36
    Early Christianity[: First Article]. | 42
    Early Christianity: Second Article. | 72
    Early Christianity: Third Article. | 117

Document 3: "Cyprian" | 166
    Cyprian[: First Article]. | 169
    Cyprian: Second Article. | 187
    Cyprian: Third Article. | 236
    Cyprian: Fourth and Last Article. | 269

Epilogue: Nevin's "Dizziness" and His Relationship to Philip Schaff | 315
    David W. Layman, General Editor

Bibliography | 327

Index | 341

Foreword

The North Atlantic world of the nineteenth century was haunted by history. The Enlightenment in many ways had wanted to leave the past behind as a land of superstition and ignorance. There was a past to be appealed to—an idealized Roman republic, certain classical philosophers—but it tended to be the past as an embodiment of timeless ideals. The variegated Romanticism of the inbreaking nineteenth century, in revolt against its fathers, found fascination in just the past the Enlightenment excoriated—Gothic ruins, Celtic and Germanic folk tales. In the following decades, attempts to recapture the past developed: neo-Gothic architecture, pre-Raphaelite painting, etc. At the same time, the pursuit of a "scientific" history which would depict "what really happened" (*was eigentlich geschehen ist*) grew in the universities.

But just what is history? Is it just "one damned thing after another"?[1] Or does it have its own logic, its own structure, its own laws? History is often organized by narratives, which tend to have more than a logic; they have a plot, a problem or question seeking resolution. How will the wrath of Achilles work itself out? What will become of Ahab's obsession with the white whale? Does history have a plot of that sort? Is it seeking some sort of resolution or answer? Theology had traditionally taken up that question, but Hegel and thinkers in his wake, most notably Karl Marx, sought philosophical answers, answers that emerged from history itself.

Theology was not immune to the historical turn. Christian thought cannot avoid history. The gospel proclaims that the eternal God who is beyond time entered history in his Son to redeem history from itself. Salvation is based on an event in history, not on an escape from history. The nineteenth-century turn to history as an overarching interpretive category was thus a challenge to theology. Easy solutions were available. One could elevate some past moment of history as a stable norm—for example, the consensus of the first centuries for the Oxford Movement, or Thomas Aquinas for some within the Catholic scholastic revival—and remove the vicissitudes of change from the equation. Or one could see history as an uncomplicated story of progress toward the

---

1. Toynbee, *A Study of History*, abridgement of volumes VII–X, 267. (Toynbee was describing the ostensible opinion of another historian.) A full exploration of the origins of the phrase can be found at Quoteresearch, "History is Just One Damn Thing after Another."

Kingdom of God on Earth, as did some proponents of the Social Gospel at the end of the nineteenth century. In either case, history becomes uncomplicated. For some of the greatest theologians of the age, however, such solutions were inadequate. History and change seemed too ingredient in the essence of Christian faith and life, even if Christ remains "the same, yesterday, today, and forever" (Heb 13:8). And so, the concept of "development" beckoned, with its combination of change yet identity over time.

America was not free from these trends, despite its occasional dreams of escape from European history and a related antagonism to the importance of history. It was an American, Henry Ford, who said that "history is more or less bunk." But as recent debates over how to teach American history in our schools show, even in America, history is never just bunk. John Williamson Nevin is a superb example of this truth. He was himself an exemplar of changes taking place in American Protestant theology in his time. The surge of German immigration into America in the mid-nineteenth century formed a significant part of the background of the Mercersburg movement, as the importance of Nevin's German colleague, Philip Schaff, indicates.

Nevin and the Mercersburg movement were also part of an understudied aspect of American theology in this period: the attempt to develop an historically informed, tradition-minded, catholic but not Roman, form of Protestantism. Similar attempts can be traced in American Lutheranism of the period, as in the work of Charles Porterfield Krauth of the Lutheran seminary in Philadelphia and, to a degree, among some high-church Episcopalians. The pursuit of such an "evangelical catholicism" has since then been a consistent, even if minority, strand in American theology.

Nevin, however, is more than an exemplar of historical trends. As the texts here collected show, he struggled throughout his life to understand history, especially the history of Christian life and thought. The subtle shifts from one writing to the next show the seriousness of his quest. History is change, but never simple rupture. The present develops out of the past and the past is never in its entirely left behind. As historical work since Nevin has shown, the Reformation was more medieval than it appears in much Protestant self-understanding.

One need not find Nevin's solutions altogether convincing to learn from his work. They have much to teach us about theology in nineteenth century America, about the possibilities and limits of the Reformed tradition, and about the speculative problem of continuity and change in the Church's understanding of its message, a problem that is still very much with us. Michael Stell and David Layman are owed our thanks for gathering these texts together and presenting them in such a helpful fashion.

    Michael Root, PhD
    Professor Emeritus
    School of Theology and Religious Studies
    The Catholic University of America

Editorial Approach and Acknowledgments

The purpose of this series is to reprint the key writings of the Mercersburg theologians in a way that is both fully faithful to the original and yet easily accessible to non-specialist modern readers. These twin goals, often in conflict, have determined our editorial approach throughout. We have sought to do justice to both by being very hesitant to make any alterations to the original but being very free with additions to the original in the form of annotations.

We have decided to leave spelling, capitalization, and emphasis exactly as in the original, except in cases of clear typographical errors, which have usually been silently corrected. We have, however, taken a few liberties in altering punctuation—primarily comma usage, which is occasionally quite idiosyncratic and awkward in the original texts, but also other punctuation conventions which are nonstandard and potentially confusing today. In several articles the volume editor has added quotation marks to the original author's quotes as required by modern conventions. We have also adopted standard modern conventions such as the italicization of book titles and foreign-language words. One major change has been made from previous editorial practice in earlier volumes: the publisher has asked the editors to no longer replicate "small caps," except in the case of "Lord" (when quoting the Hebrew Scriptures) and similar words. So we have replaced that convention with italics; when its use in the original seems significant, it has been noted in a footnote. Another of Nevin's idiosyncrasies needs to be noted: portmanteau words (e.g., "everyday," "everyone"), or terms that we hyphenate (e.g., "so-called," "well-informed"), were regularly spelled as separate words: e.g., "every day," "every one," "so called." These have not been changed. The entirety of the text has been re-typeset and re-formatted to render it as clear and accessible as possible; pagination, of course, has accordingly been changed. Original section headings have been retained; in articles which lacked any section headings in the original, we have added headings of our own in brackets.

Original footnotes are retained, though for ease of typesetting, they have been subsumed within the series of numbered footnotes which includes the annotations we have added to this edition. Our own annotations and additions, which comprise the majority of the footnotes, are wholly enclosed in brackets, whether that be within a footnote that was original, or around an entire footnote when it is one that we have added.

Source citations in the original have been retained in their original form, but where necessary, we have provided expanded citation information in brackets or numerated footnotes and have sought to direct the reader toward modern editions of these works, where they exist. Where citations are lacking in the original, we have tried as much as possible to provide them in our footnotes.

In the annotations we have added (generally in the footnotes, though very occasionally in the form of brackets in the body text), we have attempted to be comprehensive without becoming cumbersome. In addition to offering citations for works referenced in the original, these additions fall under four further headings:

1. Translation
2. Unfamiliar terms and historical figures
3. Additional source material
4. Commentary

We have attempted to be comprehensive in providing translations of any untranslated foreign-language quotations in these works and have wherever possible made use of existing translations in standard modern editions, to which the reader is referred.

Additional annotations serve to elucidate any unfamiliar words, concepts, or (especially) historical figures to which the authors refer, and where applicable, to provide references to sources where the reader may pursue further information (for these additional sources, only abbreviated citations are provided in the footnotes; for full bibliographical information, see the bibliography).

With eleven volumes of the **Mercersburg Theology Study Series** published, most of the significant Mercersburg texts are now in "**MTSS**" editions. Where available, references will be made exclusively to those editions in the form "(MTSS [volume number])." Scholars who need original bibliographical data on a text can consult the relevant volume. It is the firm belief of the editors that the MTSS series should in the future be considered the standard scholarly edition of Mercersburg Theology. The Abbreviations page immediately below indicates this and other abbreviations used for the most important sources continually cited throughout the notes. Especially significant for this volume are modern translations of the patristic texts Nevin quotes. Where possible, we have cited translations from the twentieth century; sometimes we have defaulted to the *Ante-Nicene Fathers*.

We have sought to shed light on the issues under discussion. Although most commentary on the texts has been reserved for the General Introduction, further brief commentary on specific points of importance is sometimes provided in footnotes to facilitate understanding of the significance of the arguments.

We hope that our practice throughout will help bring these remarkable texts to life again for a new century, while also allowing the authors to be heard in their own authentic voices.

Acknowledgments

Volume Editor

As volume editor, I would like to thank David Layman for asking me to be the editor of this volume. It has been my privilege to work with David on a volume which so closely ties into my research for my dissertation. His insight and knowledge of Nevin's work and the secondary literature has been invaluable. His constant encouragement to be clear and concise in my writing and arguments was especially helpful to me. He has helped guide the process of bringing this volume to fruition. The finish line many times seemed elusive, but David was always faithful to keep us on track. I thank my pastor, Justin Estrada, pastor of Redeemer Presbyterian Church, who helped with the Greek translations. Special thanks to Michael Root, my *doktorvater*, who was kind enough to write the foreword to this volume. He has been an invaluable source of advice on the process of writing and scholarship. I thank Lancaster Theological Seminary for opening their library to a visiting scholar so I could, on one fateful day, stumble upon the name John Nevin and his little book, *The Mystical Presence*. Since that day, I have made many trips to the Library and the staff has always been welcoming and accommodating. I also want to thank the archivists at Evangelical and Reformed Historical Society (ERHS) and Franklin & Marshall libraries for their help in my work with Nevin's archived materials. I thank Wipf & Stock and the Mercersburg Society for their continued support of this publishing project, now twelve volumes in length. Finally, I thank my wife Carrie Ann, without whose love and support this would not have been possible.

General Editor

It has been this editor's task to help guide the development of these volumes for the past seven years, after his own editorship of volume 6 (*Born of Water and the Spirit*). Although the founding editor, Brad Littlejohn, has moved on to other interests, his editorial philosophy (stated in the above comments) continues to guide the series editors' endeavors. My fellow series editor, Lee Barrett, Stager Professor of Theology at Lancaster Theological Seminary (now under the umbrella of Moravian University) connects the enterprise to the institution that maintains the Mercersburg vision and provides invaluable advice and encouragement. He made a final reading of the entire manuscript that enabled this editor to correct multiple infelicities and provide several needed footnotes. Each year, LTS hosts the Mercersburg Convocation that reflects on continuing relevance and application of that vision. The editors are indebted to the Mercersburg Society for its unstinting financial support of this enterprise.

I extend my gratitude to the volume editor, Michael Stell, who has been faithful to the task despite severe disruptions, both the pandemic of 2020, and his own life responsibilities. He brings fresh eyes and insights to the interpretation of these texts, which are (at the time of this writing) the focus of his doctoral work. Academicians who have published their dissertations know the special problems with making such adaptations. Mr. Stell had the weighty endeavor of simultaneously writing his dissertation and tailoring its results for the audience of this series. He should get the credit for courage in challenging the scholarly consensus.

A special note about the "Epilogue." After considerable discussion with Mr. Stell, Dr. Barrett (my co-editor) and others, it was decided that I should present this material in this manner. Besides Dr. Barrett, Dr. Linden DeBie and Dr. William Evans gave invaluable counsel. However, the general editor bears the responsibility for its content and presentation, as he does for any flaws that remain in the presentation of the volume.

Lancaster Theological Seminary and the Archives of the Evangelical and Reformed Historical Society (both in Lancaster, Pennsylvania) are the essential repositories of texts relevant to Mercersburg; Google Books and Internet Archive (archive.org) together comprise a world-class research library accessible from one's desktop. (Google's interface is easier to interact with; while Internet Archive includes more recent literature which can be digitally "checked out," and fills some crucial gaps in the former.) The general editor made constant use of the latter two resources. Readers who wish to follow up on some of the esoteric sources used by Nevin can generally find them there.

Contributors

Michael J. Stell is a PhD candidate in Systematic Theology at Catholic University of America. His dissertation is a diachronic study of Nevin's views of history from his first published work through to his lectures in the 1870s. He teaches humanities, theology, and philosophy at Redeemer Classical Christian School in Kingsville, MD.

David W. Layman earned his PhD in Religion from Temple University in 1994. Through the fall of 2023, he has been a lecturer in religious studies, philosophy, and humanities at schools in south-central Pennsylvania, and is now retired. He is editor for volume 6 of the Mercersburg Theology Study Series, *Born of Water and the Spirit: Essays on the Sacraments and Christian Formation*, and has served as a General Editor of the Series since Volume 5.

Abbreviations

ACW   Ancient Christian Writers: The Works of the Fathers in Translation. Edited by Johannes Quasten, et al. Westminster, MD: Newman Press, 1949—.

ANF   *Ante-Nicene Fathers*. Edited by Alexander Roberts and James Donaldson. American Edition. Revised by A. Cleveland Cox. Buffalo: Christian Literature, 1885–96.

Epist.   Cyprian. *Th. C. Cypriani Opera Genuina, Pars I: Epistolae*. Lipsiae: Berhn. Tauchnitz jr., 1838.

Letters   Cyprian. *Letters of St. Cyprian of Carthage*. 4 vols. Trans. G.W. Clark. Ancient Christian Writers: The Works of the Fathers in Translation. Edited by Johannes Quasten et al. New York, Newman Press, 1984.

MR   *Mercersburg Review* (1849–52, 1857–78; 1853–56: *Mercersburg Quarterly Review*)

MTSS   Mercersburg Theology Study Series. Edited by W. Bradford Littlejohn (2012–2017), Lee Barrett (2017–), and David W. Layman (2017–). Eugene, OR: Wipf & Stock, 2012–.

PG   *Patrologiæ Græca*, edited by J.-P. Migne. Lutetiæ Parisiorum: J.-P. Migne, 1857–1866.

PL   *Patrologiæ Latina*, edited by J. P. Migne. Lutetiæ Parisiorum: J.-P. Migne, 1844–1864.

PPS   St. Cyprian of Carthage. *On The Church: Select Treatises*. Popular Patristic Series, No. 32. Edited by John Behr. Translated by Allen Brent. Crestwood, NY: St. Vladimir's Seminary Press, 2006.

Tract.   Cyprian. *Th. C. Cypriani Opera Genuina, Pars II: Tractatus*. Lipsiae: Berhn. Tauchnitz jr., 1839.

WCF   Westminster Confession of Faith.

WM   *Weekly Messenger of the German Reformed Church*, New Series.

General Introduction

Michael J. Stell

"To be deep in history is to cease to be Protestant.[1]*"*

Any Protestant who has studied the history of the church prior to the Reformation, especially the most ancient history of the church, has felt the weight of Newman's words. To look at the third and fourth, or even the second, centuries hoping to find Protestantism, especially American Protestantism, is to seek in vain.[2] John Williamson Nevin, raised in the Reformed tradition and rather late to historical studies, felt this tension. This tension is familiar to many, including the editor of this volume. I was raised in the Reformed tradition and attended a Reformed seminary. Most of my historical studies were typical of the Protestant tradition in America, and my theological studies were very much in the vein of Charles Hodge and American Presbyterianism. It was not until I began my doctoral studies at a Catholic university that I began to delve into the larger history of the church, especially in the Middle Ages and earlier. I was also exploring the extensive diversity of the American Reformed traditions.[3] As I was researching John Calvin's doctrine of union with Christ, I came across multiple references to Nevin's *Mystical Presence.* Thus began a journey into Nevin's work, and I found that he was asking many of the same questions that I had been asking. Here was a kindred mind, speaking to me from a similar place; it was his insights from which

---

1. John Henry Newman, *Essay on the Development*, 8.

2. It is worth noting that one would also not find modern American Catholicism in the ancient world of the church. One of the significant elements of the essays in this volume, however, is the question of whether the earliest centuries of the church are more like American Protestantism in the nineteenth century or American Catholicism of the same period.

3. There are some who want to treat the Reformed as a singular tradition rather than a series of various national traditions which, while similar in many doctrinal loci, still have very unique expressions of what it means to be Reformed. See Crisp, *Deviant Calvinism*. Crisp discusses Nevin in a different volume where he is somewhat critical of Nevin's theological emphases: Crisp, *Retrieving Doctrine*, 156–81.

I could proceed into a deeper study of history and my own tradition. His writings were a refreshment to my soul and a renewed foundation for my own studies. Even if one does not come to the same conclusions as does Nevin, it is nevertheless necessary to come to terms with the full history of the church and the theology generated through her history. The essays of this volume of the Mercersburg Theology Study Series are where Nevin does his most important historical work, and where we also feel the tension of that history, at times in very raw personal terms. In order to fully appreciate that tension it is necessary to give some background to Nevin's "historical awakening."[4]

Nevin's Historical Awakening

Nevin's autobiographical reflections were originally published serially, and only collected in 1964 as *My Own Life*. The chapter on "Historical Awakening" describes his awakening to the reality of history as a science through the writings of Augustus Neander.[5] Nevin said he taught himself German in order to read Neander,[6] and uses very evocative imagery to describe the transformation: it was like "the valley of dry bones" coming alive in Ezekiel's vision; church history became "for me like the creations of poetry and romance."[7] Whereas the "fiery African father" Tertullian was only "known spectrally before," Neander caused "him to walk the earth again in living, intelligible form."[8]

> [T]he old Christian Fathers generally . . . appeared no longer as the freaks simply of brainless folly or diabolical madness. There was seen to be both meaning and method in their rise and progress. They had an inward, one might say necessary connection with the history of the Church; and there could be, it

---

4. Nevin, *My Own Life*, 139–49. For a fuller treatment of Nevin's life, there are four essential historical studies: Appel, *Life and Work*; Nichols, *Romanticism in American Theology*; Hart, *John Williamson Nevin: High Church Calvinist*; DeBie, *John Williamson Nevin: Evangelical Catholic*. Appel's is the oldest, written by one of his students, and includes both biographical information as well as extensive selections of his writings. Nichols, Hart, and DeBie wrote 1961, 2005, and 2023 respectively. Several introductory essays in MTSS are useful, esp. DeBie, editor's introduction to *Mystical Presence*, MTSS 1:xxiii–xlii and Layman, general introduction to *Born of Water*, MTSS 6:1–33. A good introduction to Mercersburg theology is William Evans, *Companion to the Mercersburg Theology*, 82–109.

5. Johann August Wilhelm Neander (1789–1850) was a convert from Judaism and became professor of church history at the University of Berlin. Nevin's belief in the 1830s that "religion is a life" (documented below) either came from Neander or was strengthened by his reading of *Allgemeine Geschichte der christlichen Religion und Kirche* (trans. *General History of the Christian Religion and Church*). See Schaff, *Development of the Church*, MTSS 3:361–62; Borneman, general introduction to part 1 of *Philosophy and the Contemporary World*, 10; DeBie, *John Williamson Nevin*, 78.

6. John Payne casts some doubt on this claim: "From *The Friend* one would have the impression that he learned German primarily to read the German Biblical critics" ("John Williamson Nevin: the Early Years," 31n57). *The Friend* was a weekly periodical that Nevin edited in Pittsburgh from April 1833 to February 1835. It includes several important early essays, especially "Religion a Life," quoted below.

7. Nevin, *My Own Life*, 139.

8. Nevin, *My Own Life*, 140.

was clearly shown, no right understanding of Christianity and the Church, the onward course of the mystery of godliness in the world, without an insight, at the same time, into the interior nature of its counterfeit and contradiction, the mystery of iniquity working from the beginning in this bad way.[9]

That is to say, to understand orthodoxy one had to also understand the ancient heresies.

It was an awakening of the soul for Nevin. He borrowed Kant's characterization of David Hume's writings: "'They broke up my dogmatic slumbers.'"[10] Before Neander, Nevin thought, "this sense of the historical was something which I could hardly be said to have even begun to possess at all."[11] Thus we have the standard account: Neander gave birth to Nevin's understanding of historical development.[12] It is this presentation of historical development that is on display in the essays in this volume.

Nevin's Pre-Mercersburg Historical Writings

However, this understanding did not develop in Nevin's thinking simply through reading Neander. There is some discussion among Nevin scholars on exactly how Nevin's self-understanding is reflective of his own intellectual history. Nichols and Layman remind us that scholars should have a sense of skepticism about the historicity of Nevin's recollections.[13] In his editorial work on Nevin's pre-Mercersburg writings, Layman sees a latent historical development in his "Religion A Life" essays from his days in Pittsburgh.[14] This view is challenged by others, including Nevin's earliest biographer, Theodore Appel.[15] While this essay will not resolve this disagreement, Nevin was almost certainly thinking about these historical realities before he read Neander. His historical consciousness had been germinating but did not find fruition until he read Neander and other German thinkers.[16] So, while it already in-

---

9. Nevin, *My Own Life*, 140, 141.

10. Nevin, *My Own Life*, 143.

11. Nevin, *My Own Life*, 143.

12. For variations on this account, see Nichols, *Romanticism*, 42–45; DeBie, *John Williamson Nevin*, 78; William Evans, *Companion*, 21; Hart, *John Williamson Nevin*, 75.

13. Nichols, *Romanticism*, 37; Layman, "Historicity and Unity," 28. Autobiographies have been challenged by historians when it comes to specifics. Alister McGrath argues in his biography of C. S. Lewis that Lewis's autobiography was wrong on his date of conversion (McGrath, *C.S. Lewis*, 141–46).

14. Nevin, "Religion A Life," 42n16. Layman sees some sense of development even further back in Nevin's *Biblical Antiquities*: general introduction to *Born of Water*, 15–16. Nevin was a teacher at Western Theological Seminary, a Presbyterian institution, from 1829 to 1840.

15. Appel, *Life*, 80; DeBie, editor's introduction to *Mystical Presence* MTSS 1:xxxiii, notes 44 and 46; cf. DeBie, *John Williamson Nevin*, 58.

16. Layman considers Nevin's introduction to Rauch and his "romantic idealism" as the "catalyst" which brings this latency to fruition (Layman, general introduction to *Born of Water*, 18). DeBie, *John Williamson Nevin*, 79–81, discusses the influences on Nevin immediately before he met Rauch, concluding that "no one path, event, or moment in time changed him into an idealist and historian" (79). My own experience provides a model for understanding this intellectual process: the ideas in my

cluded ideas that would be more fully expressed later, his account in *My Own Life* does express a transformation brought on by his exposure to German idealism.[17] With that in mind, we begin with two of his earliest historical treatments.

Biblical Antiquities

Nevin's first published work, *A Summary of Biblical Antiquities* was originally a two-volume work that was published by the American Sunday School Union.[18] It is an introduction to the history and culture that is encountered in reading the Scriptures. Its purpose was to educate and inform the layman through a "simple, systematic compilation, bringing together, without technical phrase or learned discussion, the most essential points of the whole subject."[19] Topics are what would be generally expected under this rubric including geography, dress, and customs. The chapter entitled "General History of Religion" will be the only one we consider.[20] Nevin begins with a retelling of the biblical narrative of Adam and Eve, who "were altogether holy." They "had a trial of their faithfulness" but "[i]n that trial they failed." The "ruin" of their fallen state was "awful," the "most deplorable that any mind can conceive," since they faced, in their rebellion, the infinite wrath of God. Only God could save them.[21] Nevin describes salvation using the covenantal language typical of Presbyterianism.

> A wonderful arrangement has been, from the beginning, made in heaven, to recover the lost. The eternal Son of God engaged to become a *sacrifice* for their guilt, and the Father consented to receive once more into favour, and by his Spirit, to restore to holiness, as many as should be willing to accept the atonement thus wonderfully secured. . . . It was determined that, in consideration of the Saviour's work, the Holy Spirit should be sent forth into the hearts of men, to enlighten and persuade them, to the end that they might become willing to be saved; . . . and that, out of the multitude of Adam's fallen children, a portion should yet gloriously rise from ruin and find a happy restoration to the great family of God. Here originated the *Church*.[22]

---

thinking that resonated with *Mystical Presence* were already present. However, I did not have a way of organizing those ideas under a unitary rubric. *Mystical Presence* brought it together for me. In my mind, Nevin's personal development can be understood in a similar fashion.

17. The most detailed explanation of this transformation is in the work of Linden DeBie. See esp. his biography *John Williamson Nevin*, 84–98; 174–83; he gives more background on the German thinkers who contributed to this new thinking in his *Speculative Theology*, 42–51.

18. Nevin, *A Summary of Biblical Antiquities*. I will be citing the second edition of this work which was republished in one volume in 1849.

19. Nevin, *Summary*, 6.

20. The entire work is a work of history, or perhaps in our modern nomenclature, an historical anthropology.

21. Nevin, *Summary*, 235.

22. Nevin, *Summary*, 235–36, emphasis original.

Therefore, the church begins in the Old Testament and continues into the New. In line with his Presbyterian training, Nevin distinguishes between the church as invisible and visible.[23] The invisible church is made up of those "who are *really* and *truly* the people of Christ."[24] The visible character of the church is a mixed body which contains some who "belong to the church as an outward body on earth, who have no part in its glorious reality."[25] History has a telos: the "advancement of the Redeemer's kingdom to its glorious consummation. This will be clearly seen, when the history of the earth shall have come to its close."[26] Nevin does not move this history beyond the sacred page. The Biblical narrative is redemptive history: the history of the coming of "*Jesus Christ crucified to save a lost world.*"[27] The telos of this history ends where the pages of Scripture end; any idea of development of history would be limited to the boundaries of Scripture.[28] *Biblical Antiquities* then does not seem to point to nascent developmental thinking about history on Nevin's part, although he may be beginning to question whether this sacred history might be extended beyond the Bible to the rest of ecclesiastical history.

"Religion A Life"

Written between 1834 and 1835 while he was in Pittsburgh at Western Seminary, "Religion A Life" briefly discusses history.[29] In the third installment he writes:

> The same proper apprehension of the nature of religion, as a matter of sentiment rather than intellection, is all-important as a key to the history of the

---

23. For this distinction, see Westminster Confession of Faith, XXV: I+II; Dabney, *Systematic Theology*, 726; Hodge, *Systematic Theology* 3:547–52. In his Mercersburg writings, Nevin will use "Actual" and "Ideal" rather than "visible" and "invisible;" e.g., Nevin, *The Church*, MTSS 5:141–48.

24. Nevin, *Summary*, 236, emphasis original.

25. Nevin, *Summary*, 236.

26. Nevin, *Summary*, 239.

27. Nevin, *Summary*, 249. Therefore, God's providential working in history is understood as being the history of the Church. "[T]he Kingdom of Christ began to be formed just after the fall; and the same kingdom has been going forward ever since, and will go forward to the end of the world" (239). Error in the Apostolic age was the influence of the Judaizers who were attempting to convert Gentiles into the Judaism (254–55). Paul's teachings in Galatians, that Christianity was not bound to its Jewish context, took time to understand and accept. The process of disconnecting the Gospel from its Jewish origins was certainly a development, but it was a development which was bound to the history limited in the canon. Nevin even calls this discussion of history in the pages of Scripture "inspired history" (249).

28. Nevin is using Presbyterian theology in this chapter without, however, using the language. There may be several reasons why Nevin does not incorporate the language of federalism in this chapter. (Federalism says that God acts through two covenants: a covenant of works, which humankind has failed to keep, and a covenant of grace, which alone can save humankind.) The simplest reason is probably that his publisher was not a Presbyterian publishing house and most likely desired a broader reach. For discussions of federalism or covenant theology, see Hodge, *Systematic Theology* 2:354–77; Witsius, *Economy of the Covenants*; Vos, *Biblical Theology*; Robertson, *Christ of the Covenants*.

29. These essays were collected and republished in *New Mercersburg Review* 17 (1995) 37–45.

church. Without entering in some measure into this idea, we cannot rightly appreciate the history of particular doctrines or men belonging to the church, nor will we be able to estimate the nature of the triumph which Christianity has achieved over all the forms of error with which it has had to struggle, as constituting the highest argument of its own heavenly origin.[30]

Nevin's concern seems to be that one cannot think of the origins of the church in the post-apostolic age in terms of speculative theology. Certainly, in a time of persecution, the thing that bound together the first believers was not merely a set of doctrines. Rather, Christianity lived and moved forward in history because it "lived, and retained its identity, from one age to another, just because it occupied the minds of its true subjects as a system of facts entering into the range of their own spiritual being, and not as a system of notions simply for abstract speculation."[31] What protected truth in the early stages of Christianity and kept the church focused on the Gospel was religion thought of in terms of a life. Nevin explained, "It lived only because it was something *more* than speculation; because it had life in itself, and entered as a living history into the experience of the souls by which it was truly embraced."[32] Christianity is not primarily a mental construction on the part of the believer. It is *life*, the life of Christ, that is central to the church. However, it is doubtful that Nevin would think that the Catholic Church of the medieval period was the carrier of this life in the way he discusses in the essays in this volume.[33] Even so, we can say that he is beginning to move toward something more dynamic and organic. Further evidence for this transition is found soon after he arrives in Mercersburg, in his writing about the Heidelberg Catechism.

Nevin's Early Mercersburg Historical Writings: "The Heidelberg Catechism"[34]

Nevin left the Presbyterian Western Seminary in 1840 and joined the faculty at Mercersburg that same year.[35] While both ecclesial communions were Reformed, the German Reformed Church held the Heidelberg Catechism as their confessional statement.[36] One of the first things that he did upon arriving at Mercersburg was start a se-

30. Nevin, "Religion A Life," 42.
31. Nevin, "Religion A Life," 42.
32. Nevin, "Religion A Life," 43, emphasis original.
33. See Nevin, translator's introduction to Schaff's *Principle of Protestantism*, MTSS 3:36–55.
34. For background, see DeBie, *John Williamson Nevin*, 103–10.
35. For discussions of this ecclesial and professional shift, see Appel, *Life*, 92–99; Hart, *John Williamson Nevin*, 58–60; DeBie, *John Williamson Nevin*, 82–84.
36. For more on the history and formation of the Heidelberg Catechism, see Barrett's general introduction to *Heidelberg Catechism*, MTSS 10. The editors of that volume made the decision not to include the *WM* essays in the volume because the content of the essays was about the history of the continental Reformation, rather than the Heidelberg Catechism as such. Thus, that volume begins with Nevin's more important *History and Genius of the Heidelberg Catechism*. The *WM* essays were

ries of articles on its history in the denomination's newspaper, *The Weekly Messenger*. These articles ran for approximately two years, although after article 17, he took a year-long intermission. Appel says this historical work gave him the opportunity to discover "what was the genius or inner spirit of the Church in whose service he was called to labor."[37] These essays express his earliest historical thinking, especially on two subjects which become so important to his theological work in just a few years: the papal office and the Eucharist.

Nevin's opening statement of historical development utilizes organic metaphors rather than the Hegelian emphasis that will become central to his discussions in just a few years. "Let us have progress, by all means; but let it be progress *upwards*, within the sphere of the original life of the Church itself, as a tree unfolds itself in growth and is the same tree still; not progress *outwards*, by which the life of the part, together with its form, is renounced, and 'another gospel' introduced in the room of the old."[38] Nevin wants to emphasize that, contra Mosheim, the Reformed church is not a schism from the Lutheran church, but is its own legitimate formulation. "[The Reformed Church] is the Extra-Lutheran protestant Church, as we find it developed and organized, in different national systems, before the time of the *Synod of Dort*."[39] "Development" here seems to lack the teleological implications that will become so important to Nevin's later historical understanding.[40]

Nevin's early focus is on Zwingli's formation and eventual movement away from Catholicism. He is attempting to demonstrate the unique history of the Reformed church. Here his interpretation will display differences from his later discussions. For instance, in the third article, he says, "Already the *lie* which [Romanism] embodied, had exhausted the freshness and vigor of its own life, and was coming to be rapidly for the hearts of men a nerveless, dying interest. So it is always with systems of error."[41] The "system of popery" had lost its life-force and was only a skeleton from which the hearts of the people were fleeing. In the fifth entry, Nevin portrays the Zurich

---

an introduction—for Nevin himself, and by Nevin to his church—to the history of the continental Reformation, as distinct from the Puritan and Presbyterian movements in the British Isles. What they show is that at the very beginning of his Mercersburg tenure, Nevin was concerned to retrieve a usable history as the basis for confessional renewal in his adopted church. Appel thought that both works should have been combined into a single volume because the *Weekly Messenger* articles contained more historical background on the Reformation—Ulrich Zwingli in particular—which was not included in subsequent *History and Genius* (Appel, *Life*, 150).

37. Appel, *Life*, 150.

38. Nevin, "Heidelberg Catechism," *WM* 6, no. 12 (December 9, 1840) 1086, emphasis original. (This entry is a preliminary "proposal" by Nevin.) "Another gospel" alludes to Gal 1:6.

39. Nevin, "Heidelberg Catechism ¶1," *WM* 6, no. 12 (December 9, 1840) 1086, emphasis original.

40. Layman specifically sees this as evidence of Nevin's thinking in his "pre-Schaff" state (general introduction to *Born of Water*, MTSS 6:23–24, n128, n129). Indeed, the organic metaphor is retained by Nevin as late as his "Catholic Unity" sermon. Idealism will also manifest itself in that sermon, as discussed below.

41. Nevin, "Heidelberg Catechism ¶3," *WM* 6, no. 14 (December 23, 1840) 1093, emphasis original.

disputations as a debate over Scripture versus Tradition. The bishop of Constance "had no idea" he would be "encountering the naked sword of God's word" in his defense of the Catholic position without the protection of his "tradition."[42] Zwingli appears before the Zurcher senate armed only with Scripture; it is the battle between "light and darkness."[43] Nevin even says that the "bible is the religion of the protestants."[44] While manifesting typical Protestant biases, he begins to express the idealism that becomes so important later:

> In the vast flow of the world's history, the particular is always comprehended and carried forward in the movement of the general; and whatever power individual mind may appear to have at times, in directing and modifying this movement, it is a power after all which grounds itself ultimately in the spirit of the general itself, and is limited and conditioned by it at every point, as the sphere within which necessarily all its activities must play.[45]

Luther and Zwingli were not firebrands plucked from the time in which they lived but were products of historical formation. "In the deep bosom of life, its forces had been working long before these men appeared, like energies of a volcano gathering themselves for a sure explosion."[46] He even hints at the idea of the twin poles of a dialectic saying that Luther's unyielding and antagonistic mind "was called to encounter in the mind of Zuingle [sic], in order that the cause in which both were engaged, might by such counteraction take a happier direction than either of them could have given to it alone."[47] Even so, Nevin continues to frame the Reformation in terms of a break from the past life of the Church, even likening it to the American and French Revolutions. This is very different from what we will see below in "Early Christianity" and "Cyprian." Nevin's awakening to the German mind is still developing.

Regarding the Lord's Supper, Nevin begins to interpret Calvin's view as a dialectical synthesis between Luther and Zwingli. He will develop this more explicitly in his later discussion with Hodge. While both sides can only see the eucharistic controversy in a partial and one-sided way, "the subject was felt to demand a deeper and more spiritual view; and this was secured to it in the end, in such a way as to unite and reconcile what was right in the Zuinglian and Lutheran theories, while the error which each included was thrust out of the way."[48] Already Calvin is central to emergent read-

---

42. Nevin, "Heidelberg Catechism ¶5," *WM* 6, no. 16 (January 13, 1841) 1105.

43. Nevin, "Heidelberg Catechism ¶6," *WM* 6, no. 17 (January 20, 1841) 1109. For a discussion of Zwingli's life and his time at Zurich, see Gäbler, *Huldrych Zwingli*.

44. Nevin, "Heidelberg Catechism ¶12," *WM* 6, no. 23 (March 3, 1841) 1133. Contrast Nevin's discussion of the Bible and Puritanism in "Early Christianity: Second Article," below, 77–90.

45. Nevin, "Heidelberg Catechism ¶3," *WM* 6, no. 14 (December 3, 1840) 1093.

46. Nevin, "Heidelberg Catechism ¶3," *WM* 6, no. 14 (December 3, 1840) 1093.

47. Nevin, "Heidelberg Catechism ¶6," *WM* 6, no. 17 (January 20, 1841) 1109.

48. Nevin, "Heidelberg Catechism ¶7," *WM* 6, no. 19 (January 27, 1841) 1013.

ing: "to understand the history of the Church, we must look into the soul of Calvin."[49] After taking a nearly yearlong break, Nevin takes up his pen again and addresses the sacramental question more in depth. While the changes are subtle, Nevin seems to have grown in his understanding.[50] He continues the idea of a synthetic union but advances his understanding of Calvin's view of Christ's presence in the Eucharist. This doctrine said there was "an actual union . . . realized on the part of the believer with the life of the Saviour's glorified body; involving a communion with him in his whole nature, as real as the bond which identifies us, in virtue of our natural birth, with the general nature, soul *and* body, of our first father Adam."[51] He already thinks that the current understanding of the Lord's Supper by many Reformed in America is not the synthesis found in Calvin (as he will argue in *Mystical Presence*), but is a reversion to the Zwinglianism.

Nevin is just beginning to feel the full weight of the historical consciousness which he had previously only intuitively understood. He broadens his historical reach, moving ever deeper into the history of the Reformation. He concludes that if the German Reformed Church "is to strike her roots deep into the earth, and fling her branches far and wide toward heaven, so that the whole land shall please itself in her shadow, it will be only by aspiring to be known and felt under her birthright title as the *Church of the Heidelberg Catechism*."[52]

Nevin's Awakening to History

Nevin does not give a clear indication in his *My Own Life* of exactly when and how this historical awakening happened in his life. As we have already seen, there is no clear demarcation between Pittsburgh and Mercersburg. *My Own Life* does not provide any specifics as to which of his earlier writings he would change or repudiate. Consequently, Nevin scholars are left trying to piece together when changes in his thinking take place.[53] Nonetheless, we can see clear movements in Nevin's thinking

---

49. Nevin, "Heidelberg Catechism ¶15," *WM* 6, no. 28 (March 31, 1841) 1149. He even likens Calvin to Moses whose soul was touched with the fire of heaven. Calvin is therefore even greater than the most powerful man in Europe in the sixteenth century, Charles V (1500–58). He also refers to Calvin's founding of "presbyterianism" in Geneva as a return to the primitive order of the New Testament. This language of repristination will be explicitly rejected in "Early Christianity" and "Cyprian."

50. He will address this in the serialized essays, "Pseudo-Protestantism" and then *The Mystical Presence*.

51. Nevin, "Heidelberg Catechism ¶18," *WM* 7, no. 32 (April 27, 1842) 1373, emphasis original.

52. Nevin, "Heidelberg Catechism, ¶29," *WM* 7, no. 49 (August 24, 1842) 1442. The italicized phrase was originally in "small caps."

53. Some important attempts: Nichols, *Romanticism*, 44–63 is classic. Hart, *John Williamson Nevin*, 71–77, 101, 108 covers the facts. One idiosyncrasy is that he interprets Nevin's organicism as an example of federal theology. There are important details in Payne, "John Williamson Nevin: The Early Years" that need further consideration. William Evans, *Imputation and Impartation*, 146–58 contrasts the origins of Nevin's theology to other major streams of American Reformed thought; in a

during this whole period (1840–53) on how to think about history. This process will culminate in the essays that are contained in this volume.

"Catholic Unity"

Two watershed documents for Nevin are his sermon, "Catholic Unity" and his introduction to Philip Schaff's *The Principle of Protestantism*. Both are connected to Schaff's text (originally a lecture), with the sermon being published as an appendix at Schaff's request. John Payne describes its major themes:

> In this sermon Nevin set forth in brief all the major features of ecclesiology which he expanded upon in future essays: He stressed the Christological ground of the Church and the mystical union, not just with the divinity but with the humanity of Christ, especially in the eucharist, and for this view he drew already on Calvin and the Heidelberg Catechism. He accented the Pauline metaphor of the Church as the body of Christ which is filled with the life of Christ, the source of the Church's unity. He argued that the Church is not an aggregate of individuals but an organic whole which precedes the individual. He adopted the Hegelian distinction between the ideal and the actual and applied it to the difference between the potency of the life of Christ, which is in process of realizing itself, and the actualization of the potency in the Church.[54]

Let's begin with the last point.[55] The Ideal precedes the Actual, yet it can only be realized though a gradual process.[56] Although everything that is necessary for the realization of the Ideal is already present in the life of Christ that is mediated to the people of God through the Church, the Actual is not yet the full realization of the Ideal. As such, there is always a struggle, a process of development, that takes place.

> But it may happen that for a long time this hidden force shall be embarrassed and repressed by untoward influences, so as not to find its adequate form and action in the actual order of the Church. Thus we behold at this time the Christian world in fact, broken into various denominations, with separate

---

less technical study, *Companion to the Mercersburg Theology*, Evans develops previous scholarship in MTSS. Linden DeBie makes the case that German mediating theology is the primary source of Nevin's thought: *John Williamson Nevin*, 79–98, 174–182; DeBie, "Germ, Genesis" gives an older version of his position. In contrast to DeBie, Layman, general introduction to *Born of Water*, MTSS 6:1–19, agrees with Hart that Nevin was a "high church Calvinist," at least in the origins of his piety. DeBie responds to Layman in *John Williamson Nevin*, 175n20 and 179.

54. Payne, "Schaff and Nevin," 170. DeBie, *John Williamson Nevin*, 132–36, gives a reading of the sermon.

55. Nevin's capitalization of Ideal and Actual is not consistent through his writings. For clarity, when referring to them in the context of Hegelian development, I will treat them as proper nouns except in quotations.

56. Nevin, "Catholic Unity," MTSS 5:120. For a more detailed discussion of these concepts see his sermon, "The Church" in MTSS 5:141–48.

confessions and creeds, among which too often polemic zeal appears far more prominent than catholic charity. Such distraction and division can never be vindicated, as suitable to the true conception of the Church.[57]

The current state of the Church as divided into various denominations does not, at least in an ultimate sense, subvert the true nature of the church as the unified body of Christ. In fact, the Ideal of full unity is constantly seeking to find actualization in the Church.[58]

> The life with which it is animated does indeed seek an outward revelation in all respects answerable to its own nature; and it can never be fully satisfied till this be happily secured; but as a process, struggling constantly towards such an end, it may be vigorously active at the same time, under forms that bear no right proportion whatever to its wants.[59]

The reality of the church in her Actual state should be a cause for lament, since it does not correspond to the life of Christ; even so, there is still hope because the Actual will always be moving toward the Ideal.

Nevin likens this movement to the development of the natural world. However, what Nevin calls "mere nature" experiences movement through a blind process.[60] In contrast, the church's development takes place through intelligence and will because this is a moral development. Thus, the obligation to seek a realized unity is the vocational duty of all Christians. "The whole Church then must be regarded as inwardly groaning over her own divisions, and striving to actualize the full import of this prayer; as though Christ were made to feel himself divided, and could not rest till such unnatural violence should come to an end."[61] The main focus of Nevin's thinking then is directed at the source of the existing divisions, the sects that were so common in American Protestantism.[62] Sectarian division is necessary only in the same sense that heresy is necessary. Neither reality is something to which the church should just quietly acquiesce. While sectarianism is a product of the spirit of the Reformation, it cannot be the end that the Reformation pointed toward.[63] The spirit of the

---

57. Nevin, "Catholic Unity," MTSS 5:121.

58. For more information on the Triennial Convention and this sermon in particular, see the editor's introduction to the sermon in Nevin, *One, Holy, Catholic, and Apostolic, Tome One*, MTSS 5:107–11.

59. Nevin, "Catholic Unity," MTSS 5:121. Nevin's theme was especially poignant since this sermon was preached at a convention that was seeking unity between the Dutch and German Reformed Churches.

60. Nevin, "Catholic Unity," MTSS 5:122.

61. Nevin, "Catholic Unity," MTSS 5:122.

62. See Nevin, "The Sect System," MTSS 5:238–71.

63. Nevin appears to still be trying to come to some understanding of how the current reality of both denominations and the sects which have withdrawn from those denominations are to be understood. It is clear that Nevin does not understand denominations and sects to be the same thing, but neither does he seem to have a clear understanding of the distinction between them. Further into

Reformation, if it is truly from God, must contain in its life the ability to move toward unity. Referencing Jesus's high priestly prayer, Nevin says "the hour is coming, though it be not now, when the prayer of Christ that his Church may be one, will appear gloriously fulfilled in its actual character and state, throughout the whole world."[64] His idealism allows him to be able to hold the two states together dynamically in the life of the church. Union of the Ideal and the Actual will not be the result of denominational machinations but must come from the life of the church in her Actual state.

In the meantime, Nevin recognizes that many of the spiritual and theological developments of Protestantism since the Reformation are "the liberty of the Reformation run mad."[65] Here he places "the modern rationalism of Germany," the Dissenters of Great Britain, and "the unbridled licentiousness of private judgment" in American sectarianism.[66] Nevin believes that we can best explain the reemergence of "the mysterious charm" of "popery," as well as the Oxford movement in Anglicanism, as a necessary "reaction" to these extremes of religious radicalism. The attraction of Catholicism and the Oxford movement are not "accident[s] or caprice," but "belong to the inmost history of the church."[67] Through these reflections, Nevin's idealism is laying the groundwork for recognizing the dialectical movement in and of *history*.

Nevin's Introduction to Schaff's *Principle of Protestantism*

While the "Catholic Unity" sermon gives evidence of Nevin's historical awakening, his introductory essay to Schaff's *Principle of Protestantism* demonstrates a fuller understanding of his thinking about historical development. This is one of the reasons that the whole of the work, including Nevin's introduction, is considered to be "the first concerted expression of the Mercersburg theology."[68] Nevin begins the introduction as an apologetic for Schaff, in light of criticisms expressed since the lectures had first

---

the essay, Nevin speaks of the communion of the Reformed in the context of the churches of Switzerland, Holland, and the Palatinate. He also speaks of Episcopalians but does not indicate whether he means American or Anglican, or how they should relate to Methodists. One thing he is clear about, the papacy and Catholicism are not the solution to the unity which the church should strive toward; Nevin still refers to the pope as Antichrist in this sermon. In a few years, Nevin will apply that term to the sects themselves (*Antichrist*, MTSS 5:163–232). In later writings on church unity, he will once again reject the papacy as the unifying reality which can bring true ecclesial union. See especially "Reply to 'An Anglican Catholic'" and "The Old Catholic Movement"—both discussed at the end of this introduction.

64. Nevin, "Catholic Unity," MTSS 5:124.
65. Nevin, "Catholic Unity," MTSS 5:130.
66. Nevin, "Catholic Unity," MTSS 5:130–31.
67. Nevin, "Catholic Unity," MTSS 5:131.
68. Bains and Trost, editors' introduction to *Principle of Protestantism*, MTSS 3:27. MTSS 3 contains the most recent edition of Schaff's *Principle*. For detailed discussions, see Nichols, *Romanticism*, 107–39 and DeBie, *John Williamson Nevin*, 138–53. "Catholic Unity" was originally published as an appendage in *The Protestant Principle*, which gives the above statement further credence.

been delivered. One complaint was that Schaff's treatment of the Protestant principle was not American enough, or stated from a different perspective, it was too German.[69] Nevin responds in terms of Schaff's own development.[70] Schaff was brought from Europe to teach in the Americas; his own personal development could replace a conflict between the German and Anglo-American cultures with a *national* theological *Entwicklung*.

> What is needed is a judicious union of both, in which the true and good on either side shall find its proper supplement in the true and good of the other, and one-sided extremes stand mutually corrected and reciprocally restrained. Realism and Idealism, practice and theory, are both—separately taken—unsound and untrue. Their truth holds—can hold only—in their union.[71]

Here dialectical development is not merely a movement of the past, but points toward a future possibility. Nevin applies this to the need for "living" theological practice, i.e., a theology that *develops*.[72]

> All great epochs in the world's development, after all, owe their presence primarily to theory and speculation. Our religious life and practice can be sound and strong only in connection with a living, vigorous theology. But to be thus living and vigorous, our theology must be more than traditional. It must keep pace with the outward course of human thought, subduing it always with renewed victory to its own power. Not by ignoring the power of error, or fulminating upon it blind ecclesiastical anathemas, can theology be saved from death; but only by meeting and overcoming it in the strength of the Lord.[73]

Here Nevin agrees with Schaff: the movement of history is built on a strong understanding of the sovereign action of God in history, moving history toward an end that he has designed.[74]

Nevin's larger argument attempts to normalize the historical understanding which Schaff presents in his address. Nevin frames this in a two-fold way: as a means of understanding the flow of history, and as a means of placing America's current ecclesial and cultural reality in an historical context. He frames historical movement by discussing the way that error functions in history. Error is not simply a nexus of wrongly held views. He writes, "To contend successfully with any error, it is all

---

69. For a discussion of the influence of German theology on American theology, see Aubert, *German Roots*.

70. Nevin uses *Entwicklung* [trans. "development," "evolution"] in the text.

71. Nevin, Translator's Introduction to *Principle*, MTSS 3:39. Nevin later discusses the union of the German and the Anglo in his discussion of the value of the newly formed Franklin & Marshall College, a union of two existing institutions. Nevin, "Address on Behalf of the Faculty," 22–32.

72. This is perhaps what Nevin means by the opening of an understanding of history which is referenced in his autobiographical *My Own Life*, which is discussed above.

73. Nevin, Translator's Introduction to *Principle*, MTSS 3:39–40.

74. For a revisionary discussion of Schaff's influence on Nevin, see Layman in this volume's Epilogue.

important that we should understand properly and acknowledge fairly the truth in which it finds its life."[75] Any wrong belief must be grasped in its context and seen as a reaction against another set of beliefs, and must be understood to have something about it, whether in the belief or in its progenitor, that draws people to follow it. No error that has grown in the Church could have done so in a context that was foreign to truths which it sought to supplant. Catholicism, for instance, could not have become what it was in the High Middle Ages if it was not connected to something in the earlier teachings of the church. It "includes generally some vast truth in every one of its vast errors;" in making "war upon the error," one must be concerned to "rescue and save" the truth which is embedded within it. "The truth which it includes must be reconciled with the truth it rejects, in a position more advanced than its own, before it can be said to be fairly overcome."[76]

As in "Catholic Unity," the opposed movements in this history are the American ecclesial reality versus Roman authority. These must be brought together in an organic union. "Both separately taken are false, or the truth only in a one-sided way; and the falsehood, sooner or later, must make itself practically felt. The full truth is the union of the two."[77] Therefore, private judgment (personal interpretation of Scripture) cannot be separated from authority and tradition. It is a "sacred right . . . but it can hold only in the element of true Church authority."[78] The solution is "an inward marriage of the two general tendencies as shall be sufficient to make them one," a union of the experiential and the Churchly, "the only form in which religion can deserve to be considered complete."[79] For the present, the current state of Protestantism is "interimistic. It can save itself only by passing beyond itself."[80] For this reason, the Reformation was a necessary moment in the movement of the Actual Church into the Ideal. The "consciousness of the Church at the beginning of the second century," was not identical to that of the Reformation.[81] The history of the church was driven forward by apostasy. "[I]n surmounting such apostasy," the new position is "an actual advance upon it that could not have been made in any other way." Therefore, the Middle Ages was the

---

75. Nevin, Translator's Introduction to *Principle*, MTSS 3:41.

76. Nevin, Translator's Introduction to *Principle*, MTSS 3:42.

77. Nevin, Translator's Introduction to *Principle*, MTSS 3:43.

78. Nevin, Translator's Introduction to *Principle*, MTSS 3:45. For Nevin's later opinion on "private judgment," see "Evangelical Radicalism," MTSS 11:313–14.

79. Nevin, Translator's Introduction to *Principle*, MTSS 3:46.

80. Nevin, Translator's Introduction to *Principle*, MTSS 3:48.

81. Nevin, Translator's Introduction to *Principle*, MTSS 3:50. We can see Neander's influence here. "Just as in the progressive evolution of Christian life, we saw Jewish and Pagan elements entering in with a corrupting influence, while yet the Christian principle preserved itself pure in the conflict with both; so we must observe the same thing again in the history of doctrines and in life, in dogmatics and in ethics, both having sprung from a common root." Neander, *General History of the Christian Religion and Church*, 1:338.

"womb in which was formed the life of the Reformation itself."[82] The Reformation in turn was the "legitimate succession from the Church life of the Middle Ages."[83] The "life of the Church in the fifth, fourth, and third centuries" was only brought to the Reformation because it was preserved and gestated, so to speak, in the "womb" of medieval Christianity.[84]

Having incorporated the historical consciousness of the mediating theologians, Nevin is prepared for his historical discussion of the Eucharist in *The Mystical Presence* and his interaction with his chief critic, Charles Hodge.

Nevin's Dialectical Historical Method: *The Mystical Presence*

The place where Nevin's dialectical method becomes most sophisticated is in his treatment of the Eucharist, especially in his only full-length book *The Mystical Presence*.[85] Nevin's decisive move is to make Calvin's eucharistic theology the standard for the Reformed faith in the sixteenth and seventeenth centuries. This is essential for Nevin, since Ulrich Zwingli (1484–1531), not Calvin, was the originator of the Reformed Church. Nevin frames this privileging of Calvin in terms of the struggle of a modified dialectic. Calvin's teaching on the presence of Christ's body in the Eucharist was an organic synthesis of two antagonistic theologies upon which a higher order could be established. After briefly considering Nevin's presentation of his doctrine in *Mystical Presence*, I will show how Nevin applies this dialectic in his rejoinder to Hodge's review of this book.

There is little doubt of the significance of this book in the formation of the Mercersburg theology. The crucial element is Nevin's understanding of two historical contexts: the development of the Reformed doctrine of the presence of Christ in the Supper in the sixteenth century, and Nevin's contemporary situation, in which American Reformed churches had all but abandoned this understanding for one Nevin called unchurchly and rationalistic. His central thesis is that while the founder of the Reformed church was Zwingli, the Reformed doctrine of the Eucharist was Calvin's. This was not to be understood in terms of actual intra-Reformed discussions on the meaning of Christ's presence in the Supper, but as an organically emerging synthesis. "Not that he [Calvin] is to be considered the creator, properly speaking, of the doctrine. It grew evidently out of the general religious life of the Church itself in its antagonism to the Lutheran dogma on the one hand and the low Socinian extreme

---

82. Nevin, Translator's Introduction to *Principle*, MTSS 3:51. It is noteworthy that Nevin, while he has accepted Schaff's understanding of historical development, speaks of the "great Roman apostasy" (51) and "the latent mystery of iniquity" (52)—still using Protestant images of Antichrist.

83. Nevin, Translator's Introduction to *Principle*, MTSS 3:52.

84. Nevin, Translator's Introduction to *Principle*, MTSS 3:52–53.

85. Nevin gives an outline of this treatment in a series entitled "Pseudo-Protestantism," in *WM*. These essays are excerpted in Appel, *Life*, 233–39 and summarized in DeBie, *John Williamson Nevin*, 160–61.

on the other."[86] Nevin is not attempting to establish some new understanding of the doctrine of the Reformed church. Rather, history discloses two contrary positions that had to be brought together in a higher order of unity. Calvin, Nevin thought, had the ability to synthesize competing ideas in a manner that grasped the essential elements of each opposing view. This was accomplished through Calvin's understanding of the participation the believer has with Christ in the eucharistic meal, which occurs in the union with the human nature of Christ. This participation is not like our participation with the human nature of Adam. It is a participation "in his own nature as a higher order of life."[87] This understanding not only allows Nevin to incorporate essential elements of existing Reformed eucharistic theology, he is also able to draw from the earlier theological tradition of the Church and at the same time critique medieval Catholicism's doctrine of transubstantiation.[88]

> It is a participation of the Saviour's life; of his life, however, as human, subsisting in a true bodily form. The living energy, the vivific virtue, as Calvin styles it, of Christ's flesh, is made to flow over into the communicant making him more and more one with Christ himself and thus more and more an heir of the same immortality that is brought to light in his person.[89]

It is not material, "local or corporal;" nevertheless it is a *"real* presence."[90] In this way, the sacrament has an objective force for worthy receivers, and the grace which is given in the sacrament is a communication of Christ's heavenly flesh. "He became flesh for the life of the world and our communion with him involves a real participation in him as the principle of life *under this form.*"[91] With this formulation, Nevin thinks Calvin affirms a real presence of Christ that truly feeds the believer with immortal life, while maintaining the Reformed critique of a corporal presence, thought to be the consequence of both transubstantiation and Lutheran consubstantiation.[92] In developing this synthesis "Calvin did not bring in a new faith at this point to supplant that which previously prevailed. He simply contributed to the right understanding and full enunciation of the faith which was already at hand."[93]

86. Nevin, *Mystical Presence*, MTSS 1:42; DeBie explains "Socianism" in note 9.

87. Nevin, *Mystical Presence*, MTSS 1:44. The difference is that the human participation with Adam is physical—today we would say in the DNA; whereas Nevin thinks that the Christian's participation with Christ's human nature (which is in heaven) is spiritual—i.e., supernatural—it is "real and yet spiritual at the same time" (MTSS 1:50).

88. Transubstantiation is the Catholic doctrine that affirms "the presence of Christ under each species, bread and wine, in Holy Communion." This is done at the words of institution by the priest meaning that "at the consecration during the Mass, the substance of the bread and wine [is] changed into the substance of the body and blood of Christ." Kelly, *The Ecumenical Councils*, 137.

89. Nevin, *Mystical Presence*, MTSS 1:51.

90. Nevin, *Mystical Presence*, MTSS 1:50, emphasis original.

91. Nevin, *Mystical Presence*, MTSS 1:52, emphasis original.

92. Nevin, *Mystical Presence*, MTSS 1:48–49.

93. Nevin, *Mystical Presence*, MTSS 1:55.

Nevin then begins a tour de force in which he traces the historical record of the sixteenth and seventeenth century divines and creedal statements to demonstrate how the Reformed communions and theologians incorporated this Calvinistic synthesis into the symbols of the Reformed churches. Nevin does not merely want to display what happened historically but manifest how that historical reality reflected a forward movement in history. This will become vital when dealing with Hodge's critique.

> The more fully we become acquainted with the historical connections and relations under which they started into life, the more shall we feel it to be impossible that they should mean anything less than the full strength of their language seems to mean. And it is hardly necessary to add that their *historical* sense, as thus determined, must be admitted to be in the end their only true sense.[94]

Nevin demonstrates the dominance of this understanding of the Eucharist by compiling sources from the sixteenth and seventeenth centuries. The difficulty that he has in the employment of the dialectic is the question of when does it end? If we accept the traditional Hegelian understanding of the dialectic, the synthesis becomes a thesis, and then a new antithesis arises.[95] However, Nevin would want to insist that new antithesis, which he deems the "Puritan Principle," is not really a new antithesis, but an attempt to return to one movement in the previous battle, the Zwinglian view. "The modern Puritan view evidently involves a material falling away, not merely from the form of the old Calvinistic doctrine, but from its inward life and force."[96] This assertion is more clearly supported in Nevin's rejoinder to Hodge.

Nevin and Hodge on Development in Reformed Theology

Nevin published *The Mystical Presence* in 1846. The work did spawn several reviews, but Nevin took none of them too seriously because they lacked academic weight. That changed in 1848 when Charles Hodge took up his pen to critique his former student. Hodge admits that he had not wanted to even read Nevin's book, but his hand was forced when he increasingly was asked about the doctrine of the Reformed Church on the question of the sacraments. Hodge's review is not merely a critique of Nevin's

---

94. Nevin, *Mystical Presence*, MTSS 1:68–69, emphasis original.

95. This pattern is not found in Hegel, and indeed, its putative existence is a "legend:" Mueller, "The Hegel Legend." "'Dialectic' does not for Hegel mean 'thesis, antithesis, and synthesis.' Dialectic means that any 'ism'—which has a polar opposite, or is a special viewpoint leaving 'the rest' to itself—must be criticized by the logic of philosophical thought, whose problem is reality as such" (411). Mueller traced this scholarly myth to Heinrich Moritz Chalybäus (see Chalybäus, *Historical Development*, 366–67). However, Nevin's implementation does not depend on Hegel, but on the later philosophical tradition, especially as he learned it from Schaff: Schaff gives his version of the dialectic in *What is Church History?*, MTSS 3:289.

96. Nevin, *Mystical Presence*, MTSS 1:111.

theology, but a wholesale critique of Nevin's historical method.⁹⁷ As such, Hodge's review and Nevin's rejoinder are competing views of historical development. In my judgment, Nevin's response is the high-water mark for his use of dialectical thinking.⁹⁸

Hodge argues that the views of the Reformed divines cannot be completely known since the sixteenth century was a transitional one. The divines were developing their own views over against Catholicism, and eventually, with the Lutherans. Even the early Reformed symbols in Hodge's mind cannot be taken as expressing the mature Reformed view, because they were "framed for the express purpose of compromise."⁹⁹ The lack of clear and sharp distinctions was not possible in the sixteenth century because there was no agreement among themselves and they desired "to prevent the schism between two branches of the Protestant church."¹⁰⁰ The kind of authority and distinction that Hodge was arguing for was found later in the Reformed Scholastics, such as Francis Turretin, whose *Institutes* was the theological text in use at Princeton.¹⁰¹ In this critique, Hodge is challenging the central argument of Nevin: that Calvin's theology of the eucharist should be understood as the synthesis between Luther and Zwingli, and is the dominant view of the Reformed Church in the sixteenth and seventeenth centuries.

Hodge attempts to establish his own historical dialectic. He begins with the Swiss divines who approximated the Zwinglian view. For Hodge, Calvin is the antithesis, not the synthesis. The synthesis would be the Reformed symbols to which both parties concurred. For Nevin, this method is "artificial" or "mechanical" because it is done retroactively. It is applied backwards to the historical record once a later generation has decided which view is correct. It is essential to Hodge to eliminate what he considers the "foreign elements" found in Calvin's thought which found their way into the early Reformed Creeds. He believes there are three creeds that establish this compromise: the *Consensus Tigurinus* (1549), the Heidelberg Catechism (1563), and the Second Helvetic Confession (1566).¹⁰² Of particular importance for Hodge is the *Consensus* because this was agreed to and signed by Calvin and Bullinger. "We have,

---

97. Hodge, "The Mystical Presence . . . by the Rev. John W. Nevin . . . ," 227–78.

98. Nevin tried to respond in Hodge's own journal (*Biblical Repertory and Princeton Review*) and was refused (Nevin and Hodge, *Coena Mystica*, MTSS 2:52). He turned to the denominational magazine of the German Reformed Church, *The Weekly Messenger*. Throughout the summer of 1848, Nevin presented, section by section, Hodge's critique and his own response. The presentation was only accessible in this obscure religious broadsheet until the entirety was published (2013) in MTTS 2, as Nevin and Hodge, *Coena Mystica*. Later, when the theological journal of Mercersburg was established, Nevin condensed the exchange: "The Doctrine of the Reformed Church on the Lord's Supper" (*MR* 2:421–548); republished in MTSS 1:225–322.

99. Nevin and Hodge, *Coena Mystica*, MTSS 2:4.

100. Nevin and Hodge, *Coena Mystica*, MTSS 2:5.

101. Turretin, *Institutes of Elenctic Theology*. On the role of Turretin, see the DeBie's commentary, *John Williamson Nevin*, 45.

102. English translations of these three creedal statements can be found in Dennison, *Reformed Confessions of the 16th and 17th Centuries*, 1:537–45; 2:769–99; 2:809–81.

therefore, in this document the well considered and solemnly announced agreement of the Zuinglian and Calvinistic portions of the Reformed church."[103] This agreement then governs the interpretation of the other two creedal statements in Hodge's list. In turn, these latter two creeds enshrine the already established compromise between the two Reformed camps. As the ensuing quotes from Nevin will show, this quasi-dialectic lacks a dynamic understanding of history. "Synthesis" takes place externally to the life of the church. It is found in the act of creating confessional statements whose purpose is to exclude rather than unite. The history of doctrine is not *historical* at all; it merely attempts to show where the "right" view existed in earlier moments of history. The false view, as Hodge sees it, dies out as the correct understanding is fixed in the church's teachings. Nevin responds:

> The idea of the past, as something which once had a real life of its own, that must needs be *reproduced*, in the spirit, from its own ground upwards, in order that it may be understood, is thrust aside in favor of the much more convenient imagination that it never had any right to be anything more than can be forcibly squeezed into modes of thought which prevail in our own time. Dr. Hodge comes to the sixteenth century, in this case, with his whole mind conformed to a certain scheme in regard to the Church and the sacraments, which is assumed with full confidence, from the start, to be the only one that can at all bear examination.[104]

For Nevin, *synthesis* is the growth of a living reality, and not merely a fixed confessional statement arrived at the end of the process. Hodge's procedure is flawed since it begins with the premise of making the *Consensus* the definitive statement of Calvin's views. In contrast, Nevin sees the *Consensus* as a capitulation on Calvin's part that brings the Swiss divines more in line with Calvin's views. He tries to establish this with the commentary Calvin wrote on the *Consensus,* which, combined with Nevin's historical survey, demonstrates a history which is radically different than Hodge's. "In *my* survey however, the Zuinglianizing element is made to give way gradually altogether to the Calvinistic, which appears at last accordingly as the acknowledged ruling life of all the leading Reformed Confessions."[105] Nevin attempts to demonstrate this in the later creeds of the Reformed church.

With the Marburg Colloquy (1530), there was a lull in the reformers' discussions surrounding the Eucharist. This allowed the opportunity for a synthesis to form from the antitheses, the poles of Luther and Zwingli: "time and opportunity were allowed for the quiet development of what may be denominated the Melancthonian and Calvinistic theory, in opposition to crass Lutheranism on the one side and crass

---

103. Nevin and Hodge, *Coena Mystica*, MTSS 2:17.
104. Nevin and Hodge, *Coena Mystica*, MTSS 2:8, emphasis original.
105. Nevin and Hodge, *Coena Mystica*, MTSS 2:25, emphasis original.

Zuinglianism on the other."[106] Zwingli's view of the Eucharist was understood in opposition to the Roman Mass and was focused on the elements in their role as symbols. Luther's view was focused the presence, mystically understood, as the means by which the grace of Christ became available to the individual believer. What is needed, Nevin thinks, is a synthesis which joins, in an organic manner, the elements of both views. This is found in the theory of Calvin and Melanchthon.[107] If this synthesis had taken place mechanically, Calvin would have taken elements from each side, much as is done in a political compromise. But Nevin thinks that is not what Calvin has done. Calvin, like Zwingli, rejects the idea of local presence of the body of Christ, but will, with Luther, insist that Christ's body is the active element that gives grace in the sacrament.[108] Nevin thinks Calvin was the instrument, prepared and used by God, to achieve this synthesis. Zwingli, on one side, insisted that sacramental presence could not be understood in any localized sense. Luther, on the other, insisted that Christ must be present locally in sacrament for the idea of "this is my body" to having real meaning. For Calvin:

> [Christ's presence] is effected, superlocally, by the spirit. Christ's flesh and blood are at hand, not in the bread and wine as such, but in the transaction; not materially or by mechanical contact in space, but *dynamically*, in the way of living substance and power; not for the outward man primarily and separately, as Luther contended, but for the *soul*, . . . as the central life of the whole person, so as to flow out from this to the *body* also as the true pabulum of immortality.[109]

The *Consensus* then is not, as Hodge claims, a movement away from Calvin's "foreign element." Rather, Bullinger, and the whole of the Reformed tradition which bore the Zwinglian elements, are as it were lifted into Calvin and the tradition which followed him. This is supported, Nevin thinks, by Calvin's signatures to both the Augsburg Confession at Strasbourg and the *Consensus* at Zurich, giving his assent to both sides. On the contrary, if Hodge is right, Calvin was being dishonest: he "played a false game either at Strasburg or Zurich."[110]

Further documentation for Nevin's understanding is found in his historical survey of the Reformed Symbols as presented in his *Mystical Presence*. Nevin argues that Hodge is prioritizing an earlier set of symbols which fit *his own* understanding of the Eucharist. Simply put, Hodge begins with his own view and uses it to judge history, to

---

106. Nevin and Hodge, *Coena Mystica*, MTSS 2:50.

107. It is important to note that Nevin does not use "synthesis."

108. For a discussion of Nevin's understanding of Calvin's views on the Eucharist, see Gerrish, *Tradition and the Modern World*, 49–70.

109. Nevin and Hodge, *Coena Mystica*, MTSS 2:55, emphases original.

110. Nevin and Hodge, *Coena Mystica*, MTSS 2:63. Later in the same paragraph, Nevin says that if Calvin's views are what Hodge claims, he "was a crafty Jesuit indeed" to played false with both sides.

determine where history is "right."[111] Nevin on the contrary, traces the conflict of ideas into the future and demonstrates how the eventual synthesis is already present in the church's doctrine and continues to influence its spiritual life.[112] Any attempt to revert to a previous pole of the antitheses, as Nevin accuses Hodge of doing, is a movement backward into a period which cannot be recovered because the church's doctrine has moved forward. Nevin believes he has shown that the Reformed community has lost something held in the earlier tradition: the conviction that the Lord's Supper is "*a mystery*, in its original and proper sense." If this is so, then Hodge's version of historical development is "'a process of decay'" rather than a "'process of growth.'"[113]

Historical Development in Nevin's Later Writings

Nevin's historical understanding itself developed from a nascent element in his earliest writings to his fully developed use of a modified dialectic in his rejoinder to Hodge. Such was the state of Nevin's thinking in 1848. In the same year, *Antichrist: or the Spirit of Sect and Schism* was published; two later essays criticize "The Sect System" in the newly formed *Mercersburg* Review in 1849.[114] His focus moves back to the patristic period in the essays contained in the present volume. The immediate context is explained in the introductions to the essays.

However, Nevin struggles to make his historical dialectic work. The full import of these essays in the larger corpus of Nevin's work is a matter of dispute among Nevin scholars. Nevin's opponents in the German Reformed Church imputed a five-year episode of "dizziness" to Nevin.[115] David Layman, one of the general editors of the MTSS

---

111. Nevin will make an analogous criticism a decade later when evaluating "Hodge on the Ephesians," MTSS 7. In Hodges's *Commentary on . . . the Ephesians*, rather than allowing the scriptural text to speak in its own language, Hodge "has his own theological system . . . that serves continually as a medium through which to study . . . the inspired text" (64).

112. Later, as a member of a committee to reform the liturgy of the German Reformed Church, Nevin and his colleagues did the historical work to see how this doctrine was found in the liturgical language of the Church. These efforts led to the formation of the Provisional Liturgy and the subsequent Revised Liturgy. For a complete discussion of the liturgical controversies, see Maxwell, *Worship and Reformed Theology* and DeBie, *John Williamson Nevin*, 292–321. For a historical survey of Reformation liturgies, see Gibson and Earngey, *Reformation Worship*.

113. Nevin and Hodge, *Coena Mystica*, MTSS 2:111, emphasis original. The last two phrases are quoting Hodge in *Coena Mystica*, MTSS 2:38. See also Nevin, *Mystical Presence*, MTSS 1:321 for Nevin's conclusion regarding Hodge's historical method.

114. The latter is less systematic, a critique of the religious pretensions of the many American sects to authority and truth. Both works are in Nevin, *One, Holy, Catholic, and Apostolic, Tome 1*, MTSS 5. See Layman, general editor's introduction to Nevin, *One, Holy, Catholic, and Apostolic, Tome 2*, MTSS 7:4–5 for a summary and possible explanation of Nevin's transition to the essays in this volume.

115. For the origins of this theory, see Good, *History*, 312. Nichols, *Romanticism*, 192–217, made it the theme of chapter 8.

and volume editor of volume six, examines the timeline and gives a fresh analysis of the "dizziness" in an epilogue to this present volume.[116]

It is not until the early 1870s that we have clear evidence for how Nevin thinks about "historical development," with the essays "The Old Catholic Movement" (1873) and "A Reply to 'An Anglican Catholic'" (1874).[117] Additionally, Nevin lectured on the philosophy of history while president of Franklin and Marshall College. These three sources give us an adequate picture into the historical thinking of Nevin as he comes to the end of his career. I will conclude with "Reply to 'An Anglican Catholic,'" since that presents the crux of the controversy. Resolving its significance will provide, I believe, a unified explanation of Nevin's later understanding.

"The Old Catholic Movement"

"The Old Catholic Movement" analyzes that movement using a historical declension narrative that Nevin had previously rejected. This does not mean that he is rejecting his previous objections to the idea of the church going into decline in the earliest centuries of the church. Rather, he is exploring how to talk about the church coming out of the Middle Ages in terms of corruption and needed reform. For Nevin, this is tied to the Petrine office and the growing power of the popes through history. Nevin does not deny the legitimacy of the papal office. He does, however, regard the Ultramontane movement[118] in nineteenth century Catholicism as a declination away from the true flow of history. Rather than a bishop among bishops, Pius IX styled himself as the sole voice of God. This focus on the singular bishop distorted the nature of the episcopal office as shared among the college of bishops. The Old Catholic Movement, which rejected the First Vatican Council's dogmatic proclamation of papal infallibility, stood as a movement that could lead to reform.[119] Papal infallibility was the historical aberration. Nevin thought that the pope's heavy-handed response to all who tried to challenge his newly minted authority demonstrated to the whole world that this

---

116. See below, 315–26. For an exposition of the situation and the conflicts internal to Nevin's theology see William Evans, *Companion*, 110–20.

117. Nevin does write several essays which have historical connections. He writes two essays on the Apostle's Creed in 1869 (MTSS 8:255–261, 262–265) and an essay on the Heidelberg Catechism for the tercentenary in 1863 (MTSS 10:267–304). These are themes which Nevin has explored previously and do not contain much which is relevant to discussions of his views on historical development. Additionally, he wrote two smaller essays on "Athanasius" and "Arianism" in 1867 (MR 14). Neither of these essays are dealing with historical development but are good examples of what Nevin will call "objective" history in his philosophy of history lectures.

118. "Ultramontanism" sought to centralize authority in the Vatican and the Curia (the administrative arm of the papacy). While it came to a head in the rule of Pius IX and his dogmatic proclamation on the Immaculate Conception (*Ineffabilis*), it has a history in the seventeenth and eighteenth centuries. See González, *Story of Christianity*, 2:164–66 and *Dictionary of the Christian Church*, 1655, 439.

119. See Moss, *Old Catholic Movement* and Bokenkotter, *Concise History*, 319–27. The dogmatic constitution, *Pastor Aeternus*, which created the doctrine, can be found in Denzinger, *Enchiridion*, 609–16 (lines 3050–75).

was not in historical continuity with Roman Catholicism as it had been. Against this, "a new race of reformers . . . has sprung up in the German Catholic Church." Their status as German is decisive for Nevin because the particular demands of the *German* science of history cannot allow this "new strange life" to enter the Catholic Church.[120]

The Old Catholic movement arose against the zenith of the Ultramontane system as an "opposite power in the Church."[121] Thus for Nevin, the Old Catholic Movement is not outside the life of the church, but represents the full manifestation of the opposite power that has been present in the church for centuries.[122] "[T]his old endeavor, the burden of the world's history for so long a time, is the same work which has now come also into the hands of these Old Catholics, and which they feel themselves commissioned of God to conduct to its triumphant end at last in a way answerable to the antichristian climax that has been reached on the other side."[123] Nevin later frames this in explicit terms of thesis and antithesis. "Authority and freedom are opposite, but not therefore contradictory conceptions; their opposition is polar: antithetic in order that it may become synthetic."[124] Pius's authoritarianism was the thesis, the Old Catholic movement was the antithesis. Thus, by attempting to trigger a synthesis, the Old Catholic movement was performing a vital function of the church, both in and for the church.

Nevin thinks that Ultramontanism shows it is possible for a false idea in the church to grow and develop. When that false idea comes out in the open and attempts to establish itself in the church as legitimate, the truth must also rise in response. The Old Catholic Movement is that response. Pius IX's consolidation of papal authority is not the historical stance of the church. His strong-arm tactics in attempting to squelch discussion,[125] and the fact that anyone who challenged the historical continuity of papal infallibility was threatened with excommunication, is in Nevin's estimation abundant evidence of the illegitimacy of the doctrine.[126] Although he does not mention Cyprian, Nevin must have recognized that the promulgation of papal infallibility exploded his optimistic reading of that church father as a resource for understanding the collegiality of bishops.[127] All unity from Vatican I forward will be "artificial mechanical uniformity."[128] Unity in this sense can only be by submission.

---

120. Nevin, "Old Catholic Movement," 251.

121. Nevin, "Old Catholic Movement," 268.

122. Nevin, "Old Catholic Movement," 268. Nevin specifically points to Luther's *Babylonian Captivity* as being in this stream of antithesis.

123. Nevin, "Old Catholic Movement," 269.

124. Nevin, "Old Catholic Movement," 270.

125. For instance, Nevin calls the "mingling of religion and the lust of power" being able to develop a force which will call forth destruction and terror (Nevin, "Old Catholic Movement," 282).

126. Nevin, "Old Catholic Movement," 275–76; "Even history, as a science, must adjust itself to this Procrustean bed."

127. See below, 197–207, 213–21, 284–89.

128. Nevin, "Old Catholic Movement," 287.

Nevin's application of the language of dialectic in the discussion of the Old Catholic Movement, its place in history, and the potential for real ecumenical unity of the divisions caused by the Reformation, seems to show that Nevin has not completely abandoned his understanding of historical development, a reading that will be supported by the next two sources.[129]

Lectures on History

In the early 1860s, Nevin begins teaching again at Franklin and Marshall College. He eventually becomes president again, serving for a decade (1867–76).[130] Multiple sets of student notes of his lectures exist in the archives, including on what Appel calls "the Philosophy or Science of History."[131] They lack the polemical edge manifested in the essays in this volume, but show that Nevin's thinking on development remained broadly Germanic: history is governed by laws that are teleologically focused. History is properly the realm of humanity and not nature. It is the realm of reason, intelligence, and freedom rather than instinct. Although man resides in nature, history proper "has a law and end of its own, as a life above and beyond nature, or the limitations set to mere animal or vegetable life."[132]

History, properly speaking, is what Nevin calls Universal or World History.[133] "In this character it is not the sum or mere aggregation of individual history, but a totality

---

129. One of the difficulties with Nevin's position here is that his anticipation about the way that history would unfold turned out to be wrong. Nevin's hope that the Old Catholic Movement would provoke a synthesis never materialized. It never gained much traction around Europe or in America. Even liberal Catholics, who most opposed the promulgation of the dogma, began to see it as an important check to liberal democratic (and often secular) states which were attempting to aggrandize their own authority (Bokenkotter, *Concise History*, 326–27). That Nevin expected otherwise shows he was still relying on the German science of history. History would unfold developmentally.

130. Appel gives the beginning of Nevin's re-entry into academia as 1861–62 (*Life*, 590). The college was in need of an experienced faculty member since their history professor had to resign due to finances and Nevin took his place. Part of his duties would be giving a series of lectures on the philosophy of history, but Appel does not say exactly when Nevin began these lectures. According to college catalogs from these years, the first year Nevin taught these lectures was in 1867. It appears that when he started teaching in the early 1860s, he was teaching German literature, aesthetics, and history. Starting in 1867, he is listed as the president of the college and professor of philosophy of history and aesthetics. The 1877 catalog still lists the lectures, but no name is attached to them since Nevin ended his career at the college in 1876.

131. Appel, *Life*, 590–91. To date, no full treatment of Nevin's philosophy of history notes have been created or published. Part of my doctoral work is to create a working set of notes using several sets of student notes as a guide. My dissertation will have an extensive discussion of this set of notes. A summary of these notes was also published in the Franklin and Marshall student newspaper, *The College Days*, beginning in January 1873. Here I will use the version anthologized and abridged in Appel, *Life*, 590–601.

132. Appel, *Life*, 591.

133. In the class notes, Nevin often uses foreign languages; here he uses both English and German—*Welt Geschichte*.

including a movement which has in it a law, tending toward a particular end."[134] History, because it is drawn from the life of men, is organic. It grows and is governed by a "vital principle" that is active and guiding it from beginning to its end. "The development must, therefore, be subject to some law, which binds all the parts together into a single whole, always tending toward some definitive end or result."[135] This means that in the midst of what seems to be the "endless confusion" of historical data, there is in reality an order that undergirds history.[136] If it were not so, there would be no rationality in humankind. History is therefore not merely what has happened; if that were the case it would be nature and not true history. History is governed by the organic laws of its telos, its end and goal.

This reading would seem to point to Hegel, but Nevin does not blindly implement his historical method here. Hegel's philosophy of history was too idealistic because it separated "the universal from the particular." In contrast, "the true idea of the science requires generally that the two should be united and proceed together." In the same way, history joins together the objective and the subjective. "History is objective in one view—*Res gestæ*—and subjective in another—written history."[137] The latter exists in human "thought or knowledge" about historical events; this is what Nevin means by "historiography." So, on the one hand, history is the movement of objective (we might say factual) events, "whilst in the other it is the representation or record of it as handed down from one generation to another."[138] In order for history to be true history,

> it must include order, law, unity and an ultimate sense or meaning; it cannot be the result of chance, or be regarded as chaotic in any sense; it is a system that has a rational constitution; we have it in the presence of intelligence, which does away with the idea of blind necessity; and in studying history, we must consequently believe in the presence of law and order working towards a rational end. In a word, we must believe that God is in history as well as man and the devil.[139]

Thus, history both moves and is moved and this movement, or *development*, follows laws.

From here, Nevin moves to the chronological understanding of history. History in this sense is progressive not cyclical. History, like a stream, does not progress evenly or regularly. It is not always continuous, and there may be "abrupt interruptions" as

---

134. Appel, *Life*, 592. In the lecture notes, Nevin utilizes his standard distinction between "all" and "whole": "all" is a mechanical unity, achieved by physically aggregating "parts," while an organic unity descends from the "whole." See Nevin, *One, Holy, Catholic, Apostolic, Tome 1*, MTSS 5:94, 118–19 for his earliest statements as applied to the church.

135. Appel, *Life*, 592.
136. Appel, *Life*, 593.
137. Appel, *Life*, 593. *Res gestæ* means "things done" or things that happened.
138. Appel, *Life*, 593.
139. Appel, *Life*, 594.

it moves "from one plane to another."[140] However, the changes in history, unlike a stream, are "always tending upwards from one to another, in which each one is higher than the preceding."[141] Nations and individuals have different roles to play in this movement of history—"a share in bringing about the grand result."

> This movement is a rational one, subject to law, and never at the mercy of mere chance, else we could have no faith in it. It is continually evolving changes, and sometimes it seems to turn backward: for having solved one problem, it must as it were go back and take up new forces which have not as yet been developed. This retrograde movement is a preparation for that which follows. The beginning of a stage or era is always an apparent retrograde.[142]

So, the movement of history is subject to a law. However, that law is not an immanent one, but is "beyond the present life and order of things,"[143] and "comes out in the Christian revelation." "Jesus Christ must be the foundation of our life, and the main stream of history must be in the Christian Church. . . . The law of history, therefore, tends toward Christianity, of which Christ is the principle or life."[144] History has a Christian telos, and it is only in knowing that Christ is the principle of life that animates it which allows any success in understanding its true goal.[145]

Did Nevin Abandon "Historical Development"?—"Reply to 'An Anglican Catholic'"

A second essay (in addition to "The Old Catholic Movement") from this later period of Nevin's life helps fill out the question of Nevin's views on history and development. Recent reading of this essay has resulted in a significant break with older scholarship.[146] "Reply to 'An Anglican Catholic'" has been interpreted as saying that Nevin has

---

140. This metaphor certainly draws on Nevin's youthful explorations of the Pennsylvanian fields and forests. See DeBie, *John Williamson Nevin*, 42.

141. Appel, *Life*, 595.

142. Appel, *Life*, 596.

143. Appel, *Life*, 596.

144. Appel, *Life*, 597.

145. Layman, in his epilogue (below, 326n66), objects that Nevin's lecture notes are not necessarily a full reflection of his views on a subject, referring to some of the differences between Nevin's essays and his seminary lectures. While that claim is worthy of consideration, some key differences are worth noting. First, these lectures are delivered to college students, not seminarians. There is a difference of focus and purpose in the education of young minds on an undergraduate level versus the preparation for young men for the gospel ministry. Second, the philosophy of history lectures appear to have been modified through the various iterations of Nevin's delivery. While some of that modification is attributable to the variations among the students taking the notes, it does imply Nevin was continuing to give careful thought to his philosophy of history. Finally, though not complete in the archives, Nevin did allow a version of these notes to be published in the F&M student paper, *College Days*. These bear remarkable consistency to the lecture notes.

146. The break was initiated with Layman, general introduction to *Born of Water*, MTSS 6:24, 31. He was supported by William Evans, *Companion*, 85, 112–16 and DeBie, *John Williamson Nevin*, 340.

left behind "development" as a functional way to understand history and has adopted in its place the concept of "movement."

This essay is part of a longer discussion on the question of ecclesial union.[147] The conversation was stimulated by the sixth General Conference of the Evangelical Alliance, held October 1873 in New York. Nevin identifies his interlocutor as "Anglican Catholic," who complains that the Alliance failed to take account of the "'old idea, that the Episcopate is the bond of union, appointed by the Lord, and transmitted by succession from the Apostles.'"[148] Nevin responds that the purpose of the Conference was *not* to create a doctrinal or ecclesial basis for fellowship among churches and professes he has "no mind to plunge at all into the dismal swamp of the controversy about bishops."[149] Yet he spends the next eleven pages doing just that.

"Anglican Catholic" complements Nevin's historical work in "Cyprian" and commends his recognition that Cyprian was in fact a bishop in the sense referred to in the above quotation. However, "Anglican Catholic" and Nevin hold this common opinion on different grounds. "Anglican Catholic" accepts the "English" understanding of the formation of the office of Bishop as a *jure divino* constitution which must be present in the church for the church to properly be a church. In contrast, Nevin thinks that such a constitution is a merely outward or external form. Nevin maintains his German philosophy of history, which requires insight into the inner life of the church, and understanding how structures and activities grow out of this life "organically," rather than "mere outward ordination."[150] The episcopate does not originate in some external demand, but out of the inner life of the church.[151]

Second, Nevin sees a significant historical problem for the "Anglican Catholic": the Petrine Office. Nevin's views in the "Old Catholic Movement" essay are still present in this essay. The question at hand, however, is can the "English" system of history truly claim Cyprian as an exemplar for their views on the episcopacy if they in turn reject the rule of the chair of St. Peter? "Historically; the view which identified the episcopate with the unity of the Church in the beginning, ran in fact from the first toward this idea of a central primacy as its proper goal, and had no power to stay itself in its course till that goal was fairly reached."[152] Nevin is still thinking developmentally: Cyprian's understanding of the episcopacy logically drives to papal authority. Nevin is using his knowledge of Cyprian to argue that Anglicans have a false understanding of

---

See also Evans, "Philosophical Idealism and the Reformed Theological Tradition," 411.

147. Nevin began the discussion with "Apollos: Or the Way of God." For the background to the essays and a reading of "Apollos," see DeBie, *John Williamson Nevin*, 342–45. "Reply" and "Apollos" are important to those who study the history of the ecumenical movement.

148. Quoted by Nevin in "Reply," 406.

149. Nevin, "Reply," 399–401, 406.

150. Nevin, "Reply," 408.

151. See Nevin's previous critique of the Anglican theology of the episcopate in "The Anglican Crisis," MTSS 11:283–88.

152. Nevin, "Reply," 414.

the flow of history. Cyprian's view placed the locus of unity in the office of the pope.[153] To be in unity, in the sense that Cyprian meant it, was to be in solidarity [*in solidum*] with the occupant of the episcopal chair of St. Peter. From Cyprian forward, to hold to the office of the bishop as the guarantor of unity was to affirm that church unity was tied to communion with the Bishop of Rome.[154] "History fell in thus with [this] logic."[155] Cyprian's position led *historically* to Petrine supremacy.

In other words, "Anglican Catholic" could not dam the flow of history at a singular point in time and ignore the historical developments that followed and were nascently present in that point. Furthermore, even if he *could* appeal to Cyprian, Nevin denies that Cyprian or his age should be understood as the "standard of absolute Christian truth and right."

> Christianity as it stood in the age of Cyprian, and as it stood in the Nicene age, can by no means be taken as a safe pattern of what Christianity should be in the present age, or as the true ideal of what the Christian world must reach after to solve in time to come the problem of Catholic unity. No protest against the ecclesiastical and theological errors of modern Romanism, I am well persuaded, can be valid or truly Protestant, which is not at the same time a protest against the principial[156] working of the same errors in the third and fourth centuries. Cyprianic Christianity is at best embryonic Romanism, as can be easily shown in many things.[157]

Cyprianic theology *organically* develops into Romanism; a Protestant who "protest[s] against the . . . errors" of the latter must, in order to be historically consistent, protest against the same errors "embryonically" present in the former. Such a perspective is still following the method of German historical science.

The section in the essay that initiates the break mentioned earlier is entitled "Organic and Historical." This section poses the question: what is the proper bond of unity? For Nevin, it is not the episcopacy as his interlocutor claims. That is to rely upon an outward abstraction that is not organically connected to the ongoing life of the church. Unity must grow, drawing life from the living power of "the one organic spiritual constitution of the Church."[158] Nevin thinks there was an error in the way the

---

153. "Hence the thought that underlies the whole tract *De unitate ecclesiae,* and meets us everywhere in Cyprian, that the true episcopate is an orb meeting together from all sides in a common centre, answerably to the relation of the general apostolate to the person of St. Peter." Nevin, "Reply," 415.

154. See "Cyprian," below, 216–19.

155. Nevin, "Reply," 415.

156. "Constituting a source or origin; primary, original." OED Online, "Principial, adj." Nevin is therefore saying that a protest against the errors of "modern Romanism" must also protest against the *source or origin* of those errors in the third and fourth centuries.

157. Nevin, "Reply," 416–17.

158. Nevin, "Reply," 418. Nevin's historiography relies upon the distinction between growth which is in nature and growth which is historical. Natural growth can never move beyond what it is. A tree moves from seed, to sprout, to full maturity, and then dies. This tree also gives to the world more of

church fathers conceived the office of bishop. While there was a time when the office was needed and the patristic understanding of the episcopal office necessitated the movement to the Petrine office, the error itself demanded that it be eventually overthrown. This agrees with what we have seen in his Lectures: history does not remain static but is always moving forward; it is always progressing.

This brings us to the crux: after discussing the historical stream of Christianity, he writes, "We need not call this development. For that is a treacherous amphibological term again, like baptismal regeneration or justification by faith, which may be taken in different senses, giving rise to endless contention. Let us call it simply historical movement. That is enough."[159] Here he is reacting to the "energetic language" of "Anglican Catholic" against the "development theory": "'Christianity is either a revelation or it is not. If it is a revelation, it was all revealed in the beginning. If it is not a revelation, it is what man chooses to make it.'"[160] If, says "Anglican Catholic," Christianity is relying upon historical development to solve its dilemmas, it becomes a thing that can be manipulated by men. The solution to this plasticity is to rely upon revelation.

Nevin's reply carries with it some of his old acerbic wit. The "Anglican Catholic" imagines "that he has it ["*his* system"] all now as a fixed historical tradition handed down to him without change from the primitive ages."[161] Nevin responds tersely, "That is not history; and that is no right view of God's revelation."[162] It makes the church a static organization with no inner life that organically grows through history. Since the Word of God (revelation) is described as having life and power (Heb 4:12), this conception of the church as historically changeless must be wrong. Christ, who is the Word of God, lives as the head of the church and is both the source and telos of history. He "impart[s] to the historical stream of Christianity itself, through the ages, a corresponding character of ever flowing and ever changing life[.]"[163]

At this point Nevin shrugs his shoulders: "We need not call this development. . . . Let us call it simply historical movement." In contrast to the simplistic reading made by Layman, he has not given up the teleological character of this "movement." Two paragraphs later he expostulates "there is not a doctrine belonging to [true Christianity], which has not had its history, its rise, its movement, its *progressive evolution*

---

itself through the giving of its own seeds. But this growth never moves beyond this cycle. History however, because it is guided toward a telos which is not found in nature, has a different kind of growth pattern. The growth of history consists of "continually evolving changes" guided by rationality which can manifest both progression and regression (Appel, *Life*, 596).

159. Nevin, "Reply," 421. "Amphibological" means "of doubtful meaning." Webster's *American Dictionary* (1846), 32.

160. Nevin, "Reply," 419, quoting "Anglican Catholic." This repeats the argument Nevin had twenty-five years earlier with Hugh Davey Evans: see below, document 1: "Historical Development." Nevin's reply (next paragraph) likewise repeats *his* prior response.

161. Nevin, "Reply," 420.

162. Nevin, "Reply," 420.

163. Nevin, "Reply," 421.

and determination."[164] This confirms what we have already seen in his lectures on the philosophy of history and the essay "Old Catholic Movement." "Movement" does not negate the teleological direction of history. Furthermore, Nevin's *apparent repudiation of "historical development" is dictated by the context of the argument.* Since the meaning is not agreed upon and using it detracts from the argument he is making against "Anglican Catholic," he discards it and puts another in its place. Nevin is content to call it "movement" so long as that contains all he means by the organic, guided flow of history. It is "an ongoing progress involving the birth of new things continually out of the bosom of old things. This is what history means; nothing less than this; and it belongs to the very idea of humanity, that it should exist in this form; and nothing which is really human can exist in any other form."[165]

Conclusion

While this survey of three important texts of Nevin's later period does not definitively answer the question of Nevin's views on historical development, it does provide the foundation for a reconsideration of his later views. It demonstrates that there is fruitful ground for further study on the notes from Nevin's philosophy of history lectures. These lectures opened the possibility of re-examining the interpretations of Nevin's later historical work. This is especially true of Nevin's meaning of the "amphibological" term, "development" itself. Most crucially, these three texts show us that Nevin is still deeply interested in history and the church's place in it. Nevin still stands as an exemplar for all who seek to find catholicity in history.

The essays in this volume display all the typical characteristics of Nevin's writings that can be seen in the other volumes of the Mercersburg Theology Study Series. Nevin can be caustic, polemical, complex, subtle, and deeply insightful—all in the same paragraph. This is the reason why, nearly two hundred years after these essays were originally published, scholars and church leaders are still drawn to his work. These essays also reveal to his readers someone who is intellectually attempting to do justice to the fullness of the history of the Church of Jesus Christ. Some looked at this history and converted to the Catholic Church—like John Henry Newman, who speaks in the opening quotation. While the essays in this volume reveal one who is struggling with this history, Nevin did not convert. He remained in his ecclesial Protestant communion, and continued to strive for evangelical, historical catholicity.

---

164. Nevin, "Reply," 421–22, emphasis added.
165. Nevin, "Reply," 421.

Document 1

"Historical Development"

Editor's Introduction

This essay is Nevin's first systematic discussion of "historical development." He opens it with a quotation from an essay by Hugh Davey Evans.[1] Although Evans commends the Mercersburg divines for their emphasis on the doctrine of the church, he does not believe one can have a historic doctrine of the church while rejecting the historic form of the church (e.g., the episcopacy). "Historic," he fears, means development of doctrine. Moreover, development of doctrine needs some criterion to determine legitimacy, such as an infallible head of the church, a fixed doctrinal position, or Scriptural revelation. The latter two criteria[2] will lead only to more sects (dividing over the meaning of the position or Scripture), the very consequence Nevin and Schaff want to avoid. But any of these options means development is meaningless. Any real development is a movement away from the criterion, and is, therefore, nothing more than sectarianism. Rather than development, we must rely upon the fixed standard of the interpretation of the Church Catholic.

Nevin responds with a short apologetic for the Mercersburg theory of development. To deny some kind of development through history is an untenable position. The modern churches of American do not look like the churches of antiquity; not all of them are apostatized, therefore there has been some kind of development. If the contrary were the case, the church that we reference in the Creed—one, holy, catholic, and apostolical—would not truly be a church. The development of the church is not merely the addition or rejection of doctrinal statements as Evans makes it out to be. Rather than denying the unity of the church, development means that unity must be tied to the life of the church through history. "Surely to be *historical* at all, Christianity

---

1. Evans (1792–1868) was a lawyer and "lay theologian and defender of high church principles." He edited *The True Catholic* from 1843 to 1856. "Evans, Hugh Davey."

2. Evans seems to think that an infallible head (a pope) *might* work, but would also be irrelevant, i.e., the head would determine "development," and so one doesn't need a theory of development.

must be in the world under the form of history, which itself implies organic life and growth."[3] Since history is a living reality[4] that moves toward a telos, the church needs to be the living body of Christ in its life. Christianity itself grows—like a human being. An adult is not the "same" as the child, even as the person maintains his or her identity over time. Thus, Nevin thinks, the Bible is the standard of the whole spiritual identity of the body of Christ (the "movement"), while allowing for real historical change in that body. "Revelation" then is that whole living reality growing in and through the "body of Christ"—neither external (e.g., a pope or Bible telling a believer what to believe) nor a past completed event. This text introduces the themes Nevin will explore in this volume.

---

3. Below, 35, emphasis original.

4. The question of what makes history "living" for Schaff and Nevin can be summarized with this quote from Schaff, "Development is properly identical with history itself; for history is life, and all life involves growth, evolution and progress" (*What is Church History?*, MTSS 3:335). Anglican claims, though different than the Puritan "repristination" model, are nevertheless a similar kind of reversion to a previous state. They point backward, not forward. Development is not merely change, but refinement or progress toward an end.

Historical Development.[1]

We fear that this phrase "historical" is connected in their minds with the doctrine of development, of which also they speak a good deal, and which we consider the thing in the world most irreconcilable to the true idea of an historical Church. We ourselves do not see how development is to work without the aid of an infallible earthly head of the Church. We think it has worked very badly with the aid of such an head; but that was because the head was not really infallible. It seems to us that continued progress requires a continual standard to which to appeal. If we have an infallible living teacher upon earth, to whom we can go, and upon whose decisions we can rely, the doctrine of development may be safe; but it will be useless. But a development, independent of such a teacher, must be continually in danger of going wrong, as we find that most actual developments of Church doctrine have. Now, if we have not an infallible living authority to protect us, we must substitute for it some fixed standard, by which the development is to be tried. But progress is of the essence of development, and it must get beyond any fixed standard. They will come to differ. Which are we to follow? If the fixed standard, why not adopt it at once, and say nothing of development? If development, how are we to know that we are right? What is theology but a science, like the human sciences? What has become of Revelation? We have no difficulty in answering these questions for ourselves. We adhere to the fixed standard, the Scriptures as interpreted by the consent of the whole Church, Catholic as well in time as in space. But this fixed standard is utterly incompatible with development. All sects, in the true sense of the word, have developed away from this standard. All "sectarianism," in the true sense of the word, is nothing but a development, which has introduced a new doctrine not conformed to this standard.—*True Catholic.*[2]

The passage here quoted, forms the conclusion of an article on "Sectarianism," in the April number of the *True Catholic* (a most respectable Episcopal Magazine published in Baltimore) which winds up with a short friendly notice of "what has been called the Mercersburg School."[3] We use it as a convenient occasion, for fixing attention on the true force of the question to which it refers.

1. [*MR* 1 (September 1849) 512–14.]
2. [Hugh Davey Evans, "Sectarianism," *True Catholic* 6 (April, 1849) 529–39.]
3. [Evans, "Sectarianism," 538.]

What is *historical* development? Not fact added to fact, or thought to thought, in an outward way. Still less movement from one position to another wholly new and different. But growth, evolution from within, organic expansion. All *life* implies such movement. History has no other sense. It is the revelation of an idea, or spiritual fact, in *time*; the very form, in which the original *wholeness* of such a fact is brought to pass, the only form in which it *can* come to pass.[4] So in the case of the single man. So in the case of every nation.[5] And shall we then hold the Church, the inmost sense of man's life, to be a dead outward *traditum*? God forbid. It is historical; not because it is the same thing forever, like a mountain or a sea; that would be the very opposite of history; but because it is the power of a divine fact, which is forever growing itself more and more into the consciousness, the interior life of the world (a process that implies new forms and stages of its apprehension continually) and which can never be complete till the whole thinking and working of humanity shall appear transfused with its glorious reconstructive power; something, God knows, to which even the Church itself, in its best and palmiest state, has never yet been able to attain.[6]

What do the friends of Christianity mean, when they deny development. Can they deny *change*? Not surely without the derision of all history itself. The Church of the fourth century is *not* one in form with that of the first; the Church of the sixteenth century again is different from both. Rome pretends the contrary, in her own favor. But the pretense is monstrous. What Protestant denomination, however, can carry through any similar plea? Is modern Presbyterianism identical with past Christianity, in all ages before the Reformation or in *any*? is modern Methodism? is modern Episcopacy? All intelligent and candid men know the contrary and are coming to confess it more and more. And what are we to say then of such change? Must it all be set down as apostacy[7] and corruption? Let those shoulder this dread alternative who see proper to do so. We gladly embrace for our part (as the only escape from it) the idea of organic development, by which, through all changes, we are allowed to believe the Church, *one*, holy, catholic and apostolical, from the beginning onward to the last

---

4. [Nevin intuited that life was a *process* in and of an *organism* before he came to Mercersburg: Layman, general introduction to *Born of Water*, MTSS 6:15–18. On the motif of "wholeness," see Nevin, "Catholic Unity," MTSS 5:114–21; Nevin, *The Church*, MTSS 5:142–44.]

5. [Nevin does not really explore the idea of development of nations in his discussions in these texts which are principally focused on the church. Nevin does speak briefly of America in historically developmental terms in "The Year 1848" (see MTSS 11:22–48) but spends more time on this in his unpublished lectures on the philosophy of history. As discussed in the general introduction, the full version is in the archives, while a greatly condensed version is in Appel, *Life*, 590–601. A slightly longer outline was published in the Franklin and Marshall *College Days* (Jan–Jun; Nov & Dec, 1873).]

6. [The thesis "it is the power of a divine fact" is fundamental to Nevin. It first became prominent in *Antichrist*, MTSS 5:179–84 and was most fully stated in Nevin, "Hodge on the Ephesians," MTSS 7:98–101.]

7. [This is Nevin's spelling. The editor will use the modern "apostasy" in his own comments.]

Document 1: Historical Development.

day.[8] Such development requires no "infallible earthly head"[9] for its direction and conduct; just as little as a living oak needs to be built up by line and compass. An outward authority of this sort, supposed to supersede the free working of the intelligence and will of the Church itself, would be the source of petrifaction and stagnation only, not of development. This implies freedom, ethical activity, life poised upon itself as a principle and centre.[10] It is just the stability system, which in every shape turns into mechanism and leads to popery.[11]

Christianity, it is true, has its "fixed standard" in the Bible. But the standard is not itself Christianity, the thing it is to try and measure. *That* is a divine fact, from Christ onward, out of the Bible and beyond it. The Bible is its norm. But what then? Must it be stationary, to be normal?[12] All life has its fixed norm, which, however, embraces it not as something fixed and at rest, but as a fact in motion, the succession of different states, and stages in time. Does the development of a plant, carry it "beyond its fixed standard"? The Bible is the fixed standard of Christianity, not as the whole depth and compass of its sense may be supposed to have been at hand in the consciousness of the Church from the beginning; for this has not been the case, and is very far from being the case even now; but as furnishing the divine mirror by which this sense is to be tried and recognized as true, through all stages of its growth into the actual life of humanity by the Church.[13] The piety of a child is very different from that of a full grown man; and yet the Bible is the *fixed* standard of the entire *movement*, by which the first gradually ripens into the second.

"What has become of Revelation?" *Can* a revelation, we ask in return, be really in the world as a *mere* outward authority, be it living pope or dead book of whatever name; but to be so in any real sense *must* it not, along with the letter, enter into the actual consciousness of the world also, the very process of its inward being, as "spirit and life"? And how is this to be effected save in a *human* way, or through a mighty process of history, by which ages shall be required to evolve into full apprehension and power, the vast interior fulness of the Christian principle, the "great and wide sea" of truth that lies before us in the Bible? Surely to be *historical* at all, Christianity must be in the world under the form of history, which itself implies organic life and growth, and not with the form simply of Pompey's Pillar[14] or the Pyramids.

---

8. [See the general introduction for the emergence and changes in this "idea of organic development."]

9. [Addressing one of the key points that Hugh Davey Evans makes in the opening quote.]

10. [See Nevin's ethical theory in "Human Freedom," in MTSS 11:54–74.]

11. [Nevin had earlier mentioned the "stability system" in *Antichrist*, MTSS 5:190n20.]

12. [Nevin here means "normal" in the sense of "being a norm."]

13. [Nevin explores this more in the second essay of "Early Christianity" in this volume (77–90).]

14. [A 67-foot-high pillar in Alexandria, Egypt. It was erected to celebrate a triumph, not by Pompey, but by Diocletian over an Alexandrian revolt in AD 297.]

Document 2

"Early Christianity"

Editor's Introduction

The three essays that comprise "Early Christianity" were written a few months after the publication of "The Anglican Crisis."[1] Like many of Nevin's writings, this was connected to a specific event: the "Gorham Case." Rev. Gorham was examined for an appointment to a vicarage but was found wanting on the matter of baptismal regeneration. When his appointment was denied, he appealed to the Judicial Committee of the Privy Council, a secular arm of oversight, which upheld his right to the post.[2] Nevin reacts with astonishment and concern: are sacraments acts of real supernatural power? Is the church itself a "supernatural constitution" to which one adheres in faith because it has been established and upheld by God?[3] As Nichols observed, this was not merely an *Anglican* crisis but "The Crisis of Protestantism."[4]

Already Nevin is laying out the alternatives, as if to sort them out in his own mind: 1. "giving up of the sacramental system altogether" which leads to "Baptistic Independency;" 2. "reconciliation . . . with Rome;" 3. "a new miraculous dispensation on the part of God himself . . . with fresh apostolical commission." If none of these are available, then the remaining possibility is "the idea of historical development" in which the contradictions between Catholicism and Protestantism are "surmount[ed]" with "true historical progress."[5] Here he utilizes Schaff's discussion of the movement of history under the rubric of the apostles Peter, Paul, and John.[6]

---

1. MR 3 (July 1851) 359–98; republished in MTSS 11:269–306.
2. *Dictionary of the Christian Church*, 692, 908.
3. Nevin, "The Anglican Crisis," MTSS 11:279–82, 286–88. "We must believe in a divine church, in order to believe in divine sacraments, or in a divine ministry under any form" (288).
4. Nichols, *Romanticism*, 197.
5. Nevin, "The Anglican Crisis," MTSS 11:303–6.
6. Schaff's theory is presented in *The Principle of Protestantism*, MTSS 3:189–91.

Document 2: "Early Christianity"

This crisis, and Nevin's (as usual) passionate thrashing out of the theological conundrums that arise from it, gives a partial explanation for "Early Christianity." What *is* the theological character of the early church? Is either evangelical Protestantism or Anglicanism consistent with it? Nevin was exploring the ancient church for the first time since he explored the eucharistic theology of the church fathers in *The Mystical Presence*.[7] Nevin's first source is a travel diary published by Leonard Bacon in *The Independent* and republished by the *American and Foreign Christian Union* in the summer of 1851. Bacon had traveled through Italy and France, commenting on the religious world that he found in these Catholic lands. Nevin also quotes extensively from Daniel Wilson's travel diary, published as *Travels on the Content of Europe . . . in the Summer of 1825*. These works, written by "Puritanizers"[8] (as Nevin thought of them), provide him with a context to explore the history of the early church. Both authors expressed surprise at the Christianity that they discovered in their travels. Especially important for Nevin is Wilson's "discovery" of the piety of Charles Borromeo, and his theological and Scriptural knowledge. Wilson exclaimed, "Oh if he had more fully studied and obeyed his Bible, and had read with honest candor the treatises of his great contemporaries, the reformers of Germany and Switzerland, he might perhaps have become the *Luther* or *Zuingle* [of Italy]."[9] The idea of a truly godly archbishop and the "idolatry" he found in the city of Milan, Borromeo's see, seem unreconcilable to Wilson. The Catholic character of Borromeo, rather than an anachronism, is in Nevin's mind the very life of piety that he and Schaff have been presenting to American readers since 1844. Borromeo—and church fathers like Ambrose and medieval divines like Anselm—can never be Protestantized. That is because there is no Protestantism in view in the history of the church that precedes them. The repristination argument, which Nevin and Schaff have decried as the basis for what they called pseudo-Protestantism,[10] will not stand up to the history of early Christianity. The rest of the first essay attempts to show this through a survey of the third, fourth, and fifth centuries. Nevin concludes that "the fathers of the fourth and fifth centuries were not Protestants of either the Anglican or the Puritan school."[11] Were they transplanted in time to the future, they would find themselves lost in the churches of modern Protestantism.

Nevin begins the second essay with a summary of the Puritan theory of what early Christianity should have been like if their historiography was correct. He observes, "There was no papacy, no episcopacy, no priesthood, no thought of a supernatural virtue in baptism, no dream of anything like the mystery of the real presence in the

---

7. MTSS 1:111–22.

8. Nevin's most succinct statement of the "Puritanism" he has in view here is "Evangelical Radicalism," MTSS 11:310–14. Note the distinction made in p. 313n11.

9. Below, 53.

10. Schaff, *What is Church History?*, MTSS 3:295, 298; Nevin, "Pseudo-Protestantism." DeBie summarizes the latter series in *John Williamson Nevin*, 160–61.

11. Below, 70.

awful sacrament of the altar."[12] How then does one explain the Christian practice of the Middle Ages? For the Puritanizers the answer is apostasy.[13] Nevin's goal in this essay is to "explode" this argument by considering the facts of history. Nevin's argument is simple in its goal, but complex in its formulation. Both sides agree that by the fourth century, the church was different than the Puritanistic model of the church. Is this discrepancy best explained by apostasy or a historical trajectory? Nevin's argument begins with an explication of the implications of Matthew 16:18 and 28:18–20.[14] If these passages are indeed the promise of Christ, they seem to imply that "the church should endure on its first foundation, that is with true historical succession from its own beginning, through all ages."[15] The Puritan idea of an apostatized church is therefore at war not just with history but with Scripture itself. To claim that the promises of Christ have been fulfilled through various schismatic sects is to deny the reality of an historic, catholic church. The church then loses any claim to visibility and can only be an invisible, individualistic reality.[16] The implications of this claim leave no hope for Protestantism to be anything other than a Christianity which is *sui generis*[17] with early Christianity. He writes, "But give up the historical succession, by taking the ground that the church had failed for a thousand years, except among sects from which it is notorious Protestantism did *not* spring," and one will be left with the claim that "the Reformation was in truth a new setting up of Christianity parallel with its first setting up by the Apostles."[18] In the latter case, the Reformation would have needed miracles to confirm its *de novo* divine commissioning. This is something that the Reformers never claimed for themselves.[19] It also means that modern Christians—if consistent with their historical theory—should have no faith in the decisions of the church of the

---

12. Below, 72.

13. Nineteenth-century writers, including Nevin, spell this "apostacy."

14. This is not new territory for Nevin. In *The Church*, Nevin gives one of the marks of the church as being "*historical*." "Once in the world by Jesus Christ, [the Church of the Creed] must continue to be in the world always to the end of time. To suppose a chasm in its continuance at any point, is in fact to overthrow its existence altogether. Nor will it do, to talk of its being present at times, in a merely invisible way" (MTSS 5:153, emphasis original). See also Nevin, translator's introduction to Schaff's *Principle*, MTSS 3:50–55.

15. Below, 78.

16. James Good, in his critique of "Nevinism," says Nevin makes two errors: he rejects "[t]he old Reformed view," which "was to leap over the Middle Ages" and make "the Reformation a return to the Apostolic Church." In its place Nevin claimed that Protestantism "developed" out of Roman Catholicism. Good, *History*, 314. (In attacking Nevin, Good ignores the role of Schaff in bringing this theory to Nevin.) The solution for Good is historical succession through the invisible church of the Middle Ages. Good relies upon the biblical imagery of leaven; however, in the end, he appeals to medieval sects as an example of how this leavening of the invisible church was to find fruition in the Reformers.

17. Literally, "of its own kind."

18. Below, 82, emphasis original.

19. See for instance, Calvin's discussion in the "Prefatory Address" to the *Institutes*, 1:15–16. Calvin gives reasons why the Protestant church does not have to provide proofs of her origin—such as miracles—because it does not claim to be a new church.

Document 2: "Early Christianity"

fourth and fifth centuries. The doctrine of the Trinity, the formation of the canon, the key Christological formulations are all to be questioned if the Puritan idea of apostasy is allowed to stand. There is also no history of the great martyrs and no global mission of the church in its earliest expansions that the Puritan can claim as his own. All Christian history between the apostolic era and the Reformation is sacrificed on the altar of a historiography which sees only apostasy.

In contrast, Nevin gives his own historical survey of early Christianity. Allowing the ancient fathers to speak for themselves, and quoting extensively from the primary literature he had available, he concludes that post-apostolic Christianity was not identical to Puritanism—certainly not in the version predominant in New England.[20] Nevin identifies six ways in which Puritanism differs from early Christianity: its failure to understand the church as an object of faith, its misunderstanding of the relationship between the people and the ministry, its denial of the true nature of the sacraments, its rejection of the rule of faith and the system of doctrine which springs from it, and its failure to have faith in the continuing reality of miracles.

With this tour de force of history complete, Nevin sets the stage for the final essay where he asks, how should we justify Protestantism in light of this history? He begins by interacting with critiques of his first essays. Nevin's basic rejoinder is that it does not matter whether what he has written is theologically true, but whether it is historically true. Nevin's pen is especially sharp when he challenges his interlocutors to demonstrate that his historical survey is incorrect, flawed, or lacking in proper conclusions. His challengers' "want of anything like true scholarship" is evident to Nevin because they are challenging his historical facts with theological convictions. In these essays, Nevin is not seeking to demonstrate what was theologically right or wrong about early Christianity. He is not attempting to provide a way of understanding history through a theological lens—he accuses his interlocutors of doing *that*. Rather, he wants to allow the voices of the past to speak in their own language and idioms. Thus, Nevin will say repeatedly that he is only presenting the facts of the historical record.[21] As much as the Puritan historical method might like history to be other than it is, Nevin insists that the facts of history are clear: the fathers of the third, fourth, and fifth centuries, including Augustine, were more Catholic than Protestant. Rewrite history if it pleases you, says Nevin, but do not pretend the historical data are not what they are.

---

20. Below, 114–16.

21. For Nevin to say he was merely presenting "facts" is to deny that he is in fact working as an historian. Nevin's historiography, and German historiography in general, does a better job of explaining the details of the historical record. But to say that the Puritans were ignoring the facts to simply make history say whatever they wanted seems heavy-handed. We can perhaps understand Nevin's vitriol because the Puritan historiography was blind to its own inadequacies. This can be seen with Joseph Berg and his complaints about the Mercersburg divines. See Bain and Trost, general introduction to Schaff, *Development*, MTSS 3:16–21 for a good summary of how this same issue impacted Nevin's colleague, Philip Schaff. A broader discussion of the conflict between Mercersburg and its "Puritan" opponents can be found in Good, *History*, 286–321 (from an anti-Mercersburg historian) and Shriver, "Philip Schaff: Heresy at Mercersburg."

The third essay spends most of its time in surveying English and German scholarship on the nature of Christianity in the earliest centuries of the church. He begins with Isaac Taylor's *Ancient Christianity*.[22] He uses Taylor to support his argument that the claim there was an idyllic Puritan period is not borne out by the facts of history. He similarly challenges the Anglican claim that *it* is in continuity with the church through the Nicene period. Anglicanism would lay claim to the necessity of bishops, and the early decisions of the ecumenical councils, but then dismiss the later church as corrupted by the papacy. Nevin attempts to cut the ground out from under both positions. History, when considered in its entirety, demonstrates that "the church, from the time it first comes into notice, to have been plainly committed to the cause of things that led onward directly to the Nicene system."[23]

The end of the third essay is Nevin's discussion of historical development as a way of solving the dilemma of the history he has presented to this point. If early Christianity is as Nevin has expressed, and if the idea of repristination is rejected, how then does one get from the fourth century to the Reformation? And beyond that, how does one get to the modern period in a way that is more than simply seeing history as events that happened in the past? If there is no substantive connection between the ancient church and the Reformation, then in Nevin's mind there is no hope for the modern church. There must be some kind of development in place to address this dilemma. Two noteworthy representatives of the historical development theory are John Henry Newman[24] and Nevin's colleague, Philip Schaff.[25] These two represent, respectively, the English and German systems of the science of history.[26]

---

22. Taylor (1787–1865) was the scion of an artistic and literary family. He began to read the writings of the church fathers in his twenties, and "is said to have coined the word patristic." In response to the Oxford Movement, he argued in *Ancient Christianity, and the Doctrines of the Oxford 'Tracts for the Times'* (1839–40) that "Puseyite doctrine was already permeated with all the errors and superstitions of the middle ages." Schnorrenberg, "Taylor, Isaac," 911–13. In the texts below, it will appear strange for Nevin to be quoting Taylor *ad nauseum*, who viewed the patristic church and piety so negatively. Nevin clarified his attitude a year later: "Much as we dislike the theological animus that reigns in it, its simply historical positions . . . are of unanswerable force" ("Anti-Creed Heresy," MTSS 8:202). It was Taylor's interpretation that the Nicene period led ineluctably to the later church. So Nevin will use these "facts" to say that just as one could not return to a "pure" apostolic church, one could not bring back an ideal Nicene Christianity.]

23. Below, 137.

24. Newman's 1845 edition of *An Essay on the Development of Doctrine* was written to discuss how the Church moved and developed from the first centuries of her history. Newman uses seven tests (in the 1878 edition he called them notes) to demonstrate legitimate changes (developments) versus illegitimate (corruptions). Before the publication of the 1845 *Essay*, Newman converted from Anglicanism to Catholicism.

25. Schaff represents the German idea of development which sees Protestantism as a growth out of late medieval Catholicism. See esp. Schaff's *Principle*, MTSS 3:63–75 (the historical preconditions that made the Reformation possible) and 75–116 (how Protestantism fulfilled those preconditions).

26. John Payne, "Schaff and Nevin," 182, gives a helpful summary: "Newman's theory posited a continuous and regular growth without violence or contradiction," while the "German theory . . . took into account opposing forces at work, separately for a time, before issuing in a higher unity."

Document 2: "Early Christianity"

Nevin also describes the theories of H. W. J. Thiersch[27] and Richard Rothe.[28] Thiersch presents history in terms of epochs with each epoch ending in a great metamorphosis, which leads into the next age. Each successive age is moving the church toward its consummative ideal. However, the ideal will only be reached through a "miraculous dispensation."[29] Rothe presents development in terms of the forward transformative movement of humanity.[30] Protestantism is a movement out of the old Catholic ecclesial understanding, ultimately resolving the church into the state: "The last and authentic goal of Christ's activity was and is—not a Christian Church but a Christian world."[31] Nevin rejects Rothe's theory as "unsound,"[32] and is skeptical of Thiersch.[33]

In any case, for Protestantism to be legitimate, Puritan historiography must be abandoned and historical catholicity must be maintained. There are three possible paths through which the contradictions of Catholicism and Protestantism can be transcended. First, Protestantism can absorb the life of Catholicism into its own ecclesial life. Second, Protestantism and Catholicism can be seen in terms of an Hegelian tension in which a higher synthesis of the two is created. The third option is a Protestantism that is performing a necessary reform of Catholicism and will eventually be united with it to fulfill the church's mission in the plan of God. Which of these is the best way to understand historical catholicity, Nevin is reluctant to stake a claim.[34] What is necessary is some historical connection between the Catholicism of early Christianity and Protestantism in the modern period. Nevin's purpose in "Early Christianity" can be characterized as a quest for this historical catholicity.

---

27. Heinrich Thiersch (1817–85) rose to the professorship of theology at Marburg but resigned because he "sincerely believed that the Lord had restored the apostolic office and the prophetic gifts of the Apostolic Church in the Irvingite community." David Schaff, "Thiersch, Heinrich Wilhelm Josias," 415–16. Irvingism, or the Catholic Apostolic Church, integrated traditional Christian liturgies and what would now be called "charismatic" phenomena. Its liturgy was a significant resource for the Provisional Liturgy of the German Reformed Church: Maxwell, *Worship and Reformed Theology*, 425–66.

28. Richard Rothe (1799–1867), theologian at Heidelberg. He thought that Christianity "has for its goal the consummation of the kingdom of God on earth." But since "the State ... is the actual realization of all moral life, ... the kingdom of God on earth can present itself only in the form of a perfected state or organism of states, wherefore the Church becomes gradually superfluous." Sieffert, "Richard Rothe," 102. In spite of Nevin's rejection of Rothe here, Rothe's doctrine of revelation had a significant impact on Nevin later in life: editorial introduction to Nevin, "Bread of Life," MTSS 6:214–15.

29. Below, 152. Thiersch came to believe this new dispensation had appeared in the Catholic Apostolic Church.

30. Rothe, *Theologische Ethik* and *Die Anfänge der christlichen Kirche und ihre Verfassung*.

31. Barth, *Protestant Theology in the Nineteenth Century*, 603.

32. Below, 154.

33. Recall that in "Anglican Crisis," a new dispensation ratified by miracles is one of the options *in addition* to historical development (MTSS 11:303). Thus, Thiersch's explanation of religious change is not Nevin's preferred alternative.

34. Besides Payne, "Schaff and Nevin," a good study of the options at the end of "Early Christianity" is Black, "A 'Vast Practical Embarrassment,'" 277–79.

Early Christianity[: First Article].[1]

[American Puritanism in Catholic Europe]

In an interesting letter of the Rev. Dr. Bacon,[2] written recently from Lyons in France and published in the N. Y. "Independent" and the "American and Foreign Christian Union," we meet with the following passages referring to the present and past religious character of that ancient and venerable city.

> Before I left home I resolved that, if it were possible, I would visit Lyons in my travels, and see for myself what *God* has wrought there for the revival and advancement of true religion. That city, as you know, is the centre of a great and powerful organization for the propagation of the Roman Catholic faith—an organization second only to the Propaganda at Rome in the extent of its missions and the amount of its resources. In that city, too, the Roman Catholic religion is more flourishing, with the indications of living zeal, and more deeply seated in the affections of the people, than in any other city on the continent of Europe. The fact, then, so often reported to us, that there a Protestant Evangelical Church has been gathered, and that in the midst of such a population evangelical labors have been crowned with signal success, is a fact which the Christian traveler may well turn aside to see.
>
> [. . .]
>
> Ever since my childhood the name of Lyons has been associated in my thoughts, with the faith and patience of the saints who suffered there as witnesses for *Christ* in the second century. The story of the sufferings and constancy of Pothinus, Blandina, Perpetua,[3] and others, is upon record in the epistle from the Christians of Lyons and Vienne, to their brethren in Asia Minor, with whom they appear to have been closely connected—a document which is familiar to the readers of Milner's Church History,[4] and which is

---

1. [*MR* 3 (September 1851) 461–90.]

2. [Rev. Leonard Bacon (1802–81), Congregational pastor and professor at Yale College and founder and editor of *The Independent*. He was an abolitionist and was famous for his travel diaries, one of which Nevin quotes here.]

3. [Pothinus (c. 87–177), Bishop of Lyons, martyred in AD 177, along with Blandina, a slave girl; Perpetua, martyred in Africa, March 7, 203.]

4. [Joseph Milner (1744–97), *History of the Church*, 1:245–60. For a contemporary discussion of

Document 2: Early Christianity[: First Article].

among the earliest and most authentic remains of Christian antiquity. It was an interesting thought that I was now for the first time upon ground that had been consecrated by the struggle of primitive Christianity, and watered with the blood of martyrs, some of whom had looked upon the faces of *Christ's* immediate followers. And now, among the 200,000 inhabitants of Lyons, are there any living remains of the Gospel for which the primitive martyrs suffered, and which gave them the victory? The archbishop of Lyons and Vienne is honored by the Roman Catholic Church as the successor of Pothinus and St. Irenaeus;[5] but how slight the resemblance between the pompous and showy worship now performed under the roof of that old cathedral, and the simple prayers and songs of the few disciples who were wont to meet here in some obscure chamber "with their bishops and deacons," seventeen hundred years ago. Where are the successors of those primitive Christians?

It was with such thoughts that I went forth on the morning of the Lord's day to find the Evangelical Chapel in the *Rue de I Arbre Sec*. I looked in at the cathedral and at other churches, splendid with pictures and images, as I past by, and beheld their devotions; and it seemed to me that the city could hardly have been more given to idolatry in the palmy days of Pagan Rome, than it is at this day. In these magnificent structures the Christian traveler looks in vain for anything like what he has learned from the New Testament. The worship, instead of being offered exclusively and directly in *Christ's* name to the one living and true *God*, is offered to deified mortals, and chiefly to Mary, "the mother of *God*."[6] Instead of being addressed only to an invisible God, who is a spirit, and who must be worshipped in spirit and in truth, it is offered to images and pictures (and those, for the most part, of no superior description) and to dead men's bones. Not in such places, nor where such worship is offered, are we to look for the true succession from the apostles and primitive martyrs, the true Catholic Church, which is the body of *Christ*.[7]

---

the reception, printing history, and a reconsideration of Milner's historical methodology, see Gutacker, "Joseph Milner."]

5. [Irenaeus (c. 130–202), Bishop of Lyons, successor to Pothinus. He is well-known for his attack on Gnosticism and is considered to be one of the last people with a living connection to an apostle, St. John, via Polycarp. He was made a doctor of the Church by Pope Francis in January, 2022.]

6. ["Mother of God" is a translation of the Greek word *theotokos*. The idea of Mary as the "mother of God" was a key part of the Christological discussions of the fifth century between Nestorianism and Eutychianism. Nestorianism held that the "Incarnate Christ" was "two separate persons" (*Dictionary of the Christian Church*, 287–91). This implied that Jesus Christ as born of Mary was not fully God and therefore Mary was not "Mother of God." Eutyches overreacted by denying not only two persons, but teaching that Christ only had one nature. The orthodox formulation came to be that Jesus Christ is one person, the Word, in two natures, divine and human. See the extended note in Nevin et al., *Born of Water*, 148–49n41. The Council of Ephesus (AD 431) officially declared the Virgin Mary to be *Theotokos*.]

7. ["Evangelical Religion in Lyons, France," *American and Foreign Christian Union* 2 (July 1851) 230, 231–32.]

Dr. Bacon's letter is addressed to an Association of Benevolent Ladies in New Haven, whose contributions have gone for a number of years past, through the Foreign Evangelical Society, (now the Am. and For. Chr. Union)[8] towards the support of an evangelical missionary in Lyons. In that city, containing with its immediate environs at least 300,000 inhabitants—next to Paris, the most populous and influential city of France—the great centre of Papal influence—the truth, according to Dr. Baird, has made greater progress within the last twenty years than in any other city of the same country.

> The work began in 1825, or even earlier, in the efforts of a pious Swiss Protestant shoemaker. In the humble apartment of this poor man little meetings were held for reading the Scriptures and prayer. It was at these meetings, we believe, that Mr. Moureton, the brave grenadier of Napoleon, (who was in the battle of Leipsic,[9] and several others in the later years of the reign of that wonderful man) was converted.[10]

There was of course a considerable body of Protestantism there before; but this unfortunately had ceased to be evangelical; like the Protestantism of France generally had glided into dead rationalistic formality. The church here noticed is a wholly new and independent movement. The pious grenadier, Mr. Moureton, in the capacity of a deacon and colporteur, has done much to promote it for a series of years by his labors among the laboring population of Lyons and its suburbs. The Rev. Adolphe Monod,[11] settled as one of the pastors of the regular Protestant church in 1829, was soon after "brought to the saving knowledge of Christ, and began to preach the true Gospel with great zeal and power;"[12] the result of which was, that the worldly-minded consistory of the church took offence, and soon after deposed him from his office. In this way he became the head of the small evangelical interest just noticed, which now assumed the character of a separate church, and has since grown into its present importance. It is remarkable however, that this improved Protestantism has derived but little of its material from the ranks of the old Protestantism.

> Mr. Monod soon found that the new church was to be increased not so much by bringing back the degenerate Protestants from their rationalism to the simplicity of the gospel, as by conversions from among the Roman Catholics. Thus his enterprise became from the outset a work of evangelism among the manufacturing population of the city and its crowded suburbs. Into that field of labor he entered with great zeal and great success. And when, on the

---

8. [American and Foreign Christian Union.]
9. [The Battle of Leipzig, October 16–19, 1813.]
10. ["Evangelical Religion," 229.]
11. [Adolphe-Louis-Frédéric-Théodore Monod (1802–56).]
12. ["Evangelical Religion," 229.]

Document 2: Early Christianity[: First Article].

removal of Mr. Monod to Paris a few years ago, he was succeeded by Mr. Fisch, the work went on with undiminished prosperity[.][13]

—that is, the work of turning Catholics into a much better sort of Protestants than could be made generally from the Protestant body itself. Dr. Bacon describes the congregation as very plain, made up for the most part of common laboring people of the lower class, but still as much resembling in its intelligent appearance and simple worship what he had been accustomed to in Puritan America; so that he felt himself, stranger though he was, among brethren of the same household of faith. In the afternoon, he attended a meeting of the brotherhood for mutual conference and inquiry.

> It was held in a school-room, and very much resembled a Congregational church meeting in New England. There was however one obvious difference. Those brethren were not merely concerned with the working of a system defined and understood in all its details, and familiar to them from their childhood. With the New Testament in their hands, they were inquiring after principles and rules of church order; and the question which then chiefly occupied their attention, and seemed somewhat to divide their opinions, was whether the government of their church should be in part committed to a body of elders, or retained entire in the hands of the assembled brethren. As I listened to the discussion, I could not but admire the free and manly yet fraternal spirit in which it was conducted. And as I saw what a school for the development of various intellectual gifts as well as for the culture of Christian affection, that church had been under its simple democratic organization, I felt quite sure that those brethren, with all their confidence in their teachers, would not be easily persuaded to subvert a system to which they were already so greatly indebted, or to divest themselves of the right of freely debating and voting on all their interests and duties as a church.[14]

The letter states, that there are now in the city and suburbs four chapels, in addition to the mother church, one with a distinct pastor the other three missionary preaching places—that four ministers, several evangelists and a number of colporteurs, are constantly employed—that the total number of communicants in 1850 was 440, while about 2500 persons were more or less directly connected with the evangelical community; whereupon the excellent and much respected writer concludes:

> I think that in these facts the ladies who formerly contributed to aid the good work at Lyons, will find evidence that their cooperation was not in vain. Rarely have I enjoyed anything more than I enjoyed my visit to that missionary and apostolical church. Nor do I know where to look for a more-satisfactory representation of the ideal of primitive Christianity than may be found in the city

---

13. ["Evangelical Religion," 265.]
14. ["Evangelical Religion," 233.]

which was made illustrious so long ago by the labors of Irenæus, and by the martyrdom of Pothinus and Blandina.[15]

In reading this, we were reminded of certain notices of the same place, in somewhat similar style, from the pen of the Rev. Daniel Wilson [1778–1858], (then of Islington, but better known since as Bishop of Calcutta) in his work entitled "Travels on the Continent of Europe in the Summer of 1823;"[16] as also of certain parallel passages in the same work, relating to the early and later Christianity of the celebrated city of Milan. Take in the case of Lyons the following extracts:

> This morning I have visited St. Irenée, the site of the ancient city, though now only a suburb. I here visited the Roman baths at the Ursuline Monastery (formerly so, for all the monasteries and convents were abolished at the Revolution.) These baths consist of a series of numerous dark vaults, communicating with each other, about twenty feet under ground; but no longer interesting, except from their antiquity. I then went to what was the garden of the Minimes, and saw the remains of the Roman Amphitheatre, where the early Christians were exposed to the wild beasts. This scene affected me extremely. The form of the Amphitheatre remains, after a lapse of sixteen or seventeen centuries. Some traces may be discovered of the rising seats of turf, and several dilapidated brick vaults seem to indicate the places where the wild beasts, and perhaps the holy martyrs, were guarded. It is capable of holding an immense assemblage—perhaps 30 or 40,000 persons. A still more elevated range of seats, to which you ascend by decayed stone steps, seem to have been the place allotted for the magistrates and regulators of the barbarous shows. A peaceful vineyard now flourishes where these scenes of horror once reigned. The tender garden shrub springs in the seats and vaults. The undisturbed wild flowers perfume the air. A stranger now and then visits the spot, and calmly inquires if that was the Amphitheatre which once filled all Christendom with lamentation. What a monster is persecution, whether Pagan, Popish, or Protestant! And yet, till the beginning of the last century, it was hardly banished from the general habits of Europe. Would to God that even now it could be said to be utterly rooted out!
>
> I visited, after this, the church of St. Irenée, built in the time of the Romans, when the liberty of public worship was refused the Christians. It is subterraneous, and contains the bones of the many thousand Christians who were martyred in the year 202, under the emperor Severus. It is of this noble army of martyrs that Milner gives such an affecting account. An inscription

---

15. ["Evangelical Religion," 266.]

16. [Daniel Wilson, *Travels on the Continent of Europe; . . . in the Summer of 1823*, 4th London ed., in *The Christian Library: A Reprint of Popular Religious Works*, vol. 7 (New York: Thomas George Jr., 1836). Wilson became "the leading Evangelical clergyman" in London. He was called to the post of Bishop of Calcutta in 1832 and continued his criticisms of Tractarianism while serving in India. *Dictionary of the Christian Church*, 1751.]

Document 2: Early Christianity[: First Article].

on the church states, that St. Pothinus was sent by Polycarp,[17] and founded it; and was martyred under the emperor Antoninus;[18] that St. Irenæus succeeded him, and converted an infinite multitude of Pagans, and suffered martyrdom, together with nineteen thousand Christians, besides women and children, in the year 202; and that in the year 470, the church was beautified. I have not an exact recollection of what Milner says, and therefore may be wrong in giving credit to some of these particulars; but I have a strong impression that the main facts agree with the tradition on the spot; and I confess, I beheld the scene with veneration. I could almost forgive the processions which are twice in the year made to this sacred place, if it were not for the excessive ignorance and superstition attending them.

Near to this church are some fine remains of a Roman aqueduct, for conveying water to the city, built at the time of Julius Caesar. A convent of three hundred nuns has arisen since the peace, in the same place, of the order of St. Michel, where many younger daughters are sent from the best families, to be got out of the way, just the same as under the ancient regime. In saying this, I do not forget that the education in many of the convents is, in some respects, excellent, and that the larger number of young persons are placed there merely for a few years for that purpose. Still the whole system is decidedly bad, and unfriendly to the highest purposes of a generous education.[19]

[. . .]

Upon looking carefully into Milner's Ecclesiastical History,[20] since I came home, I find there were two early persecutions of the Christians at Vienne and Lyons (neighboring French towns,) one about the year of our Lord 169, under the emperor Marcus Antoninus;[21] the second under Septimus Severus, about the year 202.[22] The first of these is best known, and the accounts in Milner refer to it. The scene of its cruel executions was the Amphitheatre which I visited as I have above mentioned. The second is not so credibly attested, but at the same time may on the whole be believed to have taken place. The church of St. Irenée relates exclusively to it. Pothinus was bishop of Lyons during the first

---

17. [Polycarp (c. 69–155), Bishop of Smyrna; held by tradition to be a student of John the Apostle. One letter of his survives ("To the Philippians"). At his martyrdom, he was reportedly stabbed when the flames of his pyre did not consume him.]

18. [Antoninus Pius (86–161; reigned 138–61) is considered one of the five good emperors. His relations with Christians were a continuation of the policies of Trajan and Hadrian. His personal piety, especially to his predecessor, Hadrian, meant that confrontations with Christians, who refused to sacrifice to the emperor cult were likely to face persecution. However, no mass persecutions were perpetrated during his rule.]

19. [Wilson, *Travels*, 92–93.]

20. [Milner, *History of the Church*.]

21. [Marcus Aurelius (121–80; reigned 161–80) was the last of the Five Good Emperors. He is famous for his *Meditations*, an important text of Stoic philosophy.]

22. [Septimius Severus (145–211; reigned 193–211) came to power through battle, defeating Clodius Albinus, another claimant to the throne, at the Battle of Lugdunum.]

cruelties; he had been a disciple of the blessed Polycarp, the contemporary of the apostle John. He perished about the year 169, being upwards of ninety years of age; he had been sent, in all probability, by Polycarp from Smyrna to found these French churches; for the merchants of Smyrna and Lyons were the chief navigators of the Mediterranean sea. This could not be very long before the persecution burst out. He was accompanied in his apostolical labors by Irenæus, an Asiatic Greek also, who wrote the interesting and authentic account of the first acts of the martyrs, preserved by Eusebius,[23] and given so well by Milner. Irenæus succeeded Pothinus as bishop, and suffered martyrdom in the persecution of 202.[24]

The animus of the writer in all this, the inward posture with which he looks upon the past and its relation to the present, comes out more clearly in the notice he takes of Milan and its distinguished prelates St. Ambrose and St. Charles Borromeo.[25]

Sunday morning, Sept. 14.—This is one of my melancholy Sundays. An immense Catholic town of one hundred and fifty thousand souls—the ecclesiastical apparatus enormous; about two hundred churches, eighty convents, and one hundred religious houses—compare this with the Protestant establishment of Birmingham or Manchester, which fall as far short of what such a crowded population fairly demands, as the Milan establishment exceeds it. We might surely learn something in England of the duty of greater zeal and attention to our pure form of Christianity, from the excessive diligence of the Catholics in their corrupt superstitions.

I feel a peculiar veneration for Milan on two accounts: St. Ambrose, whom Milner dwells on with such commendations, was the light of this city in the fourth century; Carlo Borromeo, whose benevolence exceeds all description, was archbishop here in the sixteenth. This last I know at present little of; but Ambrose was one of the most humble and spiritual of the fathers of the church, two or three centuries before Popery, properly speaking, began. In this city Ambrose preached: it was here Austin[26] heard him, attracted by the fame of his eloquence. It was here also, that Angilbertus,[27] bishop of Milan in the ninth century, refused to own the supremacy of the Pope; indeed, the church of Milan did not submit to the Roman see till two hundred years afterwards. May God raise up another Ambrose to purify and recall the city and churches, which he instructed thirteen or fourteen centuries ago! Nothing is impossible with God; but Popery seems to infatuate this people. On the church of Milan

---

23. [Eusebius Pamphilus (c. 260–340), bishop of Caesarea; known as the father of church history.]
24. [Wilson, *Travels*, 94.]
25. [Ambrose (c. 339–97), bishop of Milan; helped convert Augustine, and is a doctor of the Catholic Church. Charles Borromeo (1538–84), Archbishop of Milan; leader of the Counter Reformation, canonized in 1610.]
26. [Nevin's source certainly intended "Augustine."]
27. [Angilbert II, Archbishop of Milan from 824–59.]

Document 2: Early Christianity[: First Article].

notices are affixed, that whoever causes a mass to be said there, may deliver any one he chooses from purgatory. In the mean time, this debasing superstition goes hand in hand with secret infidelity and unblushing vice.[28]

[. . .]

St. Ambrose died in the year 397, in the 57th year of his age, and the 23d of his episcopate. He has been charged with leaning too much towards the incipient superstitions of his day, and thus unconsciously of helping forward the growth of monastic bondage and prelatical pride. Something of this charge may be true; but he lived and died firm and unbending in all the fundamentals of divine truth. He loved the Saviour. He depended on his merits only for justification. He relied on the illumination and grace of the Holy Spirit. He delighted in communion with God. A rich unction of godliness rests on his writings; and he was one of the most fervent, humble, laborious, and charitable of all Christian bishops.

[. . .]

I have witnessed to-day, with grief and indignation, all the superstitions of Popery in their full triumph. In other towns, the neighborhood of Protestantism has been some check on the display of idolatry; but here in Italy, where a Protestant is scarcely tolerated, except in the chapels of ambassadors, you see what things tend to; Popery has its unimpeded course; every thing follows the guidance and authority of the prevailing taste in religion.

At half-past ten this morning we went to the cathedral, where seats were obtained for us in the gallery near the altar. We saw the whole of the proceedings at High Mass—priests almost without end—incense—singing—music—processions—perpetual changes of dress—four persons with mitres, whom the people called the little bishops—a crowd of people coming in and going out, and staring around them; but not one prayer, nor one verse of the Holy Scriptures intelligible to the people, not even if they knew Latin; nor one word of a sermon; in short, it was nothing more nor less than a *Pagan show*.

We returned to our inn, and, after our English service, we went to see the catechising. This was founded by Borromeo, in the sixteenth century, and is one of the peculiarities of the diocese of Milan. The children meet in classes of ten or twenty, drawn up between the pillars of the vast cathedral, and separated from each other by curtains; the boys on one side, the girls on the other. In all the churches of the city there are classes also. Many grown people were mingled with the children. A priest, and sometimes a layman, sat in the midst of each class, and seemed to be explaining familiarly the Christian religion. The sight was quite interesting. Tables for learning to write were placed in different recesses. The children were exceedingly attentive. At the door of each school, the words, *pax vobis*, peace be unto you, were inscribed on a board; the names of the scholars were also on boards. Each school had a small pulpit, with a green cloth in front, bearing the Borromean motto, *Humilitas*.

---

28. [Wilson, *Travels*, 77–78.]

Now what can, in itself, be more excellent than all this? But mark the corruption of Popery: these poor children are all made members of a fraternity, and purchase indulgences for their sins by coming to school. A brief of the Pope, dated 1609,[29] affords a perpetual indulgence to the children in a sort of running lease of six thousand years, eight thousand years, &c., and these indulgences are applicable to the recovering of souls out of purgatory; the prayers also before school are full of error and idolatry. All this I saw with my own eyes and heard with my own ears; for I was curious to understand the bearings of these celebrated schools. Thus is the infant mind fettered and imprisoned.

Still I do not doubt that much good may be done on the whole—the Catholic catechisms contain the foundation of the Christian religion, a general view of Scripture history, explanations of the creation and redemption; of mankind, some good instructions on the moral law, sound statements on the divinity of Christ, and the Holy Trinity, some acknowledgments of the fall of man, and the necessity of the grace of God's Holy Spirit; with inculcations of repentance, contrition, humility, self-denial, watchfulness, and preparation for death and judgment. These catechisms are not brief summaries, but rather full explanations of religion; making up small volumes of fifty or more pages. In the frontispiece of the catechism for the diocese of Geneva is the following affecting sentence, under the figure of our Lord, "*Son amour et mon crime ont mis Jésus à mort*"[30]—a sentiment which cannot but produce good. Still all is wofully mixed up with superstition, and error, and human traditions; and the consequence of this mixture is, that vital truths are so associated in the mind, from early youth, with the follies of Popery, that even the most pious men of that communion do not enough distinguish between them. If you deny transubstantiation, they suppose you disbelieve the divinity of Christ; if you avow that you are not a Papist, they suppose that you are a heretic, and have renounced the faith, &c. It was thus that such eminent Christians as Pascal, Nicole, Quesnel, Fénélon,[31] and the great men of the Jansenist school, lived and died in the church of Rome.[32] "A voluntary humility," as well as the

---

29. [The exact "brief" that is being referred to here is unclear. The pope at the time, Paul V, was responsible for completing the work on St. Peter's Basilica.]

30. [Trans. "His love and my crime put Jesus to death."]

31. [Blaise Pascal (1623–62), the best known of the Jansenists (see next note), was a scientist and an apologist for the Christian faith; his most-remembered work is *Pensées*. Pierre Nicole (1625–95) and Pasquier Quesnel (1634–1719) were also involved in the Jansenist controversy. Francois Fénélon (1651–1715) defended the "Quietism" of Mme. Guyon and the teaching of "disinterested love"; when his book was put on the Index, he submitted to the pope. He was archbishop of Chambrai.]

32. [Jansenism is named for Cornelius Jansen (1585–1638), the Bishop of Ypres. The movement began with the reading of Augustine's works by Jansen and his mentor, Jean du Vergier de Hauranne (1581–1643). Jansen's posthumously published book, *Augustinus*, was very popular among Catholics in Holland, Belgium, and France. It was condemned by Pope Urban VIII as heretical and placed on the Index. Jansenism emphasized Augustinian elements such as the efficacy of grace, predestination, and the total fallenness of the human will. The Jesuits, the Jansenists' chief antagonists, accused them of

Document 2: Early Christianity[: First Article].

"worshipping of angels,"—Coloss. ii. 18—may well be noted by St. Paul as an error, which ought zealously to be excluded from the Christian church.[33]

[...]

I was vexed on returning to England, and consulting my books, that I had been so long ignorant of the history and character of Borromeo. He is considered by the Roman Catholic writers as the model of all virtues, and the great restorer of ecclesiastical discipline in the sixteenth century. I have not been able to satisfy myself in what degree he was a true Christian, in the Scriptural sense of the word. That he was devoted to the superstitions of Popery, and was a firm upholder of the Roman see, cannot be doubted; but I have no access to his sermons or letters, so as to judge whether any living embers of the faith and love of Christ were smothered at the bottom of these superstitions. His habits of devotion, his self-denial, his zeal, his fortitude, his humility, and especially his unbounded and almost unparalleled benevolence, which are ascribed to him by universal consent, would lead one to hope that, notwithstanding "the wood, and hay, and stubble," accumulated on it, he was building on the true "foundation, Christ Jesus."—1 Cor. iii. 11, 12.

He was born at Arona in 1538, in a small apartment which I saw behind the church; and was of one of the noblest and most opulent families of Italy. At the age of eleven he had several livings given him by his uncle the Cardinal de Medicis, who was elected Pope in 1549.[34] In his twenty-third year he was created cardinal by the same pontiff, and managed the proceedings of the council of Trent, as well as the chief temporal affairs of the Pope, for some years. This I consider as by far the most unfavorable part of Borromeo's life, as to the cultivation of personal piety. Such employments at Rome must have initiated him into all the system of that artful and secular court—and he who was intrusted to draw up the Trent catechism, must at that time have had little real Christian knowledge or feeling. However, in 1565 he left Rome, and went to reside at Milan, of which he had been made archbishop.

Here begins the bright part of Borromeo's history. He had now to preside over the largest diocese of Italy, consisting of not less than eight hundred and fifty parishes, many of them in the wildest regions of the Alps. He began by resigning all his other preferments, by giving up to his family his chief estates, and by dividing the revenues of his archbishopric into three parts—one for the poor—another for the building and reparation of churches—the third for his domestic expenditure as bishop; all the accounts of which he submitted annually to the examination of his clergy. He next totally renounced the splendor

---

being Calvinists. The Jansenist positions were officially declared heresy by Innocent X in the apostolic constitution, *Cum Occasione* (1653).]

33. [Wilson, *Travels*, 79–80.]

34. [Pope Pius IV (1499–1565); papal dates 1559–65; he was the pope who presided over the close of the Council of Trent and implemented many lasting reforms that were needed in late medieval Catholicism.]

in which he had lived at Rome, reduced the number of his servants, forbade the use of silk garments in his palace, rendered his household a pattern of edification, slept himself on boards, prolonged his watchings and prayer to a late hour of the night, wore an under dress coarse and common, and devoted himself to perpetual fasts and abstinences.

He then entered on the task of restoring decayed discipline and order throughout his vast diocese. To this end he was indefatigable in visiting himself every parish under his care, held frequent ecclesiastical synods, and established a permanent council, which met monthly to inspect and regulate the conduct of the priests. In this manner his contemporaries agree in asserting, that he removed various scandals which prevailed amongst all classes of the faithful, abolished many superstitious usages, and checked the ignorance and abuses of the secular and regular clergy.

His fortitude in carrying through his reforms, notwithstanding the violent opposition which he met with from all quarters, deserves remark. On one occasion an assassin was hired, who shot at him, whilst kneeling in prayer, in the archiepiscopal palace. Borromeo, unmoved, continued his devotions; and, when he rose from his knees, the bullet, which had been aimed at his back, but had been caught in the lawn sleeves of his dress, fell at his feet.

His charities were unbounded. He built ten colleges, five hospitals, and schools and public fountains without number. Besides this, he bestowed annually the sum of thirty thousand crowns on the poor; and in various cases of public distress in the course of his life, as much as two hundred thousand crowns more.

In the meantime, his personal virtues, his lowliness, his self-command, his forgiveness of injuries, his temperance, his prudence, his sanctity, the consistency of his whole character (I speak after his biographers, whose veracity, I believe, is not questioned) gave him such weight, that he not only rendered his immense diocese a model of good order and discipline, after an anarchy of eighty years, during which its archbishops had not resided, but extended his influence over the neighboring dioceses, and pushed his regulations throughout a great part of France and Germany.

Perhaps his conduct during a pestilence which raged for six months at Milan is amongst the actions of his life which may lead one the most to hope that this benevolent and tender-hearted prelate was indeed animated with the fear and love of his Saviour. Nothing could restrain him from visiting his sick and dying flock, during the raging of this fatal malady: when his clergy entreated him to consult his own safety, he replied, that nothing more became a bishop than to face danger at the call of his duty. He was continually found in the most infected spots, administering consolation both to the bodies and souls of his perishing people; and he sold all the small remains of his ancient splendor, and even his bed, to give the produce to the distressed.

Document 2: Early Christianity[: First Article].

The institution, or rather invention of Sunday schools, is again a further evidence of something more than a superstitious state of heart. Nothing could be so novel as such institutions in the sixteenth century, and nothing so beneficial. When we recollect the public admiration which has rested on such schools in our own Protestant and enlightened country, though planned scarcely fifty years back, we may estimate the piety of mind, the vigor and penetration of judgment, which could lead a Catholic archbishop and cardinal to institute them two hundred years ago, and to place them on a footing which has continued to the present day. May I not add, that possibly some of the superstitious usages now attached to these schools may have grown up since the time of Borromeo. Certainly the indulgences which I saw were of the date of 1609, five-and-twenty years after his death; for the reader must be informed that, in the year 1584, this benevolent bishop fell a victim to fever caught in the mountainous parishes of his diocese, which he was visiting in his usual course.

As a preacher he was most laborious. Though he had an impediment in his speech, and a difficulty in finding words to express readily his meaning, he overcame these hindrances, and preached most assiduously on Sundays and festivals at Milan. His biographers say, that the higher classes in the city were offended with him, and did not frequent his sermons; but that the common people flocked with eagerness to hear him. Perhaps something of what the Apostle calls "the offence of the cross," may be traced in this. It does not at all lessen my hope of Borromeo's piety, that the rich and great did not follow him.

Such is a faint sketch of some of the chief events in the life of Charles Borromeo. My materials are scanty, especially as to the spiritual state of his heart and affections. It is for God only to judge on this subject: but charity rejoices to hope all things in such a case. I acknowledge that his simple and sublime motto, *Humilitas*, is very affecting to my mind. I trust it was the expression of his real character; and that his submission to the usurpations of the Romish church may have arisen from that faulty prostration of the understanding to human authority, which is so apt to engraft itself, under circumstances like those of Borromeo, on scriptural lowliness of spirit. Oh, if he had more fully studied and obeyed his Bible, and had read with honest candor the treatise of his great contemporaries, the reformers of Germany and Switzerland, he might, perhaps, have become the *Luther* or *Zuingle* [Zwingli], instead of, what he actually was, only the *Fenelon* of Italy.[35]

The reference made in the foregoing extract to *indulgences* shows the writer, with all his education, to be one of those who stick in the vulgar notion still of this doctrine, and in spite of all evidence to the contrary insist on forcing upon the Roman church an abomination here which she continually disowns.

The idea of an indulgence to commit sin, a license in form to do wrong, is a pure fiction got up by the seething brain of fanaticism to make Popery odious; and is just as

---

35. [Wilson, *Travels*, 85–86. See above on Fénélon.]

little entitled to regard at best, as the charge brought against Presbyterians for instance of holding and teaching, that there are infants in hell not a span long. An indulgence has not even the force of a pardon for past sin, however repented of truly by the sinner. It is a wholly different conception, which we have no right to drag hither and thither to suit our own prejudice, but are bound in common honesty, if we must oppose it, to understand and handle at all events in the sense of its own system, and not in another sense.

[Anti-Catholicism and the American Sect Spirit]

One can hardly help feeling somewhat amused with the evident embarrassment, in which the good vicar of Islington finds himself with his facts. He has in his mind a certain scheme of religion, what he conceives to be the clear sense of the Gospel in regard to this great interest, which is at war with the whole idea he has formed of Romanism; to such an extent, that he feels bound to think of this last only as a system of unmitigated abominations, a wholesale apostacy from the truth, and such a tissue of foolery and impiety in the name of religion as can scarcely be reconciled with the opinion, that there are any pious persons at all within its communion. He finds it a great deal easier to admit the true godliness of ten "witnesses" opposing the church in the middle ages, even though it should be among such a sect as the Albigenses,[36] than to be entirely satisfied with that of one only, quietly submitting to the authority of this church, believing in transubstantiation, and praying to saints and images, in its bosom. And still he is a good man, anxious to find his own ideal of evangelical piety as broadly as possible diffused in the history of the world, and cordially disposed to acknowledge and honor it wherever it comes in his way. With the instance of Ambrose, in the case before us, he can get along without any *very* serious difficulty, taking Milner's *Church History* for his guide, and holding fast always to the common Anglican theory of a marked distinction, between the Christianity of the first four or five centuries and that of the thousand years following. There are things hard to understand in the piety of Ambrose and Augustine, even as we have it portrayed to us in Milner; for which however an apology is found in the supposition, that standing as they did on the borders of the great apostacy which was to follow, they came accidentally here and there within the folds of its impending shadow, without still belonging to it properly in the substance of their faith. But the idea of any similar exhibition of apostolical religion from the same see of Milan, under the full-blown Papacy and in open communion with its

36. [The Albigenses were a heretical sect which began in the eleventh Century in Albi in Southern France. They taught a form of Manichaean dualism which said that there were two eternal principles of "good" and "evil." Evil in Manichaeanism is always associated with the material world. The Albigenses denied most of the Old Testament and thought Christ was an angel with a phantom body. They also denied the sacraments, especially the Eucharist. They were declared heretics at several Councils, including the Fourth Lateran Council (1215). The Dominican Order was created specifically to stamp out the heresy which was successful; by the fourteenth century there were none in Europe.]

corruptions—and all this too in the middle of the sixteenth century, and in the person of one who had been employed to draw up the Roman Catechism for the Council of Trent—was altogether another matter, and something not provided for plainly in any way by our tourist's previous theory. The good account he hears of St. Borromeo perplexes him. He finds it impossible to unite in his mind the image of a truly holy archbishop, such as he is described to have been, with the mummery and superstition of the modern Milan (a city wholly given to idolatry) which yet hardly could have been much better in the age of the Reformation, when presided over by this canonized man. Did he not hear the trumpet of the Reformation, giving no uncertain sound just over the Alps? And how then could he refuse to make common cause with it against Rome and the Pope? The bishop that was to be of Calcutta cannot understand it; but being, as we have said a good man, he makes it a point on his return home to look into the character of this same Borromeo, with such literary helps as he can find for this purpose; when, lo, to his own great surprise, not to say amiable confusion, it appears that there is no reason whatever to question the extraordinary sanctity of the man, so far as least as the outward show of consecration to works of piety is concerned. So the Rev. Daniel Wilson, in the exercise of that charity which hopeth all things and believeth all things [1 Cor 13:7], feels himself constrained to bear open testimony to its reality; the only question being still, whether the seeming sanctity after all had any proper root in the doctrine of justification by faith, the one great principle of religion in its true Protestant form. On this point a lingering doubt remains, which could be properly dissipated only by studying the character in question in the mirror of his own written thoughts; a privilege which our author had not still enjoyed when he first published his travels. Subsequently however it came in his way to look into the soul of the Catholic saint in this way; and now every doubt as to the genuineness of his piety was forced to retire; so that in the second edition of the same book, we have finally a free, full and altogether joyful acknowledgment of the fact, that in the person of Borromeo the Roman communion actually produced, so late as the 16th century, out of its own bosom and as it were in the very face of the Reformation itself, a veritable saint of like station and piety with the great St. Ambrose of the fourth century, and worthy even to be set in some sort of comparison with the Protestant saints, Zuingli, Luther, and Calvin. Under huge incrustations of Popish superstition, may be clearly traced still, in this extraordinary case, the lineaments of a truly evangelical faith, an actual diamond of grace, formed no one can tell how in the very heart of what might seem to be most fully at war with its whole nature. The case is set down accordingly as a sort of grand exception to common history, the next thing to a *lusus naturæ* [freak of nature] in the world of grace. Anselm, Bernard, Thomas a Kempis, Fenelon,[37] and a few other

---

37. [Anselm (c. 1033–1109); Archbishop of Canterbury, known for his *Cur Deus Homo* and the so-called ontological argument for the existence of God. Bernard of Clairvaux (1090–1153), known for his mysticism rather than his theological acumen, was made a doctor of the Catholic Church in 1830. Thomas à Kempis (c. 1380–1471); an ascetical writer most well-known for his *Imitation of the Life of Christ*. Fénélon was previously mentioned.]

like celebrities perhaps, names "*rari nantes in gurgite vasto*,"[38] are referred habitually to the same convenient category or rubric. They are spiritual curiosities, which no one should be expected fully to understand or explain.

In all this, however, we have two utterly false conceptions at work in the mind of the vicar of Islington himself. In the first place, his estimate of the extent to which real piety has existed in the Catholic church, both before the Reformation and since, is in no sort of agreement with the truth. In the second place, his imagination that this piety is in no sense the proper product of the Catholic religion as such, but something violently exceptional rather to its natural course, is not a whit less visionary and unsound.

Both these notions, we know, enter largely into our common Protestant thinking. But this does not make them right. They form in conjunction a mere blind prejudice, which like every other prejudice of this sort is sure to prove hurtful, in the end, to the cause it seems to favor and serve. Of all styles of upholding Protestantism, we may say, that is absolutely the worst, which can see no sense or truth whatever in Catholicism, but holds itself bound to make it at every point as bad as possible, and to fight off with tooth and nail every word that may be spoken in its praise. Such wholesale and extreme pugnacity, may be very convenient; as it calls for no discrimination, it requires of course neither learning nor thought, but can be played off under all circumstances, by almost any polemic, with about the same good effect. Its strength consists mainly in calling nick-names, in repeating outrageous charges without regard to any contradiction from the other side, in thrumming over threadbare commonplaces received by tradition from the easy credulity of times past, in huge exaggerations, and vast distortions, and bold insulting insinuations thrown out at random in any and every direction.[39] But however convenient all this may be, requiring little reading, and less

---

38. [Trans. "rare swimmers in the vast sea." This quote from Virgil's *Aeneid* 1:118 is generally used to mean that these are rare exemplars, though Virgil means to describe the survivors of a maelstrom.]

39. As a single exemplification, take the *Ladies'* petition got up a few months since for the Legislature of Pennsylvania, in the city of Philadelphia, under the auspices of the notorious Giustiniani, calling for the suppression of nunneries, under the gross insinuation of their being only seats of licentiousness and sin. [Louis Giustiniani was an itinerant anti-Catholic rabble-rouser who would "travel about with a troupe of Germans, {purportedly} 'converting' them to Protestantism in each city" (Billington, *Protestant Crusade*, 308). His anti-Catholic diatribes include *Intrigues of Jesuitism* and *Papal Rome As It Is*.] Strange "ladies" they must have been, that could lend their names to such an infamous libel on the purity of their own sex. The like insult directed towards the Episcopalians, Methodists or Presbyterians, would have at once drawn upon itself the angry frown of society, as a breach of all decency as well as charity. But as directed against the *Catholics* only, the blackguardism of the thing was generally not felt. Certain evangelical papers caught up even with great gusto, as a capital hit, the flying report that the Legislature had referred the petition to the Committee on Vice and Immorality. Now if any ground had ever been given for scandal in the history of American nunneries, one might have some patience with such ribald ruffianism, hiding its malignity under the cloak of religion. But what well informed person needs to be told, that every apology of this sort is wanting! All attempts yet made to blast the good name of these institutions among us, have recoiled with signal discomfiture on the heads of those who have acted as leaders in the vile crusade. It is enough to refer to Charlestown, Pittsburg, and Montreal—to the *memory* of Miss Reed, Dr. Brownlee and Maria Monk. [Rebecca

thought, and no politeness nor charity whatever, it is high time to see that it is a system of tactics, which needs in truth only a slight change of circumstances at any time to work just the opposite way from that in which it is meant to work. The vanity and impotency of it must become apparent, in proportion precisely as men are brought to look at things with their own eyes; and then the result is, that sensible and well-bred people, not those who go by the text book of a sect, but such as move in a wider range of thought and have some better knowledge of the world, political and literary men, seeing how they have been imposed upon by the current slang, are very apt to be taken with a sort of quiet disgust towards the whole interest which they find to be thus badly defended, and so to look favorably in the same measure on the other side, as being at so many points plainly an injured and persecuted cause. To make our opposition to Romanism of any weight, the first condition would seem to be clearly that we should have made ourselves acquainted with it on its own ground, that we should have taken some pains to learn from the system itself what it means and wills. But of all that army of Zealots, who hold themselves perfectly prepared to demolish it at a blow through the stage or press, how few are there probably who have ever felt it necessary to get their facts from other than the most common Protestant sources? Take indeed our ministers generally. Has one in fifty of them ever examined seriously a Catholic work of divinity, whether didactic, practical or historical? An ordinary anti-popery assault implies no preparation of this sort whatever; but rather a dogged purpose only, not to hear or believe a single word the Catholics say for themselves, while everything contrary to this is forced upon them from other quarters, as the voice and sense of their system. The sooner all such fanatical indecencies can be brought to an end, the better. They help not Protestantism, but serve only to involve it in reproach.

Reed (1813–38); raised in a New England Puritan home, she joined the Ursuline Convent due to her family's money problems. She eventually escaped and wrote *Six Months in a Convent*. This book fueled anti-Catholic sentiment and lead to riots against the Ursuline Convent, which was burned down. Maria Monk (1816–49), published *Awful Disclosures of Maria Monk or the Hidden Secrets of a Nun's Life in a Convent Exposed* (1836) which claimed rampant infanticide among the nuns and priests in Montreal. It was proved to be a fabrication shortly after it was published, but continued to be widely read and even translated into several languages. William Brownlee (1784–1860) was a well-known anti-Catholic nativist and early Monk supporter, although he later repudiated her.] On the other hand, the good works of these religious houses have been too manifold and plain in every direction, to be at all rationally called in question. Now in all seriousness we ask, what right in these circumstances have people pretending to be themselves respectable and pious, to vilify and calumniate the inmates of such institutions in the way of which we now speak, as though they had forfeited all claim to the most ordinary courtesies of well bred life? Just as little right, we say confidently, as any gentleman has to outrage in the same way any Ladies' Seminary whatever that is to be found in the land.— This same Giustiniani is the apostle of German Catholicism, as it has been called, or Rongianism, in this country; whose *wonderful* success in founding churches in New York, Rochester, Buffalo and Philadelphia, has been duly trumpeted and glorified in times past by a part of our religious press; though the same papers have never considered it necessary to let us know, how completely the infidel sham has in each case run out since into clear smoke. [Rongianism was an abortive attempt at a liberal Catholicism that rejected the authority of Rome. Schaff, *Development*, MTSS 3:365.] He has now gone to Italy, we are told, to help set things right in that unfortunate part of the world. [Giustiniani died in 1855.]

To return to the two imaginations already named. It is a sheer prejudice to suppose, in the first place, that cases of sanctity and true godliness have been, or are now, of only rare and extraordinary occurrence in the Roman communion. Any one who is willing at all to look into the actual history of the church, to listen to its own voice, to study its institutions, to make himself acquainted with its works, will soon find reason enough to rejoice in a widely different and far more favorable view. The single institution of the "Sisters of Charity,"[40] with its manifold services of mercy and love, is of itself fact enough to upset, for any thoughtful mind, the vulgar idea that Romanism is without religion, and a source of evil only without any good. This is however but one among many illustrations looking the same way, which the charity, "that rejoiceth not in iniquity but in the truth [1 Cor. 13:6]," need never be at a loss to find in the same church. That must be a stout bigotry indeed, which is able to turn aside the force of all such examples, by resolving them into self-righteousness or mercenary motives of any still lower kind. It has its fit parallel only in the calumnies, that were used in the first ages to blacken the virtues of Christianity into crimes among the heathen.

But in the second place it is just as blind a prejudice again, to suppose that the piety of the Roman church, such as it is, springs not from the proper life of the system itself, but is there rather by accident, and as something out of place, and so to speak in spite of the unfriendly connections with which it is surrounded; so that if it could only be torn up from the soil in which it thus happens to stand, and transplanted into a truly evangelical liberty, it might be expected to thrive and flourish at a much better rate. The native and as it were normal tendency of Catholicism, in the view of this prejudice, is not to piety at all, but only to superstition and sin; for it is taken to be a systematic conspiracy against the doctrines of grace from the beginning; and hence when we meet with the phenomenon of a truly evangelical spirit here and there in its communion, as in the case of Pascal or Fenelon, we are bound to see in it a wonderful exception to established law, and to admire so much the more the power of the evangelical principle, which is sufficient even in such untoward circumstances to bring to pass so great a miracle. No one however can study the subject to any extent for himself, without being led to see that the very reverse of all this is the truth. Catholicism is inwardly fitted for the production of its own forms of piety, and owes them to no foreign source or influence whatever. Its saints are not exotics, that pine after other climes and skies, but products of home growth, answerable in all respects to the conditions that surround them. To place them in other relations would be, not to advance, but to cripple their life. Borromeo was constitutionally a Catholic in his piety, and not a Protestant. The same may be said of Fenelon, of Philip de Neri,[41] of

---

40. [Sisters of Charity of St. Joseph's, a community of religious women started by St. Elizabeth Ann Seton or Mother Seton, (1774–1821) in Emmitsburg, Maryland. The Sisters' foci were works of charity and education. Mother Seton founded St. Joseph's Academy and Free School in Emmitsburg and many Catholic schools around the country bear her name. There is a shrine to her in Emmitsburg near the campus of Mount Saint Mary's University.]

41. [St. Philip Neri (1515–95); known as the "Apostle of Rome." He co-founded the Confraternity

Document 2: Early Christianity[: First Article].

Anselm and Bernard, of Ambrose, and of the old church fathers generally. The piety of all of them has a complexion, which is materially different from any that we meet with in the modern Protestant world. We mean not by this to call in question the reality of this last, or its high worth; all we wish to say is, that it is of another character and order, and that what we find of saintliness in the Roman church is strictly and legitimately from itself and not from abroad. To Protestantize it even in imagination, is to turn it into caricature and to eviscerate it at last of its very life. What could the early fathers do with themselves in New England? Such an institution as that of the Sisters of Charity can never be transferred to purely Protestant ground; as no such ground either could ever have given it birth. Attempts are made in our own time to furnish a Protestant version of the same idea, under what claims to be a higher and more evangelical form; for the purpose of supplying an evident want. But nothing of this sort will ever equal the original design, or be more indeed than a weak and stunted copy of this on the most narrow and ephemeral scale. It is only in the bosom of ideas, principles and associations, which are Catholic distinctively and *not* Protestant, that charity of this sort finds itself perfectly at home. And just so it is with the piety of this church in general. It is fairly and truly native to the soil from which it springs. That church, with all its supposed errors and sins, has ever had power in its own way to produce a large amount of very lovely religion. If it has been the mother of abominations, it has been unquestionably the mother also of martyrs and saints. It is a sorry business to pretend to deny this, or to try to falsify the fact into the smallest possible dimensions, for the sake of some miserable preconception with which it will not agree. We do but belittle ourselves, when we resort to strategy so poor as that. To deal with Romanism to any purpose, we must get rid of the notion that it carries in it no truth, no grace, no principle of religious activity and life; that it is as bad as infidelity, if not a good deal worse;[42] that it lacks all the attributes of a church, and is

---

of the Most Holy Trinity which gave aid to pilgrims.]

42. We clip the following from an editorial of the *New York Observer,* called forth not long ago by a sermon which Archbishop Hughes preached on his return from Europe, as the paper sneeringly adds, "without the Cardinal's hat." It is curiously characteristic. ["The Socialist's Creed," *New-York Observer* 29, no. 27 (July 3, 1851) n. p.]

"The Tribune finds fault with Bishop Hughes, for resisting the progress of Socialism in Europe. Between Romanism and Socialism there is little to choose, so far as the moral improvement of the people is concerned. They are essentially Anti-Christian, and many wise and good men regard infidelity as the least evil of the two, when the choice must be between it and Popery. We have therefore regarded it as one of the phenomena of the times, worth observing and recording, that the leaders of the Romanizing and the Fourierite parties in this country, are now discussing the comparative worth of their two schemes, for the improvement of mankind. We regard them both with equal detestation, and in the controversy now in progress, are quite indifferent as to the issue." [Fourierism was an utopian socialism formulated by French thinker Charles Fourier (1772–1837).]

The same editorial reproaches the sermon, in the beginning, with betraying a want of sympathy with the liberty spirit that is now at work in Europe. So in general our American anti-popery is ever ready to fall in with the revolutionary tendency abroad, as though it must necessarily be both patriotic and pious—needing only plenty of *Bibles* to tame the whirlwind and keep it right. And yet notoriously this movement is prevailingly irreligious, radical, socialistic and infidel, threatening the foundations

purely a synagogue of Satan or a mere human confederacy, for worldly and unhallowed ends. One wing of the Presbyterian church has it is true openly committed itself to this bold position, in pronouncing what they stigmatize as *Romish* baptism to be without force[43]—unchurching virtually thus the whole church as it stood at the birth of the Reformation and for at least twelve hundred years before, and making such men as Augustine and Chrysostom,[44] as well as Luther and Calvin of a later day, to be no better than unbaptized heathens, so far as any idea of covenant or sacramental grace is concerned; for it is notorious, that the baptism in question goes back, with all its objectionable features, not only to the fourth century, but beyond that to the days of Cyprian even and Tertullian. But no such *brutum fulmen*[45] as this can stand. All history laughs it to scorn. The vitality of Romanism at this very time, and the evidently growing confusion of Protestantism, all the world over, show it to be idle as the passing wind. It is no time, in the crisis to which things are now coming, to think of settling the question between Protestantism and Rome, in this extravagant and fanatical way. There must be honesty enough to see and own good on the side of this *hated* church, as well as a keen scent for its sores. Take it simply as it appears in our own country, struggling finally into full organization, after years of crushing difficulty and

---

of all government and society. So it is regarded by the Catholic church; which is powerfully resisting it, and forms at this time, we verily believe, a most necessary bulwark in the old world against its terrible progress. But this the N. Y. Observer denounces, as hostility to the cause of liberty and the rights of man; while it goes on the next moment to make Catholicism just as bad as Socialism itself. We have heard before of the same sentiment being uttered in high places. But it is for all this none the less a truly abominable sentiment, that must sooner or later quail before the frown of intelligent and good men. A few years since Dr. Hengstenberg of Berlin, whose zeal for Protestantism none can question who have any knowledge of the man, was heavily pressed on this very point by a party which made a merit of treating Romanism in the same way—Protestants of the rationalistic no-religion school, who were disposed to place religion in mere opposition and contradiction to the Catholic church. [Ernst Wilhelm Theodor Hermann Hengstenberg (1802–69). Educated under Neander and Tholuck, he taught at Basel and Berlin.] But he had courage to say to such spirit, "Get thee behind me, Satan;" and to proclaim to the world that there is no comparison to be thought of between Infidelity and Catholicism, and that when it comes to a war with the first, all our affections and sympathies are bound to go joyfully with the last, as one grand division simply of the great army of faith to which all true Protestants as well as all true Catholics belong. The heartless fanaticism of the N. Y. Observer not only *infidelizes* such men as Bishops Chevereux, England, Eccleston, Hughes, Kenrick, &c, (any of them good enough to compare with the Rev. Sydney E. Morse & Co [the editor and publisher of the *New-York Observer*] any day) and Sisters of Mercy, Sisters of Charity, &c., in large number, in our own time; but goes away back to other times also, and swamps all the fathers and martyrs, after the first two centuries at least, in the same Acherontian lake. [Acheron was one of the rivers in Hades; "Acherontian" thus means "dark and dismal."]

43. [In 1845, the General Assembly of the Old School Presbyterian Church voted to say that Roman Catholic baptism was invalid. Charles Hodge of Princeton Theological Seminary agreed with Nevin's negative reaction: "The General Assembly," 444–71.]

44. [St. John Chrysostom (c. 347–407); earned his nickname, "golden-mouthed," for his preaching and rhetorical skill; he was of the Antiochene school of theology; named Patriarch of Constantinople in 398 where his reform efforts led to a confrontation with the Emperor and Empress. When he would not submit to the emperor's will, he was force marched to his death in extreme weather.]

45. [Trans. A "harmless thunderbolt"; i.e., an empty threat.]

persecution; and need we say, that it has merit and respectability enough in a religious view to give it some right to the same sort of genteel respect at least, that is felt to be proper towards almost every sect besides? Is its hierarchy at this time a whit behind that of the Episcopal church, in point of learning, piety, or official diligence and zeal? Has any church among us produced better specimens of apostolical sanctity, than the first bishop of Boston[46] for instance or the first bishop of Charleston,[47] and others also that might easily be named; men, whose virtues adorn the history of the country, and whose parallels are not so readily offered in other communions, that we can afford for this reason to pass their memory into ungrateful oblivion. It is not easy to read the writings of Bishop England, glowing with the eloquence of noble gentlemanly feeling as they do on almost every page, and not be filled with indignation, as well as moved even to tears at times, with the gross and cruel wrong which has been heaped upon the Catholics among us from the beginning, in the holy name of religion. What *right*, we ask again, have the zealots of other churches to lay aside here the laws of common courtesy, and to be just as rude and scurrilous as they please? What right have rabid pens, or still more rabid tongues, to make religion in this form the synonyme [sic] of impiety and unbelief, and when confronted with clear proofs and living examples of the contrary, to resolve all into hypocrisy, or happy inconsistency, as though it were not possible for piety to grow forth in any way from such a system? Some go so far as to tell us even, that no intelligent priest or layman in the Catholic church can seriously believe what he professes to believe. This however is such unmannerly rudeness as deserves no answer, come from what quarter it may.

But what we have in view now more particularly, is to expose the fallacy that lies in the extracts we have given from Dr. Bacon and Bishop Wilson, with regard to the nature of early Christianity, as compared with that particular modern scheme of religion, which they dignify with the title Evangelical, and which is for each of them the only true and perfect sense of the Gospel. Both writers assume, that there existed in the beginning, back of the corruptions and abuses of Romanism, and subsequently to the time of the Apostles, a certain golden age, longer or shorter, of comparatively pure religious faith, which truly represented still the simplicity and spirituality of the proper divine model of the church, as we have it plainly exhibited to us in the New Testament; and that this was in all material respects of one character precisely with what they now approve as the best style of Protestantism.[48] But never was there a more perfect mistake.

---

46. [Jean-Louis Lefebvre de Cheverus (1768–1836); served as bishop from 1808–23 before returning to his native France where he became Archbishop of Bourdeaux and was named a cardinal a few months before his death.]

47. [John England (1786–1842); originally from Cork, Ireland; he was named bishop in 1820 and served until his death. He clashed with Charleston plantation social structures when he established a school for enslaved and freed African Americans.]

48. [The prevalent Protestant belief in an ecclesial "golden age," and the desire to recapitulate that age, is the "repristination" Nevin criticizes in the next paragraph.]

[Protestant Repristinationism and the History of the Church]

It may be easy enough to show, that there are many points of difference between early Christianity and Romanism, as we find this established in later times. But this fact is by no means sufficient to show, that the first was to the same extent in agreement with modern Protestantism, whether in the Episcopalian or in the Congregational form. It is clear on the contrary, that no such agreement has ever had place, but that modern Protestantism is still farther away from this older faith than the system by which it is supposed to have been supplanted in the middle ages. No defence of Protestantism can well be more insufficient and unsound, than that by which it is set forth as a pure *repristination*[49] simply of what Christianity was at the beginning, either in the fourth century, or the third, or the second. It will always be found on examination to have no such character in fact;[50] and every attempt to force upon the world any imagination of the sort, in favor of either Episcopacy, or Presbyterianism, or Independency, in favor of all or of any one of the three score and ten sects[51] which at this time follow the Bible as their sole rule of faith, must only serve in the end by its palpable falsehood to bring suspicion and doubt on the whole cause which is thus badly upheld. Whatever differences there may be between the first ages and those that followed, it is still plain enough that the course of things was from the very start *towards* that order at least, which afterwards prevailed; that this later order therefore stands bound by true historical connection with what went before; and that Protestantism accordingly, as a still more advanced period in the general movement of history, holds a living relation to the first period only through the medium of the second, and is just as little a copy of the one in form as it is of the other.[52] This we sincerely believe is the only ground, on which may be set up any rational defence of the great revolution of the 16th century (unsupported as it stands by miracles or inspiration) in conjunction with a true faith in the Divine character of the church. It is the theory of historical development, which assumes the possibility and necessity of a transition on the part of the church through various stages of form, (as in all growth) for the very purpose of bringing out more

---

49. [Nevin's thesis is that Protestantism was not a restoration of any earlier historical period. Protestantism emerged *through* the church of the fathers and medieval "Romanism." One could not "leap over" centuries of alleged corruption and return to "true" Christianity. See the texts in Nevin, *One, Holy, Catholic, and Apostolic, Tome 1*, MTSS 5:153, 205–6, 251–52. Here the church was "organic," "historical," and a "supernatural fact"—a unitary organism with a supernatural life pervading and yet manifested in its historical diversity.]

50. [Nevin attempts to carry out this "examination" in the next article.]

51. [Nevin wrote an earlier critique against "The Sect System," MTSS 5:238–71, attacking the absurdity of the notion, held by each sect, that *it* had faithfully "repristinated" apostolic Christianity.]

52. [Compare Nevin's treatment here with his discussion of "The Old Catholic Movement," 240–94. This later discussion has a very negative view of the movement of history in the hands of the papacy and sees the Petrine office as being a negative reality in the flow of the history of the Church. The German prelates were right, in the post-Vatican I reality of the doctrine of infallibility, to break from Rome.]

Document 2: Early Christianity[: First Article].

and more fully always the true inward sense of its life, which has been one and the same from the beginning. When Romanists refuse every such view, and insist that their whole system has been handed down from the time of the Apostles, it *seems* not easy certainly to admit the pretence. But when Protestants also refuse the view, and pretend to give us things, in their several by no means harmonious systems, just as they were in the first ages of the church, the pretension is still more glaringly rash and false. However it may be with Romanism, it is certain that Protestantism can never make good its claims on any such ground. And yet it will not do, to give up all historical connection with the church as it first started, and as it stood afterwards for fifteen hundred years—at least not without an overwhelming *Thus saith the Lord* in the form of miracles.[53] The only escape then is in the formula of the same and yet not the same, legitimate growth, historical development. If this cannot stand, if it be found at war with the true idea of a Divine revelation, we for our part must give up all faith in Protestantism, and bow as we best can to the authority of the Roman church; for an interest which resolves itself virtually into infidelity, as Protestantism under every other view in which it can be put seems to us to do clearly, has no right, as in the end also it can have no power, to stand.[54]

It needs but little knowledge of history certainly, to see that Christianity as it stood in the fourth century, and in the first part of the fifth, in the time of Jerome[55] and Ambrose and Augustine, in the time of Chrysostom and Basil[56] and the Gregories,[57] was something very different from modern Protestantism, and that it bore in truth a very near resemblance in all material points to the later religion of the Roman church. This is most clear of course as regards full Puritanism, in the form it carries in New England; but it is equally true in fact of the Anglican system also, and this whether we take it in the low church or high church view. Episcopalians are indeed fond of making a great distinction, between the first four or five centuries and the ages that follow; telling us with much self-complacency, that the early church thus far was comparatively pure, that the Roman apostacy came in afterwards marring and blotting the fair face which things had before, and that the English church distinguished itself at the

---

53. [Nevin thought a new revelation should have been ratified by miracles. But the Protestant Reformation had no such miracles. Therefore, the only way it could claim divine authorization would be to show it was a *development* of apostolic Christianity, and consequently authorized by the miracles the apostles performed.]

54. [One of the things lacking in Nevin's discussion here is any connection to the history of the New Testament or apostolic era. This weakness leaves Nevin's argument open to attack because he is not truly connecting it to the period which was upheld as authoritative by his interlocutors.]

55. [St. Jerome (c. 342–420); most well-known for his translation of the Bible into Latin, the Vulgate, which became the standard Biblical text until the 16th century with the publication of Erasmus's *Novum Testamentum* (1516).]

56. [St. Basil the Great (c. 330–79). He succeeded Eusebius as the Bishop of Caesarea.]

57. [Gregory {Bishop} of Nyssa (c. 330–95); Gregory {Bishop} of Nazianzus (329–89). Together with Basil, they are known as the Cappadocian fathers, and played a central role in the victory of Nicaean orthodoxy.]

Reformation by its moderation and sound critical judgment, in discriminating here properly between the purity of the primitive faith and its subsequent adulterations. According to the most churchly view, the Reformation was for Anglicanism no revolution properly speaking at all, but the simple clearing away of some previous abuses, and a self-righting of the English church as a whole once more into its old habit and course. But this is altogether a most lame and desperate hypothesis.[58] All history gives it the lie. The boasted discrimination of the English Protestantism vanishes into thin air, the moment we come to inquire into its actual origin and rise. Never was there a great movement, in which accident, caprice, and mere human passion, more clearly prevailed as factors, over the forces of calm judgment and sound reason. If under the political auspices that ruled it, the system was indeed so fortunate as to hit the true mean in the way pretended, while all the Protestant world besides missed it, the advantage must be ascribed to its good luck far more than to its good judgment. The case however becomes still worse, when we look into the real nature of the advantage which is to be referred to this good luck. The main feature of it is episcopacy, with a king at the head of it instead of a pope. In virtue of this constitution, and some few peculiarities besides, Anglicanism piques itself on being a *jure divino* succession of the old English branch of the Church Catholic, while for want of such accidents other Protestant bodies, it is held, have no right to put in any similar claim. The charm lies in the notion of the episcopate, handed down by outward succession, as a sort of primary Divinely appointed mark and seal of the true church.

But what would such men as Cyprian, Ambrose, or Augustine, have thought of the glorification of the episcopate, with all that may go along with it in the English system besides, in any such outward style as this? They did indeed put a high value on episcopacy and some other things that Anglicanism contends for; but only as these interests were themselves comprehended in what they held to be a still wider and deeper system of truth. Episcopacy torn from the idea of that glorious unity, with which alone was felt to go the actual presence of Divine powers in the church, would have been for either of these fathers as perfectly powerless an institution for church ends, as any other scheme of government whatever.[59] The plea then of falling back here to the ground of the first four or five centuries, is for the vindication even of this *accident*[60] itself a false plea; for the episcopacy of that time, and its other points of agreement with modern Anglicanism, were mere circumstances in a wider scheme

---

58. [Nevin attempts to refute this theory in the "Third Article" below, using Isaac Taylor's *Ancient Christianity*, beginning 123.]

59. [Nevin here is rejecting the main argument for Anglicanism which he will address more clearly in "Cyprian" below, especially 213–21, 236–39.]

60. [Nevin here is using "accident" in an Aristotelian sense of a property which is not essential to the substance of something. The simplest way to think of accidents is a color of an object, like a red car. The essential properties of a car are not found in its "redness" and therefore redness is an accident. In this case, the "accident" is episcopacy separated—he thinks—from the catholicity of the church fathers.]

of thought, which this same Anglicanism disowns now as antichristian and false. If it had a right to reform thus far, and might do so without losing its identity as a part of the church, no good reason can be shown why it had not as much right, if it saw proper, to reform still farther. The rupture with Catholicism is the grand point; over against which, the accident of retaining episcopacy, and some other fragments of the old system, dwindles into insignificance.

For in truth there is no return here to anything more than fragments of the early system, even in the dead view now mentioned. It is as pure a fiction as ever entered a good man's head, to dream as Bishop Wilson does that his favorite scheme of evangelical Episcopalianism prevailed in the fourth century; and the case is not materially improved, by simply changing the dream into an Oxford or Tractarian shape. The whole idea of a marked chasm anywhere about the fifth century, dividing an older purer style of Christianity from the system that meets us in the middle ages, much as English episcopacy stands related to the papacy, is no better than a chimera; history is all against it; we might just as rationally pretend to fix any such dividing line in the eighth century or in the tenth.

According to Bishop Wilson, Ambrose was somewhat infected with the *incipient* superstitions of his day; but still "lived and died firm and unbending in all the fundamentals of divine truth;" by which is meant, that he looked to the merits of Christ for salvation, and built his religion on the doctrine of justification by faith, taking the Bible for his text book and guide, after the most approved evangelical fashion of the present time.[61] "Ambrose was one of the most humble and spiritual of the fathers of the church," we are told, "two or three centuries before Popery properly speaking began."[62] Even as late as the ninth century, the church of Milan is represented as still holding out against the claims of the Papacy; and not till two hundred years after that indeed, does the writer allow it to have submitted to the Roman see, and in this way to have been drawn fully and finally into the vortex of its corruptions. But if anything in the world can be said to be historically clear, it is the fact that with the close of the fourth century and the coming in of the fifth, the Primacy of the Roman See was admitted and acknowledged in all parts of the Christian world.[63] This is granted by Barrow himself, in his great work on the Supremacy; though he tries to set aside the force of the fact, by resolving it into motives and reasons to suit his own cause.[64] The promise of our Saviour to Peter, is always taken by the fathers in the sense that he was

---

61. [Wilson, *Travels*, 79.]

62. [Wilson, *Travels*, 77–78.]

63. [For modern discussions of the history of the papacy and papal authority, see Eno, *The Rise of the Papacy*; Collins, *Keepers of the Keys*; Schatz, *Papal Primacy*.]

64. [Barrow, *A Treatise of the Pope's Supremacy* (New York: John C. Riker, 1845). Nevin's interpretation is not transparent. Barrow recounted papal claims of supremacy beginning with Pope Sixtus V (1585) and then worked backwards to "the source" of the claim (8). By the time his account arrived at Pope Gelasius (492) however, Barrow found that the popes acknowledged the emperor as lord (9–10; 155–60). Barrow later explained how the papacy gradually aggrandized its own power (141–54).]

to be the centre of unity for the church, and in the language of Chrysostom to have the presidency of it throughout the whole earth. Ambrose and Augustine both recognise this distinction of Peter, over and over again, in the clearest and strongest terms. To be joined in communion with the see of Rome was in the view of this period to be in the bosom of the true church; to be out of that communion was to be in schism. It was not enough to be in union with any other bishop or body of bishops; the sacrament of unity was held to be of force only, as having regard to the church in its universal character; and this involved necessarily the idea of one universal centre, which by general consent was to be found in Rome only, and no where else.[65] Examples of the actual exercise of supreme power on the part of the Popes, in the fourth and fifth centuries, are so frequent and numerous, that nothing short of the most wilful obstinacy can pretend to treat them as of no account. In every great question of the time, whether rising in the East or in the West, all eyes show themselves every ready to turn towards the *cathedra Petri*, [chair of Peter] as the last resort for counsel and adjudication; all controversies, either in the way of appeal or complaint, or for the ratification of decisions given in other quarters, are made to come directly or indirectly in the end before this tribunal, and reach their final and conclusive settlement only through its intervention. The Popes, in these cases, take it for granted themselves, that the power which they exercise belongs to them of right, in virtue of the prerogative of their see; there is no appearance whatever of effort or of usurpation, in the part they allow themselves to act; it seems to fall to them as naturally, as the functions of a magistrate or judge in any case are felt to go along with the office to which they belong. And the whole world apparently regards the primacy, in the same way, as a thing of course, a matter fully settled and established in the constitution of the Christian church. We hear of no objection to it, no protest against it, as a new and daring presumption, or as a departure from the earlier order of Christianity.[66] The whole nature of the

65. "St. Ambrose relates in praise to his brother Satirus, that on reaching shore after shipwreck, he was careful to inquire, whether the bishop of the place 'agreed in faith with the Catholic bishops, that is with the Roman Church'"—assuming communion with Rome thus to be a test of orthodoxy and catholicity. [Quotation marks have been added: Ernest Silvanus Appleyard, *Claims of the Church of Rome* (London: James Darling, 1848), 38.]

66. It is common to refer to the strong terms, in which St. Gregory the Great opposed the use of the title, "Universal Bishop," on the part of John the Faster, Bishop of Constantinople, as a proof that no similar character was then thought of in favor of the Roman see. But this is altogether too late, to be of the least historical force in any such view. The evidences of the acknowledgment of the primacy of Rome long before this on all sides, are too overwhelming a great deal to be for a moment disturbed, by the mere sound of what is here paraded as a contrary testimony. Gregory disliked the pretension of the title; it had for him a haughty sound, which fell not in with his sense of the respect that was due to other bishops. Even Peter, "the first member of the holy universal church, to whom the care of the whole church was committed," was to be regarded still as one among his brethren, and not as a single and exclusive head. [This quotation joins together several phrases from Thomas William Allies, *The Church of England Cleared from the Charge of Schism* (Oxford: John Henry Parker, 1848), xviii, 313, 429.] In rejecting this title, Gregory certainly did not disclaim any superior authority in himself, as successor of Peter; for he himself affirmed the contrary in the most positive terms, and exercised in the most marked manner the powers of an actual ruler of the whole church. "Assuredly," says Mr. Allies in his attempt

case implies, as strongly as any historical conditions and relations well could, that this precisely and no other order had been handed down from a time, beyond which no memory of man to the contrary then reached.[67] So perfectly idle is the dream, that Popery, taken in the sense of an acknowledgment of the primacy of the Roman see, and of its right to be regarded as the centre of church unity, came in only some two or three centuries after the age of Ambrose, and was not fully admitted into Milan even before the eleventh century.

[The Patristic Church System]

The idea of the primacy itself however, in the view now presented, was from the first but one necessary part of that general doctrine of the church, which the modern evangelical school is ever ready to denounce, as the introduction of Romanism and a complete falling away from the primitive scheme of faith. It implies of course episcopacy; but it implies also a great deal more. At the ground of it lies the conception of a truly Divine character belonging to the Church as a whole, and not to be separated from the attributes of unity and universality, the idea of the church thus as one, holy, and catholic; the idea of an actual continuation of Christ's presence and power in the church, according to the terms of the original apostolic commission; the idea of sacramental grace, the power of absolution, the working of miracles to the end of time, and a real communion of saints extending to the departed dead as well as to those still living on the earth. It is perfectly certain accordingly, that in the fourth and fifth centuries, all these and other naturally related conceptions, running very directly into the Roman corruptions as they are called of a later period, were in full operation and force; and this in no sporadic exceptional or accidental way merely, but with universal authority and as belonging to the inmost life and substance of the great mystery of Christianity. The fathers of this glorious period did indeed hold "all the fundamentals of divine truth," as Bishop Wilson is charitable enough to suppose; but they held them in no such order and view, as they are made to carry in the theory which Bishop Wilson would fain make to be the reigning sense of their faith, in spite of the "incipient superstitions" with which it was outwardly disfigured. We owe it to ourselves here to see and own the full truth. The religion of these fathers was not of the shape and type now usually known as evangelical, and paraded commonly as the best style of Protestantism. They knew nothing of the view which makes the Bible and

---

to uphold the Church of England, "if there was any Pontiff who, like St. Leo, held the most strong and deeply rooted convictions as to the prerogatives of the Roman see, it was St. Gregory" [Allies, *Church of England Cleared*, 344]. His letters abound with admonitions, injunctions, threats, and decrees, directed to bishops in every part of the church, all of whom he treated as brethren whilst they were blameless; if they erred, admonishing them as a father; and punishing them as a judge when they proved delinquent.

67. [Nevin is probably paraphrasing a legal phrase meaning "time immemorial": Garner, *Dictionary of Modern Legal Usage*, 555.]

Private Judgment[68] the principle of Christianity or the only rule of faith. They took Christianity to be a supernatural system, propounded by the Saviour to his Apostles, and handed down from them as a living tradition (including the Bible) by the Church. The order of doctrine for them was the Apostles' Creed. They looked upon the sacraments as mysteries; taking baptism to be for the remission of sins, and seeing in the "tremendous sacrament of the altar" the real presence of the Redeemer's glorified body, and a new exhibition continually of the one sacrifice that takes away sin. All was reality, not merely shadow and type. They acknowledged the divine character of the Christian priesthood, the necessity of confession, the grace of ministerial absolution. They believed in purgatory, and considered it "a holy and wholesome thought to pray for the dead that they may be loosed from their sins."[69] They held that the intercession of saints is salutary for the living in the other world, as well as in the present; and they made it a part of their piety accordingly to seek the aid of departed saints, as well as of angels, by addressing to them direct invocations for this purpose. They counted it a part of their religion also to venerate and cherish the monuments and relics of departed saints and martyrs, and were firmly persuaded that miracles were often performed through the instrumentality of such relics, as well as on fit occasions also in other ways; for of the continuance of miracles in the church, they never dreamed of making any question. They set a high value on the merit of celibacy and voluntary poverty, chosen in the service of the kingdom of God; and both by doctrine and example did what they could to recommend the monastic life, as at once honorable to religion and eminently suited to promote the spiritual welfare of men. All these things too went together, in their view, as so many parts and constituents of a single religious system; and the only voices that ventured here and there to make them the subject of doubt or contradiction, as in the case of Aerius, Jovinian and Vigilantius,[70] were quickly cried down from every side as absolutely heretical and profane.

In the bosom of this system stood, not outwardly and by accident only, but as true representatives of its very soul and life, such men as Athanasius,[71] Chrysostom, Basil the Great, Cyril of Jerusalem,[72] Gregory of Nazianzen and Gregory of Nyssa,

---

68. ["Private Judgment" was, as interpreted by Nevin, the evangelical claim that the meaning of the Bible was determined by the reason or experience of the individual Christian. See Nevin's critiques in "The Sect System," MTSS 5:246–49, 260–65 and *Philosophy and the Contemporary World*, MTSS 11:218–20, 313–14.]

69. [2 Macc 12:46, Douay-Rheims Bible, the proof text for the Catholic view of prayer for the dead.]

70. [Aerius (4th century, exact dates unknown); none of his writings are extant. He was accused of Arianism, though no formal conviction is known. It seems that seventeenth century Anglicans made him something of a folk hero. Jovinian (died c. 405) was condemned as a heretic by two synods: Rome and Milan. Vigilantius (c. 5th century); only known through the writings of Jerome, his chief opponent. Jerome accused him of rejecting the cult of the saints and martyrs, celibacy, and monasticism.]

71. [St. Athanasius (c. 297–373); bishop of Alexandria. Defender of Nicene orthodoxy in the face of significant opposition. He was exiled several times for his refusal to compromise on the language of the Nicene Creed.]

72. [St. Cyril of Jerusalem (c. 315–86); Bishop of Jerusalem. He disliked the term "homoousios"

Document 2: Early Christianity[: First Article].

Ephraim the Syrian,[73] Hilary of Poitiers,[74] Jerome, Ambrose, and Augustine. They held the fundamentals certainly of the Gospel; but they held them in connexion with a vast deal that modern evangelical Protestantism is in the habit of denouncing as the worst Roman corruption, and what is most stumbling of all they made it a fundamental point to hold the supposed better parts of their faith just in this bad connection and no other. The piety even of Ambrose and Augustine is steeped in what this modern school sets down as rank heathenish superstition. The slightest inspection of historical documents is sufficient to convince any unprejudiced mind of this fact. No one can read attentively even the Confessions of Augustine,[75] the work in which Milner and others affect to find a full parallel to the *experience* of true religion in the modern unchurchly style, without being made to feel that there is no room in truth for any such imagination. The two orders of thought are materially different. The very *crisis* of conversion in the case of the African father, turns on the principle of absolute and unconditional submission to the supernatural authority of the *Church*, in a form that would be considered anything but evangelical with the Pietistic or Methodistic tendency of the present time.

The ground taken here then by Bishop Wilson, and by the whole low church or no church so called evangelical interest, still bent on claiming some sort of genealogical affinity with the orthodoxy and piety of the fourth and fifth centuries, is clearly and palpably false. But how is it with Puseyism[76] or Anglicanism in the high view, pretending to find in this early period its own pattern of Episcopacy, as distinguished from what it conceives to be those later innovations of the Papacy which it pompously condemns and rejects? Alas, the whole theory is brittle as glass, and falls to pieces with the first tap of the critic's hammer. Nothing can well be more arbitrary, than the way in which this system proceeds with church antiquity, choosing this feature and refusing that, just as it may happen to square or not square with the previously settled accident of its own constitution. It is stiff for the episcopate, without being able to see that the idea of its divine right rests from the start in a view of the church, which involves with equal force and often asserts the same necessity for the primacy. It builds a doctrine here and a practice there on the universal tradition of this classic time, this golden era of sound church feeling and faith; but without any reason, other than its own pleasure

---

from the Nicene Creed, but his faith was determined to be orthodox. He was a strong proponent of the sacraments and the real presence in the Eucharist.]

73. [St. Ephraem Syrus (c. 306–73); a voluminous writer who affirmed the sinlessness of the Virgin Mary and devotion to the saints.]

74. [St. Hilary of Poitiers (c. 315–67) was known as "The Athanasius of the West." His most famous work, "On the Trinity" is a standard anti-Arian treatment on Trinitarian doctrine which is referenced by both Augustine and Thomas Aquinas, the two most important trinitarian doctors of the Catholic Church.]

75. [Augustine, *Confessions*.]

76. [Edward Pusey (1800–82); leader of the Tractarians and the Anglican high church movement known as the Oxford Movement.]

and whim, thrusts out of the way other doctrines and practices embraced in the same universal tradition with even greater clearness and force.[77] The whole hypothesis is untrue. There is no such chasm between this classic period and the time following as it pretends, and least of all in the form of any such discrimination of doctrines and practices as it needs to prop up its own cause. The fathers of the fourth and fifth centuries were not Protestants of either the Anglican or the Puritan school. They would have felt themselves lost, and away from home altogether, in the arms of English Episcopalianism, as well as in the more bony and stern embrace of Scotch Presbyterianism.[78]

New England Puritanism of course, as represented by Dr. Bacon, is quite willing to admit the general truth of what has now been said in relation to the age of Ambrose and Augustine; though at times ready enough still to talk of these fathers and their fellows, as though it took them to be in the main of its own communion and faith. Much even that Episcopalian Protestantism finds to be good here, this more unchurchly system has no hesitation in treating as part and parcel of the "great apostacy," which so soon turned the whole truth of Christianity into a strange lie. The fourth century was miserably corrupt. Even the third carries in many respects a very questionable face. But still we are not to give up entirely the idea of a truly golden age, representing for a time at least, however short, the true original simplicity of the Gospel, as the same has been happily resuscitated once again in these last days, particularly among the churches of New England. In the second century somewhere, or even reaching over this a link here and there into the third, back of popery and prelacy, the theory ventures to assume what all historical documents fail to make clear, the existence namely of a strictly evangelical church, founded on Protestant principles, (the Bible the only rule of doctrine, justification by faith, the clergy of one order, the people the fountain of all church power) breathing a Protestant spirit, and carrying men to heaven without sacramental mummery or mysticism in the common sense[79] Puritan way of the

---

77. [For an appeal, several months earlier, to an "holistic" understanding of "sound church feeling and faith" (specifically as it relates to baptism), see Nevin et al., *Born of Water*, MTTS 6:81–2.]

78. "Did St. Athanasius or St. Ambrose come suddenly to life, it cannot be doubted what communion they would mistake for their own. All surely will agree that these fathers, with whatever difference of opinion, whatever protests if we will, would find themselves more at home with such men as St. Bernard or St. Ignatius Loyola, or with the lonely priest in his lodgings, or the holy sisterhood of mercy, or the unlettered crowd before the altar, than with the rulers or the members of any other religious community. And may we not add, that were the two saints, who once sojourned, in exile or on embassage, at Treves, to come more northward still, and to travel until they reached another fair city, seated among groves, green meadows, and calm streams, the holy brothers would turn from many a high aisle and solemn cloister which they found there, and ask the way to some small chapel where mass was said in the populous alley or forlorn suburb? And, on the other hand, can any one who has but heard his name, and cursorily read his history, doubt for one instant how the people of England in turn, 'we, our princes, our priests, and our prophets,' Lords and Commons, Universities, Ecclesiastical Courts, marts of commerce, great towns, country parishes, would deal with Athanasius—Athanasius who spent his long years in fighting against kings for a theological term!"—Newman, *Essay on Development* [Newman, *Essay on the Development*, 97–98].

79. [An allusion to the ruling philosophy of American Protestantism: Common Sense Realism, also called Baconianism. It assimilated Christian theology to the Baconian method of empirical

Document 2: Early Christianity[: First Article].

present time. So we have seen Dr. Bacon pleasing himself with the imagination, that the Christianity of Lyons in the second century, in the days of Pothinus and Irenæus, and of course also the faith and piety of the church generally in a still earlier part of the same century, in the days of Ignatius and Polycarp,[80] corresponded in all material respects with the modern ecclesiastical life of Connecticut and Massachusetts. Is there any more ground for this fancy, than can be urged in favor of the one we have just now dismissed? We believe not. It rests throughout on a mere hypothesis, which involves in the end a purely arbitrary construction of history, just as wild and bold, to our view, as any that has been offered to us, from a different standpoint, by Strauss or Baur.[81] Into this part of the subject however, the limits necessarily imposed on us at present will not permit us to enter. We hope to be able to return to it in a second article, some time hereafter.

J. W. N.

---

science: observation and organization of facts. For Christian thinkers, the relevant facts were the "facts" of the Bible, not religious experience or the "mysticism" of the sacraments. For discussions within Mercersburg studies, see William Evans, *Companion*, 37-40 and DeBie, *Speculative Theology*, 1-6. Nevin criticized it at length in "A Plea for Philosophy," MTSS 11:84-94.]

80. [St. Ignatius (c. 35-107), Bishop of Antioch. He is best known for seven short epistles to churches and individuals, written while traveling to Rome on his way to martyrdom, that reflect the state of the church and piety in the immediate post-apostolic period.]

81. [David Fredrich Strauss (1808-74); famous for his *Leben Jesu* {*The Life of Jesus*} in which he applied the concept of myth for the first time to the life of Christ. Ferdinand Christian Baur (1792-1860); founder of the Tübingen school. He applied the Hegelian dialectic to the New Testament and to the historical development of the early church.]

Early Christianity: Second Article.[1]

[The Puritan Theory of Early Christianity]

The general Puritan theory of Early Christianity may be reduced to the following propositions:

1st. That it started in the beginning under the same form substantially, both in doctrine and practice, which is now known and honored as Evangelical Protestantism without prelacy. The doctrine was orthodox, as distinguished from all heresies that are at war with the doctrines of the Trinity, human depravity, and the atonement. The principle of the Bible and private judgment lay at the bottom of the whole system. The worship was much in the modern style of Scotland or New England. So was it also with the government or polity of the churches. All was vastly rational and spiritual. Even Presbyterianism, according to the Congregationalists, was not yet born. The Baptists carry the nudity farther still. But all agree, that the church notions of later times were unknown. There was no papacy, no episcopacy, no priesthood, no liturgy, no thought of a supernatural virtue in baptism, no dream of anything like the mystery of the real presence in the awful sacrament of the altar. The primitive piety was quite of another order from all this. It was neither hierarchical nor mystical, but ran in the channel rather of popular freedom, democratic right, and common sense.

2nd. That this happy state of things, established under the authority of the Apostles and in their time universally prevalent in the churches, was unfortunately of only very short duration. How long it lasted is by no means clear. After the destruction of Jerusalem, we have for a time almost no historical notices whatever that serve to reveal to us the actual condition of the church; and such testimony as we have, with the going out of the first century and the coming in of the second, have so questionable a look at certain points, that it is hard to know how far they are to be trusted anywhere. It became the policy of later times to corrupt and suppress documents.[2] The theory thus is of necessity thrown here on presumption and hypothesis. Two broad facts for it however are settled and given; first, that the church started right in the beginning, and secondly, that on coming fully into view again in the third century it is found to be strangely wrong, fairly on the tide in truth of the prelatical system with its whole

---

1. [*MR* 3 (November 1851) 513–62. See DeBie's commentary, *John Williamson Nevin*, 276–78.]
2. [This idea was popularized by Dan Brown's *DaVinci Code* in both the novel and the movie.]

Document 2: Early Christianity: Second Article.

sea of corruptions and abominations. Between these dates then must be assumed an apostacy or fall, somewhat like that which turned our first parents out of paradise into the common world. When or how the doleful change took place, in the absence of all reliable historical evidence, can only be made out by conjecture; and here naturally the theory is subject in different hands to some variations. The Presbyterian, Congregational, and Baptist schemes or constructions, are not just the same. All however make the paradisiacal period of the church very short. It is hard to find even one whole century for it after the destruction of Jerusalem; though in a vague loose way it is common to speak of it, as reaching through the second century and some little distance perhaps into the third.

3d. That the change thus early commenced was in truth in full opposition to the original sense and design of Christianity, and involved in principle from the start the grand apostacy that afterwards became complete in the church of Rome, and which is graphically foretold in those passages of the New Testament that speak of antichrist, the mystical Babylon, and the man of sin.[3] The Baptists include in this corruption more than the Congregationalists; and these again include in it more than the Presbyterians, taking Presbytery itself in fact, and that idea of the church which *once* went along with it, for the first stage of the downward progress; but as to what lies beyond this, the vast world of notions and practices namely that go to make up the prelatical system as we find it in full force in the days of Cyprian, the whole Puritan body of course is but of one mind. It is throughout an usurpation only and an abuse, against the Bible, against apostolical and primitive example, against the entire genius and spirit of evangelical religion. It belongs to an order of thought and habit of life, which however countenanced by many good men in the beginning, must be regarded as constitutionally at variance with the first principles of the Gospel, as antichristian and worldly; the natural and only proper end of which, in the course of two or three centuries, was the complete failure of the church in its original form. It became the synagogue of Satan.[4] Christianity went out in dismal eclipse for a thousand years, with only a few tapers, dimly burning here and there in vallies and corners, to keep up some faint remembrance of that glorious day-spring from on high with which it had visited the nations in the beginning.[5]

4th. That the long night of this fearful captivity came to an end finally, through the great mercy of God, by the event of the Reformation; which was brought to pass by the diligent study of the Bible, the original codex of Christianity, under the awakening and guiding influence of the Holy Ghost, and consisted simply in a resuscitation of the life and doctrine of the primitive church, which had been so long buried beneath

---

3. [This even carried into twentieth century Presbyterianism; see e.g. Loraine Boettner's "Introduction" in *Roman Catholicism*, 1–18.]

4. [This was a common idea in American Protestantism. For an example contemporary with Nevin, see Dowling, *History of Romanism* (1853). Biblical allusion to Rev 2:9.]

5. [An allusion to Luke 1:78, 79.]

the corruptions of the great Roman apostacy. The Reformation, in this view, was not properly the historical product and continuation of the life of the church itself, or what was called the church, as it stood before. It was a revolutionary rebellion rather against this as something totally false and wrong, by which it was violently set aside to make room for a new order of things altogether. If it be asked, by what authority Luther and the other reformers undertook to bring in so vast a change, the answer is that they had the authority of the Bible. This and this only, is the religion of Protestants. Popery was antichrist;[6] the Bible teaches plainly a different religion, which must have prevailed in the beginning, and which Popery had contrived to suppress; and what better right than this fact then could the reformers have or need, to fight against it, to overturn it as far as they were able, and to set up the religion of the Bible, the primitive evangelical religion, in its room and place? Such was their warrant, and such as far as it went their good and excellent work. It is not strange however, coming out of such thick darkness as they had in their rear, that they were not themselves able at once to see clearly all that needed to be done in this great restoration; to say nothing of such outward political limitations as they had to contend with for instance in England.[7] Luther stuck miserably in the mud of Romanism to the last. Even Calvin had his sacramental crotchets, and talks strangely at times of the church. Anglicanism remained out and out semipopery. Hence the need of new reformation. This we have in Puritanism;[8] which itself also has required some time to come to that perfection of Bible simplicity and truth, which it now happily presents in this country, especially in New England—and most of all, if we take their own word for it, in the wide communion of the Baptists. Here finally, after so long a sleep, the fair image of original Christianity, as it once gladdened the assemblies of the faithful in the days of Ignatius, Polycarp, Irenæus, and the blessed martyrs of Lyons and Vienne, has come forth as it were from the catacombs, to put to shame that frightful mask which has for so many centuries cheated the world in its name and stead. And what is better still, there is some ground now also to hope, since we have got into the middle of the nineteenth century and Anglo-Saxon mind is in a fair way to rule the world,[9] that this second edition and experiment of a pure faith and true church will be more successful than the first; and that Christ will find it proper *now*, in these last days, to be with his church

---

6. [See for instance the original wording in the WCF.XXV.vi, "{the Pope of Rome} is that Antichrist, that man of sin and son of perdition" (Schaff, *Creeds of Christendom*, 3:658–59).]

7. [This understanding of the Reformers' lack of critical examination of their own historical period is still present. I can remember this argument being used during my undergraduate Bible college education as the rationale for why the Reformers were not "Baptists" or dispensational in their theology.]

8. [The idea of reforming the English Reformation to rid the Church of England of the vestiges of popery was a common theme among the Puritans of the late sixteenth and seventeenth centuries. It provides a needed context for some of the more extreme aspects of Puritanism such as their denial of Christmas and wedding rings.]

9. [See Schaff's *Principle* for a more developed critique of this version of history (MTSS 3:36–205).]

always, and to make good thus his own promise that the gates of hell shall not prevail against it, as they might seem to have done before, till Shiloh come or to the end of the world.[10]

Such in a general view, we say, is the Puritan theory of the past history of the church, and such is the relation in which it imagines Protestantism to stand to Primitive Christianity. The theory and the fancy we believe to be both together absolutely visionary and false. More than that, they are eminently suited to overthrow at last the credit of Protestantism itself, and along with this to upset all faith in Christianity as being really and truly such a revelation as it claims to be for the salvation of the world. Grant the premises of this wild hypothesis, and infidelity may proceed at once to draw its own conclusions with unanswerable force.

It is truly amazing, before looking at the facts of history at all, that the holders of the hypothesis are not troubled some by the very *prodigiousness* of the conceptions that enter into its composition. They appear to be quite easy and at home, for the most part, in the fabric of their peculiar historical system, as though it were the most natural and reasonable structure in the world; and yet never was fabric of this sort probably so put together, as to furnish by its very texture more just cause for anxiety and distrust. The theory, instead of being natural and reasonable, is as much against nature and reason as can well be conceived. Let any thinking man put out of his mind the mere habit of looking at the past through the medium of the theory itself, so as to bring home to himself clearly in an abstract way the elements and combinations of which it is constructed, and he must feel surely that no scheme could well be, in an *a priori* view, less probable or worthy of trust. Every presumption is against it. If believed at all by the earnestly thoughtful, it can be only through stress of overwhelming evidence, making it a sin to doubt. The unthoughtful of course feel no such difficulty. Their faith is easy, just because it is hollow and blind.

Only look at the scheme in its own light. All previous history looked to the coming of Christ, and prepared the way for it, as the grand central fact of religion and so of the world's life.[11] The Old Testament revelation, through thousands of years, made room for the magnificent and awful mystery. At length it came, the Fact of all facts, full of grace and truth, heralded by angels, surrounded with miracles, binding earth to heaven, and laying the foundations of a new creation of whose splendors and glories there should be no end. Christ died for our sins, and rose again for our justification. His apostles were solemnly commissioned to preach the gospel throughout the world. On the day of Pentecost, they were armed with supernatural power from on high for this purpose; and the history of the Christian Church was opened under a form, that carried in it the largest promise of universal victory and success in following time. With this promise corresponded in full the progress of the new cause, in the age of the apostles and for a short time afterwards. The Gospel was rapidly published throughout

10. [" . . . til Shiloh come": Gen 49:10.]
11. [For an early discussion from Nevin on biblical history see *Summary*, 237–56.]

the Roman world. The ascended Redeemer at the right hand of God, made head over all things to the church, gave proof of his exaltation and power by causing his kingdom to spread and prevail, in the face of all opposition whether Jewish or Pagan. The whole course of things seemed to show clearly, that the powers of a higher world were at work in the glorious movement, and that it embodied in itself the will and counsel of heaven itself for the full accomplishment of the end towards which it reached. It is usual indeed to make this early success of Christianity one of the external proofs of its divine origin, a real supernatural seal of its truth, like that of miracles. One would naturally suppose, that such a beginning must have led to some sound and true result, in harmony with its own heavenly conditions. But, according to the hypothesis now before us, the very opposite of this took place. Hardly had the last of the apostles gone to heaven, before signs of apostasy began to show themselves in the bosom of the infant church, threatening to overthrow and defeat entirely its original design. In the midst of its early triumphs, whilst it had still strength to perform miracles and exhibit martyrdoms on all sides in favor of the truth, the leaven of this malignant corruption went forward, strangely enough, in the most active and virulent way; infecting and poisoning, more and more, the very vitals of the church; till in the course of a single century from the death of St. John, perhaps indeed much sooner, the entire course of its life was changed from what it had been at first, and turned into a false direction. Traces of the original faith and piety are still to be found indeed in the third and fourth and fifth centuries, the echoes and reminiscences as it were, more and more faint, of the better age which had gone before; but these were exceptional now to the central tendency, rather than its true and genuine fruit; the power that prevailed, and that was fast carrying all things its own way, almost without question or protest, was the "mystery of iniquity,"[12] that same great anti-christian apostasy in principle and drift, which in due time afterwards culminated in the Pope, and brought upon the world the darkness of the middle ages. The eclipse came not at once in its full strength; but still, from the very start, it was the beginning of the total obscurity that followed, and looked to this steadily as its end. So in truth Satan in the end fairly prevailed over Christ. The church fell, not partially and transiently only, but universally, in its collective and corporate character, with an apostasy that was to reach through twelve hundred years. Had it not been for some copies of the Bible here and there, in the hands of a few obscure and persecuted witnesses for the truth, the light of Christianity would have become absolutely extinct; for the so called catholic church, in league plainly with the powers of hell, and with the sovereignty of the world in its hands, showed itself bent for ages on the accomplishment precisely of this terrible result. Never was there so glorious a morning, so suddenly lost and forgotten in think impenetrable clouds! The grandeur of the enterprise is equalled only by the greatness of its failure. And what is

---

12. [2 Thess 2:7. The "mystery of iniquity" was thought to be part of the power of evil that would finally be manifested as Antichrist. By this point, Nevin no longer identified Antichrist as the papacy, but as sectarianism: Nevin, *One, Holy, Catholic, and Apostolic, Tome One*, MTSS 5:161.]

that fearful whisper that seems to steal upon us, in view of it, from the very depths of the bottomless pit: "This man began to build, and was not *able* to finish [Luke 14:30]?" But here again the hypothesis is ready with its own answer. The failure was not final. So long as the Bible lived, there was still room for hope; and at last accordingly, "in the fulness of time" [Gal 4:4], after centuries upon centuries of ecclesiastical chaos, God was pleased to say once more, "Let there be light," and there *was* light.[13] The reformers of the 16th century drew forth from the sacred volume, by the help of God's Spirit, the true scheme and pattern of the christian faith, as it was in the beginning. The spell of ages was broken. Christ gave tokens that he was again at the head of his church. The unfinished work of the first and second centuries was once more actively and vigorously resumed. In the form of Protestantism, it may *now* be expected, after so long a time, to go forward conquering and to conquer, until all enemies are subdued under the Saviour's feet. True, Popery is not still dead, and Protestantism itself is getting into huge difficulties; but we must now have faith in Christ's headship over his church, and in his promise that the gates of hell shall never prevail against it; so as to be firmly persuaded, in spite of all fears and discouragements, that the right course which things have at last taken must certainly prove successful in the end, and that he who sits king in Zion will not rest till he shall have brought forth judgment unto victory.

[Nevin's Critique of Puritan Historiography]

Will any sober minded man pretend to say, that this, in itself considered, is not a strange and unnatural hypothesis, which it is exceedingly hard to reconcile, either with the divine origin of the church, or with its divine mission, or with the divine presence in it of Him, who is represented as having the government of the world on his shoulders for its defence and salvation?[14]

But the case becomes yet more difficult, when we look into the sacred oracles which lie back of the actual history of the church, and find that instead of lending any countenance to this scheme prospectively, they set before us in the most plain and unquestionable terms an altogether different prospect. Some few passages, we know, have been impressed by a strained and violent exegesis into the service of the theory, by being made in sound at least to foretell a general apostacy of the church, the features of which it has been pretended to identify in the Papal communion; and it is not uncommon to hear the enemies of Popery appealing to these perversions of scripture as the very voice of inspiration itself, and charging those who question the infallibility of their gloss with setting themselves against the authority of God's word. But the day for such arbitrary and unhistorical interpretation, it may be trusted, is now fast coming to an end. On the field of science at least, it is fairly and fully exploded. No real biblical scholar, in any part of the world, is found willing to endorse the vulgar anti-popery

---

13. [Often described in later discussions as "*post tenebras lux*"—after darkness comes the light.]
14. ["Government . . . shoulders": Isa 9:6.]

sense of these pet texts. On the other hand, however, there are many single passages and texts, which clearly foretell the unfailing stability of the church, through all ages, on to the end of time. And what perhaps is of still more account, the whole drift and scope of the Bible look always in the same direction, and in this direction only.

Even under the Old Testament, it was a standing article of faith that the theocracy could not fail. But this perpetuity was itself the type only of that higher and better state, in which the Jewish theocracy was to become complete finally as the New Testament church. If it lay in the conception of the old that it should not prove a failure, much more must this be taken to lie in the conception of the new. It is to the times of the Messiah in this view emphatically, that the predictions and promises of the Old Testament in relation to the coming fortunes of the church especially refer. All join in the assurance, that the kingdom then to be set up should be an everlasting kingdom, and that of its dominion and glory there should be no end.[15] Nothing could well be more foreign from the old Messianic scheme, than the imagination that the enlargement of Jacob, by the coming of Shiloh, was to give place almost immediately again to a long night of captivity and bondage, ten times worse than that of Babylon, from which there was to be no escape for more than a thousand years. And just as little can any such view be reconciled with the plan of Christianity, as it meets us in the New Testament. This proceeds everywhere on the assumption, that the kingdom of God, or the church, as now established among men, was destined, not to fall but to stand, not to pass away like the streams of the desert, but to be as the waters of the sanctuary rather, in Ezekiel's vision, an ever deepening and perpetual river.[16] There are, it is true, predictions enough of trials, heresies, apostacies and corruptions; but the idea is never for a moment allowed, that these should prevail in any such universal way as the theory before us pretends. On the contrary, the strongest assurances are given, that this should not be the case.

These stand forth most conspicuously and solemnly, in those wonderful passages from the mouth of the blessed Saviour himself, which form as it were the charter of the church and its heavenly commission to the end of time. "Thou art Peter; and upon this rock I will build my church; and the *gates of hell shall not prevail against it*" Matth. xvi. 18. The use which the Romanists make of this text, must not blind us to its true magnificence and grandeur. It is still scripture; and we are bound, as good Protestants, to pause with some reverence before it, and to inquire with seriousness what it actually does mean. Take it as we may, it looks certainly like a most explicit pledge, in terms of unusual solemnity and deliberation, that the church should endure on its first foundation, that is with true historical succession from its own beginning, through all ages. Of the same tenor again precisely is the apostolic commission, after our Saviour's resurrection and just before his ascension: "All power is given unto me in heaven and in earth: Go ye *therefore,* and teach all nations, baptizing them in the

---

15. ["Everlasting . . . no end": Dan 7:17, 27 (thought to be prophetic of Christ's kingdom).]
16. [Ezek 47:5.]

name of the Father, and of the Son, and of the Holy Ghost; teaching them to observe all things whatsoever I have commanded you: And, lo, *I am with you alway, even* unto the end of the world" Matth. xxviii: 18–20. Here again we have scripture, under a most majestic and commanding form. Has it any meaning answerable to its magnificent terms, or is it a mere flourish of Oriental figures which mean the next thing to nothing? Words could hardly be put together in a way more significantly suited to express the idea, that the object of this commission was one which could not possibly suffer failure or defeat. The enterprise in view is conditioned by the fact, that all power is in the Saviour's hands, that he is head over all things, as Paul expresses it, to the church [Eph 1:22]; and all conceivable difficulties attending it, as in the case of Moses when sent to bring Israel out of Egypt, are reduced to nothing by the one overwhelming consideration, "Lo, I am with you always," engaging the entire plenitude of this power for its never ending success. It is useless to dwell on other testimonies that look immediately in the same direction. If these capital and classical passages have no power to fix attention or constrain belief, it is not to be imagined that any amount of scriptural evidence besides will be felt to carry with it any real weight.

It is very certain, that only the most wilful and stubborn prejudice can fail to see, how utterly at war the Bible is with the notion of a quickly apostatizing and totally failing church, in any view answerable to the strange Puritan hypothesis which we have now under consideration. No such notion accordingly ever entered the mind of the primitive church itself. It was for a time supposed indeed that the end of the world was near at hand, and that the resurrection state or millenium [*sic*] would soon appear; and it was only gradually, that this view gave place to the idea of a long course of history preparing the way for Christ's second coming. But neither in the one form nor in the other, was the thought ever admitted that the church itself might collapse or go into universal dismal eclipse. That would have been counted downright infidelity. The promise to Peter and the apostolic commission were never taken but in one sense; and that appeared to be so plain, that no one but an unbeliever, it was supposed, could ever think of seriously calling it in question. It became accordingly, as we all know, an element of the primitive faith, an article of the early creed, to believe in the being of the holy catholic church as an indestructible fact, a divine mystery that could never fail or pass away.

The biblical doctrine on this subject is so clear indeed, that even the most unhistorical advocates of the Puritan theory are themselves constrained to allow it; though they take care to put it into a shape to suit their own preconceived scheme. Nothing is more common than to hear them talk of the unfailing and enduring character of the church, of its being founded on a rock, and of Christ's presence with it always for its protection and defence; they are willing to say with the ancient creed, when necessary, "We believe in the church as one, holy, catholic and apostolical." But by all this they mean in the end, not the church in any outward and visible view, not the historical organization known under this name and claiming these titles from the third century down to the sixteenth, but a supposed succession of hidden and scattered witnesses, in the so called catholic church partly, but more generally after a time on the outside of it, handing down what the theory is pleased to call a pure faith, in conflict with the reigning system, and in the way of more or less direct protest against it as an anti-christian usurpation. It is of the invisible church only, they tell us, the secret "election in Israel," that the glorious things spoken of Zion are to be understood. The church was in the wilderness for a thousand years before the Reformation, among the Waldenses,[17] Albigenses,[18] Henricians,[19] Paulicians,[20] and such like; God was never altogether without a handful of people somewhere, that refused to bow the knee to Baal. No such evasion however is of any force in truth, for getting clear of the difficulty which we have here in view. It turns in the first place on a mere arbitrary assumption, borrowed from the clouds, and got up palpably to serve a purpose, without the least regard to historical facts and dates; an assumption that is doomed therefore, by necessary consequence, to dissolve before the light of history more and more into mere fog and mist. These sects of the middle ages are bad stuff at best, for making out the romance of a pure Christianity, from the fifth century to the fifteenth, on the outside of the Roman church. But allowing them to have been as good as the theory before us affects to believe, and granting it besides a fair proportion of sporadic exceptional cases of piety, in the reigning church itself, to fill up the thin and airy succession, what sound mind can be satisfied still to take *this* for any fitting verification of the glowing predictions of the Old Testament, any true fulfilment of the high sounding promises and pledges that are contained in the New? No *such* construction of these predictions and promises certainly ever entered into the mind of the primitive church itself; the

---

17. [The Waldensians were a small Christian community which was started in Lyons, France in the twelfth century by Peter Waldo (d. 1217). Some Protestants claimed that the Waldenses and the Hussites were a unique church started by Paul during his journey to Spain. The exact origins of this theory are unknown. The group did continue without official papal recognition or episcopal oversight and appointed their own ministers and had a copy of the New Testament translated into the vernacular. The group still exists in the Piedmont region of Northern Italy.]

18. [The Albigensians were an eleventh century heretical sect in Southern France who advocated a form of Manichaean dualism. They rejected key Catholic doctrines like purgatory, the sacraments, and the bodily resurrection.]

19. [The Henricians were followers of Henry of Lausanne (d. c. 1148). Little is known of Henry's life; most of the information comes from his opponents which included Bernard of Clairvaux. He was an advocate of extreme poverty for the clergy as a means of demonstrating the corruption and worldliness of the Church. He apparently denied the efficacy of the sacraments if the priest was living an immoral life. Henry is claimed by the Jehovah's Witnesses as a genuine anointed believer.]

20. [The Paulicians were the oldest group mentioned here. The name is probably derived from Paul of Samosata (third century), Bishop of Antioch, though some have connected it to the Apostle Paul. Its founder was probably Constantine of Samosata (modern day Turkey) in the seventh century. Their history is a long one and reflects the three religious influences of the region: Catholicism, Orthodoxy, and Islam. They were dualists who had Gnostic, Manichean, and Nestorian leanings. They denied the Trinity and held to a form of adoptionism. They were iconoclasts who rejected the veneration of Mary, the crucifix, sacramentalism, and the hierarchy of the Church. Gibbon called them the precursor of the Reformation (*History of the Decline*, 10:79–84 {ch. 54}).]

construction is perfectly foreign from the sense of the ancient creed; and we may safely say, that nothing short of the most powerful prejudice in favor of a previously established theory can account in any case, for its being accepted as in the least degree satisfactory or probable. The whole is a subterfuge plainly, got up to escape the clear and proper sense of the Bible, and not an honest commentary by any means designed to meet this sense in a fair and open way.

The difficulty then stands before us still in its full strength. The helplessness of the plea thus put in to turn aside its force, only serves to give it greater weight. The more we bring the case home in an actual way to our thoughts, the more are we likely to be confounded with its palpable monstrosity. Puritanism puts an enormous tax upon our faith from the very outset, when it requires us to believe things so contradictory and mutually destructive as are here brought together in one and the same theory or scheme. That the church should have such a history behind it as that of the Old Testament, such a glorious array of miracles, types, prophecies, heralding and foreshadowing its advent, for thousands of years, as the desire of all nations, the last sense and grand fulfilment of all previous revelations; that its actual inauguration in the world should be so every way worthy of this stupendous world-embracing proem,[21] in the mystery of the incarnation itself ("God manifest in the flesh, justified in the Spirit, &c." 1 Tim. v: 16.), in "promises exceedingly great and precious" [2 Pet 1:4], and high guaranties from the throne of heaven, in signs and wonders and miracles, and in wide pentecostal triumphs throughout the Roman empire; that Christianity should start thus, under such divine auspices, the glorified Saviour head over all things for its single cause and sake, and ever present by his Spirit in the midst of it according to his own word, and by infallible tokens also making his presence known and felt on all sides; that the church in these circumstances should look upon itself as an institution founded upon a rock, and make it an article of faith that its charter could not fail: and yet, that in fact all began to fail, to go into confusion, to run towards apostacy, before the end of the second century; that this fearful tendency, in spite of Christ's headship in heaven and his, *Lo, I am with you always,* on earth, through fires of martyrdom and unheard of sacrifices for the faith once delivered to the saints, so far prevailed actually as in the course of two or three centuries more to turn this whole faith into a lie; that the church in short, under its original corporate character, ran out historically into a complete and universal failure, so as to be for a whole millennium of the most horrible spiritual darkness and desolation, a mere synagogue of Satan, the enemy of all truth and righteousness, seeking only to pull down and destroy what Christ (King in Zion Ps. ii: 1–6) was still trying to build here and there, by such people as the Paulicians and Albigenses: All this taken together, we say, requires such a cormorant[22] credulity for its full reception, that the most careless minds, when brought to think only a little for themselves, are very likely to start back aghast from the scheme, and may well be

21. ["Preamble."]
22. [Apparently here meaning "insatiably greedy or rapacious." OED Online, "Cormorant, n."]

excused for gently asking, By what authority and right does it pretend so to lord it over our faith?

It would seem reasonable to expect in so improbable a case, that the main positions of the theory at least would be so supported by clear historical proof, as to carry with them some sort of coercive force for such as are willing and anxious to know the truth. An apostasy so profound and total should be properly attested in some way, by historical testimonies and monuments. Allowing it to have come in gradually, this only gives us the more right to expect and demand the evidence of which we now speak. So vast a revolution, in such view, implies of necessity a moral struggle, a conflict of principles and aims, a tumult of inharmonious and opposing forces. To say that the primitive church yielded passively to the great apostasy from the beginning, without contradiction or protest, is to make it from the very first, not "the pillar and ground of the truth," [I Tim 3:15] but the mother of error itself; to conceive of it as built, not on a rock beating back the strong floods of hell, but on the mere sand at the mercy of all winds and waves [Matt 7:26–27]. The least we can ask then, is to have set before us in history some traces of this grand ecclesiastical catastrophe, by which all our *a priori* conceptions of Christianity are so confounded, and our faith in its divine origin and heavenly commission is so terribly tried.[23] And as we should have clear proof in this way of the failure of the church in the beginning, it would seem but reasonable also that we should not be left to take the Reformation on trust subsequently as a merely human work. Allow the continuous stability of the church, as a divine institution carrying in itself down to that time the promises and gifts with which it was freighted in the beginning, and we may at least try to justify Protestantism as a true product of this historical life itself; in which view it might need no higher warrant perhaps for its vindication. But give up the historical succession, by taking the ground that the church had failed for a thousand years, except among sects from which it is notorious Protestantism did *not* spring, and that the Reformation was in truth a new setting up of Christianity parallel with its first setting up by the Apostles; and then really we see not, why the proper credentials of a truly apostolical commission should be wanting in the second case more than in the first. Luther himself did not hesitate

---

23. [Part of the issue which Nevin is dealing with is the question of how declensions take place. Rather than the "grand catastrophe" (as Nevin's interlocutor interpreted early Christianity), most declines in cultures or institutions happen gradually, and are seldom complete through all aspects of a culture or nation. His overall point, that God did not abandon his promises to maintain the church, even through the Middle Ages, is still valid and an important rejoinder to a false view of history. However, as the history of the Old Testament demonstrates (which Nevin discussed in his *Summary of Biblical Antiquities*, see the general introduction), *God's people can devolve, even to the place of the worship of idols*. It is also worth noting here that Nevin's insistence on any decline being a sharp and total decline seems at odds with his earlier understanding of decline (see e.g., Nevin, "The Heidelberg Catechism" in *WM* [December 1840–August 1841]). Even in *The Mystical Presence*, Nevin could speak of decline, though he addresses that in light of his understanding of development, as explored in the introduction. The concept of decline, at least in a modified form, is addressed when Nevin takes up the Old Catholic Movement which is formulated in Germany in reaction to the First Vatican Council's decree on papal infallibility ("The Old Catholic Movement").]

to pose the radicalism of the Anabaptists with this test: "If they have a commission from God, let them prove it by *miracles*."[24] But if the Reformation itself is to be taken for what this Puritan theory makes it, we must say it was quite as much a new church as the enterprise of Storck and Munzer,[25] and needed quite as much the argument of miracles for its support.

But now when we look into the actual course of history, we find it in no agreement whatever with these reasonable presumptions and anticipations, as directed either towards the end of this supposed failure of the church or towards its beginning. The Reformation, we all know, lacked entirely the seal of miracles, the only truly apostolical warrant for a really apostolical work. In this respect it bore no resemblance to the mission of Elijah, the restorer of Moses in the apostate kingdom of Israel. That such an apostasy, reaching through a thousand years, should finally be set right in this way, is not a little strange. On the other hand however, the coming in of the apostasy is more strangely conditioned still. Never was a revolution so vast and important, so broad and deep in its course, so sweepingly disastrous in its effects. We may apply to it without exaggeration the strong figure: "In those days the sun shall be darkened, and the moon shall not give her light, and the stars of heaven shall fall, and the powers that are in heaven shall be shaken [Mark 13:24–25]." The church, having in charge the most vital interests of a fallen world, proved recreant to her solemn trust, fell from her high estate, and became literally the seat of Antichrist and a synagogue of Satan.[26] Thus fearfully radical, the revolution was at the same time no less dreadfully universal. And yet, strange to say, no one can tell when or how it came to pass. We have indeed certain schemes that pretend to be such an explanation. But these, when examined, are found to be purely fanciful attempts to solve the demands of a theory already adopted, rather than the exhibition of actual historical grounds for the theory itself. It is assumed in the first place that a certain form of religion, Puritanism for instance, is taught in the New Testament, and therefore that it must have prevailed in the apostolical and primitive church; it is very evident in the next place, that a wholly different form of religion prevailed in the church of the third and fourth centuries, a system intrinsically at war with Puritanism and leading directly towards full Catholicism; here then the fact of an apostasy is supposed to be historically established, and any combination now is taken to be rational and legitimate that serves at all to bind

---

24. [See Calvin's third point in his "Prefatory Address," *Institutes* 1:14–18 for a discussion on miracles.]

25. [Nicholas Storch (d. 1530); a German Anabaptist and leader of the Zwincken Prophets who sought to establish a community of the elect only. The group never settled anywhere for very long. Storch died in Bavaria. Thomas Müntzer (c. 1490–1520); a German Anabaptist who claimed special direct inspiration by the Holy Spirit. After he was expelled from Bohemia and the Holy Roman Empire, he helped lead the Peasants Revolt (1525). He was captured at the Battle of Frankenhausen and executed.]

26. ["Synagogue of Satan": Rev 2:9; "seat of Antichrist" might be an assimilation of the popular images of Antichrist to Rev 2:13; 13:2; 16:10.]

the two sides of it plausibly together. So we have various pretty plans or methods, that of the Quakers, that of the Baptists, that of the Independents, that of the Presbyterians, and coming down somewhat farther that also of the Episcopalians,[27] setting forth with more or less particularity how the corruption of pure Christianity in the first ages took place, first one step and then another, till at last the face of it was totally altered and changed; but if we call for the direct proof of these fine spun constructions, we find it to be either wanting altogether, or at best to consist in a few stray words, picked up here and there without regard to the general formation from which they are taken, and of such slippery and extremely brittle sense, that one may well feel astounded to see what weight they are made to bear. It seems to be counted sufficient for the most part, if no direct proof can be quoted the other way, or if the force of any such quotation can be ingeniously set aside. If Irenæus speak not of infant baptism in terms that cut off all captious debate, the Baptists hold it a good argument that the baptism of infants in his time was unknown. If Justin Martyr[28] teach not diocesan episcopacy in the same terms with Cyprian, the Presbyterians lay hold of him as a good witness that the ambition of prelacy was not yet born. If the primacy of the Roman see be not positively declared by the earliest fathers in round set phrase, the Episcopalians take it as so much testimony that this usurpation, as they call it, came in at a later day. If it appear that the Apostles' Creed is not quoted in its full present form before the fourth century, Puritanism chuckles over the nice discovery, and on the strength of it proceeds at once to deny its apostolical and primitive authority, treating its article of the church as a figment, and seeing in it the germs at least of all sorts of Popish error and delusion.[29] And so it goes throughout the chapter. It never seems to enter the head of these self-complacent theorizers, that the burden of proof lies of right first and foremost upon themselves; that the difficulty of making out clear and plain testimony in every case for the negative of their arbitrary positions, is not in and of itself any testimony whatever in favor of these positions; that the *indifference* of the argument in this form, the mere want of positive and direct testimony either way, is itself in truth a most powerful presumption, not in favor of their theories, but against them, and in favor only of the cause to which they are variously opposed. The grand difficulty is just to see, how so great an apostacy as is here supposed to have had place, turning the fair

---

27. [The Quakers, or The Society of Friends, were founded by George Fox (1624–91). The Independents are the Congregationalists of English Puritanism. The Baptists began in England in the seventeenth century as an off-shoot of the Congregationalists. The Presbyterians were the English Puritans who gained power in the English Civil War and formalized their creedal statements at the Westminster Assembly (1643–53). The Episcopalians are the American Church which become independent from the Anglican Church in 1783. All of these sects are derived from the Church of England.]

28. [Justin Martyr (c. 100–69), one of the earliest Christian apologists. He was trained as a philosopher and continued to wear the philosopher's cloak after his conversion. His apologetic writings were attempts to defend Christian faith and practice against popular misconceptions which were circulating through the empire. He was martyred during the reign of Marcus Aurelius (121–80).]

29. [Nevin, "Puritanism and the Creed," MTSS 8:103–21.]

Document 2: Early Christianity: Second Article.

bride of the Lamb in so short a time into the similitude of a harlot, should have gone forward through its several stages or steps, as laid down in either of these schemes, and yet have left no trace of its dire revolutionary march on the historic page!

That false tendencies might begin to work in a pure state of the church, is not hard to believe. But the case before us involves immeasurably more than this. These tendencies are taken to be from the start in full opposition to the genius and spirit of the Gospel; they work rapidly in fact towards its overthrow; they bring in by degrees new ideas and practices altogether, the fruit of cunning secular pride and borrowed from Judaism or Paganism, that go directly to undermine and break up the simple evangelical system of earlier times; and yet they provoke no opposition, excite no alarm, but make an easy prey of the whole church, as it would seem, without a protesting cry or a contradictory stroke. The ministers took the lead in the bad movement, and the people fell in passively with their wrong guidance. All sorts of pious lies and forgeries were resorted to for its support; and the daughter of Zion was either too silly to perceive the fraud, or too sleepy to lay it seriously to heart. The old faith died thus, and gave no sign. The apostacy came in without an effort or a struggle. True, as we are told, it had stages and degrees. But each new stage found a generation ready to accept it, as the undoubted sense of the faith they had received from their fathers. The work went silently but surely forward always in the same false direction. It carried along with it the universal church. When this comes fully into view in the fourth century, we find, not a part of it merely, but the entire body fully committed to the sacramental, liturgical, churchly and priestly system, with the full persuasion that the whole of it had come down from the earliest times. All history may be defied, to furnish any parallel to such a revolution, any change political or religious at once so vast and yet so entirely without noise. It passes before us like a scene of magic. As some one has observed, it is as though the world on some one night had gone to bed Protestant or Puritan, and on waking the next morning found itself thoroughly and universally Catholic.

Only, think of a single province, such as modern New England for instance, in the course of one or two hundred years throwing off the whole type of its religion in this way, and with general consent accepting another of diametrically opposite character and cast, without a single monument to inform posterity how the thing was done. Think of her associations and consociations, with their system of parity and rank democracy, passing over in so short a time to a well ordered hierarchy, revolving round a single centre. Think of her free prayers losing themselves in liturgical forms, her naked spiritualism stooping to clothe itself with the mummery of outward ceremonies and rites, crossings, bowings, sprinklings, with all the paraphernalia of a truly pontifical worship. Think of her sacraments turning from barren signs into supernatural mysteries, of the simple memorial of the Lord's supper in particular assuming the character of a real sacrifice for the sins of the living and the dead, and running into the bold and utterly confounding tenet of transubstantiation. Think of her mission of worldly prudence, utility, materialism and common sense, running out into the glorification of monasticism, voluntary poverty, the angelical life of celibates and virgins. Imagine these and other kindred transformations, we say, accomplished between the days of Dr. Increase Mather[30] and those of President Dwight,[31] and all so smoothly and quietly as to leave no trace, not a solitary record or sign of resistance, protestation, division or dissent, to inform posterity in any case when or how the change took place. Would it not be a moral miracle, transcending entirely the common order of history? But in the hypothesis before us, the miracle goes far beyond this. It embraces not one province only, but many, widely separated in space, and differing in every social and national respect. It is universal Christendom, from Britain to Africa, from Spain to India, that is found to have yielded simultaneously to the spirit of defection and revolt, as though it had been animated through all its borders with one and the same principle of evil, bewildering its senses and hurrying it among the tombs. Nothing could better show the universality of the supposed apostasy, and the deep root it had taken previously in the mind and life of the church, than the grand divisions that took place in the fourth and fifth centuries; giving rise to rival communions on a vast scale, some of which have upheld themselves down to the present time. These could not of course consent in any such innovation after they fell asunder; on the contrary, the laws of party and sect would have been sure to bring out a loud complaint of the change, if anything of the sort lay within the reach of knowledge before. But the Arians and Donatists brought no charge here against the Catholics.[32] The Nestorians and Monophysites went out and founded new churches, which remain to this day;[33] but they carried along with the characteristic peculiarities of the Roman system, which they have never ceased since to regard as of truly apostolic force and date. These have indeed become for the most part mere petrifactions or dead fossil remains; but in this character they still bear powerful and unanswerable testimony to the fact of which we now speak, the universal and unquestioned authority of this system throughout Christendom in the fourth century. No language written on rocks for this purpose, could be more sure or plain.

30. [Increase Mather (1639–1723); New England Puritan pastor and president of Harvard College.]

31. [Timothy Dwight IV (1752–1817); Congregationalist pastor and president of Yale College. He was Jonathan Edwards' (1703–58) grandson.]

32. [Arianism, a Trinitarian heresy that arose in the fourth century based on the teachings of Arius (c. 250–336), denied the full deity of the Son as being of the same nature as the Father and was condemned as a heresy at the Council of Nicaea (325). The Donatists were a schismatic group which broke from the Catholic Church in Africa. They held to the absolute purity of the Church especially in regard to the lapsed (those who capitulated during the times of persecution). It was formally condemned at the Council of Carthage (411).]

33. [Nestorianism was a Christological heresy which claimed the two natures of the incarnate Christ demanded that there be two persons as well. It was named for Nestorius (d. 451) and condemned as a heresy at the Council of Ephesus (431). They formed a church based in Persia and are today known at the Assyrian Church of the East. Monophysitism was a Christological heresy that posited that the incarnate Christ had only one nature (Gk. *phusis*) rather than a human and a divine nature. Some of its forms were known as Eutychianism for Eutyches (d. 454), its chief proponent, and condemned at the Council of Chalcedon (451). After Chalcedon, the Monophysites formed their own church which settled in Armenia and is today known at the Armenian Apostolic Church.]

Document 2: Early Christianity: Second Article.

The contrast in which this noiseless revolution stands with the known vigilance of the church in other things, serves to make it still more striking and strange. Christianity in the beginning was anything but a passive and inert system, which offered itself like wax to every impression from abroad. It had a most intense life of its own, power to assimilate and reject in self-conservation over against all dissolving agencies, as never any system of thought or life before. It is just this organific and all subduing character that forms the grand argument from history, for its divine origins and heavenly truth. Neander has it continually in view.[34] What subtle speculations were not tried, in the first centuries on the part of the Gnostics, Manicheans, Sabellians, Arians, and others, to corrupt the truth;[35] and yet how promptly and vigorously all these innovations were met and repelled. It was not reflection either that led the way in the contests with heresy, but a fine tact rather and living instinct for the orthodoxy to which they were always opposed. Danger was felt with keen inward sensibility even afar off, and no time was lost in sounding an alarm. There is no lack accordingly of historical witnesses and monuments to show here what actually took place. They abound in the form of controversies, councils, heretical parties, and wide-spread long enduring schisms. And yet in the midst of all this vigilant activity, if we are to believe our Puritan hypothesis, the great apostacy of Popery came in upon the universal church so quietly that no one now can lay his hand on the origin of a single one of all its manifold forms of corruption and abuse. It gave rise to no controversy, created no party, led to no schism. The Argus-eyed[36] jealousy of the heretical sects themselves was blinded and deceived. They saw not the wholesale treason which was going forward in such bold and impudent style; and it was allowed by all of them accordingly to pass, without one syllable of remonstrance or rebuke.

But this is not all. The prodigiousness of the theory goes still farther. It is by the Bible it pretends to be sure that the church started on the Puritan model, and that this later state of it therefore must be counted a grand falling away from its first and only true form. But now the Bible itself comes down to us through the hands of this same apostate church, which made no conscience, we are sometimes told, of forging and falsifying documents, to almost any extent, for the purpose of carrying out its own wrong; and we have absolutely to take it on trust from the credit solely of this suspicious source. This is particularly clear, in the case of the New Testament, the main authority of course

---

34. [Johann August Wilhelm Neander (1789–1850) was fundamental to Nevin's (and Mercersburg's) view of history. See this volume's general introduction for details and sources.]

35. [Gnosticism was a second and third century Christian heresy which attempted to reconcile Greek dualistic philosophy with the Christian message. Nevin frequently used "Gnosticism" to refer to modern thinkers who deny the full implications of the incarnation. Manicheanism was a Gnostic sect founded by Mani the Persian (c. 215–75), which emphasized a form of extreme dualism and asceticism. Sabellianism was a Trinitarian heresy known as modalism. Little is known of the founder, Sabellius, other than he lived sometime in the third century.]

36. [Argus Panoptes ("All-Seeing") had one hundred eyes over his head or body (*Encyclopedia Britannica*, "Argus").]

for the question here in debate. What authority was it that fixed the sacred canon, determining in the beginning what books were to be taken as inspired, and what other books not a few were to be rejected as apocryphal or false? The authority precisely of that very organization, which these same canonical writings are now brought forward to convict of palpable wholesale unfaithfulness to its own trust; and which was in the full career of such sad apostasy indeed, while diligently and as it would seem most faithfully fulfilling this great commission, for the use of the world in later ages. The work of settling the canon began in the second century, but was not fully completed before the fourth; and then it was by the tradition and authority of the church simply that the work, regarded through all this time as one and the same, was brought thus to its final consummation. We have already seen however, where the church stood in the fourth century, and in what direction all its forces were tending in the third. Is it not strange, that we should be under obligation to such a growing mystery of iniquity for so excellent and holy a gift, and that coming to us in this way we can still be so sure that every line of it is inspired, so as to make it the only rule of our faith? Is it not strange that the very Church, which had still divine tact enough for the delicate function of settling the canon, had at the same time no power to see or feel her own glaring departures from the light of this infallible rule, but actually gloried in it as the oracle and voucher of her claims;—not dreaming how, after the lapse of twelve hundred years, it should blaze forth into quite another signification, and be a swift witness against herself, as the whore of Babylon, the mother of abominations and lies.[37]

Nor does the wonder stop here. The faithful execution of this most responsible task of settling the canon, and handing down an uncorrupted Bible, for the use of all following time, is not the only merit of the ancient church. These ages of apostasy, as they are here considered, were at the same time, by general acknowledgment, ages of extraordinary faith and power. Miracles abounded. Charity had no limits. Zeal stopped at no sacrifices, however hard or great. The blood of martyrs flowed in torrents. The heroism of confessors braved every danger. Bishops ruled at the peril of their lives. In the catalogue of Roman popes, no less than thirty before the time of Constantine, that is, the whole list that for with only two or three exceptions, wear the crown of martyrdom. Nor was this zeal outward only, the fanaticism of a name or a sect. Along with it burned, as we have seen before, a glowing interest in the truth, an inextinguishable ardor in maintaining the faith once delivered to the saints. Heresies quailed from its presence. Schisms withered under its blasting rebuke. Thus, in the midst of all opposition, it went forward from strength to strength, till in the beginning of the fourth century finally we behold it fairly seated on the throne of the Cesars. And this outward victory, as Neander will tell us, was but a faint symbol of the far more important revolution it had already accomplished in the empire of human thought, the interior world of the spirit. Here was brought to pass, in the same time, a true creation from the bosom of chaos, such as the world had never seen before, over

---

37. [The figure of Rev 17:1–18, generally held by Protestants to be identical with the papacy.]

which the morning stars sang together and the sons of God shouted for joy [Job 38:7]. In foundation and principle at least, old things, whether of philosophy, or of art, or of morality and social life, were passed away, and, lo, all things had become new [2 Cor 5:17]. This is the grand argument for Christianity from its *miraculous success*; of which Puritanism, when it suits, is ready to make as loud use as any part of the church besides, as though it really believed this ancient glory to be in some way after all truly and properly its own. And yet by the same Puritanism we are told again, when another object is in view, that the cause which thus conquered the world by manifest supernatural power, was itself so deserted and abandoned by its glorified King, as to be all the while rushing at the same time towards universal apostacy and ruin, by the mystery of sin which it carried in its own womb!

And then again, when this mystery came fully out, and the apostacy stood completely revealed in the form of full grown and undisguised Popery, followed as we all know by the long deep night of the middle ages, there was still no end to the moral wonders of which we now speak. The Papacy itself is a wonder of wonders. There is nothing like it in all history besides. So all will feel, who stop to *think* about it in more than a fool's way. History too, even in Protestant hands, is coming more and more to do justice to the vast and mighty merits of the system in past times, bringing in light upon it, and scaring away the owls and bats that have so long been accustomed to hoot and flit here at their own will. These ages of darkness as they are called, were still, to an extent now hard to understand, ages also of faith. The church still had, as in earlier days, her miracles, her martyrdoms, her missionary zeal, her holy bishops and saints, her works of charity and love, her care for sound doctrine, her sense of a heavenly commission, and her more than human power to convert and subdue nations. True, the world was dark, very dark and very wild; and its corruptions were powerfully felt at times in her own bosom; but no one but a simpleton or a knave will pretend to make this barbarism *her* work, or to lay it as a crime to *her* charge. She was the rock that beat back its proud waves. She was the power of order and law, the fountain of a new civilization, in the midst of its tumultuating chaos. Take the conversion of Saxon England in the time of Gregory the Great, and the long work of moral organization with which it was followed in succeeding centuries. Look at the missionaries that proceeded from this island, apostolical bishops and holy monks, in the seventh and eighth centuries, planting churches successfully in the countries of the Rhine. Consider the entire evangelization of the new barbarous Europe.[38] Is it not a work fairly parallel, to say the least, with the conquest of the old Roman empire in the first ages? Is not the argument of "miraculous success" quite as strong here as there? Think again of the theology of this old Catholic church, of its body of ethics, of its canon law. The cathedral of Cologne is no such work as this last; the dome of St. Peter is less sublimely grand than the first. How wonderful, that the theological determinations of the fifth and sixth centuries, in the midst of endless agitation and strife, should fall so steadily the right way; and

---

38. [See the contemporary study in Fletcher, *Barbarian Conversions*.]

also that these true conclusions should seem to hang so constantly, in the last instance, on the mind and voice of Rome. And then in the ages that followed, how wonderful again, that when there was but small power to build, nothing should be done at least to unsettle and pull down the edifice of sound doctrine as it stood before. However much of rubbish the Reformation found occasion to remove, it was still compelled to do homage to the main body of the Roman theology as orthodox and right; and to this day Protestantism has no valid mission in the world, any farther than it is willing to build on this old foundation. Its distinctive doctrines are of no force, except in organic union with the grand scheme of truth, which is exhibited in the ancient creeds and in the decisions of the first general councils. Cut off from this root, taken out from the stream of this only sure and safe tradition, even the authority of the Bible becomes uncertain, and the article of justification by faith itself is turned into a perilous lie. In every view, we may say, the work and mission of the church after the fourth century continue to be, as they were before, the most wonderful and solemn fact in the world. And yet, according to the theory now in hand, it was no longer an apostatizing church merely, but a body fully apostate, fallen from the truth, opposed to righteousness, in league with Satan, and systematically bent on destroying all that Christ came into the world to build. Antichrist, the man of sin, reigned terribly supreme, "sitting in the temple of God, and opposing and exalting himself above all that is called God or that is worshipped [2 Thess 2:4 modified]." How truly confounding the incongruous combination! How perfectly self-satirical the incoherent face of the contradiction!

[Puritanism's Empty Ecclesiology]

The theory is false. It rests on no historical bottom. The scriptures are against it. All sound religious feeling is at war with it. Facts of every sort conspire to prove it untrue. It is a sheer hypothesis, a sort of Protestant myth we may call it, got up to serve a purpose, and hardened by time and tradition now into the form of a sacred prejudice; or rather it is an arbitrary construction, that seeks to turn into mere myth and fable the true history of the church. In this view we have said, that it may fairly challenge comparison with the famous critical systems of such men as Strauss and Baur.[39] Indeed these are in some respects more plausible. They take the ground, that Christianity as we have it now in the New Testament is a product properly of the second century, rather than the true birth historically of the first; that the original facts and doctrines were far more simple; that the religious imagination of the infant church, or the spirit of controversy among its Jewish and Gentile parties, idealized all into new shape and

---

39. [Ferdinand Christian Baur (1792–1860) and David Friedrich Strauss (1808–74) applied Hegel's concept of historical development to the interpretation of the New Testament and early Christianity, so as to remove any sense of supernatural origins. Strauss's *Life of Jesus* "rejected the historicity of all supernatural elements" in the gospels, a view that has influenced certain strands of what has been called "the quest for the historical Jesus." Schaff, *Development*, MTSS 3:344–45, 368–69.]

Document 2: Early Christianity: Second Article.

form; and that most of our canonical books were then forged according to this new and higher scheme, and piously fathered upon the apostles to give them more credit and weight. Monstrous as this representation is, it is truly wonderful what a show of learning, critical and historical, can be urged in its favor, enough almost to deceive at times the very elect themselves [Matt 24:24]. And yet it is a wild theory, which needs no other force to upset it in the end than the simple persuasion, that the church itself is of divine origin, and not the most abominable imposture that ever has appeared in the world. The article: "I believe in the holy catholic church," which must ever precede in the order of faith, as Augustine tells us,[40] that other article: "I believe in the holy inspired bible," wherever it really prevails in the heart, scatters to the wind all imaginable sophistries and subtleties in this form. The logic of Hegel[41] before it, becomes no better than a spider's web. The true answer to Strauss, as well as to the whole Tübingen school,[42] is an act of faith in the mystery of Christianity itself, as we have this concretely set forth in the ancient creed.[43] But now what better after all, as tried by the touchstone of such faith, is the Puritan theory at which we are now looking? Is it not equally borrowed from the clouds, and at the same time equally fatal to all firm and full confidence in the supernatural origin and mission of the church, whose history it pretends to follow in so strange a way? To allow the suppositions of Strauss or of Baur, is from the very outset to drag down Christianity from the skies, and to make its whole signification not only human merely and earthly, but grossly carnal also and devilish. It is morally impossible to conceive of its rise and growth in any such style, and yet look upon it as a direct revelation in any way from heaven. The two conceptions are incompatible, and go at once to destroy each other. And just so also, we say, to allow the historical suppositions of Puritanism, is to convert the divine origin of the church into a fiction or a dream. Even such a scheme of history as we have in Mosheim for instance, or in the text book of Gieseler[44] with all its show of authorities, is intrinsically at war with any real faith in this mystery, and can never fail

---

40. [Nevin might have had in mind Augustine's "*Ego vero evangelio non crederem, nisi me Catholicae ecclesiae commoveret auctoritas.*" {Trans. "I would not have believed the gospel had I not been moved by the authority of the Catholic church." Augustine, *Against the Epistle of Manichæus*, in *Nicene and Post-Nicene Fathers*, 4:131.} Nevin quoted this a year later in "The Anti-Creed Heresy," MTSS 8:201n12.]

41. [For Hegel and his "logic," see above, 17n95, as well as Borneman, general introduction, part 1 to *Philosophy and the Contemporary World*, MTSS 11:3n1, 9–10.]

42. [The academic home of Baur and Strauss.]

43. [On the Church as an object of faith, see Nevin, *The Church*, MTSS 5:146–56; "Catholicism," MTSS 7:11–32; "The Apostles' Creed," MTSS 8:84–87.]

44. [Johann Lorenz von Mosheim (1694–1755) "introduced objectivity to the study of church history with his *Institutiones historiae ecclesiasticae* (1729)" (Schaff, *Development*, MTSS 3:361). Johann Karl Ludwig Gieseler (1792–1854) was a German Protestant church historian known among English-speaking theologians for *Lehrbuch der Kirchengeschichte*; trans. *A Compendium of Ecclesiastical History* (New York: Harper & Brothers, 1849). Nevin thought Mosheim needed to be "sanctif{ied}" with more pious sources. He regarded Gieseler as "rationalistically cold and dry," but the text was "accompanied" with "full extracts from original sources" that made it especially valuable. Nevin, *My Own Life*, 144.]

to undermine it where no antidote is in the way. The sense of authorities, the force even of facts, turns always on the standpoint from which they are viewed. An infidel hypothesis necessarily sees all persons and things in the light of its own evil and false eye. Both Mosheim and Gieseler in this way are very little better than Gibbon.[45] To accept their disposition and combination of facts, is of necessity to give up secretly the whole idea, that the glorious things spoken of Zion in the beginning ever had any truth [Ps 87:2–3]. But the common Puritan scheme goes farther still in this infidel direction. It outrages all moral verisimilitude, and joins together such contraries as by no possibility *can* cohere in the same real and firm belief. What sane mind can bring its theory of the wholesale errors and corruptions of the early church, into any sort of harmony with the assured feeling, that the heavenly and supernatural conditions of its presence in the world were ever in any real sense what they are described as being, either in the New Testament or in the ancient creeds? There is not the least doubt, but that the theory in fact tends directly to destroy all such assurance, by the monstrous and violent incompatibility of its own terms. This does not imply indeed a formal giving up of the point in question, as an article of so called faith. That is the true logical end of the contradiction. But all men have not logic; and it is quite possible to carry out the rationalism in another form. The article may be shorn of all historical connections, and thrust out from the real world altogether, so that the supernatural in the case shall have no actual being whatever in the bosom of the natural, but be only as a cloud or dream floating over it and beyond it in Gnostic or Nestorian style.[46] In such shape it may be possible still, to believe in a holy catholic church, which was from the very start the mere foot ball of Satan.[47] But in the same way it is possible also to believe, that the moon is made of green cheese.

And so we come finally to the conclusion, towards which this discussion has been looking and reaching all along, that there never was in truth any such identity as Puritanism dreams between the early church and its own modern self. Its hypothesis of the vast and terrible revolution by which all is taken to have fallen so soon into another type, is unnatural, unhistorical, irreligious, and fairly incredible; and we have a right to infer accordingly that its primary premise is false. No such primeval state ever existed, as makes it necessary to consider the whole subsequent history of the church an apostacy only and a grand universal lie. Dr. Bacon[48] and others are entirely mistaken, when they imagine any counterpart to New England Congregationalism in the days of Ignatius and Polycarp, or please themselves with the thought that the

---

45. [Edward Gibbon (1737–94), famous for his *Decline and Fall of the Roman Empire*, an event that he blamed on Christianity. He thus became for Nevin a prime example of anti-Christian skepticism.]

46. [See Nevin, *Antichrist*, MTSS 5:192–97 for his critique of Gnosticism and Nestorianism.]

47. [Most likely a reference to an early version of soccer since American football was not yet an organized sport. For information on the history of the football, see http://www.antiquefootball.com/football_evolution.htm.]

48. [Quoted at length above, 42–46.]

martyrs of Lyons and Vienne, in the second century, suffered for just such views of truth as are now preached in the pulpits of Connecticut and Massachusetts. An overwhelming presumption of the contrary lies before us in the later history of the church; and it needs only some proper freedom from prejudice, we will now add, to find this presumption abundantly confirmed by the historical data of this older period itself. True, these are comparatively sparse, and often a good deal indefinite and vague; and it is not impossible for an adroit criticism, on this account, to twist them to its own mind—especially if it have *carte blanche* to treat as interpolation or corruption every passage that may prove refractory in the process. But the violence of all such criticism appears plainly enough on its own front, and when it has made the most of its cause in this way, the proofs that stand in clear force against it are still amply sufficient for the purpose now affirmed. The force of the argument is sometimes enfeebled and obscured, by fixing attention too exclusively on single points and particular phrases and texts. But what the case requires, is a steady regard to the broad issue in question as a whole, and a fair estimate of the testimony or evidence concerned under the like universal view. It is not necessary to stickle for this or that point separately considered; nor is it worth while to waste either ink or breath, in settling the credit or fixing the sense of one clause here and another there, in the remains of Clemens Romanus, Ignatius, or Irenæus.[49] The main question in controversy is of far wider scope and range than any such particular eddies raised in its bosom, and is capable of being brought to some general conclusion in a much more comprehensive and summary way. It regards not so much mere prelacy, or the use of a liturgy in this or that particular form, or the positive practice of infant baptism at a given time, or the mode in which the water was applied in this sacrament whether in the case of infants or adults, or the acknowledgment of transubstantiation and the sacrifice of the mass—it regards not so much any one or all of these and such like points separately taken, we say, as it does rather the whole idea and scheme of the church, in which all such points are comprehended, and from which they derive necessarily in the end their proper significance and import. The determination of these single points, we know, is of no small consequence, where it can be fairly reached, for the settlement also of this general and main question. But what we wish to say is, that in the case before us the main question is not thrown absolutely or conclusively on any particular issues of this sort, which it may be possible for a small criticism to envelope here and there in dust or smoke. The general spirit and form of early Christianity are capable of being understood from its few historical remains, especially when taken in connection with the tradition of following times, in such manner as fairly to overwhelm the nibbling of such mouse-like criticism at particular points, instead of being dependent upon it at all in any way for their own authority. The sense of the whole here is so clear and plain, that we have the best

---

49. [Clement of Rome (exact dates unknown), Bishop of Rome, considered to be the third bishop of Rome. He wrote an epistle to the church at Corinth, which is his only known work, though others bear his name.]

right to use it as a key or guide for the interpretation of the parts. Take for instance the Baptistic points of immersion and the exclusion of infants from the church; all turns finally on the light in which the sacrament of baptism itself was regarded, and so on the view taken of the supernatural constitution of Christianity;[50] and it requires nothing more than the most general acquaintance with the first age of the church, and the writings that have come down to us from that time, to see and feel surely that the whole standpoint of Christianity then was completely different from that of the Baptists in the present day; so that no proof they may ever seem to have for their favorite hobbies[51] can have any force at all to identify the one position with the other. Allowing the points of correspondence they claim to be real, to what can it amount still so long as it is plain, that the whole inward posture of the early church was in contradiction to the unmystical, unsacramental and unchurchly system, in which the Baptists now glory as pre-eminently their own? The best and most sufficient defence against this system after all, is simply to be somewhat imbued with the general soul of the primitive church, as it looks forth upon us from the writings of Ignatius, Justin Martyr, Irenaeus and Tertullian. With any such preparation, no one can be in danger of mistaking the modern fiction for the ancient truth. They belong to different worlds; and only to be at home in the one, is necessarily to feel the other in the same measure foreign and strange.[52]

[The Church Fathers Against the Puritans]

It is in this general way that we propose now, to try briefly the whole question here offered for our consideration. May the Puritan system as a whole, whether carried out in the Baptistic or in the Congregational or in the Presbyterian form, or allowed even to get as far as low-church Episcopalianism, be regarded as constitutionally one and the same with what Christianity was in the second century, and so by implication in the latter part also of the first?[53] To settle this question, we need not go minutely into the Ignatian controversy, or any other of like accidental and mechanical character. Strike out as an interpolation every passage in Ignatius that goes directly for episcopacy, and for the argument now in hand but little is lost from the weight that truly and properly belongs to him as a witness. For a really thoughtful mind, this weight lies in no such texts nakedly taken, but in the reigning drift and complexion of the epistles as

---

50. [Nevin has just made this argument in "Noel on Baptism," MTSS 6:97–101.]

51. [Short for "hobby horse."]

52. [In this long paragraph, Nevin has simply been saying that to understand the church fathers aright, we must be able to see "the whole," or as we would say today, understand their teaching and practices "holistically." See further Nevin, "Thoughts on the Church," MTSS 7.]

53. [This is the central question to the whole of Nevin's historical project in these essays. The way one answers this question determines both how one understands history and how one understands the church. Thus, at least at this stage of Nevin's life, the key question which must be answered correctly is, "what is the church?"]

Document 2: Early Christianity: Second Article.

a whole. A very short writing in this way, such for instance as Pliny's celebrated letter to Trajan,[54] where there is any power whatever to reproduce in the mind its historical surroundings, may convey by its total representation far more than any criticism can reach by mere verbal dissection. In this way it is very easy, we think, to bring the question here propounded to a full and conclusive settlement. Whatever Christianity may have been in the second century, and in the age immediately following that of the Apostles, it was not the system that is now known and honored as Puritanism, and least of all was it this system under its most approved and complete form as it reigns at the present time in New England.

I. In the first place, it rested throughout on a wholly different conception of the *Church*. With Puritanism, the church is acknowledged to be divine, as having been founded originally by Christ, and as standing still in some way under the superintendence of his Spirit. But this supernatural character, in the end, resolves itself very much into an unhistorical abstraction. The church is not conceived of as a real outward as well as inward constitution, having in such view of its own organism as a single whole, and keeping up a true identity with itself in space and time. It is of the nature rather of a school; the divinity of it falls back entirely upon its doctrine; or rather on the Bible which is taken to contain this doctrine, while men are left to draw it from this source, as they best can, in a perfectly human way. The only realization of the church after all in the world, thus, is in the form of an invisible communion, representing all those who are happy enough, under the guidance of the Holy Ghost, to find the truth. In the way of such inward spiritual experience, on the part of individuals, there is room to speak still of supernatural operations reaching over into the sphere of our present life; but to dream of any other supernaturalism in the church than this, is counted dangerous superstition. The idea of the church in this way is stripped of all mystery; it falls to the level of any other social or political institution; to believe in it is just as easy, as to believe in the Copernican system or the Parliament of Great Britain. It is neither catholic nor apostolical, except as Aristotle's philosophy may be called Aristotelian for all who are satisfied that he was the author of it. No divine obligation, no supernatural necessity, accordingly, is felt to go along with any actual organization bearing this name; a thousand organizations, wholly independent of one another, may have equal right to such distinction; and though all should fail even for centuries, it would be perfectly possible to restore the machinery again in full force, at any time, and with all its original powers, by the help simply of the Bible, the true *magna charta* of man's rights and privileges in this form. The divine character of the church is in no sense parallel, for Puritanism, with the divine character of the bible. It holds it for a sort of profanity to make any such account of its heavenly authority. Theoretically and practically,

---

54. [In which Pliny, governor of a province in Asia Minor inquired (c. 112) of the emperor Trajan what to do with Christians. In short, Trajan replied, they were not to be sought out, and if they denounced Christianity, were to be pardoned. Pliny gave a brief description of Christian worship, as his information had it. *Dictionary of the Christian Church*, 1301.]

Puritanism treats the actual church[55] as a simply human institution, the work of man's hands, and of divine force at the last only as civil government is of such force, or in the sense rather of the republican maxim, "The voice of the people is the voice of God." The powers of the organization, and so of course the offices by which they are to be executed, are held to come, not from above, but from below. It is made the glory of Christianity to be purely and intensely democratic. No *jure divino* constitution is to be allowed to the ministry, no superhuman force to its functions. The people are the fountain of right, and the basis of all order and law. Congregationalism completes itself in full Independency. All comes thus to the platform of common sense; all goes by popular judgment and popular vote.[56]

Now it is not the truth or worth of this theory, in itself considered, that we are here required to discuss; we merely affirm, that it is in no sort of harmony with the idea of the church which prevailed in the second century. This might be confidently inferred indeed from the simple fact, acknowledged on all sides, that the ruling features of the later church system come fully into view in the next century, as the only scheme known or thought of throughout the Christian world. To imagine the Puritan ideal, as we have it now exemplified in New England, turning itself over, by complete somerset,[57] in the course of one century, into the pattern of things presented for instance in Cyprian or the Apostolical Constitutions,[58] without so much as a historical whisper to show when or how the prodigious revolution was brought to pass, is much like pretending to take Gulliver's travels or the stories of Sinbad the Sailor for sober truth. But besides this, the authorities of the second century itself are full against the whole fancy which is here in question. The drift and spirit of every writing that has come down to us from this time, look quite a different way. To read Ignatius, or Polycarp, or Justin Martyr, or Irenæus, or Tertullian, is to feel ourselves surrounded in the very act with a churchly element, a sense of the mystical and supernatural, which falls in easily enough with the later faith of the primitive church, but not at all with the keen clear air of modern Puritanism, as this sweeps either the heaths of Scotland or the bleak hills of New England. We need not stop here to settle the precise polity of the church at every point, in the age after the Apostles. It is enough to know, that all proceeded on a view of its supernatural rights and powers, which was exactly the

55. [See general introduction for Nevin's use of "Ideal" and "Actual" church. Sometime after the essays in the volume were completed, he returned to the subject in a more tentative way in "Thoughts on the Church," MTSS 7:131–171.]

56. [Hatch, *Democratization*, discusses the impact of democratic principles on America's understanding of the church; see Wentz, *John Williamson Nevin* for a specific discussion of Nevin's thinking. As noted earlier, "common sense" is an allusion to the predominant American philosophy of Common Sense realism, which found Christian truth in the "facts" of the Bible, understood as a supernaturally-revealed textbook. See further Nevin, "Evangelical Radicalism," MTSS 11:310–14 for this mode of religious democracy.]

57. [That is, "somersault."]

58. ["A collection of ecclesiastical law dating from *c.* 350–80, and almost certainly of Syrian provenance" (*Dictionary of the Christian Church*, 90). It was written from an Arian point of view.]

Document 2: Early Christianity: Second Article.

reverse of what we have found to be the Puritan scheme. The church was considered a mystery, an object of faith, a supernatural fact in the world, not based at all on the will of men, but on the commission of Christ, the force of which it was held extended from the Apostles forward through all time. It was taken to rest on the ministry, which was regarded accordingly as having its origin and authority, not from the people, but from God. The idea of a democratic or simply popular constitution in the case finds no countenance in the New Testament; this proceeds throughout on the assumption rather that the powers both of doctrine and government for the church, start from above and not from below; the apostolate is the root of all following ministerial offices and functions. And fully conformable with this, is the theory and the actual order of the church in the period of which we now speak. We may appeal here even to Clement of Rome in the latter part of the first century, who in a memorable passage (*Ep. I. ad Corinth,* c. 42–44) urges the duty of submission to church rulers, on the ground of a divine order in their office, parallel with that of the Levitical priesthood under the Old Testament, of which God had shown himself so jealous through the ministry of his servant Moses.[59] To quote Ignatius on the same general point, may be taken as perfectly superfluous. It is not merely where he bears direct witness for episcopacy, that his testimony is of weight; the force of it lies rather in the universal tone of his several epistles. It is sometimes said, that the episcopal passages have the air of being interpolations, thrust into the text from a later age. But any one may readily see the contrary, who will take the trouble of reading the text with his own eyes, for the purpose of getting out of it its own sense instead of putting into it a sense to suit himself. There is nothing whatever in these passages at variance with the reigning tone of the epistles, but on the contrary they are in full keeping with this throughout.[60] There is hardly a sentence or a line indeed in Ignatius, that is not in spirit fully opposite to Puritanism, on the great question of the church. He has in his mind always the mystical order of the creed, according to which the fact of the incarnation underlies in a real way the fact of the church, as the carrying out of the same wonder for faith. In correspondence with the real union of divinity and humanity in Christ, his mystical body must have a real historical and visible being in the world as well as an invisible spiritual character,

---

59. "The apostles had their office from Christ," he tells us, "Christ from God; they were sent by him as he was sent by God. Both in right order according to God's will [42.1–2]." Clothed with full power after his resurrection, they went forth and founded churches on all sides, appointing tried men to preside over them as bishops and deacons, which was only fulfilling the sense of ancient prophecy, Is. lx: 17. This they did, in virtue of their own commission, to prevent contentions such as they knew were likely to arise; and not only did they appoint these first officers, but "they made arrangement also for the future, that when these should die other approved men should succeed to their place [44.2]." [Nevin's source—which he uses in "Cyprian" below—may have been *Patrum apostolicorum opera*; see 112–17. For a modern English version, see Clement, *Epistle to the Corinthians*, ACW 1:34–36.]

60. This is well shown by that most profound and acute critic, Dr. *Richard Rothe,* in his work entitled *Die Anfänge der christlichen Kirche,* where the authority of these epistles, and the whole subject of the constitution of the early church, are handled in a truly masterly style [Richard Rothe, *Die Anfänge der Christlichen Kirche und ihrer Verfassung*, vol. 1 (Wittenberg: Zimmermann'schen, 1837)].

and this must of necessity carry along with it in such view the attributes of unity and catholicity, as the signature of its superhuman authority. Hence the stress laid on the hierarchy, as the bond, not from below but from above, of that glorious *sacramentum unitatis* [unifying sacrament] on which was felt to hang the virtue and value of all grace in the church besides. Hence the holy martyr's horror of all schism. Obedience to the church is, in his view, obedience to Christ; to be out of communion with the bishop, in rupture with the one altar he guards and represents, is to have no part at the same time in the kingdom of God.[61] The unity must be somatic, as well as spiritual.[62] To fall away from this bond, is taken to be a falling away to the same extent from the lively sense of the mystery of the incarnation, a species of Gnosticism which turned the flesh of the Son of God into a mere phantom, and so robbed the Gospel of its heavenly power. For those who resolve Christ in this way into a phantom or abstraction, according to Ignatius, make themselves in the end to be without either substance or strength; all true christian strength comes from an apprehension of the whole mystery here in view as something historically and enduringly real. With this agrees again, as all know, the teaching of Irenæus in the latter part of the second century, as it has come down to us particularly in his celebrated work against heretics; and the same views substantially are presented to us also by Tertullian and Clement of Alexandria.

II. The contrary schemes of the church just noticed, involve with a sort of inward logical necessity different and contrary views also of the *ministry,* and of its relations to the body of the people. Puritanism makes the ministers of religion to be much like county or town officers, or sees in them at best only good religious counsellors and teachers, whom the people create for their own use and follow as far as to themselves may seem good. It spurns the whole idea of a divinely established hierarchy, drawing its rights and powers from heaven, and forming in its corporate character the bond of unity for the church, the ground of its perpetual stability, and the channel of all communications of grace to it from Him who is its glorified head. Every view of this sort runs counter to the democracy of the system, and does violence to its rationalism and common sense. It has no power constitutionally to believe in any really supernatural order reaching here below the time of the Apostles; and it must have accordingly the same guaranties for freedom precisely, which it is accustomed to ask and lean upon in the case of purely human and civil relations. Hence the vast account it makes of the popular element in all ecclesiastical interests and concerns, its zeal for the parity of the clergy, its deep seated hostility to the idea of the priesthood, as well as to all pontifical allusions or associations, in any connection with the work of the christian ministry.

---

61. Μη πλανασθε ἀδελφοι [με'] ἐι τις σχιζοντι ακουλουθει βασιλειαν Θεου οὐ κληρονομει, Ad Philad. c. 3 [trans. "Do not be deceived, my brethren: if a man runs after a schismatic, *he will not inherit the kingdom of God*" {Ignatius, *Epistles*, ACW 1:86, emphasis original}]. [Here Nevin was probably using Möhler's *Patrologie*, which he cites later: J. A. Möhler, *Patrologie, oder christliche Literärgeschichte*, vol. 1, ed. F. X. Reithmayr (Regensburg: G. Joseph Manz, 1840), 141n.]

62. ἱνα ἑνωσις ῃ σωματικη τε και πνεθματικη, Ad Magnes. c. 1, 13 [Möhler, *Patrologie*, 138n; trans. "so that there may be a oneness both of flesh and spirit" {Ignatius, *Epistles*, ACW 1:73}].

Document 2: Early Christianity: Second Article.

But now how different from all such thinking, is the light in which the ministry is found to stand in the second century. We need not go into any minute examination of the ecclesiastical polity which then prevailed. The question is not primarily whether there were three orders of clergy, or two, or only one; whether the bishops of Ignatius were diocesan in the modern sense, or simply parochial; but this rather, What relation did the overseership of the church bear to the mass of its members? And this, we say confidently, was neither Congregational *nor* Presbyterian, in the established sense of these distinctions at the present time. Let any one look into the writers already named, especially Ignatius and Irenæus, so as to catch at all their general tone and spirit, and he will feel it to be no better than burlesque, when Dr. Bacon allows himself to transfer to the scene of Smyrna or Lyons, in the second century, the picture he himself gives us of what he takes to be the repristination of the primitive church in this latter city in our own day.[63] The imagination of any such ecclesiastical republicanism, is completely foreign we may say from the whole spirit of this ancient period. Only look at the way in which Irenæus speaks of the episcopate and the apostolical succession, as the grand bulwark of truth against all heresy and schism; not once or twice merely, but whenever the subject comes in his way; showing the view to be inseparably joined with the entire scheme of Christianity in his mind. It is not to be disguised moreover, that the episcopate is viewed by him as a general corporation, having its centre of unity in the church of Rome. Against the novelty of heretics, he appeals to the clear succession of the catholic sees generally from the time of the Apostles; but then sums all up, by singling out the Roman church, founded by the most glorious apostles Peter and Paul, and having a certain principality for the church at large, as furnishing in its line of bishops a sure tradition of the faith held by the universal body from the beginning.[64] Take this system of church government as we may, it is the very reverse of all

63. "The meeting which I attended was a meeting of the brotherhood for mutual conference and inquiry. It was held in a school-room, and very much resembled a Congregational church meeting in New England. There was, however, one obvious difference. Those brethren were not merely concerned with the working of a system defined and understood in all its details, and familiar to them from their childhood. With the New Testament in their hands, they were inquiring after principles and rules of church order; and the question which then chiefly occupied their attention, and seemed somewhat to divide their opinions, was whether the government of their church should be in part committed to a body of elders, or remain entire in the hands of the assembled brethren. As I listened to the discussions, I could not but admire the free and manly, yet fraternal spirit in which it was conducted. And as I saw what a school for the development of various intellectual gifts, as well as for the culture of Christian affection, that church had been under its simple democratic organization, I felt quite sure that those brethren, with all their confidence in their teachers, would not be easily persuaded to subvert a system to which they were already so greatly indebted, or to divest themselves of the right of freely debating and voting on all their interests and duties as a church. [. . .] Rarely, have I enjoyed anything more than I enjoyed my visit to that missionary and apostolical church. Nor do I know where to look for a more satisfactory representation of the ideal and primitive Christianity, than in the city which was made illustrious so long ago by the labors of Irenæus, and by the martyrdom of Pothinus and Blandina."—*Letter from Lyons* ["Evangelical Religion in Lyons, France," (July 1851) 233, 266].

64. "*Sed quoniam valde longum est, in hoc tali volumine omnium ecclesiarum enumerare successiones: maximae et antiquissimae et omnibus cognitae, a gloriosissimis duobus Apostolis Petro et Paulo Romae*

such independency and popularity as are made to be the basis of ecclesiastical order in New England. Congregationalism lays no such stress on the episcopate or overseership of the church, regarded as an organic corporation, bound together always by a common centre, and having authority by unbroken tradition from the Apostles. And just as little have we here the type of modern Presbyterianism. The bishops of Ignatius, Polycarp, and Irenæus, however small may have been their charges, were not simply Presbyterian pastors. They have altogether a different look, and hold an entirely different relation to the people over whom they preside. Their rule is not indeed lordly, but neither is it simply representative and democratic; it is patriarchal rather, but at the same time an actual episcopate or oversight, derived from the chief Shepherd, at once supreme and self-sacrificing, in the full spirit of 1 Pet. v: 1–4. The order altogether is that of a hierarchy. The pastors are at the same time priests; and pontifical ideas fall in with their ministry easily and naturally from every side. The altar at which they serve is not merely a cold metaphor; and the sacrifice they offer upon it is mystical indeed, but nevertheless awfully and sublimely real. In one word, the system contains in element and germ at least the whole theory of the church that is more fully presented to us afterwards, in the writings of Cyprian and Augustine. There is no contradiction between the two schemes. The first flows over without any sort of violence or effort into the last; and becomes hard to understand, only when inquisitorial theorists put it to the rack, for the purpose of forcing from it a sense and voice which are not its own.[65]

III. This leads us naturally to the consideration of a third general and broadly palpable difference, between Puritanism and the early church, that namely which appears in the view they take of the *holy sacraments*. The modern system owns no real mystery either in baptism or the Lord's supper. It takes them indeed for divine institutions; but the sense of them is altogether natural only and human. They carry in them no objective force, have no power whatever to present what they represent; they are taken to be signs only or pictures of a grace, which exists not in the sacraments themselves, but out of them and beyond them under a wholly different form. Any virtue they have

---

fundatae et constitutae ecclesiae, eam quam habet ab Apostolis traditionem et annuntiatam hominibus fidem per successiones episcoporum pervenientem usque ad nos indicantes, confundimus omnes eos, &c.— *Ad hanc enim ecclesiam* propter potiorim principalitatem necesse est omnem convenire ecclesiam, &c."— Adv. haeres. III. 3. §. 2. [Irenaeus, *Adversus Haereses*, in *PG* 7:848–49. Trans. "Since, however, in a volume of this kind it would be too long to list the successions of all the Churches, we shall here address the tradition of the greatest and most ancient Church, known to all, founded and built up at Rome by the two most glorious apostles, Peter and Paul—the tradition receive from the apostles, as well as *the faith proclaimed* to men, which has come down even to us through the successions of the bishops. In this way we confound all those who in any way whatever, either because of an evil self-complacency, or of vainglory, or of blindness and evil-mindedness, gather in unauthorized assemblies. *For with this Church, because of her greater authority, it is necessary that every Church, that is, the faithful who are everywhere, should agree, because in her the apostolic tradition has always been safeguarded by those who are everywhere*" (Irenaeus, *Against the Heresies: Book 3*, ACW 64:32, latter emphasis Nevin's).]

65. This is shown, with what appears to us to be the most triumphant evidence, by Richard Rothe, in the great work to which we have before referred, *Die Anfänge d. chr. Kirche*, particularly in the third book [555–711].

is from the activity of the worshipper's mind, moved it may be by the Spirit of God to make good use of the outward and natural help to devotional thoughts and affections, which is thus placed within its reach. All beyond this is held to be superstition; and the sacramental system in particular of the Catholic church, as well as the whole doctrine of the real presence in its Protestant form also, is denounced and discarded as a purely diabolical figment, brought in under the Papacy in complete contradiction to the original sense of the Gospel, and without the least ground or reason in the practice of the church as it stood in the beginning.

It might seem plain to any child, that if any such low view had prevailed in the second century, it must have required a miracle to place the entire church, in its doctrine of the sacraments, where we find it to be in the fourth century, or to lead it over even in half a dozen centuries to so astounding a tenet as that of transubstantiation, with like universal and at the same time profoundly noiseless and peaceful revolution. But the second century can easily enough speak here for itself. And so clear and full in truth is its voice on the whole subject, that we venture to say no one can listen to it attentively, having any sort of confidence at the same time in the true apostolicity of its faith, and not be inspired with a feeling of downright horror, in view of the deep yawning gulph by which this is found to be sundered from what we have just now seen to be the modern system. Right or wrong, Puritanism is in its sacramental doctrine a grand apostacy, not only from what Protestantism was designed to be in the beginning, but also from the faith of the early church as it stood in the days of Pothinus and Irenæus. The martyrs of Lyons must have drawn back aghast from the view of baptism and the holy eucharist now commonly prevalent in New England; while their venerable bishops, no doubt, would have placed it in one category with the numerous heresies of the time, that went directly to overthrow the real appearance of Christ in the flesh.

Passing over baptism, let us fix our attention on the sacrament of the blessed eucharist. Nothing can be clearer at first glance, than that the fathers of this period make vastly more of the institution than is at all answerable to the natural and simple light in which it is regarded by Puritanism. They lay great stress on its doctrinal significance, as being in some vital way related to the mystery of the incarnation, and conditioning the whole faith and life of the church; and they seldom refer to it, without bringing into view the idea of its mystical supernatural import. Ignatius takes the real presence of the eucharist to be organically related to the truth and realness of the Saviour's humanity, and upbraids the docetic Gnostics, (who acknowledged thus also the force of the connection) with abstaining from the institution, because they would not believe that Christ had ever assumed anything more than the show of a human body. "They refrain from the service," he writes, "on account of their not confessing *that the eucharist is the flesh of our Saviour Jesus Christ,* which suffered for our sins and which the Father in his goodness raised from the dead. Contradicting the gift of God they die in their contention; but it would be their interest to love, so that they too might rise again."⁶⁶ In another place, (ad Ephes. c. 20.)⁶⁷ Ignatius calls the eucharist the "medicine of immortality" (φαρμακον ἀθανασιας) and the "antidote of death" (ἀντιδοτον του μη ἀποθανειν); phrases that are sufficiently explained by the last clause of the foregoing quotation, where the risen flesh of the Saviour is made to be the power that is to reanimate also our mortal bodies. But if there were any doubt as to the doctrine of Ignatius here, or as to its agreement with the reigning faith of the church at the time, it must vanish certainly before the ample and plain testimony of Irenæus.

With this father again, the doctrine of the eucharist is made to be of extraordinary practical and theoretical account. It is not a circumstance merely in the general system of faith, but appears as a truly living and divinely efficacious link, between the mystery of the incarnation on one side and the coming resurrection of our bodies on another; showing plainly that these connections as suggested by Ignatius, were not fanciful or casual, but rooted in the reigning belief of the church. The Gnostics generally held the material world to be intrinsically evil, and so not capable of coming into any real union with the new creation by Christ. They would not allow accordingly that the Saviour took a real human body; and they could not admit of course then the resurrection of the body, in the case of his people. It was a principle with them, that the body as such constitutionally excluded the idea of immortality. Against these errors Irenæus affirms the goodness of the natural creation, the truth of Christ's incarnation, and the commensurateness of his redemption with the whole nature of man, as being able to save the body in the way of future resurrection no less than the soul. One grand source of argument is found in the mystery of the holy supper, which it is taken for granted that these heretics, in common with the church, acknowledged to be a bond of communication with Christ's substantial flesh and blood. However disposed they might be by their spiritualistic system to take these terms in an improper and merely figurative sense, it seems that they were still compelled to yield here to the pressure of the catholic faith, and to admit thus an actual presence of the Saviour's glorified body, whatever that might be, in this sublime mystery; and no evidence could well be stronger than this, for the universal and vital authority of this faith in the church itself at the time. To deny the possibility of the resurrection, according to Irenaeus, involves this consequence: "That neither the cup of the eucharist is the communication of his blood, nor the bread which we break the communication of his body; for it is not

---

66. Εὐχαριστιας και προσευχης ἀπεχονται, δια τὸ μὴ ὁμολογειν τὴν εὐχαριστιαν σαρκα εἶναι του σωτηρος ἡμῶν Ἰησου Χριστου τὴν ὑπερ ἁμαρτιων ἡμων παθουσαν, ἥν τη χρηστοτητι ὁ πατηρ ἡγειρεν. Οἱ ἀντιλεγοντες τη δωρεα του Θεου συζητουντες ἀποθνησουσι συνεφερεν δὲ αὐτοις ἀγαπαν, ἱνα και ἀναστωσιν.—Ad Smyrn. c. 7. [Möhler, *Patrologie*, 145n; trans. "From the Eucharist and prayer they hold aloof, because they do not confess that the Eucharist is the Flesh of our Savior Jesus Christ, which suffered for our sins, and which the Father in His loving-kindness raised from the dead. And so, those who question *the gift of God* perish in their contentiousness. It would be better for them to have love, so as to share in the resurrection" (Ignatius, *Epistles*, ACW 1:92, emphasis original). Emphasis in text is Nevin's.]

67. [Möhler, *Patrologie*, 147; Ignatius, *Epistles*, ACW 1:67–68.]

blood, unless it be from his veins and his flesh, and the rest of that human substance, by which he became truly the Word of God."[68] Again:

> Since we are members of him, and live from the natural creation, which he furnishes to us for this end, causing his sun to rise and sending rain according to his own pleasure; he has proclaimed the cup which is of the natural creation to be his own blood, from which he moistens our blood, and has established the bread which is of this creation to be his own body from which he nourishes our bodies.[69]

And still farther:

> When therefore the natural cup and bread, by receiving the word of God at consecration, are made the eucharist of the blood and body of Christ, by which the substance of our flesh is advanced and upheld, how can they deny that the flesh is capable of the gift of God, which is eternal life, since it is nourished by the blood and body of Christ and is his member? Even as the blessed Apostle says in his Epistle to the Ephesians, *We are members of his body, of his flesh and of his bones*; not speaking of the spiritual and invisible man, (for spirit has neither bones nor flesh) but of that constitution which is truly human, consisting of flesh and nerves and bones, which is nourished from the cup that is his blood and from the bread that is his body. And as the slip of the vine laid in the ground brings forth fruit in its time, and the grain of wheat falling into the earth and undergoing decomposition rises manifoldly by God's Spirit, through which all things are upheld; which then by the wisdom of God come to be for the use of man, and receiving the word of consecration become the eucharist, which is the body and blood of Christ: so also our bodies nourished by this, and laid away in the earth and dissolved into it shall rise again in their time, the Word of God bestowing the resurrection upon them to the glory of God the Father."[70]

In another place, Irenaeus calls upon the heretics either to give up the errors now noticed, or else to abstain from the eucharist, as some of the earlier Docetae[71] actually did in the time of Ignatius, according to what we have seen before. "How can they say," he exclaims,

> that the flesh perishes and attains not to life, which is nourished by the body and blood of the Lord? Let them change their view, or refrain from offering these things. Our view, on the contrary, agrees with the eucharist, and the eucharist again confirms our view. For we offer to him things that are his

---

68. [Möhler, *Patrologie*, 378; ANF 1:528.]
69. [Möhler, *Patrologie*, 379; ANF 1:528.]
70. Adv. haeres. v. 2, §. 2, 3 [5.2.3; Möhler, *Patrologie*, 380; ANF 1:528].
71. [Literally, "illusionists," adherents of Docetism, who held that salvation did not take place through Jesus' humanity, since his body was an "illusion."]

own, setting forth congruously the communion and unity, and confessing the resurrection of the flesh and spirit. For as the bread from the earth, when it has received the invocation of God, is now no longer bread, but the eucharist consisting of two things, an earthly and a celestial; so also our bodies receiving the eucharist are no longer corruptible, having the hope of the resurrection to everlasting life.[72]

So much for the real presence of the Saviour's glorified humanity in the holy supper. Can there be any doubt in the face of these passages, whether such a mystery was held by the early church, or whether it was considered to be of necessary force as a part of the faith originally delivered to the saints? We see too, how the service was regarded as carrying in it the force of a sacrifice or oblation, analogous with the offerings of the altar under the Old Testament; an idea which Irenæus elsewhere utters in full and distinct terms, applying to the case, in the spirit of later centuries, the memorable passage, Mal. i: 10, 11, where it is said: "From the rising of the sun even unto the going down of the same, my name shall be great among the Gentiles; and in every place incense shall be offered unto my name, and a pure offering; for my name shall be great among the heathen, saith the Lord of Hosts." But what student of antiquity needs to be told, that the eucharist in this early period carried in it a significance and solemnity, of which no rational account can be given, except on the ground that such powers as those now mentioned were supposed to go along with its celebration?[73]

We inquire not now into the truth of this old sacramental doctrine; neither is it necessary to define in what mode precisely it understood the mystery of the real presence to take place. It is enough to know, that the mystery itself was universally received, as of fundamental consequence in the christian system; and that the doctrine therefore stood in no sort of harmony with the common Puritan view of the present time. The martyrs of Lyons and Vienne died in full hope of the resurrection; but this hope was based on a species of realistic sacramentalism here, which we feel very sure would bring upon them now through all New England the charge of gross superstition, and leave no room for them whatever within the magic ring of its "evangelical sects."

IV. A like wide contrast between the early system and the modern comes into view, in the next place, when we look at their different theories in regard to the *rule of faith*.

It is a primary maxim with Puritanism, that the Bible alone is the rule and ground of all religion, of all that men are required to believe or do in the service of God. In this sacred volume, we are told, God has been pleased to place his word in full, by special inspiration, as a supernatural directory for the use of the world to the end of time; for the very purpose of providing a sufficient authority for faith, that might be independent of all human judgment and will. If it be asked, how the Bible is to be interpreted

---

72. Adv. haeres. iv. 18 §. 5 [4.18.5; Möhler, *Patrologie*, 383–84; *ANF* 1:486].

73. See an interesting and clear representation of the testimony of Irenæus on the whole subject in Möhler's *Patrologie*, pp. 377–391.

and made available as a rule of faith, the answer is that every man must interpret it as he best can for his own use, under the guidance of God's Spirit, and with such helps as he may happen to have at his command. In other words, the ultimate tribunal for the exposition of God's word is private judgment. No other tribunal can be regarded as of any legitimate authority or right. All tradition especially, pretending in any way to over-rule private judgment, is to be firmly rejected as something inimical to the rights of reason and conscience. What men can see to be taught in the scriptures is to be of force for them as revelation, and what they cannot see to be so taught there is to be of no such force. The great matter accordingly is to place the bible in every man's hands, and to have him able to read it, that he may then follow it in his own way. The idea seems to be, that the bible was published in the first place as a sort of divine formulary or text book for the world to follow in matters of religion, and that the church rested on no other ground in the beginning for its practices or doctrines, appealing to it and building upon it in a perfectly free and original way after the fashion of our modern sects; in which view it is to be counted still the foundation and pillar of the truth, so that the dissemination of its printed text throughout the world, without note or comment, is the one thing specially needful and specially to be relied upon for the full victory of Christianity, from sea to sea and from the river to the ends of the earth.[74]

This theory has many difficulties. To place a divine text at the mercy of private judgment, looks very much like making it a mere nose of wax. Men deal not thus with the authority of other laws and constitutions. All the world over the sense of written statutes is ruled more or less by the power of an unwritten living tradition, (such as the "common law" of England and this country) which at the same time is applied to the case by some public tribunal, and *not* by every man at his own pleasure. So deeply seated indeed is this order in our very nature, that it is never surmounted even by those who in the case before us pretend to set it aside. Puritanism never in truth allows the bible *alone* to be the religion of Protestants. Every sect has its tradition,[75] its system of opinions and habits, handed forward by education, just as much as the Catholic church itself, through which as a medium the written word is studied and understood at every point. In no other way could it exist as a historical body at all. The private judgment of a good Presbyterian is always carried, from infancy on to old age, in the bosom of a general Presbyterian stream of thought, that has been flowing in its own separate channel from the origin of this communion in the days of John Knox;[76] and the same thing precisely is true of the Methodists, as well as of all the

---

74. [For more on this "Bible alone" and "private judgment" hermeneutic, see Nevin, *Philosophy and the Contemporary World*, MTSS 11:218–222, 310–14.]

75. [Nevin developed this theme in "The Sect System," MTSS 5:250. Nevin was reacting to Winebrenner, *History of all the Religious Denominations in the United States*. This volume was edited by one of Nevin's detractors and consisted of the "traditions" of the various denominations in the middle of the nineteenth century, most of them written by their own adherents.]

76. [Knox (c. 1513–72), leader of the Scottish Reformation. He served in England during the reign of Edward VI, was exiled in Geneva for a time during the reign of Mary Queen of Scots and returned

other scores of sects that in as many variant ways follow the same infallible rule of faith and practice. It cannot well escape observation again, that the bible itself lends no sort of countenance to the hypothesis, which turns it thus in such abstract style into the sum total of all God's mind and will, mechanically laid down for man's use, like the directions for the building of the tabernacle in the book of Exodus. It never speaks of itself as being either a system of divinity or a confession of faith. It has no such form, but shows as clearly as possible an altogether different construction and design. Nay more, it is perfectly certain from the New Testament itself, that Christianity was *not* made to rest on any such foundation in the beginning, but on a living authority, which started in Christ and passed over from him to the ministry of the church. This is as plain as words could well make it, from Matth. xvi: 18, 19; Matth. xxviii: 18, 20; Eph. ii: 19, 22, and 1 Tim. iii: 15, 16. On the basis of the apostolical commission, backed by heavenly miraculous authority, and entering into no negotiation whatever with the world's private judgment, the early church was in fact planted and built throughout the Roman empire. The books of the New Testament came afterwards as part and parcel of the glorious revelation committed to her hands; and it was not till the fourth century, as we have before seen, that the arduous and responsible task of settling the canon was brought to a complete close, although the main parts of it were acknowledged and in general use probably before the middle of the second.

These are difficulties, we say, which from the Puritan standpoint it is by no means easy to meet. But we do not press them at present. What we wish to hold up to view is the clearly evident fact, that the church of the second century was not Puritan but Catholic, in its conception of the rule of faith, concurring here in its whole habit of thought with the order that actually prevailed, as just now stated, in the first planting of Christianity in the world. The sacred books are indeed referred to with high veneration in this age, as they are in all subsequent times of the Catholic church, but never under any such abstract and independent view, as they are made to carry in the private-judgment sect system of the present day. Of a bible, out of which every man was to fetch the doctrines and practices of religion as he best could with the bucket of his own common sense, these early Christians had not so much as the most remote imagination. They own the inspiration of the scriptures and appeal to them as the norm and measure of their faith; but it is only and always as they are taken to be comprehended in that general tradition of infallible truth, which had come down from the Apostles in a living way by the church. The bible was for them the word of God, not on the outside of the church, and as a book dropped from the skies for all sorts of men to use in their own way, but in the bosom of the church alone, and in organic union with that great system of revelation of which this was acknowledged to be the pillar and ground. Sundered from that organism, cut off from the living stream of catholic tradition, the holy oracles in the hands of heretics were considered as shorn of all their force. Such men as Irenæus and Tertullian had no idea of sitting

---

from his exile to lead the Scottish break from Rome in 1560.]

down, and debating points of doctrine with the Gnostics out of the bible, in any way owning at all their right to appeal to it as an independent rule; just as little as it ever entered into their heads probably to put the people, "with the New Testament in their hands," on inquiring "into the principles and rules of church government," after the democratic fashion of the nineteenth century.[77] They will not allow the heretics to put their cause on any ground of this sort; they cut them off by prescription, that is, by the clear title of the regular church to the succession or tradition of Christianity, as it had been handed down, under the broad seal of its original charter, from the time of the Apostles. Some notice has been taken before of the way, in which Irenæus appeals to the known apostolical succession of the bishops in his time, and their collective voice in favor of the truth, bringing all to centre and culminate in Rome as the principal see. This constitution, and no other, is with him the organ of unity both in doctrine and government; all else is heresy and schism. "It is necessary to hearken to the presbyters in the church," he tells us (Adv. haer. iv. c. 20), "who have the succession from the Apostles, and along with the succession of the episcopate have received the certain gift of truth according to the good pleasure of the Father."[78] Again (iv. c. 33, §. 8.):

> The true knowledge (γνῶσις) is the doctrine of the Apostles, and the ancient constitution (συστημα) of the church in the whole world, and the character of the body of Christ according to the successions of the bishops, to whom they (the Apostles) have committed the church in every place.[79]

The paths of heresy are many and variable, but the doctrine of the church is one and unchanging all over the world;

> she preserves the traditionary faith, though spread throughout the earth, with the greatest care, as if she occupied but one house; and believes it, as if she had but one soul and one heart; and proclaims, teaches, hands it forward, with marvellous agreement, as if she had but one mouth. The languages used are indeed different, but the matter of the tradition is still one and the same (i. 10. 2. comp. v. 20. §. 1.).[80]

Again (iii. 4. §. 1[–2].):

> If the Apostles had left us no writings, ought we not still to follow the rule of that tradition, which they handed over to those to whom they committed the churches? To this rule many nations of barbarians do hold in fact, which

---

77. ["Evangelical Religion," 233. Nevin has quoted these phrases in their full context twice before.]

78. [Correction: 4.26.2. In this sequence of quotes Nevin follows the order of Möhler, *Patrologie*, beginning 349–50. He translates Möhler's German renderings. See Irenaeus, *Adversus Haereses*, in *PG* 7:1053–54; *ANF* 1:497.]

79. [Irenaeus, *Adversus Haereses*, in *PG* 7:1077; Möhler, *Patrologie*, 349 (συστημα is in Möhler; Nevin might have picked up γνῶσις from elsewhere); *ANF* 1:508.]

80. [Irenaeus, *Adversus Haereses*, in *PG* 7:551–52; Möhler, *Patrologie*, 351; *ANF* 1:331.]

believe in Christ, and have his salvation inscribed by the Holy Ghost without ink or paper on their hearts, carefully following the tradition &c.[81]

Specially striking is the passage, L. iii. c. 24. §. 1., where this tradition is made to carry in it a divine element, rendering it infallible; gathering itself up into the mystery of that faith "which we have received and hold from our church, and which the Spirit of God continually renovates, like a precious jewel in a good casket, imparting to it the quality of his own perennial youth."[82] Such is the testimony of Irenæus. Tertullian is, if possible, still stronger in the same churchly strain. He will know nothing of any private argumentation, from the scriptures or any other source; all must yield to the smashing weight of ecclesiastical tradition. Christianity is built, not on a book, but on a living system handed down from the day of Pentecost. Truth is fellowship with the churches derived by regular succession from the Apostles; they have collectively but one doctrine; and whatever disowns this order, is without farther examination to be rejected as false. His whole tract on the *Prescription of Heretics* rests on this view, and might be quoted here with effect. The heretics have no right to appeal to the scriptures. These belong only to the church. She may say to them:

> "Who are you? Whence do you come? What business have you strangers with my property? By what right are you, Marcion, felling my trees? By what authority are you, Valentine, turning the course of my streams? Under what pretence are you, Apelles, removing my land-marks? The estate is mine; why do you other persons presume to work it and use it at your pleasure? The estate is mine; I have the ancient, prior possession of it; have the title deeds from the original owners. I am the heir of the Apostles; they made their will, with all proper solemnities, in my favor, while they disinherited and cast you off as strangers and enemies."[83]

Tertullian had no idea of making exegesis the mother of faith.[84]

Is it necessary to say that the faith of the second century, as here portrayed, is something very different from the reigning evangelical scheme of the present day? No honest student of history, we think, can fail to see and confess, that the doctrine of Irenæus and Tertullian on the relation of the bible to the church is essentially one and the same with that which is clearly presented afterwards by Chrysostom and Augustine, and that in sound at least it is very much like the Catholic doctrine as opposed to Protestantism in modern times.

---

81. [Irenaeus, *Adversus Haereses*, in *PG* 7:855; Möhler, *Patrologie*, 356; *ANF* 1:417.]

82. [Irenaeus, *Adversus Haereses*, in *PG* 7:966; Möhler, *Patrologie*, 356; *ANF* 1:458.]

83. [John Milner, *End of Religious Controversy*, vol. 1, 2nd ed. (London: Keating, Brown, 1819), 90, citing {Tertullian,} *Præscrip. Advers. Hæres.*, ed. Rhenan{us}, 36, 37. (The quotation marks represent Tertullian's imaginary interrogation of the heretics.) See *ANF* 3:261.]

84. See Rothe's work [*Anfänge*] before quoted; [see] also Möhler's *Patrologie*, pp. 344–357, 737–748.

Document 2: Early Christianity: Second Article.

V. Take next the *order of doctrine*. Single truths have their proper value and force, not merely in themselves separately taken, but in the place they occupy as parts of the whole system to which they belong. Much depends then on the order in which they are held. The doctrinal scheme of the early church has come down to us in the Apostles' Creed. Into the question of the origin of this symbol, it is not necessary now to enter.[85] Its universal prevalence in the fourth century is itself argument enough for a thinking mind, that it must have come down from time immemorial before in substantially the same form; but independently of this, it is abundantly plain from the writers of the second century, that the whole theology of that period was shaped in the mind of the church on this model at least, and on no other. But this at once conditions and determines its universal character, setting it in close affinity with the later theology of the Catholic church, and placing it in broad contrariety to the Puritan scheme of doctrine as we now meet with it in New England. Puritanism, by its abstract spiritualistic character, has lost the power to a great extent of understanding both the old creed, and the catholic theology of which it was the foundation; and with a certain feeling of superior maturity is disposed generally to put the whole away as somewhat childish and out of date. The objection is not so much to single points in themselves considered; for most of these may be translated into some good modern sense; but it holds rather against the order in which they are put together, the architecture of the creed, its reigning animus, its [sic] too much of one thing and its too little or nothing at all of another. The sound of it is uncomfortably mystical, sacramental and churchly. Puritanism knows very well in its inmost soul, that no *such* creed is the symbol exactly of that form of belief which it now parades as its own, and as being at the same time the only true and perfect sense of the bible. It would never have produced any creed of this sort. It sees all truth in a different order, and holds it in quite other proportions and relations. When it undertakes to give us a creed in fact, (as it is ready to do commonly at a moment's warning and to any order) the product is something very different from the ancient symbol of the Apostles.[86]

85. [Nevin had previously examined this topic in "The Apostle's Creed," MTSS 8:35–54.]

86. See an article entitled "Puritanism and the Creed," in the Mercersburg Review for November 1849, published at the same time also as a separate tract. [Nevin, "Puritanism and the Creed," in *The Early Creeds* MTSS 8:103–21.] It will be remembered, that the *Puritan Recorder*, of Boston, plainly acknowledged "that the Creed and Puritanism have not a kindred spirit," and that only by courtesy it found a place originally in Puritan formularies and catechisms. "Its life and spirit," it was said, "never entered into the life of the Puritan churches; and consequently it now exists among us as some fossil relic of by-gone ages. And we look with a sort of pity upon those who are laboring to infuse life into it, and to set it up as a living ruler in the church. We are free to confess, that this Creed has forsaken the Puritans, and gone over to become the idol and strength of all branches of anti-puritanism. And there are good reasons; for Puritanism builds on the Scriptures, and this Creed teaches, in several respects, anti-scriptural doctrines." [A lengthy quotation is found in the same essay, MTSS 8:105.] It should have been said rather, that Puritanism has forsaken the Creed; breaking away at the same time from the faith of the universal church as it stood in the second century, and while it accepts the bible from the hands of this same church, cooly turning round and saying to it: You never understood your own scriptures; *we* know what they mean, and you and your creed may go to the tomb of the Capulets.

There is a real difference, as regards the *tout ensemble*[87] of Christian doctrine between the Patristic system and Protestantism in its original proper form. More than one has felt something of the experience given in the following striking passage from Thiersch. "It is a strange impression," he remarks in his work on the *Canon,* p. 280,

> that the church fathers make on one who first enters on the study of them, under the full force of a merely Protestant consciousness. So fared it with the writer himself. Nurtured on the best that the old Protestant books of devotion contain, and trained theologically in the doctrines and interpretations of the orthodox period of Protestantism, he turned finally to the fathers. Well does he remember how strange it appeared to him in the beginning, to find here nothing of those truths, which formed the spring of his whole religious life, nothing of the way the sinner must tread to arrive at peace and an assurance of the Divine favor, nothing of Christ's merit as the only ground of forgiveness, nothing of continual repentance and ever new recourse to the fountain of free grace, nothing of the high confidence of the justified believer. Instead of this, he found that all weight was laid on the incarnation of the Divine Logos, on the right knowledge of the great object of worship, on the objective mystery of the Trinity and of Christ's Person, on the connection between creation, redemption, and the future restoration of the creature along with the glorification also of man's body on the freedom of man and on the reality of the operations of Divine grace in the sacraments. But he was enabled gradually to live himself into this old mode of thought, and without giving up what is true and inalienable in the Lutheran Protestant consciousness, to correct its onesidedness by a living appropriation of the theology of the fathers. He soon saw, that over against the errors of the present time, its pantheism and fatalism, its spiritualism and misapprehension of the significance of the corporeal, the church needs a decided taking up again of what is true in the Patristic scheme of thought, and an assimilation of her whole life to the ancient model—in spirit and idea first, as outward relations are not at once under human control. This old primitive church stood out to his view more and more in its full splendor, in its sublime beauty, of which only fragmentary lineaments are to be recognised in the churches, confessions and sects, of the present day.[88]

Thiersch here finds Protestantism itself materially different from early Christianity; while he holds it however, in its legitimate character, capable of a living conjunction with the ancient faith, though carrying in itself a fearful tendency to fall away

---

We have never heard of any repudiation of this monstrous sentiment, on the part of the interest thus represented by the Puritan Recorder, and take it for granted therefore that it is nothing more than a true picture after all of what must be considered here a general falling away from the *regula fidei* of the primitive church.

87. [Trans. "all together," but here seeming to mean "the whole assemblage."]

88. [Heinrich W. J. Thiersch, *Versuch zur Herstellung des historischen Standpuncts für die Kritik der neutestamentlichen Schriften* (Erlangen: Heyder, 1845), 280–81.]

Document 2: Early Christianity: Second Article.

from it altogether; a tendency, which is now getting the mastery of it in truth in many places, and that needs to be counteracted by a return to former ideas. What he has his eye upon immediately is the rationalism surrounding him in Germany. But the tendency is not limited to that form of open unbelief. It lies in all unchurchly religion. It animates the whole sect system. It forms the proper soul of Puritanism. This is not original Protestantism, carrying in it the *possibility* merely of a full dissociation from the mind of the ancient church; but it is this possibility actually realized. It is a growth completely to the one side, which refuses now all organic agreement with the trunk of Christian doctrine as this stood in the beginning. The two schemes of thought are quite apart, and can never be made to fit together with any sort of symmetry or ease. Puritanism, by its very constitution, ignores and abjures the *old* sense of the Apostles' Creed.

VI. Look finally at the subject of *faith in miracles*. It is well known, that the early church not only believed firmly in the miracles of Christ and his Apostles, as well as in those of the Old Testament, but had a most firm persuasion also that the same power was still actively displayed in her own bosom, and that it lay in her commission in truth to look for its revelation, as occasion might require, "always to the end of the world." It is generally admitted even among Protestants not openly rationalistic, (though some feel it necessary with the celebrated Dr. Conyers Middleton[89] to take different ground through fear of Popery) that many supernatural signs and wonders were wrought in the service of Christianity during the first three ages. But what we have to do with just now is not so much the actual truth of these miracles, as the state of mind on the part of the church itself, by which they were considered possible, and which led to their being readily received on all sides as nothing more than the natural and proper fruit of the new religion. The apologists appeal to them boldly as notorious facts. Both Irenæus and Tertullian challenge the heretics to prove their authority by miracles, as the church did hers in every direction; and the proofs mentioned are such as giving sight to the blind and hearing to the deaf, casting out devils, healing sicknesses, and even raising the dead to life. To question the fact of miracles in the church, would have been in this period equivalent to downright infidelity. It lay in the whole sense the church then had of the realness and nearness of the supernatural world, in her felt apprehension of the living communion in which she stood with it through Christ, that such demonstrations of its presence should be regarded as most perfectly possible, and in some sort as a matter of course. Her idea of *faith* was such, as of itself involved this from the very start.

But who needs to be told, how different from all this the tone of thought is that now pervades the universal empire of Puritanism? The difference is not in the mere

89. [Disappointments over failure to obtain desired posts, and a self-admitted "taste of Pagan sense," led Middleton (1683–1750) to attack the "testimonies of miracles given by patristic authorities," while claiming not to deny the miracles of the apostolic period. He ridiculed "primitive" exorcists as "quackery and imposture." He has been interpreted as contributing to the rise of "higher criticism." Dussinger, "Middleton, Conyers," 55, 56.]

want of miracles; though that is something too for a thoughtful mind; it appears rather, under a more alarming and affecting view, in the want of power to exercise faith in anything of the sort. Puritanism pretends indeed to great faith in the invisible and supernatural; just as the Gnostics did also in ancient times. But its faith, like theirs, is in the language of Ignatius wonderfully asomatic and unreal. The action of the supernatural is remanded by it to the world of mere thought. God works miracles now in the souls of his people; and away back in the shadow land of the past, he wrought them by special dispensation also under a more outward form. But the age of such proper wonders is long since past. It is unsafe to speak of them after the third century, and not very wise to lay much stress on them even in the second. All pretensions to anything of the sort may be set down at once, and without any examination, as purely "lying wonders." Such we all know to be the reigning habit of thought here, with this popular system. Dr. Middleton's theory suits it to a tittle, and is drawn as it were from its very soul. Puritanism has no faith in miracles answerable at all to what prevailed in the early church, no power we may say to believe them in the same way. Its inward relation to the world from which miracles come, is by no means the same. The difference is not in the judgment exercised in regard to this particular miracle or that, but in the total frame of the mind with regard to the universal subject. This is not faith, but absolute scepticism, just as complete as anything we meet with in Gibbon, Voltaire, or Hume.[90]

The martyrs of Lyons knew nothing of such scepticism. It required another sense of the "powers of the world to come [Heb 6:5]," to carry so many simple and plain persons, with such triumphant courage, through the scenes that are described in the account of their martyrdom. They had no difficulty in admitting the reality of signs and wonders in the church. Nay, these had place in connexion with their own sufferings, and are reported by Irenæus, (the supposed writer of the account) as carrying in them nothing incredible whatever. Blandina, a weak slave, was regarded as being upheld, quite beyond the common course of nature, in the terrible torments through which she was made to pass, from the break of day till night. The deacon Sanctus was tortured with hot plates of brass and in other ways, till his body became so covered with wounds and bruises that the very figure of it was lost; a few days after which he

---

90. Both the *N. Y. Observer* and the *N. Y. Churchman*, representing but too faithfully we fear the spirit of their respective communions, noticed not long since with pure derision a sermon by Dr. Forbes, the late convert to Romanism, in defence of the idea that Christ has continued to fulfil his promise of miracles in the later ages of the church. [The exact numbers of these notices have not been located.] The misery of all this is, not that this or that wonder of popular belief in the Catholic church may be shown to be false and ridiculous, but that the basis on which alone any such popular beliefs are made possible, the sense namely of the supernatural order of Christianity as a real and ever present fountain of the miraculous in the church, is rationalistically undermined and destroyed. [Major critics of the miraculous in Christianity in the early modern period include Gibbon, famous for his *Decline and Fall of the Roman Empire*; Voltaire, pseudonym of François-Maria Arouet (1694–1778), French Enlightenment thinker who was very critical of religion, especially in his satirical *Candide*; David Hume (1711–76), Scottish philosopher and historian who was famous for his skepticism, especially of religion. His *Essay upon Miracles* was a challenge to the Christian understanding of miracles.]

was brought out again, when it was supposed that the inflammation of his sores would cause him, under the repetition of the same cruelties, either to yield at once or expire. But "to the amazement of all, his body under the latter torments recovered its former strength and shape, and the exact use of all his limbs was restored; so that by this miracle of the grace of Jesus Christ, what was designed as an additional pain, proved an absolute and effectual cure."[91] The martyrs appeared to move in a perfect nimbus of supernatural grace; even "their bodies sent forth such an agreeable and pleasant savor, as gave occasion to think that they used perfumes."[92] The wild beasts of the amphitheatre, to which she was exposed, could not be provoked to touch Blandina. One of the martyrs "had a revelation" in regard to another, which this last made it his business dutifully to follow.[93] What remained of the bodies, after the terrible tragedy, was burned to ashes, and thrown into the waters of the Rhone; but it was believed, that a part of these ashes was afterwards miraculously recovered, and the relics were deposited under the altar of the church which anciently bore the name of the Apostles of Lyons.[94]

We say nothing of the credibility of these statements, nothing of the opinion we should have of what they pretend to describe. We hold them up simply as a picture of the mind that was in the church in the days of Pothinus and Irenæus; and in view of it we have no hesitation in saying, that Dr. Bacon is altogether mistaken, when he finds its *facsimile,* either in Mr. Fisch's evangelical congregation of the present Lyons, or under the keen sharp features of Puritanism in any part of New England. It would be easy to extend this contrast to other points. Veneration for the *relics* of deceased saints comes into view, as far back as our eye can reach. The bones of Ignatius, who was martyred at Rome under Trajan in the beginning of the second century, were carefully gathered up after his death, we ate told, and carried back to Antioch his episcopal see. According to Chrysostom, they were borne in triumph on the shoulders of all the cities through Asia Minor. In Antioch they were placed finally in a church distinguished by his name, which St. Chrysostom encourages people in his day to visit, as having been to many the means of undoubted help both spiritually and corporally. In the case of Polycarp, the church of Smyrna writes that the malice of the devil was exerted to prevent his relics being carried off by the Christians; "for as many desired to do it,

91. [Alban Butler, *The Lives of the Primitive Fathers, Martyrs, and other Principal Saints: compiled from original monuments, and other authentic records*, 3rd ed. (Edinburgh: J. Moir, 1799), 6:26. Nevin's exact edition cannot be determined.]

92. [Butler, *Lives of the Primitive Fathers*, 6:28.] It is related in the acts of the martyrdom of St. Polycarp, written by the church of Smyrna, that when fire was set to the pile prepared to burn him the "flames forming themselves into an arch, like the sails of a ship swelled with the wind, gently encircled the body of the martyr, which stood in the middle, resembling not roasted flesh, but purified gold or silver, appearing bright through the flames; and his body *sending forth such a fragrancy,* that we seemed to smell *precious spices.*" [Butler, *Lives of the Primitive Fathers*, 1:298, emphases Nevin's.]

93. [Probably referring to the episode of Attalus and Alcibiades: Butler, *Lives of the Primitive Fathers*, 6:31.]

94. [Butler, *Lives of the Primitive Fathers*, 6:34, 35.]

to show their respect to his body."[95] At the suggestion of the Jews, the proconsul was advised not to give the body into their hands, lest they should pass from the worship of the crucified one to the worship of Polycarp; "not knowing," say the acts, "that we can never forsake Christ, nor adore any other, though we love the martyrs, as his disciples and imitators, for the great love they bore their king and master."[96] The corpse accordingly was reduced to ashes. "We afterwards took up the bones," the church adds, "more precious than the richest jewels or gold, and deposited them decently in a place, at which may God grant us to assemble with joy, to celebrate the birthday of the martyr."[97] How different all this is from the spirit of modern Puritanism, even a child may see and feel. But the veneration for relics is itself only the proof and sign of a great deal more, embraced in the article of the "communion of saints" as it was held in the early church, every vestige of which has disappeared from the thinking of this later system. It is equally evident again, that the church of the second century attributed a peculiar merit to the state of celibacy and virginity, embraced for the glory of God and in the service of religion, which falls in fully with the tone of thought we find afterwards established in the Roman Catholic communion, but is as much at war as can well be imagined with the entire genius of Puritanism in every form and shape. It is not necessary, however, to push the comparison any farther, in the consideration of these or of other kindred points. Our general purpose is abundantly answered, our cause more than made out, by the topics of proof and illustration already presented.

[The Failure of Puritanism Concluded]

The Puritan hypothesis, we now repeat, is false. There never was any such period of unchurchly evangelicalism as it assumes, in the history of early Christianity. Its whole dream of a golden age, answerable to its own taste and fashion, after the time of the New Testament and back of what it takes to be the grand apostacy that comes into view in the third century, is as perfectly baseless as any vision could well be. It rests upon mere air. It has not a syllable of true historical evidence in its favor; while the universal drift of proof is directly against it. Those then who will have it that New England Puritanism is the true image of what Christianity was at the start, and that the church tendency as it appears in universal force afterwards was from the start a corruption only, must take still higher ground than even this dizzy imagination; they must make up their mind, with the heroic Baptists, to look upon the history of the church as a grand falling away from its original design and type, as soon as it passed out of the hands of the Apostles, and long before the last of these in fact had gone to his rest. To this the theory comes in the end; and with the great body of those who hold it, this probably is the sense that always lurks in it at the bottom. But we need

---

95. [Butler, *Lives of the Primitive Fathers*, 1:298. See *ANF* 1:42.]
96. [Butler, *Lives of the Primitive Fathers*, 1:298–99. See *ANF* 1:43.]
97. [Butler, *Lives of the Primitive Fathers*, 1:299. See *ANF* 1:43.]

Document 2: Early Christianity: Second Article.

have no hesitation surely in saying, that every view of *this* sort is fatal to the credibility of the Gospel. It is only Gnosticism in disguise.

Our faith in the realness of Christianity will not allow us to bear the thought, that it fell from the very outset into the gulph-stream of a total apostacy, which carried the universal church, without resistance or knowledge, right onward always to the shipwreck of a thousand years—while Christ was showing himself by infallible signs both present and awake in the vessel,[98] and miracles of faith and zeal prevailed on every side. It will not do; the whole supposition is monstrous. Puritanism is mistaken. It is a thousand times safer to interpret the meaning of Christianity from its own actual history in the beginning, than it is to sit at the feet now of any such modern authority, spinning the sense of it from the clouds. As to the likelihood of apostacy and wholesale error, in the main difference between the two forms of teaching, we believe the chances to be immeasurably in favor of antiquity and against the modern authority. It is far easier to believe Puritanism an apostacy, in its rejection of the *mystery* of the church and its sacraments, than it is to brand the universal faith of the second and third centuries with any such character, for the acknowledgment of this mystery as something quite above the range of reason and common sense. We choose to go here with the early church. We do not believe that it fell into apostacy, as a whole, from the very outset of its course; that it mistook fundamentally the sense and meaning of the faith delivered to it by the Apostles; that it was almost immediately overpowered by a new and foreign idea, a "mystery of iniquity" that turned it finally into the synagogue of Satan.[99] We detest and abhor any imagination of this sort; and pray God that our children may be kept from every such miserable tradition, as a true snare of the Devil that looks directly to rationalism and infidelity. There were faults and corruptions no doubt in the history of the church; but there was no such falling away from its own proper and primitive idea, as Puritanism finds it necessary constantly to assert. The reigning course of Christianity was right, and in full conformity with the will of Him who so visibly presided over it "on the right hand of the Majesty on high [Heb 1:3]." The habit of doctrine and worship in which such men as Augustine, Ambrose, Chrysostom, Cyprian stood, which animated the martyrs of Lyons and Vienne, and glowed in the seraphic ardor of Polycarp and Ignatius, must have been in the main, not diabolical, not superstitious, but true to the genius of the Gospel as it was "first spoken by the Lord and confirmed by them that heard him—God also bearing them witness both with signs and wonders, and with divers miracles, and gifts of the Holy Ghost, according to his own will [Heb 2:3, 4]." This implies of course that even the Papacy itself, *towards* which at least the whole system was carried with intrinsic necessity from the beginning, came in with reason and right, and had a mission to fulfil in the service of Christianity that could not have been fulfilled as well in any other way.

98. [Probably an allusion to Matt 8:24, 25. Nevin was confident that Jesus has always been "present and awake" in the church.]

99. [WCF 25.5. Scriptural allusions to 2 Thess 2:7 and Rev 2:9; 3:9.]

No one indeed can study the history of the church soberly, it seems to us, without seeing this in the actual course of events. The grand bulwark of the true religion, through the whole period of the middle ages, was beyond all question the ecclesiastical organization that centered in the popes or bishops of Rome. Without this, the church would have fallen to pieces, hundreds of years before the Reformation. Only suppose the Papacy to have been overwhelmed by Mohammedanism, or by the German emperors,[100] or by the wild fury of the Albigenses and other such Manichean sects, and what would there have been left of the glorious mystery of Christianity as it first stood, either to reform or mend in the sixteenth century?

If the cause of Protestantism then is to be successfully maintained, it must be on some other ground than the common Puritan assumption, that it is just what Christianity was in the beginning, and that all variations from it in antiquity are to be set to the account of a devilish apostacy, of which Popery was at last the consummation and end. Come what may of the Reformation, there are certain general maxims of faith here which we can never safely renounce. We must hold fast to the divine origin of the church, and to its divine continuity from the beginning down to the present time. We must see and admit, that Protestantism is no return simply to Primitive Christianity. Its connection with this is *through* the Roman Catholic church only, as the real continuation of the older system. In no other view can it be acknowledged, as the historical and legitimate succession of this ancient faith. This implies, however, that the life of Protestantism must be one with the life of the church as it stood previously. It is to be taken as different from this indeed in the rejection of many accidental corruptions, but not in distinctive substance and spirit. Its doctrines and habits must be felt to grow forth, with true inward vitality, from the faith that has been accredited as divine from the beginning, by the promise and miraculous providence of Christ. Puritanism then, by abjuring this historical and organic relationship to the ancient church, does what it can in truth to ruin the cause of genuine Protestantism. It brings in another Gospel. It throws us on the terrible dilemma: "Either ancient Christianity was intrinsically false, or Protestantism is a bold imposture";[101] for it makes this last to be the pure negation and contradiction of the first. But when it comes to this, what sound mind can pause in its choice? To create such a dilemma, we say then, is to fight against the Reformation. Puritanism, carrying upon its hard front these formidable horns, is no better than treason and death to Protestantism.

J. W. N.

---

100. [The Holy Roman Emperors.]

101. [Not a quotation, but Nevin's summary of the historical thesis he is considering.]

Early Christianity: Third Article.[1]

[Recapitulation and Response to Critics]

To make our discussion properly complete, it is still necessary to bring into view, more particularly than has yet been done, the practical bearings and issues of the whole subject.

It is rather a sorry commentary on the reigning knowledge of ecclesiastical history among us, that the statements made in our first article with regard to the Christianity of the fourth and fifth centuries, should have given rise in certain quarters to so much scandal and offence. We have been represented as betraying the cause of Protestantism, and making huge strides towards Romanism, by the mere fact of venturing such statements themselves; as though they were of either novel or questionable character, or must necessarily and at once imply a full approval of the points which as a matter of simple history they are found to grant and allow. Our positions here are not theological, but purely historical.[2] They relate to a question of outward fact, to be settled in such form by proper testimony. How the fact may suit this or that theory of divinity, is

---

1. [MR 4 (January 1852) 1–54. DeBie exposits this article in *John Williamson Nevin*, 279–82.]

1. [Isaac Taylor,] *Ancient Christianity, and the Doctrines of the Oxford Tracts for the Times,* By the Author of "Spiritual Despotism." Fourth Edition. London, 1844. 2 vols. 8vo.

2. *Die Anfänge der Christlichen Kirche und ihrer Verfassung.* Ein geschichtlicher Versuch von *Richard Rothe* [1799–1867], Professor der Theol. &c. Erster Band. Wittemberg, 1837.

3. *The Principle of Protestantism as related to the Present State of the Church.* By *Philip Schaff,* Ph. D. Chambersburg, 1845. [See MTSS 3.]

4. *What is Church History? A Vindication of the idea of Historical Development.* By *Philip Schaff.* Philadelphia, 1846. [See MTSS 3.]

5. *An Essay on the Development of Christian Doctrine.* By *John Henry Newman.* American Edition, [New York: D. Appleton,] 1846. [John Henry Newman (1801–90), *An Essay on the Development of Christian Doctrine* (Notre Dame: University of Notre Dame Press, 1989).]

6. *Vorlesungen über Katholicismus und Protestantismus.* Von *Heinrich W. J. Thiersch,* Doctor der Philosophie und Theologie, ordentl. Prof. d. Theol. an der Universität Marburg. Erlangen[: Heyder], 1848.

2. [Both here and in "Cyprian," Nevin's argument is presented as being merely a question of historical fact and not a question of theological superiority/inferiority. However, Nevin is clearly arguing for a particular understanding of history against the understanding of history which sees the early centuries of the church as being a kind of early Protestantism. Nevin, whatever else his agenda in these essays, clearly wants to reject that understanding. The question which he struggles to answer remains: how does Protestantism fit in his understanding of history? The tension which Nevin creates historically, theologically, and personally remains unresolved at the end of this essay.]

another question altogether; and nothing can well be more childish and absurd, than to think of making this second inquiry the rule and measure of the other. Is our theology then to regulate and decide the meaning of history? Must this last have no voice whatever, save as it can be forced to speak in agreement with the first? Shall facts be concealed or denied, because they fall not in with a given scheme of belief? Ridiculous pretension. It breathes the very spirit that is ordinarily attributed to the inquisition. We have heard of the case of Galileo; forced to do penance, as the story goes, for teaching that the earth moves round the sun, while the honor of the reigning theology was supposed to require rather, that the sun should be taken to move round the earth. The case before us is precisely of the same tyrannical complexion. Nay it is in some respects worse; for the facts of the Copernican system are by no means so near to us, and so capable of full verification in their own order, as the facts of history with which we are here concerned. The first may always be questioned with some show at least of reason; whereas to question these last is like pretending to call white black or black white.

We refer to what we have said of the religious system of the days of Ambrose and Augustine. "You tell us," exclaims some evangelical inquisitor, doing his best to look calm and mild as well as more than commonly pious, "that Christianity as it stood in the fourth century, and in the first part of the fifth, was something very different from modern Protestantism, and that it bore in truth a very near resemblance in all material points to the later religion of the Roman church."—That, Sir, is what we have said; and such precisely is our opinion.—"You go so far as to add, that were the fathers who then lived to return to the world in our time, they would find themselves more at home in the Papal than in the Protestant communion."—We have not the least doubt of it, Sir, supposing them to return as they were when they died; their first movement would be towards Romanism, and the most we could hope would be that, after some time taken to understand the present state of things, they might be prepared perhaps to pass forward to Protestantism, as after all better and higher ground.—"You hold that these fathers, whom the whole Protestant world is accustomed to venerate and laud as the glory of the ancient church, knew nothing of the view which makes the bible and private judgment the principle of Christianity and the only source and rule of faith, acknowledged the central dignity of the bishop of Rome, believed in baptismal regeneration, the mystery of the real presence, purgatory and prayers for the dead, venerated relics, had full faith in the continuation of miracles, and glorified celibacy, voluntary poverty, and the monastic life, as at once honorable to religion and eminently suited to promote the spiritual welfare of men." —Certainly, Sir, we do hold all this, and are prepared to furnish any amount of proof for it that may be reasonably required.— "Then you endorse the worst abominations of the Roman system."— Softly, Sir Inquisitor, not quite so fast; that is not the question in any way under consideration. The matter here to be settled is not what we or you may think of these points. The simple inquiry is, Are the positions true? Whatever may be thought of them theologically, are they *historically* true? They are merely historical positions.

They affirm certain facts of history as facts, and in no other way. If the positions in this view are wrong, if it can be shown that the facts were not as they affirm, let us have proof of it, proper historical proof, and we shall consider it a privilege to acknowledge and retract our mistake. But are *you* prepared, Inquisitorial Sir, for this reasonable task? Alas, no. You have never read a page of one of these early fathers; and you have never given any serious attention to the history of the church in this period as it may be studied from other sources; for if you had done so, it would not be possible for you to assume the ridiculous attitude in which you now stand. You have never studied the subject; know nothing about it; and yet here you are, in spite of all such ignorance, pretending to dispose of it in the most dogmatical and wholesale style, without the least regard whatever to actual facts. The Romanizing spirit of the fourth and fifth centuries is too clear, to admit of any sort of question or doubt. You simply expose your own want of everything like true scholarship, on the field of church history, by imagining that there is any room for controversy in the case of so plain a fact.

[Modern Historians and Church History]

Any respectable church historian may be appealed to as a witness in regard to this point. Gieseler, Neander, Mosheim, though not with the same spirit exactly, agree here in the same general representation, so far as the main fact is concerned. Quotations are unnecessary. It is agreed all round, that the prelatical and pontifical system was in full force in this period, that the sacraments were regarded as supernatural mysteries, that purgatory, prayers for the dead, and the worship of saints, were part and parcel of the reigning faith, that celibacy and monasticism were held in the highest honor, that an unbounded veneration for relics everywhere prevailed, and that miracles were received on all sides as events by no means uncommon or incredible in the church. Who indeed can be ignorant of this, who has only read Gibbon's *History of the Decline and Fall of the Roman Empire*?[3] We may put what construction we please on the facts. We may explain them as we please. But it is perfectly idle to dispute them, or to pretend to set them aside. We might just as well quarrel with the constitution of nature. The fathers of the fourth and fifth centuries were not Puritan nor Protestant. They stood in the bosom of the Catholic system, the very same order of thought that completed itself afterwards in the Roman or Papal church. And their position there was not by accident merely or in a simply external way. It belonged to the very substance of their faith. Their christianity was constructed throughout from this standpoint alone. The strong supposition then of Dr. Newman is not a whit too strong for the actual character of the case. If Ambrose or Athanasius should now revisit the earth, with their old habit of mind, neither of them would be able to feel himself at home in any of our Protestant churches. They would fall in much more

---

3. [Thus, even the skeptic Gibbon becomes a witness to the early church's belief in the supernatural.]

readily, for a time at least, with the doctrine and worship of the Catholics. And so on the other hand, neither of them would find the least toleration in any Protestant sect. Anglicans, Low Episcopalians, Presbyterians, Methodists, Congregationalists, Baptists, United Brethren, Quakers, and so on to the end of the chapter, would exclude them alike from their communion, or take them in at best as novices and babes requiring to be taught again the first principles of the doctrine of Christ. Let any one appear in New England, at the present time, in the spirit precisely and power of Athanasius, or Chrysostom, or Ambrose, or Augustine, and it is perfectly certain that he would find no countenance or favor in any quarter. Orthodoxy and Unitarians would join hands in trying to put him down, as a pestilent fellow bent only on corrupting the faith of the churches. No evangelical sect would think of extending to him the right hand of fellowship. His name would be cast out as evil, he would be regarded as a Papist and an enemy of all true religion, in every direction. Such men as Jovinian and Vigilantius would find far more favor. These were the true Protestants, as Neander styles them, of the fourth century. But for this very reason they appeared wholly out of place in its bosom. The whole tone and temper of the time was against them. They were fairly overwhelmed as rationalistic heretics.[4]

We may charge all this, if we choose, to the ignorance and superstition of the age. We may be sorry or angry, as best suits our humor, that the facts of history should come before us in such disagreeable form. It is easy enough also to renounce the authority of the whole Christianity of this period, and to throw ourselves at once back upon the authority of the Bible. The fathers of the fourth and fifth centuries were not infallible; why should we then trouble ourselves with their fancies and ways, when we have the sure word of revelation itself to make us acquainted with all necessary truth? Such ground certainly we have a right to take, if we see proper. Only, in doing so, let us see and know clearly what we are about. Let us not pretend in this way to set aside the fact itself, from the force of which we thus try to make our escape. This is all we are concerned with at present; and this is something entirely independent of

---

4. "The most eminent of these worthy opposers of the reigning superstitions was *Jovinian,* an Italian monk, who, towards the conclusion of this century, taught first at Rome, and afterwards at Milan, that all those who kept the vows they made to Christ at their baptism, and lived according to those rules of piety and virtue laid down in the gospel, had an equal title to the rewards of futurity; and that, consequently, those who passed their days in unsociable celibacy, and severe mortifications and fastings, were in no respect more acceptable in the eye of God, than those who lived virtuously in the bonds of marriage, and nourished their bodies with moderation and temperance. These judicious opinions, which many began to adopt, were first condemned by the church of Rome, and afterwards by Ambrose, in a council held at Milan in the year 390. The emperor Honorius seconded the authoritative proceedings of the bishops by the violence of the secular arm, answered the judicious reasonings of Jovinian by the terror of coercive and penal laws, and banished this pretended heretic to the island *Boa.* Jovinian published his opinions in a book, against which Jerome, in the following century, wrote a most bitter and abusive treatise, which is still extant."—Mosheim, *Eccles. Hist.* Cent. IV. Part II. Chapt. III [Johann Lorenz von Mosheim, *An Ecclesiastical History, from the Birth of Christ, to the Beginning of the Eighteenth Century,* trans. Archibald Maclaine, vol. 1 (London: Thomas Tegg, 1838), 191–92].

any construction that may be put upon it, or of any theological use to which it may be turned, in one direction or in another.

Make what we may of it, we owe it to truth here to acknowledge and confess the full existence of the fact itself. The Christianity of the fourth and fifth centuries was more Roman Catholic a great deal than Protestant. The best piety of this period, as it meets us in such saints as Athanasius, Chrysostom and Ambrose, is fairly steeped in what would be counted by the common Puritanism of the present time rank heathenish superstition. Let us at all events have honesty enough to own here what is the simple truth. Let us look the fact fairly and steadily in the face, and then *as a fact* we may deal with it as seems best.

We had no idea indeed, that what we have said with regard to this point was likely to be disputed at all, or even to be found particularly startling, in any section at least of Puritan Christianity. We thought it was a matter conceded and granted on all hands, that not only the prelatical system, but all sorts of Romanizing tendencies besides, were in full play as early as the fourth century; and that no account was to be made of this period accordingly, as a source of testimony or evidence for any other form of faith that might be supposed to have prevailed at an earlier day. Puritanism, we thought, had settled it as a fixed maxim, that the seeds of Popery were not only sown, but actively sprouting also and bearing most ugly fruit on all sides, in the fourth and fifth centuries, the time of Ambrose and Augustine; and that *therefore* exactly no stress was to be laid on the voice of any such fathers, wherever it seems to be pitched on the Catholic key and to carry in it a plainly Catholic sound. Nothing is more familiar to us certainly than this line of argument. What Independent is disturbed by the hierarchical ideas, that are everywhere current in the age of Athanasius? What Baptist cares a fig for the usages of "time immemorial," that are brought into view in the controversy between Pelagius and Augustine? What Presbyterian is put out of countenance in the least, by any amount of proof urged against his favorite system, from creeds or liturgies that date from the days of Arius or Nestorius? The ever ready answer to all such authority is, that it is quite too late to be of any significance or force. The period is given up as an age of wholesale departure from the truth.[5] The fathers of the fourth and fifth centuries, we are told,

---

5. "We can then admit, with Dr. N., that the Christianity of the fourth century was something 'very different from modern Protestantism'—and very different too from the truth and piety taught in the New Testament. We can readily admit that those fathers, were they now to rise from the dead with the same views they had when they fell asleep, would hardly 'find their home' in any of our Protestant churches. They would still have a hankering after the imaginary virtues of celibacy, and asceticism, and mystical interpretations, and baptism for the remission of original sin, and an insatiate passion for relics, and for the pretended miracles of monkery. We grant that the elements of Romanism were fermenting and growing rank in the ancient Church—the church of the fourth century;—and we also admit in these elements, the development of the great Apostacy predicted by the Apostle.—If men cannot see evidences of the Apostacy, 'the falling away,' in the teaching and monkery and fanaticism of that age, it must be for the want of eyes to see, or power to discriminate between the graceful form of truth and its hideous caricatures; or they must be the victims of a blinding credulity, which regards with reverential awe, every relic of antiquity."—*Christian Observer*, (Philadelphia) Nov, 1851. [The editors have not located this specific article. This periodical was edited by Amasa Converse. He started

were all woefully infected with superstition and under the dominion of error. Patristic testimony in any case is not of much account, except as it falls in with what we may take to be the sense of the Bible; but borrowed from the time now mentioned it is worth, on all points here in consideration, the next thing to nothing.

Take in exemplification a single passage from Dr. Miller's Letters on Episcopacy. "In examining the writings of the Fathers," he tells us,

> I shall admit only the testimony of those who wrote within the *first two centuries*. Immediately after this period so many corruptions began to creep into the church; so many of the most respectable Christian writers are known to have been heterodox in their opinions; so much evidence appears, that even before the commencement of the third century, the Papacy began to exhibit its pretensions; and such multiplied proofs of wide spreading degeneracy crowd into view, that the testimony of every subsequent writer is to be received with suspicion.[6]

This is the only proper Presbyterian view. Presbyterianism *must* take this ground, in order to have any solid bottom whatever. And still more must Congregationalism do

---

a journal in Richmond in 1827, and moved it to Philadelphia in 1839, merging it with *Philadelphia Observer*. "Death of the Rev. Dr. Amasa Converse—9 December 1872."]

This is curious enough in its connexions. The occasion is Mr. Helffenstein's circular, calling on sister sects to take part with Dr. Berg and himself in their protest against the G. R. [German Reformed] Synod, for not choosing to make our first article on *Early Christianity* cause for a process of Lynch law at our capital expense. [Jacob Helffenstein and Joseph F. Berg were two opponents of Mercersburg theology in the German Reformed Church in the 1840s. The "circular" is described in Nichols, *Romanticism*, 208. Helffenstein became a New School Presbyterian and Berg joined the Dutch Reformed Church. Hart, *John Williamson Nevin*, 169; Nichols, *Romanticism*, 86–89, 219; William Evans, *Companion*, 27; Appel, *Life and Work*, 227–28.] Our amiable friend Dr. Converse, so well known for his zeal against the assumptions of the Old School section of Presbyterianism, though too delicate to "intermeddle" with the ecclesiastical difficulties of another body, holds this a fair opportunity and call notwithstanding for stepping forward, in the character at once of both judge and jury, to regulate the affairs of the G. R. church. The body is not competent, it would seem, to act for itself. It has no right to its own historical character. It must be tried by a foreign standard, by Puritanism, by New School Presbyterianism, by "*American* Lutheranism," by all that is unsacramental and unchurchly in the land. [In Nevin's mind, these churches were revivalistic perversions of older Reformation inheritances. "American Lutheranism" was identified with Benjamin Kurtz, a supporter of revivalism, and an antagonist of Nevin ever since his *Anxious Bench* (1833/34; MTSS 5, see esp. p. 36n2).] And if it abide not *this* test, then all must be wrong. But what is it now that Mr. Helffenstein's circular finds to be so dreadful in the article on Early Christianity? Simply this, that it makes the leading elements of Romanism to have been at work in the Nicene church, and denies the existence of any golden period answerable to modern Puritanism after the age of the N. Testament. And yet, what so horrifies Mr. H. here is fully granted, in the foregoing extract by the Philadelphia observer itself. With what then does the editor quarrel? Had he read our article with his own eyes? We presume not. And yet he undertakes to deal with it, and with the whole G. R. church besides, in this magisterial way, on the strength of the first wrong impression caught up from the *ex parte* statement of a foiled and passionate appellant, flying to his Editorial Bench for redress! If this be either honorable or honest, there is need in truth that we should go to school again to learn "which be the first principles" of Christian Ethics.

6. [Samuel Miller, *Letters Concerning the Constitution and Order of the Christian Ministry* (New York: Hopkins and Seymour, 1807), 126.]

so, under every form and shape. The universal voice of the fourth and fifth centuries looks wholly another way. The least that can be said of it is, that it goes in full for the prelatical and high church system at all points; and Presbyterians and Independents are generally willing to allow that it goes for a great deal more than this system under its common Episcopalian form; that it goes in fact for many of the leading features of Romanism, and that for Episcopalians therefore as an argument which proves too much it may be said properly to prove nothing.

In this light we find the subject handled indeed, even in the Episcopal church itself, by one of its parties in controversy with the other. The Puseyites, as they are called, and the High church party in general, have been disposed to build the authority of their system very much on the Nicene period of ecclesiastical antiquity; taking it for granted, that while it exhibits, with unmistakeable clearness, all the traces of their theory as distinguished from every less churchly scheme, it may be regarded as standing equally clear from the abuses of Romanism, as these come into view along with the growth of the Papacy in later centuries. On the other side however it has been well and ably shown, that there is no room whatever for this last distinction in any such pretended form. In particular, the work entitled "Ancient Christianity," by Isaac Taylor,[7] Esq., the author of "Spiritual Despotism"[8] and other well known volumes, is wholly devoted to the object of proving that it is a most perfect mistake, to imagine anything like the counterpart of Anglican Protestantism as having existed in the fourth century, and that in truth what are usually considered the worst abuses of Romanism were already fully at work in this period; nay, that in many respects the form under which they then appeared was decidedly worse altogether, than that which they carried subsequently in the middle ages. So far as the mere question of history goes, no one will pretend to question the competency of Mr. Taylor, as a truly learned and faithful witness. His testimony is given as the result of a very full and laborious personal examination of the writings of the early fathers themselves, and is supported throughout with a weight of authorities and examples that a man must be rash indeed to think of setting aside. The evidence is absolutely overwhelming, that the Nicene church was in all essential points of one mind and character with the Papal church of later times, and that where any difference is to be found, it was for the most part not in favor of the first, but against it rather, and in favor of this last. Let a few extracts serve here to show the ground taken and triumphantly maintained by this author, on the relation of these older and later schemes of Christianity, viewed thus as a question of simple historical fact and nothing more.

---

7. [At this point, Nevin begins his argument that just as "Puritanism" cannot repristinate apostolic Christianity, so likewise "Puseyism," or high church Anglicanism, cannot repristinate Nicene Christianity. On Taylor, see prior annotation, 40n22.]

8. [*Spiritual Despotism* (1835) was one in a series of monographs critiquing religious enthusiasm. Schnorrenberg, "Taylor, Isaac," 912.]

Our ears have been so much and so long used to the sound (repeated by Protestant writers, one after another, and without any distinct reference to facts, and probably without any direct knowledge of them,) of the *progressive corruption* of Christianity, and the slow and steady advances of superstition and spiritual tyranny, that we are little prepared to admit a contrary statement, better sustained by evidence, as well as more significant in itself—namely, that, although councils, or the papal authority, from age to age, followed up, embodied and legalized certain opinions, usages, and practices, which had already been long prevalent in an undefined form, it very rarely pushed on far in advance of the feeling and custom of the times: but that, on the contrary, it rather followed in the wake of ancient superstitions, expressing in bulls, decretals, and canons (which were not seldom of a corrective kind) the inherited principles of the ecclesiastical body. Or to state the same general fact, as it is seen from another point of view, it will be found true that, if the sentiment and opinion of the church at different eras be regarded apart from the authorized expressions of the same, there will appear to have been far less of *progression* than we have been taught to suppose; and that, on the contrary, the notions and usages of a later, differ extremely little from those of an earlier age; or that, so far as they do differ, the advantage, in respect of morality and piety, is quite as often on the side of the later as of the earlier ages. If particular points be had in view, it may be affirmed that Popery is a practicable form, and a corrected expression, of the Christianity of the Nicene age.—[Taylor,] *Ancient Christianity, Vol. I. p.* 63.

[...]

A well-defined and authoritative system (involving elements of evil) is, I think, much to be preferred to an undefined system, involving the very same elements; and I firmly believe that it were, on the whole, better for a community to submit itself, without conditions, to the well-known Tridentine Popery, than to take up the Christianity of Ambrose, Basil, Gregory Nyssen, Chrysostom, Jerome, and Augustine. Personally, I would rather be a Christian after the fashion of Pascal and Arnold,[9] than after that of Cyprian or Cyril; but how much rather, after that of our own protestant worthies, who, although entangled by fond notions about the ancient church, were, in heart, and in the main bent of their lives, followers, not of the fathers, but of the apostles!—[Taylor, *Ancient Christianity*,] *Vol. I. p.* 124, 125.

[...]

In *this* sense then, and how much soever it may jar with notions that have been generally entertained, and whatever high offence the assertion may give to certain persons, I here distinctly repeat my affirmation that Romanism was

---

9. [The former list consists of Nicene and post-Nicene fathers, identified in earlier notes. Pascal is the noted Catholic apologist and Jansenist. Arnold is probably Arnold of Brescia, a twelfth century critic of the church's worldliness. His opposition to the temporal dominion of the popes led to his death at the hands of Frederick Barbarossa. *Dictionary of the Christian Church*, 109–10.]

Document 2: Early Christianity: Third Article.

a reform, (or if there be any other word of nearly the same meaning, but more agreeable to our ears,) a reform, or a correction of the Nicene church system. In thus reiterating this unacceptable assertion, I am prepared, if required to do so, to defend my ground by copious citations of historical and ecclesiastical evidence; and particularly by an appeal to the writings of the early popes and to the acts of councils.[10] As an inference from this advisedly-made assertion, I am prepared to say, that considered as a question affecting the morals of the people, it were better for us to return without reserve to the church of Rome, (horrid supposition as it is) than to surrender ourselves to the system which Basil, Ambrose, Chrysostom, the Gregories, and Augustine bequeathed to the nations. Nicene church principles, as now attempted to be put in the room of the principles of the Reformation, if in some points *theologically* better, or less encumbered, than the Popery of the council of Trent, would as I verily believe more quickly and certainly deluge England with fanatical debauchery, than would *such* Romanism as the church of Rome would at this moment, gladly establish among us.— [Taylor, *Ancient Christianity*,] Vol. II. p. 69. 70.

[...]

Popery then was a reform of the antecedent church system; inasmuch as it created and employed a force, counteractive of the evils which that system, and which itself too, could not but generate. The great men of the fourth century believed, that the system contained within itself a counteractive power. A few years furnished lamentable evidence of the fallacy of such a belief. The popes snatched at the only alternative—the creating a power *exterior* to the system, and assuming to be independent of it, by virtue of the special authority vested in the successors of Peter. *This* scheme was practicable; and Time has pronounced its eulogium. Terrible as is Popery, it is infinitely less terrible than its own naked substance, apart from its form. If at the present moment there are Popish nations in a moral condition almost as degraded as that into which Christendom at large had sunk in the fifth century, it is because the corrective energies of the papal hierarchy have long been dormant.— [Taylor, *Ancient Christianity*,] Vol. II. p. 71, 72.

[...]

I have undertaken to show, by numerous and varied citations, not merely that the doctrine and practice of religious celibacy occupied a prominent place in the theological and ecclesiastical system of the Nicene church, a fact hardly needing to be proved, but that the institute was intimately and inseparably connected with, and that it powerfully affected, every other element of ancient Christianity, whether dogmatic, ethical, ritual, or hierarchical. If, then, such a connexion can be proved to have existed, we must either adopt its notions and usages in this essential particular, or must surrender very much of our veneration for ancient Christianity.

---

10. [Paragraph break in the original.]

The fact of the intimate connexion here affirmed is really not less obvious or easily established than that of the mere existence of the institute itself. Modern church writers may, indeed, have thrown the unpleasing subject into the back-ground, and so it may have attracted much less attention than its importance deserves; but we no sooner open the patristic folios than we find it confronting us, on almost every page; and if either the general averment were questioned, or the bearing of the celibate upon every part of ancient Christianity were denied, volumes might be filled with the proofs that attest the one as well as the other. Both these facts must be admitted by all unprejudiced inquirers who shall take the pains to look into the extant remains of Christian antiquity.— [Taylor, *Ancient Christianity*,] *Vol. I. p.* 131.[11]

[. . .]

Do not the fathers then worship God? do they not adore the Son of God? Assuredly: but when they muster all the forces of their eloquence, when they catch fire, and swell, as if inspired, whenever (I must be permitted to make the allusion, for it is really appropriate,) whenever they take their seat upon the tripod and begin to foam,[12] the subject of the rhapsody is sure to be—"a blessed martyr," it may be an apostle; or a recently departed "doctor," or, "a virgin confessor;" or it is the relics of such a one, and the miraculous virtues of his sacred dust. If, in turning over these folios, the eye is any where caught by the frequency of interjections, such a page is quite as likely to be found to sparkle and flash with the commendations of the mother of God, or of her companion saints, as with the praises of the Son; and more often does the flood-tide of eloquence swell with the mysterious virtues of the sacraments than with the power and grace of the Saviour. The Saviour does indeed sit enthroned within the veil of the Christian temple; but what the Christian populace hear most about, is—the temple itself, and its embroideries, and its gildings, and its ministers, and its rites, and the saints that fill its niches. In a word, what was visible, and what was human, stood in front of what is invisible and divine: and when we find a system of blasphemous idolatry fully expanded in the middle ages, this system cannot, in any equity, be spoken of as any thing else than a following out of the adulatory rhapsodies of the great writers and preachers of the Nicene church.— [Taylor, *Ancient Christianity*,] *Vol. I. p.* 188.

[. . .]

Let not the Protestant reader, who may lately have heard Ambrose named as one of the great three, to whom we are to look for our idea of finished Christianity, let him not be startled at this praying to a saint. Ambrose in the west, as well as [Gregory] Nazianzen, [Gregory] Nyssen, Chrysostom, in the east, and others, too many to name, had convinced himself that no prayers were so

---

11. [Correction: pp. 133–34. The final phrase in this edition reads: " . . . who shall take the pains to look into the books where the evidence is to be found."]

12. [An allusion to the reported technique of the Delphic Oracle, the most important oracle of Greco-Roman polytheism.]

Document 2: Early Christianity: Third Article.

well expedited on high, as those which were presented by a saint and martyr already in the skies! In fact, a good choice as to the "patrocinium,"[13] was the main point in the business of prayer. These matters were, however, regulated by a certain propriety and conventional usage—may we say, etiquette: it was not on every sort of occasion that the Virgin was to be troubled with the wants and wishes of mortals: each saint had, indeed, come to have his department; and each was applied to in his particular line.[14] In connexion with subjects such as this how can one be serious? unless indeed considerations are admitted that agitate the mind with emotions of indignation and disgust.—[Taylor, *Ancient Christianity*,] Vol. I. p. 212.

[...]

It was, however, a consolation to Ambrose, in the loss of his brother, that he had lived to return to Milan, where the sacred dust would be at all times accessible, affording to him means of devotion of no ordinary value—"*habeo sepulcrum,*" says he, "*super quod jaceam, et* commendabiliorem *Deo futurum esse me credam, quod supra sancti corporis ossa requiescam.*"[15] Ambrose was truly a gainer by the death of his brother: for in place of his mere bodily presence, as a living coadjutor, he had the justifying merits of his bones, and the benefit of his intercession in heaven! Ungracious task indeed is it to adduce these instances of blasphemous superstition, as attaching to a name like that of Ambrose; but what choice is left us when, as now, the Christian community, little suspecting what is implied in the advice, are enjoined to take their faith and practice from the divines of the Nicene age, and from Ambrose, Athanasius, and Basil, especially?—*Ib.* [Taylor, *Ancient Christianity*, 1:212].

[...]

The florid orators, bishops and great divines of the fourth century, we find, one and all, throughout the east, throughout the west, throughout the African church, lauding and lifting to the skies whatever is formal in religion, whatever is external, accessory, ritual, ecclesiastical: it was upon *these* things that they spent their strength: it was these that strung their energies, these that fired their souls. Virginity they put first and foremost; then came maceration of the body, tears, psalm-singing, prostrations on the bare earth, humiliations, alms-giving, expiatory labours and sufferings, the kind offices of the saints in heaven, the wonder-working efficacy of the sacraments, the unutterable powers of the clergy: these were the rife and favoured themes of animated sermons, and of prolix treatises; and such was the style, temper, spirit, and practice of the church, from the banks of the Tigris, to the shores of the Atlantic, and from the Scandinavian morasses, to the burning sands of the great desert; such, so far as our extant materials give us any information. And all

---

13. [That is, "patronage."]

14. [For a modern study of this manifestation of patristic piety, see Brown, *The Cult of the Saints.*]

15. [Trans. "I have a sepulchre, upon which I may lie, and I believe that I shall be *more commendable* to God, that I shall rest upon the bones of a holy body."]

this was what it should have been! and this is what now we should be tending toward!— [Taylor, *Ancient Christianity,*] Vol. I. p. 265.

These are strong statements. But so far as historical facts are concerned, they are placed by our author beyond all contradiction. The Nicene Christianity bore no resemblance whatever to Protestantism. It carried in it all the principles of Romanism; so that this is to be considered in many respects an improvement on the older system, a regulation and correction of its abuses, and not by any means the bringing in of something always progressively worse. The model saint of the period is presented to us in the person of St. Antony, the "Patriarch of Monks."[16] Asceticism is made to be the highest style of piety. The merit of celibacy, the glorification of virginity, veneration for relics, all sorts of miracles, the idea of purgatory, the worship of saints, prayers for the dead, submission to the authority of the church, and faith in the sacraments as truly supernatural mysteries, come everywhere into view as the universal staple of religious thought. All this is so clearly established by the historical monuments which have come down to us from this age, that he who runs may read—unless indeed he choose rather to shut his own eyes. And what are we to think then of those, who are ready to take offence with the declaration of so plain a truth, as though it involved a deadly stab at the whole cause of Protestantism, and were the next thing in fact to a full acknowledgment of the claims of Rome! Alas for our Protestantism, if it is to stand by the feeble arm of *such* defenders. The noise they make is found to be at last, the proclamation simply of their own shame.

It is simply ridiculous then to make any question about the reigning state of the church in the fourth and fifth centuries, as related to Romanism and Popery. Our representation has not been a whit too strong for the actual truth of the case, but may lie considered as falling short of this altogether. It is the merest romance, when such a man as Bishop Wilson,[17] or any other Evangelical Protestant of the present day, allows himself to dream that such men as Ambrose and Augustine were orthodox and pious after his own fashion, that the main elements of their religion were of a truly Protestant cast, and that they were in a great measure free from the ideas which afterwards took full possession of the church under what is called the Roman apostasy. Every imagination of this sort is a perfect illusion. These fathers, and along with them the entire church of their time, were in all material respects fully committed to the later Roman system; and at some points indeed stood farther off from Evangelical Protestantism than the full grown Popery of the eleventh and twelfth centuries.[18] Let this truth then

16. [St. Anthony of the Desert (c. 251–356), an Egyptian hermit credited with innovating a monastic community living under a rule. He intervened in the Arian controversy and drew many persons to monastic solitude in the desert.]

17. [Daniel Wilson, evangelical Bishop of Calcutta, who Nevin quoted at length in the first article.]

18. [This argument is key to Nevin's overall project in the whole of the essay, but especially in this third part. Nevin's argument, that there was a trajectory in the third, fourth, and fifth centuries which pointed toward the eleventh and twelfth centuries, considered by most Protestants to be the height of the Roman apostasy, creates a lot of pressure on his historical understanding of the Reformation. It

be known and kept in mind. Here at least is a fixed fact in church history, which only the most disgraceful ignorance can pretend to dispute. Let it be made familiar to our thoughts. Nicene Christianity, the system which the fourth century inherited from the third and handed forward to the fifth, was not Protestantism; much less Puritanism; bore no resemblance to this whatever; but in all essential principles and characteristics was nothing more nor less than Romanism itself. The great Athanasius, now in London or New York, would be found worshipping only at Catholic altars. Augustine would not be acknowledged by any evangelical sect. Chrysostom would feel the Puritanism of New England more inhospitable and dry than the Egyptian desert.

For his own immediate and main object then, the argument of Mr. Isaac Taylor, it seems to us, is unanswerably conclusive and overwhelming. Anglicanism builds its pretensions throughout on the position, that antiquity as far down as to the fifth century is in its favor, and at the same time against those features of Romanism which go beyond its measure; that these Roman features came in gradually at a later period, along with the rise of the Papacy, as innovations and corruptions; and that it is possible now to cast them all off as purely outward excrescences or incrustations, and so to find in the Nicene system a true picture of what the church was in the beginning, and the fair pattern at the same time of modern Episcopacy after the Oxford scheme. This whole position, it is perfectly certain, cannot stand. It is historically false. To trust it is only to lean upon a broken reed. There is no such distinction here as it asserts, between the older and later church systems. The Nicene Christianity was in its whole constitution of one order with Romanism. The worst corruptions, as they are usually called, of this later system, were all at work in the older system. They are not by any means the inventions and devices of the Papacy, as distinguished from the supposed Patriarchal or Episcopal order of more ancient times. The idea of a steadily growing apostacy and defection from such primitive state of the church, under the usurped dominion of Rome, is a purely arbitrary fiction, which the least true study of antiquity must soon scatter to the winds. In many things, the later order was a decided improvement on the order that went before. The Papacy was a wholesome reformatory and regulative power for the most part, in its relation to what are called Popish abuses and corruptions, rather than the proper fountain itself of these evils. They belonged to the inheritance it received from the Nicene age, the period in which modern Anglicanism now affects to glory as the model and pattern of an uncorrupted Christianity just like its own. All this, we say, Mr. Taylor makes perfectly clear. Puseyism, in his hands, is convicted of miserable pedantry. Its rule is too wide a great deal for its own pretensions. The line it pretends to draw between Nicene Episcopacy and *Popery* for the purpose of marking off a *jure divino* system of church principles to suit itself, is one that exists only in hypothesis and dream, and not at all in true history.[19] Both

also challenges the historical understanding of the Reformers themselves who were clearly involved in the project of the reform of the Church.]

19. [Schaff makes similar comments in *Principle*, MTSS 3:144–48.]

historically and logically the premises of the fourth century complete themselves in the full Papal system, and under any form short of this are something, not better than such proper conclusion, but in all respects worse.

As far too as an argument may seem to hold in the relation of the church at different times to the reigning moral and social life in the midst of which it appears, the Nicene Christianity has nothing to plead in its own recommendation. It is a most gloomy picture in this view that Mr. Taylor gives us particularly of the fifth century, from Salvian[20] and other writers. All sorts of immorality prevailed throughout the nominally Christian church. Society showed itself rotten to the core. The Goths and Vandals surpassed, in many cases, the morality of those who professed the true religion and participated in its sacraments. It is evident enough too from Chrysostom and others, that the state of things in the fourth century was much the same, the visible church being literally flooded with immorality and vice. Mr. Taylor brings this forward, as an exemplification of the natural and necessary operation of the Nicene theology. This is plainly a false use of the case. It had other causes sufficiently intelligible in the social state of the world at the time. But the fact is one, which on many accounts it is important to understand and hold in mind. Romanism in later times was not embosomed generally in moral associations so bad as those of this older period; and its worst social phases at the present time, as we are accustomed to think of them in connection with such countries as Spain or Italy or Austria, are far less revolting than the life of nominal Christendom in Europe generally, and throughout North Africa, in the days of Augustine. If modern Catholicism may be convicted of being a false religion on this ground, it is certain that the whole Christianity of the Nicene age is open to like condemnation, and with still greater effect, in precisely the same view.

So much for the Nicene age, according to the judgment of this learned author. But he does not confine his view to this period. His knowledge of the laws of history could not permit him to doubt its organic union with the life of the period that went before; and his actual study of that earlier age has been of a kind to place this reasonable conclusion beyond all question. He confirms in full, accordingly, the general statement we have already made in relation to the Christianity also of the second and third centuries, as tried by the standard of modern Protestantism. The fourth century was a true continuation of the ecclesiastical forms and views of the third; and this again grew, by natural and legitimate birth, out of the bosom of the second.[21] As far

20. [Author of the fifth century, who "contrast[ed] the vices of decadent Roman civilization with the virtues of the victorious barbarians." *Dictionary of the Christian Church*, 1448–49.]

21. [This is a key argument in Nevin's understanding of historical development and central to his challenge of the "Puritanizing" elements who are attempting to argue for a repristination of a time before the corruption of the church began. Nevin's historical framing essentially leaves no room open for such a time to have existed, thereby eliminating the possibility of any historical restart as Nevin's opponents are attempting to create. For Nevin, all attempts to create a New Testament equivalent to American Puritanism is denied by the historical records as we have them. The difficulty that Nevin will encounter in the remainder of the essay, is that he does not establish what that something might look like. As we will see at the end of this essay, Nevin's solution is to allow time to pass to establish the proper

Document 2: Early Christianity: Third Article.

back as our historical notices reach, we find no trace this side of the New Testament of any church system at all answering to any Puritan scheme of the present time; no room or space however small in which to locate the hypothesis even of any such scheme; but very sufficient proof rather that the prevailing habit of thought looked all quite another way, and that in principle and tendency at least the infant church was carried from the very start towards the order of the third and fourth centuries, and through this, we may say, towards the medieval Catholicism in which that older system finally became complete. Listen for a moment again to the strong testimony of our English writer.

> At a time not more remote from the Apostolic age than we, of this generation, are from the times of Barrow, Tillotson, Taylor, Baxter,[22] we find every element of the abuses of the twelfth century, and not the elements only, but some of those abuses in a ripened, nay, in a putrescent condition.—[Taylor, *Ancient Christianity,*] *Vol. I. p. 70.*
>
> [. . .]
>
> I cannot however proceed to call in my next pair of witnesses, without adverting to a fact which forces itself upon every well informed and reflecting reader of the early Christian writers, I mean the much higher moral condition, and the more effective discipline of the Romish church in later times, than can with any truth be claimed for the ancient church, even during its era of suffering and depression. Our ears are stunned with the outcry against the "corruptions of Popery." I boldly say that Popery, foul as it is, and has ever been, in the mass, might yet fairly represent itself as a *reform upon*[23] *early Christianity*. Do not accuse me of the wish to startle you with paradoxes. I will not swell my pages (which will have enough to bear) with quotations from modern books that are in the hands of most religious readers. In truth, volumes of unimpeachable evidence might be produced, establishing the fact, that the *later* Romish church has had to boast eminent virtues, in connexion with her monastic institutions; and I think virtues, better compared,[24] and more consistent than belonged to the earlier church. [. . .] Nothing can be more inequitable than to charge these horrors upon Romanism. The church of Rome has done, in these instances, *the best it could,* to bring the cumbrous abomination bequeathed to it by the saints and doctors and martyrs of the pristine age into a manageable condition. And if we are to hear much more of the "corruptions of popery," as opposed to "primitive purity," there will be no alternative but freely to lay open the sewers of the early church, and to a[l]low them to disgorge their contents upon the wholesome air. [. . .] Before we reprobate popes, councils, and Romanist saints, let us fairly see what sort

---

theory of development, which he does not have, is unwilling to publish, or is unable to determine.]

22. [That is, 150–200 years.]
23. [Taylor's text reads "regulated form of."]
24. [Taylor's text reads "compacted."]

of system it was which the doctors and martyrs of the highest antiquity had delivered into their care and custody. We Protestants are prompt enough to condemn the pontiffs, or St. Bernard;[25] but let inquiry be made concerning the Christianity embodied in the writings of those to whom popes and doctors looked up, as their undoubted masters.— [Taylor, *Ancient Christianity*,] Vol. I. p. 77–79.

[...]

I have undertaken to adduce proof of the assertion, not only that the doctrine of the merit of celibacy, and the consequent practices, are found in a mature state at an early age; but also—That, at the earliest period at which we find this doctrine, and these practices, distinctly mentioned, they are referred to in such a manner as to make it certain that they were, at that time, no novelties or recent innovations. Now I am aware that a statement such as this, if it shall appear to be borne out by evidence, will excite alarm in some minds; the dissipation of erroneous impressions, is always a critical and somewhat perilous operation; nevertheless dangers much more to be feared, are incurred by a refusal to admit the full and simple truth. Yet the alarm that may be felt in this instance, at the first, may soon be removed; for although it were to appear that certain capital errors of feeling, and practice, had seized the church universal, at the very moment when the personal influence of the apostles was withdrawn, yet such an admission will shake no principle really important to our faith or comfort. In fact, too many have been attaching their faith and comfort to a supposition, concerning pristine Christianity, which is totally illusory, and such as can bear no examination—a supposition which must long ago have been dispelled from all well-informed minds, by the influence of rational modes of dealing with historical materials, if it had not been for the *conservative*[26] *accident,* that the materials, which belong to this particular department of history, have lain imbedded in repulsive folios of Latin and Greek, to which very few, and those not the most independent, or energetic in their habits of mind, have had access. Certain utterly unfounded generalities, very delightful had they possessed the recommendation of truth, have been a thousand times repeated, and seldom scrutinized.

But the times of this ignorance are now passing away: and I think the zeal of the Oxford writers will have the effect, as an indirect means, of disabusing effectively, and for ever, the religious mind, in this country, and perhaps throughout Europe, of the inveterate illusions that have so long hung over the fields of Christian antiquity. It will be utterly impossible, much longer to make those things believed which we have been taught to consider as unquestionable; and the result must be, (how desirable a result) the compelling the

---

25. [Bernard of Clairvaux (1090–1153).]

26. ["Conservative" refers to the alleged manner in which these materials were "conserved," i.e., in "repulsive folios," such that few scholars were able to, or desired to, access them.]

Document 2: Early Christianity: Third Article.

Christian church, henceforward, to rest its faith and practice on the only solid foundation.

The actual impression, moral and spiritual, made upon the Jewish and Pagan world by the preaching of the Apostles themselves, and of their personal colleagues, has, I fear, been overrated by the generality of Christians.[27] [. . .] And then, as to the period immediately following the death of the apostles, and of the men whom they personally appointed to govern the churches, we have too easily, and without any sufficient evidence, assumed the belief that a brightness and purity belonged to it, only a shade or two less than what we have attributed to the apostolic times. This belief, is, in fact, merely the correlative of the common Protestant notion concerning the progressive corruptions of Popery, it being a natural supposition that the higher we ascend toward the apostolic age, so much the more truth, simplicity, purity, must there have been in the church. Thus it is that we have allowed ourselves to theorize, when what we should have done, was simply to examine our documents.

The opinion that has forced itself upon my own mind, is to this effect, that the period dating its commencement from the death of the last of the apostles, or apostolic men, was, altogether, as little deserving to be selected and proposed *as a pattern*, as any one of the first five of church history;—it had indeed its single points of excellence, and of a high order, but by no means shone in those consistent and exemplary qualities which should entitle it to the honour of being considered as a model to after ages. We need therefore neither feel surprise nor alarm, when we find, in particular instances, that the grossest errors of theory and practice, are to be traced to their origin in the first century. In such instances, for my own part, I can wonder at nothing but the infatuation of those who, fully informed as they must be of the actual facts, and benefited moreover by modern modes of thinking, can nevertheless so prostrate their understandings before the phantom—venerable antiquity, as to be inflamed with the desire of inducing the Christian world to imitate what really asks for apology and extenuation.— [Taylor, *Ancient Christianity*,] Vol. I, p. 102–104.

[. . .]

In fact, I think, there are very few points of difference, distinguishing the Nicene church from either the earlier or the later church, within the compass of two hundred years on either side, which modern controvertists of any class would much care to insist upon, as of material consequence to their particular opinions.— [Taylor, *Ancient Christianity*,] Vol. I. p. 144.

These are serious admissions; and coming from such a source, they are entitled certainly to serious consideration. Let it be borne in mind, that we quote them simply

---

27. [Taylor's claim is corroborated by the modern statistical work of Rodney Stark in *Rise of Christianity*. See 3–13 on "The Arithmetic of Growth," which yields an estimate of 7500 Christians in the year 100, and little more than 40,000 a half-century later (13: Table 1.2). Stark argues that "[t]he projections reveal that Christianity could easily have reached half the population by the middle of the fourth century *without* miracles or conversions en masse" (14, emphasis added).]

in confirmation of a historical fact, without any regard now to the light in which this fact may be viewed, either by Mr. Taylor himself or by others, in its theological connections.[28] It is of the highest importance, that we should make here a clear distinction, between what actually had place and what construction should be put upon it in a theory of church history. All we are concerned with at present, is the simple fact, (explain it or judge of it as we may) that the Christianity of the second century was in no sense of one and the same order with modern Puritanism. How far precisely it may have anticipated the several features of the later Nicene system, is not entirely clear; but that it carried in it the elements and germs of this system, and looked towards it from the first with inward natural tendency, would seem to be beyond all doubt. The third century could not be what we find it to be in Cyprian and the Apostolical Constitutions, without some corresponding preparation at least in the age immediately preceding; and both the fact of such preparation, and its general nature, can be easily enough traced, as we have already shown, not merely to the time of Tertullian and Irenæus, but away back even to the days also of Polycarp and Ignatius. Let the *fact* then be fairly and honestly acknowledged; or else let it be disputed and set aside, if possible, on proper historical grounds. We present it as a simple point of history. We might wish it to be otherwise; but we feel that we have no power to make it otherwise, any more than we have to stop the earth from rolling round the sun, or to hush the alphabet of geology into dead silence. Facts themselves must not be treated as heresies, however we may feel disposed to treat the conclusions which are drawn from them.

[Patristic or Apostolic?]

But—we hear some one say—our appeal as to what constituted Early Christianity, in its oldest form, is to the New Testament itself. Let the writings of the Apostles themselves speak. The fathers sadly corrupted the truth, and mingled with it the dreams of pagan philosophy. Let those who choose rest in such false doubtful authority; *we* go at once to the original founders of the church, and are content to learn what it was in the beginning from their lips.

All very good, we say in reply; all very good. But the point before us just now, is not the Christianity that may be taught in the New Testament, or that may have prevailed in the Apostolical age.[29] Our inquiry, as historical, has been directed throughout to the determination of what Christianity was *after* the age of the Apostles, first in

---

28. [On Nevin's opinion of Taylor see above, 40n22.]

29. Those who take us to task for not ascending at once to the original records of Christianity, for the determination of what it was in its earliest and purest form, ought to remember that this whole discussion has had for its object from the beginning an altogether different inquiry—prompted in the first place by a particular position taken in the Rev. Dr. Bacon's Letter from Lyons ["Evangelical Religion in Lyons, France"]; this namely, that the system of religion now prevalent in New England, is to be regarded as in all material points the same with that which existed at Lyons, and throughout the church generally, in the days of Pothinus and Irenæus.

the Nicene age, and then back of that again in the middle and first part of the second century. The facts regarded in these two cases, are by no means just the same; and our idea of the first must not be allowed to blind or distort our vision, as directed towards this last. *You* may not care indeed for any later state of the church; but that is no reason why such later state should not be allowed, as a fact of history at least, to appear in its own place and under its own form. If we do not need it for our faith, let us at all events not quarrel with it as a matter of simple knowledge.

The fact itself however, in whatever light we regard it theologically, is one of the greatest practical account, as necessarily conditioning our whole theory of church history, and more particularly the view we may take of the relation that holds between Catholicism and Protestantism.

We have from it first of all this general result, that Protestantism is not at all identical with early Christianity, in the form at least which it carries after the time of the Apostles. We do not of course urge this as an objection to Protestantism. There are, as we shall see presently, different ways of reconciling the fact with the supposition that it is after all the purest and best style of Christianity. If we except Newman, all the distinguished writers whose works are quoted at the beginning of the present article, have in view the vindication of the Protestant Reformation, over against the pretensions of the Roman church; and yet all of them agree with Newman himself, in believing the modern form of religion to be in many respects very different from that which prevailed either in the fourth century or in the second. Newman's own theory indeed makes the mere fact of the disagreement to be of no conclusive force; since he himself allows the idea of a real historical movement in the life of the church, and must consider Protestantism therefore to be sufficiently justified on his own principles, if only it can be shown to be a legitimate development out of the bosom of Christianity as this stood before.[30]

[History and Protestantism—A Corrective]

The general truth is clear. Protestantism and Early Christianity are not the same. Let it be observed, we speak not now of early Christianity as it may be supposed to have been in the age of the Apostles, but of its manifestation in the period following that age, as far back as our historical notices reach this side of the New Testament. We speak not of what it may have been before the destruction of Jerusalem, or for a short time afterwards, in the first century; but of what it is found to have been, as a fact of history, in the second century as well as in the third and fourth. Let it be observed

---

30. [The details of Newman's thinking regarding Protestantism were most likely not fully known to Nevin. An important piece of his thinking— Newman's *Apologia Pro Vita Sua* (1865)—was not yet published. A new critical edition of the *Apologia*, edited by Frank Turner, is available. This reveals that Newman would most likely have taken a negative view of Nevin's assessment here. There is no indication that Newman ever interacted with Nevin's ideas, though Schaff did have opportunity to meet with Newman at the Birmingham Oratory in his world travels.]

again also, that we speak now not of inward essence but of outward form. There may be wide differences in the latter view, where a real sameness has place after all under the former view. All we say is, that Protestantism outwardly considered does not agree, in its general constitution and form, with what we find Christianity to have been after the time of the New Testament, as far back as the middle of the second century as well as in the fourth and third. No one of our modern sects can show itself to be identical with this ancient church. They may fall upon the still older period of the New Testament, and claim to be in full agreement with this; to all that we have nothing just now to say; but they are not any of them what the church was in the days either of Athanasius or of Cyprian or of Irenæus. The church from the fourth century back to the first part of the second was not Congregationalism, nor Presbyterianism, nor Methodism, nor Anglican Episcopalianism, nor any other phase of Protestantism as it now stands. It had its own changes great and serious during this period; but through them all it bears a certain sameness of character peculiar to itself, with which none of these modern systems is found to agree. It carries in it from the beginning elements and tendencies, from whatever source derived, that look steadily towards Romanism, the later system in which all at last actually reached their natural end.[31] Protestantism is not the repristination simply of any such ecclesiastical antiquity, (this side of the New Testament) whether under its later or its earlier form. Its right to exist can never be put safely on any test of this sort.

So much we ought to see and openly confess. Nothing is gained, but much lost rather, by pretending to consider our modern position the same that was occupied by the primitive post-apostolical church. We cannot force facts; and it is always rash and impolitic to take ground directly or indirectly, that makes any such violence necessary for the support of our cause.

Granting then, as all who know anything of church history must, that Protestantism is not the restoration strictly of early (post-apostolical) Christianity, but that this ran naturally rather first into the Nicene system, and then through that again into the later Roman Catholic system, how is the cause of the Reformation to be vindicated as just and right? What view shall we take of this disagreement, (solemn historical fact as it is and not to be disguised nor ignored) which shall not compromise the credit of Protestantism, but allow us to regard it still as worthy of our confidence and trust? Such is the great question, with the solution of which not a few of the best minds of our age are now seriously wrestling, as a problem of the deepest interest for the world. Only the superficial can fail to look upon it in this light.

---

31. [As much as Nevin relies heavily on the German historical science for his understanding of development, this line of reasoning is very close to Newman's presentation in the *Essay*. Perhaps that is simply because he was discussing Newman in the paragraph above. In the end, Nevin and Newman differ, most likely because of Nevin's reliance on the German historiography; Nevin is at least somewhat content to allow time for the movement of history to bend. Newman famously was not able to make space in his thinking for that possibility and he subsequently converted to Catholicism. For a critique of Newman's understanding of development, see Schaff, *Principle* MTSS 3:141–48.]

DOCUMENT 2: EARLY CHRISTIANITY: THIRD ARTICLE.

Shall we cut the whole matter short, by casting off entirely the authority of the post-apostolical church from the second century down to the sixteenth and by throwing ourselves exclusively on the New Testament, as a sufficient warrant for the modern system, not only without antiquity, but against it also, to any extent that the case may require? This is the ground taken by Puritanism.[32] Its theory is, that Protestantism stands in no organic historical connection with the life of the Catholic church as we find it before the Reformation; that the relation between the two was one of simple contradiction; that the old church was an entire apostacy from the Christianity of the New Testament; and that this was reproduced in the sixteenth century, as an absolutely new creation, directly from its own original fountain and source. The assumption is, that the church at an early period fell away from its primitive purity, and came under the power of a strange and dreadful apostacy, which completed itself formally in the Papacy and all the abominations usually charged upon the church of Rome.[33] The theory involves the idea of a steadily growing corruption, a continual progress from bad to worse. The fourth century thus is taken to have been far more pure than the twelfth. Still its general corruption also is not to be denied. The third century too must have been strongly set in the same false direction. But is there no part of the second, that may be claimed as the pattern of evangelical piety in its modern Protestant style? This is frequently taken for granted in a quiet way, for the purpose of effect. But we have found the assumption to be groundless. History knows nothing of any such period, after the age of the Apostles, but on the contrary shows the church, from the time it first comes into notice, to have been plainly committed to the course of things that led onward directly to the Nicene system. So this Puritan theory, to be fully true to itself, is willing in the end to give up *all* post-apostolical antiquity. It is enough for

---

32. It is hardly necessary to say, that Puritanism, as we always take it, is by no means the same thing with Protestantism. It is of later appearance, a sort of *second growth* upon the original work of the Reformation; and its distinctive features in this view are by no means hard to understand. It is one side simply of the original whole of Protestantism, the Reformed tendency; not in polar union as this was at first with the Lutheran tendency, and so in organic connection with the proper historical life of the old Catholic church; but cut off from both these relations, and under such miserable unhistorical and unchurchly abstraction, now claiming pedantically to be the truth, the whole truth, and nothing but the truth, of all that Christianity has ever been in the world. It resolves all religion into private reason, by making this to be the only oracle of what is to be considered the divine sense of the Bible. It is always in this way rationalistic, even when it may seem to be most orthodox. It has no sense of a supernatural church, no faith in the holy sacraments, no sympathy with the reigning drift and tone of the ancient creed. It makes no account of Catholic Christianity. Anglicanism, in its eyes, is sheer foolery and falsehood. The sense of Lutheranism—*true* Lutheranism, and not the bastard spawn of Puritanism itself usurping this venerable name—it has no power even to comprehend; the whole system is a *terra incognita* to its brain. Even the old Calvinism or Reformed faith has passed quite beyond its horizon. And yet it now claims to be the whole fact of Protestantism, and as such the whole truth of Christianity! Preposterous assumption. Puritanism is indeed a great fact too in its way; but it is not proper Protestantism. This is something older, wider, greater, and as we believe also a great deal better.

33. [There has been some movement among contemporary Protestants to address the critique Nevin brings here. Two examples are Emerson et al., *Baptists and the Christian Tradition* and Allen and Swain, *Reformed Catholicity*.]

it, to be certain that the pattern of Protestantism is found in the New Testament. Grant that a different order of religion is found to be at work immediately afterwards, in the ancient church, to what does the fact amount in the face of this original rule, which the world can now interpret for itself? So far as any such difference goes, we have only to set it down from the first for an apostacy, the coming in of that grand catastrophe which afterwards turned the church into a synagogue of hell. Protestantism sets the whole process aside, overleaps the entire interval between the sixteenth century and the first, abjures antiquity clear back to the beginning, and claims to be a new and fresh copy simply of what Christianity was in the days of the Apostles.

This theory we have examined and found wanting. Its disposition of facts, in the first place, is loose and blind in the extreme. There is no such difference as it pretends, in the order of corruption, between the Popery of the middle ages and the period going before. We agree fully with Mr. Taylor, that this was in many respects an improvement on the older system. Then again, the main hypothesis in the case is in the highest degree unnatural and violent. It assumes a full *principial*[34] failure of the church from the very start, an actual triumph of Satan over Christ in the very heart and bosom of his own kingdom, in the face of all God's promises to the contrary, in the face of the original charter and commission of this same church from Christ's own lips, and in spite of his continual headship over it at the right hand of the Father, with all power given unto him in heaven and in earth, to make good his word that the gates of hell should not prevail against it through all time [Matt 28:18; 16:18]. For the idea is, that the ancient church *did* fail, so as to lose finally the life with which it started; and that Protestantism therefore is no continuation of this life in any really historical way, but an actual return to the beginning, for the purpose of a new experiment of Christianity under a better and safer form. In this way Protestantism is made to be the contradiction and negation of all previous Christianity, back to the age of the Apostles. Its justification requires us to denounce and condemn all church antiquity. To be on good terms with it, we must renounce everything like hearty fellowship—if not with the names—at least with the real persons of the fathers, martyrs, and saints, of the first centuries, everything like true sympathy with their actual spirit and life. Then farther, the use which the theory makes of the Bible is by no means satisfactory;[35] and is of such a wilful and arbitrary character indeed, as may well inspire a terrible doubt of its being more free from mistake after all than the use made of it by the ancient church. If all antiquity could so blunder here, for fifteen centuries, as to miss the entire sense of God's word, who will go bail for us that Puritanism may be trusted and followed now as a truly infallible guide? Finally, the scheme refuses to come into any sort of intelligible harmony with the course of church history. It supposes such a state of things as

---

34. ["Constituting a source or origin; primary, original." OED Online, "Principial, adj."]

35. [For Nevin's response to evangelical biblicism, see *Philosophy and the Contemporary World*, MTSS 11: 218–21, 310–14; for a later treatment, see Nevin, "Inspiration of the Bible." See also DiPuccio, *The Interior Sense of Scripture*.]

leaves no room for the idea of a divine life in the church, and makes it in fact to have been the enemy of all truth and righteousness. And yet the church has never been without the signs and proofs of Christ's supernatural presence in her midst (according to his promise) from the beginning.

Altogether thus, this Puritan theory runs directly towards infidelity. It puts together terms which are in their own nature incompatible; and in asking us to believe them, necessarily remands our faith into the world of mere abstractions and notions. On this account it is, that we have denounced it as secretly the foe of Protestantism. We say most deliberately, that a christianity which is not historical, not the continuation organically of the proper life of the church as it has existed from the beginning—but which abjures all connection with this life as something false, and sets itself in contradiction to it as a totally new and different existence—can have no right whatever to challenge our faith, as being the same supernatural fact that is set before us by the article of the church in the ancient creed. It seeks to turn that fact into a wholesale lie, by making such supposition the only alternative to its own truth. No defence of Protestantism in this form can stand. To make the Reformation a mere rebellion, a radical revolution, a violent breaking away from the whole authority of the past, is to give it a purely human or rather an actually diabolical character. It comes then just to this, that either the rebellion was diabolical or else the ancient church back to the second century was the work of the Devil and not Christ's work. We are shut up to the necessity of rejecting one, in order that we may choose the other; for they are opposite interests, and the case will not allow us to acknowledge both at once. But who that has any faith in the supernatural mystery of the church, as it came from Christ in the beginning, can submit to the claims of Protestantism put into any such shape as this? Who of any sound christian feeling will bear to give up all antiquity in such radical style, for the sake of a wholly new system starting only in the sixteenth century? This is Puritanism; but we are not willing to allow that it is Protestantism, that it expresses the meaning of the Reformation in its true original sense. Puritanism is absolutely unhistorical by principle and profession; but Protestantism, if it have any right to exist at all, is the true historical continuation of the ancient church. To force the other character upon it, is to kill it root and branch.

We are sorry to find that Mr. Isaac Taylor, with all his learning and good sense, is not able to clear himself of this false and untenable ground, in his controversy with the Oxford theology. He sets out indeed with what might seem to a very strong acknowledgment, of the dependence of the modern church upon that of antiquity. The following passages are of great point and force certainly, against the whole spirit of our reigning sect system at the present time, (wiser in its own conceit than seven men that can render a reason [Prov 26:16]) which only laughs at every sort of authority in such form, and counts *itself* to be nothing less than the direct embodiment of the bible over against all that the church has ever been before.

Looking at the Christian world at large, it is my full conviction, that there is just now a far more urgent need of persuasives to the study of Christian history and literature, than of cautions against the abuse of such studies. Too many feel and speak as if they thought there were no continuity in their religion; or as if there were no universal church; or as if the individual Christian, with his packet bible in his hand, need fix his eyes upon nothing but the little eddy of his personal emotions; or as if Christianity were not what it is its glory and its characteristic to be—*a religion of history.*

Christianity, the pledge to man of eternity, is the occupant of all time; and not merely was it, itself, the ripening of the dispensations that had gone before it, but it was to be the home companion of the successive generations of man, until the consummation of all things. Not to know Christianity as the religion of all ages—as that which grasps and interprets the cycles of time, is to be in a condition like that of the man whose gloomy chamber admits only a single pencil[36] of the universal radiance of noon.—[Taylor, *Ancient Christianity*,] Vol. I. p. 21, 22.

[. . .]

If it be true that the general complexion of church history, through the course of long centuries, is such as to offend our preconceived notions, and to shock our spiritual tastes, and if, while we bend over the records of those dim eras, the promise of the Lord to be with his servants, still rings in our ears, as a doleful knell of hopes broken; if it be so, or as far as such may be the fact, the motive becomes more impressive and serious which impels us to acquire an authentic knowledge of this course of events, in all its details,—and if there are any who must acknowledge that they feel a peculiar repugnance in regard to church history, they are the very persons, more than any other, who it behooves to school themselves in this kind of learning; for it seems more than barely probable, that this distaste springs from some ill affection of their own minds, demanding to be exposed and remedied. Such persons may well admit the supposition that they have hastily assumed certain notions of their Lord's principles of government, which are in fact unlike what, at length, they will find themselves to be subject to; and if so, the sooner they dispel any such false impressions, the better. On the face of the instance supposed, one should say, that any perplexities we may feel in regard to that course of events which constitutes the history of Christianity, probably spring from some deep-seated error of feeling, or of opinion, which, for our own sakes, we should carefully analyze.—[Taylor, *Ancient Christianity*, vol. 1,] P. 25.

[. . .]

These indispensable studies, have, in fact, been revived of late, to a great extent, in our own, as well as other countries; while the use and necessity of them are forced anew upon the minds of all by the rapid and unexpected advances of Romanism, whose ministers are taking advantage of that ignorance

---

36. [Taylor's text reads "ray."]

Document 2: Early Christianity: Third Article.

of antiquity which has too long been the reproach of Protestantism.— [Taylor, *Ancient Christianity*, vol. 1,] P. 28.

[. . .]

Those "fathers," thus grouped as a little band, by the objectors, were some of them men of as brilliant genius as any age has produced: some, commanding a flowing and vigorous eloquence, some, an extensive erudition, some, conversant with the great world, some, whose meditations had been ripened by years of seclusion, some of them the only historians of the times in which they lived, some, the chiefs of the philosophy of their age; and, if we are to speak of the whole, as a series or body of writers, they are the men who, during a long era of deepening barbarism, still held the lamp of knowledge and learning, and, in fact, afford us almost all that we can now know, intimately, of the condition of the nations surrounding the Mediterranean, from the extinction of the classic fire, to the time of its rekindling in the fourteenth century. The church was the ark of all things that had life, during a deluge of a thousand years.— [Taylor, *Ancient Christianity*, vol. 1,] P. 34, 35.

[. . .]

Nearly of the same quality, and usually advanced by the same parties, is the portentous insinuation, or the bold and appalling averment, that there was little or no genuine Christianity in the world from the times of Justin Martyr to those of Wicliffe [Wycliffe], or of Luther! and the inference from this assumption is, that we are far more likely to be led astray than edified by looking into the literature of this vast territory of religious darkness.

I must leave it to those who entertain any such sombre belief as this, to repel, in the best manner they are able, those fiery darts of infidelity which will not fail to be hurled at Christianity itself, as often as the opinion is professed. Such persons, too, must expound as they can, our Lord's parting promise to his servants.— [Taylor, *Ancient Christianity*, vol. 1,] P. 35.

[. . .]

Christianity is absolute truth, bearing with various effect, from age to age, upon our distorted and discoloured human nature, but never so powerfully pervading the foreign substance it enters as to undergo no deflections itself, or to take no stains; and as its influence varies, from age to age, in intensity, as well as in the particular direction it may take, so does it exhibit, from age to age, great variations of form and hue. But the men of any one age indulge too much the overweening temper that attaches always to human nature, when they say to themselves—*our* Christianity is absolute Christianity; but that of such or such an age, was a mere shadow of it.— [Taylor, *Ancient Christianity*, vol. 1,] P. 36.

[. . .]

The modern spirit of self-sufficiency seems to reach its climax in the contempt thrown by some upon those who, endowed with as much learning and acumen as ourselves, read the scriptures while the ink of the apostolic autographs had hardly faded.— [Taylor, *Ancient Christianity*, vol. 1,] P. 40.

[. . .]

It is in fact a circumstance worthy to be noticed, that even the most ultra-protestant of ultra-protestants, if it happens to him to meet with a real or apparent confirmation of his peculiar views, within the circle of ecclesiastical antiquity, shows no reluctance whatever in snatching at it, and in turning it to the best account he can, piously quoting Irenæus, or Tertullian, or Ignatius, like any good Romanist! It is—"the bible, and the bible alone,["] just when the evidence afforded, on some disputed point, by the writings of Ignatius, or Irenæus, or Tertullian, happens to tell in the wrong direction; otherwise, these "papistical authorities" are good enough. —[Taylor, *Ancient Christianity*, vol. 1,] P. 52.

[. . .]

It has been nothing so much as this inconsiderate "bible alone" outcry, that has given modern Popery so long a reprieve in the heart of Protestant countries; and it is now the very same zeal, without discretion, that opens a fair field for the spread of the doctrines of the Oxford Tracts.— [Taylor, *Ancient Christianity*, vol. 1,] P. 54.

These, we say, are sound and true sentiments. But they are not well sustained by Mr. Taylor's own work. The only use he sees proper to make of ecclesiastical history after all, is such as is made of the testimony of a common witness in a court of law. The voice of the church is to him only as the voice of the profane world, the authority of the fathers of one and the same order with the authority of Tacitus, or Pliny.[37] Antiquity may help us to the knowledge of some facts, but nothing more; to sit in judgment on the facts, to make out their true value, to accept them as grains of gold or reject them as heaps of trash, is the high prerogative of modern reason, acting in its triple office of lawyer, juryman, and judge. The rule or standard of judgment is indeed professedly the bible, God's infallible word; but the *tribunal* for interpreting and applying it, the highest and last resort therefore in all cases of controversy and appeal, is always the mind of the present age as distinguished from every age that has gone before. Mr. Taylor's standpoint is completely subjective. It is not the right position for doing justice to any history; but least of all, for doing justice to the history of God's church. For if the church be what it professed to be at the start, and what it is acknowledged by the whole christian world to be in the creed, it is a supernatural constitution, and in such view must have a supernatural history.[38] A divine church with a purely human history, is for faith a contradiction in terms. In any such view however, it is something fairly monstrous to think of turning the whole process into the play of simply human factors, and then requiring it to bend every where to the measure of our modern judgment.

37. [Two Roman historians from the first and early second centuries.]

38. [Nevin's use of "supernatural constitution" is first found in *The Church*, MTSS 5:149, 156 and *Antichrist*, MTSS 5:202–3.]

Document 2: Early Christianity: Third Article.

But this precisely is what Mr. Isaac Taylor allows himself to do. With the bible in hand, he finds it a most easy and reasonable thing to rule out of court the universal voice of the church, from the second century if need be to the sixteenth, wherever it refuses to chime in with his own mind. In this way he falls in fact into the theory and method of Puritanism, under the most perfectly arbitrary form. Protestantism in his hands ceases to be historical altogether, and stands forward in direct antagonism to the life of the early church. The relation between the two systems is made to be one of violent contradiction and opposition. It admits of no organic reconciliation. To make good the modern cause, antiquity is presented to us under attributes that destroy its whole title to our confidence and respect. It becomes indeed an unintelligible riddle. It is the church of Christ in the habiliments of hell; or shall we call it rather a hideous vision of Satan himself, transformed for the time into an angel of light [2 Cor 11:14]?

"Our brethren of the early church," Mr. Taylor himself tells us (*Ancient Christianity*, Vol. I. p. 37),

> challenge our respect, as well as affection; for theirs was the fervour of a steady faith in things unseen and eternal; theirs often a meek patience and humility, under the most grievous wrongs; theirs the courage to maintain a good profession before the frowning face of philosophy, of secular tyranny, and of splendid superstition; theirs was abstractedness from the world, and a painful self-denial; theirs the most arduous and costly labours of love; theirs a munificence in charity, altogether without example; theirs was a reverent and scrupulous care of the sacred writings, and this merit, if they had had no other, is of a superlative degree, and should entitle them to the veneration and grateful regards of the modern church. How little do many readers of the Bible, now-a-days, think of what it cost the Christians of the second and third centuries, merely to rescue and hide the sacred treasure from the rage of the heathen!

This is a beautiful and bright picture. But, alas, the historical analysis that follows turns it all into shame. Nothing can well be more gloomy and oppressive to a truly christian mind, than the light in which the fathers of these first centuries, together with the theology and piety of the ancient church generally, are made to show themselves beneath the pencil of this brilliant and fluent writer. False principles came in from the start, not affecting simply the surface of the new religion, but carrying the poison of death into its very heart. Gnosticism, though resisted and conquered on the outside of the church, had a full triumph within. Out of it grew the ascetic system, false views of marriage, the glorification of virginity, monasticism, and all kindred views. The celibate corrupted the whole scheme of theology. Christianity itself is opposed to the Oriental theosophy, proceeding throughout on a different view of the world; and it vanquished this enemy in fact. But only, we are told, to take it again into its own bosom. "The catholic church opposed its substantial truths to these baseless and malignant speculations; and triumphed: but alas, it fell in triumphing."[39] Gnosticism thus infused its own antichristian soul into the entire body of the Nicene theology.[40] Parallel with this doctrinal corruption, ran a corresponding corruption of the whole life of religion practically considered. The true scheme of salvation was to a great extent lost. Repentance and justification by faith sunk out of sight, overwhelmed completely by a factitious religion of outward forms and rites. The sacraments were exaggerated into saving mysteries. Polytheism, expelled and subdued under its heathen character, rose into power again as Christian demonolatry, the worship of saints, relics and images; all in pure contradiction to the original genius of the gospel. Along with this system went the universal noise of prodigies and miracles. These were "lying wonders," piously contrived to keep up the credit of the reigning superstitions. They are not insulated instances merely of alleged supernatural agency, but form a *miraculous dispensation,* running on from year to year, and carrying along with it the ostensible faith and homage of the whole church. At the same time it is plain enough to modern common sense, that the dispensation was throughout an enormous cheat, kept up by the priesthood for their own ends. Even the best men of the church, such as the Nicene fathers generally, must have been more or less privy to these awfully wicked frauds.[41] St. Ambrose, for instance, must have first buried the skeletons, during the night, which he pretended to discover the next day, by divine revelation, as the remains of the martyrs Gervasius and Protasius;[42] must have hired men to act the part of demoniacs, who should bear testimony to the truth of the discovery, drilling them well into their diabolical parts; must have engaged Severus, the butcher, to feign himself restored to sight by touching the covering of the relics, as they were borne in solemn procession to their new resting place beneath the altar of the Ambrosian church. And yet Ambrose was one of the best and greatest men, belonging to the history of the ancient church.

---

39. [Taylor, *Ancient Christianity*, 1:152.]

40. "The massive walls of the church, like a hastily constructed coffer-dam, had repelled, from age to age, the angry billows of the Gnostic heresy, which could never open a free passage for themselves within the sacred enclosure. Nevertheless these waters, bitter and turbid, no sooner rose high around the shattered structure, than, through a thousand fissures, they penetrated, and in fact stood at one and the same mean level, within, where they were silently stagnant, as without, where they were in angry commotion."—*Vol. I. p.* 176 [corrected: Taylor, *Ancient Christianity*, 1:175].

41. "It will be my painful task, to lay open the shameless frauds and impious miracle-mongering, by means of which the trade of the priests at these magnificent shrines was kept a-going;—frauds incomparably more discreditable than were any that had been practised in the heathen oracular temples. This is indeed a heavy theme; and how sorrowful—how sickening, when a man like Chrysostom is found acting as the Hierophant of these mysteries of iniquity!"—*Vol. II. p.* 307 [corrected: Taylor, *Ancient Christianity*, 2:207].

42. [The remains in question were found in the ground beneath the new church Ambrose was having built in Milan. Directed by a dream, Ambrose instigated a search. He identified them as the martyrs, which then evoked miraculous healings. *Dictionary of the Christian Church*, 671. Here Nevin describes Taylor's cynical debunking of the episode.]

Document 2: Early Christianity: Third Article.

With such a view of the theology and life of the fourth century, Mr. Taylor finds it natural and easy to charge the system directly with the universal decay of morals, that marked the last stage of the old Roman civilization. All came, by necessary derivation, from the "church principles" of the third and fourth centuries. The cause which Christ had founded for the salvation of the world, proved in the end like the breath of the Sirocco, sweeping it with an immeasurable curse.[43]

This may suffice for our present purpose; which is not to discuss directly the merit of our author's positions; but simply to set them in contrast with the other side of his own picture of this same ancient Christianity, in argument and proof of the perfectly unhistorical character of his general scheme. A man may talk as he pleases about the glories of the early church, Christ's presence in it, and its victories over error and sin; if he couple with it the idea of such wholesale falsehood and corruption as is here laid to its charge, all this praise is made absolutely void.[44] The two thoughts refuse to stand together. One necessarily excludes the other. Common history will not endure any such gross contradiction. But still less can it be reconciled with any faith in the history of the church, as a supernatural order. If Ambrose could so lend himself to the Devil, he was no saint. If the church generally was so terribly corrupt both in doctrine and practice, embodying in itself the worst principles of heathenism, God surely was not in the midst of it as a Saviour and King. It was, clear back to the third and even to the second century, the synagogue in truth of Satan, the unclean temple and home of Antichrist.

For the errors and corruptions here set to its account, are not represented as partial only or relative, the exaggerations or distortions merely of acknowledged truth and sound christian feeling. In that view, they might still be reconciled with the idea of a truly historical church, bearing in its bosom the supernatural presence of its glorified Head. Faith in the continuity of the church as a divine fact (the proper mystery of the creed) by no means requires us to overlook or deny the frailties and follies that necessarily belong to the human side of its history.[45] But in the case before us, the human, which left to itself is always the diabolical also, is made absolutely to overwhelm

---

43. "Christianity, as restored by the Reformers, has gradually regenerated the countries which have freely entertained it; while, on the contrary, Christianity, as debased by the Nicene divines, after quickly spending its healthful forces, only served to hurry the nations downward into—to use Salvin's language—'a sink of debauchery.'"— [Taylor, *Ancient Christianity*], Vol. II. p. 37.

44. "The ancient church having compromised the greatest truths, and thereby forfeited the guidance of the Spirit of Truth, rushed forward, without a check on every path of artificial excitement; and being at the same time urged by the circumstances of its precarious conflict with the expiring paganism, as well as with innumerable new-born heresies, to strengthen itself by the nefarious arts of popular influence—by factitious terrors, hopes, wonders, it regarded no scruples of honor, and threw the reins on the neck of fanatical extravagance."— [Taylor, *Ancient Christianity*,] Vol. II. 157. If this be true, what nonsense to speak of *such* a heaven-forsaken church, as being in any sense the ark of religion or the pillar and ground of the truth!

45. [The "actual Church . . . supposes imperfection and defect at every point of its progress . . . ." Nevin, *The Church*, MTSS 5:145.]

the divine. All resolves itself pragmatically into the play of worldly factors, often of the most ignoble kind, in no real union whatever with heavenly factors in any way answerable to the promise, "Lo, I am with you always to the end of the world [Matt 28:20]." At best the heavenly is sublimated into the notion only of God's providence, as it floats over *all* human history—a Gnostic conception, that falls immeasurably short of the mystery set before us in the creed. The errors and corruptions charged upon the church here, are such as strike at the very root of its inmost sanctuary, we may say, of its universal constitution and life. They are false, not by excess or distortion merely, but by principle; being nothing less, in truth, than the introduction of another gospel altogether, whose swift triumphs soon supplanted the original and proper sense of Christianity, from one end of its broad domain to the other.

[On the Need for Historical Development]

If Protestantism then is to be defended successfully it can be neither on the ground that it is a repristination simply of early post-apostolical christianity, nor on the ground that it is an absolute nullification of this ancient faith, leaping over it with a single bound to the age of the Apostles.

We are shut up thus to the idea of *historical development*, as the only possible way of escape from the difficulty with which we are met in bringing the present here into comparison with the past. If the modern church must be the same in substance with the ancient church, a true continuation of its life as this has been in the world by divine promise from the beginning, while it is perfectly plain at the same time that a wide difference holds between the two systems as to form, the relation binding them together can only be one of living progress or growth. No other will satisfy these opposite conditions. Growth implies unity in the midst of change. That precisely is what we are to understand by historical development. We do not say now, that it is actually the true key to the problem of Protestantism. We say merely, that if this interest be at all capable of rational apology, in the face of its notorious disagreement with ancient christianity, it can be in this way only and in no other. If we are not at liberty to apply the law of organic progress to the case, there is no help for the cause of the Reformation, the facts being what we find them to be in actual history. Let those look to it, who pretend to be the most staunch friends of Protestantism by scouting[46] the entire idea of any such law; who will have it either that their own small version of Christianity in this form, as given in some one of our sects, is a true picture of what the church was in the beginning of the second century, or that it is against this altogether, and above it, as being the re-assertion at last of the original and proper sense of the New Testament, from which the whole course of history immediately afterwards fell away. Neither of

---

46. [Here having an especially nineteenth-century meaning: "To reject with scorn." OED Online, "scout, v.2."]

Document 2: Early Christianity: Third Article.

these alternatives can stand. The present here is plainly not one with the past; but just as little may it pretend to be the nullification of the past, or its plump contradiction.

Some pretend to identify this doctrine of development with the system of Romanism itself; as though the only occasion for it were found in the variations through which it is supposed to have passed in reaching its present form. Nor have Romanists themselves been unwilling always, to allow it a certain amount of truth. It is not easy to deny certainly, that very considerable changes had place in the history of Christianity before the time of the Reformation; and this might seem to be a natural and ready view, for surmounting the objection drawn from them against the stability and unity of the Catholic church. Mr. Newman, it is well known, has tried to turn the idea to account in this way, in his memorable *Essay on the Development of Christian Doctrine*. Few theological tracts, in the English language are more worthy of being read, or more likely to reward a diligent perusal with lasting benefit and fruit. The author holds christianity to be an objective fact in the world, that must be throughout identical with itself.[47] Still that it has undergone serious modifications in its outward form and aspect, he considers to be no less certain and clear. To reconcile this semblance of discrepancy then, he has recourse to what he calls the *theory of developments*. It is of the nature of a living idea to expand itself, to take new form, as it comes by the course of history into new relations requiring its application in new ways. At the same time

---

47. "Christianity is no dream of the study or the cloister. It has long since passed beyond the letter of documents and the reasonings of individual minds, and has become public property—It has from the first had an objective existence.—Its home is in the world. The hypothesis, indeed, has met with wide reception in these latter ages, that Christianity does not fall within the province of history, that it is to each man what each man thinks it to be, and nothing else.—Or again, it has been maintained, or implied, that all existing denominations of christianity are wrong, none representing it as taught by Christ and his Apostles; that it died out of the world at its birth, and was forthwith succeeded by a counterfeit or counterfeits which assumed its name, though they inherited but a portion of its teaching; that it has existed indeed among men ever since, and exists at this day, but as a secret and hidden doctrine, which does but revive here and there under a supernatural influence in the hearts of individuals, and is manifested to the world only by glimpses or in gleams, according to the number or the station of the illuminated, and their connexion with the history of their times" [Newman, *Essay*, 3, 4; Newman's 1878 edition reads as follows, after "Christ and his Apostles . . .": "that the original religion has gradually decayed or became hopeless corrupt; nay that it died out of the world at its birth, and was forthwith succeeded by a counterfeit or counterfeits which assumed its name, though they inherited at best but some fragments of its teaching; or rather that it cannot even be said either to have decayed or to have died, because historically it has no substance of its own, but from the first onwards it has, on the stage of the world, been nothing more than a mere assemblage of doctrines and practices derived from without, from Oriental, Platonic, Polytheistic sources, from Buddhism, Essenism, Manicheeism; or that allowing true Christianity still to exist, it has but a hidden and isolated life in the hearts of the elect, or again as a literature or philosophy, not certified in any way, must less guaranteed, to come from above . . . " (1878 ed., p. 4)]. All this however, the writer tells us truly, is at best in itself a *hypothesis* only. The only natural assumption is the contrary, namely, "to take it for granted that the christianity of the second, fourth, seventh, twelfth, sixteenth, and intermediate centuries, is in its substance the very religion which Christ and his Apostles taught in the first, whatever may be the modifications for good or for evil, which lapse of years, or the vicissitudes of human affairs have impressed upon it. . . . The *onus probandi* is with those who assert what it is unnatural to expect; to be just able to doubt is no warrant for disbelieving" [Newman, *Essay*, 5, 6].—*Introduction*.

however it carries in itself, from the start, the type and norm of all that it is subsequently to become. We must distinguish accordingly between a true development in such view and a corruption which transforms the very substance of the idea itself into something else. Mr. Newman lays down no less than seven tests, by which we may be guided and assisted in making this important distinction; and then goes on to apply the subject, by illustrations drawn with great force and effect from the actual history of the church in past ages. The whole theory, however, has been condemned by other Romanists, as being at war with the true genius of the Catholic religion. Mr. Brownson of our own country in particular, it will be remembered, set himself in vigorous opposition to it from the start. Catholicism, as he will have it, has known no change. It is only Protestantism that has moved away from what the church was in the beginning, and that is still always in motion and never at rest. It is only Protestantism, that needs any such law of development to account for its changes; and to Protestantism alone, accordingly, the whole theory legitimately and of right belongs.[48]

Be this as it may, Protestantism at all events is still less able to get along without the help of some such theory than Romanism. In no other way possibly, can it make good its claim to be the historical continuance at all of the supernatural fact which the church is allowed to have been in the beginning.[49] This is now felt by all, who deserve to be considered of any authority in the sphere of church history. The whole progress of this science at the present time, under the new impulse which has been given to it by Neander and others, is making it more and more ridiculous to think of upholding the cause of the Reformation under any other view. It *must* be one with the ancient church, to have any valid claim to its prerogatives and powers; but this it *can* be only in

---

48. Mr. Brownson's judgment in this case is not to be taken, of course, as at once final and conclusive for the Catholic church. Mr. Newman's book was written before he became a Romanist in form; but it has been defended by some in that communion; and we do not find, that Mr. Newman himself, since his conversion, has renounced the general doctrine of it as wrong. On the contrary, if we understand him rightly, it is distinctly affirmed still in some of his recent lectures. Möhler has the same thought. [For Nevin's extensive interaction with Brownson, see Nevin, "Brownson's Quarterly Review" and "Brownson's Review Again" (1850) in MTSS 11.]

49. Mr. Newman will tell us, that even in *this* way it is perfectly indefensible, as being not a true development at all of what Christianity was in the beginning, but its radical corruption. "Whatever be historical Christianity, it is not Protestantism; if ever there were a safe truth it is this.—Protestants can as little bear its Ante-nicene as its Post-tridentine period [post Council of Trent] [*Essay*, 7]. . . . So much must the Protestant grant, that if such a system of doctrine as he would now introduce ever existed in early times, it has been clean swept away as if by a deluge, suddenly, silently, and without memorial; by a deluge coming in a night, and utterly soaking, rotting, heaving up, and hurrying off every vestige of what it found in the church, before cock-crowing; so that 'when they rose in the morning,' her true seed 'were all dead corpses'—nay dead and buried—and without a grave-stone [*Essay*, 8; a hypothetical metaphor, with allusion to Isa 37:36]." This we may consider to be exaggeration and mistake; since it amounts to a full condemnation of Protestantism in every view, as being without all real root in the past life of the church. But it only shows the more strongly, what necessity there is of making out the line of a true historical succession in its favor, by a deeper and better apprehension if possible of this idea of development.

the way of historical growth. Give that up, and all is gone. Without the idea of development, the whole fact of Protestantism resolves itself into a fearful lie.

Those who wish to see this subject ably and happily handled, are referred to Professor Schaff's *Principle of Protestantism*, the special object of which is to exhibit and defend the idea of historical development in its application to the Protestant movement.[50] This work we have noticed at some length on a former occasion. It was decried, on its first appearance, by a certain class of Protestants, as being inimical to the very cause it professed to defend. But it was only because the author had a far deeper insight into the necessities of his subject, than these who thus judged him were able to understand. They belonged to the unchurchly, unhistorical school, for which Christianity is a mere matter of opinion or notion, and which has no difficulty accordingly in setting all the laws of real history, as well as all the conditions of a truly supernatural church, at the most perfect defiance, in order to carry out its own dogmatical abstractions. Dr. Schaff had entered too far into the modern sense of history and the proper idea of the church, to be satisfied with any such poor and superficial habit of thought. He saw the absolute necessity of showing Protestantism to be historical, in the full modern force of this most significant term, for the purpose of vindicating its right to exist; and his work accordingly is a most honest and vigorous attempt to defend it on this ground. We have said before, what we now deliberately repeat, that it is the best apology for the cause of the Reformation which has yet appeared in this country. If this cause is to be successfully upheld at all, it can only be, we believe, on the general ground taken in this book. However it may be as regards details, the argument in its main course and scheme may be considered identical now with the very life of Protestantism. It is approved and endorsed in such view, we may say, by the whole weight of German theological science, as it appears in its best representatives at the present time. The Reformation, according to this scheme, was not a revolution, radically upsetting the church as it stood before. In that view it must have been a new religion, and would have needed miracles to support its claims. It was merely a disengagement of the old life of the church from the abuses, with which it became burdened in the course of time, and its advancement to a form more congenial, than that which it carried before, with the wants of the modern world. It was no nullification thus of previous history, no return simply to what christianity was supposed to have been in the beginning; its connection with that was still through the intervening history of the old Catholic church; and from the bosom of this church it sprang by true living derivation and birth. Protestantism is no repudiation then of ancient christianity, nor of the proper religious life of the middle ages. It owes its being to this old life, which was engaged for centuries before with its painful parturition. Here is the idea of historical development. But the theory goes farther still. Protestantism, the favorite child of Catholicism, is not itself a full realization of the true idea of Christianity. It has terrible defects upon it, malignant diseases, belonging as would seem to its very

50. [See Schaff, *Principle*, MTTS 3:148–91, for his positive theory.]

blood, which are growing always worse and worse, and threaten to bring upon it in the end full dissolution. It will not do then to rest in it as the absolute consummation of the church. To take it for that, is again to turn it palpably into a lie. As it was not the first form of Christianity, so neither may it be considered the last. It is itself a process of transition only towards a higher and better state of the church, which is still future though probably now near at hand, and the coming in of which may be expected to form an epoch in history quite as great at least as that of the Reformation itself.[51] The result of this new development will be the recovery of Protestantism itself from the evils under which it now suffers, and in this way its full and final vindication by the judgment of history. It will be however, at the same time, a vindication of Catholicism also, as having been of true historical necessity in its day for the full working out of the problem which shall thus be conducted at last to its glorious solution. Such, we say, is the theory of *historical development,* as we have it applied in this interesting and able tract to the great question here brought into view; the question, namely, how Protestantism is to be set in harmony with the past history of the church, and with its true ideal as the kingdom of God, a supernatural polity of truth and righteousness among men.

This German idea of development, as we may call it, is not the same with that presented to us by Dr. Newman.[52] The last is a continuous expansion and enlargement under the same form and in the same general direction; the process involves no disorder or contradiction in its own movement; it is the full sense always, as far as it goes, of what the church was in fact and intention from the beginning; it is the simple coming out of this sense, in a view answerable to the new relations of its history from age to age; each stage of development is by itself normal and full, and so of force for all time; all moves thus in the line of Catholicism only, without the possibility of growing into anything like Protestantism; on which account, accordingly, this must be regarded as a corruption of the original idea of Christianity, by which it is changed into another type and fashion altogether. It is not easy in truth to conceive of the old Catholic system blossoming into Protestantism, in the way of any such regular and direct growth; and there seems to be no room therefore, for the supposition, that Dr. Newman's conception of development goes against the pretensions of the Roman church.[53] The German

---

51. [Nevin uses the "epoch" language in his "The Year 1848," MTSS 11:23–24, 28, 32, and in his lecture notes on the philosophy of history (Appel, *Life*, 591–601; see the discussion in the general introduction to this volume).]

52. [See John Payne, "Schaff and Nevin," 182, for a summary of the contrast between the two systems. In short, in Newman's version, the development is continuous; whereas in the German version, it works through contradiction, i.e., the Hegelian concept of *aufheben*, "sublation": nullification of some past moment and its transmogrification into something new. See Schaff's definition, *What is Church History*, MTSS 3:289.]

53. We meet with the same thought in Tertullian. "There is nothing," he tells us, "which does not advance by age. All things wait upon time; as the preacher saith, there is a time for every thing. Look at the natural world, and see the plant gradually ripening to its fruit, first a mere grain; from the grain arises the green stalk, and from the stalk shoots up the shrub; than the boughs and branches

Document 2: Early Christianity: Third Article.

theory however does do so, in the most emphatic manner. Its idea of growth is that of a process carried forward, by the action of different forces, working separately to some extent, and so it may be even onesidedly and contradictorily for a time, towards a concrete result representing in full unity at last the true meaning and power of the whole. Each part of the process then is regarded as necessary and right in its own order and time; but still only as *relatively* right, and as having need thus to complete itself, by passing ultimately into a higher form. Catholicism in this view is justified as a true and legitimate movement of the church; but it is taken to have been the explication of one side of Christianity mainly, rather than a full and proper representation of the fact as a whole; a process thus that naturally became excessive, and so wrong, in its own direction, preparing the way for a powerful reaction finally in the opposite direction. This reaction we have in Protestantism; which in such view springs from the old church, not just by uniform progress, but with a certain measure of violence, while yet it is found to be the product really and truly of its deeper life. Here again however, as before, the first result is only relatively good. The new tendency has become itself one-sided, exorbitant, and full of wrong. Hence the need of still another crisis (the signs of whose advent many seem already to see) which may arrest and correct this abuse, and open the way for a higher and better state of the church, in which both these great tendencies shall be brought at length happily to unite, revealing to the world the full sense of Christianity in a form now absolute and complete.

For a truly learned representation of this whole view, in its relations to other older schemes of ecclesiastical history (for there has been a remarkable exemplification of the law of development in the progress of this science itself) we beg leave to refer our readers to Professor Schaff's tract entitled, *What is Church History?*[54] They will find it well worthy of their most careful and diligent perusal.

We have spoken before of Thiersch's "Lectures on Catholicism and Protestantism."[55] They abound in original and fresh thought, pervaded throughout with a tone of the most earnest piety, though not altogether free at times from the excesses of an erratic fancy. The history of the church is with him also a grand and

---

get strength, and the tree is complete; thence the swelling bud, and from the bud the blossom, and from the flower the fruit; which at the first crude and shapeless by little and little proceeds, and attains its ripe softness and flavor. And so in religion, for it is the same God of nature and of religion; at first in its rudiments only, nature surmising something concerning God; then by the law and the prophets advanced to its infant state; then by the Gospel it reached the heats of youth; and now by the Comforter is moulded to its maturity" [quoted in Taylor, *Ancient Christianity*, 1:93–94]. Tertullian speaks here as a Montanist, but the thought itself may be applied to the gradual expansion of the Catholic system [a paraphrase of Taylor, *Ancient Christianity*, 1:93n]. Isaac Taylor sets it down, in this view, as the foundation principle of Humanism (Vol. I. p. 93–98). He wrongs the church however, by charging it with the introduction of new revelations. The supposed innovations of the system came in always as the growth merely of what was at hand before. The expansion thus claimed to be organic, the actualization simply of the previously potential. It was a development in every case, professedly, and not a proper apocalypse.

54. [Schaff, *What is Church History?*, MTSS 3:232–316.]
55. [Thiersch, *Vorlesungen über Katholicismus und Protestantismus.*]

complicated process, exposed to powerful corruptions, and yet moving onward always towards the full consummation of its own original idea; which is not to be reached however without the intervention of a new supernatural apostolate, in all respects parallel with that which was employed for the first establishment of Christianity in the beginning. The church, he thinks, has passed through four great metamorphoses already, in coming to its present condition. First we have it under its *Old Catholic* form, as it existed between the age of the Apostles and the time of Constantine. Then it appears as the *Imperial (Græco-Roman)* church, in close connection with the state, and undergoing many corruptions and changes. Next it becomes the *Roman Catholic* church of the middle ages. Last of all it stands before us as the *Protestant* church. This was called forth, with a sort of inward necessity, by the corruptions and abuses of the Roman system; and it has its full historical justification, in the actual religious benefits it has conferred upon the world; benefits that may be said to show themselves even in the improved character of Romanism itself. Still it is but too plain, that Protestantism is not the full-successful solution of the problem of Christianity. It has not fulfilled the promise of its own beginning; and it carries in it no pledge now of any true religious millenium [sic] in time to come. Evils of tremendous character are lodged within its bosom. A reign of rationalism and unbelief has sprung out of it, for which the present course of things, in the view of Thiersch, offers no prospect of recovery or help. It is no relief, in such case, to know that the Catholic church, in countries where it has no Protestantism as a rival at its side, such for instance as South America[56] or Spain, is in a moral condition equally if not still more deplorable. It is only the more sad, that neither *here* nor *there* the proper face of the true church is to be discerned.

> Whether the Reformers, could they have seen the present posture of the church that goes by their name, would have regretted and cursed their own work, as has been often said, we know not; but it is certain that a keen eye and a strong faith are needed, in view of the general declension that prevails, not to overlook the good which is still left, and to see in it the germ of a better future. Of such future however one of the most necessary conditions is just this, that we should learn to maintain a proper bearing [*das richtige Verhalten*] towards the Catholic church and its peculiarities [*alles Einzelne*].[57]

The self-sufficiency of both systems must come to an end, before room can be made for that higher state of the church, which God may be expected then to bring in by miraculous dispensation, restoring all things to their proper form.

Professor Rothe takes a different view, conditioned by his speculative construction of Christianity in its relations to Nature and Humanity, as we have this fully

---

56. [The historical situation in South America is very different than when Nevin (paraphrasing Thiersch, *Vorlesungen*, 1:291) penned these words. There is a strong Protestant presence in the Global South and especially in Latin and South America. See Stanley, *Christianity in the Twentieth Century* and Schwaller, *History of the Catholic Church in Latin America*.]

57. [Thiersch, *Vorlesungen*, 1:291, German phrases added by editor.]

Document 2: Early Christianity: Third Article.

brought out, with unparalleled architectonic power, in his *Theological Ethics*.[58] The idea of the church he takes to be accidental, rather than essential, to the religious life of the world. The ultimate and only fully normal order of man's existence is the state, the organism of his moral relations, which can never be complete save as they are brought in the end to embrace all that is included also in the sense of religion. Such will be at last the actual consummation of the process, by which our world is now fulfilling its original destiny and design. The process itself however is conditioned now by the fact of redemption, made necessary through sin. This implies a new power brought into the world for its sanctification; a power in such view different from the natural life of the world, but fited [sic] at the same time to take possession of this life always more and more, and finally to transform it fully into its own image. So far as Christianity continues in such distinction from the world naturally considered, it must have its own organization as something distinct from the state, and as something necessarily also in conflict to a certain extent with its very conception. This organization gives us the proper fact of the church. Its relation to the state is at first one of broad opposition; but in the nature of the case it is in this respect a changing and flowing relation; for as the state receives into it more and more the power of the christian life, through the agency of the church, the mission and work of this last over against it shrink always into narrower bounds, so that the assertion of its authority becomes at last a source of oppression and restraint. In the end thus it comes naturally to a rebellion against the idea of the church, as an exclusive institute for the purposes of religion. This was the true sense of the Reformation. It involved the breaking up of the old Catholic doctrine of the church, as something good in its time but no longer answerable to the advanced age of the world, for the necessary purpose of securing free room and scope for the forces of religion under a different form, that namely which is presented to us in the constitution of the state. There is still indeed a demand for the action of the church, and but little prospect as yet that this demand will soon come to an end; but the first step has been taken towards what is to be at last the true order of religion; the vanishing nature of the church has begun to be apparent; its former attributes are passing away; we find it in a chaos of dissolution, the result of which will be in due time its universal absorption into the political organism which has been its rival from the beginning.[59]

58. [Rothe, *Theologische Ethik*.]

59. "There is bitter complaint made in our day, especially in Evangelical Christendom, of the decline of the church. With right and without right, as we choose to take it. With right; for the church, *as a church*, is in reality falling always more and more into ruins, and how it may or can be helped up again, even with the best will on the side of government, is in no wise to be seen. Without right; for this collapse of the church is just the consequence of the maturity and independence of the christian life, which thus breaks the old form that has become too strait for it, and escaping from its restraints runs joyfully towards its true element, the state. We will acknowledge unreservedly the decline of the church, but in the complaint which is made on this account we will take no part. As it seems to us, the general position in which we have tried to set the reader is the only one, from which one can survey the whole course of church history, without danger of falling out with its movement. From this

This is truly a startling way of bringing the problem of Protestantism to a solution; and it is no wonder perhaps that the religious world, even in Germany itself, where the church might seem indeed to be fast tumbling into ruins, has not been able yet to look upon the view with much favor. Still it is the view of a most earnestly religious man, who is at the same time one of the profoundest thinkers and most learned scholars of the age, grappling here in all his strength with what he feels to be the very life question of Protestantism itself; and it well deserves attention in such light, if for no other reason yet at least for this, that it goes to show how real and serious the general problem is, which is here offered for our consideration. Puritanism, with its ordinary want of historical sensibility and its most superficial conception of the mystery of the church, may affect to find no difficulty in the whole subject, and can easily afford to dismiss every theory of this sort as a vain and superfluous speculation. It needs no solution for a knot, which it has no power to see. But for all this, the knot itself is there, and it is one of no common intricacy and force. Puritanism is ready at once to reject Rothe's resolution of the church into the state; but only because it does not admit at all the idea of the church in his sense, and in the old christian sense, as distinguished from the idea of the state. That whole idea is for it from the start a falsehood, the very *proton-pseudos* [the original error] we may say of Romanism. Its highest order is only the state throughout, or man in the form of natural political society. The church has no absolute necessity; it is not of the essence of religion in any way; this holds in humanity as such under the political order; and it is the glory of Protestantism, as well as its only true sense, to assert such independence to the fullest extent. Hence many churches instead of one; any number of them indeed, to suit the world's taste; till the whole conception runs out finally into the open sea of no church whatever. And what less is this, we ask, than Rothe's version of the Reformation—the breaking up, namely, of the old doctrine of the holy catholic church, as we find it in the creed, and the first grand step towards its full formal dissolution at last in the all devouring idea of the state?

The whole theory, with all our respect for Rothe, *we* of course at once repudiate as unsound and false. How could the idea of the church be an object of faith, that is a supernatural mystery of like order with the other articles of the creed, if it were after all any such merely provisional and transient fact, (a downright *"figment"* the Puritan Recorder would say rather) designed to pass away finally in another conception altogether? We might just as well resolve the resurrection of the body, with Hymeneus and Philetus,[60] into the idea of a new moral life begun in the present world. It will not do

---

standpoint alone also, do we first reach a real justification of the Reformation against Catholicism. So long as the *church* is considered to be the highest and only proper realization of the christian life, the act must in truth be set down for a crime, by which the unity of the church, and so the church itself, has been and only could be dashed to pieces."—*Die Anfänge d. chr. Kirchr* [Rothe, *Die Anfänge der Christlichen Kirche*], *p.* 88.

60. [2 Tim 2:17, 18; Nevin misspells Hymenaeus.]

to defend Protestantism, by surrendering Christianity. We are not willing to give up for it either history or the creed.

Rothe's error, we think, lies in the assumption, that the economy of the world naturally considered must be regarded as carrying in itself, from the beginning, all the necessary elements and conditions of a perfect humanity; in which view a real redemption must complete its work under the form of our present telluric life, (though not of course without the resurrection) keeping itself to the organism of earth where the law of sin and death now reigns, and achieving a true and proper victory here on the theatre of the actual curse, instead of translating its subjects for this purpose, in a violent way, over into some altogether new and different order of being. A scientific apprehension of what the world is as a historical process or *cosmos,* would seem indeed to require that it should not be defeated in its highest end, the glorification of humanity, by the disorder of sin—that with reference to this it should not turn out a hopeless failure, an irrecoverable wreck, from which man must be extricated by an act of sheer power for the accomplishment of his salvation somewhere else. But we have no right to assume in this way, that the proper sense of the world in its natural order lies wholly in itself as an independent and separate system. The overshadowing embrace of a higher economy—the absolutely supernatural —we must believe rather to have been needed from the first to complete its process in the life of man. In such view, redemption is more than the carrying out of the natural order of the world to any merely natural end; and the church, as the medium of its work, is more than a provisionary institute simply for perfecting the scheme of the state, the highest form of man's life on the basis of nature as it now stands. The true destination of this lies beyond the present economy of nature in the sphere of the supernatural, in an order of thing that fairly outleaps and transcends the whole system out of which grows now the constitution of political kingdoms and states. In the kingdom of heaven, the last and most perfect order of humanity, as "they neither marry nor are given in marriage," so also there will be neither Greek nor Jew [Matt 22:30; Gal 3:28], but the whole idea of nationality is to be taken up, as it would appear, into a far higher and wider conception rooted not in nature but in grace.[61] The church will not lose itself in the state; but it will be the state rather that shall be found then to have vanished away in the church.

We have then this result. Since Protestantism is not the same thing with primitive post-apostolical Christianity, but this last looks rather directly towards Romanism; and since, at the same time, Protestantism cannot be historically divorced from the first life of the church, and set in full rebellion against it (if the church was originally what it claimed to be, a divine supernatural fact and not a hellish imposture) without forfeiting all title to our faith and trust; there is but one view only in which it is possible to uphold rationally the modern system, and that is the view of historical

---

61. [For more discussion of Nevin's understanding of the relationship between grace and nature, see Nevin, "Man's True Destiny" and "Natural and Supernatural" (both in MTSS 11); "Nature and Grace;" and Layman, "Nevin's Holistic Supernaturalism."]

development; which however must be so taken, that it shall not on the one side remain hopelessly bound to the limits of the Roman system, as in the hands of Dr. Newman, nor yet on the other side run itself out into a fair dissolution of the very idea with which it started, whether this be by the Hegelian dialectics of a man like Baur or by such more respectable theories as we have from the hands of Rothe and Thiersch. A development into sheer vacuity, is only another word for annihilation. If *that* be the true sense of Protestantism as related to the old mystery of the church, all defence of it for faith is gone. It must be a real historical continuation of the church, in the verity of its old supernatural existence, carrying along with it a true participation in its prerogatives and powers, or it is nothing.[62]

[Protestant Catholicity and the History of the Church]

It is not necessary now that we should be prepared to determine positively the true construction and proper significance of Protestantism beyond the result now stated, in order to make this result itself of practical account. It is of high account at all events to see what are the necessary conditions of the question which is to be solved, what are the terms and limits within which the solution must move, whatever view we may choose to take of it afterwards as restrained to such bounds. It is much only to have it settled in our minds, that the defence of Protestantism, if it is to be made good at all, must be conducted in a certain general way, whether any particular plan of such defence may be counted satisfactory or not. We propose at present no positive doctrine on the subject one way or another. That has not been the object at all of these articles. We have wished merely to show that the nature of Christianity, and the facts of history, require the argument for Protestantism to run in a certain line, if it is to be of any force; and that no different form of apology, in which this general necessity is overlooked or trampled under foot, can deserve to be regarded with respect. No view of Protestantism can be either sound or safe, which by setting it in absolute universal opposition to Catholicism makes it to be unhistorical, and so cuts it off from all lot or part in the inheritance of the past life of the church.

Nothing more than the sense of this plain truth is needed, to expose the vanity of all that system of polemics against the church of Rome, which proceeds on the assumption that it is purely and entirely false and corrupt, and that it deserves no

---

62. [Nevin has clearly been moving his argument toward this point and yet now that he is here, he does not resolve the tension with a clear understanding of what he means by historical development. Rather, he ends up saying that one of the systems of development which he has discussed must be the way forward with no real indication of which he privileges. Thus, Nevin creates a new kind of tension while seeking to remove a different one. In Nevin's "Cyprian" essay (below, 311–14), this tension will be even more evident for him, as he begins to despair of finding an adequate or workable solution to the developmental tension that is evident here. Andrew Black describes Nevin's later answer to the "church question" as "restoration without resolution" ("A 'Vast Practical Embarrassment,'" 279).]

Document 2: Early Christianity: Third Article.

hearing in truth, and much less anything like calm respect, whatever it may pretend to urge in its own defence.

We are all familiar with the anti-popery spirit under this radical and fanatical form.[63] Our common religious press may be said to teem with it every week. It meets us on the street and in all public places. Our very piety is infected with it to a large extent, both in the sanctuary and in the domestic circle. The fountains of our charity are turned by it too often into wormwood and gall. Many appear to look upon it as one main part of their religion, a necessary evidence of their evangelical temper and habit, to hate and curse the Catholics. However it may be in any other direction, here at least they feel that they do well, as it would seem, to be angry, to show contempt, and to indulge misrepresentation and abuse, to their heart's full content. Nicknames are so pat to the tongue, that they flow from it like the poison of asps without effort or thought. All too in Christ's sweet and holy name. The most abominable charges and criminations are trumpeted without proof, as though the bold repetition of them simply were enough, in the end to make them good. No pains are taken to understand any doctrine or practice of the church, in the light of its own historical or theological relations; it is counted quite sufficient to drag every article in the most rude and vulgar way before the tribunal of the world's common sense[64] (alas, how *common* in many cases) and to take the measure of its merits accordingly; as though the deepest mysteries of religion might be settled by such superficial and profane judgment, as it were at a moment's glance. All runs out easily thus into the most wholesale censure and reproach. Romanism is found to be, from beginning to end, a tissue of impiety and folly, at war with the most sacred interests of humanity, and in full contradiction to the will of God. It is a diabolical conspiracy against truth and righteousness. There is no reason in any of its institutions; they are founded on falsehood throughout; they subvert the whole sense of the gospel, and in their source and operation are purely antichristian, of one order we may say with infidelity itself. Such in general is the tenor of this popular theory.

But no such style of thinking can be maintained, where anything like a sound historical feeling has been brought into exercise in regard to the church. Those who look at Romanism only in this rabid and fanatical way, show themselves by the very fact to have no sense of the divine organization of Christianity as a perpetual living constitution in the world, and no apprehension of the necessity there is that Protestantism should be strictly and truly the product of this life, if it can have any right to exist at all. They make no account of history. Their view of Protestantism is such as cuts it off entirely from the concrete mystery of the church in past ages, and turns it thus into a mere abstraction. In this way it is essentially rationalistic and infidel; and it is ever ready accordingly to make common cause with open unbelief, in treating the

---

63. [For Nevin's reaction to radical Protestant anti-Romanism, see Hart, *John Williamson Nevin*, 156, 163.]

64. [Again, the ruling American philosophy of "Common Sense Realism."]

whole real past of the church as a sort of universal cheat and lie. Faith in historical christianity at once upsets every such habit of thought; and in doing so necessarily begets a more just and tolerant spirit towards the present Catholic church. It does so in a two-fold view, first as it regards the past, and secondly as it throws its eye forward into the future.

As regards the past, the faith now mentioned feels itself bound to derive the life of Protestantism, genealogically, from the historical church of previous ages; which at the same time is clearly seen to carry in it the leading features of Romanism away back to the Nicene age, and in element or germ at least beyond that also up to the very middle of the second century. Now it need not follow from this, that all such features are to be approved as right and good for all time; nor even that they were in all cases right and good at any time. The very idea of the Reformation implies the contrary; for the meaning of it is, that many things belonging to the old church were either abuses in their own nature, or had grown to be such by the progress of history, which it was necessary at last to thrust wholly out of the way. But no one who has any sense of the divine constitution of the church can bring himself to look upon its whole past order and spirit, for this reason, as false and wrong; nor can he think of denouncing even what he may not be able to approve, in any such style of vituperation as our modern anti-popery sees fit to indulge in towards what it calls the abominations of Romanism. Here then it becomes at once impossible for any person of this sort, to sympathize with the vulgar method of fighting the Roman Catholics which we have now under consideration. Take it, for instance, as it comes before us in "Kirwan,"[65] or in the pages of the "Protestant Quarterly Review."[66] It not only fights Romanism, but fights at the same time with fully equal effect the whole ancient church. The points on which it expends mainly its indignation, or ridicule, or scorn, are to a great extent distinctive, not of modern Romanism as such, but of the church as it has existed back to the fourth century, if not indeed to the first part of the second. The argument goes too far, and proves a great deal too much. It becomes immediately profane, by striking at all that has been esteemed most holy for the faith of christians, not simply in the middle ages, but in the ages also that went before. It turns the fathers into knaves and fools. It covers all ecclesiastical antiquity with disgrace. This is more than any sound mind, imbued with the slightest tinge of right historical feeling, can be expected patiently to endure. It is infidelity pretending to preach to us in the name of evangelical religion. If anti-popery is to be at the same time anti-christianity, in this blind irreverent style, the less we have to do with it the better. No such zeal for Protestantism can be entitled

---

65. ["Kirwan" was an anti-Catholic polemicist, a pseudonym for Nicholas Murray. Nichols, *Romanticism*, 249. Nevin reviewed his book in "Kirwan's Letters."]

66. [*Protestant Quarterly Review* was the journal of Joseph F. Berg, a German Reformed leader who had always expressed strong anti-Catholic opinions. It was Nevin (under Schaff's influence) who changed. Soon after these essays were completed, Berg moved to the Dutch Reformed Church. See Appel, *Life*, 396, and 398–401 for samples of Berg's anti-Catholic bias. Nichols, in *Romanticism*, fairly describes Berg's side of the longstanding feud: esp. 86–89, 176–77, 208–9.]

to any sort of respect. It carries the evidence of its own impotency on its very front. To have any knowledge of the past, and to perceive at all the organic continuity that must necessarily hold in the life of the church from age to age, through all transformations and changes, involves at once the clear perception also that this vulgar feeling towards Romanism is from beneath and not from above. We need not be slavishly bound by the authority of the past; but as believers in the divine reality of the church, we must consider it one of our first duties to treat its ancient history with reverence and respect. We may not join hands here with Ham, the father of Canaan. Those who do so, and who thus make Christianity vile, while they pretend to be spitting only upon the errors and superstitions of Rome, prove by this very fact that they are blind witnesses and teachers even in regard to Romanism itself. Whatever may be wrong here, *they* are not the men whom it is safe to follow as guides and leaders into a better way. They do not understand what they condemn. There is neither light nor love in their zeal. If our war against Romanism is to be so managed that it must be at the same time a war against all church antiquity, we may as well give up the contest. But to have any intelligent regard for the ancient church on the other hand, any feeling of religious fellowship with it, is to see that Romanism itself is no fair object for persecution in this radical and ribald style. We may oppose it still; but we will have some sense also of its just claims and merits. We will not spit upon it, nor cover it with spiteful and malignant slang. We will not feel, that love to Christ and hatred of the Pope are precisely one and the same thing.

But the future also comes in, through the medium of a right historical feeling, along with the past, to promote this same equitable and moderate tone of thought towards the Catholic church. To have faith in Protestantism at all as a development out of Catholicism (the only view that allows any real faith in it whatever) is to feel at the same time that it is not in and of itself the last full result of the process to which it owes its birth; that it has not carried away with it the *whole* life of the church as it stood before; that what it lacks accordingly in this respect, can only be made up to it hereafter in some way from the other side of Christianity, as the same is still extant in the church of Rome. The actual course of history is proving this, for all thinking men, more and more. Protestantism, as it now stands, is not the end of the Reformation. Who will dare to say of it, that any one of its sects separately, or that all of its sects collectively, may be taken for the full and whole sense of the holy catholic church, the original mystery of the creed? It is but too plain, that it falls far short of the proper idea of this mystery. The sect system,[67] say what we may of it, is constitutionally at war with the true being of the church, and tends always towards its dissolution. It can never stand therefore as a fixed and ultimate fact, in the history of Christianity. If it be required in the progress of this history at all, it can only be for the sake of some ulterior order in which it is destined finally to pass away; and so, no system in which it is comprehended can ever be enduring, under any such form. In the case of

67. [Nevin, "The Sect System," MTSS 5:238–71.]

Protestantism, this constitutional instability is now a simple matter of fact which has become too plain to be denied. The system is not fixed, but in motion; and the motion is for the time in the direction of complete self-dissolution. Fools and bigots may shut their eyes, to the truth; but it is none the less clear for all this to such as are earnestly thoughtful and truly wise. The fashion of this system passeth away. We can have no rational faith in it then as an abiding order, but only as we take it for a transitory scheme, whose breaking up is to make room in due time for another and for more perfect state of the church, in which its disorders and miseries shall finally be brought to an end. But to feel this, with any sense of the historical rights of the ancient church, and with any apprehension of what the Roman communion still is as distinguished from the Protestant, is to see and feel at the same time that the new order in which Protestantism is to become thus complete cannot be reached without the co-operation and help of Romanism. However faulty this may be in its separate character, it still embodies in itself nevertheless certain principles and forms of life, derived from the past history of the church, which are wanting to Protestantism as it now stands, and which need to be incorporated with it in some way as the proper and necessary complement of its own nature. The interest of Romanism is not so left behind, as to be no longer of any account; it must come in hereafter to counterbalance and correct again the disorder and excess of the other system. To this issue it comes necessarily, we say, with the historical scheme now under consideration.

The issue itself however may be conceived of is coming to pass in different ways, accordingly as greater or less stress is laid on one or the other of the factors concerned in its production.

First, Protestantism may be taken for the grand reigning stream of Christianity, (though not the whole of it by any means) into which finally the life of Catholicism is to pour itself as a wholesome qualifying power, yielding to it the palm of superior right and strength.

Or secondly, the two forces may be viewed as contrary sides merely of a dialectic process, in the Hegelian sense, which must be both alike taken up and so brought to an end (*aufgehoben*) in a new form of existence, that shall be at once the truth of both and yet something far higher and better than either.[68]

Or lastly, it may be supposed that the principal succession of the proper church life lies after all in the channel of the Roman Catholic communion; while Protestantism is to be regarded still as a true outflow of the same life, legitimate and necessary in its time, which however must in the end fall back into the old Catholic stream in order to fulfil its own mission, bringing into the universal church thus a new spiritual tone which only such a crisis could enable it to reach.

Of these three hypotheses, the first of course falls in best with the natural presumption of all Protestants in favor of their own system. But so far as the vindication

---

68. [Nevin would have followed Schaff's presentation of this Hegelian concept: *What is Church History?*, MTSS 3:289.]

of Protestantism itself is concerned, on the scheme of historical development, it would hold good under any of the views now mentioned; for even the last implies the necessity of its presence, and the reality of its vocation, as a vast and mighty factor in the work by which the church is to be made finally complete. It is no part of our business now, however, to discuss the merits either of all or of any of these hypothetical constructions; what we have in view is simply to show, how the general historical view here in question, by which Protestantism is seen to be in its very nature a movement towards something more complete than its present state, and something which is to be reached only in the direction of Catholicism, must necessarily beget towards the Roman church a much more tolerant and favorable feeling than that which usually actuates the enemies of this communion.

We know well, what sort of offence some are likely to take with any statement of this kind. They count it for no small part of their righteousness, to hate the Roman Catholic church with a perfect hatred; and they are ready to make it a grievous heresy in others, if they fall not in at once with this want of charity, or presume to take any view of the case that is less intolerant than their own. We have only to say however, that we have not so learned Christ [Eph 4:20]; and we know of no reason why we should passively succumb to the authority of any such arbitrary and intemperate spirit. It is no article of faith with us, no term of orthodoxy, to believe that the Pope as such is Antichrist, that the Roman church is Babylon, that a certain scheme of exegesis or a certain construction of church history, brought in to prop up this view, is to be received as of one and the same force with the authority of God's word itself. We have yet to learn, by what right any pretend to set up their exegetical or historical hobbies in such shape, the shibboleths at best of a mere party, for the universal law of Protestantism and the only measure of its faith. We claim for ourselves, and for all Protestants, the exercise here of some independent thought, and full liberty to judge of this whole subject as the case itself may seem to require. It is high time indeed, that the school to which we now refer should itself begin to see, that its Procrustean rule[69] here is one that cannot stand. Anti-popery, in this absolutely radical and unhistorical style, is not the whole and only true sense of Protestantism. Its fanatical war-whoop belongs to the outskirts of this camp at best, and not to its proper centre. The best Protestant piety, and we may say the entire Protestant learning, of the present time, fall not in at all with any such senseless yell, but stand in doubt of it more and more as being too often of the very same sound with open infidelity itself. Philology and history are working now mightily against this narrow school, all over the world, and not at all in its favor. Its only strength lies in its determination to ignore and resist, as it best can, the progress of true theological science. But this must soon prove also a crumbling trust. Historical studies in particular are already fast undermining its foundations, by the new trains of

---

69. [The mythical giant Procrustes forced people to fit his bed, whether by stretching or cutting off body parts; thus the phrase means arbitrarily compelled conformity.]

thought they are forcing on the mind of the world. The actual course of events too in our own age, is full of ominous meaning in the same direction.

Certain it is, that the present especially is no time for yielding tamely to the madness of any spirit, that seeks to build up Protestantism as the work of God, by denouncing Catholicism as purely and wholly the work of the Devil. Never before perhaps was the principle of unbelief so actively at work in the nominally christian world, for the overthrow of religion under every supernatural view. To make the matter worse, this principle is affecting to be itself the deepest and last sense of Christianity, the true end of its high and glorious mission for the redemption of the human race. Here undoubtedly we meet the real Antichrist of the present age, in a form that may well fill the world with apprehension and dread. It is at once rationalism (with the sect spirit) in the church, and radicalism in the state.[70] Against this formidable enemy, the cause of Protestantism and the cause of Romanism are one and the same; and wo be to us as Protestants, if we refuse to see and acknowledge the fact.[71] To make Romanism itself infidelity, to deride its supernatural pretensions, to treat its mysteries as diabolical and profane, and to own no fellowship with its faith whatever (in the common anti-popery style) is almost unavoidably to come to a sort of truce at least, if not indeed open friendship, with the real infidelity to which it stands opposed, and that is now notoriously making war upon it in precisely the same form and fashion. It is a sad spectacle in truth, when any part of the Protestant church is seen smiling on the enemies of all religion, and even cheering them forward it may be in their work of destruction, simply because it is directed immediately against the church of Rome, as though *any* opposition to this were at once a service rendered to the other side. According to this style of thinking, it would be a gain for the cause of religion if Romanism were at once swept, by some sudden revolution, from the face of the earth, even if open infidelity for the time should be left in its place.[72] Shall we join hands with those who thus think

70. [Nevin had already interpreted "the sect spirit" as Antichrist in *Antichrist*, MTSS 5:177–232. On political radicalism, see below second note following.]

71. [This is similar in many ways to the claim of J. Gresham Machen in *Christianity and Liberalism*, 52: " . . . how great is the common heritage which unites the Roman Catholic Church, with its maintenance of the authority of Holy Scripture and with its acceptance of the great early creeds, to devout Protestants today! We would not indeed obscure the difference which divides us from Rome. The gulf is indeed profound. But profound as it is, it seems almost trifling compared to the abyss which stands between us and many ministers of our own Church. The Church of Rome may represent a perversion of the Christian religion; but naturalistic liberalism is not Christianity at all."]

72. The want of spiritual discernment here with many Protestants is truly amazing. They are ready to bid God speed to any agency, however low and vile, that is turned against the Catholic church. Every vagabond that sets up the trade of abusing the Pope, finds some favor. Ronge, [a liberal, anti-Roman, Catholic] a few years since, was at once hailed as a second Luther, though his whole cause now lies in the gutter of infidelity. And how was Giustiniani [the anti-Catholic demagogue noted earlier] lauded for his work, in getting up German churches of the same stamp in our own country. There is a fearful tendency among us even to make common cause with the revolutionary spirit in Europe, under its worst forms, just because it seeks to destroy priests as well as to put down kings. True, we all condemn Rationalism and Socialism in the abstract; but we are wonderfully prone notwithstanding to look upon the cause in which they are enlisted as in itself a very good cause, which it becomes us as

and talk? God forbid. They are traitors to the cause of Protestantism, if this be indeed the cause of true Christianity. We abhor every such unholy alliance as is here offered to our view. We go with Rome against Infidelity, a thousand times more readily than with Infidelity against Rome.[73] We are very sure too, that any Protestant feeling which is differently constituted at this point, must be throughout miserably defective and false. It proceeds on a wrong apprehension altogether of the true relation between Protestantism and Romanism; it stands in no sympathy or fellowship whatever with the Catholic life of other ages; it shows itself to be wanting thus in a material element of Christianity itself. Plume itself as it may on its own worth, it is of counterfeit quality in its very nature. Its elective affinities prove it to be false.

[Conclusion]

We now bring these articles to a close. In the way of general recapitulation, our whole subject may be exhibited in the following propositions.

1. It is an error to suppose, that Nicene Christianity as it existed in the fourth and fifth centuries was in any sense identical with modern Protestantism. It was in all material respects the same system that is presented to us in the later Roman church.

2. It is an error to suppose, that the Christianity of the second century, as we find it in the time of Irenæus or even in the days of Ignatius and Polycarp, was of one and the same order with modern Protestantism. Especially was it unlike this in the Puritan form. However it may have differed from the Nicene system, it was made up of elements and tendencies plainly which looked towards this all along as their logical end. It was the later system at least in principle and germ.

3. The difference which exists in the whole case turns not merely on any single outward institution, such as episcopacy, but extends to the ecclesiastical life as a

---

Republicans [Nevin means here the political philosophy] and Protestants to cheer and help. The cry of liberty and social rights deceives us. It becomes part of our religion to pray for the success of every revolution got up in the name of freedom, whatever else may be its merits. We fall in with the cant and slang of humanitarian patriotism on this subject, as though it were the true sense of Christ's blessed evangel; and are prepared then to denounce every voice that refuses to take up the same song, as false to the genius of America. Such religious papers as the *N. Y. Observer* make common chime here with the *Tribune* and *Herald* of the same city; and the very pulpit rings in many cases, with no uncertain sound, in the same direction. But what can be more shallow than all this? Europe may need reform; no doubt does need it greatly. But how idle is it to look for anything of this sort, from the revolutionary spirit that is now bent on overturning its governments and institutions? To expect the regeneration of society from any such spirit, is itself a species of infidelity not to be excused. [A year later, Nevin presented a scathing (and prescient) critique of the conflation of religion and the "cry of liberty" as expressed in the reception by the American church of Louis Kossuth, the Hungarian revolutionary leader ("Man's True Destiny," MTSS 11:338–44).]

73. [For a discussion of the Catholic fight against modernism, see Bokenkotter, *Concise History*, 294–308.]

whole. It is a vain pretence therefore, by which Anglicanism affects to be on this score a true and full copy of what the church was in the first ages. The universal posture and genius of the ancient church, its scheme of thought and modes of action, were different. Its life was constitutionally Catholic and not Protestant.

4. No scheme of Protestantism then can be vindicated, on the ground of its being a repristination simply of what Christianity was immediately after the age of the Apostles.

5. On the other hand however, to pretend that this post-apostolical Christianity was in no view the legitimate continuation of the New Testament church, but a full apostacy from this in principle from the very start; so that Protestantism is to be considered a new fact altogether, rooting itself in the bible, without any regard to history; is such an assumption, as goes to upset completely the supernatural mystery of the holy catholic church, in the form under which it is made to challenge our faith in the Apostles' Creed. To take away from the church its divine historical existence, is to turn it into a wretched Gnostic abstraction. To conceive of it as the mere foot-ball of Satan from the beginning, is to suppose Christ either totally unmindful of his own word that the gates of hell should not prevail against it, or else unable to make his word good. No theory can stand, which thus overthrows the truth of the church from the beginning.

6. Protestantism then, if it is to be rationally vindicated at all on the platform of faith, must be set in union with the original fact of Christianity through the medium of the actual history of this fact, as we have it in the progress of the old Catholic church from the second century down to the sixteenth. It must be historical, the product of the previous life of the church, in order to be true and worthy of trust. Whatever line of sects it may be possible to trump up on the outside of the church proper, down to the time of the Waldenses, it is well known that Protestantism was not derived from any such poor source in fact; and one of the greatest wrongs that can well be done to it, is to seek its apology in any such jejune and hollow succession. If it be not the genuine fruit of the best life that belonged to the old church itself, as Luther and his compeers believed, it can admit of no valid defence.

7. This however involves of necessity the idea of historical development; by which both Romanism and Protestantism are to be regarded as falling short of the full idea of Christianity, and as needing something beyond themselves for their own completion.

8. No opposition to Romanism can deserve respect, or carry with it any true weight, which is not based on some proper sense of its historical relations to early Christianity and to modern Protestantism, in the view now stated. Without this qualification, anti-popery becomes altogether negative and destructive

Document 2: Early Christianity: Third Article.

towards the Roman church, and is simply blind unhistorical radicalism of the very worst kind. Its war with Romanism, is a rude profane assault in truth upon all ecclesiastical antiquity. No such controversy can stand. History and theology must in due time sweep it from the field.

J. W. N.

DOCUMENT 3

"Cyprian"

Editor's Introduction

Nevin's four essays on the life and thought of Cyprian are a continuation of his work in the "Early Christianity" essays. The latter series was completed in January of 1852; "Cyprian" was started in May, the third number of that year. In "Early Christianity," Nevin had introduced the question of what the church was like in the second and third centuries. He now expands that exploration by reading one of the most important church fathers of that period: Cyprian, who was martyred AD 258, after about a decade as bishop of Carthage.[1]

The first essay is focused on Cyprian's biography and his journey toward martyrdom. Corollary themes include reverence for the martyrs and the question of the lapsed. The lapsed were those believers who capitulated to the imperial command to offer oblation to the emperor, which was a seen as a denial of the faith. The status of the lapsed allows Nevin to explore important questions in Cyprian's ecclesiology. The lapsed were sinful, but they still "believed Christianity to be true, and saw in the church the only ark of salvation for a ruined world."[2] This is key for Nevin, since it gave clear testimony that even people who had allegedly betrayed their faith were convinced that they could only find salvation in reconciliation and return to the life-giving bosom of the church.

The second essay begins with a more-detailed exploration of how the lapsed could be readmitted into the fellowship and life of the church. This also allows Nevin to explore the serious disagreements among the various churches about how they should respond, especially how this reconciliation was to be effected. He wrote, "However desirable it was for those who had fallen to be restored to the peace of the church, this could be done effectively only through real humiliation and penance on their own part, making room for ecclesiastical absolution afterwards in a regular and valid

---

1. DeBie introduces this series of essays in *John Williamson Nevin*, 282.
2. P. 181 below.

form."³ This provides the foundation of the later doctrines of penance and absolution in the church, and once again supports Nevin's thesis that the church is a supernatural institution with powers to provide salvation. Cyprian thought the lapsed should be brought back into the church, but not immediately. The magnitude of their lapse needed to be matched in magnitude by their penance. Nevin uses this discussion to powerfully illuminate Cyprian's doctrine of the church. He also explores the Cyprianic doctrine of episcopal authority and the meaning of schism, which arose over the proper procedure for readmitting the lapsed. Nevin sees the struggle that arose from these schismatics as being ultimately beneficial because it forced the church to think about the nature of the church and its authority. It forced the church to develop more clarity about her supernatural constitution and reality as one catholic church.

At the end of the second essay, Nevin asks if Protestantism can legitimately lay claim to being the church based on the Cyprianic understanding of the church; the third essay develops his argument. He begins by asking whether the Anglican or Episcopalian claim to apostolic continuity rescues Protestantism.⁴ To the contrary, he explains, "The question between those who receive and those who reject episcopacy on Protestant ground is a mere circumstance, over against the broad deep issue by which in the nature of the case both are sundered from the Church of Rome."⁵ The real question for Nevin comes down to what is Protestantism in relation to the Catholic Church? Is Protestantism merely a schism from the one true church? Or has Protestantism lost something integral thus betraying the essence of what it means to be a church as a supernatural power? One can feel the weight of Nevin's dilemma:

> Protestantism, it is plain, involves an entire departure from the theory or scheme of Cyprian here, not simply as it may reject this or that form of ecclesiastical polity, this or that ecclesiastical use, but as it refuses to see in the church the actual presence of the Christian salvation under the same outwardly real and objective view.⁶

Nevin's worry, especially as he proceeds in the Cyprian essays, is that Protestantism is irreparable. He extends his survey beyond Cyprian to his contemporaries and predecessors. It leads him to conclude, "the Cyprianic doctrine of the church falls back thus, in its fundamental conception, to the earliest Christian time."⁷ Nevin then contrasts this conclusion with modern Protestantism. Evangelical Puritanism is not merely different from the earliest ages of the church, it is diametrically opposed to it. Nevin ends the third essay with a poignant question: is there any future hope for

---

3. Pp. 188–89 below.

4. Nevin explores this question in "The Anglican Crisis" (MTSS 11:269–306) and comes back to it in "Reply to 'An Anglican Catholic.'" Schaff also discusses this in *Principle* (MTSS 3:141–48).

5. P. 237 below.

6. Pp. 239–40 below.

7. P. 260 below.

Protestantism? With that question left hanging without answer, one might hope that Nevin would do something similar to his final essay in "Early Christianity." In the fourth essay however, Nevin continues with his historical survey of Cyprian's theology. This is not merely a rehashing of previous material. He is exploring some of the other issues in Cyprian's writing that manifest the supernatural character of the church. Especially interesting is the question of the baptism of heretics. This allows Nevin to simultaneously explore discussions of the efficacy of baptism and the authority of the pope.[8] Cyprian famously battled with Stephen, bishop of Rome at the time, over the question of the efficacy of baptisms done by heretics and schismatics. Stephen said that they were valid while Cyprian took the opposite view. Nevin does find affinity with Cyprian's position even as he acknowledges that it was rejected by the church.

Nevin concludes the essay with the question that has been looming throughout these essays: is the version of Christianity in Cyprian's era legitimate or illegitimate? This is vital because it goes to the on-going battles that he is having in the American ecclesial environment, the all-consuming "church question." One can truly begin to feel the weight that he is struggling with. If Cyprianic Christianity is authentic ("true" to whatever standard validates *Christianity*), how can Protestantism be authentic? How does one move from Cyprian in the third century to the plethora of sects in the American nineteenth century? How can both realities be legitimate expressions of the same Christianity? These questions adumbrate Nevin's struggle. His thesis remains: "Early Christianity was in its constitutional elements, not Protestantism but Catholicism."[9] How then should we justify the continuation of Protestantism rather than convert to Catholicism? He has two possible answers: whole cloth apostasy from the time of the apostles or historical development. Nevin recounts the various views he explored in the third essay of "Early Christianity." While Nevin presents the same theories of development, he is more agnostic about which method will solve the dilemma. Payne says that Nevin, while ultimately suspending judgment, favors either Schaff's view or the final view, which we might call the "reabsorption" theory.[10] While Nevin demurs on a solution, he is insistent that his purpose in these essays was merely to present the historical information and allow it to provoke the reader on its own. We are left where he leaves the essays, in the dilemma of the history he has recounted, hoping that there is a way to make historical development function.[11]

---

8. Nevin's views on baptism are presented in Nevin et al., *Born of Water*, MTSS 6.

9. P. 312 below.

10. See Payne, "Schaff and Nevin," 182. Payne argues that "Early Christianity" and "Cyprian" are essentially arguing for the same conclusion: there must be some kind of historical development of which there are three options. Both essays reject the traditional Puritan version of history which sees the vast history of the church to be a great nullity. Layman sees a deeper despair in the Cyprian essay which gives lip service to the idea of historical development (Layman, "Revelation in the Praxis," 128–29).

11. Good says that the publication of Cyprian gave his enemies the material they needed to be able to prove their accusations against Nevin in regard to his weak stance on Catholicism (Good, *History*, 284).

Cyprian[: First Article].[1]

[Cyprian's Conversion and Call to the Episcopate]

Thascius Cecilius Cyprian, the great ornament of the Latin Church in the third century, was born at Carthage, about the beginning, probably, of this period, of a highly respectable and wealthy family. His father, we are told, was one of the principal senators of that place. Of his secular relations, however, including his education and many years afterwards of prosperous worldly life, almost nothing is now known; his biographer, the Deacon Pontius, having judged all this to be of no consideration, and so not worthy of any historical mention, "in view of that spiritual greatness" by which he became so illustrious in the end.[2] We know only that he was possessed of good natural parts; that he enjoyed the best opportunities for intellectual culture; that these were diligently and successfully turned to account; that he applied himself particularly to the study of oratory and eloquence; that he became professor of rhetoric subsequently in his native city, a highly honorable as well as lucrative employment in that age; that he prosecuted his profession with great reputation and success, ("*gloriose rhetoricam docuit*,"[3] according to Jerome); that he lived in elegant and genteel affluence, as a man of the world, devoted it would seem to mere pleasure and ambition, the lust of the eye and the pride of life, without God and without hope. He was a Pagan; and with all his secular cultivation the vices of Paganism held him firmly in their power.

In this condition however, according to his own confession, he was by no means happy. Amid the pleasures and honors of the world, he had a keen sense also of its unutterable vanity, and sighed frequently after higher and more enduring good. Christianity no doubt had some influence upon him in this way, long before he was brought to yield himself to its power. He could not but approve in his conscience its high purposes and aims; and there were aspirations in him at times, that would fain

---

1. [*MR* 4 (May 1852) 259–77. Nevin's primary source for Cyprian's works was the "Tauchnitz" edition: *Th. C. Cypriani Opera Genuina* (Lipsiae: Berhn. Tauchnitz jr., 1838, 1839). The volume is paginated in two parts; in these notes they are abbreviated as "*Epist.*" {*Epistles*} and "*Tract.*" {*Treatises*}.]

2. [*De Vita et Passione* in PL 3:1481–98; trans. as Pontius, *The Life of Cecil Cyprian*, in *Early Christian Biographies*, 5–24. Nevin's primary source for Pontius seems to have been Butler, *Lives of the Primitive Fathers*, 9:179–222. Pontius dismisses Cyprian's "secular relations" in §2, but the quoted words do not appear in any known translation.]

3. [Trans. "he taught rhetoric magnificently;" see *Letters*, 1:125n67.]

have burst the chains of sense and flesh, to make common cause with this divine philosophy in its heaven-ward flight. But he had no power to persuade himself, that what Christianity proposed in this case was in any way truly practicable. He saw that no merely natural ability or effort would be sufficient for any such end, the eradication of worldly affections and desires, the conquest of self, and a true surrendry of the heart to heavenly and eternal things; and it fell not in with his carnal wisdom, his natural experience and common sense to believe in any real provision for the purpose under a supernatural form. He knew, indeed, that the claims of the Church included the idea of such supernatural help; that powers more than human were supposed to be embraced in her constitution, for the accomplishment of its more than human ends; that her sacrament of regeneration in particular, was held to be not a powerless baptism with water merely, but an actual new birth by the Spirit into such a state of grace as brought with it the real possibility of righteousness and salvation, in a form wholly beyond and above the reach of nature. Of all this he had often heard; for it was part of the daily talk and universal faith of the Christian world at the time; but to his worldly judgment the thing appeared incredible. He was not able to acknowledge the mystery of any such supernatural grace; it appeared to him no better then [sic] a fanciful dream; and thus all his better thoughts and aspirations served only to fill him in the end with a more perfect feeling of despair, a sense of hopeless bondage to the power of this present world for which religion itself could offer no relief.

In his tract *Da Gratia Dei*, addressed to his friend Donatus, soon after his conversion, he has himself given us a picture of the spiritual state in which he found himself, for some time at least, previously to that event. "I lay in darkness," he writes,

> and floated on the world's boisterous sea, with no resting place for my feet, ignorant of my proper life, and estranged from truth and light. Circumstanced as I then was, I found it hard and impracticable to receive the promise held out by the divine goodness for my salvation; namely, that a man might be born again, and that being animated into a new life, through the laver of saving water, he might lay aside what he had been before, and though retaining the same bodily frame put on an entirely new mind and spirit. How is so great a conversion possible, I said to myself, that one should suddenly and at once put off what has either hardened upon him from his own nature or has become inveterate through long custom? These things are wrought, as it were with a firm and deep root, into his very constitution. When does one learn frugality, who has been accustomed to rich and sumptuous entertainments? And when does one who has been used to costly raiment, shining in gold and purple, descend contentedly to plain and simple apparel? He who has prided himself in honors and the insignia of power, cannot stoop to a private and inglorious state. He who has been surrounded with the officious attendance of numerous retainers and clients, considers it a calamity to be left alone. So universally, it seems to be necessary, that through the seductive force of custom wine should

Document 3: Cyprian[: First Article].

> continue to invite, pride to inflate, anger to inflame, covetousness to disquiet, cruelty to stimulate, ambition to please, and lust to hurry headlong in its own course. Such were often my private thoughts. For being deeply entangled in the manifold errors of my own previous life, which I considered it impossible for me to lay aside, I yielded thus to my besetting sins, and through despair of any thing better gave myself up to their power as an evil belonging to me by native and proper right.[4]

This description refers particularly to the period immediately before his conversion, when he was led to think seriously of embracing the Christian salvation. He had formed an acquaintance with an aged and excellent priest in Carthage, named Cecilius, who gradually won his entire confidence, and whose influence on him was happily employed at the same time to engage his favorable attention to the claims of the Gospel. By him he was led to devote himself to the study of the Holy Scriptures, and finally to offer himself as a catechumen for admission into the Christian church. In this state of preparation, according to his biographer, he proposed to himself the highest ideal of Christian perfection; though he was far from being able at once to secure the victory over himself and over the world, to which his ardent spirit aspired. The full crisis of his conversion he himself refers to his baptism, which carried in it for his subsequent faith always the character of a real gift of life bestowed upon him by God. "When by means of the regenerating wave," he says,

> the stain of my former life was washed away, and the serene and pure light of heaven descended into my sin-cleansed bosom; as soon as the second birth, by the Spirit derived from on high, had transformed me into a new man, presently in a wonderful way doubts began to be settled, perplexities to solve themselves, and obscurities to grow plain; there arose strength, for what before seemed difficult, and power to do what was before held to be impossible; making it clear, that the first natural life in the service of sin was of the earth, and that what the Holy Ghost had now breathed into me was of God.[5]

Cyprian's baptism took place about the year 245 or 246, when perhaps he was not much less than fifty years old. He always regarded the priest Cecilius afterwards as under God the author of his spiritual life; and in token of his grateful affection towards him took his name into union with his own, calling himself from the time of his conversion Thascius *Cecilius* Cyprian.

He adopted at once what was then regarded as the highest rule of piety, devoting himself in a life of celibacy and voluntary poverty to the service of God. The Scriptures were made his favorite and constant study. He sold his estate, and gave the money as well as almost all he possessed besides, for the support of the poor; "by which," says Pontius, "he gained two ends of principal importance; renouncing and despising all

---

4. [*Ad Donatum De Gratia Dei* in Tract., 2; PPS 32:49–51, 52.]
5. [*Ad Donatum* in Tract., 2–3; PPS 32:52.]

secular views, (than which nothing is more fatal to the true interests of piety and religion) and fulfilling at the same time, the law of charity, which God himself prefers to all sacrifices."[6] With the study of the Scriptures he joined also that of the best ecclesiastical writers then known. Among these his great favorite was Tertullian, his own countryman, out of whose writings he made it a point to read something almost every day; calling for them as Jerome relates, with the simple word: "Hand me the Master."[7] In a very short time, he was favorably known, we may say even distinguished, for his Christian knowledge and piety, on all sides.

This good reputation created a general desire, on the part of the people, to have him raised to the priesthood; and he was accordingly consecrated, while still a neophyte or recent convert, to this holy office; his extraordinary merit being considered a sufficient reason, for dispensing in his case with the rule, which forbade the ordination of persons of this class. Soon after Donatus, the bishop of Carthage died; and now there was a general cry, on the part of both clergy and laity, that Cyprian should become his successor. Of this dignity however he felt himself to be altogether unworthy; and protesting against his own nomination, with unaffected humility, went so far even as to hide himself by flight, that he might avoid the public pressure. But the place of his retreat was soon discovered; when the people laid siege literally to the house where he was, closing up every avenue of escape, and refusing to withdraw till he should yield himself to their will. He bowed himself accordingly in the end to the necessity which seemed to be imposed upon him so evidently by God himself, and thus became bishop of Carthage not more perhaps than two years after the time of his conversion. His consecration took place, with the unanimous approbation of the bishops of the province, in the year 248. With all this popular enthusiasm however, there was not a universal satisfaction with the appointment. A few of the presbyters, including Fortunatus and Donatus who had themselves aspired to the dignity, with some of their friends among the laity, opposed the election as being in favor of one who was still only a novice in the church. Cyprian treated this party with great kindness, and bestowed upon them indeed special marks of his friendship and confidence; for the purpose partly of placing them on good terms with the body of the people, who were highly offended with their conduct. But they were not to be subdued in this way. All kindness was lost upon them; a deep grudge was still harbored in their bosoms against the new bishop, which only waited a favorable opportunity to break forth afterwards into open insubordination of the most active and violent kind.

---

6. [Butler, *Lives of the Primitive Fathers*, 9:182, slightly altered. The full quote: "By distributing his goods to maintain the peace of many needy people and thus dispensing almost all his wealth, he combined two virtues: contempt for worldly ambition, than which nothing is more harmful, and the conferring of mercy. The latter God preferred even to sacrifices, and he who said that he had observe all the commandments of the law did not fulfill it." Pontius, *Life*, 7.]

7. [See Jerome, *On Illustrious Men*, 74, 75n6, paraphrased in Butler, *Lives of the Primitive Fathers*, 9:182. In Latin, it was indeed a "simple word," *da Magistrum*.]

Document 3: Cyprian[: First Article].

Cyprian entered upon his episcopal duties with the greatest resolution and vigor. However backward he had been to undertake the office, there was no lack of zeal with him, when it had been undertaken, to carry out in full the proper sense of its functions. The energetic, uncompromising spirit, with which he insisted thus on what he conceived to be its rightful prerogatives and claims, has sometimes been regarded as the sign of a hierarchical nature, a disposition to lord it over God's heritage; in which view, to a carnal worldly mind, his previous deprecation of the episcopate must appear to have been no better than a politic feint or sham, a mere piece of mock modesty at best, in no true keeping with the ambition which actually reigned in his soul. Such also is the construction, which this carnal judgment is ever prone to put upon all similar instances of the *nolo episcopari*,[8] as they come before us in the history of the ancient church. But let it be felt that Christianity is what it claims to be, and all this sort of thinking is at once reduced to its proper miserable worth. There is in truth no contradiction whatever, between the backwardness of Cyprian to become bishop, and the high church style in which he afterwards acted as a bishop. On the contrary, both exhibitions of character sprang from the same ground, the firm faith namely which he had in the divine origin of the church, and in the reality of the apostolical commission as something always of force in the succession of its priesthood. His humility led him to shrink in the first place from the honor and responsibility of a ministry, which he felt to be so directly from heaven; and the very same feeling substantially, the sense of what was due to such an office over against all simply private and personal ends, engaged him afterwards to use its resources, and assert its rights, with the most uncompromising zeal. He became in an important sense the organ of the high trust with which he was clothed. However humbly he thought of himself, he could not too much magnify his office. This was, not of man, but of God. However much his election to it might have been due to the people, he never thought of resolving the office itself, its powers, resources, or rights, into any such popular vote. That would have been to his mind nothing short of absolute blasphemy. Every true bishop, in his view, was a successor of the apostles, and a real bearer of the commission which they received originally from the Lord Jesus Christ Himself. This was the consciousness in which he stood, and that actuated we may say his universal ministry. It is easy to see, how it might impart to this at times an air of something like pontifical assumption, as viewed from the standpoint of the common unbelieving world. But it needs only a slight knowledge of his life, a cursory acquaintance with the spirit that breathes through all his epistles and tracts, to be fully satisfied that his character was the very reverse in fact of every such unfavorable imagination. His hierarchichal ideas were all based, like those of St. Paul, on the renunciation and sacrifice of self. Never perhaps was there a bishop more truly humble, more self-denying, more gentle and affectionate, more ready to render himself up as a holocaust of love for the welfare of men or for the glory of God.

8. [Trans: "I do not want to be bishop."]

It is not too much to say of him, that he was the complete ideal of a true Christian bishop. His piety, his humility, his charity and benevolence, his gentleness combined with firmness and courage, his unsleeping vigilance and unbending resolution in the exercise of church discipline, were all deserving of the highest admiration. His very countenance, says Pontius,[9] was at once venerable and full of grace, beyond what could well be expressed; so that no one could look upon him, without being inspired with a certain feeling of respectful awe. Cheerfulness and gravity were happily blended together in his looks; and his whole air and manner were such as to make it doubtful whether love or respect should preponderate in his presence; only this was certain, that he deserved the largest measure of both. His dress corresponded with the dignity and propriety of his appearance in other respects; it was simple, without being either ostentatious or mean. His liberality towards the poor, which had been so great before he became a bishop, formed afterwards also a leading ornament of his life. With his presbyters and people, he lived in relations of the tenderest sympathy and regard; dwelling among them as a father; taking counsel with them in all the concerns of the church; and seeking in every way especially to make them sharers of his own spirit, and full partners with himself in the heavenly calling of the gospel. He stood in the most intimate and active spiritual *rapport* with his flock; rejoicing with those that rejoiced and weeping with those that wept; making common cause with them in their trials; even bearing their sins in a certain sense and carrying their sicknesses and griefs, as though they had been his own. He could say of them literally in the strong language of Paul: "Who is weak, and I am not weak? Who is offended and I burn not? [...] We live, if ye stand fast in the Lord. [...] For what is our hope, or joy, or crown of rejoicing? Are not even ye in the presence of our Lord Jesus Christ at his coming? For ye are our glory and joy."[10] He lived, not merely to rule and teach his people, but still more to make continual intercession for them before God. With prayers and tears they were borne upon his priestly heart, we may say, in the solemn ministrations of the altar, day and night.

[The Decian Persecution, Cyprian's Exile, and the "Lapsed"]

It was not long till large and extraordinary occasion was afforded in the providence of God, for trying these virtues of the new bishop to the fullest extent. He had not enjoyed his dignity much more than a single year in peace, when the terrible Decian persecution, as it is called, burst like an avalanche upon the Church.[11] The cruel edict reached Carthage about the beginning of the year 250. In such cases, the bishops, as being the acknowledged leaders of the Christian community, were always liable to

9. [The following description paraphrases Butler, *Lives of the Primitive Fathers*, 9:187–88; see *PL* 3:1487; Pontius, *Life*, 10–11.]

10. [2 Cor 11:29; 1 Thess 3:8; 1 Thess 2:19–20.]

11. [For details on the Decian persecution, see González, *Story of Christianity*, 1:85–90.]

Document 3: Cyprian[: First Article].

become the first objects of attack. Cyprian however was especially obnoxious to the heathen party, as being so conspicuous a deserter from its ranks in the last part of his life, and now placed in the fore-front of the opposite cause.[12] The fanaticism of the mob, accordingly, at once fixed upon him for its prey. Circus amphitheatre and market, resounded with the cry: *"Cyprian to the lions!"* Not being found at once, he was proscribed, and all persons were forbidden to give him shelter or help. The rage of his enemies, however, was at this time disappointed. He saved himself by flight.[13]

This was a momentous step in the circumstances, which was not taken without the most full and earnest deliberation. It was not a question of easy determination at once, to decide in view of all points between the two alternatives of flight or death. The crown of martyrdom was in many cases an object of ambition in the early church; some were in danger of even rashly throwing themselves in its way; although the rule was not overlooked at the same time, by which our Saviour Himself allowed his disciples, when persecuted in one city or country, to save themselves by fleeing to another [Matt 10:23]. Cyprian had no difficulty in approving the course of others, who went into banishment, suffering the loss of their property, to avoid death. But his own case was not just of this general sort. He was the shepherd of the flock; and the question was mainly, what he owed in this fearful crisis to the welfare of his people. Would it not be the part of a hireling, to quit his post and forsake his charge, just when the wolf seemed ready to fall upon it and tear it in pieces? On the other hand, however, the presence of the bishop provoked persecution.[14] And then what was to be gained for the flock itself, by allowing the shepherd to be smitten, and the sheep to be scattered abroad, by the very first blast of the storm which was now at hand? Was the church properly prepared to meet the hurricane in that way. Alas, Cyprian knew but too well, that this was not the case; and facts enough of a deplorable kind were soon offered to confirm his apprehension. His clergy wished him to retire, for the sake of the church. Still he seems to have hesitated for a time; being "in a strait betwixt two [Phil 1:23];" till in answer finally to his earnest prayers, he received what he considered a direct monition from heaven, ordering him to withdraw. So at least his own language in one

---

12. In derision, and popular spite, they called him *Coprianus,* playing on the sense of a Greek word which signifies dung [Butler, *Lives of the Primitive Fathers*, 9:188].

13. [Butler, *Lives of the Primitive Fathers*, 9:188–89. Nevin is relying heavily on Butler's loose use of Pontius. Pontius presents the flight of Cyprian more in terms of obedience to God when he would have preferred to receive the martyr's crown. To fail in his obedience to God would have been sinful, and so in a spirit of humble obedience, Cyprian went into temporary exile. Pontius, *Life*, 11, 12.]

14. In his letter on the subject to the Roman presbyters and deacons (ep. 20, ed. Tauchn.) he says: "*Cum me clamore violento frequenter populus flagitasset, non tam meam salutem quam quietem fratrum publicam cogitans interim secessi, ne per inverecundam praesentiam nostram seditio, quae coeperat, plus provocaretur* [*Epist.*, 42]." [Trans. " . . . when the populace clamoured for me violently and repeatedly, I . . . withdrew for the time being. I was thinking not so much of my own safety as the general peace of our brethren; I was concerned that if I brazenly continued to show myself in Carthage I might aggravate even further the disturbance that had begun" (*Letters* 1:101).]

place would seem to imply;[15] and the fact is asserted also by his biographer Pontius. In this way the question was conclusively settled; and with a few confidential attendants, he went into retirement some distance from Carthage, hiding himself at once from both the knowledge and the power of his enemies. But his pastoral relations to his flock were not dissolved by this absence. During the whole time of his recess, though absent in body, he was still with them in spirit; maintaining constant communication with them by messengers and letters; watching over their affairs with intense sympathy and concern; administering counsels, admonitions, instructions and exhortations, suited to their circumstances and wants; and above all assisting them continually by his intercessions and prayers.

The simple fact of this earnest pastoral supervision, thus firmly and steadily asserted on the one side and met with reciprocal confidence and trust on the other, through the entire period of his retreat, is enough of itself to shield him from the suspicion of having been actuated in the step, by the motive of mere fear or an unworthy regard in any way to the preservation of his own life. If there was any room for this reproach, says Neander, his subsequent behavior showed at least that he was able to overcome the dread of death, while the calm and candid tone with which he gives account of the course he took in his letter to the Roman clergy, must be considered enough for his justification.[16] But no such doubtful apology does proper justice to the case. To admit the possibility of the weakness in question, is to overthrow the truth of the whole moral relation in which Cyprian is here exhibited to our view. A pious man might shrink from death, and choose flight as the more easy alternative for saving his faith; but he could not in these circumstances, without hypocrisy and guilt, assume a tone and air which would virtually imply the exact contrary of this, as we find Cyprian doing continually in his correspondence with the flock he had left behind him at Carthage. Nowhere does he betray the slightest sense of any such infirmity in what he had done, or the least anxiety to make his position right in the eyes of his own people. On the contrary, he uses towards them from first to last the tone of one, who felt that he had done nothing to forfeit their confidence, nothing to invalidate his pastoral right, nothing to embarrass the exercise of this right in the smallest degree. He places himself right in the midst of the bloody conflict which is going forward; makes common cause with the confessors and martyrs; acts throughout in the spirit of a general at the head of his troops; with trumpet tongue calls them to battle; triumphs in the "coronation" of such as were faithful unto death, as though it had been his own; weeps over the fall of the "lapsed," like a mother in bitterness for the loss of her children; insists

---

15. Ep. 16. ed. Tauchn. "*Audietis omnia, quando ad vos reducem me Dominus fecerit,* qui ut secederem jussit [*Epist.,* 38, emphasis Nevin's]." [Trans. "And you shall hear all of these things when the Lord *who bade me withdraw* has brought me back to you (*Letters,* 1:95)."] This might mean simply a scriptural or providential direction; but for one familiar with Cyprian's faith it refers more readily to a strictly supernatural order, by vision or in some other way.

16. [Neander, *General History of the Christian Religion and Church,* trans. Joseph Torrey, 2nd American ed. (Boston: Crocker and Brewster, 1849) 1:134.]

Document 3: Cyprian[: First Article].

afterwards on the discipline of the church, as the necessary remedy for such vast ruin; and at the risk of his own credit and popularity shows himself inexorable in asserting its most severe claims, in the face of a party violently bent on setting aside his authority, and supported to a certain extent by the voice even of confessors and martyrs themselves. Such deportment in such relations is not to be reconciled with the idea of a pusillanimous shrinking from martyrdom in the mind of Cyprian himself, without the supposition either of vast self-ignorance or else great conscious duplicity. He must have been in one way or the other totally undeserving of moral respect, if he could act the part he did in this style, without an inward consciousness fully answerable to what it implied. And then again, how could any such acted part have engaged the confidence of his people? Those who knew him best, gave him full credit practically for being all that this high bearing continually assumed. The entire relation between him and his church, as it comes out in his letters, is such as should silence at once every imagination of anything like pusillanimity in his conduct. Every such thought, even in the hypothetical and guarded form it carries with Neander, destroys in fact the true verisimilitude of the picture in view; reduces all to the play of mere human and worldly factors; caricatures the supernatural side of Christianity, and in the end, we may say, turns the divine itself into the diabolical. We might as well charge St. Paul with selfishness and affectation in his ministry, and yet pretend to honor him notwithstanding as a glorious representative and true apostle of Christ.

The wisdom and propriety of Cyprian's secession were abundantly shown, in the salutary fruit which grew out of it for the church, both while it lasted and after it was over. Though outwardly absent, he was still the soul of the Christian cause at Carthage, throughout the entire ordeal of the Decian persecution. The faithful were encouraged and animated, by the assurance that he was still at their head and ready to die with them in the end for their common faith. Martyrs and confessors fought their good fight more joyfully, from knowing that his eye was upon them, and his heart with them, in the deadly struggle. When peace returned, there was no one so well fitted to restore the disorders, and repair the breaches, which had been caused by the overflowing scourge. Not only his own diocese, but the church at large, derived the greatest advantage while he lived from his truly apostolical vigilance and zeal; while his writings have proved a large source of instruction and benefit to the whole Christian world, through all ages since.

It has been intimated already, that the church was not properly prepared for the fearful trial which came upon her under the Emperor Decius.[17] A comparatively long season of outward prosperity and rest previously had led as usual to much worldliness

---

17. [Decius (d. 251), declared emperor in 249. He was the first emperor to undertake a systematic persecution of Christians throughout the empire. He executed the Bishop of Rome, Fabian, in 250. The focus of the persecution was the emperor cult. Christians who had means could often purchase fake certifications of cultic participation. Those who could not faced the dilemma of capitulating, which meant offering oblation to the emperor, or martyrdom. Those who capitulated were known as "the lapsed."]

and carnal security in her communion. Multitudes professing the Christian name, and not a few even who served at the altar, had come to be perfectly secular in their character, differing but little either in spirit or life from the Pagan world with which they were surrounded. It is a gloomy picture Cyprian himself draws of this dismal fact, in the first part of his tract *De Lapsis;* a picture, which for the honor of Christianity one might wish to keep out of view; but which, for the right understanding of Christianity at the same time, it is very important in truth that we should be brought to look steadily in the face. In the end, the actual here forms a better commentary on the mystery of godliness, the proper nature of the church in the world, than any ideal that may lie substituted for it by the human imagination. The persecution, says Cyprian, was an exploration, mercifully ordained by God to revive discipline and restore faith. Both had fallen into sad decay.

> Many, unmindful of what believers had been in the age of the apostles and should be always, had given themselves up to the pursuit of wealth, and were bent only on increasing their worldly estate. Devotion was wanting among the priests, and faith among the deacons; there was no charity in men's works, no strictness in their manners. Men dressed their beards; women painted their persons; both eyes and hair, God's work, were falsified by art into a new form. Cunning deceptions were practised on the simple, and advantage taken of brethren by dishonest tricks. Marriages were formed with unbelievers, by which Christ's members were prostituted to the Gentiles. Oaths were taken not only rashly, but falsely, those in authority were treated with proud insolence; curses flowed from poisoned lips; discords were kept up with lasting mutual hatred. Many bishops even, who should have been a lesson and example to others, renouncing the service of God for the care of worldly things, forsook their sees, and left their people, wandering into other parts of the country in quest of markets for profitable trade, anxious to have money largely while brethren in the church were in extreme want, grasping farms by trading and fraud, and multiplying their gains by interest.[18]

This, be it remembered, in the third century, and before the Church had come to enjoy any toleration by law in the Roman empire.[19] The picture of course sets before us a part only of the Christianity to which it refers; there was embraced in this a large amount besides of very different character. Still there is reason to believe, that this bad side of the case reached very far, and that there was an amount of worldliness and ungodliness in the church far beyond what is commonly imagined of these primitive times. And yet all this was strangely joined, as we shall see, with the proper superhuman power of faith, and a corresponding presence of true supernatural grace, in the same church, to an extent which was found fully sufficient to carry it triumphantly

---

18. [Cyprian, *De Lapsis*, in *Tract.*, 137; ACW 25:16–17; PPS 32:107.]
19. [Granted by Constantine the Great in the Edict of Milan (AD 313).]

Document 3: Cyprian[: First Article].

through the fires of persecution, and to give it soon after the mastery of the Roman world.

The first effects of the Decian trial were terribly disastrous. A large portion of the Christian profession was at once swept away by it, like chaff before the wind. The imperial order required all to conform to the religion of the state, by taking part in some idolatrous ceremony, prescribed by the magistrate in the way of test. In the first place there was a proclamation merely, calling upon all persons to come forward within a certain time, and prove themselves good subjects of the government in that easy way. Only those who refused to do so, exposed themselves afterwards to more active persecution. They might quit the country before the term was up. In that case, their property was confiscated, and they were forbidden to return on pain of death; but they saved their faith. Such as chose not to fly, saw themselves at the mercy of the populace and the civil power, and in danger always of being called to the most severe account. They might be cited at any time to answer for their faith; when if they refused to deny Christ, by doing homage to idols, they were cast into prison, and subjected to sharp torture from time to time for the purpose of overcoming their resolution. Those who stood this trial were honored in the church as *confessors*. In the case of some, the process was carried sooner or later to the issue of a violent death. They were then known and revered as *martyrs*. To the disgrace however of a large number calling themselves Christians at this time in Carthage, they did not even wait till such confession and suffering were required at their hands, as the price of their fidelity to the Saviour; but showed themselves eager rather, on the first noise of the coming danger, to place themselves beyond its reach, and to save both life and property, by submitting of their own accord to the idolatrous test through which this bad security was to be gained. "At the first word of the threatening foe," Cyprian writes, "a very large portion of the brotherhood (maximus *fratrum numerus*) betrayed their faith, prostrated not by the violence of persecution, but by their own voluntary fall."[20] All admonitions and engagements, the hopes of heaven and the terrors of hell, seemed to be at once forgotten.

> They did not wait to go up to the Capitol at least by compulsion, to deny on interrogation. Many [were] conquered before the battle, overthrown without conflict, retained not even this credit, that they seemed to sacrifice to idols unwillingly. They ran to the forum of their own accord, hastened to death freely, as though they had before wished this, and but embraced now an opportunity which they had always desired. How many were put off by the magistrates through the close of day; how many even begged that their own ruin might not be thus postponed![21]

More than this.

---

20. [Cyprian, *De Lapsis*, 138, Nevin's emphasis; ACW 25:18; PPS 32:109.]
21. [Cyprian, *De Lapsis*, 138–39; ACW 25:19; PPS 32:110.]

> For many their own destruction was not enough; they urged one another with mutual exhortations to perdition, pledged one another reciprocally in bumpers of death. And that nothing might be wanting to the fulness of crime, children also, carried or led by the hand of their parents, lost what they had acquired in the beginning of their life.[22]

The great body of the "lapsed" probably were of this sort. Others however fell with less inexcusable disgrace; yielding only when they were brought to trial; or it may be not till nature was well nigh worn out by long privations and horrible torments. Some allowed themselves to take a sort of middle course, which amounted, in fact however to the sin they endeavored in this way to avoid. They did not themselves actually sacrifice; but by paying a fee they procured certificates, declaring that they had complied with the edict; or it might be, without this, and even without personally appearing before the magistrate, had their names enrolled simply on the official list of those who were thus approved. It was easy to frame a plausible apology for these evasions, especially under this latter form; but they were condemned by the church as tacit treason to the cause of Christ.

Altogether the fall of so large a portion of his flock was a calamity, that filled the soul of Cyprian with keen mortification and distress. It is to him as though the raging foe had torn away from the church a part of her own bowels. "What shall I do here, beloved brethren?" we hear him pathetically say.

> In such tumultuating inward commotion, what or how shall I speak? It needs tears rather than words, to express the grief with which the wound of our body is to be bewailed, the manifold loss of our once numerous community to be deplored. For who can be so hard and iron hearted, who so unmindful of fraternal charity, as to be able to stand in the midst of such vast wreck, such dismal and squalid ruins, with dry eyes, and not at once be forced rather to burst into tears, weeping forth his sorrow before it can he spoken? I mourn, brethren, I mourn together with you; nor is personal soundness and private health enough, in my case, to assuage my griefs; since the pastor is most wounded in the wound of his flock. I join my bosom severally with all, I share their various loads of desolation and grief. I wail with those that wail, and weep with those that weep, and feel myself fallen with those that fall. Those darts of the raging enemy have pierced at the same time my members, those cruel swords have entered my bowels. My mind has no exemption or freedom from the pressure of the persecution; I too am prostrated, by affection, in the prostration of my brethren.[23]

We might be ready to suppose, that where it cost so little to fall there would be little or no care afterwards to come to terms with the church, and that the fall would

22. [Cyprian, *De Lapsis*, 139; ACW 25:20; PPS 32:111. "{B}umpers of death" is an image of people drinking together; ACW reads: "with poisoned cup they toasted each other's death!"]

23. [Cyprian, *De Lapsis*, 136–37; ACW 25:15–16; PPS 32:104–5.]

easily prove thus for many a total and final apostacy. This however was not the case. The lapsed generally, it would seem, did not mean this, or at least were not able to carry things out to this extremity. Their compliance with idolatry was an expedient merely for avoiding persecution. They still believed Christianity to be true, and saw in the church the only ark of salvation for a ruined world. No sooner were they free from secular danger, accordingly, by means of their defection, than they began to show an anxiety, many of them at least, to be restored again to the state from which they had fallen. The reconciliation of the lapsed, their return into the bosom of the church, became thus a difficult and embarrassing question, before the persecution itself which gave rise to it had come to an end.

Deplorable as the defection seemed however, it was by no means a defeat of the Christian cause. While some fell, others stood. The true life and vigor of the church came more conspicuously into view, by, contrast with such partial desolation; and were found amply sufficient to sustain, and in the end to turn back, the full weight of the shock with which they were now tried. Many witnessed a good confession before the magistrate, and went joyfully into prison for the name of Christ; many went into voluntary exile, forsaking their property to save their lives with their faith; while a large number besides, who were not called upon to do so, showed themselves willing to face persecution for the same cause, if it were necessary, by simply refusing to do what was required by the government. The honor of the confessors was still farther advanced by the sharp tortures, that were employed without effect to subdue their constancy; and in the case of a number it came to its full consummation in martyrdom. To this whole army of the faithful Cyprian refers (*De Lapsis*, § 2. 3.), in tones of almost rapturous exultation. Speaking of the joy with which he looked forward to his meeting with the confessors, on his return from exile, he exclaims:

> Lo! the white robed cohort of Christ's soldiers, who have broken with firm front the impetuous shock of urgent persecution, prepared to suffer imprisonment, armed to endure death! Bravely ye have withstood the world, a glorious spectacle to God, an example for brethren to follow. The religious tongue owned Christ, in whom it had before professed to believe; the illustrious hands, which had been used only to divine works, refused now sacrilegious sacrifices; mouths sanctified by celestial food, after the body and blood of the Lord rejected the contamination of meat offered to idols; from the impious and wicked veil, with which the captive heads of the sacrifices were there bound, your heads remained free; the forehead made pure by God's sign could not brook the Devil's crown, but reserved itself for the crown of the Lord. With what delight does the church, as a mother, receive you to her bosom returning from battle! With what sense of blessedness and joy she throws open her gates, that you may enter, in serried ranks, bearing back trophies from the prostrate foe! Along with triumphing men come women also, who in this warfare with the world have conquered at the same time the weakness of their own sex.

> There too are virgins, in service now doubly glorious, and boys superior in virtue to their years. Nor is the multitude around you without part in this triumph, following close in the footsteps of your own conspicuous praise. In them is found also the same sincerity of heart, the same firm integrity of faith. Rooted immovably in the heavenly precepts, and established in the evangelical traditions, they were not dismayed by the prospect of banishment, torture, loss of properly, or loss of life. A term was set for the trial of faith. But he who remembers that he has renounced this world, regards no day of the world; nor does he now calculate times on earth, who looks for eternity from God. Let no one, beloved brethren, detract from this glory, or disparage the credit of those who have thus kept the faith by invidious remark. When the term set for renouncing was up, every one who had not renounced, in fact proclaimed himself a Christian. The first title of victory, is to have confessed the Lord when apprehended by the hands of the Gentiles. A second degree of glory, is to be reserved to the Lord by a cautious retreat. The first, is a public confession, the second private; that conquers the secular magistrate, this is content to keep a pure conscience before God who sees the heart.[24]

In another place (Ep. 10.), he gives us a glimpse of the severe character of the ordeal, through which these heroes and heroines of the cross were required to pass. He is writing to the martyrs and confessors themselves, yet in prison.

> I exult and rejoice, O most brave and blessed brethren, to hear of your faith and courage, in which our mother the church glories. She gloried not long since indeed, when the constancy of those who confessed Christ led them to accept voluntary banishment for his name. This present confession however, as it excels in suffering, is in proportion more illustrious in honor. With the thickening of the fight, the glory of the soldiers has also increased. Nor were ye deterred from the battle through fear of torments, but these served rather to provoke your zeal, so that ye returned still courageously to the terrible contest with unfaltering devotion. Some of your number, I learn, are already crowned; some the next thing to the same victorious coronation; while all, whose glorious company fills the prison, are animated with similar and equal ardent resolution for carrying on the contest; as becomes soldiers in the divine camp of Christ, whose firm faith no blandishments should deceive, no threats terrify, no pains and tortures overcome, since greater is he who is in us than he who is in this world, and no earthly punishment can be so mighty to cast down as the divine protection is to raise and uphold. Proof of this has been had in the glorious engagement of our brethren, who leading the way to others in overcoming torments have confronted the battle with an example of courage and faith, till the battle itself has been conquered and forced to yield. With what praises shall I proclaim your merit, most brave brethren? How sufficiently extol the strength of your resolution, the perseverance of your faith?

---

24. [Cyprian, *De Lapsis*, 135–36; ACW 25:13–15; PPS 32:100–104.]

Document 3: Cyprian[: First Article].

> Ye bore to the completion of glory the most excruciating torture, and yielded not to punishments which might be said rather to yield at last to you. Crowns brought pains to an end, which torments failed to reach. Torture was increased and protracted, not so as to break down the constancy of faith, but only to bear the men of God more speedily to the Lord. The admiring crowd of witnesses, saw the celestial conflict, the conflict of God, the spiritual contest, the battle of Christ, where his servants stood with free voice, with uncorrupted mind, with divine courage, naked indeed of secular armor, but equipped as believers in the arms of faith. The tortured stood stronger than their tormentors, and beaten and torn limbs vanquished those who beat and tore. Faith showed itself insuperable to the long sustained fury of the assault, even when at last, the body a broken wreck, it was not limbs now so much as wounds that were tortured in the servants of God. Blood flowed that might extinguish the conflagration of persecution, that might quench with glorious gore the flames and fires of hell. O what a sight was that to the Lord, how sublime, how great, how acceptable in God's eyes through the consecrated faithfulness of his soldiery; as it is written in the Psalms, the Holy Ghost addressing and admonishing us also in like words: *Precious in the sight of the Lord is the death of his saints.* Precious truly is that death, which buys immortality with the price of its blood, which wins a crown by the completion of virtue.[25]

The man who could write in this style was actuated certainly by no selfish worldly consideration, in holding himself personally aloof from the scene of conflict whose triumphs he describes in such glowing terms. We are bound to believe him, when he declares (Ep. 7.)[26] his anxiety to be back among his suffering people, and represents himself as engaged by a sense of duty only to delay his return. His whole soul was with his flock. He makes the cause of the martyrs and confessors his own, and seems to share with them the glory of their testimony for Christ. It is a subject for congratulation only that one and another, from time to time, are brought to seal this testimony with death. Let those who are still left behind in prison, be ambitious only of the same illustrious coronation.

> If the hour of conflict calls, face it boldly, fight bravely, knowing that ye fight under the eyes of your present Lord, and by the confession of his name are advancing to his own glory; who moreover is no mere spectator of his contending servants, but also wrestles and contends in us, and while he crowns is at the same time crowned himself in the issue of our combat.[27]

Such martyrdom, and such readiness for martyrdom, are regarded as the highest ornament of the cause to which they belong.

---

25. [*Epist.*, 18–19; *Letters*, 1:71–73; quoting Ps 116:15.]
26. [*Epist.*, 14–15; *Letters*, 1:67.]
27. [*Epist.*, 21; *Letters*, 1:74.]

> O blessed church ours, to be so irradiated with the rays of divine favor, to be made so illustrious by the glorious blood of martyrs in our own days. It was white before by the good works of the brethren; now it has become purple through martyr's blood. Its garlands lack neither lilies nor roses. Let all strive now for the ample dignity of either distinction; let them lay hold of crowns, either white by work or purple by suffering. In the heavenly camp both peace and war have their own flowers, to crown the glory of the Christian soldier.[28]

While he magnifies in this way the honor of the martyrs, he is by no means unmindful of their wants while still in the body. The presbyters and deacons are urged to keep a continual eye on the necessities, both of those who were thrown into prison, and of others also who in their poverty continued faithful to Christ. The funds of the church must be steadily applied to their relief. For this the clergy held such money in their hands. His own portion of course was not to be spared. "I beg of you," he writes in one place (Ep. 7.),

> to have good care of the widows, of infirm persons, and of all the poor. Also let strangers, if any are in need, be helped out of my own amount placed in charge of our colleague Rogatianus; to whom, lest this may possibly be already all laid out, I now send also by the acolyth [acolyte] Naricus another sum, that cases of distress may be the more readily and largely helped.[29]

Due regard must be had still more to spiritual wants. The confessors are urged to give themselves to heavenly meditations and prayers. By the daily sacrifice of the altar especially, they must arm themselves for the great conflict. The priests must visit them in turns, one at a time with his assisting deacon, to "offer" in their behalf; going thus singly and alternately to avoid exciting attention; for which reason also the brethren generally must not go to see them in crowds; lest it should rouse jealousy, and lead to a denial of access to them altogether. "Would that my situation and office," he exclaims in one of his letters (Ep. 12),

> allowed me to be now present. Most readily and cheerfully would I fulfil, with solemn ministry, all the duties of love towards our most brave brethren. But let your diligence be a substitute for my care, and do all that should be done for those, who are distinguished through the divine favor by such merits of faith and virtue. Let the bodies also of any, who though not put to the torture in prison yet depart this life there by a glorious end, receive attention and affectionate care. For neither courage nor honor are wanting in their case, to place them on the roll of the blessed martyrs. For themselves, they have suffered all that they showed themselves ready and willing to suffer. [. . .] They have endured, faithful, and firm, and unconquerable, even unto death. Where to will and confession in prison and bonds is added the term of dying, the martyr's

28. [*Epist.*, 21; *Letters*, 1:75.]
29. [*Epist.*, 15; *Letters*, 1:67.]

> glory is complete. Finally take note also of the days on which they depart, that we may be able to celebrate their commemoration among the memories of the martyrs. Although Tertullus, our most faithful and devoted brother, who with his other care shown toward the brethren in every active service is not wanting in attention to this object also, will continue to inform me of the days on which our blessed brethren in prison pass into immortality by the end of a glorious death, that we may celebrate oblations and sacrifices here for their commemoration; which we hope soon to celebrate with you also, by the protection of the Lord.[30]

The style in which Cyprian addresses these sufferers for the name of Christ, it has sometimes been remarked, is not just according to modern evangelical rule. There is often what we can hardly help feeling to be an undue glorification, not only of the martyrs already dead, but of those also who were steadfastly aspiring after the same crown. It seems to be taken too easily for granted, that this crown formed as a matter of course a direct passport to the abodes of bliss. The grand point is made to be simply enduring to the end. We hear no warnings on the danger of self-deception, no calls to anxious self-examination. The subjective side of the Christian salvation is most completely merged in the objective. Then there is a strange want of caution or reserve, in speaking of personal merit. Secular soldiers could hardly be stimulated more directly, by the idea of high desert, or by the prospect of glory and renown. And yet it would be a great mistake, to suppose that this implied no sense of the need of humility and vigilant diligence on the part of these confessors, no apprehension of the spiritual dangers to which they were still exposed. Cyprian in fact often refers to this. He felt that the merit of a good confession, and the praises bestowed upon it, might become a snare; and he abounds in exhortations accordingly, enforcing the necessity of a subsequently pious walk and conversation to make such credit full and complete. We learn from him too, that there was but too much in the actual course of events to justify such anxious solicitude. Some few of the confessors at least fell into gross irregularities and sins. "I hear that some disgrace your number," he writes *Ep.* 13,

> and destroy the praise of your excellent name by their corrupt conduct; whom ye yourselves, as lovers and defenders of your own renown, are bound to rebuke, restrain, and correct. What reproach is it to your name, when one lives only to become intemperate or lascivious; another returns into the world, from which he had been expatriated, to be apprehended and punished afterwards, not now as a Christian, but as a malefactor! I hear too that some are inflated and proud.[31]

---

30. [*Epist.*, 27–28; *Letters*, 1:81–82.]
31. [*Epist.*, 30; *Letters*, 1:84–85.]

It is a strange glimpse we have in this way, into the interior life of the church in these ancient times. There is much in it, which it is not easy at once to understand, but from which, rightly considered, there may be for this very reason a great deal also to learn.

The object of this sketch is, not merely to give some account of Cyprian, but to illustrate at the same time, from the mirror of his life and writings, the Christianity of the third century. The subject will be resumed hereafter.

J. W. N.

Cyprian: Second Article.[1]

[The Discipline of the "Lapsed"]

It has been already mentioned, that those who renounced their faith, under the sore pressure of the Decian persecution, were not willing for the most part to continue in this dreadful renunciation. Their sin of itself excluded them from the privileges and hopes of the Church. They professed repentance however, and sought to be restored to its communion. In many cases, this was without any proper evidence of such inward humiliation, and true change of mind, as the solemnity of the offence required. The very number of the delinquents stood in the way of a just regard to discipline. It was easy to make light account of an offence, into which it had been found so easy to fall, and in which so many were concerned. The system of discipline too was not definitely settled at all points, in regard to the treatment of those who were brought into such condemnation. The cases of transgression also were by no means all of one and the same moral enormity. There was room for distinctions, and so for pleas of special indulgence and favor. Most of all however, reliance was placed on the intercession of the confessors and martyrs. It had long been a standing belief in the Church, that such faithful witnesses for Christ, besides winning an extraordinary crown for themselves, had power by their prayers and merits to recommend in a peculiar way the cause of others also who applied to them for such help. Many felt that a recommendation from this quarter, was equivalent to a full right and title to the privilege it enforced. The lapsed in particular, who had forfeited all mark of their own, considered it a powerful advantage to come in for a sort of partnership interest, in this way, in the merit of those who by their sufferings might be said to have made good in some sense to the Church, the failure and fall of her less constant children. Recourse was had to them accordingly in prison, for letters of peace, as they were called, or written testimonials, recommending such as received them to pardon and reconciliation with the Church. Such intercession was supposed to be specially of force, when obtained from one who was on the point of sealing his testimony with blood; the crown of actual martyrdom gave additional weight to the patronage, which was thus transferred from earth to heaven. Something of the same authority however was felt to belong to all the

1. [*MR* 4 (July 1852) 335–87. For DeBie's analysis of this essay, see *John Williamson Nevin*, 283–86.]

confessors. By showing themselves willing and ready to die for Christ, if necessary, they were all regarded as standing high in the Divine favor, and as having special and extraordinary claims to respect among men. To the exercise of such patronage as we have now in consideration, so long as it was kept within proper bounds, there could be no reasonable objection. There was a true deep and solid ground for it in the mysterious constitution of Christianity itself. But in the nature of the case, it was very liable to run into the form of an abuse. The confessors were by no means all wise and discreet. Many of them in fact were very ignorant. Their very zeal for the salvation of souls might betray them into a false compassion. To some of them too, there could hardly fail to be a snare in the function of authority itself, which they were called to exercise in this high spiritual form. It carried in it a dangerous aliment for pride in one direction, as well as for something like religious fanaticism in another. Certificates and recommendations were liable to be given in this way with too much facility and freedom, and to be so used afterwards as to interfere seriously with the proper ends of church discipline. Such was the abuse that actually followed on no inconsiderable scale. Through the weakness or levity of some of the confessors, these indulgences, or letters of peace, were given to applicants of every character and class, in the greatest profusion and without any sort of discrimination or judgment. In some cases, they were put into so loose a form as to be tickets of admission into the church, not simply for the holder, but for his family also or friends, as many as he might choose to embrace under the convenient privilege, "*Communicet ille cum suis.*[2]" Armed with such powerful recommendation, a great crowd of temporary apostates, now anxious professedly to repair their past fault, knocked loudly at the door of the church, demanding rather than begging to be restored to its privileges. To make the matter still worse, a portion of the clergy showed, a disposition to yield to the pressure, and allowed themselves to communicate with the lapsed, on terms which overthrew in truth all order and discipline. This served of course to encourage their violent impatience, and made it more difficult than it would have been otherwise to deal with the case in the right way.

The occasion was serious and trying. The cause of the lapsed might be said to be a popular one, in view of the numbers who were concerned in it, and in view also of the great credit of the confessors and martyrs who seemed to be enlisted to a certain extent on its side. It required no little courage to face it with direct opposition. This however Cyprian did not hesitate to do, with all the authority which he felt to belong to him in the character of a bishop. He saw the whole discipline of the church at stake, in the course things were threatening to take. But it was no hierarchical feeling merely, no zeal simply for the honor of his own order, that engaged him to take his stand. He saw in this relaxation of discipline, an extreme danger at the same time for the souls of those, in whose favor the deceitful privilege was sought. However desirable it was for those who had fallen to be restored to the peace of the church,

2. [Trans. "that he might commune with them."]

this could be done effectually only through real humiliation and penance on their own part, making room for ecclesiastical absolution afterwards in a regular and valid form. Such was the necessary wholesome medicine, which God had provided for the healing of sin. There must be on the one side an *exomologesis* or confession, going to the bottom of the offence and carrying along with it the force of a real penitential expiation or satisfaction in some form; and then on the other side, to complete this, a solemn formal release under the hand of the ministering priest, bringing relief to the conscience from God himself. Uniting in it itself both these conditions, reconciliation with the church might be regarded as something more than an empty outward ceremony; it carried in it the force of a really Divine transaction, which served actually to reconcile the subject at the same time with Christ and with God, and gave him a title sacramentally to all the blessings of heaven. But the abuse before us tended towards the destruction of this salutary order on both sides. It turned the exomologesis into a superficial sham on one side; while on the other it obscured the proper sense of the grace of absolution, as a power proceeding through the priesthood only from the general church. It was under this view especially, that Cyprian set himself with all his might in opposition to the irregularity; sending letter upon letter from the place of his retreat, now to the clergy, now to the people, and now to the confessors themselves, full of instruction and warning with regard to the whole case. His tract, *De Lapsis,* is taken up mainly with the same subject. With great earnestness and firmness, he insists that the lapsed should not be at once restored to the peace of the church. They were not indeed to be rejected without mercy, as persons for whom there was no hope. On the contrary, they must be received as penitents, and encouraged in this character to desire and seek, as also to expect in the end, a release from church censure; but in the nature of the case, this course of penitential trial, where the offence had been so great, ought to be of long duration, and in a form to show true inward grief and humiliation. The terms of restoration must be governed in some measure by the character of the offence in different cases; but to fix and determine them was no business for private judgment merely or hasty particular decision. Let the persecution first come fairly to an end. Then the bishops might come together in council, and after suitable deliberation adopt such rules and decrees, as would secure uniform practice and meet all the exigencies of the case. In the mean time, the confessors must exercise their prerogative with becoming humility, and not in such a way as to do violence to the Divine order of the church; lest the merit of their good confession should be again neutralized and made of no account, by what must be regarded as an act of treason to the very cause in whose behalf it had taken place.

Addressing the general body of the people, Cyprian writes on the subject as follows:[3]

---

3. Ep. 17, ed. Tauchn. [*Epist.*, 38–40; *Letters*, 1:96–98].

That you mourn and grieve over the ruin of our brethren, I know from myself, most dearly beloved, who also groan with you on their account, and am in great sorrow and pain, and feel what the beloved apostle has said, (2 Cor. xi: 29): "Who is weak, and I am not weak? Who is offended, and I burn not?" Or as he has it in another place, (1 Cor. xii: 26): "Whether one member suffer, all the members suffer with it; or one member be honoured, all the members rejoice with it." So I suffer and grieve for our brethren, who fallen and prostrated by the stress of persecution have carried away with them a part of our bowels, inflicting on us thus the sharp pain of their own wounds; which nevertheless the Divine mercy is able to cure. The case however, in my judgment, calls for deliberation and caution, lest by a too forward usurpation of peace more heavy occasion only be given for the Divine displeasure. The blessed martyrs have written to us with regard to certain persons, commending their desires to our consideration. When the Lord shall first have given us all peace restoring us to the church, the cases will be examined severally along with your presence and judgment. I hear however that some of the presbyters, unmindful of the gospel, and not heeding what the martyrs have written to us, nor reserving to the bishop the honor of his priesthood and see, have already begun to communicate with the lapsed, and to offer for them and give them the eucharist—things that should be reached only in due course and order. For whereas in smaller offences which are not committed directly against God, penance is performed for a suitable time, and confession is made with proper probation of life in the case of the penitent, and no one can come to communication unless through the imposition of hands upon him first by the bishop and clergy; how much more is it needful, in the case of these most heavy and extreme offences, that all things should be conducted cautiously and wisely according to the discipline of the Lord! This indeed our presbyters and deacons ought to have urged, for the welfare of the sheep committed to their care, and to guide them by the divine rule into the way of sueing for salvation. I know both the tractableness and the reverence of our people, who would have given themselves diligently to the work of satisfaction and deprecation towards God, had not some of the presbyters to please them led them astray. Be it your part then to exercise over the minds of the lapsed severally a wise and wholesome influence, in conformity with the divine precepts. Let no one unseasonably pluck fruit which is still unripe; let no one commit to the deep again his vessel battered and pierced by the waves, before it has been diligently repaired; let no one hasten to receive and put on a rent garment, if he see it not mended by a skilful workman and made fit to wear by the art of the fuller. Let them listen patiently, I pray, to our counsel; let them wait for our return; that when we shall have come to you through the mercy of God, we may be able in a council of our fellow bishops to examine the letters and requests of the blessed martyrs, according to the discipline of the Lord, in the presence of the confessors and with the assistance also of your judgment. In regard to this, I have

Document 3: Cyprian: Second Article.

written letters both to the clergy and to the martyrs and confessors, which I have directed to be read also in your hearing. My desire is, brethren dearly beloved and longed for, that ye may always prosper in the Lord and bear us in mind. Farewell.

In his letter to the clergy, (Ep. 16, ed. Tauchn.), he refers still more sharply to the conduct of those presbyters, who had encouraged the disorder of which he complains. They had been treating his authority with contempt before. He had held his peace for a time; but the case now had become too serious for silence; not only the honor of the episcopate was invaded; that might be overlooked; but the safety of souls also was in question. The case of the lapsed was in danger of being made worse, instead of better, by a hollow and groundless restoration of peace. Their offence had been of the heaviest kind, and called for corresponding remedy and help.

> He who conceals this from our brethren, deceives them deplorably; so that those who might do true penance and satisfy the paternal and merciful God by their prayers and works, are seduced into greater perdition, and those who might rise experience a still deeper fall. For while in the case of smaller sins the offenders do penance for proper time, and in the order of discipline come to confession, and by the imposition of the hands of the bishop and clergy receive the right of communicating; now in an unripe time, the persecution still continuing and the church itself not yet restored to peace, these are admitted to communion, and their name is offered; and no penance yet done, no confession yet made, no hand yet laid upon them by the bishop and clergy, they are allowed to receive the eucharist; of which it is written: "Whosoever shall eat this bread, or drink this cup of the Lord, unworthily, shall be guilty of the body and blood of the Lord" (1 Cor. xi: 27).[4]

The fault of all this lay with those, whose business it was to instruct the people, and to keep them to a proper observance of the divine precepts. The blessed martyrs too were wronged by what was done. *They* had, with becoming regard for the rights of the bishop, referred the case to him for favorable judgment, after peace should have been restored to the suffering church; these unruly priests, on the contrary,

> refusing us the honor allowed by the martyrs along with the confessors, and disregarding the law and rule of the Lord the observance of which is enjoined by these same martyrs and confessors, before the fear of persecution is over, before our return, almost before the decease itself of the martyrs, communicate with the lapsed, and offer and give the eucharist; whereas if even the martyrs, overlooking scripture in the heat of their zeal, had desired anything going against the law of the Lord, they ought to have been set right by the admonition of the presbyters and deacons, according to usage in time past.[5]

4. [*Epist.*, 37; *Letters*, 1:94.]
5. [*Epist.*, 37–38; *Letters*, 1:95.]

Writing to the martyrs and confessors, (Ep. 15), he takes occasion to say:

> Official concern and the fear of the Lord compels us to admonish you by letter, most brave and blessed brethren, that ye who have so devotedly and courageously kept the faith of the Lord, may show like care for the observance also of the Lord's discipline and law. For whilst all the soldiers of Christ should be true to the orders of their leader, it is most of all fit that they should be obeyed by you, who have become an example to others of virtue and piety. And I had supposed indeed, that the presbyters and deacons, who are on the ground, would admonish and instruct you fully with regard to the law of the gospel; as it was always the custom, under our predecessors, for the deacons to assist and guide the wishes of the martyrs in prison by counsel and scriptural rule. But now with the greatest grief I learn, not only that there has been no such suggestion to you of the divine precepts, but that even what ye yourselves proposed in the way of caution towards God and honor towards his priest, is made of no effect by some of the presbyters, who forget what is due both to God and the bishop. For whereas you had written to me, desiring your prayer to be examined, and peace to be restored to certain lapsed persons, when we should be able to meet with the clergy at the close of the persecution, these unfaithful ministers—against the rule of the gospel, against your respectful petition also, before the doing of penance, before confession made of the most serious and extreme offence, before the imposition of hands by the bishop and clergy for repentance—dare to offer for them, and to give them the eucharist, that is, to profane the sacred body of the Lord; since it is written: "Whosoever shall eat this bread, or drink this cup of the Lord, unworthily, shall be guilty of the body and blood of the Lord." And in this there may be some excuse indeed for the lapsed. For who that is dead may not in haste to be made alive? Who may not be eager to run to his own salvation? But it is the business of the rulers to keep the law, and to instruct the hasty or ignorant, lest they become butchers, who should be shepherds, of the sheep. For when they concede what tends to destruction they do but deceive; and the fallen are not raised thus, but by offending God are urged into greater ruin. Let them then learn from you, what they ought rather themselves to have taught; let them reserve your petitions and wishes for the bishop, and wait a mature and quiet time for giving the peace for which you intercede. First let the mother have peace from the Lord; then may your petitions be considered for the peace of the children.[6]

They must not suffer themselves, he goes on to say, to be overcome by the importunity of those who sought their aid. The case called for the greatest care and circumspection. As the friends of the Lord, hereafter along with him to judge the world [1 Cor 6:2], they should look diligently into the circumstances and merits of each single case; that no occasion for reproach might be given to the surrounding heathen world.

---

6. [*Epist.*, 34–35; *Letters*, 1:90–91; quoting 1 Cor 11:27.]

Document 3: Cyprian: Second Article.

In the tract *De Lapsis,* we have the case put into the same form still more at large.

> The priest of God must not deceive with false concessions, but provide for salutary remedies. He is a poor physician, who handles the tumid recesses of wounds with sparing hand, and by saving exaggerates the virus which is seated in the interior depths of the body. The wound must be opened and cut, the amputation of diseased parts must make room for a more vigorous cure. However the patient may complain and cry out for pain, he will give thanks afterwards, when he comes to the sense of health.[7]

The neglect of such salutary discipline forms, in the eyes of Cyprian, a new calamity full as deplorable as the apostacy which had gone before.

> A new form of desolation, dearly beloved brethren, has broken forth; and as if the storm of persecution had been a light thing, treacherous mischief and flattering ruin are carried to their height under the name of mercy. Against the vigor of the gospel, against the law of the Lord and of God, communication is thrown open by the temerity of certain persons to the unprepared—an empty and false peace, dangerous to those who give it, and of no worth to such as receive it. They require not patience in order to health, nor true medicine by satisfaction; penitence is driven from the breast, the recollection of the most grave and extreme offence is put out of the way. The wounds of the dying are covered, the deadly plague seated in the inmost vitals is hid under a feigned sorrow. Those who return from the altars of the Devil approach the holy place of the Lord with tainted and unclean hands; still reeking as it were from the deadly food of idols, their throats yet exhaling their own crime and breathing the smell of dire contagion, they invade the Lord's body, in the face of the scripture which exclaims: "The soul that eateth of the flesh of the sacrifice of peace-offerings, that pertain unto the Lord, having his uncleanness upon him, even that soul shall be cut off from his people" (Lev. vii: 20). So the Apostle testifies: "Ye cannot drink the cup of the Lord and the cup of devils; ye cannot be partakers of the Lord's table, and of the table of devils" (1 Cor. x: 21); as he threatens also the disobedient with this denunciation: "Whosoever shall eat this bread, or drink this cup of the Lord, unworthily, shall be guilty of the body and blood of the Lord" (1 Cor. xi: 27). In contempt of all this, before expiation of offence, before confession made of crime, before the purgation of conscience by sacrifice and the hand of the priest, before any pacification of the displeasure of an angry threatening Saviour, violence is done to his body and blood, and they sin now more against the Lord with hands and mouth, than when they denied him before. They take that for peace, which some trade off to them with fallacious words. It is however not peace, but war; no one can be joined to the church, who is separated from the gospel. What? Do they call injury a benefit? Do they set forth impiety under the name of piety? Are

---

7. [Cyprian, *De Lapsis*, 142; ACW 25:24; PPS 32:118.]

> those who should be weeping and calling upon their Lord continuously, to be stopped in their penitential lamentations by the pretence of communication? To such lapsed persons this is what hail is to fruit, a whirlwind to trees, a destroying murrain to cattle, a cruel tempest to ships.[8]

All such agencies work, not to cure and save, but only to kill and destroy. It is another persecution in truth, by which the subtle adversary seeks to cut off the last hope for the lapsed, by silencing their grief, causing them to forget their sin, and so preventing them from the use of a long and thorough course of tears and prayers, the only penance that could bring them to a true peace with their offended Lord.

> Let no one deceive himself or fall into mistake. The Lord alone can exercise mercy; he only can pardon sins committed against himself, who has carried our sins, who has suffered for us, whom God has given for our iniquities. Man cannot be greater than God; neither can the servant by his indulgence remit or pardon, what has been committed in the way of heavy offence against the Lord; such thought rather must add to the crime of the offender, by his forgetting the word: "Cursed be the man that trusteth in man [Jer 17:5]." The Lord is to be entreated, the Lord is to be appeased by our satisfaction, who has said that he will deny those that deny him to whom alone all judgment has been committed by the Father. We believe indeed, that the merits of the martyrs and works of the righteous are of much avail with the Judge; but when the day of judgment shall have come, when after the close of the present life and world the people of Christ shall stand before his tribunal.[9]

The firm position taken by the bishop served to control to a certain extent the disorder here brought into view, and might have corrected it entirely perhaps, if it had not been for the advantage taken of it by the small party which had been secretly opposed to him, as we have before seen, from the time of his election to the episcopate. At the head of the faction stood now the deacon Felicissimus.[10] The time seemed favorable for an insurrectionary movement; and occasion was taken accordingly from a particular church visitation, which Cyprian had ordered by commission previously to his own return, to raise the standard of open revolt. Felicissimus, with Novatian and four other presbyters, refused to acknowledge the authority which it was attempted to exercise in this form, and undertook to establish in fact a separate and independent church: into which the lapsed were encouraged to enter without farther difficulty or delay.[11] Many of them, impatient of the discipline to which they were required to

---

8. [Cyprian, *De Lapsis*, 142–43; ACW 25:24–26; PPS 32:119–21.]

9. [Cyprian, *De Lapsis*, 144; ACW 25:27; PPS 32:121–22.]

10. [Felicissimus (dates unknown), was the leader of the group who opposed Cyprian on the reinstatement of the lapsed. He was able to gain a following while Cyprian was absent from his office.]

11. [This schism is known as Novatianism. Of the life of its founder, Novatian, few details are known. He seems to have had a significant following of those who agreed that Pope Cornelius was too lax in his acceptance of the lapsed back into fellowship. Novatian was likely martyred under a renewed

Document 3: Cyprian: Second Article.

submit in the regular church, fell but too easily into the snare. Some of the confessors also, who had become involved as patrons in the cause of these bad clients, were led away unhappily by the same spirit of defection. Altogether the movement amounted in a short time to quite a serious schism. Cyprian brings the whole case before us, in a letter addressed to the people of his charge, (Ep. 43), as follows:

> Although, beloved brethren, the most faithful and exemplary presbyter Virtius, the presbyters Rogatianus and Numidicus,[12] confessors made illustrious by divine distinction, as also the deacons, good men and devoted in all obedience to ecclesiastical order, with the other ministers, give you the full attention of their presence, and cease not to confirm you severally by assiduous exhortations, as well as to direct and reform the minds of the lapsed with salutary counsels—so far as I can nevertheless I also admonish you, and in such way as I can visit you, by letter. By letter I say, dearly beloved brethren. For it is made inexpedient for me to return to you personally before Easter, through the malignity and treachery of certain presbyters; who mindful of their former conspiracy, and retaining their old grudge against my episcopate, that is against your vote and God's judgment, renew of late their ancient opposition, profanely plotting against our authority in their usual insidious style. And herein truly the providence of God appears, that without will or wish on our part, nay in the midst of our indulgence and silence, they have paid the penalty they deserved, by expelling themselves without expulsion from us, giving sentence against themselves in their own conscience, excommunicating themselves from the church, as wicked conspirators against your will and that of God, by their own voluntary act. Now the faction of Felicissimus is disclosed, whence it came, and wherein it has had its root and strength. These before encouraged and urged some of the confessors, not to abide in concord with their bishop and observe the ecclesiastical discipline with faith and quietness according to the precepts of the Lord, not to maintain the glory of their confession by a corresponding blameless walk and conversation. And as though it had been a small thing, to have corrupted the minds of some confessors, and to have aimed at arming a portion of the ruptured brotherhood against the priesthood of God, they have now turned themselves with venomous deception to the destruction of the lapsed, seeking to turn them away, sick and wounded as they are and by the calamity of their fall disabled for vigorous counsels, from the cure of their wound, and by the interruption of their prayers and deprecations, by which God should be appeased with long continuous satisfaction, seducing them into deadly presumption by the show of a false and deceitful peace.

---

persecution under the Emperor Valerian (199–260) in 257–58.]

12. [These presbyters—of which nothing further is known—were faithful to the instructions which Cyprian had given on the administration of the church in contrast to those who followed Novatus of Carthage who opposed him and eventually joined the Novatians.]

But I beseech you, brethren, be on your guard against the snares of the Devil, and diligently watch for your own salvation against the mortal delusion. This is another persecution, another trial. These five presbyters are nothing different from those five officers, whom the late edict joined with the magistracy, that they might subvert our faith, that they might entangle in deadly snares the weak hearts of brethren by leading them to deny the truth. The case is now the same, the same subversion is again at work to the ruin of souls through the five presbyters joined with Felicissimus; in this namely, that God is not entreated, that he who has denied Christ is not led to deprecate the anger of Christ thus denied, that after the guilt of crime penance also is done away, that there is no satisfaction to the Lord through the bishops and priests, but that with the desertion of the Lord's priests, against the evangelical rule, a new tradition of sacrilegious institution is set up and made of force. And whereas it had been before agreed upon both by us and by the clergy, and confessors of the metropolis [Rome],[13] as well as by the bishops generally whether in our province or beyond the sea, that no new regulation should be made in regard to the cause of the lapsed, until we should all come together, and with joint consultation settle upon a course in which both discipline and mercy should be properly regarded, this our judgment is rebelled against, and a factious conspiracy formed to overthrow all sacerdotal authority and power. What distress do I not suffer now, beloved brethren, that I cannot come to you in person, to address you severally myself, and to exhort you after the rule of our Lord and his gospel! It was not enough—the exile now of a second year and mournful separation from your face and sight, the incessant grief that gives me away from you no rest in my sore lamentations, the tears that flow day and night because the priest, whom ye created with so much love and zeal, is not yet allowed to salute you and meet your affectionate embrace. To our languishing mind is added now this farther distress, that in so great anxiety and need I cannot myself run to your aid, lest through the passion and craft of the traitors our presence should give rise to new tumult, and that the bishop, who ought to consult in all things for peace and tranquillity may not appear to have himself given occasion for sedition, and to have provoked fresh persecution. From where I am however, beloved brethren, I counsel and warn you, trust not rashly pernicious words, assent not lightly to declarations which are false, take not darkness for light, night for day, famine for food, thirst for drink, poison for medicine, death for salvation. Let neither their age nor authority deceive you, who resembling in wickedness the two elders, that of old sought to corrupt and violate the chaste Susannah,[14] endeavour by spurious doctrines to corrupt the purity of the church and violate evangelical truth.

13. ["Rome" was in the notes in the original; Nevin inserted it in the text.]

14. [Dan 13 (Greek version): when Susannah rejects the advances of two elders, they falsely accuse her of immorality and have her condemned to death. Daniel exposes them by inquiring what tree they saw Susannah sin under; they give different answers.]

Document 3: Cyprian: Second Article.

The Lord cries aloud and says: "Hearken not unto the words of the false prophets, who speak a vision of their own heart, and not out of the mouth of the Lord; who say to them that reject the word of the Lord, Ye shall have peace" (Jer. xxiii: 16, 17). Those now offer peace, who themselves have no peace; those pretend to bring back the lapsed into the church, who have themselves withdrawn from the church. God is one, and Christ is one, and there is one church, and one cathedra founded on the rock by the Lord's voice. No other altar can be set up, there can be no new priesthood, by reason of the one altar and one priesthood. He who gathers elsewhere, scatters. Adulterous, impious, sacrilegious is whatever human passion may institute, in violation of a Divine arrangement. Keep far away from the contagion of such men, and avoid their word as you would flee from a cancer or plague, mindful of the Lord's warning; "They be blind leaders of the blind; and if the blind lead the blind, both shall fall into the ditch" [Matt 15:14]. They intercept your prayers, which with us you pour forth to God day and night, that you may appease him with just satisfaction; they intercept your tears, by which you wash away the guilt of the offence which has been committed; they intercept the peace, which ye seek truly and faithfully from the mercy of the Lord, not knowing that it is written: "That prophet, or that dreamer of dreams, which hath spoken to turn you away from the Lord your God shall be put to death" (Deut. xiii: 5). Let no one, dear brethren, turn you aside from the ways of the Lord, let no one force you Christians from the gospel of Christ, let no one sunder the children of the church from the church. Let those perish alone, who have willed to perish; let those remain alone on the outside of the church, who have withdrawn from the church; let those alone be separate from the bishops, who have rebelled against the bishops; let those alone suffer the penalty of their conspiracy, who by your vote formerly and God's judgment now have deserved such condemnation.[15]

Here we are introduced to Cyprian's doctrine of the Church, which may be said to underlie and condition his whole theological system. Opportunity was soon given for bringing it into view, with yet clearer as well as more ample representation, and in terms of still more commanding decision and force.

[Cyprian's Return and The Unity of the Church]

His return to Carthage took place soon after Easter a. 251, after an absence of about fourteen months. The persecution had run its course; and the way was now open for the re-appearance of the bishop, in the full exercise of his episcopal functions, without danger of new commotion. The first great concern was to settle, in provincial council, the course to be pursued throughout the Church in regard to the lapsed. Such

---

15. [*Epist.*, 83–86; *Letters*, 2:61–65.]

a system was adopted, as the necessities of the whole case, in the united judgment of the assembled bishops, appeared to require and demand. Those who had so grievously sinned, were not to be lightly set free from the bonds of their guilt. They must submit to a long and severe course of humiliation and sorrow, making satisfaction to God, and proving the sincerity of their repentance, by patient continuance in prayers and tears. With this however was held out, for their encouragement, the hope and prospect of reconciliation with the church at some future time; that they might not be thrown into despair, and so be led to fall back as hopeless outcasts from the church into the life of the heathen world. Regard was to be had, at the same time, to the nature and circumstances of each particular case of offence, some being entitled in this view of course to much greater indulgence than others. It was still farther provided, that where there was danger of death, in the case of a penitent who seemed to be sincere, an earlier reconciliation should take place, so that none thus earnestly seeking the peace of the church might be doomed to the great calamity of leaving the world without it. Some time after, as we shall see, a general relaxation or indulgence was allowed on this principle, in view of a new persecution under the Emperor Gallus;[16] for which, it was held, the penitents could not be properly prepared, without the aids of grace that were to be found only in the bosom of the church.

In the same council, judgment was solemnly given against the schism of Felicissimus, with sentence of excommunication upon all who had joined themselves to his party and cause. Some attempts were still made afterwards to carry forward the rebellious movement. Among other measures, the party set up in the end a new bishop of Carthage, in opposition to Cyprian, and made a special effort to have the appointment acknowledged and approved at Rome. But all proved of small account. In the course of a few years, the new church seems to have ended in nothing.

In the mean time, however, a more serious schism had taken place in another part of the church. Novatian, a presbyter of the church of Rome, had come to stand at the head of a party, which set itself in opposition to the regular bishop Cornelius.[17] Ostensibly, the main question of controversy was the course of treatment to be pursued in regard to the lapsed. Novatian took the ground, that those who had thus fallen from the faith could in no case properly be received back again into the bosom of the church, but must be left to the uncovenanted mercy of God. In this respect, the schismatical movement at Rome was the direct opposite of that at Carthage; it taxed the discipline of the church with the want of that very severity, the exercise of which it was charged in the other case with carrying to excess. And yet that same Novatus, whose name figures in the Carthaginian faction, having made his way soon after to Rome, found no difficulty in making himself just as mischievously active here in the

---

16. [Trebonianus Gallus (206–53); the emperor who succeeded Decius. His reign was troubled and short. He was likely killed by his successor, Publius Licinius Valeriansus.]

17. [Cornelius (d. 253); elected as pope in 251 after the bishopric of Rome had been vacant for 14 months due to intense persecution. He was sent into exile by Gallus where he died as a martyr.]

Document 3: Cyprian: Second Article.

cause of Novatian as he had been before in that of Felicissimus. He seems to have been one of those restless spirits, with whom it is a sort of principle or maxim to go for any agitation that is against the existing order of things, and to whom the right of disorganization and revolution is especially *sacred*, whatever may be the occasion for its exercise. Cyprian, in one of his letters to Cornelius (Ep. 52),[18] gives him a very bad character. In Rome now, however, he was all zeal for the cause of strict and severe discipline in the church; and it seems to have been through his turbulent activity in a good measure, that this cause was brought to take the form of an organized schism, by the pretended elevation of Novatian to the episcopate, in opposition to the regular bishop Cornelius. Efforts were made subsequently to carry out the organization in a wide form, and to have it acknowledged in other provinces. The body in communion with Cornelius was charged with corruption. This was to be on the contrary a pure church. Such plausible pretension in fact deceived many. The Novatian schism carried for a time quite a formidable aspect. Its day however was short. It had no power to stand against the authority of the Catholic Church. Excommunicated first by a council at Rome, the party labored in vain to have the sentence reversed or nullified abroad. Great pains were taken especially to gain the interest of the African bishops. But Cyprian took measures to have the case fully understood; and the result was that the African church went fully in favor of Cornelius, and joined in the excommunication of the Novatians. The main significance of the schism was, in this way, that it formed a striking occasion for the development of the true idea of the Church, in its character of unity and wholeness, and furnished at the same time a powerful and most instructive exemplification of the divine strength that belongs to this heavenly constitution, under such view, for the accomplishment of its own ends. The occasion did not create the doctrine of the Church, for which it became for all ages so conspicuous a theatre. It merely brought into view the fact, which it is the object of that doctrine to affirm and assert. The unity of the Church was the actual rock, on which the Novatian schism was dashed to pieces. The controversy lay between the authority of this supernatural constitution, regarded as a real historical fact in the world,[19] and a simply human movement which affected to treat it as no fact by presumptuously thrusting itself into its place. No one saw this more clearly than Cyprian; and no one contributed more largely, or with greater effect, to place the controversy in its true light, and to bring out, in doing so, the high and solemn sense of that holy "sacrament of unity," as he terms it, in which is comprehended emphatically for all time the unconquerable strength of the true Catholic Church. Most of the letters we have from him during the pontificate of Cornelius, fifteen in number, are mainly occupied, directly or indirectly, with this great subject. It gave occasion also to his celebrated tract *De Unitate Ecclesiae*.[20]

18. [*Epist.*, 99–101; *Letters*, 2:82–85.]

19. [On this terminology, see above "Early Christianity," 142.]

20. [The full title of the tract is *De catholicae ecclesiae unitate. On the Unity of the Church*, in PPS 32:146–81.]

"Cornelius was made bishop," he says (Ep. 55),

> by the judgment of God and his Christ, by the almost unanimous voice of the clergy, by the vote of the people as far as present, and by the collegiate action of a number of the best older bishops, when no one had been appointed before him, when the place of Fabian [his martyred predecessor],[21] that is when the place of Peter and the dignity of the sacerdotal seat, was vacant; which having been thus occupied by the will of God and the firm consent of all of us, whoever may now pretend to be made bishop, he must be made necessarily on the outside, and can have no ecclesiastical ordination, as not holding the unity of the church. Be he who he may, and how much so ever he may arrogate to himself, he is profane, he is foreign, he is without. And since after the first there can be no second, whoever is made after one, who ought to be alone, he is not second now but none.[22]

Afterwards, coming to the person of Novatian he says:

> It is not necessary to ask *what* he teaches, since he teaches without. Whoever and whatever he may be, he is no Christian who is not in Christ's church. Boast as he may of his philosophy, or make vain parade of his eloquence, the man who has not kept brotherly charity and ecclesiastical unity, has lost even all that he was before. Or shall he be counted a bishop, who, where there was a regular bishop in the church consecrated by sixteen fellow bishops, intriguingly seeks to be raised to this dignity in a false and foreign form, by the help of deserters; and whereas there is from Christ one church divided throughout the world into many members, likewise one episcopate spread abroad by a concordant multitude of many bishops, *he,* after the order handed down by God, after this compact full unity of the catholic church everywhere settled, undertakes to create a human church, and sends out his new apostles to many cities to plant the authority of this recent institution, and while through all provinces and cities bishops have long since been ordained, venerable in age, sound in faith, tried in times of pressure and persecution, dares to create over these other spurious bishops of his own fabrication! As if he could overrun the whole world with the obstinacy of his new attempt, or dissolve the compact organization of the church by the dissemination of his discord; not knowing, that schismatics are always fervid at the start, but have no power to grow, or to carry on what they have unlawfully begun, wearing out with the failure of their own bad zeal.[23]

---

21. [Fabian (d. 250); he was a long serving pope (236–50), though little is known of his personal life. He was martyred on January 20, 250 at the beginning of the Decian persecution. The bracketed text is Nevin's.]

22. [*Epist.,* 108; *Letters,* 3:38.]

23. [*Epist.,* 116–17; *Letters,* 3:48–49.]

Document 3: Cyprian: Second Article.

Even if he had been regularly elected and consecrated at first, he goes on to say, and had afterwards withdrawn from the unity of the church, his episcopate would by this fact alone have been made of no force. Only in the unity of the office, universally taken, can any single bishop have true jurisdiction or lawful power.

The tract *De Unitate Ecclesiae* is a formal exhibition and defence of this general proposition, that the Church in its universal catholic character is the one only Divinely constituted medium and channel of salvation, and that schism therefore, or separation from it, involves necessarily at the same time separation from Christ also and exposure to everlasting death. Open outward persecution, the author tells us, is not the only nor the worst form in which Christians have reason to fear the assaults of Satan. Such direct war is less dangerous, and more easy to be met and overcome, than his insidious approaches under the garb of friendship and peace. It is in this latter view especially, that he is called the Serpent. So he deceived our first parents. So he tried to deceive Christ also; but was defeated and foiled. We are required to avoid the first of these examples, and to follow the second. Thus only shall we win immortality in the footsteps of the Prince of Life. But how can we do this, unless we keep his commandments, hold fast to his prescribed rules? This alone is to be truly grounded on a rock, such as no storms or tempests can shake. To believe in Christ, we must do what he orders and requires; we must keep to the true way of salvation. Without such inward settlement, we shall be as chaff before the wind. What could be more subtle than the machinations of Satan, as now put forth in the name and under the show of Christianity itself? Seeing himself vanquished in the form of open heathenism, his altars forsaken, his temples deserted, through the growth of the new religion, he seeks now to reach by fraud what he has not been able to effect by force.

> He invents heresies and schisms, to overturn faith, corrupt truth, rend unity. Those whom he cannot retain in the blindness of the old way, he circumvents and deceives by the error of a new course. He bears away men from the Church itself, and while they seem to themselves to have already come to the light and left the darkness of this world, he infuses into them again without their knowing it other shades of night; so that although not standing with the gospel of Christ, and with his rule and law, they nevertheless call themselves Christians, and walking in darkness fancy that they have light, through the blandishing false art of the adversary; who, according to the word of the Apostle, transforms himself into an angel of light [2 Cor 11:14], and passes off his emissaries as ministers of righteousness, asserting night for day, perdition for salvation, despair under pretence of hope, Antichrist in the name of Christ, so as by plausible lies cunningly to make void the truth. This comes, beloved brethren, by not going back to the origin of the truth, not seeking the head, not observing the teaching of the heavenly master.[24]

---

24. [Cyprian, *De Unitate Ecclesiae*, in *Tract.*, 119 (§3); PPS 32:148–49.]

For the determination of this rule, Cyprian goes on to say, there is no need of long discourse and argument.

> A summary test of truth is at once at hand for faith. The Lord addresses Peter: "I say unto thee that thou art Peter, and on this rock I will build my Church, and the gates of hell shall not prevail against it. And I will give unto thee the keys of the kingdom of heaven; and whatsoever thou shalt bind on earth, shall be bound in heaven; and whatsoever thou shall loose on earth, shall be loosed in heaven" (Matth. xvi: 18, 19). Again he says to the same, after his resurrection: "Feed my sheep" (John xxi: 15, 17). [On that one he builds his church, and commits his sheep to him to be fed.][25] And although, after his resurrection, he gives like power to all the Apostles, and says: "As my Father hath sent me, even so send I you. Receive ye the Holy Ghost; whosoever sins ye remit, they are remitted unto them; and whosesoever sins ye retain, they are retained" (John xx: 21–23); still to make the unity clear, he provided by his authority that the origin of this same unity should start from one (*unitatis ejusdem originem ab uno incipientem sua auctoritate disposuit*). {The other Apostles were also indeed what Peter was, endowed with like partnership both of honor and power, but the beginning proceeds from unity,} [and the primacy is given to Peter, that there might be shown to be one church of Christ and one cathedra. They are all pastors, and there is shown to be one flock, which is fed by all the Apostles with unanimous consent,] that the Church of Christ may be demonstrated one. Which one Church also the Holy Spirit describes in the Song of songs, personating the Lord, where it is said: "My dove, my undefiled is but one; she is the only one of her mother, she is the choice one of her that bare her" (Cant, vi: 9). Can one who holds not this unity of the Church, believe that he holds the faith? Will he, who withstands and resists the Church, [who deserts the cathedra of Peter on which the Church is founded,] presume still that he is in the Church, when the blessed Apostle Paul also sets forth the sacrament of unity in like style, where he says: "There is one body and one Spirit, one hope of your calling, one Lord, one faith, one baptism, one God" (Eph. iv: 4–6)?[26]

25. [Bracketed texts here and below are Nevin's.]

26. [Cyprian, *De Unitate Ecclesiae*, in *Tract.*, 118–19 (§4, second edition); PPS 32:151–53. As Nevin indicates below, there is a textual variant between two textual traditions. The PPS edition labels these textual traditions as "Received" and "Primacy." Nevin's square brackets [ ] mark phrases from "Received." The phrase surrounded by curly brackets { } is also from "Received," but was not marked by Nevin.] The clauses which we have put into brackets in this passage have been regarded by some as spurious; although it is by no means sealed, that the suspicion is correct. As to any theological interest that may seem to be at stake, however, the question is not of any account, since as Neander remarks, no less than Möhler [Johann Adam Möhler (1796–38)], the clauses contain nothing that is not elsewhere affirmed by Cyprian, even more distinctly than here. [The probable source for this interpretation is Neander, *Allgemeine Geschichte*, 365–66 or *General History*, 1:212–13.] They add but little indeed to the necessary sense, and plain purport, of their own context. [Some have said that the longer text, which is designated the Primacy text in the PPS, points to a later addition to the Cyprianic corpus in support of the primacy of the chair of Peter. Allen Brent in his commentary takes a view

Document 3: Cyprian: Second Article.

This unity the bishops especially are bound firmly to assert and maintain, so as to show clearly that the Episcopate itself also is one and indivisible.

> Let no one deceive the brotherhood, let no one corrupt the truth of faith by treacherous falsehood. The Episcopate is one, the parts of which hold severally from the whole (*eujus a singulis in solidum pars tenetur*). The Church also is one, which is extended into multitude by the force of its own fecundity; just as there are many rays of the sun, but only one light; and many boughs of a tree, but one trunk only firmly rooted in the ground; and as in the case of many streams flowing from a single fountain, however widely diffused the plentiful supply may appear, the unity is still preserved in the source. Tear a sunbeam from its place; the unity of the light suffers no division. Break off a bough from a tree; it has no further power of growth. Cut off a stream from its fountain; it must soon become dry. So the Church of the Lord also, irradiated with light, sends out her rays over all the earth; still there is but one light, which is everywhere diffused, and the unity of the body is not divided. She spreads forth her boughs with exuberant growth through the whole world; she sends her abundant streams abroad, far and wide in every direction; yet is there but one head, one origin, one mother of continually prolific grace. Of her womb we are born; by her milk we are nourished; with her spirit we are animated.[27]

The Church is the spouse of Christ. She only can bear children to God. Whoever is out of her, can have no part in the blessings of the Gospel. "He is a stranger, he is profane, he is an enemy. No one can have God for his father, who has not the Church for his mother. If one might escape who was out of Noah's ark, then may he also escape who is out of the Church."[28] Not to gather with the Lord, is of itself to scatter.

This sacrament of unity, the writer tells us, was typically represented by the seamless garment of the Saviour, for which the soldiers cast lots. It is in truth, a mystery, closely related to the awful and glorious fact of the Trinity. The terrestrial constitution here has its root and force, we may say, in the celestial. Not to hold the unity of the Church, is not to hold the faith of the Father and the Son, not to hold life and salvation.

Thus we see the terrible nature of the sin of *schism*. It is full against the universal voice of the Scriptures. It is at war with the whole habit of faith, the whole mind of Christ. The temper which leads to it, is not of God but of the world; though it may be in the Church outwardly for a time, it forms no part of its true and proper life; it is there by accident; and when it comes to actual separation and secession, the process is only an act of self-judgment, a critical elimination from the body of Christ of an element which has been all along foreign and false.

---

similar to Nevin's, even pointing to Ep 33 (*Letters*, 2:40–42) in support of this view (PPS 32:151).]

27. [Cyprian, *De Unitate Ecclesiae*, in *Tract.*, 120–21 (§5); PPS 32:154–55.]

28. [Cyprian, *De Unitate Ecclesiae*, in *Tract.*, 121 (§6); PPS 32:157. In the last sentence, both clauses are negative hypotheticals: *if it were possible* . . . .]

> Let no one imagine, that the good can depart from the Church. It is not the wheat which is carried away by the wind, nor a well rooted tree that is overthrown by the storm. Empty chaff is thus driven, and trees of small strength are thus violently laid low. To such the doom pronounced by the Apostle John refers: "They went out from us, but they were not of us; for if they had been of us, they would no doubt have continued with us" (I John ii: 19).[29]

Heresies and schisms come from the working of human corruption, refusing to own the obedience of faith; and they serve, as St. Paul says 1 Cor. xi: 19, to make manifest those who are approved, to separate the chaff from the wheat.

Let all then, who value their salvation, give good heed to the voice of God, charging and commanding them not to listen to the words of such false prophets. They prophesy, and cry peace; but it is not from the Lord. They have not been sent.

> These the Lord describes, when he says: "They have forsaken me, the fountain of living waters and hewed them out cisterns, broken cisterns, that can hold no water" (Jer. ii: 13). When there can be no baptism save one, they nevertheless pretend to baptize; while the fountain of life is deserted, they notwithstanding promise the grace of life giving and saving water. Men however are not washed there, but defiled rather; their sins are not purged, but only accumulated. That is no nativity to God, but a generation of children to the Devil.[30]

No such spurious filiation can bring with it true grace, or lead to heavenly life.

In vindication of their divisions, some quoted the passage which is so often abused for the same bad end in modern times: "Where two or three are gathered together in my name, there am I in the midst of them" (Matth. xviii: 20). Cyprian however charges them with wronging the true sense of these words, by overlooking and keeping out of sight their occasion and connection. They rend the text, as they try also to rend the Church. The object of the passage, as the previous context shows, is to enforce unity, not division. The Saviour is speaking of the authority and power the Church has to bind and loose on earth, as being the organ and medium of a corresponding power in heaven. This goes so far, he adds, "that if two of you shall agree on earth as touching any thing that they shall ask, it shall be done for them of my Father which is in heaven. For where two or three &c. [Matt 18:19–20]." The stress of the thought lies on the idea of that Divine concord, which is itself but another name for the life of the Church in union with her glorious Head.

> Not multitude, but unanimity, is made to be of such vast account. If two of you, he says, shall agree on earth; the unanimity is put first, the concord of peace is made to go before, that we may agree with faith and firm effect. But how can he agree thus with any one else, who agrees not with the body of the Church itself and with the universal brotherhood? How can two or three

29. [Cyprian, *De Unitate Ecclesiae*, in *Tract.*, 123 (§9); PPS 32:161.]
30. [Cyprian, *De Unitate Ecclesiae*, in *Tract.*, 124 (§11); PPS 32:162–63.]

Document 3: Cyprian: Second Article.

> come together in Christ's name, who are in palpable separation from Christ and his Gospel? For we have not separated from them, but they have separated from us, and inasmuch as heresies and schisms are of later birth, by setting up separate conventicles for themselves, they have forsaken the head and fountain of truth. Our Lord, however, speaks of his Church, and says to those who are in the Church, that if they should be in concord, if they should when met together, though only two or three, unitedly pray according to his command and direction, they would be able, though but two or three, to obtain from the Divine majesty what they should ask. Wherever two or three are gathered together in my name, he says, I am in the midst of them; in the midst of such, namely, as are simple and peaceful, such as fear God and keep his commandments. With such though only two or three he promises to be, as he was with the three youths in the fiery furnace, and because they continued simple towards God and of one mind among themselves, refreshed them with the spirit of dew in the midst of surrounding flames [Dan 3:49–50 (LXX)]; as he was with the two Apostles shut up in prison, who also were of like single and united mind, opening the doors of the prison, and placing them in public again to speak to the people the word they faithfully preached [Acts 16:16–34; 5:17–32]. When he lays down the rule then, "Where two or three are gathered together in my name, there am I in the midst of them," he does not sunder men from the Church, who has himself established and formed the Church; but reproving discord to the unfaithful, and commending peace to the faithful, his language shows, that he is more with two or three only praying in unity than with the greatest number in dissent, that more may be obtained by the concordant supplication of a few than by the inharmonious prayer of many.[31]

How can they meet together with Christ among them, who come together on the outside of his Church? That posture is of itself fatal to all faith and piety.

> Though such should be slain for the confession of the Saviour's name, this stain is not washed out even by blood; the inexpiable and dreadful guilt of discord is not purged even by such passion. He cannot be a martyr, who is not in the Church; he cannot win the kingdom, who forsakes her that is destined to reign.[32]

Schism breaks the law of peace and charity, which is of no less force than the law of faith. The greatness of this grace is set before us in full by St. Paul, in the thirteenth chapter of his First Epistle to the Corinthians. How can one have God, who has not charity? He may give his body to be burned, but the sacrifice will profit him nothing. "Such an one may be slain, but he cannot be crowned."[33] Even to prophesy, cast out

---

31. [Cyprian, *De Unitate Ecclesiae*, in *Tract.*, 125–26 (§12); PPS 32:164–65.]
32. [Cyprian, *De Unitate Ecclesiae*, in *Tract.*, 126 (§14); PPS 32:166.]
33. [Cyprian, *De Unitate Ecclesiae*, in *Tract.*, 127 (§14); PPS 32:167.]

devils, and do miracles, is not enough to insure salvation. There must be righteousness, to gain the favor of the Judge; obedience to his precepts, that we may merit reward.

The spirit of schism, according to Cyprian, was no new thing, but it had assumed latterly a more than usually bold and active form—a proof, as he sees it, that the "perilous times of the last days," foretold by the Apostle, were now actually at hand, and the world drawing towards an end. The faithful, however, should not be disturbed by this. Let them see in these apostacies and insurrections the clear fulfilment of prophecy, and be only the more firmly resolved to keep clear of all fellowship with every such unbelieving movement, however outwardly bold and strong.[34] Let them bear in mind the judgment of Korah, Dathan and Abiram, and the punishment of King Uzziah, as monuments of the crime and danger of such rebellious independence to the end of time. Those who now pretended to set up a new jurisdiction in the Church, usurping the powers of the priesthood which God had himself established, must be regarded as falling into the same fearful condemnation with these ancient examples.[35] To such applies the Lord's word: "'Ye reject the commandment of God, that ye may keep your own tradition.' This crime is worse than that of the lapsed, so far as they are brought afterwards to do penance and make full satisfaction for their sin."[36] It is a more full alienation from the Church; not through compulsion, but of deliberate choice; not transiently but perseveringly; carried out by principle and maxim, and seeking to involve others in its own perdition. It leads, not to penitence, but to pride only and every new disorder. It is a lapse, not once merely, but every day; and martyrdom itself, which may be a passport to heaven in the other case, is shorn hereof all worth and power.

Some confessors had been carried away by the false movement. But let not this create wonder or doubt. The merit of confession formed no security against the snares of the Devil afterwards, no immunity from temptation and sin. Of this, there were painful proofs in the disorderly and wicked conduct of some of the confessors under other forms. Solomon lost the grace he once had.[37] A confessor may do so too. His confession is only the beginning of glory, not its end. It is an engagement to be true to Christ, which can continue to be meritorious only so far as it is sacredly kept, by a faithful observance of his institutions and precepts. Without this, what can it be but a source of greater guilt and heavier condemnation?[38] The glory of the confessors as a body is not overthrown by such cases of defection; as the fall of Judas, the traitor, shook not the credit of the Apostolic college to which he had once belonged.[39]

---

34. [Cyprian, *De Unitate Ecclesiae*, in *Tract.*, 128–29 (§§16–17); PPS 32:169–71.]
35. [Cyprian, *De Unitate Ecclesiae*, in *Tract.*, 129 (§18); PPS 32:172.]
36. [Cyprian, *De Unitate Ecclesiae*, in *Tract.*, 130 (§19); PPS 32:172–73. Mark 7:9.]
37. [Cyprian, *De Unitate Ecclesiae*, in *Tract.*, 130 (§20); PPS 32:174–75.]
38. [Cyprian, *De Unitate Ecclesiae*, in *Tract.*, 130–31 (§21); PPS 32:175–76.]
39. [Cyprian, *De Unitate Ecclesiae*, in *Tract.*, 131–32 (§22); PPS 32:177.]

Document 3: Cyprian: Second Article.

The conclusion is an earnest and powerful exhortation, to maintain unity, as the fundamental law of Christ's house, the necessary condition of charity and faith, in the observance of which only it is possible to be rightly prepared for the coming of the Lord. This is the posture of those, who wait for this glorious advent, with their loins girded and their lamps burning [Matt 25:1–13].

> Let our light shine by good works, that it may lead us out of the darkness of this world into the light of eternal day. Let us anxiously and preparedly expect the sudden coming of our Lord, that when he should knock, our waking faith may receive from him the reward of vigilance. If these commandments are kept, if these admonitions and precepts are observed, we cannot be overwhelmed asleep by the false power of the Devil, we shall reign as watchful servants in the kingdom of Christ.[40]

Such is the general scope and sense of this remarkable tract of Cyprian, *On the Unity of the Church*. The same doctrine runs through all his works. We are made to feel its presence, indirectly at least and by implication, if not in a more open way, in almost everything he wrote. It was not with him an accidental opinion merely. As already remarked, it lay at the foundation of his whole theology. It entered into the inmost core and heart of his faith. He holds it not as a theory, resting on argument or speculation. His genius and taste lay not that way. The whole is with him an object of faith, a fact flowing with overwhelming force out of the constitution of Christianity itself, and clearly established by the voice of inspiration in the Holy Scriptures. He deals with it always in this universal view. It is for him the necessary form of the mystery of salvation. It conditions all his sense of what is comprehended in the glorious gospel of the Blessed God.

[Cyprian's Theology of the Church]

Cyprian's theology, like that of all the Fathers, is cast in the type or mould of the Apostles' Creed. All turns on the mystery of the Holy Trinity, exhibited in the way of real revelation through the mystery of the Incarnation. This stupendous *fact* carries in it the redemption of the world, by bringing into it a new and higher order of life, in the bosom of which it is made possible for the fallen posterity of Adam to surmount the law of sin and death, to which they are subject without hope in their natural state. The Word made Flesh is the ground and foundation of the whole constitution; which is thus throughout of a strictly supernatural character, and in such form is not to be apprehended without faith. By descending into the Virgin, we are told in the tract *De Idolorum Vanitate* §. 11, God so united himself with man, as to form a real mediation through the Son, by which men are conducted to the Father. "Christ consented to become what man was, in order that man also might have power to be what Christ

---

40. [Cyprian, *De Unitate Ecclesiae*, in *Tract.*, 134 (§27); PPS 32:181.]

is."[41] The Gospel thus is not a doctrine or theory merely of salvation; it is a revelation of *grace* and *truth* in living form, an actual economy of redemption brought to pass through the mystery of the Incarnation, and to be found nowhere else. As such an objective reality exhibited in this concrete way, men can have part in it only by surrendering themselves truly to its power. This they do by *faith* and *love,* which simply express the proper counterpart in such case of the truth and grace presented on the other side. These accordingly are the ground factors of Christianity and the Church.[42] It is easy to see how such surrendry to the power of such a supernatural fact, if this itself be no dream and faith and love no delusion or hypocritical pretense, must draw after it with necessary consequence the character of unity in the Christian life, and how too such unity becomes a necessary mark and test of the reality of this life in its proper form. How shall the truth and grace of Christ, of whose fulness we are all required to receive and in whom only we can be complete, be ever otherwise than in full harmony with themselves? Or how shall faith and love stand in real, and not simply notional and visionary, communication with this new order of life, and not be the source of a corresponding unity? To receive here, is actually to pass over into the form of that which is received; and the receptivity must be ruled and filled absolutely by its object, in both forms; so as to be a full bowing of faith to the authority of it as truth in one direction, and a full submission of love to its claims as grace in another. To be out of unity thus, in either view, is to be out of Christ. Schism is as regards love, precisely what heresy is as regards faith; an act, which implies an inward falling away from what may be termed the fundamental law of Christianity, the law of implicit surrendry to the living fact of the Gospel, as the true end and proper whole of man's life. The unity of the Church comes then from its constitution. It does not depend on the thought and will of men. It is not such a union as results from the voluntary agreement of a number of persons, who happen to be of the same mind. The foundation of it is in God, in the mystery of the Trinity, in the fact of the Incarnation, back of all piety among men in its individual forms. Such individual piety comes only through the acknowledgment and appropriation of the truth and grace, which go before it in the mystery of godliness under its general and universal form. This is the true idea of the Holy Catholic Church, as an article of faith. It is a real constitution, of supernatural origin and force, which as such carries in itself its own laws, its own attributes, its own prerogatives and powers, and refuses to come into subjection in any way to human opinion or human plan.

Of such constitution in its very nature, the Church is at the same time, according to Cyprian, not an idea simply or principle committed to the mind of the world and left to actualize itself afterwards in its own way, but a most positive creation like the

---

41. [Cyprian, *De Idolorum Vanitate*, in *Tract.*, 15; ANF 5:468.]

42. [Faith and love as "ground factors" of Christianity anticipates a theological structure Nevin developed after 1870. It is outlined in Nevin et al., *Born of Water*, MTSS 6:216–17 (see 216n16), and briefly manifested in Nevin, "The Bread of Life," MTSS 6:229–30.]

world of nature, starting directly from God, and asserting its supernatural presence and power, from the beginning onward to the end of time, under a most real outward and historical form. As the Word, in becoming Flesh, was no Gnostic vision merely, but a real manifestation of God in human form, such as might be looked upon with the eyes and felt by the hands, so the new order of life which followed could not be without a corresponding organization, it was supposed, in and through which it should make itself felt among men through all ages. Such organization, to meet the demands of the case, must be not of men but of God; for only in such view could it truly contain and put forth the heavenly powers of which it is to be the outward body and form. The Church, accordingly, is of Divine institution outwardly as well as inwardly; fully as much so, according to this view, as the economy of the Old Testament. It is a system of law and precept starting from Christ, to which the blessings of the gospel are bound by heavenly ordination, and which men are required to acknowledge and obey as the necessary condition and only real medium of grace. Christ laid the foundations of the Church first in his own person, by his life, sufferings, death, resurrection, and glorification; and then in the mission of his Apostles, who after proper training were solemnly appointed to carry forward his work, and received power from on high at the same time for doing so with effect. The Apostolic commission was no doctrine merely, but a most real creation or constitution under a living outward form; which moreover, it was expressly declared, was to be of force to the end of time. As the living Father hath sent me, the Founder of Christianity says, even so send I you; the one mission is just the continuation of the other, and carries with it the same authority and force; he that heareth you, heareth me, and he that despiseth you despiseth me, and he that despiseth me despiseth him that sent me [John 20:21; Luke 10:16]. All power, he tells them after his resurrection, is given unto me in heaven and in earth: Go ye *therefore*—because it is so, and ye are to go in my name—and teach all nations, baptizing them in the name of the Father, and of the Son, and of the Holy Ghost; teaching them to observe all things whatsoever I have commanded you; and, lo, I am with you alway, even unto the end of the world [Matt 28:19, 20]. This was the guarantee, that their mission and work would not be in vain. He breathed on them, we are told in another place, and said, Receive ye the Holy Ghost; whose soever sins ye remit, they are remitted unto them, and whose soever sins ye retain, they are retained [John 20:22, 23]. This commission was followed soon after by a corresponding inauguration. Behold I send the promise of my Father upon you, the Saviour said before his ascension; tarry ye in the city of Jerusalem, until ye be endowed with power from on high [Luke 24:49]. The appointment, the solemn commission, the commandments and instructions which went along with it, were not enough; there must be a real communication of supernatural power answerable to all this, by which the Ministry thus divinely constituted should become the channel, not in word only but in very deed and fact, of the new order of life which was now made complete for the world. This took place, as we all know, on the day of Pentecost; when the Spirit which could not be given previously "because that Jesus was not yet glorified" (John vii: 39), descended in full measure on the waiting and expecting disciples, as with the sound of a mighty rushing wind and in flames of fire, proclaiming by these sensible symbols that the promise was fulfilled, and immediately confirming by the gift of tongues the all sufficient nature of the grace it brought along with it for its own ends. Such, according to the evangelical narrative, was the origin and first constitution of the Christian Church. It is hard indeed to conceive of a polity more outwardly real, more objectively historical, having less the show of a mere doctrine, or carrying more completely the form of a living concrete fact.

So it was always regarded by Cyprian. He saw in the Church a real constitution, carrying in itself by Divine appointment actual supernatural and heavenly powers, of one order with the grace and truth brought to light by the mystery of godliness in Christ, and not to be found in the world under any other form. He took in earnest the conception of Head and Body, so frequently applied by St. Paul to this mystical relation; looking upon the Church as in truth the fulness in this way of him that filleth all in all, and honoring it as the organ through which he is pleased to make his saving power known and felt among men [Eph 1:23]. The whole economy, body and head, was for him a single grand fact, a new and extraordinary order of life with its own prerogatives, functions and powers, the origin of which was altogether above nature and only in God.

The notion of a simply human organization of the Church, a constitution founded on the will of men, and carrying with it no higher powers than such as might be taken to flow from the people for whose spiritual use it was established, was as far removed as possible from his thinking. The principle of Independency, the theory of Congregationalism, the idea of everything like ecclesiastical democracy or republicanism, lay heaven wide apart from the whole posture and habit of his mind. To found the kingdom of God in such style on the voice and will of men, like a confraternity of Free Masons, he would have considered the very perfection of rationalism and unbelief. To be the Divine reality it claims to be, it must come from above and not from below, its powers must proceed immediately from God and not from the people. Even the Presbyterian scheme was not enough for Cyprian, in this view. That scheme as it *once* stood (not adulterated as we find it now for the most part by the Puritan idea of church democracy) acknowledges a Ministry of divine origin, but not in the form of a hierarchy, with one order of office and power rising by divine right above another. It contends for the parity of the clergy, makes bishops to be of secondary growth and mere human arrangement, *(primi* [sic] *inter pares*,[43] as the word goes) with no rights or powers save such as have come to them by concession or usurpation from the body over which they are placed. We sometimes hear the *republicanism* of this system also paraded, on such account, as one of its special titles to confidence and praise.[44] That

---

43. [Trans. "first among equals."]

44. [For background on republicanism in American Christianity, see Hamstra, general introduction to *One, Holy, Catholic, and Apostolic, Tome One*, MTSS 5:8–10.]

Document 3: Cyprian: Second Article.

precisely would have formed its condemnation in the eyes of Cyprian. He had no conception of an upward movement of powers here, whether by clerical or popular vote. The church pyramid, in his view, started from its own summit, not from its base. The only true order of its constitution, and so of the derivation of its functions and powers, was: Christ first, the head of the universal organism; then the Apostolate continued by regular succession in the Episcopate; then the Ministry in its lower orders; and finally the body of the people held in connection with the head through the medium of this hierarchy, which is thus Divinely ordained to be the one only channel of all descending communications of life and grace.

This excludes of course, not merely such rank rationalism as resolves the life of the Church into the will of mere natural humanity, in the style of such religious reformers as Kossuth, Kinkel, Mazzini,[45] (who generously propose to settle by the world's vote what Christianity shall be, after they have cleared the world of what it pretends to be now); but it shuts out also, what Cyprian would have regarded as only a more refined and plausible species of the same unhappy rationalism, the imagination, namely, that the supernatural economy of which Christ is the fountain and head comes to its actualization in some way or other first in the mass of believers, who then *as such* democratically organize the ecclesiastical polity in its higher forms—just as natural men are supposed to have the power of creating, in their own sphere, the corresponding polity of the State.[46] This is the conception of the so called *universal priesthood* of Christians, which plays so important a part in certain schemes of theology.[47] Cyprian knew nothing of it, in any such republican sense. All believers are indeed priests in his view, as they are prophets also and kings; but their prerogative in this respect forms in no sense the foundation or ground, from which the powers and rights of the Holy Ministry may be said to grow. The only order here is downwards, not upwards. The universal priesthood is not first under Christ, but last; it is not the basis of the proper hierarchy, but that in which this comes to its end. The bishops hold from Christ; the presbyters and deacons from the bishops; and *through* this constitution all priestly, prophetical, and kingly character, in any real form, descends to the people. The entire constitution in this view is held to be *jure divino* in the fullest sense,

---

45. [Lajos Kossuth (1802–94); a leader in the Hungarian revolution in 1848. Johann Gottfried Kinkel (1815–82); German revolutionary who led the Prussian revolution with this wife, Joanna Mockel. Giuseppe Mazzini (1805–72); a leader in the Italian unification movement and was a leader, with Garibaldi, of the 1848 revolution in Italy. For Nevin's views on the revolutions of 1848, see "The Year 1848," MTSS 11:26–33; he critiques Kossuth and the response of American religious leaders in "Man's True Destiny," MTSS 11:339–42.]

46. [The concept of a social contract originated among Enlightenment political thinkers and was very influential in the formation of the American republic. See for instance Locke, *Concerning Civil Government, Second Essay* in *Locke: The Political Writings*.]

47. [Nevin later critiqued this conception in "The Christian Ministry," MTSS 7:45–47. It continues to be debated whether in these essays Nevin *accepted* Cyprian's view as normative, or merely presented it as one historical option: Nichols, *Romanticism*, 275–80; William Evans, *Companion*, 112–17; Littlejohn, "Sectarianism," 410n20.]

not a matter in any way of human policy or convention. The idea of a hierarchy of man's device, whether this be considered wise or foolish, upsets the whole sense of the institution; for then it must be regarded as having all its force from below, and not from above; and its pretensions to anything higher, if it make them, become then in truth both an usurpation and a sham. Cyprian had no thought of any such mournful pedantry as that. He was not a man to rest quietly in shadows and shams. He cared for no mock episcopacy, with mock powers, cocktail pretensions ending in mere sound and show. The entire force of the system lay, to his mind, in its *jure divino* character, in its supernatural authority, in its being a constitution which started from God, and carried in itself corresponding heavenly powers, under a real and not simply imaginary form, for the accomplishment of its own heavenly and supernatural ends.

In all this, there was no want of proper regard to the people. Their rights and privileges were fully recognized. They had a voice especially in the election of their chief pastors. Cyprian himself was in some sense forced to become a bishop, by the popular will. This however was at most only a nomination to office; the actual investiture came from another quarter. All real ecclesiastical jurisdiction and power, it was well understood on all sides, came not from below but from above, not from the people nor through the people, but by the hands of the Ministry with strict apostolical succession from Christ.

With such real constitution, the Church is not to be regarded of course as springing from the Bible; as though God had given the revelation of Christianity only in such written form, and left it for men then to turn this text or copy into life as they best could. It is perfectly certain from the New Testament itself, that the great mystery of godliness was never committed in the beginning to any such helpless and wretchedly mechanical plan. It is as plain as the written text itself can make it, that the world was *not* thrown upon the Bible in the first place, to construct from it as to its own sapient mind might seem best the scheme of Christianity, to manufacture out of it the glorious fact of the Church in a form to suit its own judgment and taste. There is not a word in the Bible, which goes legitimately to support this monstrously rationalistic supposition; while the *Apostolical Commission* must ever be enough of itself for all truly believing and thoughtful minds, to cover it with confusion and shame. The Church is itself, according to the New Testament, a living constitution, not made of men after a supposed Divine prescription merely, but Divinely made, not an inspired doctrine simply but a supernatural reality and fact, built in a real outward way on the foundation of the Apostles and Prophets, Jesus Christ himself being the chief cornerstone. So it is viewed always by Cyprian. No man could well make more account than he did of the Holy Scriptures. They were his continual study. He appeals to them as law and testimony on every occasion. His three books entitled *Testimonia*,[48] addressed to Quirinus, are made up almost entirely of passages quoted from the Bible. But with all this, it never enters into his mind to make the Bible a fountain and rule of truth for the world

---

48. [Known as "The Three Books of Testimony Against the Jews" in *ANF* 5:507–57.]

Document 3: Cyprian: Second Article.

as such, for the world *on the outside of the Church*, for the world in no union with the *living tradition of Christianity*, as a Divine fact handed down from the Apostles. On the contrary, he is of one mind here precisely with Tertullian and Irenaeus. The Bible is for him of authority only in the bosom of the Church. The New Testament grew out of this living revelation, supposes everywhere its supernatural presence, belongs to it exclusively in the way of rightful property, and can never be used safely except in believing submission to its authority and communion with its life. Heretics and schismatics, in this view, have no right to appeal to the Bible. It has to do with an actual economy, in which they have no part, a world of positive realities which is for them as though it did not exist. What indeed can be more absurd, than to dream of separating the letter of Christianity from its own proper life? It is as though the blind should undertake to correct by the science of optics, the familiar experience of those who see; or as if some bold and pertinacious somnambulist might pretend to set aside by logic, the verities of the waking world. Natural philosophy and logic as related to the system of nature are of force only in the bosom of this system, as an actual felt and acknowledged fact; and just so we may say, that the proper use of the Bible, as a rule of faith and practice, in its relation to the sphere of grace, is necessarily conditioned also by the authority of this higher order of things, or in other words by the living tradition of the Church, felt and acknowledged to be a fact in the same way.[49]

Starting in this way from the Apostolical commission, and bearing throughout the character of an independent supernatural constitution, the entire structure of the Church rests, for Cyprian, on the *Episcopate*. This he holds to be the strict succession of the Apostolate. The powers of the Church are carried forward by this channel alone. Here is the foundation of its unity and strength. Every bishop, in his proper sphere, is a representative and organ of the Divine Head, from which the whole body derives its life. He is the regular bond of union and communion thus, between Christ and the congregation over which lie presides. To despise his authority, is the very spirit of heresy, and schism. "Our Lord in the Gospel," Cyprian writes *(Ep. 66, ad Pupianum)*,

> when many of his disciples left him, turning to the twelve said: "Will ye also go away?" Peter answered him: "Lord, to whom shall we go? Thou hast the words of eternal life; and we believe and are sure that thou art the Son of the Living God [John 6:67–69]." Peter speaks there, on whom the church was to be built, teaching and showing in the name of the church, that however the rebellious and proud multitude of those who are unwilling to obey may depart, still the church does not turn away from Christ, and the church for him is the people in union with the priest, the flock adhering to its own pastor. Whence you ought to know, that the bishop is in the church and the church in the bishop, and that if any one be not with the bishop he is not in the church; and that

---

49. [Nevin here seems to be laying the groundwork, at least philosophically, for the creation of a magisterial teaching office. See Nevin, "The Christian Ministry," MTSS 7; and the interpretations in Nichols, *Romanticism*, 275–80; William Evans, *Companion*, 112–13; Littlejohn, "Sectarianism," 410–12.]

> those flatter themselves in vain, who not having peace with the priests of God pretend to communicate with certain persons in a surreptitious way, since the church, which is catholic and one, is not rent nor divided, but is in truth firmly joined and soldered together by the close mutual conjunction of the priests.[50]

In another place (Ep. 33, addressed to the Lapsed) he says:

> Our Lord, whose precepts and directions we are bound to obey, settling the honor of the bishop and the plan of his church, in the Gospel, thus addresses Peter: "I say unto thee, that thou art Peter, and on this rock, etc." Matth. xvi: 18, 19. From hence flows down through the change of times and successions the ordination of bishops and constitution of the church, that the church may rest upon the bishops, and every act of the church be governed by these rulers. Such then being the order established by Divine law, I marvel, that some of you have audaciously presumed to write to me *as in the name of the church,* when the church is constituted by the bishop and clergy with all who are in good standing.[51]

The same general thought we meet with in Cyprian's writings over and over again. The divine right of Episcopacy is perpetually asserted, or taken for granted, as a fact lying at the very foundation of the universal, scheme and constitution of the Christian Church.

To be the foundation of unity for the Church however, in this broad view, the Episcopate must be in unity with itself. No bishop can be said to be the organ and representative of Christ, in virtue of what he is simply in his single and separate capacity. To be such an organ, he must be comprehended in the whole organism of which Christ is the head, His office can never be of force, except in union and harmony with the entire office of which it is only a part. "*Episcopatus unus est,*" we are told, "*cujus a singulis in solidum pars tenetur*" (De Unit. §. 5).[52] Again it is: "*Episcopatus unus, episcoporum multorum concordi numerositate diffusus*" (Ep. 55, ad Antonianum);[53] so that Novatian's attempt to bring in new bishops, to get up a hierarchy in certain places in opposition to the one already established, was perfectly absurd as well as profane. Even if he had been himself regularly consecrated, (which was not the case) he could have no power to start another ministry in any such irregular style. "No one can have either the power or the honor of the episcopate, who retains neither the unity of the episcopate nor its peace."[54] So, writing to Stephen of Rome (Ep. 68) in reference to a

---

50. [*Epist.*, 178; *Letters*, 3:121.]

51. [*Epist.*, 67, emphasis Nevin's; *Letters*, 2:40.]

52. [Cyprian, *De Unitate Ecclesiae*, in *Tract.*, 120; PPS 32:154; trans. "The episcopate is one, an individual share in which individual bishops hold as owner of a common property." See n. 8 in PPS for an explanation of the legal implications of *in solidum*.]

53. [*Epist.*, 116; *Letters*, 3:48; trans. "There is but one episcopate, but it is spread amongst the harmonious host of all the numerous bishops."]

54. [*Epist.*, 117; *Letters*, 3:49.]

Document 3: Cyprian: Second Article.

certain Marcian, one of the bishops of Gaul, who was reported to have given in his adhesion to Novatian "forsaking the unity of the catholic church and the harmonious consent of its priesthood,"[55] Cyprian urges him to address letters to the other bishops of that province requiring them to take measures for the proper care of his flock in some other way.

> For the numerous body of the priests is joined together by the cement of mutual concord and chain of unity on this account, that if anyone of our college shall attempt to create heresy and so to lacerate and waste the flock of Christ, the rest may bring help and as good and compassionate pastors gather the Lord's sheep into the flock. [. . .] For although we are many pastors, we feed nevertheless one flock, and are bound to look after all the sheep which Christ has purchased by his blood and passion.[56]

The solidarity of the Episcopate then is no division properly speaking of its powers; it does not weaken the force of the office in single cases, but only makes it full and complete; every bishop in his sphere is armed with the jurisdiction of the universal college, and is to be regarded in fact as an overseer of the whole church; just as the Apostolate was not the sum simply of the several trusts belonging to its membership, but belonged to each Apostle in full as his own commission. In both cases, however, the trust in such form was strictly collegiate. It could have no force, save in the solidarity of the Divine constitution, out of which it sprung, and from which alone also it derived all its significance and truth.

Cyprian has a very high sense, in this view, of the prerogatives and rights of each bishop in his own see; and he is often appealed to by modern Episcopalians, accordingly, as a powerful witness for what is sometimes called the independency of the common episcopal office, over against the pretensions of the see of Rome. No one indeed could well go farther than he does, in magnifying this office, as one directly representing among men the supreme authority of Christ. In this respect, all bishops are for him of like dignity and co-ordinate power. He writes to Stephen, bishop of Rome, in the tone of a colleague possessing the same rank with himself; and he did not hesitate even, when the question arose concerning the baptism of heretics, to take ground openly against him, as Paul withstood Peter to the face, charging him with error and overbearing presumption.

All this, it must be allowed, is not answerable exactly to the order of the Papal system, as we find it established in later times. The relation between the see of Rome and the other sees would appear to have been more free and independent altogether, than it came to be afterwards. The supremacy of the Pope was not in Cyprian's mind, or at least is not in his writings, as it rules for instance in our day the thinking of

---

55. [*Epist.*, 186; *Letters*, 4:28.]
56. [*Epist.*, 187, 188; *Letters*, 4:29–30, 31.]

Wiseman or Hughes.[57] But we must not make more of this point than it will properly bear. The idea of a strict independency in the jurisdiction of bishops, we have already seen to be most perfectly at war with Cyprian's scheme. The Episcopate is one first, and then manifold; the unity must go before the distribution; the independence can hold only in union with the solid corporation out of which it grows. Sundered from this, it becomes at once schism and death. It can never generate or uphold a true and valid church life, in the form of Novatianism say, *or Anglicanism.* The first condition of all real episcopal jurisdiction and power, is that it shall be truly of collegiate force, the exercise of the office under its universal or catholic view. But this now, in the nature of the case, implies and demands an actual outward order or system of some kind, by which the conception of such wholeness shall be properly secured and made good. The idea here, if it is not to end in an empty abstraction, must take the form of fact. As the church at large must be held together by a real bond in the episcopate, so this again must be bound like an orb or sphere to some single centre, that shall be the principle or beginning of its unity in a like actual view. So much is at once implied by the solidarity of the office. There can be no such consolidation even in the way of outward league merely, and still less in the way of inward living organism, without a real primacy at some point to support and represent the whole.[58] Such an actual primacy and real centre of unity for the universal Episcopal college, there can be no reasonable question or doubt, Cyprian habitually saw and acknowledged in the pontificate of the Bishop of Rome; which was regarded as flowing, with such right of priority, from the place originally assigned to Peter by our Blessed Lord himself in the joint commission of the Apostles.

[The Church's Unity and the Claims of Rome]

This is plainly intimated, in what we have quoted from the tract *De Unitate Ecclesiae*. It lies in the universal argument of this tract; since the real unity it asserts necessarily requires the supposition of an actual centre somewhere, and all goes at once to fix it at Rome and nowhere else. We may say the same of Cyprian's doctrine of the Church, wherever it comes into view. It runs always with inevitable logic to this conclusion. Without it, the doctrine is a mere solecism.[59] But what is thus implied is also amply

---

57. [Nicholas P.S. Wiseman (1802–65), an English Cardinal of the Ultramontane school; John Joseph Hughes (1797–1864); first archbishop of New York, founder of Fordham University.]

58. The Anglican Episcopate finds its centre to some extent in the See of Canterbury, but still more effectually in the Royal Supremacy. The King or Queen, as the case may be, is with most terrible reality, and not simply by fiction of law, Head of the Established Church. Our American Episcopacy has not yet got a fixed centre of any sort. It is Congregational. But this is a suicidal anomaly; which the hierarchy must overcome in some way hereafter, if it is to be of any lasting account. [The previous year Nevin had stated this critique in more detail in "The Anglican Crisis," MTSS 11:283–91; 298–300. See also Black, "A 'Vast Practical Embarrassment,'" 264–73.]

59. [A grammatical mistake.]

Document 3: Cyprian: Second Article.

enough expressed, not only in this tract, but also in other places. So in his letter to the people of his charge on the faction of Felicissimus, which we have before quoted, we hear him say, that "there is one church, and one cathedra founded by the Lord's voice upon the rock,"[60] and no room on account of the one altar and one priesthood for the establishment of any other. So, Ep. 70, to Januarius and others: "There is one baptism, and one Holy Ghost, and one church founded by Christ the Lord on Peter with origin and plan of unity (*super Petrum origine unitatis et ratione fundata*)."[61] Again, Ep. 73, to Jubaian:

> It is plain where and by whom the remission of sins can be given, which is granted in baptism. For to Peter first, on whom he built his church and from whom he instituted and shows the origin of unity, our Lord gave that power that what he loosed on earth should be loosed in heaven. And after his resurrection, he addresses also the Apostles, saying, As the Father hath sent me, etc."[62]

In the same epistle afterwards we are told, that the church "is one, and has been founded by the Lord's voice upon one, who also received his keys."[63] Peter is the centre of the Apostolate, and so the real beginning of the actual organization of the Church; but this was no temporary order only; the Episcopate finds a corresponding centre in the *Cathedra Petri* at Rome, as the necessary starting point of unity in the same way. Thus, writing to Cornelius, bishop of Rome, of the attempt made by Felicissimus and his party to get up a new bishop at Carthage, (Ep. 59) Cyprian says; "They dare to make voyage, with letters from profane schismatics to the see of Peter and the chief church, whence the sacerdotal unity is derived, etc."[64] Again in another letter to the same Cornelius (Ep. 48), he says expressly that the Roman church was to be acknowledged as "the root and mother (*radix et matrix*) of the catholic church," and that communion with its bishop was the test of abiding in catholic unity and charity.[65]

---

60. Or as a different and better reading gives it, *super Petrum*, "on Peter." [*Epist.*, 85; *Letters*, 2:64. The textual variant is "*super petram*." However, as Nevin points out that is not considered the most likely reading of the text.]

61. [*Epist.*, 202; *Letters*, 4:47.]

62. [*Epist.*, 211; *Letters*, 4:58.]

63. [*Epist.*, 213; *Letters*, 4:60.]

64. [*Epist.*, 144; *Letters*, 3:82.]

65. "*Nos enim singulis navigantibus, ne cum scandalo ullo navigarent, rationem reddentes, scimus, nos hortatos eos esse,* ut ecclesiae catholicae radicem et matricem *agnoscerent ac tenerent.*" [. . .] "[P]lacuit, ut per episcopos . . . per omnes omnino in provincia ista positos literae fierent, sicuti fiunt, ut te universe [universi] collegae nostri et communicationem tuam, id est catholicae ecclesiae unitatem *pariter et caritatem probarent firmiter ac tenerent* [*Epist.*, 94 {trans. "To all who were sailing away we explained to them the situation individually so that they should not be scandalized on their travels, exhorting them to discern *the womb and root of the Catholic Church* and to cleave to it. . . . It was accordingly, the resolution of the bishops to prevent any perplexity being created in the minds of our far-distant brethren through uncertain information about a schism in Rome. . . . Thus, all our colleagues should together unequivocally express their approval of, and attach themselves to, you, and your communion, that is to say, abide by *the unity* and, along with that, the charity *of the Catholic Church*" (*Letters*, 2:75,

The point is too plain to admit of any doubt. But this is not all. It is no less certain, that the view of Cyprian here was no peculiarity properly speaking of his own; it belonged to the age. He may have led the way in asserting the full sense of the church system at some points; but the elements of the system were all previously at hand in the actual constitution of the church as it then stood. The very title *cathedra Petri*, in such familiar use, is one proof of this. Neander thinks it may have been first used in a merely ideal sense for the episcopate as a whole;[66] but the supposition rests on no historical evidence whatever, and is in its own nature highly improbable. It grew, no doubt, from the notion of an actual continuation of Peter's primacy in what was regarded from the beginning as Peter's see. The celebrated letter of the Oriental bishop Firmilian against Stephen, translated and preserved in Cyprian,[67] though sometimes quoted to show the contrary, goes in fact fully to establish this affirmation. His whole argument turns on the unity of the church; which Stephen is charged with forgetting and disregarding because he acknowledged the baptism of heretics to be valid. The blindness of this must be felt, he thinks, when it is remembered that in founding his Church the Saviour gave the power of remitting sins first to Peter alone, and afterwards to the Apostles only; which accordingly was confirmed to the churches established by his legates, "and the bishops who have succeeded them by vicarious ordination."[68] All who set up any other altar or priesthood on the outside of this "one catholic church of apostolical succession," are involved in the guilt of Korah, Dathan and Abiram [Num 16:1–25], and must look for like punishment.[69] "And in this view," he goes on to say,

> I feel indignant at the plain, palpable folly of Stephen, that he, who thus glories in the place of his episcopate and claims to hold the succession of Peter, on whom the foundations of the church are laid, should bring in many other rocks and establish many new church structures, by maintaining with his authority that baptism his place there.[70]

This is not certainly to dispute the primacy of Stephen, or to charge him with usurping for his see as the *cathedra Petri* a dignity which did not belong to it in fact. It is just the reverse. All goes to show, that Stephen was known to claim such central relation to the universal episcopal college, by right of succession from Peter, and that, this claim was sustained by the general consent and tradition of the church. What offends Firmilian, and brings him to speak disrespectfully of the bishop of Rome, is that he should turn the weight of his high station in favor of the baptism of heretics; and pains are taken to make it appear, that by so doing he virtually stultified his own prerogative, by doing

---

Nevin's emphases retained; to convey the fuller sense, additional text was added)}].

66. [Neander, *Allgemeine Geschichte*, 364–65; *General History*, 1:211–12.]
67. [*Epist.*, 229–44; *Letters*, 4:78–94.]
68. [*Epist.*, 238; *Letters*, 4:88.]
69. [*Epist.*, 238–39; *Letters*, 4:88.]
70. [*Epist.*, 239; *Letters*, 4:88–89.]

Document 3: Cyprian: Second Article.

away with the very foundation on which it was taken to rest. For if there could be a valid baptism on the outside of that one catholic church which was built upon Peter, it would follow that there might be other churches also on other foundations; and what must become then of the famous primacy of Rome? The argument involves an unbecoming sneer; but it is by no means simply *ad hominem*; the whole force of it turns on the assumption, that the theory of the catholic church which gave rise to Stephen's pretensions was in itself true, and known and acknowledged to be so on all sides.

The Church then, of which such vast account is made by Cyprian, was no idea merely or theory, but a well defined objective and historical reality, a most real corporation of which the whole world had knowledge and might take account. It was the so called *Catholic Church,* which held its rights by direct succession from the Apostles, (a succession about which there could be *then* certainly no possible mistake) held together throughout the world by a common Apostolical Episcopate, and having its acknowledged centre through this in the See of Peter at Rome. It is to this most real corporation, and not to any abstraction of vague and indeterminate bounds, that the law of unity, which he takes to be so essential to the idea of Christianity, is applied by him in all its uncompromising force. This precisely is the *Noah's Ark,* on the outside of which there is no salvation.[71] Here, in this empirical catholic church, thus openly defined and circumscribed as a body in harmony with itself, and here only, were to be sought and found all the Divine properties and supernatural powers, which belong of necessity to the true idea of the church as an object of faith. This is the glorious constitution founded on Peter. This is that illustrious *Mother*, the Immaculate Spouse of the Incarnate Word, of whom it is said: "*Illius foetu nascimur, illius lacte nutrimur, spiritu ejus animamur;*"[72] and to whom is at once referred the awfully solemn and most pregnantly significant old oracle: "*Habere jam non potest Deum patrem, qui Ecclesiam non habet matrem.*"[73] Here reside all grace and truth. The mystery of godliness is there in both forms, to be submitted to by men with corresponding self-surrendry of charity and faith. Not to own it, is to fall into heresy or schism; which involve each other in the end, and either of which must be regarded as fatal to that whole posture of "obedience to the faith," in which St. Paul makes the idea of Christianity so comprehensively to stand [Rom 1:5]. To be separated from the church, is to be separated from the promises, to have no part nor lot in the privileges or hopes of the gospel. No one in such state can be a true friend or sincere follower of Christ. "*Alienus est, profanus est, hostis est.*"[74] Schism is always damnable and damning. It strikes at the root of the *Christian*

71. [The metaphor of the church as "Noah's Ark" stayed with Nevin. See "The Christian Ministry" and "Hodge on the Ephesians," MTSS 7:50, 98, 101–2, 121.]

72. [Cyprian, *De Unitate Ecclesiae*, in *Tract.*, 121; PPS 32:155; trans. "From her womb we are born, by her milk we are nurtured, by her spirit we are given life."]

73. [Cyprian, *De Unitate Ecclesiae*, in *Tract.*, 121; PPS 32:157; trans. "He cannot have God as his Father who does not have the Church as his Mother."]

74. [Cyprian, *De Unitate Ecclesiae*, in *Tract.*, 121; PPS 32:157; trans. "He is a foreigner, he is deconsecrated, and he is an enemy." Concerning the translation of *profanes* as "deconsecrated," the editor of

Fact; for that Fact is not confined to the mystery of salvation in Him who is the Head of the Church, but must be of perennial force in the Body also over which he thus presides, as the proper continuation of this same mystery "always even unto the end of the world" [Matt 28:20]. Schism destroys the very substance of grace. "*Quidquid a matrice discesserit seorsum vivere et spirare non poterit, substantiam salutis amittit.*"[75] It is a sin, for which not even the merit of martyrdom itself can make any satisfaction. It is a perpetual apostacy, which makes all acts of religion, while it lasts, absolutely worthless and vain; for it is in truth the full verification, we are told, of what St. Paul says 1 *Cor. xiii:* 1–3: "Though I speak with the tongues of men and of angels—have all gifts—give my body to be burned, and have not *Charity*; I am as sounding brass; it profiteth me nothing."

The maxim, *No salvation out of the Church* (*extra ecclesiam salus nulla*),[76] amounts of course at the same time to an assertion, that full salvation is to be found in the Church, that what is needed for this object is here really and truly at hand under a supernatural form. In Cyprian's scheme, accordingly, all that is embraced in this proposition holds good of the empirical catholic communion, in which only the church had for his faith the character of objective reality. Separation from this real constitution brought with it guilt and perdition, just because truth and grace were actually comprehended in it, under the most real view, for the purposes of salvation. In the bosom of the Church, answerably to the figure of Noah's ark, was wafted, as it were, on the face of the deep and high above the surrounding desolation of nature, the mysterious presence of a new and higher order of life. The whole constitution was above nature, a sacrament, a Divine mystery; which however was really in the world under an outward and historical form, and carried in itself really and truly the supernatural powers that were needed for the accomplishment of its own more than natural ends. These powers start in Christ, and can never be absolutely divorced from his person. But from him as the Head, they

---

the PPS references the Ciceronian tradition (PPS 32:157n12).]

75. [Cyprian, *De Unitate Ecclesiae*, in *Tract.*, 133; PPS 32:178; trans. "Whatever splits off from the parent tree is not able to live and breathe apart from it. It loses the essential nature of health."]

76. [The history of this doctrine in Catholicism and Protestantism is a long one (see for instance WCF XXV.2 for a Protestant understanding). The Latin phrase appears to have originated with Origen but the doctrine finds its most important understanding with Augustine. Since the Church was understood to be the vehicle through which God administers grace, it seemed to be implied that the Church was the ordinary means or mediating agency by which people come to God. This doctrine, well-developed in the Middle Ages, was challenged with the discovery of the new world. This teaching is still official dogma in the Catholic Church, and in many Protestant creedal statements. In America, with its plurality of churches, this idea was growing increasingly foreign, even in Nevin's day, especially with the advent of revivalism (see Nevin's critique in *Anxious Bench*, MTSS 5:33–103). Nevin's discussion here would have been to many others an indication of his softness on Rome. This discussion of the Cyprianic principle is, however, not really new ground for Nevin as he has previously discussed the idea of the Church as a mediating agency (see also Calvin's discussion of the church in *Institutes*, Book IV). For a current discussion of the Catholic understanding of this phrase, see Kasper, *The Catholic Church*.]

flow over into his Body, τό πλήρωμα τοῦ τά πάντα ἐν πᾶσι πληρουμένου.[77] The channel of this communication is the Apostolic Ministry; whose original commission remains always in force, and must be taken as a full guaranty, to the end of time, of the actual sufficiency of the office for such high purpose and design. No bishop, no church, is with Cyprian, as we have seen, a fixed und settled rule. Not to hear and obey the bishop, is to despise the authority of Christ. Not to be in communion with the bishop, is to be out of communion with the fountain of all grace and life. The bishop is the source of power to the common priesthood; by the intervention of which then, the word is made to take effect, the sacraments have force, and all spiritual blessings are conveyed in a real and not simply imaginary way to the people.

[Unity and Baptism]

This whole view comes out most amply and explicitly, in the controversy which was raised concerning the baptism of heretics. With our present Protestant habit of thought, that old controversy altogether is apt to seem of no great interest or account. With the doctrine of the church which prevailed in the third century, however, it was in fact of the very highest significance; and all that is needed to make it of interest still, is that we should be able to reproduce in our minds in some living way the idea of this doctrine as now explained. The controversy throws light on the doctrine, and shows at the same time how extensively and profoundly it had entered into the mind of the universal early church. Could there be any valid baptism among heretics? That was the question. A huge and respectable party took the ground, that no such baptism had any force, and that heretics coming into the church must be baptized over again, as being in truth before without the sacrament altogether. Cyprian went zealously for this view. Stephen, Bishop of Rome, took the other side, governed as he said by previous tradition; and in the end, as is well known, this Roman decision prevailed, and became the acknowledged law of the Catholic Church. With the history of the controversy, and its proper merits, we are not now concerned. Its bearing on the subject before us is all we care about at present. This is at once full and plain. Cyprian argues at large against the validity of baptism among heretics from the familiar view that all grace in the church is bound to its catholic organization, and must flow through the channel of the regular episcopate and priesthood. This is the basis of his whole opposition. The thought comes up from all sides, and in all forms. Baptism, he assumes, involves of necessity the present action of the Holy Ghost, which is to be found only in the Church of the Apostolic Succession; and to this, it then follows, the sacrament must be necessarily confined.

"It is absurd," he writes Ep. *74, ad Pompeium,*

---

77. [Trans., " . . . the fulness of him that filleth all in all {Eph 1:23}." The Greek text as quoted by Nevin differs slightly from the standard text.]

> that whereas the second nativity is spiritual, by which we are born in Christ through the laver of regeneration, they should say one may be spiritually born among heretics, where they deny that the Spirit is. For water alone cannot purge sins and sanctify a man, if it have not also the Holy Spirit. Whence, either they must concede that the Holy Spirit is there where they say baptism is, or else there is no baptism either where the Holy Spirit is not, because baptism cannot be without the Spirit. But what a thing is it to assert and contend, that they may be the sons of God who are not born in the church. For that it is baptism by which the old man dies and the new is born, the blessed Apostle shows and proves when he says: "He hath saved us by the washing of regeneration" (Tit. iii: 5). But if regeneration be by washing, that is by baptism, how can heresy generate sons to God through Christ, not being the spouse of Christ? For it is the Church alone, which by conjunction and union with Christ generates children spiritually, according to the word of the same Apostle: "Christ hath loved the church, and gave himself for it, that he might sanctify it, cleansing it with the washing of water" (Eph. v: 25, 26). If this therefore be his beloved spouse, which is alone sanctified by him and alone cleansed by his washing, it is manifest that heresy, which is not the spouse of Christ and cannot be either sanctified or cleansed by his washing, is not able to generate children to God.[78]

Again:

> It has been handed down to us, that there is one God, one Christ, one hope and one faith, one church and one baptism established in this one church; from which unity if any one depart, he must be found necessarily with heretics, by defending whose cause against the church he makes war upon the sacrament of divine tradition. This sacrament of unity is represented to us in the Song of songs: "A garden inclosed is my sister, my spouse, &c" (iv: 12). But if the church be an inclosed garden and sealed fountain, how can he enter into the same garden or drink of its fountain, who is not in the church? So Peter himself also, in demonstration of unity, has taught us that we cannot be saved except by the one baptism only of one church. In the ark of Noah, he says, "a few, that is, eight souls, were saved by water; the like figure whereunto even baptism doth also now save us" (I Pet. iii: 20, 21). How brief and spiritual a compend,[79] to exhibit the sacrament of unity! For as in that baptism of the world, by which its old iniquity was purged away, whosoever was not in the ark of Noah could not be saved through water, so now also no one can be saved by baptism who has not been baptized in the church, which our Lord has founded in unity after the sacrament of one ark.[80]

---

78. [*Epist.*, 225; *Letters*, 4:73–74.]
79. [That is, "compendium."]
80. [*Epist.*, 228–29; *Letters*, 4:77.]

Document 3: Cyprian: Second Article.

Again in the epistle *ad Jubaianum* [Ep. 73], after the passage before quoted, showing that the power of remitting sins in baptism flows from the commission of our Lord, given first to Peter, "*super quem aedificavit ecclesiam et unde unitatis originem instituit et ostendit*,"[81] and then after his resurrection to the Apostles generally, it is added: "We see from this, that only those who are set over the church by evangelical law and the Lord's ordination can baptize and give remission of sins, while nothing can be bound or loosed on the outside, where there is no one who has power either to bind or loose."[82] Then follow the familiar examples of Korah and his company, and of Aaron's sons offering strange fire on the altar. Afterwards the church is compared[83] to the garden of Eden; its members to trees, of which any that fail to bring forth good fruit must be hewn down and cast into the fire.

> These trees she waters with four rivers, that is, the four Gospels, by which she bestows with heavenly inundation the grace of salutary baptism. Can he irrigate from the fountains of the church, who is not within the church? Shall he be able to impart to any one the salubrious and saving draughts of paradise, who disobedient, and of himself condemned and banished from the fountains of paradise, pines away and dies with the drought of eternal thirst?[84]

This shows strikingly the relation, in which the use of the Scriptures, as well as of the means of grace generally, is regarded by Cyprian as standing to the Divine constitution of the Church. These streams of life are *not* for private judgment, and independent use, on the outside of this sacred inclosure; they belong to the garden, whose walls are obedience and faith, and only *there* can they serve truly their heavenly purpose. "The Lord cries," our author proceeds,

> that if any one thirsts he should come and drink of the rivers of living water that flow from his person. Whither shall he come who thus thirsts? To heretics, where the fountain and river of living water is wholly wanting, or to the church, which is one, and has been by the Lord's voice founded upon one, who received also his keys. One she is, who holds and possesses all the power of her Spouse and Lord. In her we preside, for her honor and unity we contend, her grace as well as glory with faithful devotion we maintain. We by Divine permission water the thirsting people of God, we keep the bounds of the living fountains.[85]

Elsewhere we are told, that no supposed soundness of doctrine, on the part of those who are out of the church, can be taken here as of any account; it is simple alienation

---

81. [*Epist.*, 211; *Letters*, 4:58; trans. "... upon whom the Lord built the Church, establishing him visibly to be the source of its unity."]
82. [*Epist.*, 212; *Letters*, 4:58.]
83. [In the original, strokes of "a" and "r" are missing, giving the appearance of "comp u ed."]
84. [*Epist.*, 213; *Letters*, 4:59–60.]
85. [*Epist.*, 213; *Letters*, 4:60.]

from the church itself, that makes all ministrations on the outside of it to be of no force or worth whatever. "Should any one object," (Ep. 69, *ad Magnum*)

> that Novatian holds the same law which the catholic church holds, baptizes with the same symbol that we also use, acknowledges the same God the Father, the same Christ the Son, the same Holy Ghost, and that so he may usurp the power of baptizing because he seems not to differ from us in the interrogation of baptism—let such an objector know first, that there is *not* one law of the symbol common to us with heretics, nor the same interrogation. For when they say: "Dost thou believe the remission of sins and the life everlasting by the holy church," they lie in the interrogation, since they have no church. Then again they confess themselves with their own voice, that remission of sins cannot be given except through the holy church, and not having this they show that with them no sins can be forgiven.[86]

These passages may serve as specimens. Many pages might be filled with quotations in the same general strain. No salvation out of the church; full possibility of salvation in the church, because *there,* and there only, the supernatural grace required for this end was, by Divine constitution, exhibited and made present for the obedient use of faith in an actual and real way. This is everywhere Cyprian's doctrine, and it is referred to everywhere as the reigning doctrine of the age. That it was so in fact, there is no room for even the shadow of a doubt. Firmilian's long letter [Ep. 75], before mentioned, presents in full the same view as common to the Oriental church with the Latin; for it may be said to echo every sentiment on the subject, that is to be found in Cyprian. "All power and grace," he says in particular,

> are established in the church, where the elders preside, who also possess the power of baptizing and laying on hands and ordaining. For as it is not lawful for a heretic to ordain, so neither also to baptize, nor to perform any sacred and spiritual function, as being estranged from the source of sanctity (*quando alienus sit a spiritali et deifica sanctitate*). All which we some time since affirmed, in council at Iconium in Phrygia, assembled from Galatia and Cilicia and other neighboring regions, as something to be firmly held and asserted against heretics—a doubt having been raised in regard to it by some persons.[87]

It was a public decision thus, made by a large portion of the Church in Asia Minor. "The power of remitting sins," he says, after quoting the commission first to Peter and then to the Apostles as a body,

> was given thus to the Apostles, and to the churches founded by them as Christ's legates and the bishops who have succeeded them by vicarious ordination. When now enemies of the one catholic church in which we are, and

---

86. [*Epist.*, 193–94; *Letters*, 4:37.]
87. [*Epist.*, 233–34; *Letters*, 4:83; trans. "he is an outcast from all spiritual and sanctifying holiness."]

Document 3: Cyprian: Second Article.

adversaries of us who have succeeded the Apostles, arrogate to themselves illegal priesthoods in opposition to us, and set up profane altars, what else are they than Korah and Dathan and Abiram, sacrilegious with like crime, and doomed to like punishment, along with all who favor their cause—as *their* friends and partizans also shared their miserable fate![88]

The same general theory is premised to us again, in the broadest and strongest terms, by the *Apostolical Constitutions,* a work which is generally supposed to have taken its present form about the middle of the third century.[89]

The idea of a Church which is thus the organ and medium of grace in a real way, whose office it is, not simply to proclaim salvation, but with supernatural power also to bring it actually to pass, involves at once a corresponding view of the Holy Sacraments. They must be, not signs and pictures only, but seals and vehicles of the grace they represent. What *Baptism* in particular was to the faith of Cyprian in this view, our quotations have already plainly enough shown. These however are a mere fraction of the testimony to the same purport, which it would be easy to furnish from his writings. Baptism is for him everywhere the sacrament of regeneration, the mystery of the new birth, the real ground and foundation of spiritual life. It never seems so much as to enter his mind, that there can be any question made of this in the Church. To doubt it, would be, in his system, to doubt the supernatural realness of Christianity itself. This assumes throughout, that nature in man is fallen, without strength and under a curse; that what is born of the flesh is flesh; and that provision is made for his redemption by a new and higher order of life, which no less real than nature itself, but of another form altogether, starting from Christ and sustained by the Holy Ghost, is of force to set aside the old curse, and to "condemn sin in the flesh, that the righteousness of the law may be fulfilled in those who walk not after the flesh but after the Spirit [Rom 8:4]." The true conception of the new birth thus, is not the stimulation of mere nature in anyway as such, whether by human or supposed divine influence, but the actual introduction of the natural man into this higher order of life, the *supernatural* sphere of the Spirit, bringing along with it the real possibility of salvation. This supposes at once a Divine act, which was regarded always by the early Church, accordingly, as having place in the mystery of Baptism. He that believeth and is baptized, the Apostolical commission runs, shall be saved [Mark 16:16]. Faith is submission to the new order of life supernaturally offered in the Church; and its proper complement is the heavenly reality of this grace itself, meeting it as God's act and seal in the laver of regeneration. Baptism in such view is of course, as the old creeds have it, "for the

---

88. [*Epist.*, 238–39; *Letters*, 4:88.]

89. [*The Apostolical Constitutions* is a collection of ecclesiastical law which dates from the second half of the fourth century. Exact authorship is unknown, but much of the text is a reworking of other texts from the second and third centuries. The text probably originates in Syria, perhaps specifically Antioch. The text does have historical value especially for its liturgical information. An English translation can be found in *Ante-Nicene Christian Library* 17:15–269.]

remission of sins."⁹⁰ It is a real translation from the sphere of nature, the fallen life of Adam, over into the sphere of truth and grace, the full possibility of righteousness and eternal life, which is revealed in Christ.

How real all this was to Cyprian is shown, most impressively and affectingly, by the account he gives of his own conversion, in the passage we have already quoted on this subject from his tract *De Gratia Dei*. He had felt the darkness and misery of nature; but despaired of help; till he was brought finally to bow to the hope set before him by the Church, and to offer himself, as a catechumen nearly fifty years old, for admission into its mystic inclosure. He had found it hard to believe, "that a man might be born again, and that being animated into a new life, through the laver of saving water, he might lay aside what he had been before, and though retaining the same bodily frame put on an entirely new mind and spirit."⁹¹ But this great mystery became real to him, through the actual experiment of submitting as a little child to the authority of Christianity in its own proper form. He believed, and was baptized; and his baptism was to his faith a real response of grace on the part of heaven, bringing with it the complete power of salvation.

> When by means of the regenerating wave (*undae genitalis auxilio*), the stain of my former life was washed away, and the serene and pure light of heaven descended into my sin cleansed bosom; as soon as the second birth, by the Spirit derived from on high had transformed me into a new man (*postquam coelitus spiritu hausto in novum me hominem nativitas secunda reparavit*); presently in a wonderful way doubts began to be settled, perplexities to solve themselves, and obscurities to grow plain; there arose strength for what before seemed difficult, and power to do what was before held to be impossible; making it clear, that the first natural life in the service of sin was of the earth, and that what the Holy Ghost had now breathed into me was of God.⁹²

How it may be with others, we know not; but on our own mind, we confess, such a testimony, on such a subject, coming from such a man, falls with uncommonly powerful and solemn impression. In what startling contrast it stands, with the reigning so-called *evangelical* tone and style of the present day! Which is to be regarded as right, and which wrong, the voice of the ancient church in Cyprian, or this unsacramental modern voice? We pretend not here to answer the question. It is one however of most profound significance and interest, which the thoughtful may well be asked to lay seriously to heart. "He that hath *ears* to hear, *let him hear* [Matt 11:15]."

That Cyprian's voice here was in fact that of the universal ancient church, is beyond all doubt. The controversy concerning the baptism of heretics proceeds throughout, as we have already seen, on the supposition, that the sacrament is of real force

90. [This language is from the Nicene Creed.]

91. [Cyprian, *Ad Donatum De Gratia Dei*, in *Tract.*, 2; PPS 32:50]

92. [Cyprian, *Ad Donatum De Gratia*, in *Tract.*, 2–3; PPS 32:52; the Latin phrases follow the English translations.]

Document 3: Cyprian: Second Article.

for the remission of sins, and carries in it objectively the sense and power of the new birth. The question also in regard to the forgiveness of mortal sin after baptism, which was a source likewise of no small difficulty to the early church, turned always, as we may at once see, on the same theory. For our modern Puritan habit of thought, there is no meaning in either of these old Catholic questions. Both of them are felt to be of antiquated interest, of no real difficulty, and of only small account. All that is needed however to make us feel their ancient significance, is some due apprehension of what baptism was held to be in the period to which they belong. In the age of Cyprian, no one questioned its power to take away sin and to produce regeneration, who did not mean at the same time to question the whole fact of Christianity. It was a settled maxim: "*Omnia delicta in baptismo deponi*" (*Test. III.* §. 65).[93] It was a thing understood and acknowledged on every side, that all "*qui ad divinum munus et patrimonium baptismi sanctificatione perveniunt,*" all who are made Christians by the sanctification of baptism, "*hominem illic veterem gratia lavacri salutaris exponunt, et innovati Spiritu sancto a sordibus contagionis antiquae iterata nativitate purgantur,*" put off there the old man through the grace of the salutary laver, and being renewed by the Holy Ghost are cleansed from the defilement of the old contagion by a second birth.[94]

Infant Baptism, in this view, comes to its proper significance. Infants need the grace which the sacrament brings as much as others, and no age is to be shut out from the benefit of a salvation which God has provided for all; "*Deus, ut personam non accipit, sic nec aetatem.*"[95] If even the greatest sinners of full age are not to be refused the grace of baptism for the remission of sins,

> how much less should it be refused to an infant, which being recently born has not sinned at all, except as by natural generation from Adam it has brought along with it in its first birth the contagion of the old death, and for which the way to obtaining the remission of sins is so much the more easy, as the sins to be remitted are not its own but those of another.[96]

So Cyprian writes (Ep. 61 [64], *ad Fidum*) in the name of a whole council of African bishops, in resolution of the doubt, not whether infants might be baptized at all, (nobody then, it seems, made any question of *that*) but whether it was necessary to defer their baptism till the eighth day, as in the case of circumcision among the Jews. The unanimous judgment is, that no such limitation was to be allowed. "*Nulla anima perdenda est,*" they say; on which account, "*universi judicamus nulli homini*

---

93. [Cyprian, *Testimonia Adversus Iudaeos*, in *Tract.*, 93; trans. "All these faults were removed in baptism." §65 alludes to 1 Cor. 6:9–11. The maxim is not found in the biblical text but can be derived from it. *ANF* 5:551.]

94. [Cyprian, *De Habitu Virginum*, in *Tract.*, 116; Nevin's translations follow the Latin phrases. *ANF* 5:436.]

95. [*Epist.*, 169; trans. "{just as} God draws no distinction between persons, so neither does He between ages" (*Letters*, 3:111).]

96. [*Epist.*, 170; *Letters*, 3:112.]

nato misericordiam Dei et gratiam denegandam."[97] The first birth makes room and creates occasion immediately for the second.

[The Sacramental Force of the Eucharist]

The same real force Cyprian sees always in the mystery of the *Holy Eucharist.* It is for his faith an actual sacrament, and not merely an outward monument or sign. As regards the mode of the communication it offers with the body and blood of Christ, his language is indeed more general than precise; but it is abundantly clear as to the fact. Writing on the petition in the Lord's Prayer, *Give us this day our daily bread, (De Oratione Dominica* §. 18), he says that Christ is the bread of life for his people, "*qui corpus ejus contingunt,*" and so we are to pray that no serious sin may intervene to hinder our daily participation of the heavenly bread of the eucharist, and so of his body or flesh which he declares to be given for the life of the world.[98]

> Since then to eat of this bread is to live forever, as it is plain that those live who touch his body and receive the eucharist by right of communication, so on the other hand we must fear and pray lest any one, by being separated from Christ's body through prohibition, remain far from salvation, since he himself warns us, *Except ye eat the flesh of the Son of man, and drink his blood, ye shall have no life in you* [John 6:53]. And so we pray that our bread, that is Christ, may be given to us daily, that we who abide and live in him may not recede from his sanctification and body.[99]

This makes the eucharist at once the communion of the real flesh and blood of the Son of Man, according to the awful mystery of his own words in the sixth chapter of John. Hence the stress we find laid on it, as a real Divine viaticum, a source of strength and fortification against evil, for all great emergencies in the Christian life. A striking exemplification of this we have in the course pursued with regard to excommunicated penitents. Their probation was long and severe. But the danger of death in any case might bring it to an end. They must be strengthened for the last conflict by receiving the Lord's body. So when a new persecution was expected, we find this indulgence made general. "It was proper," Cyprian writes (Ep. 57, *ad Cornelium*),

> that the term of penance should be protracted, with relief to the infirm at death, whilst there was rest and tranquillity allowing such delay with the tears

---

97. [*Epist.*, 169; trans. "we all formed the judgment that it is not right to deny the mercy and grace of God to any man that is born. . . . {in order to} prevent the destruction of any soul (*Letters*, 3:110)." The text reads "universi *potius* judicamus."]

98. [Cyprian, *De Oratione Dominica*, in *Tract.*, 165; PPS 29:78; *ANF* 5:452. *ANF* translates the text as "in union with His body," but gives an alternative rendering as "in contact with His body" (n. 4). Cf. Simonetti, ed., *Ancient Christian Commentary . . . , New Testament* 1A:135. Nevin later made use of Cyprian's application of "daily bread" to eucharistic bread in "Bread of Life," MTSS 6:224 and note 10.]

99. [Cyprian, *De Oratione Dominica*, in *Tract.*,, 165; PPS 29:78, 79; *ANF* 5:452.]

Document 3: Cyprian: Second Article.

of mourners and such succor to the dying at the last hour. But now peace is needed, not for the infirm, but for the strong, and communication is to be given by us, not to the dying, but to the living; in order that we may not leave unarmed and naked but may fortify with the protection of Christ's body and blood, those, whom we excite and exhort to battle; and that, inasmuch as the eucharist is for the purpose of a defence (*tutela*) to those who receive it, we may arm those whom we wish to be safe against the enemy with the fortification of the Lord's fulness. For how can we teach or urge them to shed *their blood* in the confession of Christ's name, if *his blood be* not allowed them for the struggle? Or how shall we prepare them for the cup of martyrdom, if we do not admit them first to drink the Lord's cup by right of communication in the church?[100]

Intimately connected with this idea of the mystical presence of Christ's body and blood in the sacrament of the Supper, as the bread of life, is the persuasion and belief that the service carried in it the force of a sacrifice or offering. In whatever sense the mystery involves communion with Christ's body and blood, it is with his body, we know, as broken, and with his blood as shed for the remission of sins. It is as comprehending in them always the force of the atonement wrought out by his bloody death, that his flesh is thus meat indeed, and his blood drink indeed, for the use of a dying world. That atonement, in such view, is no past transaction merely, but a fact "once for all," the power of a perennial indissoluble life, always of force in the Saviour's person [Heb 10:10].[101] In such form, it must of necessity go along with the sacramental exhibition of his "flesh given for the life of the world" [John 6:51]. It will be there, so far as the exhibition itself is a reality and no dream, not as a remembered doctrine merely but in its own actual virtue and power as a sacrifice always well pleasing unto God. In this way no idea is more familiar to the mind of the ancient church, than that by which the eucharist is regarded as a service analogous with the offerings of the Old Testament. The passage: "In every place incense shall he offered unto my name, and *a pure offering*" (Mal. i: 11), is taken to be thus literally fulfilled. We have seen how Cyprian speaks continually of the "altar" and "priesthood" in this relation, and of "offering" or "sacrificing" as terms of one import with the celebration of the Lord's supper, in the known and familiar church phraseology of the time. Memorable especially is the language he employs on the subject, Ep. 63, *ad Caecilium*. With reference to the typical priesthood of Melchisedek, he says: "Who is more a priest of the Most High God than our Lord Jesus Christ, who offered sacrifice to his Father, and this the same that Melchisedek offered, that is, bread and wine, namely his own body and blood;" after which we are told, that Melchisedek offered an anticipatory image of Christ's sacrifice in the form of bread and wine, "*quam rem perficiens et adimplens Dominus panem et calicem mixtum vino obtulit, et qui est plenitudo veritatis, veritatem prefiguratae imaginis adimplevit;*" language that looks at once to the eucharist, as the

100. [*Epist.*, 123; *Letters*, 3:56.]
101. [Nevin later treats this theme in "Once for All."]

abiding verification of what in the other case was only picture and shadow.¹⁰² Then further on it is said:

> If it is not lawful to alter the least of our Lord's commandments, how much less may we thus make free with such great and weighty regulations relating to the very mystery itself of the Lord's passion and our redemption, or change them by human authority into anything else than what God has appointed. For since Jesus Christ, our Lord and God, is himself the High Priest of God the Father, and has offered himself first as a sacrifice to the Father, and commanded to do this in remembrance of him; that priest, it is plain, truly officiates in Christ's place, who imitates what Christ did; *and he then offers in the church a true and full sacrifice to God the Father,* when he sets himself to offer according to what he sees to have been offered by Christ himself.¹⁰³

The sacrament of the altar in this way becomes the centre of the universal Christian worship. All is a solemn λειτουργια¹⁰⁴ revolving round the shekinah¹⁰⁵ of this mysterious presence. The unutterably glorious as well as awful *reality* which is here brought into view, is felt to underlie and bind together the whole new order of life to which it belongs; sending its pulsations, like a mighty heart, over the mystical body, and making it to be in truth the "communion of saints." Hence those "commemorations" of the martyrs, which Cyprian made so much account of celebrating in this way.¹⁰⁶ Hence the idea of a certain benefit to the dead, through the power of this sacrifice performed on their account. Cyprian refers in one place to an established ecclesiastical rule, denying such posthumous privilege in a particular case of offence. The case itself is characteristic. It was that of nominating a priest, by last will and testament, to act as a secular trustee or guardian. This was regarded as something profane; for which reason, "there must be no offering made for the offender, no sacrifice rendered for his repose; he deserves not to have his name mentioned at the altar of God in the prayer of the priests, who has sought to call off from the altar the priests and ministers of God."¹⁰⁷ The same idea of reconciling power was attached to the use

---

102. [*Epist.*, 158–59; *Letters*, 3:99–100; trans. "And when the Lord brought to fulfillment and completion that symbolic action, He offered bread and a cup mixed with wine, and so He who is Fullness itself fulfilled the truth of that prefigured symbol" (*Letters*, 3:100). Melchisedek is presented as a type of Christ in Heb 7.]

103. [*Epist.*, 165, Nevin's emphasis; *Letters*, 3:106.]

104. [Lit., "service," but here with the connotation of "liturgy."]

105. ["God's presence in the world." Not a biblical term but used in post-biblical Jewish literature. See Harrelson, "Shekinah," 222.]

106. *Ep.* 39. *Sacrificia pro eis semper, ut meministis offerimus, quoties martyrum passiones et dies anniversaria commemoratione celebramus* [*Epist.*, 78; trans. "As you recall, we never fail to offer sacrifices on their behalf every time we celebrate in commemoration the anniversary dates of the sufferings of these martyrs" (*Letters*, 2:55)].—So also *Ep.* 1[digit unreadable] before quoted.

107. *Ep.* 1 [*Epist.*, 2]. "*Quod episcopi, antecessores nostri religiose considerantes et salubriter providentes censuerunt, ne quis frater excedens ad tutelam vel curam clericum nominaret, ac si quis hoc fecisset, non offerretur pro eo, nec sacrificium pro dormitione ejus celebraretur. Neque enim apud altare Dei*

of the eucharist, as we have already seen, in the restoration of penitents to the peace of the church. The conscience must be purged "with sacrifice and under the hand of the priest."[108] All prayers and supplications, as well as alms and good works of every sort, were regarded as acquiring new force when backed and supported by these altar solemnities, as truly as a like real benefit was believed to have been derived in such cases from the more ancient shadowy sacrifices of the Jewish law.

[Penance and Absolution in the Return of the "Lapsed"]

It is in full agreement with this whole doctrine of what the Church is as the real organ and medium of salvation, that Cyprian lays so much stress on the solemnity of penance and absolution in the case of the lapsed, as the necessary condition of their being restored to her communion and peace. There was a terrible reality in such a fall. The excommunication it brought with it was felt as a present actual calamity and curse. In these circumstances it became as much a necessity to be reconciled to the church, as it was to be brought into it at first by baptism. The case was not one for mere private repentance. It was not enough for the offender to think of settling it between his own conscience and God. There must be an application to the church for help; there must be full confession made to the ministers of religion; there must be a long course of contrition, with deprecatory prayers and other signs of grief; and then in the end, after all this, must come the priestly absolution, opening the way to the life giving communion of the Redeemer's body and blood. All this was held to be something vastly more than simple ceremony or show. It was the order which God had been pleased to establish, for the actual recovery of men from the guilt and power of sin. It carried in it the force of a real remedy, for what must prove otherwise a mortal and wholly incurable disease. Cyprian does not call it a sacrament exactly, as we now use the term; but it has for him undoubtedly all the elements of what is called the sacrament of penance in the Roman Church. Absolution in this way was held to be of force on earth for the actual forgiveness of sins in heaven. It must be secured accordingly by all means, before passing out of the world by death. Hence the indulgence granted to penitents *in extremis*; "because there is no exomologesis in hades (*apud inferos*), and to encourage penance, it must be made sure of its *fruit*" (*Ep.* 55, *ad Antonianum*).[109]

---

meretur nominari in sacerdotum prece, qui ab altari sacerdotes et ministros Dei voluit avocare." [Trans. "The bishops who preceded us after holy deliberation on this question decreed the following salutary provisions for the future: no brother should nominate on his death one of the clergy as guardian or trustee, and should anyone do this *the offering should not be made on his behalf nor should the sacrifice be celebrated for his repose*. For he does not deserve to be named at the altar of God in the prayer of the bishop seeing that he was prepared to distract away from that altar bishops and ministers of religion" (*Letters*, 1:52, Nevin's emphasis).] We may see at once, how this goes to show a general unquestioning consent on the part of the church, as it then stood, in the Catholic maxim, that prayer and the offering of the eucharist in behalf of the faithful dead are of true wholesome account for their repose.

108. [Cyprian, *De Lapsis*, in *Tract.*, 143; ACW 25:26.]
109. [*Epist.*, 119; *Letters*, 3:52.]

Just as infants are to be baptized *(Ep. 64)*, because "*quantum in nobis est, si fieri potest, nulla anima perdenda est.*"[110]

And yet Cyprian taught no magical or merely mechanical salvation. The absolution of the church might be gained by false pretences; it might be granted rashly; but then it would have no force in the other world. Hence the danger of hasty restorations, in the case of the lapsed. Such indulgence tended to destruction, not to salvation. The wound must be thoroughly probed and cleansed, in order that there might be a radical cure. Dying penitents must indeed be absolved; in which case, however, "the Lord will ratify our judgment here only if he find the penitence of the sinner full and right; but should any one have deceived us by a feigned repentance, let God, who is not mocked and who sees the heart, perfect our defective inquisition, and the Lord make good the judgment of his servants."[111] Over against all undue regard to the intercession of the confessors and martyrs, the people are reminded *(De Lapsis)*, "that the Lord alone can have mercy upon men, and he only impart forgiveness of sins committed against himself, who has borne our sins and suffered on their account;"[112] and also *(Ep. 27)*, "that the martyrs make not the gospel but the gospel makes the martyrs."[113] So the sacraments used unworthily, we are continually told, produce death only and not life.

Some may find here a contradiction in Cyprian's system. Neander seems to charge him in this way with some want of consistency. But the difficulty comes from a false apprehension of what is to be understood by objective grace, or the *opus operatum* rightly so called, in the ministrations of the church. To say that certain conditions are required on the part of the subject to make such grace of effect, and that the failure of these may turn it into a nullity or something worse, by no means implies that the same grace is without real power for the accomplishment of its own ends where conditional room is made for its action in this way. In the sphere of nature, causation and condition come before as under such necessary connection on all sides;[114] and no good reason can be assigned, why a similar realistic order should not be allowed to have place also in the supernatural economy of the Holy Catholic Church.

Neander however sees a falling away from the original genius of the Gospel, in this whole Cyprianic doctrine of the outward church. The mind of the age, he thinks, had taken a wrong direction, and Cyprian became a leading organ in helping it forward in what he is pleased to denominate "a relapse to the Old Testament standpoint," which had been at first happily left behind. Bursting the shell of Judaism, we are told, Christianity had in the beginning, with the help of St. Paul especially, triumphed over

---

110. [*Epist.*, 169, Nevin's emphasis; trans. "we must do everything we possibly can *to prevent the destruction of any soul*" (*Letters*, 3:110).]

111. [*Epist.*, 112; *Letters*, 3:43–44.]

112. [Cyprian, *De Lapsis*, in *Tract.*, 144; PPS 32:121.]

113. [*Epist.*, 53; *Letters*, 1:114.]

114. [Even in nature, there are causes that fail to accomplish their effect because some condition is lacking; e.g., a seed may fail to produce a plant because it lacks the condition of sufficient rain.]

Document 3: Cyprian: Second Article.

the Jewish tendency and asserted successfully the proper freedom and spirituality of its own nature.

> In the Gentile congregations the new creation was fairly revealed. But the surmounted Jewish view forced its way in again from another side. Humanity could not yet maintain itself on this height of a purely spiritual religion; for the mass who were to be educated first into the apprehension of pure Christianity, weaned first from Paganism, the Jewish standpoint was more near; out of Christianity accordingly, after it had reached its independence, a standpoint was again evolved analogous with that of the Old Testament, a new externalization of the kingdom of God, a new discipline of law, that should serve afterwards for the training of barbarous nations, a new guardianship for the mind of humanity till it should attain to full grown manhood in Christ.[115]

This rehabilitation, once commenced, proved to be of most fruitful progress, our historian tells us; and so we have a ready rule at once in hand, if we trust his guidance, for disposing of all the pontifical, churchly, and sacramental ideas, that come before us so thickly in the religious life of the third century. They are to be set to the account simply of this old most unfortunate, though it would seem highly necessary, *Rückfall*, on the part of Spiritual Pauline Christianity, *auf den alttestamentlichen Standpunkt*.[116]

This is characteristic. The great German master of church history has a theory of his own with regard to the true nature of Christianity, which he reads of course without difficulty into the New Testament, and particularly into the writings of St. Paul. It is eminently spiritualistic, much of one sort in truth with the mysticism of the Quakers, and not far removed at times from the dry rationalism of the Baptists. But the church life of the third century is plainly enough constructed throughout, on an altogether different scheme. So far as this variation goes, Neander now must necessarily find it by his own rule out of right form and shape; and so the next thing is a hypothetical speculation, to account smoothly for the somewhat remarkable fact. This, it will be observed, rests on no historical basis whatever. It is taken from the cloud land simply of his own brain, like a vast deal more that we meet with in the landscape painting of the same distinguished writer. All comes to this only, that Neander's preconception here is contradicted by the actual state of things in the time of Cyprian, and *therefore* the time of Cyprian must be a departure, in the direction of this difference, from the original sense and spirit of the Gospel. It never seems to enter the mind of the great man, that the false reckoning might be on his own side possibly, and not with the age which is thus conveniently put in the wrong. Why should the judgment of Neander after all be taken as at once conclusive in such a case, against the judgment of Cyprian and the whole early church? The matter speaks for itself, we are

---

115. [Neander, *Allgemeine Geschichte*, 331; *General History*, 194.]

116. K. G. B. I. S. 330. ff. (2te Aufl.) [trans. "relapse to an Old Testament standpoint;" Neander, *Allgemeine Geschichte*, 330–34 (heading); *General History*, 193–97 translates it "Formation of a Sacerdotal Caste"].

told; this Cyprianic system carries in it evidently a strong analogy with the religious polity of the Old Testament. Suppose it does. Was not this polity then of Divine constitution? Was it not a real theocracy? Was it not ordered and framed with reference to the Gospel? And why then should that be taken at once for a false construction of Christianity, by which it is made to appear a true completion of Judaism, carrying out the sense of its shadows in the form of corresponding glorious realities? But the genius of the new religion, we are told again, is spiritual and free. That is most true. Must it follow from this, however, that it is Gnostic, a thing of mere subjective experience and dreamy speculation? What if the very idea of spirituality and freedom here be, not the unbound action simply of man's mind in the sphere of nature, but its introduction by faith into the sphere of truth and grace, as a higher order of life brought home to it in an objective way by the power of the Holy Ghost? Cyprian saw just this mystery in the Church. It was to him a real revelation of the grace it proclaimed. Its charter was taken to be, not fiction, but fact. It was a true supernatural polity, starting from the skies but permanently settled upon the earth. Under its forms went the active presence of what they were employed to exhibit and represent, the very substance of the things which had been presented before only in the way of shadow and type. And who will say, that such a real revelation of the Spirit, if a simple actuality and no dream, would not be something sufficiently spiritual, or that the power of acknowledging it by faith might not be after all the best kind of freedom, and not a necessary falling back merely upon the Jewish standpoint for the education of unripe nations? We question much if Paul ever thought of asserting any other spirituality and freedom than this, in the name of the Gospel. The issue before us regards then just the truth of this ancient conception of the mystery of the Church. Neander's criticism assumes that the conception was visionary and false; that no such Divine polity, as Cyprian fondly dreamed, with heavenly functions and supernatural powers, was ever really at hand in its historical constitution. Grant that, and the rest follows easily enough. But other consequences also come painfully into view, for a thoughtful mind. Are we prepared for any such ominous concession? If not, what becomes of this whole judgment; Cyprian may be right after all, we repeat, and Neander wrong.

Conclusion

The church question as forced upon us by the writings of Cyprian, it is plain to see, is something a good deal deeper and more solemn than the controversy between Anglican Episcopacy and the rest of the Protestant world. We do not deny at all the importance of this controversy in its proper place; and for Episcopalianism as a system, it is hardly necessary for us to say, we entertain no small amount of veneration and regard. We do not deny too that Cyprian, who has been called the Ignatius of the West, bears ample testimony, like his predecessor of this name in the East, to the existence of Episcopacy, as an institution held to be of Apostolical origin, in the early church. But it is most plain at the same time, that we are not carried by it as a separate interest, in any way, to the last ground of the system to which it originally belonged. Mere episcopacy was not enough by any means, in the judgment of these ancient times, to uphold a true church succession; it must be the office in unity with itself under a catholic form; the office as representing the undivided and indivisible Apostolical commission, on which as a rock centering in Peter the Church was to be built to the end of time. Along with this go corresponding apprehensions of the attributes and powers of the Church, which our modem Protestant Episcopacy either rejects altogether, or turns into affectation and sham. The two systems are of altogether different constitution; and it is perfectly idle to think of establishing an identity between them, on the ground simply of their having in common the office of bishops. What charm can there be in an episcopate, that this rather than any other fragment of Peter's ship as it originally sailed towards heaven, should be taken to carry away with it now, *as a fragment,* the power of a true church life? No. Anglicanism is not Cyprianic Christianity. The question of Episcopacy is in truth of only secondary and very subordinate account. The grand issue always, is that which lies between Protestantism and Romanism. This we are bound to look solemnly in the face.

J. W. N.

Cyprian: Third Article.[1]

[Review of Cyprian's Doctrine of the Church and the Episcopal Office]

Cyprian's doctrine of the *Church* we have found to be fundamental to his whole theology and religious life. In proportion as this is the case, it becomes important to understand well in what relation, it stood to the faith and life of the Christian world generally in the first ages. To do justice to the man, as well as to judge properly of the doctrine, we must inquire how far this was peculiar to himself and to the time when he lived, or is to be regarded as having come down by legitimate inheritance and tradition from a still older period, as part of the faith which was supposed to have been originally delivered to the saints. To feel the full significance of such an inquiry, we need only to bring to mind distinctly the leading features of the Cyprianic doctrine of the church, and to observe at the same time the broad contrast and contradiction in which they may be seen at once to stand, with the thinking of a large portion of the modern so called evangelical world on the same subject.

What is most necessary to be kept in view in the Cyprianic doctrine, is not this or that feature of it taken in a separate abstract light, the point of episcopacy for instance or the point of baptismal regeneration, but the universal idea rather, the conception of the church as a whole, out of which all such particular features flow, and in the presence and power of which alone they can be said to have any real force. The Campbellite Baptists, in their style, run away with the notion of an objective power of some sort belonging to the sacrament of baptism; and then claim to be what the church was in the beginning, by laying all stress on the ordinance in such view, as was done in primitive times.[2] Their theory is, that the sacrament, as a Divine appointment, may be torn away from the living constitution to which it originally appertained, without losing its force, and so that the use of it by any class of men professing to obey the Gospel may be taken as sufficiently valid at all times for its original purposes and ends. The

---

1. [*MR* 4 (September 1852) 417–52.]

2. [An American movement initiated by Thomas (1763–1854) and Alexander Campbell (1788–1866), father and son. They claimed to restore New Testament Christianity, an example of the "repristinationism" critiqued in this volume. At first, they worked with the Baptists, since they baptized by immersion; but their further affirmation that baptism was "'for remission of sins'" led to a gradual separation. They also practiced weekly communion. Today the tradition continues in three "Christian Church/Disciples of Christ" denominations. *Dictionary of Christianity in America*, 214–15, 1007–8.]

Document 3: Cyprian: Third Article.

pedantry is much the same, it seems to us, when Episcopalians run away in similar style with mere episcopacy, or with the notion of a liturgy; and on the ground of such distinction simply pretend to be in union here with what the Church was in the first ages, with a certain affectation of exclusive completeness over against all other Protestant bodies which happen not to be possessed of the same advantage. What charm is there, we ask again as we have asked before, in a ministry of bishops, that it should be considered sufficient to bear away with it, wherever found, the original powers and prerogatives of the church, without regard to the whole constitution of the church as it stood in the beginning? Or what talismanic virtue for any such end shall be supposed to reside in the use of a liturgy, kept up in the same isolated way? We grant at once the argument for episcopacy drawn from the practice of the church in the third century; as we allow also the full force of the argument in the same form for the use of liturgies. Nothing short of the most bull-necked obstinacy, can refuse to see and admit what is so perfectly clear. In these points, separately viewed, Episcopalians undoubtedly come nearer to the Christianity of Cyprian's time, than the bodies they affect to exclude and condemn. We may say as much however of the Gospel according to Alexander Campbell. It approaches the primitive scheme of Christianity here and there, more closely than most of the sects which agree in denouncing it as rationalistic and false. And yet rightly no such advantage in this case, is allowed to be of any account; just because the resemblances rested upon show themselves to be not living but dead, are not rooted in the presence of the same life, but owe their appearance altogether to outward artificial imitation. Mechanical similitude in this way is something widely different from organical communion. It is quite possible to conceive of an identity of life under great variations of outward form, while it may be wanting entirely where the outward show of variation is the least. No figure in wax can stand truly for the life it represents. No parts brought outwardly together can constitute a living whole. So in the case before us, we say, Episcopalians are quite too fast, when from the single fact of their agreement with the primitive church in the matter of episcopacy, and one or two other like separate points, they at once jump to the conclusion that they alone have preserved under a Protestant form the true succession of what Christianity was in the beginning, and that all other Protestant bodies are without authority and right. This, we are fully persuaded, is to bring the whole cause of Protestantism into peril. The question between those who receive and those who reject episcopacy on Protestant ground is a mere circumstance, over against the broad deep issue by which in the nature of the case both are sundered from the Church of Rome; and as related to this, it is a mere circumstance in the problem of making out for Protestantism a real historical derivation from the Christianity of the first ages. For one who is brought to understand the actual state of the case, it is easy enough to see that if Episcopalian Protestantism can be successfully justified in its measure of variation from the old order of the church, Protestantism without episcopacy also may be justified in the like general predicament; the difference in the degree of variation in the two cases being after all nearly as nothing, in comparison with what is of common amount. The grand question regards the right of Protestantism in its whole view.³ Has it been possible at all to maintain a true succession of the ancient church life, under this form? Let us feel only that an intelligent affirmative answer can be returned to this question, and we shall feel at the same time that the possibility cannot be held reasonably to the narrow limits of the Anglican scheme. To be of any real force that far, it must be of force still farther. By seeking to fix it within any such purely arbitrary and mechanical bounds, we in fact destroy it altogether.

The Cyprianic doctrine of the church made vast account indeed of episcopacy; but not of episcopacy in any and every view. The significance of the whole institution was conditioned by the universal scheme to which it belonged. It was felt to be of fundamental account in its organic relation to this scheme; while out of such connection it was held to be of no importance whatever.⁴ What we need then to understand and keep in view, as we have said, is the conception or idea as a whole, which the doctrine before us exhibits as the true theory of the church. With regard to this, there is no room for any serious mistake. We may call in question, if we please, the truth of the theory. We may say that Cyprian and his age were in error. But the fact of the theory itself is too plain to be made the subject of any dispute, so far at least as its general form is concerned.

The theory is,⁵ that the Church was literally a Divine constitution, built on the foundation of the apostles and prophets, Jesus Christ himself being the chief corner stone; that it grew out of the mystery of the Incarnation, and had its perpetual charter in the living power of the Apostolical Commission; that it bore thus the character of a true historical organization in the bosom of the world's present life; that under such outwardly visible and historical form, it carried in itself at the same time real heavenly and supernatural powers, actual virtue and force above nature for its own more than earthly and natural ends; that the exercise of these powers was through functions and organs ordained of God, and centering in the ministry of the episcopate, which was derived by clear succession from the office of the Apostles, and in the character of a solid corporation formed at once the basis and the bond of unity for the universal organism; and that there was no room consequently to think of salvation, except in the bosom of this most real system and through its instrumental mediation and help.

---

3. [See Calvin, *Institutes* 2:1068–1149 {IV.iv–vii} for a discussion of the history of the office of bishop and the formation of the papacy.]

4. [E.g., just because the heretics had bishops did not change the fact that they were outside the "true" church.]

5. [Nevin here begins to restate the "theory" of the church as he finds it in Cyprian. It is "holistic" because it attempts to describe the "whole" spiritual organism, the "organic" character of the church. A modern church might have some "bits"—e.g., episcopacy, baptismal regeneration, weekly eucharist—and still not be identical with the church as Cyprian understands it. For a version that Nevin identifies with later, see "Hodge on the Ephesians," MTSS 7:98–101; for the need to understand ecclesiology "holistically," see "Thoughts on the Church," MTSS 7:132–34.]

Document 3: Cyprian: Third Article.

It is easy to see, in such view, that all faith must start as an act of submission on the part of men to the authority with which they were supposed to be thus objectively confronted. Where a real constitution of this sort was allowed to be at hand, it is plain that no acknowledgment of Christianity could be regarded as true and valid, that fell short of an actual bowing of the soul to its claims in this form. Only to question these claims, to make them a matter for debate, was to refuse for the time the objective reality to which by Divine right they were taken to appertain. To talk of faith on the outside of the church was at once a contradiction in terms. No faith could be honest and sound, which was not ready to submit to the mystery which here challenged its submission. To believe, was of necessity thus to be also *baptized*, or in other words to come under the power in this real way of that real supernatural system, into the bosom of which baptism was considered always to be the solemn act of introduction, the sacrament of a new birth. And then we need be at no loss to understand the vast stress which was laid on the sin of schism. With this theory of the church, it becomes at once an offence in full parallel with heresy, simply the obverse side in truth of that sin. It rests necessarily on the assumption, that there is no Holy Catholic Church, in the sense now under consideration—no real objective constitution, embodying in itself by Divine ordination the mystery of the Christian salvation under a supernatural form, and carrying in itself in such view the full guaranty of its proper infallible sufficiency for its own ends—and that Christianity therefore is by no means bound to any such order and method of revelation in the world, but may be carried into effect and made of force for the purposes of salvation, by the mere judgment and will of men, in some other form altogether. But who may not see, that for the doctrine before us every assumption of this sort, however tacitly and silently made, must be at once the negation of the whole fact of Christianity, the opposite exactly of all true faith? It strikes at the root of the whole mystery, which faith is required here to embrace; and in the bosom of which only as a Divine reality it can have any power to save. Schism then, in the very nature of the case, must be wholesale heresy also and death. It is the most fundamental of all forms of insurrection against the authority of the Gospel. It aims at its universal subversion.

[The Modern Protestant Doctrine Compared and Contrasted]

Such, we say, is the Cyprianic doctrine of the church. Our modern Protestant scheme, it is painfully evident, is altogether different. The difference does not turn by any means on the question of episcopacy, or on any such point as purgatory, transubstantiation, or the worship of the saints. It lies deeper than all this. The true last ground of it opens upon us in the doctrine of the church. Protestantism, it is plain, involves an entire departure from the theory or scheme of Cyprian here, not simply as it may reject this or that form of ecclesiastical polity, this or that ecclesiastical usage, but as it refuses to see in the church the actual presence of the Christian salvation under the same outwardly real and objective view. Let no one take offence at this, as though it were a reproach cast upon Protestantism. We have to do with it at present only as a simple fact of history. As such, we are bound to see it, to acknowledge it, to make it the subject of earnest and solemn consideration. It is a fact which needs to be understood and satisfactorily explained, to make good our common boast that Protestantism seeks only the light.

So far as Puritanism is concerned, the difference now mentioned is immediately palpable. It openly repudiates the whole idea of the church, which is exhibited to us by Cyprian, considers it a figment, part indeed of the mystery of iniquity [2 Thess 2:7], and something diametrically opposed to the notion of evangelical piety after its own approved style. It never grows tired of harping on the string, that to trust in the church is to have no proper sense of the spirituality of the Gospel, and that a religion of sacraments is puerile and unsafe. It sets Christianity on the outside of the church. This is not of the essence and constitution of the awful mystery in any way, but only an outward accident attached to it, which men may order and shape as they best can, with help of the Bible, to suit their own taste. The church is not the medium of the Christian salvation in any real sense. Faith stands not primarily in any act of submission to it in any such view; but has regard to truth under an altogether different form, and may be complete under a character of most perfect abstraction from its claims, and indeed must be so to make the acknowledgment of these claims afterwards, such as they are, of any actual account. Schism, on this scheme, becomes a very venial offence, is no longer at all intelligible indeed in its ancient sense. The universal sect system is based, of course, on the absolute want of everything like faith in the article of the Holy Catholic Church as it once stood; and the tendency of this system always is towards its own natural end of full Baptistic Independency, which boldly resolves the whole mystery into the notion of an indefinite multitude of churches formed by "social contract," in Jean Jacques Rousseau style,[6] without the remotest imagination of any supernatural right or force whatever.

But the Puritan system in this case is not alone. The difference before us extends also, as already intimated, to Anglican Episcopalianism. Its theory of the church is not that of Cyprian. Whether right or wrong, this last makes no room for the legitimate entrance of any such fact as the Reformation, owns no possibility whatever of a valid hierarchy aside from the unity of the apostolical succession as a solid whole, and asserts with unfaltering precision the presence of supernatural powers objectively at hand in the church and to be found nowhere else.

The difference is with Protestantism as a whole. It is not to be disguised, that this rests upon a doctrine of the church, which is broadly at variance with the doctrine of

---

6. [Jean-Jacques Rousseau (1712–78), a French philosopher, whose *Social Contract* (1762) held that political bodies or societies are formed by a kind of agreement by the members of the body which is generated out of the freely accepted obligations of otherwise isolated individuals. This is to be understood as "a philosophical fiction . . . to show how political obligation rests on individual consent" (*Oxford Companion to Philosophy*, 174).]

Cyprian. It becomes then a most interesting and momentous inquiry: *In what relation does this Cyprianic doctrine stand to the life and faith of the Christian world generally in the first ages?* The man who can be indifferent to the practical solemnity of this inquiry, may be very sure that he has himself no real faith in the Divine realness of Christianity, but is mistaking for it always a hollow phantom only of his own brain.

[The Origin of the Doctrine of the Church in Earlier Christianity]

May it be successfully pretended, in the first place, that Cyprian's doctrine was in any material view peculiar to himself, or that it gained ground and credit in the Christian world mainly through his authority and influence. This is a favorite fancy with some; and it receives a certain measure of countenance even from such a man as Neander. He talks of a gradual rise of hierarchical views by defection from the first simplicity of the Gospel, and sees in the schisms of Felicissimus and Novatian the last unsuccessful efforts of an older more free and spiritual tendency to maintain itself in opposition to this new movement, which was now bearing all in its own wrong direction. Cyprian, it is admitted, was not strictly the author of the movement; he found himself rather borne upon its bosom. But his personality fitted him to become beyond all other men of the time its representative and organ; and the supposition is accordingly, that it owed its triumph in the third century very largely to his active and uncompromising zeal. We have already seen however, to some extent, how little foundation there is for any hypothesis of this sort, in the actual facts of the age. The evidence is most ample and full, that Cyprian's doctrine of the church was, in all its essential features, the doctrine held in his time by the whole Christian world. East and West here were substantially of one and the same mind. Everywhere we find episcopacy, not only established, but acknowledged also to be of Divine right, by direct continuation down from the time of the Apostles. Along with this we find moreover, on all sides, the idea of the necessary unity of the church, the conception of its supernatural real constitution as an object of faith, in the sense of the Apostles' Creed, the acknowledgment of its essential relation to all true godliness, as being the body of Christ and so the medium through which he carries forward his glorious salvation in the world. Faith was held to stand primarily in this very habit of mind. It was obedience to the claims of the Christian fact, exhibited precisely in this outwardly objective and historical form. Hence baptism was owned to be regeneration; the eucharist was felt to involve the mystery of a real communication with the Saviour's flesh and blood; priestly absolution, following penance and confession, was relied upon as of true force for the remission of sin. Schism was regarded a deadly offence, just because it turned the fact of the Church into a lie, and was in this way a standing act of disobedience to the truth Divinely lodged in her constitution. We may set all this down, if we see proper, for rank superstition; but we can have no right to deny, that so at all events the faith of the Christian world stood in the third century, and that it was of one complexion thus with what we have found to be the general church system of Cyprian. Christianity, as it then prevailed, was conditioned absolutely and essentially by this system. The church was made to be the pillar and ground of the universal fact. We see this, not merely in the direct statements which are made on the subject, but in some respects more impressively still in forms of thought and life by which in an indirect way it is continually taken for granted. The doctrine is not met in the form of an outward accident only; we find it wrought into the whole religious mind of the age; it is of one growth with this, concrete with its very existence, we might almost say, at every point. It is implied in the controversy concerning the restoration of the lapsed. It lies in all the premises, which entered into the reigning system of church discipline, in the eagerness of penitents to secure the peace of the church, in the forms and rules which governed its mysterious communication. It formed the soul of the question concerning the baptism of heretics. It lay at the foundation of the views which were entertained of the vast merit of martyrdom, of the communion of saints, of the power of the holy sacraments, and we may say indeed of the universal theology of the age. All is constructed on the assumption of the Divine constitution of the Church, under such form of objective reality as we have now in consideration. Cyprian's writings are everywhere an appeal to this fact. He deals in no speculation; brings in no theory of his own; but throws himself perpetually on what he holds to be the living sense of Christianity, in the consciousness of that world of faith generally to which the mystery belonged. And this precisely it was, that clothed his writings with power. They came home to the heart and mind of the church, as an echo for the most part of its universally acknowledged faith.

But such a faith thus universally established in the middle of the third century, could not have sprung up like a mushroom in the night, could not have been the growth of a single day or year. It creates of itself at once a mighty presumption, that it had come down by general tradition from the time going before; and if there be no clear evidence to the contrary, this tradition or handing down must be taken to reach away back to the earliest date of ecclesiastical history. It is asking a great deal too much, in such a case, when we are required to set out with just the opposite presumption; and are gravely told that, not the fact of variation here, but the fact of identity, is that which needs to be made out at every upward step of such inquiry by direct overwhelming proof. The only truly logical and philosophical view is that which takes the sameness for granted, till the fact of some actual change is demonstrated. Such a state of things as we meet with, throughout the length and breadth of the Christian world, in the time of Cyprian, whose own life reached back to the beginning of the century, and who stood in such close theological relation with Tertullian, the great connecting link between the third century and the second, most conclusively implies that substantially the same order of thought and life had prevailed also in this earlier period.[7] It is not possible to account satisfactorily for the later known fact on any other hypothesis. And more especially must this be felt to be the case, when it is borne

---

7. [See DeBie's commentary, *John Williamson Nevin*, 287.]

in mind that the authority of such a tradition, in favor of the later system, was always boldly asserted, and that so far as we know the assertion never met with contradiction in any quarter. For even Neander has not pretended to say, that either Novatian or Felicissimus ever appealed to any older doctrine or practice, as being in opposition to the high church pretensions by which they were resisted in their schismatical designs; as they would have done certainly in their own defence, if the thing had been at all possible; and it seems to us therefore to be no better than the most puerile romance, when the great historian chooses to make their factions notwithstanding, especially that of the last, the representation of a hypothetical anti-hierarchical interest in the church, which with the advantage of antiquity and right religious feeling on its side, was no longer able now to maintain its ground. So far as episcopacy was concerned, the tradition of which we now speak carried it back distinctly, as we have before said, to the age of the Apostles. The bishops were held to be their successors in office, the bearers of the same commission which these had received in the beginning to teach all nations; and the line of this succession, in the case of the different sees, was in fact traced up to the very time when they were first established; a task, which was then just as easy as it would be now to carry back the succession of any well established civil magistracy for a like comparatively short period of years.

But we are not left to this form of proof alone, strong as it must be allowed to be in the full posture of the case. We can appeal directly to the voice of the second century itself.

[The Church as Catholic and Apostolic]

All the writers of this period speak familiarly of the government of the church by bishops, who were regarded as holding their office by legitimate succession from the Apostles. Tertullian and Irenaeus, in controversy with the heretics of their time, appeal to the course of this succession in the case of certain prominent sees as an open clearly established fact, which could be verified for any inquirer without the least difficulty or trouble. And what right can any one have now, to call in question the credibility of their statement, or to suppose that it was founded on some sort of mistake? It would be just as reasonable to question an appeal, at the present time, to the Gubernatorial succession of Pennsylvania, or Massachusetts, or New-York, since the date of the American Revolution, in proof of the historical identity of the government of either of these notable Commonwealths between the years 1776 and 1852. There was just as little room for uncertainty in the one case as in the other. "Come then," says Tertullian in his celebrated tract on *Prescription*,

> you who wish to exercise your curiosity to more advantage in the affair of salvation, go through the apostolic churches, in which the very chairs of the apostles continue aloft in their places, in which their very original letters are

> recited, sounding forth the voice and representing the countenance of each one. Is Achaia near you? You have Corinth. If you are not far from Macedon, you have Philippi, you have Thessalonica. if you can go to Asia, you have Ephesus. If you are near Italy, you have Rome, whence we also derive our origin. How happy is this church, to which the apostles poured forth their whole doctrine with their blood! where Peter is assimilated to the Lord in his martyrdom: where Paul is crowned with a death like that of John: where John the apostle, after he had been dipped in boiling oil without suffering injury, is banished to the island: let us see what she learned, what she taught, what she professed in her symbol in common with the African churches (c. 36).[8]

The heretics are boldly challenged to produce any similar warrant for their pretensions.

> Let them then give us the origin of their churches;[9] let them unfold the series of their bishops, [they too, it seems, knew of no other form of church polity] coming down from the beginning in succession, so that the first bishop shall appear to have been appointed and preceded by some one of the apostles or apostolic men, without having fallen off subsequently from their communion. For in this way the apostolic churches trace their descent; as the church of Smyrna, for instance, refers to Polycarp constituted by John, and the church of the Romans to Clement ordained by Peter. In like manner also the other churches show those who were appointed to the episcopate by the apostles, and so made channels of the apostolic seed. Let the heretics feign anything like this (c. 32).[10]

Irenaeus, the disciple of Polycarp, had argued against the false teachers of his time in precisely the same strain. "All who wish to see the truth," he says,

> may see in the entire Church the tradition of the apostles, manifested throughout the whole world; and we can enumerate the bishops who have been ordained by the apostles, and their successors down to our time, who taught or knew no such doctrine as they madly dream of. But since it would be very tedious to enumerate in this work the succession of all the churches, by pointing to the tradition of the greatest and most ancient church, known to all, founded and established at Rome by the two most glorious apostles Peter and Paul, and to her faith announced to men which comes down to us also by the succession of bishops, we confound all those who in any improper manner

---

8. [In this and the next two quotes, Nevin appears to have used Kenrick, *Primacy of the Apostolic See Vindicated*, 86–87. Kenrick provided the original Latin in notes, so Nevin was able to modify the translations. See also *ANF* 3:260.]

9. [The Latin word translated "origins" is *"origines"* which is better translated as "originals." *ANF* translates "Let them produce the original records of their churches" (3:258n5). The "unrolling" of the list of bishops then could be either a list, or a verbal recounting of the succession of bishops. This relates to Nevin's earlier analogy of the succession of governors in the Commonwealths of Pennsylvania and Massachusetts.]

10. [Quoted in Kenrick, *Primacy*, 88; text in brackets inserted by Nevin. *ANF* 3:258.]

Document 3: Cyprian: Third Article.

gather together, either through self-complacency, or vain-glory, or blindness and perverse disposition. For with this church, on account of her more powerful principality, it is necessary that every church, that is the faithful on all sides round, should agree, in which the apostolic tradition has been always preserved by those on all sides (l. iii. c. 3).[11]

No one needs to be informed of the doctrine of Ignatius on the same subject, which itself sets us almost in felt contact with the last of the Apostles, His glorification of episcopacy, as the ground of all stability and the channel of all grace in the church, is an old topic, familiar to all who have bestowed on the Episcopalian controversy of modern times even the least attention. The very fulness and force of his testimony are made, by those who cannot bear it, a reason for disputing its truth. Their own foregone conclusion would be at once upset by its clear distinct voice; and so, to save their conclusion, they set themselves to smother the voice as they best can, by taking it for granted that it is surreptitious and false, something palmed upon the real Ignatius by the pious fraud of a later age. Professor Rothe, in his great work *Die Aufänge der Christlichen Kirche*,[12] has well exposed the arbitrary and absurd character of this wholesale scepticism. The truth is the Episcopal passages of Ignatius, as they may be called, have not as such the slightest air of forgery or interpolation; they fall in naturally and easily with his general train of thought, and stand in close connection with the whole form and habit of his theology. This will be shown presently, when we come to consider more particularly the view he takes of the Church. And just as little room is there to say, that the style of thinking here brought into view does not agree with the age of Ignatius, but is made to anticipate unnaturally what belongs of right only to the next century. It is easy to see, that it is not identical in any such way with the thinking of this later time, that it bears upon it the marks of an earlier stage of the Christian life, and that it fits well with the ecclesiastical and theological connections of the period to which it is thus referred, so far as we have any knowledge of them from other sources. The Epistles of Ignatius, in their generally accepted form, are just such a light in truth as we need to find our way in ecclesiastical history, with any sort of intelligence, from the first century over into the bosom of the second, from the age of the Apostles onward to the order of things which stares us in the face in the days of Irenaeus and Tertullian. Extinguish this light, refuse to acknowledge what it reveals, violently *theorize* into the place of this another scheme of church facts altogether; and it is not too much to say, that the whole history of the second century must be brought at the same time into inextricable confusion.

We are not concerned particularly at present, however, with the question of Episcopacy. It is plain enough, that the government of the church, in the second century,

---

11. [Quoted in Kenrick, *Primacy*, 84–85; translation modified by Nevin. Irenaeus, *Against the Heresies: Book 3*, ACW 64:32.]

12. [Richard Rothe, *Die Anfänge der Christlichen Kirche und ihrer Verfassung*, vol 1 (Wittenberg: Zimmermann'schen, 1837).]

was in this form; and we think it sufficiently clear also, that the See of Rome was regarded as possessing a central dignity in the system, a sort of actual *principality,* derived from the original primacy of St. Peter. But for our main purpose just now, this is of only secondary account. What we seek, is to determine the view taken of the constitution of the Church itself inwardly considered. This is something back of all questions concerning its outward polity, even though such polity be regarded as Divine, and as essentially blended thus with the very existence of the organization to which it may belong. Waiving then the abstract controversy between Presbytery as such and Prelacy,[13] as well as that between both of these together and the Papacy, we go on to show that the second century throughout held the same view of the general nature and constitution of the Church, which we have already found to underlie the scheme of Cyprian in the third. According to this view, the Church is a supernatural fact in the world under an outward historical form, a real constitution established by extraordinary Divine commission and destined to endure to the end of time, with powers and functions answerable to such high character. It grows at the same time with inward necessity, from the mystery of the Saviour's incarnation, including his resurrection and glorification, according to the order exhibited in the Apostles' Creed.[14] In such view, it is the actual home of the grace and truth here brought to light for the salvation of dying men, not an external accident simply of Christianity, but a fundamental part of its very constitution, the medium by which it is made actual, the body through which as an organ it works, in the world. Submission to this outwardly real constitution is the true obedience of faith, in which all salvation begins, and baptism as a true objective response to such act of submission is a sacrament of regeneration introducing the subject into the heavenly order of life to which it belongs, and giving him a title to all its privileges, with the full real possibility of eternal salvation. So constituted, the Church is necessarily one, and catholic, and holy, and apostolical, carrying in it the positive whole of Christianity, and absolutely excluding as false and profane all that is external to its own communion. Schism becomes thus at once a mortal sin, of one nature with heresy; to be out of the church is to be cut off from the fountains of salvation in every other form; the bible, the sacraments, the ministry, are streams of life only within this mystical paradise, not on the outside of it; no one can have God for his father, who has not this visible and actual Church for his mother. Such, we say, is the general theory. We are not presenting it now as necessarily right and true. We propose only to show, that it was universally held in the second century.

The truth is, however, it is not easy to know where to begin with the evidence, or how to arrange it, just because it is so abundant and full. So soon as we lay aside all stubborn preconceptions, and endeavor simply to take the age on its own standpoint, we shall find that its whole theological life is constructed on the basis precisely

13. [Nevin either forgets or does not know that a key part of Calvin's discussion of ecclesiology of the early church rests on this very point. See Calvin, *Institutes,* 2:1069–70 {IV.iv.2}.]

14. [See Nevin's discussion of the history and formation of "The Apostle's Creed," MTSS 8:35–97.]

Document 3: Cyprian: Third Article.

of the scheme now stated, and that its utterances become clear and intelligible only in proportion as we make it a key for their interpretation. To understand Tertullian, Irenaeus, or Ignatius, to be able to read their writings, with any true religious interest or satisfaction, the most indispensable of all conditions is just that we should have power to perceive this fact, and power at the same time to make ourselves at home—hypothetically at least if not by conviction of its truth—in the animus of their faith as exercised in such intensely realistic style.

On the apostolicity of the church, its Divine commission, the realness of its constitution as a fact handed down by unbroken continuous succession from the beginning, Tertullian's tract in particular on the *Prescription of Heretics* might be given at large. He puts down all heresies, by asserting in favor of the church the right of possession and regular inheritance, over against which every later claim must be held at once for a false and unlawful usurpation. Christ, he tells us, who knew his own doctrine, chose twelve of his leading disciples to be the teachers of it to the nations.

> These apostles, whose name signifies *sent* . . . having obtained the promised power of the Holy Ghost for miracles and speech, and having preached the faith and established churches first in Judea, afterwards went forth into the world at large and proclaimed the same teaching of the same faith to the nations; and then they founded churches in every city from which other churches afterwards borrowed the graft of faith and seed of doctrine, and are continually doing so still in order to become churches. And in this way these also are reckoned apostolical, as being the progeny of apostolical churches. Every kind must of course be referred to its origin. Hence however many churches there may be, that which was first from the apostles is one, of which come all. Thus all are the first and apostolical, whilst all as one show their unity, by communication of peace, and title of brotherhood and mutual pledge of hospitality; rights, which no other reason regulates save one tradition of the same sacrament. [ch. 21.] From this then we draw the prescription: that if our Lord Jesus Christ sent apostles to preach, no other preachers are to be received than those whom he commissioned, because no other has known the Father but the Son and he to whom the Son has revealed him, and to no others does the Son appear to have made such revelation but to the apostles, whom he sent to preach of course what he revealed. But what they preached, that is, what Christ revealed to them, I will here also lay down the rule, ought not to be proved otherwise than by the same churches, which the apostles themselves founded, by preaching to them with the living voice as they call it, as well as afterwards by their letters. If these things be so, it is clear thence that all doctrine which agrees with those apostolical churches, the matrices and originals of the faith, is to be reckoned as true, exhibiting without doubt what the churches received from the apostles, the apostles from Christ, and Christ from God; but that all other doctrine is to be forejudged as false, the taste of which is against the truth of the churches, and of the apostles, and of Christ,

and of God. It remains then that we show, whether our doctrine, whose rule we have already given, is to be reckoned of apostolical tradition, and from this itself whether all besides must be referred to falsehood. We communicate with the apostolical churches, which is done by no different doctrine: this is the test of truth (c. 20, 21).[15]

This passage brings into view also Tertullian's idea of the necessary unity of the church. However many particular churches there may be, they are all in truth one by virtue of their common apostolical origin and life. Each one is what it professes to be, in the bosom only of the general organization of which it is thus a part. So in other places, he speaks of such churches as bound together, in distinction from all heretical assemblies, by a common "right of peace and title of brotherhood;" they have "one faith, one God, the same Christ, the same hope, the same sacramental laver." What belongs to one belongs to all; "*nostrum est quodcunque nostrorum est.*"[16] They are all "confederated by sacramental association" (*de societate sacramenti confoederantur*).[17] Unity implies exclusiveness, in other words the restriction of the Christian salvation to the church, as being its real medium and organ. This thought also is familiar to Tertullian. He lays stress on the maternity of church; and makes use of the subsequently classic symbol of Noah's ark, to express its relation to the surrounding world.

On all these points, the still older testimony of Irenaeus is yet more explicit and direct, as well as far more large and full. He too puts down the cause of all heretics by the plea of prescription, original occupancy and prior right on the part of the church, which he views always as a single corporation, in full unity with itself and of unbroken succession from the time of the apostles. The church is universal, "diffused through the whole world to the ends of the earth."[18] As such again it is exclusive, allowing no rivalry with its proper functions under any different form. He sees in it always the definite and only channel of the historical progress of the work of redemption, the only organ of Christ's redeeming activity in the world, the only possessor of the powers of the Christian salvation, that is, in one word, of the Holy Ghost. Here alone are deposited all the treasures of grace; and here accordingly they are, at the same time, in absolutely full measure. In the church only is to be found the complete truth. She is the only possessor and guardian of the true holy scriptures. She is, in the most manifold relations, the mother, and the only mother, of all who belong to Christ. To be out of her bosom, by heresy or schism, is death. In the remarkable passage, *Adv. Haer.* l. iii. c. 24, §. 1 [3.24.1], he speaks of the whole economy of the Gospel, as an objective system set forth everywhere under the same form, which we comprehend in our faith, as we receive this to keep from the church, where the Spirit of God always resides, like some

---

15. [Tertullian, *Liber De Præscriptionibus*, in *PL* 2:32; *ANF* 3:252–53.]

16. [Tertullian, *Liber De Virginibus Velandis*, in *PL* 2:891; *ANF* 4:28.]

17. [Tertullian, *Adversus Marcionem*, in *PL* 2:366; *ANF* 3:350 {trans. "united with them in the fellowship of the mystery"}.]

18. [Irenaeus, *Adversus Haereses*, in *PG* 7:550; *ANF* 1:330.]

rich unguent in a good vessel, "*juvenescens et juvenescere faciens ipsum vas in quo est*,"[19] the source of a perennially new and fresh life.

> For this gift of God is bestowed upon the church, like the breath of life to the natural man, that all the members by partaking of it may be made alive; and in her is arranged the communication of Christ, that is the Holy Ghost, the pledge of incorruption, and the confirmation of our faith, and the scale of ascension to God. For in the church, it is said, God has placed apostles, prophets, teachers, and every other operation of the Spirit; of which all fail to partake, who have not recourse to the church, but cheat themselves of life by wrong judgment and pernicious work. For where the church is, there is also the Spirit of God, and where the Spirit of God is, there is the church and all grace; but the Spirit is truth. Wherefore such as fail to partake of him are neither nourished by the breasts of the mother into life, nor participate in the most pure fountain that proceeds from the body of Christ, but dig out for themselves broken cisterns of the earth, and drink water filled with mud, avoiding the faith of the church so as not to be converted, and rejecting the Spirit so as not to be amended.[20]

Again, l. v. c. 20. §. 2 [5.20.2]:

> We must then flee the opinions of heretics, and carefully watch against their infestations; but must take refuge in the church, and be educated in her bosom and nourished by the Lord's scriptures. For the church is planted as a paradise or garden in this world. So of every tree of the garden ye shall eat, saith the Spirit of God, that is, eat ye of every scripture of the Lord; but ye shall not eat of knowledge pretending to be above this, nor touch the whole dissent of heretics. For they themselves avow, that they have the knowledge of good and evil, and set up their impious sense above God who made them. They think thus above the measure of thought. Wherefore also the Apostle says, we must not think more highly than we ought to think, but should think soberly; that we may not, by eating of their knowledge, that namely which is thus too high, be thrust out from the paradise of life, into which the Lord brings those who obey his command, "gathering together in one all things in himself both which are in heaven and which are on earth [Eph 1:10]." But what is in heaven are spiritual things, what is on earth is the economy of man. Gathering these into one therefore in himself, uniting man to the Spirit and placing the Spirit in man, he has become the head of the Spirit, and gives the Spirit to be the head of man: for through him we see, and have heard and do speak.[21]

So again, l. iii. c. 4, §. 1 [3.4.1]:

---

19. [Irenaeus, *Adversus Haereses*, in *PG* 7:966 {trans. "renewing its youth . . . causes the vessel itself containing it to renew its youth also" (*ANF* 1:458)}.]
20. [Irenaeus, *Adversus Haereses*, in *PG* 7:966–67; *ANF* 1:458.]
21. [Irenaeus, *Adversus Haereses*, in *PG* 7:1178; *ANF* 1:548.]

> It is not necessary to seek from others the truth which it is so easy to receive from the church, since the apostles have most fully committed to her, as a rich depository, all that is of the truth, that every one who will may take thence the water of life. For she is the entrance into life, while all others are thieves and robbers. On which account, we are to shun them, and to regard with diligent affection what is of the church, holding fast the tradition of truth.[22]

On the unity of the church, the same writer, as is well known to all who have any knowledge of him, is particularly clear and emphatic. He makes it to consist in identity of doctrine and confession, in community of faith, in the participation of the same Holy Ghost, and expressly also in the power of a common ecclesiastical organization, held together by the general bond of the episcopate in its collective or consolidated view.

> Though spread over the whole world to the ends of the earth, the church still holds one faith received from the apostles and their disciples. . . . This proclamation and this creed so received, she sedulously guards, notwithstanding her diffusion throughout the world, as if she occupied but one house; she believes them alike as if she had one soul and the same heart, and harmoniously proclaims and teaches them, and hands them down, as though she were possessed of but a single voice. The dialects, as regards the world, are indeed different; but the force of the tradition is one and the same. . . . For as the sun, God's creature, is through the whole world one and the same, so also the proclamation of the truth shines in every direction, and enlightens all men who are willing to come to the knowledge of the truth. *Adv. Haer.* I. 10, §. 1, 2 [1.10.1, 2].[23]

> Wherefore it is necessary to hearken to the presbyters in the church, to those who have the succession from the apostles, as we have shown, who along with the succession of the episcopate have received the sure gift of truth according to the good pleasure of the Father; while all others, who stand aside from the reigning succession, and convene together in any place, are to be held in suspicion, either as heretics of bad doctrine, or as proud and self-pleasing schismatics, or finally as hypocrites actuated by the desire of gain and vain glory. All such are fallen from the truth. . . . From all such therefore it is a duty to abstain, but to adhere to those, who both keep the doctrine of the apostles, as we have said before, and along with the order of the eldership exhibit sound speech and a life without offence for the confirmation and reproof of others. Ib. iv. c. 20, §. 2, 4 [4.26.2, 4].[24]

The true Christian gnosis is represented as resting, iv. c. 33, §. 8 [4.33.8], in two elements, the doctrine of the apostles and the church system derived from them, by

---

22. [Irenaeus, *Adversus Haereses*, in *PG* 7:855; *ANF* 1:416–17].
23. [[renaeus, *Adversus Haereses*, in *PG* 7:550, 551, 554; *ANF* 1:330, 331.]
24. [Chapter 26, not 20: Irenaeus, *Adversus Haereses*, in *PG* 7:1053–55; *ANF* 1:497.]

Document 3: Cyprian: Third Article.

episcopal succession, throughout the world. *"Agnitio vera est apostolorum doctrina et antiquus ecclesiae status in universo mundo et character corporis Christi secundum successiones episcoporum, quibus illi eam, quae in uno quoque loco est, ecclesiam tradiderunt."*[25]

How deeply seated this whole view of the unity and exclusiveness of the church was in the faith of this early time, is strikingly shown in the usual mode of denouncing heretics and heresies. The two conceptions of heresy and schism are always regarded as flowing more or less together. The error of judgment is always taken to be something, that grows out of an evil heart of disobedience towards an actual teaching authority, which all are required at once to acknowledge and obey. The truth as it is in Christ is never viewed as the sense simply of a written revelation, which men are expected to understand as they best can and so set up as an object of faith. It is primarily a *tradition*, a system handed down from the apostles under a tangible objective form, in the bosom of a constitution which is itself part of the revelation, and which challenges to itself the homage and submission of all in such view, as the indispensable condition of their having any lot or part in the grace which is thus placed within their reach. It is continually taken for granted, that this outward authority is clearly defined and constantly at hand, so as to leave no apology or excuse for falling into heresy in any form. Heretics are necessarily and at once rebels against a regularly constituted authority, which they are bound to obey; and this rebellion, in the circumstances, amounts to a virtual renunciation of the Divine supremacy of Christianity itself. It involves the guilt of schism, rupture with the evangelical tradition, a violent breaking away from the actual living order of the Gospel; and this, of course, can be nothing less in the end than down right infidelity. Such, we say, is the light in which it is regarded and spoken of always by the early fathers. We have seen already how Tertullian and Irenaeus make use of the argument from prescription. They put down all heresies as innovations and invasions upon long established right. The church is in actual possession of the truth; it belongs to her by inheritance; her title deeds reach back plainly to the original charter of Christianity. What right then can any other party have, to come in and dispute her authority? Heresy is, by its very conception, the setting up of mere private will against law and right. It expresses precisely the opposite of the attribute *catholic*, as this enters necessarily into the constitution of the real and true church. It carries in it at once the notion of sect, something cut off from the proper whole of Christianity, the substitution of what is private and subjective, matter of wilful choice, αἵρεσις, for what is objective and general.[26] All such particularism, in the sphere of Christianity, must

---

25. [Irenaeus, *Adversus Haereses*, in *PG* 7:1077; trans. "True knowledge is [that which consists in] the doctrine of the apostles, and the ancient constitution of the Church throughout all the world, and the distinctive manifestation of the body of Christ according to the successions of the bishops, by which they have handed down the Church which exists in every place" (*ANF* 1:508).]

26. So Athanasius: Πόθεν λέγεται αἵρεσις; Απο του αἱρεῖσθαι τι ἴδιον, καὶ τοῦτο ἐξακολουθεῖν [trans. "Why is it called heresy? Because his opinion is created privately {apart from the church} and he follows this opinion {seeking others to follow him}"]. [Migne placed this quote among Athanasius's

be irreligious, a work of the flesh (Gal. v: 20), a virtual denial and abandonment of the faith. The heretic is to be considered αὐτοκατάκριτος, self condemned (Tit. iii: 10, 11); as one who voluntarily disowns and gives up the Christian principle, the fundamental maxim of the obedience of faith. He is condemned, says Tertullian, "*in quo* [. . .] *sibi elegit*," by the matter of his own election. "We have no right," he adds, "to bring in anything of our own will, nor yet to choose what any one else may have brought in of his mere will" (*De Praesc.* c. 6). That is his notion of religious liberty and private judgment; which he backs by the authority of our Lord's apostles; for even they, he tells us, did not choose what they should teach, but "faithfully delivered to the nations the discipline they had received from Christ."[27] Heresies are in this way always the fruit of the fleshly mind as such, acting in opposition to the mind of the Spirit. "Wo to those," cries Origen, "who despise the church, and trust in the arrogance and swelling words of heretics."[28] There are three habits of the soul, according to Clemens Alexandrinus,[29] ignorance, opinion, knowledge; the first is that of the heathen, the last belongs to the true church, while the character of heresy is found in the second.[30] It puts the merely subjective into the room of the objective, mistakes its own fancies for heavenly realities. Christianity in this form ceased to be a church, and became a school. The attributes belonging to it as the body of Christ, were lost in the narrow conception of mere human party or sect. This is often held up by the early fathers in the way of reproach. Heretics, according to Tertullian, seemed to have no sense at all for unity or catholicity; and just for this reason, they were uncommonly liberal and tolerant, planting themselves on the ground that there should be free inquiry in religion, and liberty also to change opinion as often as it might be found necessary. "They join peace on all sides," says Tertullian, "and make no account of their own differences, whilst they band themselves together to make war upon the one truth."[31]

> They can hardly be said to have any schisms; because when they exist, they come not into view. Schism is their unity. They do not even adhere among themselves to their own systems, but every one modifies by private judgment what he has received, just as this was concocted by private judgment on the

---

"spurious" writings: *Quæstiones in Scripturam*, in *PL* 28:724.]—So Tertullian: *Haereses dictae graeca voce ex interpretation* electionis, *qua quis, sive ad instituendas sive ad suscipiendas eas, utitur* [Tertullian, *Liber De Præscriptionibus*, in *PL* 2:18 {trans. "called in Greek *heresies*, a word used in the sense of that *choice* which a man makes when he either teaches them (to others) or takes up with them (for himself)" (*ANF* 3:245)}].

27. [Tertullian, *Liber De Præscriptionibus*, in *PL* 2:18. *ANF* 3:245–46.]

28. ["*Væ his qui spernunt Ecclesiam, et confidunt super arrogantia et verbis tumentibus haereticorum* . . . ." Jerome, *Translatio Homiliarum Origenis in Ezechielem*, in *PL* 25:755.]

29. [Clement of Alexandria (c. 150–215); head of the catechetical school at Alexandria; his pupil, Origen, succeeded him as leader at Alexandria.]

30. [John Kaye, *Some Account of the Writings and Opinions of Clement of Alexandria* (London: J. G. & F. Rivington, 1835), 321.]

31. [Tertullian, *Liber De Præscriptionibus*, in *PL* 2:56. *ANF* 3:263.]

part of his teacher. The course the thing takes tells its nature and the manner of its commencement. The Valentinians have as much light as Valentinus, the Marcionites as much as Marcion,[32] to alter the faith at their own pleasure. And so all heresies, when carefully examined, are found to disagree in many things with their authors (*De Praesc.* c. 41, 42).[33]

They showed a common tendency, according to the Apostolical Constitutions, vi: 10, to treat religious differences as of no material account.[34] They affected to care only for practical piety. They laid great stress on following the Scriptures; and were fond of appealing to such texts as, "Seek, and ye shall find," "Prove all things, etc.," in justification of their restless unsettled habit. "They are forever pretending to *seek*," says Irenaeus, "as persons without sight, but are never able to find."[35] All with them is matter of opinion; whereas the idea of faith requires something fixed and sure, in the way of outward objective tradition, that may be submitted to in such view as the firm ground of the Christian life.

Holding such relation to the Catholic Church, heresies are condemned always in the most unsparing terms. By no possibility can they be either safe or right. It is common to refer them directly to the instigation of the Devil. "Heretics are all apostates from the truth," according to Irenaeus, *Adv haer.* iv: 26, §. 2;

> and as they offer strange fire on the altar of God, that is strange doctrines, they shall be consumed by fire from heaven, like Nadab and Abihu. As rising up against the truth, and exhorting others against the church, they abide in hell, swallowed up of the opening earth, like the company of Korah, Dathan and Abiram. As dividing and separating the church, they fall into the punishment of Jeroboam.[36]

Origen on Rom. xiv: 22, 23, *Hast thou faith? have it to thyself before God, &c.*, proceeds in the following strain:

> Some one may ask, if heretics also, because they act according to what they believe, may be supposed to act from faith. In my view, we should call it their

---

32. [Marcion (d. c. 160); a heretic who thought the Christian Scriptures should exclude the OT and nearly all of the NT books because of their depiction of a God of justice and vengeance. Valentinus (2nd century); founded a Gnostic sect. Widely influential as a teacher, his theological system was the most developed of the Gnostic cults and several of his students went on to found their own schools.]

33. [Tertullian, *Liber De Præscriptionibus*, in *PL* 2:57–58; *ANF* 3:264. Nevin's translation gives a different sense. "Private judgment" is a hobby-horse of his, but not suggested in *ANF*. *ANF* also clarifies that the non-schismatic character of the heretics is a mere supposition.]

34. [See *Ante-Nicene Christian Library* 17:151–52. The actual argument of this section is simply a description of the conflicting diversity of the heresies.]

35. [Source uncertain, but perhaps Irenaeus, *Adversus Haereses*, in *PG* 7:967; *ANF* 1:458 {§2}: "Wherefore they also imagine many gods, and they always have the excuse of searching [after truth] (for they are blind), but never succeed in finding it." The scriptural quotations are from Matt 7:7 and 1 Thess 5:21.]

36. [Irenaeus, *Adversus Haereses*, in *PG* 7:1054; *ANF* 1:497.]

credulity rather than faith. For as false prophets are sometimes improperly called prophets, and false science is said to be science, and false wisdom is termed wisdom; so the credulity of heretics is by a false name designated faith. Whence it is to be considered, whether even if any good work may seem to have place among them, it is not perhaps converted into sin, as it is said of one, *Let his prayer be turned into sin.* There is a chastity at times, which is not of faith, &c., &c. There is thus a false faith of such as *concerning faith have made shipwreck,* there is a false wisdom also *of this world and of the princes of this world,* which shall be destroyed. For as pirates are accustomed to kindle a fire under cover of night, near shallow and rocky parts of the sea, by which they may draw mariners, through hope of reaching a safe haven, into ruinous shipwreck; so also is that light of false wisdom or false faith kindled by the princes of the world and the powers of the air, not that men may escape, but that they may perish, in their voyage on the sea of life and through the waves of this present world.[37]

What we need to observe, is the opposition in which heresy is made to stand to the idea of the church, as something individual and private, in the form of opinion or speculation, over against an authority which is assumed to be at hand under the character of a known positive constitution, demanding submission not as a matter of opinion but as an act of faith. The sense of this opposition, and this particular conception of the nature of faith, may be said to enter into the universal thinking of the ancient church, and come into view more or less clearly wherever the subject of heresy is brought in any way under consideration.

What Irenaeus relates of Polycarp, and his well known story concerning St. John, falls in exactly with this habit of thought, and must be taken as a true picture here at all events of the mind of the first half of the second century, whatever may be made of the story in question; which itself, however, would seem to be open to no reasonable doubt. Polycarp, we are told, during his visit to Rome in the time of Anicetus,[38] converted many heretics to the church, by simply announcing the truth he had been accustomed to teach in Asia as having been received and delivered to him by the Apostles. "And there are those," Irenaeus adds,

> who have heard him say, that John, the disciple of the Lord, having entered a bathing house in Ephesus, when he learned that Cerinthus[39] was also within, hastened out of the place before he had washed, saying he feared the building might fall having Cerinthus in it, the enemy of the truth. Polycarp himself also, when Marcion once met him and asked, *Dost thou know us?* replied, *I do know thee as the first born of Satan.* Such fear had the Apostles and their

37. [Origen, *Commentariorum . . . ad Romanos,* in *PG* 14:1256; *Commentary on . . . Romans, Books 6–10,* 262–63.]

38. [Bishop of Rome from 157–68; disagreed with Polycarp on when Easter would be celebrated.]

39. [Cerinthus (c. 50–100) was an early proponent of Gnosticism.]

Document 3: Cyprian: Third Article.

disciples of communicating, even to a word, with any of those who corrupted the truth.[40]

The whole thinking of this early period, we say, is based upon the idea of the church, which we have now under consideration. No quotation in regard to particular points can do the subject any sort of justice. There is danger rather of their serving to enfeeble the argument they should support, by their necessarily partial character and isolated form. Their full proper force can be felt only in the bosom of the living connections, from the midst of which they are taken. To understand the theology or worship of the primitive church, as it comes before us in the most ancient fathers, at almost any point, we must be able to throw our minds into the posture of this idea, and to conceive of the church, hypothetically at least, as a Divine constitution, embodying in itself in a real way the powers of the Christian salvation, "the fulness of him that filleth all in all [Eph 1:23]." Take, for example, the single point of baptismal regeneration.[41] No thought is more familiar to this early Christianity, than that baptism is of force really and truly for the remission of sins, and to bring men into saving relation with God. It is spoken of continually as an illuminating, cleansing, renovating sacrament. It is made everywhere to be the basis and foundation of the Christian life. All this too, without the least sign of hesitation or embarrassment, in the most ready and matter of course style, as though the point were open to no difficulty and understood all round to be a first principle of the doctrine of Christ. To say, that such phraseology was mere rhetoric, or flourish of high sounding words known to be hollow figure and falsehood at last, is an insult on the ancient church worthy only the pen of Gibbon or the tongue of Voltaire.[42] It simply shows, what earnest was then made with the objective realness of the church. Suppose Christianity a doctrine only, a simply spiritualistic system in the modern Puritan or Methodistic sense, and then indeed all such phraseology becomes more or less unmeaning bombast, the credit of which can be saved only by such violent qualification as must turn the whole of it at last into frigid nonsense. But *suppose* only the actual presence of righteousness and salvation in the church, as a known outward and historical corporation, the full possibility of redemption brought home *there* to all who can be led to believe and embrace the joyful intelligence, and who may not see that the difficulty of all these startling forms of speech is at once brought comparatively to an end? In proportion precisely as this view can be reproduced in any modern mind in a lively way, it will be found to carry in it all the key that is needed, to solve the otherwise inexplicable enigma of the old ecclesiastical *usus loquendi*,[43] on the subject of holy baptism. And so with regard

---

40. [Irenaeus, *Adversus Haereses*, in *PG* 7:853–54; *ANF* 1:416.]

41. [Mercersburg's thought on this topic is presented in Nevin et al., *Born of Water and the Spirit*, MTSS 6. Nevin interprets Chrysostom in "The Old Doctrine," MTSS 6:196–213.]

42. [Gibbon and Voltaire were mentioned in "Early Christianity" as major anti-Christian skeptics in the early modern period.]

43. ["Usual mode of speaking" or "common usage at the time."]

to other points. All are conditioned by faith in the article of the Holy Catholic and Apostolic Church, as being the spouse of God, the mother of saints, the real medium of salvation and fountain of life to a dying world. That is the universal standpoint of Christian antiquity; and to understand it, or do it any sort of justice, we must be able, both in mind and heart, to *think* ourselves into the same position. With regard to this whole subject, there is too much reason to apprehend, antiquity might say to most of us, as St. Paul says to the Corinthians: "Ye are not straitened in us, but ye are straitened in your own bowels [2 Cor 6:12]!"

[The Doctrine of the Church in the Apostolic Fathers[44]]

When we look into the Apostolical Fathers, as they are called, we find plainly enough this same general view of the church, which is carried back thus to the very feet, as it were, of the Blessed Apostles themselves. The question, let it be still kept well in mind, is not immediately concerning episcopacy or any other such single interest separately considered. Much has been done to darken the subject, by taking it in this way. The grand point is the conception of the church, and the view taken of its relations to the Christian salvation. Here, we say, all is plain. There is not the least evidence of any real contradiction, so far as this great subject is concerned, between the commencement and the close of the second century. No violent chasm appears, sundering the period of Polycarp, Ignatius and the Roman Clement, from that of Irenaeus and Tertullian. Few as our notices are of the ecclesiastical life of this older time, they are abundantly sufficient to show that the idea of the church, as we find it afterwards everywhere received, was then in full force, ruling both the theory and the practice of religion on all sides. It was held to be a Divine constitution; it was regarded as the real home of the Spirit, and the organ and channel thus of all grace. It was in this view one, universal, and alone, the *Catholic Church* in the full sense of this most significant name, the grand and glorious mystery of the Creed. Men must bow to its authority in this form, in order to be saved. To do so, is faith; not to do so, involves at once the full condemnation of disobedience and unbelief. This clearly is the theory, whether true or false, which underlies all the religious thinking of the Apostolical Fathers.[45]

The church of Smyrna, in its Epistle on the martyrdom of Polycarp, speaks of all the παροικίαι [trans. "sojourning"] of the "holy catholic church" in every place; and tells how Polycarp remembered, in his last prayer, "the whole catholic church throughout the world."[46] Hermas represents the same conception by his symbolical

---

44. ["Apostolic Fathers" are writers and surviving texts immediately following the New Testament.]

45. [Nevin's source for the Apostolic Fathers in this part of his text is almost certainly *Patrum apostolicorum opera*, ed. Karl Joseph von Hefele, 3rd ed. (Tubingae: Henrici Laupp, 1847).]

46. [*De Martyrio Sancti Polycarpi Epistola Circularis* {trans. *Martyrdom of Polycarp*}, in *Patrum apostolicorum*, 274, 276; See ANF 1:40. There is no further mention of the "catholic church" in Polycarp's prayer (see ANF 1:42).]

Document 3: Cyprian: Third Article.

tower, "which appeared throughout of one color, shining like the brightness of the sun," though made up of believers from all nations under heaven, made to be of one mind by their common faith. The whole is as though made of one stone. Not to be in the structure of the tower, is to be reprobate. The rejected stones lying around it signify "such as have known the truth, but have not continued in it, and are not joined with the saints."[47] The ideas of heresy and schism run into each other, as a common falling away from the historical fact of the church, carrying along with it in some way its own determinate outward form. "It is better," says Clement of Rome, "that you should be found small and have place in the flock of Christ, than that you should be thrust out from his hope in aspiring to be high."[48] This is addressed to those who opposed the presbyters in Corinth, and is a call upon them to submit to the church in its proper ministry; in which view, it is plain, exclusion from the hope of Christ, is made to be just one and the same thing with excommunication from his flock in this outward form.

Ignatius is much more explicit and full. His system is clearly the same with that of Cyprian, though bearing evidently enough also the characteristic marks of an earlier age. All depends, with him, on being in union with the bishop, and so with the church over which he presides, in the name and with the authority of Christ. "Let no one deceive himself," he writes to the Ephesians, c. 5, "if any one be not within the altar, he is destitute of the bread of God."[49] Again *ad Trall,* c. 7: "He that is within the altar is clean, he that is without is not clean; that is, whoever does anything apart from the bishop and the presbytery and the deacon, he is not clean in his conscience."[50] Heretics are stigmatised, *ad Philad. c.* 3, as "evil plants on which Christ bestows no care, because they are not of the Father's planting," and then it follows: "If any one follow a schismatic, he has no inheritance in the kingdom of God."[51] Again, *ad Smyrn. c.* 4, heretics are denounced as "wild beasts in human shape, whom we are not only not to receive, but if possible not even to meet; praying for them only, if perchance they may come to repentance; which indeed is difficult; but still not beyond the power of Jesus Christ, our true life."[52] Afterwards they are described as bringing in other opinions (heterodoxies) against the grace of Jesus Christ, contradicting the mind of God, and making no account of charity; and then it is added, c. 7:

> They abstain from the eucharist and prayer, as not acknowledging the eucharist to be the flesh of our Saviour Jesus Christ, given for our sins and raised

---

47. [Hermas, *Hermae Pastor*, in *Patrum apostolicorum*, 429 {3.9.17}, 339 {1.3.6}; see *ANF* 2:50; 2:14.]

48. [Clement of Rome, *Epistola ad Corinthios I* {trans. *First Epistle to the Corinthians*}, in *Patrum apostolicorum*, 134; *ANF* 1:20 {chapter 57}.]

49. [In *Patrum apostolicorum*, 160; *ANF* 1:51.]

50. [In *Patrum apostolicorum*, 194; *ANF* 1:69.]

51. [In *Patrum apostolicorum*, 214; *ANF* 1:80.]

52. [In *Patrum apostolicorum*, 226; *ANF* 1:88.]

again through the goodness of the Father. Opposing the gift of God disputatiously they die, whereas to continue in charity would be better for them that they might rise again. It is proper therefore to have nothing to do with such.[53]

Here plainly heresy is the setting up of private opinion against what is at hand for faith in the form of known outward authority, which necessarily involves therefore a breach of charity, the rupture of unity, and so a falling away from the real life and immortality which Christ has lodged in the church exclusively under its whole form, as his own mystical body. *Heterodoxy* thus comes to its full sense. It is not one opinion merely pitted against another *opinion*; but opinion as such, in any and every shape, over against faith, and the fixed outward tradition which this is required to receive and obey.

Three topics mainly make up the argument or theme of the Ignatian Epistles; first, the danger to be apprehended from heretics, particularly such as turned the fact of the incarnation into a Gnostic dream; secondly, the vast importance of maintaining the unity of the church; and finally, the great duty of cleaving firmly to the bishop, at the head of his presbyters and deacons, with absolute subjection to his authority. These heads are not brought forward in separate and distinct form; they are made continually to flow into one another, and are so woven together as to show that they are, in the mind of the writer, inwardly related always in the way of cause and effect. The danger of heresy leads him to press the object of church unity, as the only effectual security against its seductive power; and zeal for this interest of unity again becomes a motive to enforce unconditional obedience to the bishops, as the means specially ordained and required for its preservation. No mistake can be greater than to suppose that the glorification of the episcopate with Ignatius is lugged in without other reason for the mere sake of the office itself, or to promote a simply hierarchical interest. It flows as naturally as possible from the burden of his zeal for the spiritual welfare of the churches to which he wrote; and to understand it fully, we need only to make ourselves familiar with the general conception of Christianity in which his spirit moved and had its home. All faith with him, it is plain, stands primarily in an act of submission to the Christian salvation as an outward fact, starting in the mystery of the incarnation and reaching forward from this under a form of existence altogether peculiar to itself in the church. So apprehended it must be necessarily one and whole, in unity and harmony always with itself. The objective, in the nature of the case, must rule and condition the subjective, the new creation can owe nothing to private judgment or private will. The setting up of any such pretension is at once heresy, αἵρεσις, something insurrectionary and rebellious over against the concrete fact of Christianity in its own form. It is to be deprecated and resisted, accordingly, just on this account. The force of the evil is not merely nor primarily in its error of doctrine theoretically considered; it lies rather in the attempt to substitute opinion in some form for the authority of tradition. This, whether the opinion be in one form or in another, strikes at the very

---

53. [In *Patrum apostolicorum*, 228, 230; *ANF* 1:89.]

Document 3: Cyprian: Third Article.

foundation of the Christian mystery, and includes in itself necessarily the idea of division and schism. To hold fast the unity of the church, becomes then the indispensable and only sufficient means of preserving and maintaining the truth. The ground and bond of this unity, Ignatius sees in the episcopate.[54] The bishops represent the authority of Christ, and each of them may be said to gather up in himself as a centre the religious life of the particular church over which he presides. Their general charge is at the same time collegiate, like that of the original Apostles from whom they hold their powers in the way of legitimate succession. To be in unity then with itself, and so with the universal or catholic church, and to be secure thus against the invasions of heresy, each particular congregation must remain in close communion with its own bishop and in absolute submission to his authority. This becomes with Ignatius, in such view, a cardinal and fundamental interest. Both the other interests depend upon it; and for this reason, he lays upon it everywhere the main stress of his exhortation, in a way that is apt to strike much of our modern thinking as extravagant and ridiculously absurd.

It would carry us too far to exemplify what we have now said by quotations. Nor is it necessary. No one who knows anything of Ignatius can need to be informed, what constant stress he lays on submission to the bishop, with his presbyters and deacons, as the very ideal of perfection and prosperity in the condition of every church. His general strain is:

> Do nothing without the bishop; keep your flesh as the temple of God; love unity and flee divisions; be ye imitators of Christ, as he is also of the Father. [8] I have done my part, as a man set for unity. Where there is division and wrath, God abides not. To all who repent the Lord will grant forgiveness, if they repent to the unity of God and communication with the bishop *(ad Philad. c. 7, 8)*.
> [...]
> Hold to the bishops, that God may be with you. I go bail for those who are in subjection to the bishop, the presbyters, the deacons; and with them let me have my part in God *(ad Polyc. c. 6)*.[55]

Our concern here is not just with Episcopacy. It is with the idea of the church, which must be taken necessarily to lie at the bottom of this view. It is not the episcopate, under any and every view, that carries in it such title to respect. The case supposes a real Divine constitution, in the bosom of which only the office can be of any heavenly force, and where at the same time it must be in some way the power of a single fact, an office through all its parts in unity with itself, representing thus, not in figure only but in fact, the authority of Jesus Christ in its own proper undivided form. If the Church were a human organization simply, or subject to the limitations and conditions of our human life naturally considered, it would be indeed absurd to talk of its Ministry in

---

54. [Nevin addresses the question of the episcopacy as the basis for ecclesial unity later in "Reply to 'An Anglican Catholic,'" 406–17.]

55. [In *Patrum apostolicorum*, 218, 240; *ANF* 1:84, 95.]

this style, and such exaltation of the duty of obedience to it, as the great law of unity and so of security against heresy, might well be considered anything but reasonable and safe. But Ignatius looked upon the case in no such light. All his language implies, that he took the Church to be in truth a supernatural constitution, which as such was to be regarded as of absolute and supreme sufficiency within itself for its own ends. The first duty of all men accordingly is to submit to it in such outwardly objective form. All the ends of righteousness and salvation depend upon acknowledging it, and bowing to it, precisely in this view. Nothing can well be more remote from the independent sectarian notion of religion, that prevails so extensively at the present day. But it falls in with the universal thinking of the church in the first ages.

[The Continuation of the Cyprianic Doctrine in Later Christianity]

The Cyprianic doctrine of the church falls back thus, in its fundamental conception, to the earliest Christian time. It was no innovation of the third century upon the faith of the second.[56] However it may have been with the age of the New Testament, it is certain that as soon as we pass beyond that we find ourselves surrounded on all sides with modes of thought, and forms of religious life, which involve at bottom this very scheme as carrying in it the true sense and force of the Christian salvation. So after the third century, its authority continued to be universal. The piety of the fourth and fifth centuries, the religion of such men as Athanasius, Chrysostom, Basil, the Gregories, Jerome, Ambrose, Augustine, is conditioned from beginning to end by the conception of the church, as the necessary organ and medium of grace. Augustine in particular, over against the heresies of his time, became the great expositor and spokesman of the doctrine for his own and all following ages. With him, it remained no longer an article simply of faith and strong theological feeling. No one indeed had ever a deeper sense of its glorious significance, in this form. It lay at the foundation of his spiritual life. It formed the very hinge of his conversion. His whole Christian experience was pervaded by the power of it at every point. But what came to him in this way as a fact of faith, he endeavored also to master in the way of knowledge; and the result was, that the doctrine was brought to assume, through his wonderfully vigorous mind, a form of scientific consistency and completeness which it had not possessed before. This however was all. He added nothing, properly speaking, to the contents of the doctrine itself.

"Most inwardly was he filled," according to Professor Rothe,

> with the thought of the *exclusiveness* of the Catholic Church. In the painful struggles of his own religious history, the ideas of Christianity and the Catholic Church had become for his consciousness completely commensurate

---

56. [Nevin justifies his long digression as an attempt to show that Cyprian's ecclesiology (c. 250) was continuous with that of the period immediately following the apostles. In the present section, he will extend this into the fourth and fifth centuries.]

Document 3: Cyprian: Third Article.

and identical. The hold, by which he saved himself from the shipwreck of his interior life, and on which he fastened spasmodically with the whole energy of his powerful spirit, was the absolute conviction that the Catholic Church, and this alone, was a historical revelation, in which the Christian spirit could express and actualize itself in a real way, by which it had a living powerful organism for its operation; the consciousness in short of the specific and exclusive suitableness of the Catholic Church to the Christian life as its proper form.[57] He knew, that it was only by the Catholic Church, and in her, he had himself been able to lay hold of Christianity, that only in communion with her he had found Christian life, healing for his deeply unsettled nature and the satisfaction of all its wants. Before his mind the Catholic Church stood, as the compassionate and loving guide of man, otherwise helplessly abandoned to himself and his errors, with miserable desolation; as the never failing fountain, out of which alone flowed for him the streams of Divine grace and life; as the real communion of God on earth, in which alone was to be reached a true life of holy love; and as the sheltering paternal home, where every one might find, according to his individual need, true care for his infirmities and failings, and a right field at the same time for his religious activity. All these impressions flowed together for him in the general thought—so familiar also already to Cyprian—of the *motherhood* of the Catholic Church, into which he poured the whole inwardness and tenderness of his deep sensibility. This of itself expresses exclusiveness. Christ is to him altogether identical with the Catholic Church, his life with hers; and without communion with her he holds communion with him to be impossible.[58]

The universal authority of the doctrine, finally, meets us under the most impressive form in the ancient symbols or creeds. These differ in some particulars; but never so as to contradict one another; never so as to fall away in the least from the same fundamental scheme or type. This we have in what is known generally as the Apostles' Creed. Here the article of the church forms a special object of faith, which as such must be received of course in the character of a supernatural mystery.[59] All the old church creeds acknowledge it in the same view. There can be no question moreover, but that the sense of the article was in full harmony always with what we have now found to be the doctrine held by the Fathers from the end of the first century on to

---

57. This consciousness is very beautifully and forcibly expressed, particularly in his tract *De moribus Ecclesiae catholicae et de moribus Manichaeorum* [trans. The Manners of the Catholic Church and the Manners of the Manichaeans], L. I. §. 62–64 [see *Nicene and Post-Nicene Fathers*, 4:58–59], and in the passage *Contra Epistolam Manichaei* [trans. Against the Epistle of Manichaeus], §. 5 [see *Nicene and Post-Nicene Fathers*, 4:130–31], where he gives the grounds of his confidence in the truth and divinity of the Catholic Church. He says here expressly, that the feeling described in the text outweighs with him all single difficulties that might still remain for the understanding.—*Note by Rothe* [Rothe, *Anfänge*, 680n94].

58. Die Anf d. christl. Kirche [Rothe, *Anfänge*], p. 680, 681 [Rothe's emphases].

59. [See Nevin, "The Apostles' Creed," MTSS 8:58–71.]

the beginning of the fifth. We speak not of episcopacy, whether in the Anglican or in the Roman form; what we mean, is the idea of the church as a necessary constituent in the great fact of Christianity, as the Divinely established and exclusively valid form of its actualization in the world, as the real organ and medium of all its power for the salvation of men—an outward historical constitution in this view, which in the nature of the case must be in unity with itself, and to which men must submit by faith, in the spirit of little children, in order to be saved. Nothing less than this, we say, is the sense of the article, as it comes before us in the old creeds. Our modern thinking may give it another sense; may understand it to refer to an abstraction only, the notion of the so called invisible church; but in doing so it ceases to be historical altogether, and will be found in fact to occupy a different standpoint entirely from that of the ancient Christian world, over against the universal sense and spirit of these early creeds. The doctrine, or fact rather, of the holy catholic church, grows here out of the mystery of the incarnation, completing itself in the glorification of the Saviour and the mission of the Holy Ghost; it is a living concrete revelation, founded on the Apostolical commission, and carrying along with it corresponding heavenly powers; it defines itself, with inward necessity, as one, holy, universal, and exclusive, the all sufficient and the only ark of righteousness and salvation. It is a mystery thus for faith. Nothing can be more perfectly foreign from the genius of the old creeds, as well as from the religious life universally of the ancient church, than the notion of an experimental religion in the modern sectarian sense, which completes itself on the outside of the church, and without its help, and values this as a sort of outward machinery merely that may become auxiliary afterwards to the working of piety in the other view. From no such standpoint, we may depend upon it, is it possible to fathom the deep meaning of the Apostles' Creed. Every such standpoint is, in truth, the direct negation of the faith to which it gives utterance, contradicts in every position the mystery it was framed to assert and affirm. It holds this mystery for a lie, and sets up another notion altogether, the figment of natural reason simply, in its room and place; and so repeating the old symbol, pretends perhaps to be of one mind still, with this form of sound words originally delivered to the saints. Alas, for the delusion. There is however no excuse for any such mistake. The case is plain, for all who care to understand the truth. The doctrine of the Apostles' Creed in regard to the church, is the same that is presented to us by Irenaeus, by Cyprian, by Athanasius, by Augustine. We owe it both to antiquity and to ourselves, to see and acknowledge here the full truth. The voice of ecclesiastical history is clear. The structure of the creed itself, for one who has gained any true insight whatever into its constitution, is abundantly conclusive. What it affirms, as a foundation principle of faith, is the existence of the church under its outward historical form, as a Divine fact, as the supernatural carrying forward of the work of redemption, as the actual revelation and home of the Spirit, as the real medium of grace, in the bosom of which only, but there surely, may be wrought out the full process of man's salvation, from the remission of sins onward to the resurrection of the body and life everlasting.

Document 3: Cyprian: Third Article.

The church is made to be, without a figure, the organ of the new creation. There it is held to take place. There the heavenly forces on which it depends are considered to be all actually at hand. There the ministry, the bible, the sacraments carry with them a saving power, which can belong to them no where else. This is the very mystery, which gives the article its place in the creed. In what other view could it be an object of faith? How else could men be required to bow to its authority, as a necessary part of the mystery of godliness brought to pass by the Gospel?

[The Modern Protestant Theory of Patristic Apostasy]

In what wide contrast with all this old habit of thought much at least of our modern Protestantism stands, is too plain to require any sort of proof. The evidence of it is thrown in our way continually from all sides. Take in exemplification the following significant and characteristic passage, which happens to meet our eye while we write, as a passing editorial in a late number of the *New York Observer*, (July 28) under the somewhat equivocal caption, "Tampering with the Truth."

> In the history of the rise and progress of the great apostasy, we have an illustration of the danger of the slightest deviations from fundamental truth. This giant system of iniquity may be traced to the early introduction of what, at first view, appears to be a slight error in doctrine. The apostle Paul informs us that, even in his day, the "mystery of iniquity" was already at work [2 Thess 2:7]. And almost up to the apostolic age, we may trace the specious error of sacramental grace, which lies at the foundation of that vast superstructure of spiritual tyranny, which, for ages, spread desolation over both the Eastern and Western churches. The difference between this, as at first taught, and the true doctrine, was apparently so slight that the minds of the multitude, not accustomed to discriminate, might not perceive it. A sacrament is an outward and visible sign of an inward and spiritual grace, sealing the covenant relation of believers to God. But, according to this doctrine, grace is communicated to the soul in some mysterious manner, under the form of an outward rite. This is very agreeable to the carnal heart. It saves the necessity of the personal exercise of repentance and faith, relieves of the necessity of self-scrutiny, in order to discern the "inward spiritual grace," of which the sacrament is a sign, and turns the whole matter over to the priest.
>
> This error, in its inception, was so specious, so much in harmony with the prevalent mystical philosophy, and so conformed to the taste of a superstitious age, that it was received by a declining church without suspicion. But there soon grew out of it the doctrine of *baptismal regeneration*. Then followed an increase of sacraments, in order to cover all the supposed wants of the human soul. *Confirmation* was made a sacrament to impart grace for *sanctification*; *Penance*, to secure the pardon of sins committed after baptism; the *Eucharist* was transformed into the real body and blood of Christ, to provide a ground

of confidence for the superstitious multitude, without personal piety; and to this is added *extreme unction,* that dying grace may be imparted by anointing the five senses with holy oil. To crown the whole, there is the sacrament of *Orders,* which lays the foundation of the hierarchy, by imparting to the priest the power of conferring grace, in the administration of the sacraments.

Thus we have a complete perversion of the gospel, by the introduction of a *sacramental religion,* which removes the necessity of an intelligent reception of the truth, and dispenses with faith, repentance, and holy obedience, and puts the whole affair into the hands of the priest, making his office indispensable to the right exercise of religion. Thus, the whole of Oriental and Papal Christendom lie at the feet of the Priesthood.

The *germ* from which has grown up this deadly Bohon Upas tree,[60] whose wide spreading branches overshadow the world, diffusing everywhere the malaria of spiritual death, was this same doctrine of *sacramental grace,* which some learned men in the Protestant churches are seeking to exhume from the catacombs of a past age, and impose upon the wonder-loving credulity of the nineteenth century. Though it must be obvious to the impartial student of history, that from the time of the introduction of this doctrine into the primitive churches, may be traced the gradual departure of the Holy Spirit; till at length the temple of Christ, deserted of his presence became the temple of idols, "Babylon the Great, the mother of harlots and abominations of the earth."[61]

The quotation speaks for itself. It must be confessed too, that it represents well and fairly a large portion of the religious thinking of the present time. Our universal sect system is ready to take up the same key. This precisely is what multitudes mean by the conception of *evangelical religion,* as distinguished from what they hold to be a religion of rites and forms. Our object here is not to have any controversy with the scheme. Let it pass for what it is worth. What we wish is simply to bring into clear view, the relation in which it stands to what was supposed to be Christianity in the first ages. This all should be willing to see and understand, as a matter at least of simple history. It is the character of truth to love the light. What then, in the case before us, is the clear form of fact? Here is a theory of religion, claiming to be the true sense of Protestantism, which boldly repudiates as an apostacy and mystery of iniquity the whole sense of what Christianity was taken to be in the beginning, back at least to the very age next following that of the Apostles [2 Thess 2:7]. To be on good terms with it, as the self-constituted exponent now of the true meaning of the bible over against

---

60. [A tree that supposedly grew in Java, which produced a highly desirable poison. The air around the tree was so dangerous that only condemned criminals were used to gather it, and most died in the attempt. This was based on the oft-reprinted "Account of the Bohon-Upas." So sacramental grace is a subtle but deadly poison.]

61. ["Tampering with the Truth," *New-York Observer* 30, no. 31 (July 29, 1852) 2 (Nevin recorded the wrong date). Most of Nevin's Protestant contemporaries thought "Babylon the Great" was embodied in the Papacy. Rev 7:5.]

the blundering ignorance of all past centuries, we are required to give up to Satan not only the church of the middle ages, but the church also of earlier times from the fifth century up to the very beginning of the second. For it is not with this or that questionable point only, that the issue of the *N. Y. Observer* is concerned. It goes at once to the very foundations of the ancient faith. The idea of a sacramental religion, we are told, overturns the Gospel. A ministry exercising in any true sense Divine powers, is taken to be such a conception as opens the way at once for the full reign of Antichrist. Why? Only of course because the *Church,* the proper home of such a ministry and sacraments of such supernatural force, is not believed to be the grand and awfully solemn mystery which it was held to be in the beginning. All comes to this at last. The idea of a Divine church takes away all difficulty from the idea of sacramental grace, as well as from the idea of a ministry possessed of more than human powers; whereas the want of faith in the church under any such supernatural view, as being the form and medium of the Christian salvation in the world, necessarily involves the want of power to honor the ministry and the holy sacraments under any corresponding view. If the sense of a higher order of life in this form as something actual and real be not at hand, if the church itself be after all a natural constitution only, part of the system of this world in its natural form and nothing more, then indeed it is easy to see how all that belongs to it must sink down to the same region of mere naturalism, and how it must appear no better than miserable pedantry and affectation to think of talking it into any higher sense. Alexander Campbell's "baptismal regeneration,"[62] sundered from the idea of a real historical polity bearing along with it from age to age, by strict Apostolical succession, the more than human powers with which the church started in the beginning, is in truth a most pitiful and melancholy sham. And so to the judgment now before us all sacramental religion seems, just because it has no faith in the existence of any such church either now or in time past. But, as we have seen, this faith, right or wrong, enters into the universal Christianity of the first ages. It is not there by accident either or unseemly excrescence. We find it prominently inserted in the Creed. The piety of the second century, as well as that of the third and fourth, is based upon it, and constructed upon it, from beginning to end. The religion of the whole period was beyond all controversy just what is here denounced by the *N. Y. Observer*, as the complete perversion of the Gospel. The Fathers all believed in the Holy Catholic Church, and showed themselves to be in earnest with this faith, by ascribing to the church Divine functions and powers. If *this* be the grand apostacy, the "mystery of iniquity," they were all hopelessly involved in it from the very start, and the Creed itself becomes the "masterpiece of the Devil."[63]

---

62. [A founder of the restorationist movement known as the "Disciples of Christ." Campbell maintained "baptismal regeneration," but Nevin thought he separated it from the "real historical polity" in which it had its spiritual life.]

63. [For Evangelical Puritans, the allegedly sudden loss of apostolic purity was itself "the mystery of iniquity" (2 Thess 2:7). The last phrase is likely Nevin's self-invented commonplace.]

To this end it must indeed necessarily come, with Protestantism in the unchurchly and unsacramental form. *The Puritan Recorder* was only a fair exponent of the true inward sense of the system, when it ventured to say openly some time ago, "that the Creed and Puritanism have not a kindred spirit," and that the life and spirit of the venerable formulary, notwithstanding the place allowed to it "by a sort of courtesy" in the New England Primer, "never entered into the life of the Puritan churches," so that it exists among them now only "as some fossil relic of by-gone ages." Every attempt to restore its buried authority, the *Recorder* views with pity and contempt. "We are free to confess," it tells us again,

> that this Creed has forsaken the Puritans, and gone over to become the idol and strength of all branches of Anti-puritanism. And there are good reasons; for Puritanism builds on the Scriptures, and this Creed teaches, in several respects, anti-scriptural doctrines. It is true, that most of it is *capable of a sense* which harmonizes with the Scriptures, and so the Puritans received it, in *a sense consonant with their theology*—either leaving out, or putting a strained sense upon the passage, which asserts that Christ descended into hell. But it is neither safe nor expedient to receive such a document *in such a perverted sense*. For the document once being admitted, and its authority being made to bind the conscience, then the way is open for those who hold the *errors held by its authors*, to plead that we are bound to receive it *in the sense which its authors gave to it*, and this makes it an instrument of *corrupting the faith of the gospel*.[64]

Here we have the cloven foot disclosed without any sort of reserve. Some of the "heretical points" of the creed, as they are called, the Puritan Recorder went on afterwards to expose in form, namely, the descent to hades, the communion of saints, and the holy catholic church. This last it dared to brand as "*a figment*." But as we have just said, Puritanism is fairly expounded here by the unbelieving voice of the Recorder. It has never yet raised any protest against the disclosure thus made at its heavy expense; and we presume it will not do so in time to come. Its whole standpoint is theologically different from that of the primitive church. The faith of this last, as we have it in the creed, is not its faith. It has brought in, beyond all contradiction, *another gospel*; so that the question is now, which is to be regarded as apostolically right and true, the gospel of Puritanism as it rules New England, and much of the world besides in the nineteenth century, or the gospel in which the second century gloried and trusted as a Divine gift handed down from the first. The two systems are not the same. The platform of faith on which the one rests, is by the other openly disowned as unscriptural and contrary to truth.

Here is something surely, which well deserves our most solemn attention and consideration. We do not present it now for any purpose of controversy or debate. We

---

64. [*The Puritan Recorder*, no. 34, August 23, 1849. This text had been quoted three years earlier in Nevin, "Puritanism and the Creed," MTSS 8:105. Nevin added the italics in the present version.]

do not pretend to condemn dogmatically in one direction, or to approve in another. What we wish, is merely to bring into view the historical fact, which must remain the same whatever construction we may put upon it, and which needs first of all to be distinctly perceived and acknowledged that it may be construed with intelligence in any way. Evangelical Puritanism, the modern sect system generally, is at war with what was considered to be Christianity in the first ages. The controversy between present and past here regards not simply the order of things in the Nicene period, and afterwards, but reaches up to the age next following that of the Apostles; and it has to do, not with a few accidents only of the old faith, but with its universal form and constitution. The question, in the last instance, is not of the Papacy as such, nor of Episcopacy, nor of Presbytery, nor of Sacramental Grace, nor of the authority of the Holy Scriptures. All falls back just to this: Has there ever been in the world such a Divine constitution as the Holy Catholic Church, in the sense of the ancient creeds? It is another question, which we need carefully to distinguish from this, whether there be any such Divine organization, with supernatural functions and powers, actually at hand in the world *now*. We may dispose of this second question afterwards as shall seem best; before it comes plainly the other: Was there *ever* any order of this sort in Christian history? Were the first ages right, or were they wrong, in making the existence of it an article of faith, and in grounding upon it the entire weight of the world's salvation? Here it is, that the chasm which yawns so fearfully between the past and the present comes fairly and fully into view. Puritanism does not believe, what was believed most firmly in the days of Ignatius and Polycarp, that the Church stood among men as an actual polity, created by Divine commission, and endowed with corresponding heavenly powers for its own ends. What was a foundation mystery of faith in the one case, is scouted[65] as a dangerous unscriptural "figment" in the other. In this way, Puritanism breaks with the universal Christianity of the first ages; turns its *Creed* into a grand *Lie*; for all must go together, if any regard is to be had to the original sense of the symbol; and so literally converts the course of church history into a wholesale radical apostasy and delusion from the very start.[66]

Such is the simple historical fact. Who will deny, that it is full of unutterable solemnity and interest? Here is the question of questions surely at this time, for all who can rise above the paltry prejudices of party and sect, so as to take any interest in the truth for its own sake. Alas, that the number of such should be so few! Is the old church doctrine of the Apostles' Creed—or *was* it rather—fact or figment, a reality or a dream? Was it a true "heavenly vision" to which fathers, martyrs and saints, did well "not to be disobedient;" or must it be regarded, on the contrary, as the most melancholy hallucination that ever took possession of the human mind, the art of Satan playing himself off as an angel of light, the mystery of iniquity "leading captivity

---

65. ["To reject with scorn." OED Online, "scout, v.2."]
66. [See Nevin's "Puritanism and the Creed," MTSS 8:103–21.]

captive,"[67] in a new downward sense now, most horrible to think of, for at least fourteen hundred years? What are all other questions, with the everlasting din that is made about them in our Babel of sects, as compared with this?

Was there ever among men a *Church,* in the sense of the Creed, a Divine constitution, carrying in itself real grace as an order of existence *above nature,* and rightly challenging in such view the "obedience of faith?"

That is the first question. Only where it is answered in the affirmative, of course, can there be any room for the second; which *then,* however, cannot fail to come home with like awful solemnity—as a waking and not merely sleep-walking interest—to every mind that is seriously bent on being saved:

Is the mystery of a *Divine Church* in this old sense still at work in the world? Are the glorious things once spoken of Zion yet true and real, as they were held to be in the first ages? Or has that heavenly vision dissolved long since into thin air and mere Gnostic idealism, like the baseless fabric of a dream which leaves no wreck behind?

J. W. N.

---

67. [Acts 26:19; 2 Cor 11:14; 2 Thess 2:7; Eph 4:8.]

Cyprian: Fourth and Last Article.[1]

[The Renewal of Persecution and the Plague]

The year 252 brought with it new trials for the Christian Church. There would seem to be a mysterious sympathy between the moral and physical worlds, by which every great catastrophe or crisis in the first is found to be marked more or less distinctly by corresponding tokens and signs in the second. When the foundations of society are about to give way, men's hearts are made often to faint and fear by strange signs of wrath in the course of nature. So it was before the destruction of Jerusalem; and something of the same sort we meet with in the last period of the old Pagan empire of Rome. The decline of the state, the breaking up of the ancient order of life, seemed to draw along with it calamity and disaster in all conceivable forms. The universal course of the world was so ordered, as to proclaim continually its own vanity and misery. On this subject we may learn much from Augustine.[2] Long before his time however, these signs of wrath had begun to show themselves in the economy of God's providence, filling whole lands with apprehension and fear. Wars, rumors of wars, famine, pestilence, and flood, united with the sense of perpetual political insecurity, to make men weary of the present, and to beget within them a feeling of desperation at the same time with regard to the future. At the time of which we now speak, under the reign of Gallus and Volusianus[3], a most fearful plague was moving, like a Divine curse, over the length and breadth of the civilized world. With this were joined in some parts of the empire other public calamities, such as drought and famine. As usual, these visitations served to inflame the popular heathen mind against the followers of Christ. They were regarded always as the enemies of the reigning order of things; they refused to take part in the religious sacrifices that were ordered to propitiate the gods; and it became a merit accordingly, in the eyes of fanaticism, to stir up the magistrates against them as a class of persons who had no right to live. The way was opened thus for a new persecution.

---

1. [*MR* 4 (November 1852) 513–63.]
2. [Augustine, *Concerning the City of God*.]
3. [Father and son, ruling 251–53. They followed Decius, who had initiated the Decian persecutions, and was killed in war with the Goths. The plague might have been smallpox or measles.]

It was in reference to this, that the term of penitential discipline was cut short, as already remarked, in the case of those who had before fallen and were now seeking to be restored again to the peace of the church. "Inasmuch as we see," Cyprian writes to Cornelius of Rome in the name of a whole African council (Ep. 57),

> that the day of another persecution is close at hand, and are admonished by many urgent signs to arm and prepare ourselves for the conflict set before us by the enemy, as also by our exhortations to get in readiness the people whom God has deigned to commit to our charge, and to gather within the Lord's camp all his soldiers who call for arms and ask to be led to battle—we have judged, in obedience to necessity, that reconciliation should be given to such as have not forsaken the church, but have persevered since the first day of their fall in doing penance, bewailing their sin and imploring mercy of the Lord, and that they ought to be equipped and furnished for the struggle which is drawing near. For heed must be given to the fair signs and warnings of the time, that the sheep may not be left exposed by the shepherds, but the whole flock be collected together, and the Lord's army made ready for the contest of the heavenly war.[4]

In such circumstances it might be trusted, that no improper advantage would be taken of this indulgence. It was to be hoped that penitents thus restored would be found ready now, with others, to die for their faith; in which case the reconciliation would turn out to have been on the part of the bishops, "whose office it was as priests to celebrate daily sacrifices to God,"[5] a true priestly function preparing victims for the glorious altar of martyrdom. If however any should seek restoration without this mind, they must be left to the judgment of the Lord. It was not meet that their fault should stand in the way of so great a benefit, in favor of others who might be ready in truth to embrace the martyr's crown. "Nor let any one object," the epistle goes on to say,

> that he who receives martyrdom is baptized in his own blood, and needs no peace from the bishop, having in prospect the crown of a higher acceptance and more glorious reward from the Lord. For in the first place, no one can be equal to martyrdom, who is not armed for battle by the church, and the mind must fail which is not raised and inflamed by the participation of the eucharist. Our Lord says in his Gospel: "When they deliver you up, take no thought how or what ye shall speak; for it shall be given you in that same hour what ye shall speak; for it is not ye that speak, but the Spirit of your Father that speaketh in you" (Matth. x: 19, 20). But when it is said that the Spirit of the Father speaks in those who are delivered up and called to confess the Saviour's name, how can any one be found ready and prepared for such confession, who shall

---

4. [*Epist.*, 122; *Letters*, 3:55–56.]
5. [*Epist.*, 123; *Letters*, 3:57.]

Document 3: Cyprian: Fourth and Last Article.

not first have received by the peace of the church the Spirit of the Father, who himself speaks and confesses in us by the strength he imparts to his servants?[6]

Then in the second place, if flight were chosen instead of the martyr's crown, and the penitent should be cut off by untimely death in the period of his exile, "must it not be laid to our account that so good a soldier, who gave up all and forsook house and parents and children to follow his Lord, has departed this life without peace and communion?"[7] May not the shepherds be charged in the day of judgment with unfaithfulness to their trust, who thus neglect the sheep so solemnly committed to their hands?

No military chief, on the eve of battle, could be more solicitous for the good conduct of his soldiers, than Cyprian was that the professed servants of Christ should quit themselves valiantly for the faith in this new trial. His care and zeal extended to places at a distance, as well as to his own immediate charge. We have a long admirable letter from him addressed to the people of Thibaris,[8] which sounds still like the voice of a heavenly trumpet, calling upon men to forsake all joyfully for Christ. He sees the fashion of the world passing away, the last time evidently at hand, the power of Antichrist ready to appear in full revelation; and finds in all this only the stronger reason for renouncing its expectations in every form, and making full earnest with the promise of life and immortality contained in the Gospel. Let persecutions come. They were to be expected, they had been foretold. They grow necessarily out of the relation the church bears to the world. They serve to promote our fellowship with Christ; who bids us rejoice and exult accordingly, when we are called thus to suffer for his name. Why? "Because when persecutions have place, then crowns of faith are given, then the soldiers of God are proved, then heaven is opened to the martyrs."[9] Let God be glorified by death or by flight—the leaving of all for the Saviour's name. Exile in such form involved no real separation from the church. He is not alone who, wherever he wanders or hides in mountains or dismal deserts, has Christ always for his companion. And should he fall, by robber or wild beast, by hunger or thirst or cold, or by storm at sea, it will be still under his leader's eye, a merit sure to find from him its promised reward in the resurrection. "The glory of martyrdom is not less for its being out of public view, if only it be death really for the Saviour's sake. Enough that it be attested by that one witness, who awards to martyrs their final plaudit and crown."[10] Then follow the animating examples of righteous Abel, the first martyr, of Abraham called to sacrifice his son Isaac, of the three youth whom Nebuchadnezar cast into the fiery furnace, and of others mentioned in sacred history, whose faith it should be counted a privilege to follow in the same path to everlasting glory. In the end, victory

---

6. [*Epist.*, 124; *Letters*, 3:57–58.]
7. [*Epist.*, 124; *Letters*, 3:58.]
8. [Little is known of the ancient city whose ruins are in modern Tunisia.]
9. [*Epist.*, 128; *Letters*, 3:62.]
10. [*Epist.*, 128; *Letters*, 3:63.]

must declare itself on the side of Christ, and shame and defeat be the portion of all who should join hands with Antichrist and the world. He that loveth his life must lose it, while to hate it in this world was to save it forever.

> Men are trained and exercised for secular contests, and count it greatly to their honor if it may fall to them to be crowned before a multitude of spectators and in the presence of the emperor. See what a grand and sublime contest, glorious by the reward of a celestial crown, is here, that God should behold us striving, and take a lively interest in the spectacle of our struggle, following with his eyes those whom he has deigned to make his own sons. While we fight and do battle for the faith, God beholds, his angels behold, Christ also beholds. What weight of glory is it, and what vast happiness, to contend in the presence of God, and to be crowned by Christ as Judge! Let us arm ourselves, dearly beloved brethren, with all our strength, and prepare for the contest with pure mind, sound, faith, and devoted resolution. Let the camp of God move forward to the battle, to which we are summoned. Let the sound arm themselves, that none such may lose their past integrity. Let the lapsed also arm themselves, that such may recover what has been lost. Let the sound be provoked to battle by honor, the lapsed by grief. The blessed apostle Paul exhorts us to arm and prepare in this way, when he says: "We wrestle not against flesh and blood, &c." (Eph. vi: 12–17). These arms let us take, with these spiritual and heavenly defences let us fortify ourselves, that we may be able to withstand and repel in the evil day the assaults of the Devil.[11]

Then follows a glowing picture of the final triumph of the saints, in contrast with the tearful doom of all rebels and traitors, after which the epistle concludes:

> Let these things, dearly beloved brethren, sink into our hearts. Let this be the preparation of our arms, this our meditation day and night, to keep before our eyes, and to revolve in thought and feeling continually, the punishments of the wicked and the rewards and merits of the just, what the Lord threatens in the way of penalty to those who deny him, and what on the other hand he promises to those who confess him in the way of glory. Should the day of persecution overtake us in the midst of such thoughts and meditations, the soldier of Christ, instructed by his precepts and admonitions, will not quail from battle, but be ready for the crown.[12]

The tract *De Exhortatione Martyrii*,[13] addressed to Fortunatus, is a general encouragement to martyrdom, in like earnest and vigorous strain, made up mainly of texts and examples drawn from the Holy Scriptures. It is not enough in this war to be summoned to battle by man's voice; the precepts and promises of God, as they are

---

11. [*Epist.*, 130–31; *Letters*, 3:66 {"withstand . . . in the evil day" (Eph 6:13)}.]
12. [*Epist.*, 132; *Letters*, 3:68.]
13. [In *Tract.*, 189–210; *ANF* 5:496–507.]

Document 3: Cyprian: Fourth and Last Article.

to be found in his own word, need to be well laid up and continually revolved in the mind. These are the sounds of the trumpet, that inspire the soldier with his best courage, and most surely conduct him to victory. Of such force however the Scriptures are to Cyprian's mind, as a matter of course, only in the bosom of the *Church*. As we have seen before, martyrdom itself had no value in his eyes, no proper reality we may say, under any other view. The subject is presented under a succession of leading heads, such as: That the idols of the heathen are no gods; That God only is to be worshipped; God's threatenings against such as sacrifice to idols, &c. Sufferings and persecutions are shown to be the natural lot of the righteous and pious. But Christ is greater and stronger than the world; he can sustain his people here, and he will bring them to everlasting glory hereafter—an exceeding weight of glory that may well cause all suffering and affliction in this world to appear by comparison insignificant and light. Then comes the stirring peroration:

> If it be glorious for secular soldiers, after the enemy has been conquered, to come back with triumph into their country, how much more great and illustrious is it to return triumphing, from the defeat of Satan, into Paradise; and there, from whence Adam the sinner was once cast out, to bring back victorious trophies by the prostration of him who before caused such ruinous fall; to offer unto God his most acceptable sacrifice of incorruptible faith and inward virtue without blemish; to attend him, with illustrious devotion, when he shall come to take vengeance on his enemies; to stand by his side, when he shall sit in judgment; to be joint heir with Christ; to be made equal with the angels; to rejoice, with patriarchs, with apostles, with prophets, in the profession of the heavenly kingdom! Such thoughts what persecution can conquer, what torments overcome? The mind which is settled by religious meditations remains fixed and firm, and no terrors of the Devil, no threats of the world, can shake the soul that is made strong by the sure and steady faith of things to come. The world is shut in persecutions, but heaven is thrown open. Antichrist threatens, but Christ defends. Death comes, but immortality follows. Earth disappears to the slain, but paradise meets the restored. Temporal life is extinguished, but life eternal takes its place. What dignity is it, and what security, to depart hence joyfully, to depart gloriously in the midst of affliction and pain, to close at one moment the eyes that look upon men and the world, and to open them the next on God and on Christ! How rapid so bright a transition! You are hurried suddenly from below, to rest in glory above. Lay hold of these things; think of them day and night. Found in such frame by the day of persecution, the soldier of God will be fully prepared for battle. Or if called away before, the faith which was thus prepared for martyrdom will not lose its reward. Where God is judge, merit hangs not on the accident of time. In persecution martyrdom is crowned, in peace the martyr's mind.[14]

---

14. [Cyprian, *De Exhortatione*, in *Tract.*, 209–10; *ANF* 5:506–7.]

The bishops of Rome, under the immediate eye of the emperors, were naturally the first object always of imperial persecution. The see was filled almost wholly, for three centuries, by a succession of martyrs. Cornelius, who had entered on the office at the risk of his life under Decius, was now banished, and afterwards condemned to death. Lucius, his courageous successor, soon shared the same fate. We have a letter from Cyprian to Cornelius on the occasion of his good confession, which breathes the martyr's spirit, burns with the martyr's fire, we might almost say in every line. "We have learned the glorious proofs of your faith and virtue, dearest brother," he writes,

> we have heard of the honor of your confession, with the exultation of those who feel themselves to be partners also and sharers of your meritorious praise. For since the church for us is one, and our mind also in undivided harmony, what priest must not triumph in the praises of his fellow priest as though they were his own, or what brotherhood not rejoice in the joy of brethren everywhere? It is not possible fully to express, what exultation and joy there was here, when we were informed of the prosperous and brave course of things among you—that you had led the way there in confession for the brethren, and that the confession of the leader had been swelled by their concurrence, so that in going before to glory you have made many to be companions of your glory, and have engaged the people to become confessors by being first ready to confess for all; leaving us at a loss which most to extol among you, your own ready and firm faith or the unyielding love of the brethren. There was publicly proved the virtue of the bishop going before, with the devotion of the brotherhood cleaving to his steps. As there is among you one mind and one voice, the whole Roman church has confessed.[15]

It was a splendid illustration of the faith which had been commended in the same church long before by the blessed St. Paul; an example full of instruction and encouragement to all churches throughout the world, showing the invincible nature of true Christian unity, where priest and people hold firmly together in the fear of God, and the power it has to prevail in the end over the worst designs of the enemy. The readiness shown by the whole church in this case to make common cause with the confession of the bishop, served to baffle and confound the persecuting power from the very start. Many even who had before fallen now stood firm, deriving strength from their penance, and recovering what had been lost by a glorious confession. The epistle closes with an exhortation of love, in view of what was still to come.

> Let us not cease to give ourselves, with all the people, to fastings, watchings, and prayers. Let us be instant in groanings and deprecations. These are the celestial arms for us, which cause us bravely to stand and persevere. These are the spiritual defences and divine weapons, by which we are protected. Let us be mutually mindful of each other, in concord and harmony; let us pray always

---

15. [*Epist.*, 149–50; *Letters*, 3:88–89.]

Document 3: Cyprian: Fourth and Last Article.

one for the other; let us relieve our trials and distresses by mutual charity; and which ever of us may first depart hence by the speedy favor of the Lord, let our love continue in his presence, let not prayer cease for our brethren and sisters before the mercy of the Father.[16]

Here we have a plain recognition of the thought, as one familiar on all sides, that the prayers of the saints in heaven are not without effect on earth, and that they are to be desired and made account of accordingly, by those who are still in the body, in this view. We meet the same thought at the close of the tract *De Habitu Virginum*: "*Mementote tunc nostri, cum incipiet in vobis virginitas coronari.*"[17]

Persecution served to distinguish, we are told, between the true church and schism pretending to usurp its name. Novatian and his party in Rome were now safe. So in Carthage the faction which was trying to set up a new church under Fortunatus. Antichrist knows his proper enemy, and cares not to waste his strength on those who are already in fact on his own side. "The adversary and foe of the church despises and passes by as conquered captives those whom he has already alienated and led off from the church, and turns his rage against those in whom Christ is seen to dwell."[18] The world would seem indeed in every such case, to have a most quick apprehension in some way of what is and what is not of one spirit with itself. Sects and schisms it can understand. They bring religion into its own sphere, make it a matter of private judgment, place it under the control of human will. That is something to be borne with and endured. It is only the presence of the true *Catholic Church*, with its real heavenly assumptions and powers, and its jurisdiction higher than any which belongs to the kings of the earth, that provokes its hostility and wrath. This the world has no power to comprehend. But it can feel the opposition in which it stands to its own darkness and vanity, and on this ground is ready always to fight against its claims wherever they may be exhibited in their true form.

---

16. [*Epist.*, 152; *Letters*, 3:91–92.]

17. [Cyprian, *De Habitu Virginum*, in *Tract.*, 117. In the original, the last word is "*honorari,*" not "*coronari*"; trans. "Only remember us at that time, when virginity shall begin to be rewarded {or crowned} in you" (*ANF* 5:436).]

18. *Inimicus et hostis ecclesiae, quos alienavit ab ecclesia et foras duxit, ut captivos et victos contemnit et praeterit, eos pergit lacessere in quibus Christum cernit habitare. Quanquam etsi aliquis ex talibus fuerit apprehensus, non est, quod sibi quasi in confessione nominis blandiatur,* &c." *Ep.* 60, *ad Cornelium* [*Epist.*, 151–52; *Letters*, 3:91]. So again, *Ep.* 61, *ad Lucium*, the persecution in Rome is said to have been Divinely intended to distinguish the true church from the false and to confound heretics by showing which cause the Devil was disposed to destroy and which to spare. "*Neque enim persequitur et impugnat Christi adversarius nisi castra et milites Christi; haereticos prostratos semel et suos factos contemnit et praeterit. Eos quaerit dejicere, quos videt stare*" [*Epist.*, 153–54; trans. "For the adversary of Christ pursues and assaults only the camp and army of Christ; heretics, already laid low in the dust and now belonging to him, he passes by in scorn, seeking to cast down those whom he sees to be still standing" (*Letters*, 3:94)].

[The Christian Response to the Plague]

The plague also made room for a striking argument in favor of the Catholic Church, by bringing the spirit with which it was actuated into lively contrast with the reigning spirit of the world.[19] The fear of death destroyed in the breasts of the heathen all sentiments of kindness and love. Those who could fled, to save their own lives. The sick were abandoned, in the most merciless style, to their hard fate. The dying, and the dead, were cast out upon the highways and streets. On all sides corpses were left unburied, poisoning the air still more with their pestilential putrefaction. A sort of desperation ruled the public mind; which however, instead of bringing men to acknowledge their sins and humble themselves in the way of religion, led many rather to blaspheme the only true religion itself as being the cause of this sore calamity, as well as of the other public miseries of the time. In these circumstances, Cyprian published two tracts; one, *De Mortalitate,* designed to instruct and animate Christians in their duty;[20] the other, *Ad Demetrianum,* in the way of apology and defence over against this mad charge of the Pagan world.[21] The effect of the first, along with the other exhortations of the chief pastor, backed by his own brave and noble example, seems to have been all that could have been wished or desired. The faltering were made firm, while the strong were inspired with new resolution and zeal. Not only did the Christians take care of their own sick, and show becoming regard to their own dead; but in the spirit of that heroic, self-sacrificing and self-forgetting charity, which no other religion save that of the cross has ever been able to inspire, they took upon them the care also of others. "If we are the children of God," said Cyprian to his people,

> who causes his sun to shine and sends rain upon the just and unjust, not confining his gifts and benefits to his own merely, but extending to those also who are alienated from him in the spirit of their mind, we must show it in act and deed, endeavoring to be perfect as our Father in heaven is perfect, by blessing those that curse us and doing good to those by whom we are persecuted.[22]

The church resolved itself, accordingly, into an organization of mercy and charity for the whole city. The rich made generous contributions in money; the poor lent their personal service. The sick, who had been abandoned by their heathen relatives and friends, were taken in and nursed at the risk of life. The streets were cleared of exposed corpses, and the air relieved from contagion, by their proper burial. Thus did the church heap coals of fire on the head of her enemy [Rom 12:20]. The Pagan world

---

19. [For a contemporary description, see Stark, *Triumph of Christianity*, 105–19.]
20. [In *Tract.*, 176–89; ANF 5:469–75.]
21. [In *Tract.*, 210–25; ANF 5:457–65.]
22. [The location of this paraphrase of a familiar text (Matt 5:44–48) cannot be determined. See ANF 5:495, 452 for partial quotations.]

Document 3: Cyprian: Fourth and Last Article.

looked on with astonishment, and for the moment at least was forced to admire what it had no power rightly to comprehend.[23]

The tract *De Mortalitate* has regard specially to the miseries of its own age; which Cyprian felt to be in a certain sense the consummation of the world's vanity, making room for the full advent of Antichrist, and so for the final collapse and fall of its whole present state, in the way of preparation for the second coming of Christ. The relation of the world, however, this present *saeculum,* the order of nature as such, to the economy of grace and the true kingdom of God, is always substantially the same. It remains always equally true, that the scheme or fashion of this world passeth away; that it is in itself a shadow and a dream; that the proper destiny of man lies beyond it, in a form which he is now required to embrace by faith; that this involves and requires necessarily the solemn renunciation of the life that now is for that which is to come; that those who thus set faith above sense must be hated, and charged with folly, by the mass of men who have no faith, but are bent on living only for the present time; that such moral disorder on the part of the world, added to its natural vanity, and attended with special judgments on the part of God, must make it always a scene of discipline and trial for the righteous; and that the only proper posture and habit of the believer, therefore, is that by which he is led to look upon it as a state that is ever rushing towards its own dissolution, and to wait for the revelation of the Son of God from heaven, when he shall come to be glorified in his saints and admired in all them that believe. In such view, the tract before us is of eloquent application and force for all times. These are the topics in substance, on which it dwells. Let the soldiers of the cross consider well the terms of their warfare. They are called to meet trials. These show that the world is passing away, and that the kingdom of heaven is at hand. We live by faith. Why should we not be ready joyfully to quit this life, if God calls, full as it is of temptation and sorrow—unless it be because the glorious promises of God concerning the life to come, are not firmly believed? While in the body, Christians

---

23. Compare with this the following picture, which has been preserved to us from Dionysius of Alexandria [also known as Dionysius the Great (d. c. 264), a pupil of Origen], in a notice of the plague that prevailed in that city some years later, in the reign of the Emperor Gallien: "The visitation filled the heathen with the utmost dismay, as an evil that left no hope; but it had no such terror for us, to whom it came only as a special discipline and probation. The most of our brethren spared not themselves in the fulness of their brotherly love, but cared only for one another, and by attending upon the sick without regard to their own safety, serving them willingly for Christ's sake, showed themselves ready to give their lives for them if need be with joy. Many died, after they had restored others by their care, the best among us, a number of presbyters, deacons, and distinguished laymen, ended their lives in this way—a form of death, which seems, as the fruit of great piety and vigorous faith, not to fall short of the glory of martyrdom itself. Many handled the bodies of dying; Christian brethren, closed their mouths and eyes, buried them with all decency and respect, and then followed them in death. Among the heathen, all was different. Those who took sick were thrust out; the dearest friends were forsaken; the dying were exposed in the street; the dead were left unburied. [*Historiae ecclesiasticae scriptores: Eusebius Pamphilus . . .* , 1:304–5 {Eusebius, *History,* 305–6 [7.22]}; Eusebius's source was Dionysius's "To the Alexandrians:" see *Ante-Nicene Christian Library* 20:236–38. As is often the case, Nevin's translation is paraphrastic.] [For a modern description of the role of the church in the plague, see Stark, *Rise of Christianity,* 73–94.]

are necessarily under the same law of suffering with others. Nay, they must endure more than the common world. This is part of their discipline; which is to be met with corresponding humility and patience; and which is to make room finally for their victory and crown. The plague should be terrible only to such as were not "born again of water and the Spirit,"[24] who stood exposed thus to the second death. To the servants of God, death in any form was to be counted salvation. When such were called away, it was not proper that their friends should mourn as those who had no hope—"clothing themselves in black garments here, for those who are now arrayed there in white."[25] Let the heathen see, that we really believe what we say, and do not mourn as lost those whom we profess to regard as living with God. Death is the necessary passage to immortality. Who should not desire to be thus transformed into the image of the Saviour and translated into his glory? Let those seek to stay in the world, on whom the world smiles, and who make it their confidence and life. *Our* rest and hope are not here. We have here no abiding city, but seek one to come [Heb 13:14]. Now especially all may be said to urge us forwards and upwards in our thoughts. The world is evidently tottering towards its own fall. The sorrows of the last time are near at hand. To die now, is for the righteous emphatically to be taken away from the evil to come. Let us welcome such deliverance then, as strangers and pilgrims anxious to reach their proper home.

> Paradise we consider our country, the patriarchs are our parents; and why should we not hasten forward to behold the first and salute the last? A vast collection of friends await us there; a large crowd of parents, brothers, sons, secure now of their own salvation but anxious still for ours, expect our presence. To meet and embrace these, what joy will it be on both sides! What will be the pleasure of those celestial regions, without the fear of dying, felicity supreme in a life without end! There will be the glorious choir of the apostles, there the exulting company of the prophets, there the innumerable throng of martyrs crowded for the victory of their conflict and passion, there the triumphal virgins which subdued the concupiscence of the flesh and body by the power of continence, there the merciful in the possession of their reward, who performed works of righteousness by their alms and gifts to the poor, and following the Lord's directions converted their earthly patrimony into treasures in heaven. To these, beloved brethren, let us hasten with ardent desire; let it be our wish, that we may reach there soon, that we may soon be with Christ. Let God behold in us this mind, let Christ the Lord see such to be the purpose of our faith, who maybe expected to bestow the rewards of his glory most largely on those who have had towards him the strongest desires.[26]

---

24. [John 3:5, paraphrased.]
25. [Cyprian, *De Mortalitate*, in *Tract.*, 185–86; ANF 5:474.]
26. [Cyprian, *De Mortalitate*, in *Tract.*, 188–89; ANF 5:475.]

Document 3: Cyprian: Fourth and Last Article.

[Apology to the Pagans]

The tract addressed to *Demetrianus* is written with like animation, and in a similar tone of firm and vigorous faith. It is a bold apology for Christianity over against the charges of this insulting representative of heathenism, in which the vanity and misery of the reigning Pagan life are brought out with unmerciful exposure, and the solemn truths of the Gospel proclaimed in opposition to it with Elijah-like severity and zeal. Again we have the idea of the world in its decrepitude and old age, a system now ready to pass away. War, dearth, famine, pestilence, were all in order for such a state of palpable decay. They had been foretold, as signs of the approaching end of the world. They were however, at the same time, signs of Divine wrath. God was angry with the heathen world for its sins. What right had those to complain of his judgments, who wearied him with their provocations. "Ye are angry at God's anger; as though ye had merited something good by your bad lives; as though all your calamities were not still less in number and more light than your sins."[27] Then follows a scathing censure of the reigning manners of the time, revealing to us a gloomy insight into the social state of the old Roman world in these last days of its life and power. And now as if all other crimes were not enough, the guilt must be added to them of persecuting the servants of the Most High. All other forms of religion they could tolerate; only not the service of the true God.

> Crocodiles, and baboons, and stones, and serpents, are worshipped by you; God alone is either not worshipped anywhere, or else worshipped at risk of punishment. The innocent, the righteous, the friends of God, ye deprive of their home, rob of their patrimony, load with chains, cast into prison, deliver to the sword, to wild beasts, to flames. Neither are ye content to inflict upon us such pains in any simple and compendious form. Protracted torments are applied to our racked bodies, manifold excruciations to our lacerated bowels; your savage inhumanity is not satisfied with ordinary forms of torture; it becomes a matter of ingenuity to excogitate such as new.[28]

What lust of cruelty? What gratuitous rage? In other cases, torture was applied to draw out confession. But here the confession was offered freely, and yet the torture was made to follow; showing plainly what diabolical spirit ruled and governed the whole process.

> But why turn to the infirmity of the body? Why contend with the imbecility of mortal flesh? Engage with the power of the soul, assail the force of the mind, overthrow faith, conquer by disputation if you can, conquer with reason. Or if there be anything of divinity and power in your gods, let *them* rise in their own cause, and defend themselves by their own majesty.[29]

---

27. [Cyprian, *Ad Demetrianum*, in *Tract.*, 215; ANF 5:460.]
28. [Cyprian, *Ad Demetrianum*, in *Tract.*, 217; ANF 5:461.]
29. [Cyprian, *Ad Demetrianum*, in *Tract.*, 217–18; ANF 5:461.]

But the impotency of these gods was shown, in the power which Christians had over them, through the name of Christ, in the cure of demoniacal possessions. On the other hand, God is the avenger of his people, and all who are his enemies must perish. There may seem to be indeed in this world one lot to the righteous with the wicked; but it is only in appearance. The calamities which come upon the last as a curse only, are to the first a source of discipline and so of salvation. The issue in the one case is eternal death, while in the other it is everlasting life. Let the enemies of the Church then be warned in time, and seek salvation before it be forever too late. Let them come forth from the deep night of superstition into the clear light of day.

> We grudge not your good, and hoard not up for ourselves the Divine gift. We return kindness for your hatred; and for the pains and torments you inflict upon us, we show unto you the way of salvation. Believe and live, that having persecuted us in time ye may rejoice with us in eternity. When this world is left, there is no room for penitence, no force in satisfaction. Here life is either lost or gained.[30]

Here repentance is never too late; and no one need despair of salvation, who even at the last hour applies to God with a true heart for mercy.

[Another Example of Christian Charity]

Another interesting exemplification of Christian charity on the part of Cyprian and his church, is presented to us about the same time in their cheerful and liberal response to a call that was made upon them from Numidia, for the relief a heavy calamity which had befallen the churches in that country. In an irruption of some neighboring barbarous tribe, a number of Christians, of both sexes, were carried away into captivity; and a sum of money was now required for their ransom, which the poverty of the Numidian churches found itself unable to raise. Letters were sent to Carthage, reporting the case and imploring help. We have Cyprian's epistle in reply, *(Ep. 62, ad Januarium et al.)* full of the most tender sympathy and concern. "With the greatest inward commotion," he writes,

> and not without tears, we have read what you have written to us, dear brethren, in the solicitude of your love, concerning the captivity of our brethren and sisters. For who must not grieve in such a case, who must not reckon the calamity of his brother to be his own, when the Apostle Paul says: "If one member suffer, &c." (1 Cor. xii: 26); and in another place: "Who is weak and I am not weak" (2 Cor. xi: 29). So now the captivity of our brethren is to be considered *our* captivity also, and the affliction of those in danger is to be regarded as our affliction; since we are united in truth in one body, and not love merely, but religion also should excite and engage us to ransom brethren who are our members. For

---

30. [Cyprian, *Ad Demetrianum*, in *Tract.*, 224; ANF 5:465.]

Document 3: Cyprian: Fourth and Last Article.

> since the Apostle Paul again says: "Know ye not that ye are the temple of God, and that the Spirit of God dwelleth in you" (1 Cor. iii: 16), if even love were not enough, to urge us to the help of our brethren, we should yet reflect in this case that they are temples of God which are carried away captive, and that we ought not patiently to endure the long continuance of such disgrace, but should lay out actively and promptly such strength as we have, to deserve well by our service of Christ our Divine Lord and Judge. For whereas the Apostle Paul says: "As many of you as have been baptized into Christ, have put on Christ" (Gal. iii: 27), we are to see in our captive brethren Christ himself, and to redeem from the peril of captivity Him who has redeemed us from the peril of death; that he who has rescued us from the jaws of the Devil, and who abides and dwells in us, may now himself be rescued from the hands of barbarians, and he be redeemed by a sum of money who has redeemed us by the cross and by blood; who moreover allows this to happen, that our faith may be tried, whether each one is ready to do for another what he would wish to be done for himself, if he were himself a captive in the hands of barbarians.[31]

With many thanks for the opportunity given to participate in so good a work, the epistle then goes on to state, that the case had been laid before the church in Carthage, and that a collection had been readily and freely made amounting to a "hundred thousand sesterces," (several thousand dollars) which was now forwarded to the Numidian bishops, to be applied as they might see proper to the object in view.[32] The wish is expressed that no similar calamity might again occur; but it is nobly added at the same time: "If however anything of the sort *should* take place, to prove our love and try our faith, fail not to inform us of it at once by letter, as you rest assured that, whilst our whole church and brotherhood here pray that no such event may happen, they are ready in case it should to contribute large and liberal aid."[33] In conclusion another feature of this early Christianity comes into view, which is not undeserving of our thoughtful notice:

> That our brethren and sisters who have contributed heartily and freely to this necessary work, as they are ready to do always, may be had in mind in your prayers, and a recompense be made them for their good deed in your *sacrifices and supplications,* I have subjoined their several names; as I have added also the names of certain of our colleagues in the priesthood, who being present have also contributed something in their own name and in that of their people according to their ability—noting and forwarding also their amounts besides our own proper remittance; all of whom, as faith and charity demand, ye are bound to remember in your offices of prayer.[34]

---

31. [*Epist.*, 155–56; *Letters*, 3:95–96.]
32. [*Epist.*, 156; *Letters*, 3:97.]
33. [*Epist.*, 157; *Letters*, 3:97, Nevin's emphasis.]
34. [*Epist.*, 157; *Letters*, 3:97, Nevin's emphasis.]

The persecution under Gallus proved after all less serious than was apprehended. Wars and insurrections, throughout his reign, gave him no time to carry it vigorously forward in the provinces; and his death, which took place by violence in the summer of a. 253, brought it altogether to an end. For a few years subsequently, the Church was permitted to enjoy again general rest and peace.

[The Baptism of Heretics[35] and the Authority of the Bishop of Rome]

It was towards the close of this period, that the unhappy controversy arose concerning the baptism of heretics, of which we have already taken some notice. As we have seen before, it grew entirely out of the high view which then universally prevailed of the Divine nature of the Church, as being the body of Christ, and thus the one only medium of salvation for a guilty and fallen world. All saving grace for men was held to be by the action of the Spirit, not as influencing their minds in what may be called a general natural way, but only as comprehended in this supernatural constitution, made to be historically present in the world under such outward and real form. Here was the mystery precisely, which faith, as distinguished from sense and natural reason, was required to own and embrace in the Holy Catholic Church—a new world of light and power namely, by the resurrection of Christ, actually at hand through the Holy Ghost for all the purposes of man's redemption and sanctification. In the bosom of this heavenly constitution, it was held, and nowhere else in the wide world, there was "power on earth to forgive sins [Matt 5:6]." Here the Apostolic commission was still in full force, carrying along with it corresponding endowments and prerogatives of grace. Here were real sacraments, not shadows merely but types. Here accordingly baptism by water, was at the same time baptism by the Holy Ghost, answerable in full to our Saviour's word to Nicodemus: "Except a man be born of water and of the Spirit, he cannot enter into the kingdom of God [John 3:5]." It was for the remission of sins, and carried in it the mystery of a new birth to righteousness and salvation. Such force the sacrament was considered to have, of course, not as a mechanical or magical charm, not in virtue of its own outward form merely nakedly and separately taken, but in union only with the presence of the Spirit and the fulness of the new creation. From this it would seem naturally to follow, that it could never be validly administered on the outside of the church, and that the baptism of heretics and schismatics, therefore, must be rejected as of no force.

This view in fact gained wide ground in different parts of the church. It prevailed particularly in Asia Minor and Northern Africa. In Rome however it was all along

---

35. [The controversy was initiated by (firstly) the large number of Christians who had lapsed during the Decian persecution, and (secondly) the schism of Novatian. These events generated two issues: firstly, if one had been baptized *by* a heretic or schismatic, was the baptism valid; secondly, did a person coming into the orthodox church from a heretical or schismatic community need to be *re*-baptized? See discussions in *Letters*, 4:4–8; Schaff, *History of the Christian Church*, 2:262–65; Arnold, *Cyprian of Carthage*, 84–89; González, *History of Christian Thought*, 1:238–46.]

Document 3: Cyprian: Fourth and Last Article.

held, that such baptism might be valid, and that it was not necessary therefore to baptize over again in all cases those who came from heretical associations into the true church. For some time the question was not brought to any decision. Each region was allowed to follow quietly its own tradition and custom. But now, in the middle of the third century, the difference broke out into an open and violent controversy, the result of which was a complete rupture for a season between the see of Rome and those portions of the church which stood opposed to it in this dispute.

Towards the end of the year 253, the Roman bishop Stephen went so far as to place the churches of Asia Minor under sentence of excommunication, on the charge of their being Anabaptists,[36] in insisting as they did on the re-baptism of heretics. From Asia the difficulty soon after extended itself to Northern Africa. Cyprian entered with zeal into the Asiatic view, and in doing so was brought at once into full collision with the Roman pontiff. Two councils, the first composed of eighteen and the second of seventy-one bishops, were held at Carthage in the year 255, which united in the declaration that the baptism of heretics was not to be regarded as valid. We have several letters from Cyprian on the subject, some of them quite long, all taking the same ground and breathing the same earnest and decided tone. Among the rest, one to Stephen himself, reporting to him respectfully but firmly the judgment of the larger Carthaginian council.[37]

The argument is always of one form. All grace resides in the church; heretics and schismatics are on the outside of this sacred, communion; consequently they have not the Spirit; and how then can they confer any spiritual benefit on others? Their sacraments must be, like themselves, false and void. It is not enough to say, that the Spirit is given afterwards, by confirmation or the imposition of hands, when any of them are received into the true church. It belongs to the idea of baptism, that this sacrament itself should include the grace of the Spirit;

> for remission of sins is granted to every one in baptism, and the declaration of our Lord in the Gospel shows that sins can be remitted by those only who have the Holy Spirit; since when he sent forth his disciples after his resurrection, saying, "As the Father hath sent me, even so send I you," we are told that he breathed on them, and said: "Receive ye the Holy Ghost; whose soever sins ye remit they are remitted unto them, and whose soever ye retain they are retained." This proves, that he only can baptize and give remission of sins, who may have the Holy Ghost.[38]

How then can the baptism of heretics carry with it any force (Ep. 69)? "How shall he be able to give remission of sins to another, who himself has no power to put off his

---

36. [Here understood literally: they were charged with being "re-baptizers."]

37. [For background on this episode, see *Letters*, 4:4–8. The letter sent to Stephen is 68 (*Letters*, 4:28–32).]

38. [*Epist.*, 195–96, quoting John 20:23; *Letters*, 4:40.]

own sins, as being out of the church?"[39] The interrogation made in baptism involves clearly this sense;

> for when we say, "Dost thou believe in life eternal and the remission of sins by the holy church?" it is understood that the remission of sins is not given except in the church, and that with heretics, where the church is not, sins cannot be discharged. Let those then who assert that heretics can baptize either change the interrogation, or else vindicate its truth—unless they allow them the church also, for whom they thus claim baptism.[40]

Along with baptism must go also the holy chrism or anointing with consecrated oil. "But there can be no sanctification of creature oil, where there is neither altar nor church" (Ep. 70).[41]

It is easy enough to see that Cyprian has in his eye always the position taken by Stephen and the Roman church, and that he feels it to be more than anything else in his way. He has to allow too, that this had the weight of previous custom and tradition in its favor. The contrary view, in Africa at least, had begun to acquire authority only about the close of the previous century, and was still not universally received. So far as previous practice is appealed to in this case accordingly, it is for the purpose only of establishing a provincial liberty, the right to following a special usage and custom; while pains are taken, in a way which seems to be almost Protestant at times, to break the authority of the other and more general tradition, by an appeal to what is taken to be the voice of reason and the clear sense of the Gospel. The old usage, it is supposed, may have grown out of the fact, that those who went off in the first heresies and schisms had been previously baptized in the church, and so did not need to be baptized over again if they afterwards returned to its bosom. It became an abuse, only when the same rule was extended to such as had their first baptism with heretics, which was to be considered in truth no baptism at all.

> We are not to go by custom however, but by force of reason. For even Peter, whom the Lord chose to be first and on whom he built his church, when Paul afterwards contended with him about circumcision, did not arrogate anything to himself with insolent assumption, so as to say that he held the primacy and ought rather to have deference from such as came after him, neither did he despise Paul because he had once been a persecutor of the church, but admitted the counsel of truth, and readily yielded to right reason as vindicated by Paul; leaving us thus a lesson of concord and patience, that we may not pertinaciously cleave to our own mind, but may embrace and make to be our own

---

39. [Epistle 70, not 69: *Epist.*, 201; *Letters*, 4:46.]

40. [*Epist.*, 201; *Letters*, 4:46.]

41. [*Epist.*, 201; *Letters*, 4:47. Nevin's translation here is particularly poor. He translates *olei creaturam* as "creature oil," instead of "the material substance of oil" (as rendered in *Letters*).]

Document 3: Cyprian: Fourth and Last Article.

rather what is usefully and wholesomely suggested at times by our brethren and colleagues, if it be found true and right (Ep. 71).[42]

This looks to Stephen, and may be considered pretty free in its manner of dealing with his pontifical claims; but it is not hard to see that it carries in it notwithstanding a silent acknowledgment of the truth of these claims. It is not a protest against authority absolutely in the name of reason, but a plea rather which seeks to bend authority to reason as its proper rule. "In vain do they who are vanquished by reason oppose custom to us," it is said in another place (Ep. 72 [73]) "as though custom were greater than truth, or that were not to be followed in spiritual things which is revealed for the better by the Holy Spirit."[43] Error in ignorance may be pardoned, as it was in the case of St Paul; but to continue in it, after the truth has been made clear, is obstinacy without excuse. Such passages have it must be confessed a sufficiently independent sound, and may seem at first not to be in full harmony with Cyprian's general theory of the church. But we are bound in common justice to take them in connection with this theory; and when we do so, they will be found to assert after all nothing more than this, that the authority of the church in its own sphere ought to be governed by a proper regard to the nature of things, and not simply by blind custom. To suppose that the author of the tract *De Unitate Ecclesiae* could seriously intend, for one moment, to set up private judgment as such in any case of this sort against the whole idea of church authority, or to make any particular and separate construction of the original sense of Christianity of more force than the tradition of the church itself in its absolute and fully settled form, is perfectly absurd. The more so too, we may add, as the object of Cyprian's zeal here was itself only a sort of corollary always in his mind from that very doctrine of the church, which he would be made by this supposition to hold in so poor account.

With like qualification must we take those passages, in which he seems to assert the right of every bishop to follow in his own diocese any practice which to himself may seem best, under responsibility to God alone at the last day. So Ep. 69, *ad Magnum,* he gives his judgment, imposing it however on no one, "as each overseer must give account of his conduct to the Lord, as the blessed Paul writes: 'Every one of us shall give account of himself to God; let us not therefore judge one another any more,' (Rom. xiv: 12, 13)."[44] Again Ep. 72, to Stephen himself:

> These things, very dear brother, we have reported to you, both out of official regard and from private affection, believing that you too, in the sincerity of your piety and faith, will be pleased with what is agreeable at once to both piety and truth. We know however, that some are not willing to lay aside what they have once imbibed, and cannot easily change their own mind, but without

---

42. [*Epist.*, 204–5; *Letters*, 4:50.]
43. [*Epist.*, 214; *Letters*, 4:60–61.]
44. [*Epist.*, 200; *Letters*, 4:45.]

> prejudice to the bond of peace and concord with their colleagues choose to retain certain peculiarities which have become established for themselves by use. In which matter also neither do we pretend to coerce any one or to create law, since every bishop in the government of the church has the free use of his own will, under responsibility for what he does to the Lord.[45]

Again, Ep. 72 [73], *ad Jubaianum:*

> These things, dear brother, we have written to you, after our mediocrity, not prescribing or prejudging for any one, so as that every bishop may not do what he thinks best, having the power of his own will. We, so far as in us lies, do not quarrel for the sake of heretics with our colleagues and fellow bishops, with whom we hold concord and peace in the Lord; more especially as the apostle says, "If any man seem to be contentious, we have no such custom, neither the church of God" (1 Cor. xi: 16). Patiently and mildly we maintain the spirit of charity, the honor of our college, the bond of faith and concord of the priesthood.[46]

To infer from all this, that Cyprian considered every bishop absolutely independent in his own charge, would be ridiculously foolish. The office for him had no force in any case, except in union with the organization of the church as a single whole. All he can mean here then is, that within this acknowledged general jurisdiction, and under the condition of being true to its proper authority, however this might be exercised, each member of the episcopal college was to be regarded as an independent functionary, at liberty to manage his particular trust as to himself should appear best. This question concerning the baptism of heretics accordingly he affects to look upon as one not yet absolutely settled, as one that should for the present be left open; in the case of which, at the same time he trusts, that what he takes to be the necessary sense of the true doctrine of the church, would yet be able to triumph in the end over all contrary present usage, if only it were not pretended now to force it to a general public decision. What he is provoked with in Stephen's conduct, is that he should insist on taking the point out of the sphere of freedom, and be bent on turning it into fixed law, in a form which was supposed not to express fairly at last the true mind of the church and the proper sense of the Christian tradition.

Be this as it might however, Stephen refused to recede from the ground he had already been led to take, in opposition to the churches of Asia Minor. With the delegates which were sent to him by the African council he refused to have any conference whatever, and even directed his people not to receive them into their houses, by way of testifying his displeasure with the cause they represented. Cyprian's letter was answered; but only to let him know that the position he had taken was wrong. "Let

---

45. [*Epist.*, 208; *Letters*, 4:53–54.]

46. [*Epist.*, 221–22; *Letters*, 4:69. The first sentence is awkwardly translated; *Letters* gives the middle phrase as "we do not wish to prevent any bishop from doing what he thinks right."]

Document 3: Cyprian: Fourth and Last Article.

there be no innovation," it was said, "on the rule handed down, that such as come from heretical bodies should be received by imposition of hands only to repentance." Cyprian speaks of the communication as proud and self-contradictory (Ep. 74, *ad Pompeium*);[47] but he was not in the right posture and mood exactly, to judge fairly in the case; it may have been simply strong and firm in its tone, while it refused to reason on the subject, but cut the whole question short by the stern plea of usage and tradition.

Another council, consisting of seventy-eight bishops, was convened in Carthage towards the close of the year 256, which in the face of this Roman decision solemnly re-affirmed the previous judgment of the African church.[48] The difficulty was carried thus to an actual and open breach of ecclesiastical peace.

In these circumstances, it became an object with Cyprian to have a common understanding with the churches of Asia Minor. A special communication on the subject was made accordingly to Firmilian of Cesarea [*sic*] in Cappadocia, one of the leading bishops of that region; which drew forth in return the celebrated letter of this prelate preserved among Cyprian's writings.[49] It makes common cause of course with the African bishops; echoes the sentiments and arguments of Cyprian; and speaks at the same time in the most disrespectful terms of the course pursued by Stephen. Over against the Roman plea of tradition, it is maintained that the strong terms of reprobation employed by the apostles towards heretics show plainly that they could not have admitted the validity of their baptism, and that the alleged contrary custom therefore must have crept in without right, and so should not now be allowed to contravene what was manifestly the true sense of the Gospel. The Roman tradition in some other points also was not strictly apostolical, as might be seen in its variation from what was observed at Jerusalem; so in other provinces local peculiarities of worship were to be found; which however disturbed not the proper unity of the church; an evil now forced upon it by the intolerance of Stephen, which of itself showed this tradition

---

47. [The response in the previous sentence is quoted and then characterized by Cyprian in *Epist.*, 222; *Letters*, 4:70.]

48. In the introduction to the proceedings of this synod, from Cyprian's pen, it is said with plain reference to Stephen: "*Neque enim quisquam nostrum episcopum se esse episcoporum constituit, aut tyrannico terrore ad obsequendi necessitatem collegas suos adijit, quando habeat omnis episcopus pro licentia libertatis et potestatis suae arbitrium proprium tamque judicari ab alio non possit, quam nec ipse potest alium judicare. Sed exspectemus universi judicium Domini nostri Jesu Christi, qui unus et solus habet potestatem et praeponendi nos in ecclesiae suae gubernatione et de actu nostro judicandi*" [Cyprian, *De Haereticis Baptizandis*, in *Tract.*, 266]. [Trans. "For neither does any of us set himself up as a bishop of bishops, nor by tyrannical terror does any compel his colleague to the necessity of obedience; since every bishop, according to the allowance of his liberty and power, has his own proper right of judgment, and can no more be judged by another than he himself can judge another. But let us all wait for the judgment of our Lord Jesus Christ, who is the only one that has the power both of preferring us in the government of His Church, and of judging us in our conduct there" (*ANF* 5:565).] This is carrying the tone of episcopal independence very far indeed; but the nature of the case requires, that it should still be taken with the general qualification to which we have already referred.

49. [*Epist.*, 229–44; *Letters*, 4:78–94.]

human only and not Divine. In Asia, they had always followed the other practice. One church and so only one baptism, had been their maxim. To admit baptism on the outside of the true church, was in the end to suppose other real churches also besides that founded on Peter, and so to turn into a farce the very primacy of which Stephen was now disposed to make such high-handed use. This was to be worse than the heretics themselves, by keeping them back from the laver of regeneration, and withholding from them the remission of sins, even when they were led to renounce their errors and to seek salvation as something which is to be found only in the church. And yet the Roman pontiff must be offended. The patron of heretics, God's enemies, is indignant with those who oppose them and maintain the truth of the church! Hence what strifes and dissensions has he not brought to pass?

> But what sin hast thou not accumulated on thyself, in cutting thyself off from so many flocks! For it is thyself thou has exscinded, be well assured; since he is the true schismatic, who makes himself an apostate from the communion of ecclesiastical unity. For in pretending to cut off all from thy communion thou hast only put thyself out of communion with all.[50]

What a specimen of evangelical charity and humility! A fine way truly to keep the unity of the Spirit in the bond of peace—thus to make common cause with heretics, and break with the household of faith in all parts of the world! To refuse all negotiation on the subject with the delegates of a sister province! "To call Cyprian besides a pseudo-christian, a pseudo-apostle, and a deceitful workman!"

The letter is deeply tinged with passion throughout. All is discolored, distorted and exaggerated, by the medium of excited feeling and partizan interest through which it is viewed. We see in it not so much Stephen's real spirit, or his real behavior, as the construction put upon both by the offended humor of Firmilian. Stephen never certainly applied any such abusive epithets to Cyprian. Firmilian merely construes in this way, after the fashion of heated brains, the pontiff's general procedure. It amounted to this, he means, in its virtual import; as one may flare up, when he is contradicted in some opinion by another, and say: "Do you then call me a *liar*?" This one specimen is enough to show, with how much caution and reserve the statements generally of such a witness are to be received, in this unfortunate case. It is to be regretted, that the whole controversy is set before us only under an *ex parte* and completely onesided representation. We have no version of the affair from the side of Stephen. If we had, it would no doubt be made to appear in a very different light.

As it is, the whole case tells strongly in favor of the supremacy of the Roman see, and not against it as is sometimes pretended. How came Stephen to assert such authority, in opposition to whole provinces of the church east and west, if it were not on the ground of previously acknowledged prerogative and right? Or how could the pretension do more than call forth derision, if no such ground existed for it in fact in

50. [*Epist.*, 242; Letters, 4:93.]

Document 3: Cyprian: Fourth and Last Article.

the general mind of the church? It is easy to talk of his presumption and pride, and of a regular system of usurpation kept up with success on the part of the Roman pontiffs generally. But that is simply to beg the whole question in dispute. The hypothesis is too violent. It destroys itself. Stephen was neither fool nor knave; and yet he must have been both on a grand scale, to play the part he did here out of mere wanton ambition, usurping powers to which he himself well knew, as all the world knew besides, he had no lawful claim whatever. Both Cyprian and Firmilian are themselves witnesses in fact, that a true central authority did belong to the bishop of Rome. What they complain of is its supposed abuse. They feel the force of it very plainly in spite of themselves. This is just what makes them so restive under its exercise. Had it been mere false pretension, they could have afforded to let it pass by them as the idle wind. They knew it however to be more than that. Then again, it turned out in the end that Stephen was in truth right. His judgment proved to be, with proper distinctions afterwards, the real voice of the Catholic Church, and has remained in full force down to the present time. There is reason to believe too, that it includes deep wisdom, that it is of vast practical importance, and that it was highly necessary at the same time to have the case settled in this way. Even those who are most ready to resolve the whole proceeding into the worst motives, are constrained generally to admit all this in its favor. But now what makes the case most of all remarkable perhaps, is the way in which so wise and correct a decision was reached. It was not by any theological speculation. It must be granted, that there seemed to be much more reason in the view taken of the subject by Cyprian. To this day it is by no means easy to answer his general argument. It would appear to lie really in the conception of the church, as it was then universally held, that no baptism on the outside of its visible communion could be valid; and that to pretend the contrary must necessarily bring into peril the entire doctrine, as an article of faith. And yet just this seeming contradiction the judgment of Stephen, setting at full defiance the cogency of the reasoning employed on the other side, is made to embrace. Not however through any more profound analysis of the Christian theory. Nothing of that sort was pretended. All was made to turn on tradition. The wisdom of the decision, whatever it might be, lay altogether in the fact,[51] with which what was taken to be the true sense of the Church in this form was discerned and affirmed, in distinction from all merely accidental variations with which it might have been observed in particular places. On this ground only the whole judgment was made to rest. Stephen acted in the case, not as a legislator, but simply as a judge expounding the common law of the church. This is truly characteristic, and forms one of the most interesting features of the whole transaction.

How far Cyprian may have been deserving of blame in this affair, we shall not pretend to give any opinion. Augustine, who was his great admirer, and who in a certain sense carried out his doctrine of the Church to its proper scientific perfection, considers that he fell here into serious fault; which he trusts however was surmounted

51. [The printing reads "tact."]

by his better mind afterwards, as it may be said to have been fully washed out at last by his glorious martyrdom. Of his honesty and pure zeal for the glory of God, no one can have any doubt. It is easy enough to see also, that the controversy gave him no small amount of uneasiness and grief.

In the midst of it, as he himself informs us in his epistle to Jubaianus, he wrote his tract *De Bono Patientiae*.[52] It is an exhortation to endure manfully the sorrows and trials of life, enforced by the general long-suffering of God, and by the particular pattern of Christ, as well as by the example of the patriarchs, prophets, and saints of every age, who have borne his image and walked in his spirit. The world in any view is full of vanity and grief; our present mortal state is by reason of sin a discipline of affliction throughout. All need to arm themselves with patience for the battle of life. But how much more the followers of Christ, who in addition to those natural evils were required to meet special tribulations on account of their faith; who were exposed to special and extraordinary assaults of the Devil;

> who, besides other manifold and various temptations, were called upon, by the dreadful stress of persecution, to forsake their property, to undergo imprisonment, to bear chains, to put life at stake, to endure the sword, wild beasts, flames, crucifixion, in a word all sorts of torments and pains, by faith and the virtue of patience—according to the word of the Lord: "These things have I spoken unto you, that in me ye might have peace; in the world ye shall have tribulation; but be of good cheer; I have overcome the world" (John xvi: 33).[53]

All true patience springs from a firm apprehension of the reality and glory of the life to come. We are saved by hope. God reigns. In the end, all will be right. He who is now silent will in due time be revealed in power and glory, to give rest to his people and to punish his enemies with everlasting destruction. Such is the general strain of this tract, like the music of Ossian,[54] mournful and yet pleasant to the soul. It came in good time. The hour for the patience of confessors and martyrs was once more close at hand.

[The Valerian Persecution and the Martyrdom of Cyprian]

A new persecution broke forth under Valerian in the year 257. The controversy between the bishops of Rome and Carthage was hushed, in their common sufferings for

---

52. [Cyprian, *De Bono Patientiae* in *Tract.*, 241–55.] Also, as it would seem, the tract entitled *De Zelo et Livore* [in *Tract.*, 255–65]; which some have supposed to be a sort of practical improvement in some way of the trying experience through which the author was called to pass in this controversy; though without any good reason that we can find, either in the title of the piece or in its contents.

53. [Cyprian, *De Bono Patientiae*, in *Tract.*, 247–48; ANF 5:487.]

54. [Ossian was the purported author of a cycle of Gaelic epic poetry. It was published by James Macpherson, who was later shown to have been its author. The "stories are of endless battles and unhappy loves.... No happiness is possible here, only the 'sweet joy of grief.'" Okun, "Ossian in Painting," 328.]

Document 3: Cyprian: Fourth and Last Article.

the faith. Stephen had the honor of laying down his life first, with the usual fortune and courage of his exalted see. Cyprian stood prepared in his own mind for the same fate. The persecution however was not at once carried generally to blood. It was hoped that by depriving the congregations of their pastors, and then forbidding them to meet, the object in view might be gained without resorting to this extremity. Cyprian was called before the proconsul Paternus, and required to answer for his faith. "I am a Christian and a bishop," he replied; "I acknowledge only the one true God, who has made heaven and earth and sea, and all that they contain. This God we Christians serve; and to Him we pray day and night for ourselves, for all men, and for the welfare of the emperors themselves." *Proconsul:* "Do you persist in this purpose?" *Cyprian:* "A good purpose, proceeding from the knowledge of God, may not be changed." The proconsul then pronounced sentence of banishment upon him, according to the imperial edict; and as this had regard to presbyters as well as bishops, he demanded the names of any such then living in Carthage. Cyprian refused to give them; the Roman law, he said, did not allow him to become an informer; neither was it right that they should come forward and report themselves; but let them be sought in the places of their ministry; there they might easily be found. Thus ended this good confession. Cyprian was sent to Curubis; and an order was issued at the same time prohibiting all Christian assemblies, and the common practice of visiting Christian burial places, under penalty of death.[55]

The work of proscription spread throughout Africa. In a short time we find, among other forms of punishment, many thrown into chains, and condemned to labor in the mines—bishops and other ecclesiastics mainly, but along with them also some of the laity, including even females and small boys. From the place of his exile, Cyprian forwarded to these fellow sufferers for the testimony of Jesus a large sum of money, from such means as he had still at command, accompanying the gift with a glowing letter of congratulation and encouragement, which well serves at the same time to show the ardor and courageous zeal of his own mind in the near prospect of martyrdom. For to this issue he now confidently expected to come. He had received notice of it in a vision.[56] The oracle however inspired him with no dread. On the contrary, it was to him a source only of joy and strength. The letter to which we have just referred breathes this spirit, in almost every line. "Your glory would require, most blessed and beloved brethren," it begins,

> that I should myself come to see and embrace you, were it not that I also am bound as an exile to fixed limits for the confession of the Name. But in such way as I can, I present myself before you; though not with outward bodily

---

55. [This account is based on *Acta Proconsularia Sancti Cypriani*, in PL 3:1497–1506. A modern translation is *The Acts of St. Cyprian*, in Musurillo, *Acts of the Christian Martyrs*, 168–75.]

56. Supernatural communications of this sort, in one form or another, would seem to have been not unfrequent in his experience; and he refers to them, from time to time, in a way which shows them to have been looked upon as by no means out of course in the life of the Church as it then stood.

approach, yet in affection and spirit I come, expressing by letter the mind with which I triumphantly exult in those virtues and praises which are yours, reckoning myself a partner with you, in the fellowship of love, though not in bodily passion. How indeed can I hold my voice in silence, when I hear of those who are so very dear to me so many glorious things, proceeding from the Divine favor; that a part of you, by the consummation of their martyrdom, should have already gone before to receive from the Lord the crown of their merits; while a part still tarry in the confinement of prisons, or in the mines and chains, furnishing by these very delays a larger amount of example to confirm and animate others, advancing by protracted torments to more ample titles of merit, about to have hereafter for reward celestial compensations answering to the days which are now numbered in pain?[57]

Then, after remarking that such distinction at the end well befitted the exemplary character of their previous Christian life, the epistle goes on:

That you should have been grievously beaten first of all with cudgels, as the beginning of your glorious confession, is not for us a matter of horror. Sticks could not terrify the Christian body, whose whole hope is in the wood. The servant of Christ owns the symbol of his salvation; he who has been by the wood redeemed to eternal life, is here advanced by the wood towards his crown. And what marvel is it that vessels of gold and silver should be yielded to the mines, the place where gold and silver dwell, except that the order is now reversed, so that the mines have begun to receive the precious metals, which they were before wont only to give? They have imposed fetters also on your feet, and have bound your sacred persons, the temples of God, with ignominious chains—as if with the body the spirit too might be bound, or your gold could be sullied by the contact of iron. For men dedicated to God, and religiously maintaining the testimony of their faith, these are ornaments, not bonds, the feet of Christians are not put to shame by them, but made illustrious rather for coronation. O feet happily bound, that are to be set free, not by the smith, but by the Lord! O feet happily bound, which move in the way of salvation towards paradise! O feet bound for the present in the world, that they may be free with the Lord forever! O feet held back for a time by fetters and gyves,[58] about to run swiftly with glorious course to Christ! Let cruelty and malice hold you in chains here at their pleasure, soon shall ye pass from the earth and these pains to the realms of heaven. The body is not indulged in the mines with bed and pillows, but it is refreshed with the consolations of Christ. The limbs weary with labor lie on the ground, but it is no punishment to lie there with Christ. The person, externally unwashed and squalid, is the more purified by the Spirit within. There is but little bread there; but man lives not by bread alone, but also by the word of God. There is lack of clothing

57. [*Epist.*, 244; *Letters*, 4:95.]
58. [That is, shackles or handcuffs.]

Document 3: Cyprian: Fourth and Last Article.

against the cold; but he who has put on Christ has both raiment and ornament enough. The half-shaven head looks frightful; but since the head of the man is Christ, the head which is thus distinguished for the Lord's name must be honorable in any form.[59]

It might seem hard, that "no opportunity was had there for the priests of God to offer and celebrate Divine sacrifices."[60] They must however consider their sufferings themselves a sacrifice to God of the most precious and acceptable kind, that was sure also to be followed with the largest return of heavenly profit. The priests had gloriously led the way in this service, presenting themselves as victims holy and without spot on the altar of God; and the fruit of their consecration was now seen in the similar devotion also of their flocks.

> Following your example, a large portion of the people have made with you a like confession and won a like crown, joined with you in the strongest bond of love, and not to be separated from their pastors either by prisons or mines. Among these are not wanting virgins, to whose sixty-fold fruit is now added the hundred-fold, and who are borne thus with double glory towards the celestial crown. Boys also have earned the praise of confession by a virtue beyond their years.[61]

In conclusion, they are exhorted to wait joyfully for the hour of their triumphant departure; while an interest is begged in their prayers in the mean time, as now likely to be of special force and effect, in behalf of Cyprian himself and others, whose testimony had not yet come so nearly to the like glorious end;

> that God may deign to consummate the confession of us all, that he may set us safely and gloriously free, along with you, from the darkness and snares of the world, so that we who have stood joined together in the bonds of charity and peace, both against the assaults of heretics and the pressure of the heathen, may rejoice together likewise in the regions of bliss.[62]

In answer to this we have three different letters, written from different locations in the mines, in which these sufferers acknowledge in the warmest terms the kindness of Cyprian, reciprocate his expressions of love, and modestly return his praises as properly less theirs than his own. "*Es enim omnibus in tractatu major,*" they say, "*in sermone facundior, in consilio sapientior, in patientia simplicior, in operibus largior, in abstinentia sanctior, in obsequio humilior, et in actu bono innocentior.*"[63] They were

---

59. [*Epist.*, 245–46; *Letters*, 4:96–97.]
60. [*Epist.*, 246; *Letters*, 4:97.]
61. [*Epist.*, 247; *Letters*, 4:99.]
62. [*Epist.*, 248; *Letters*, 4:100.]
63. [*Epist.*, 248–49; trans. "For there is no man your match in teaching, none more eloquent in language, more wise in counsel, more penetrating in wisdom, more generous in charity, more saintly in abstinence, more humble in obedience, more selfless in virtuous conduct" (*Letters*, 4:100).]

only his disciples. His confession before the proconsul, followed by his banishment, had been like the sound of a trumpet, summoning the soldiers of God to battle. This first shock, so well sustained, must carry with it the merit in some sense of all that had followed. They hoped only to share with him the crown of his confession by following its steps. They were now helped by his animating words; let him go on still to help them with his continual prayers.

Under a new provincial governor, Cyprian was recalled after nearly a year's absence, and directed to keep himself in the mean time to a retired country residence in the neighborhood of Carthage, till his fate should be farther sealed[64] by a new rescript which was now expected from Rome. Valerian had determined to proceed to more rigorous measures for the suppression of Christianity. For bishops, priests and deacons, the penalty was now to be at once death; senators and knights were to have their property confiscated first, and then if they still persisted in their Christian confession must likewise lose their lives; in certain other classes of persons again confiscation was to be joined with banishment and chains. The policy was to remove the clergy, and arrest the spread of Christianity among the higher classes. Pope Sixtus,[65] who had lately dared to take the post of honor made vacant by the death of Stephen, and with him four deacons of the Roman church, were the first victims of this new bloody proclamation. They suffered martyrdom on the sixth of August 258. In Carthage, as Cyprian writes in a letter to Successus (Ep. 80), all the clergy stood to their place, "ready for the brunt of battle, and fully made up in mind for immortality and glory."[66] By private messengers, he had learned the true nature of the late edict. Despatches were on the way now from the Emperor to the proconsul; "the coming of which we hope for every day," he adds, "with firm faith looking towards the hour of our passion, and expecting through the help and mercy of the Lord the crown of everlasting life."[67] Then follows a request that this information might be conveyed to the bishops of the province generally;

> in order that by their exhortation the brotherhood may be everywhere strengthened and prepared for the spiritual conflict, so that all may think less of death than of immortality, and being consecrated to the Lord with full faith and entire heart may rejoice rather than fear in this confession, in which as they know the soldiers of God and of Christ are not killed but crowned.[68]

The rescript came. Soon after it was understood that lictors were sent to bring Cyprian to Utica, where the proconsul had gone at the time to hold his court. With the advice of his friends, however, he withdrew, and kept himself concealed, till the

---

64. [Missing strokes in the printing makes "farther sealed" uncertain.]
65. [Sixtus II, d. 258.]
66. [*Epist.*, 252; *Letters*, 4:104.]
67. [*Epist.*, 252; *Letters*, 4:104–5.]
68. [*Epist.*, 253; *Letters*, 4:105.]

Document 3: Cyprian: Fourth and Last Article.

procurator came back to Carthage; in order that he might have the privilege of laying down his life among his own people. So he himself explains the matter in the last letter we have from him (Ep. 81), addressed at this time to the presbyters, deacons, and universal people of his charge. "It is meet and proper," he writes,

> that a bishop should confess the Lord in the place where he has presided over the Lord's church, and the whole flock be made illustrious by the testimony of the pastor in their midst. For whatever the confessing bishop speaks in the moment of confession, he speaks by God's inspiration with the mouth of all. But the honor of our glorious church must suffer damage, if I the regular bishop of another charge should, after sentence, received on confession at Utica, go as a martyr from thence to the Lord; whereas it is my continual prayer and most earnest wish, both for my own sake and for yours, to confess among you, to suffer there, and thence to depart to the Lord. We wait accordingly in this retreat the return of the proconsul to Carthage, ready to hear from him the imperial instructions in regard to those who bear the Christian name, and to speak what it may be the Lord's will to have spoken at the time.[69]

With the return of the proconsul, the illustrious bishop of Carthage again made his appearance, and was immediately afterwards taken into custody. The whole church in that city was thrown into commotion. A large multitude of people accompanied him to the place of judgment and kept watch through the night in dense crowd before the house in which he was kept confined. When brought before the magistrate, he witnessed a firm, good confession; which drew after it at once his doom to a violent death. The sentence was pronounced: *Let Thascius Cyprian be executed with the sword.* "God be praised!" responded the bishop, and said no more. He was then led, in the midst of a vast body of people, to the spot where his execution was to take place. Here he disrobed himself, kneeled down, and prayed. When the executioner approached, he directed twenty five pieces of gold to be paid to him for what he chose to regard in this way as a service of love. He then bandaged his own eyes; two of his clergy bound his arms; with trembling hand the executioner raised the fatal sword; the venerable head fell. So ended the tragic, but triumphant scene. The object of the saint's ambition was reached. The glorious crown of martyrdom was at last fully and forever won.[70]

The Christians, we are told, spread napkins and handkerchiefs on the ground, that they might be consecrated as relics, it would seem, by coming into contact with the baptism of blood.

The execution took place on the 14th of September a. 258, in the midst of a plain, thickly set with trees, a short distance out from the city. The body was buried privately, during the following night, on the Mappalian way. Two churches were afterwards raised to his memory; one under the name *Mappalia* on the spot where he

---

69. [*Epist.*, 253; *Letters*, 4:105–6.]
70. [*Acts of St. Cyprian*, 173–75.]

was buried; the other on the place of his execution, which received the name of *Mensa Cypriana*—that is, the *table* or altar where he was offered as a sacrifice to God. His bones were transferred long after, in the time of Charlemagne, to France.[71]

[A Synopsis of Cyprian's Religion]

We shall not pretend to follow this general account of Cyprian's life, with any separate portrait of his character. Our sketch has been so framed, as to allow this to speak for itself. No one can doubt especially the reality and strength of his piety. Religion with him was no form merely, no empty theory or notion, but a living power which possessed and ruled the entire man. He has been charged with a disposition to make too much of the simply outward. But no mistake could be greater than to suppose, that the outward was of any worth or force for him in any merely external view. There was nothing mechanical in his religion, nothing magical or superstitious. He did make account of the outward; but it was only as he held it to be joined, by Divine supernatural association, with the real presence and invisible action of the Spirit. He had no sense for what is sometimes taken to be the highest order of spirituality in modern times—that religious experience, which affects to be independent of all outward supports and helps, and claims the power of entering into communion directly with the Most High, by virtue simply of its own upward endeavors and flights. Where such habit of thought prevails, the relation between the outward and inward in religion is always felt to be more accidental than necessary, and it becomes accordingly a sort of principle and maxim that the one can be exalted only at the expence [sic] of the other. To be spiritual then is regarded as one and the same thing with being lifted by the activity of the mind, (assisted it is presumed by the Holy Ghost) out of the world of sense into that of pure thought and feeling; whilst to make account of the objective, in the character of any outward institutions or forms, considered either as human or divine, is taken to be just the opposite of spirituality in its true and best sense. Those who are in this way of thinking can never understand the necessity of laying much stress on the idea of the church and the holy sacraments. They are terribly afraid of what they call reproachfully the sacramental system. The sacraments may be good enough in their place, they think, and the church too is to be honored, particularly under its *invisible* character; but there is a constant tendency in the human mind to make such outward things a substitute for evangelical piety, that is, for the action of the soul as such conversing with God directly in an inward way; and so it is necessary to be very jealous of any view which seems to ascribe to them more than a simply rational and natural force. With this whole mode of thought, it is most certain that Cyprian had no sympathy whatever. His religion was not *evangelical,* in any such technical Baptistic or Puritanic sense.[72] The idea of any opposition between the Gospel and the Church, lay as far as

---

71. [Butler, *Lives of the Primitive Fathers*, 9:220–21.]
72. [For this "sense," see Nevin, "Evangelical Radicalism," MTSS 11:310–14.]

Document 3: Cyprian: Fourth and Last Article.

possible from his mind. Christianity with him was essentially churchly and sacramental. He could have had no patience with any spirituality, which might have plumed itself on being indifferent to this side of the mystery of godliness, under the dream of moving in a higher and more ethereal region. All *such* spirituality he would have denounced at once, beyond every sort of doubt, as false spiritualism only, Gnostic hallucination, the action of the simply natural mind in the way of religion substituted for the operations of grace under its proper supernatural form. To be in the Spirit was not in his view any exaltation merely of the natural mind as such; that would be after all something born only of *flesh*, which can never by any stimulation, we are told, produce any thing higher than itself (John iii: 6); it implied the presence and action of the Holy Ghost in the world under a real form, which was taken to be above nature, and which was felt to involve thus necessarily the idea of an actual constitution, in the bosom of which only, as distinguished from the world in its common form, it could be possible to have part in the grace it was supposed to comprehend. This constitution presented itself to his mind, as an object of faith, according to the Creed, in the mystery of the Holy Catholic Church. There accordingly, and not in the sphere of our natural life on the outside of this Divine constitution, the Spirit was regarded as dwelling and working in a most real objective way, for the sanctification and salvation of sinful men. All true spirituality then, in the view of Cyprian, was conditioned by the believing acknowledgment of this mystery, and an actual submission to the power of it in its own place and under its own proper form. He made vast account certainly of the outward church, of the regular priesthood, of the holy sacraments, of ecclesiastical institutions and forms generally; but it was just because he made all in all of the action of the Spirit, and believed at the same time that such supernatural grace was not to be found in the order of nature, but offered itself for the use of men only in the church, and so through the ministrations and forms of the church—that it was a mystery in such view, which men are bound to take as they find it by faith, and the whole sense of which is lost the moment they pretend to deal with it as an object of mere natural sense and reason.

All falls back then to the question, Was this conception of Christianity true or false? To say that Cyprian laid undue stress on outward institutions and forms, is at bottom simply to call in question the soundness of his whole theory of religion, which was at the same time, as we have seen, the universal theory of the early church—the same too that the church of all ages has professed to accept, in the repetition of the creed. Let this theory be supposed wrong—let the mystery of the Spirit, as a power working in the church under such real supernatural form, (*foolishness* to the natural mind always of course [I Cor 1:20–27]) fall to the ground, or, which is the same thing, resolve itself into the spiritualism of Quakers, Baptists or Deists, and then it will be easy enough certainly to make out here a most serious defect in the constitution of our martyr's piety. The only difficulty will be to see, how he could have had any true and genuine piety at all. But on the other hand, simply reverse the supposition just made.

Instead of taking it for granted that no supernatural grace belonged to the outward church, through the real presence of the Holy Ghost in its organization, imagine hypothetically the precise opposite of this—that the Holy Ghost namely *was* present and active in the church as a mystery for faith, and that what Cyprian believed here was objectively real and true; and who cannot see, that the whole force of the objection now under consideration is at once overthrown. *That* is all that is wanted, to set a religion of sacraments and priestly forms in perfect harmony with the demands of inward piety. Who will pretend, that such a mode of being in the Spirit—if only the mystery itself be no fiction or dream, and faith be brought to yield itself heartily to its power—is not after all something quite as evangelical and spiritual, if we look at it properly, as the highest flights of devotion under any altogether inward and exclusively subjective form? We may, if we choose, question the reality of this objective grace, the presence of any such actual shekinah[73] in the outward Christian temple. But we are bound at least to allow to Cyprian and his age, the benefit of the imagination. We must judge the early church from the standpoint of its own faith, and not from a position which assumes that this faith was a lie. We must be willing to plant ourselves, for this purpose, on the premises of the ancient creed, taken in its proper original sense. In no other form, can our judgment possibly be entitled to the least respect. Either these premises were true, or they were false. Admit them to have been true, and you can have no right to charge the sacramental system of the ancients with superstition, or to say that they lost sight of the Spirit, the only real source of the truly spiritual as distinguished from the merely *spiritualistic*, in magnifying and exalting ecclesiastical forms; just as little as you may impute superstition or formality to Moses for acknowledging reverentially the presence of God in the burning bush, instead of turning away from it to converse with Him only in his own spirit. Will it be said then that the premises of the creed are false? Very well. That is at all events clear and fair. Then the charge in question has indeed full force. The sacramentalism of the ancients was in sober truth superstition, formalism, miserable mummery, the dead mechanical service of the flesh substituted for the living service of the spirit. But what then becomes of their whole Christianity? How preposterous to speak of it or think of it still, as a Divine fact, as a mystery which carried, in it really and truly the power of the world's salvation. To such issue must the whole question come at last.

We have seen already to some extent, how Cyprian's doctrine of the church gave character and form to his theological system at other points. Along with the idea of a real Divine polity, as truly present in the world as the Jewish theocracy by which it was foreshadowed, went in his mind the conception also of a ministry exercising really Divine functions, of a proper priesthood, of sacraments powerful to take away sin and forward the soul in the way of everlasting life. Baptism, confirmation, the mystical presence of the holy eucharist, the awful sacrifice of the altar, penance, including confession and absolution, the sacrament of orders, consecrations and holy rites generally,

---

73. ["God's presence in the world." Harrelson, "Shekinah," 222.]

Document 3: Cyprian: Fourth and Last Article.

derived for him their significance and force from this article of the Holy Catholic Church. Here only the Bible could have its right authority and proper use. Here only any virtue could have true Christian merit. The idea of the church determined the view taken of heresy and schism. We have seen how it carried the sense of the communion of saints beyond the grave also, leading naturally to sacrifices and prayers for the dead, and encouraging the belief that the saints in heaven make intercession for their brethren who are still in the world. The veneration for relics, which we find in the church from the earliest times, must be referred to the same general sentiment. All these conceptions belong predominantly, we may say, to one general side of the system before us. It remains now to notice briefly the same scheme of Christianity under a second general aspect, in the view it takes of what may be considered more particularly and directly the experimental practical side of the Christian salvation. This will be found to be also conditioned and determined throughout, by the realistic apprehension of the church that enters so universally into the ancient faith. All rests on the basis, and falls into the order, of the Apostles' Creed.[74]

[The Natural State of Man]

We have in the first place a corresponding view of the natural state of man since the fall. Cyprian has indeed but little to say directly of original sin and its consequences. The controversy with Pelagianism belongs to a later time. But it would be a great mistake to suppose, for this reason, that he had no apprehension or sense of the truth which this controversy afterwards brought into full view. The fact of the fall, and of the consequent moral helplessness of the race, may be said to enter as a sort of quiet substratum into his whole system of religion. This in truth is the case necessarily with any theory of Christianity, in which earnest is made with the mystery of a supernatural church, as was done always in the beginning. The Creed itself, as we all know, is silent on the subject of original sin. But is it this for reason of any uncertain sound as regards Pelagianism? By no means. Puritanism, in its modern form, may affect to find in it here a serious ellipsis, and a reason for tinkering it into new and more orthodox shape. But in the end the very silence of the old Creed on this point is of deeper and more solemn force, than any amount of strained articulation, brought out in the abstract angular style of this unchurchly school. Is it asked why? The answer is easily and immediately at hand. The fact of the fall must of necessity be interpreted always by the fact of redemption. Let this last resolve itself into an abstraction, a mere Gnostic philosophem [sic],[75] as it must always do where Christianity ceases to be churchly and sacramental, and the felt realness of the other will be lost for faith precisely to the same

---

74. [Nevin made much of the "order" (the sequence of ideas) of the Creed. See "Apostles' Creed," and "Origin and Structure," MTSS 8:71–88; 259–61.]

75. [Nevin likely means "philosopheme," defined in Webster's *American Dictionary* (1846) as "a principle of reasoning; a theorem."]

extent. In place of the fact, we shall have a notion, a philosophical myth, in the end a Calvinistic or Hegelian *necessity* simply in the constitution of our natural human life. The only effectual protection from such error, is to be found in the right apprehension of the mystery of the Holy Catholic Church; for this at once brings into view the order of grace as something really in the world, through Christ, under a form above nature—a supernatural mystery—in the bosom of which only the redemption of the race is to be reached; a fact which it is impossible to see and acknowledge heartily, without being made to see and feel at the same time the reality of the fall, as a moral and not simply physical calamity, and the terrible nature of the consequences in which the race has come to be involved by reason of it. No testimony against Pelagianism can be stronger than that of the Creed, regarded in this view. It goes full against all modern theories of the perfectibility of man, considered in the order of nature only. It lays the axe at the root of all humanitarian dreams, by proclaiming the necessity and actual presence of another higher order of life for the accomplishment of man's true destiny. To have any living sense of the mystery that is comprehended for faith in the Church, with its remission of sins, communion of saints, resurrection from the dead and life everlasting, is necessarily to be penetrated to the same extent with the feeling that the life of nature as it lies on the outside of this most real constitution of the Spirit, is absolutely under the power of sin and death; and it is not too much to say, that without such faith in the mystery of the Church, (the world in which the saints *live* on both sides of the grave, and whose powers miraculously transcend the whole reach of the natural understanding) no sense of what humanity is naturally, and apart from the range of this new creation, can ever be properly sufficient and complete. Faith in the objective realness of supernatural grace in the church, is the indispensable condition of faith in the objective realness of the fall in the sphere of nature.

Those who make the church a human corporation only, and baptism a mere sign, will be found always to wrong in some way the true significance of the state in which the world has been brought by the fall.[76]

With Cyprian, as we have had full opportunity to see, the world on the outside of the church was altogether without light and hope. The relation between the two states, the order of grace here and the order of nature there, was that of the ark in the time of Noah to the universal desolation with which it was surrounded. The same character of most intense realism extended itself in his mind, to both sides of the awfully solemn contrast. Hence came the saving force of baptism in one direction, the damning power of schism in mother. He saw in the first a real translation from the power of darkness into the kingdom of God's dear Son; in the last a no less real abandonment of this kingdom for the empire of Satan, the god of the present world, the spirit that now worketh in the children of disobedience and wrath. He took in strict sense all those passages of the New Testament, in which the world in its natural state is represented as

---

76. [Nevin earlier argued for the interconnection of a proper view of the fall and the significance of (infant) baptism in "Noel on Baptism," MTSS 6:108 and n42.]

being under the dominion of Satan, as alienated from the life of God through the ignorance that is in it by reason of sin, and as doomed to perish and pass away in its own vanity; while the true end of man's life is to be sought and found only in a higher order of existence, brought to pass for him through the resurrection of Jesus Christ from the dead, and offered to him now as a Divine word or promise, which he is required to embrace wholly by faith. The whole poverty and misery of nature, as thus opposed to grace and the hope of everlasting life in Christ, come together for Cyprian in the conception of what he calls the "seculum," the course of our general human existence as related simply to the present world. This in its best estate is altogether vanity. It is blind, dark, prone to all evil, and powerless to all good. It lies under the curse of the fall. It is a state of dismal exclusion and exile from paradise. Those who belong to it walk continually in a vain show. Their life is a false and empty dream; from which they are to wake hereafter only to shame and everlasting contempt.

[Salvation and the Church]

All salvation, in these circumstances is held to be only and wholly of God's free grace. It can be in no part the fruit of human activity or counsel, going before this grace or working aside from it in any way of separate merit and power. The Creed rests throughout on the idea, that redemption in the case of men is possible only in an order of things above nature, in the bosom of a supernatural system. The ancient theory of the church and sacraments, rightly apprehended, here again cuts up all Pelagianism by the roots. It takes in the most real sense the declaration, "That which is born of the flesh is flesh, and that which is born of the Spirit is spirit [John 3:6]." Mere nature or flesh is held to be absolutely impotent for all purposes of righteousness and life. We must be saved by grace, descending upon us from heaven under another mode of existence altogether. For this great mystery room is made only through the death and resurrection of Christ. No other foundation can be laid. He is the propitiation for our sins. He is the second Adam.[77] Through him only is it possible to have access to the Father. Cyprian is every where full and explicit in the acknowledgement of all this. He is of one mind in regard to it with St. Paul.

On the question moreover of the personal appropriation of this objective salvation, he would have been ready to answer promptly: "By grace are we saved *through faith*; and that not of yourselves; it is the gift of God [Eph 2:8]." The subjective side of this new creation, no less than the objective, was for him undoubtedly something that sprang, not from nature as such, but only from the new order of life itself which it was required to embrace. But it is hardly necessary to say, that the doctrine of justification

---

77. [Christ as the "second Adam" is central to Nevin's Christology. For examples see Nevin, *One, Holy, Catholic, and Apostolic, Tome 1*, MTSS 5:91–2; 116–19; 174–75; also *Mystical Presence*, MTSS 1:183–85. For background, see William Evans's general introduction to *The Incarnate Word*, MTSS 4:xxvii–xxviii; William Evans, *Companion*, 63–68.]

by faith, as we have it brought out by Luther at a later day, is not to be found anywhere in Cyprian's writings; for it is now generally understood and admitted, that it was unknown in this form to the ancient church universally. This does not at once show the doctrine to be at war with the ancient faith. Theology may require in a later stage of its history distinctions and determinations, which were not called for in the period going before.[78] The two conceptions of justification and sanctification, which it has been found so important to hold apart in our Protestant confessions and catechisms, flow always more or less together in the Bible; and in the thinking of the early church they come before us continually in the same concrete form. The objective side of the process is never so sundered from the actual life of the personal subject, as to be considered his property, without being at the same time a real quality of his life itself in some way. Cyprian, as we have seen, makes vast account of faith. But it is not just in the Lutheran view of this grace. Faith with him is simply the acknowledgment of the mystery of the Christian salvation as something actually present in the church, and a firm reliance on it in such view for the accomplishment of its own ends. It is the power of owning practically, as certain and true, the supernatural realities of the Gospel, the solemn assurances of God's word, which the natural mind is able at best to embrace only as unsubstantial notions. The declaration that the just shall live by faith is taken to mean in this way, that the lively apprehension of heavenly and eternal things enables the righteous man, the true follower of Christ, to overcome the world and lay hold on everlasting life. This would seem to be the same view that is taken of the subject in the eleventh chapter of the Epistle to the Hebrews; where the examples brought forward from the Old Testament go singly to show the power which this supernatural principle has in the just, to enable them to do what would be impossible to mere nature, by making sure to them, on the authority of some Divine word, things that have no certainty in any other form. Faith in this case is not the instrument simply, by which righteousness is received in a purely outward way; it is regarded rather as the very form of righteousness itself in the believer's soul; as where St. Paul says: "We walk by faith [2 Cor 5:8];" or St. John: "This is the victory that overcometh the world, even our faith [1 John 5:4]." In Cyprian's scheme of theology the efficient cause of justification is the mercy of God, the meritorious cause the righteousness of Christ, the instrumental cause the sacrament of baptism, while what has been called the formal cause is the actual appropriation of this objective grace on the part of the sinner himself.[79] The power of such appropriation is something above nature, a gift from God which goes along with the grace that is offered to it in the church; the exercise of it however is necessarily an active state of the personal subject in whom it is found, and

---

78. [Nevin is introducing the idea of development here and then demonstrating how the principle of development might work in a later period differently than it does in an earlier period.]

79. [Here Nevin adapts a broadly Aristotelian schema: "efficient cause" is simply what produces or brings about an effect and is closest to our modern notion of "cause." The "instrumental cause" is the means ("instrument") through which the effect is realized; "formal cause" is the end or goal of the process, the "form" or essence of the produced effect.]

Document 3: Cyprian: Fourth and Last Article.

must set what it appropriates in real union with his life. It makes him just, implants in him a real principle of righteousness, by the new living relation into which he is thus brought with the redemption that is found in Christ. This justice or righteousness supposes faith throughout; involves it; holds in the power of it continually as its necessary subjective form. Faith so joined with its proper object is of itself a state of justification. In such view again however, it is at once more than mere faith. It includes also charity or love, by which it becomes at the same time the germ of sanctification, the principle of all good works.

In this way we may easily comprehend how Cyprian comes, in the full spirit of the whole patristic theology, to lay so much emphasis and stress on the necessity and merit of good works. On this subject he abounds in a style of speaking, which is apt to strike modern evangelical ears as being, to say the least, very unguarded and by no means safe. His language sounds often like a downright contradiction of what many take to be the sense of St. Paul, on the doctrine of salvation by faith. It seems to make all hang rather on works; and taken in connection especially with the virtue he attributes to the sacraments, may readily enough be construed as lending countenance to a merely legal religion of the most outward and mechanical sort. No one however can enter into Cyprian's spirit, or make himself at home in his actual world of thought, without feeling that no such judgment can be relied upon as intelligent and just. Cyprian is no dealer in mere forms and dead works. If his piety seem to us of this cast, there is fair room to suspect something wrong in ourselves. We are bound at all events to believe, that we have not penetrated fully the sense of his system; and should consider it worth our serious pains, to cultivate some better acquaintance with it in its own proper form.

He himself, it is certain, never dreamed of being in the least opposition here to the doctrine of St. Paul. The idea of good works, of works acceptable to God and deserving heaven, on the part of the simply natural man, never entered into his mind. They are considered possible only in the case of one who is already made just to some extent, by being united to Christ through the glorious power of the gospel. They are the fruit of supernatural grace. They own their whole possibility and worth to the "obedience of faith,"[80] and the actual mystery of righteousness which is made to meet and fill this habit of the soul in a real way through the church. Hence they can have no place on the outside of this Divine constitution. Even martyrdom, in a state of schism, has no merit. In the church however, such works are but the necessary product of the Christian life itself. Without them, faith must be dead. If it live and act at all, it must *work by love.* It completes itself in the form of good works; which then are not another different kind of righteousness, but serve simply to bring into view the full meaning and force of the inward habit from which they spring; just as the branches of the vine bring forth fruit, in virtue of the life which unites them to the parent stock. As such

---

80. [Nevin picks up this phrase in "Christian Ministry" (1854) and later. See *One, Holy, Catholic, and Apostolic,* Tome 2, MTSS 7:52, 64, 108–9, 159.]

fruit, the real produce of the branches, detracts nothing from the proper dignity of the vine, but sets this rather in the most conspicuous light; for what would the vine be without foliage and fruit; so says our blessed Lord himself: "Herein is my Father glorified, that *ye bear much fruit*; so shall ye be my disciples [John 15:8]." And as good works are necessary in this way, so may they easily be seen to carry with them actual merit also; not of course in the way of any original or independent desert on the part of the believer; all thought of that is excluded by the relation in which they stand necessarily to the only source and fountain of all righteousness in Christ; but yet as really and truly laying a foundation for reward, through God's mercy, in the new world of grace to which they belong. They are in this view a qualification for glory and honor and immortality [Rom 2:7], and may be said to deserve accordingly the crown they are hereafter to receive [Jas 1:12].

[Charity and Works of Mercy]

Very special virtue is attributed, in particular, to the giving of alms and to works of mercy in every form. Prayer, we are told (*De Oratione Dominica*, §. 32 [–33]) in order that it may be efficacious, must not be naked and alone.

> Sterile supplications to God have no power. As every tree that bringeth not forth good fruit is hewn down and cast into the fire, so prayer without fruit can have no merit with God, being divorced from work. This Divine Scripture teaches, when it says (Tob. xii: 8): "Prayer is good with fasting and alms." For he who will render a reward in the day of judgment for works and alms, inclines now also graciously to him who joins work to prayer. Thus at last Cornelius, the Centurion, when he prayed, was found worthy to be heard. He gave much alms to the people, and prayed to God alway; and so an angel stood by him as he was praying about the ninth hour, with this testimony to his work: Cornelius, thy prayers and thine alms have come up for a memorial before God [Acts 10:2, 4]. Swiftly those prayers ascend to God, which are borne to him by the merit of our good works.[81]

The tract *De Opere et Eleemosynis*, as its title shows, is entirely devoted to this subject. We learn at once from its introduction, in what light works of mercy are regarded, and in what relation they are supposed to stand to the great interest of salvation.

"Many and great are the divine benefits," it runs,

> which the abounding kindness of God the Father and of Christ has wrought and is still working for our salvation; that the Father sent his Son to restore us and give us life, and that the Son was willing to be sent and to become the Son of Man, in order to make us the sons of God—humbled himself, that he might raise those who were before prostrate—was wounded, that he might cure our

---

81. [Cyprian, *De Oratione Dominica*, in *Tract.*, 172–73; ANF 5:456.]

Document 3: Cyprian: Fourth and Last Article.

wounds—became a servant, that he might bring liberty to those who were in bondage—endured death, that he might bestow on mortals immortality. These are manifold and great gifts of Divine mercy. But what providence is it besides this, and how great clemency, that salutary counsel has been taken prospectively for the full preservation of man when thus redeemed. For when the Lord, coming into the world, had healed those wounds which Adam carried, and cured the old poison of the serpent, he laid down the law, that he who was made whole should sin no more, lest something worse should happen to him. We were shut up and confined to close bounds by the injunction of innocence. Nor would there have been any help for the lapses of human frailty, if the Divine goodness had not again interposed, by pointing to works of justice and mercy, to open for us a way of maintaining salvation—that whatever stains should afterwards be contracted, we might wash them away *by alms*. The Holy Spirit declares in the Divine Scriptures: "By alms and faith sins are purged" (Prov. xvi: 6). Not of course those sins which were first contracted; for these are purged by the blood and sanctification of Christ. So again he says: "Water will quench a flaming fire; and alms maketh an atonement for sins" (Sir. iii: 30). Here also it is shown and proved, that as by the laver of saving water the fire of hell is quenched, so the flame of sins is set at rest by alms and good works. And whereas remission of sins is given once in baptism, continuance in such well doing afterwards as a certain semblance of baptism again procures the Divine indulgence. This our Lord also teaches in the Gospel. For when his disciples were noticed for eating without having first washed their hands, he answered and said: "Did not he that made that which is without make that which is within also? But rather give alms of such things as ye have, and behold all things are clean unto you" (Luke xi: 40, 41); showing and teaching thus, that not the hands are to be washed, but the breast, and that stains within are to be removed rather than such as are without—that he who has purged that which is within may be said to have purged also that which is without, and with the cleansing of the mind to have begun to be clean also in his outward person. And then to show how we may be pure and clean, he added that we must give alms. The Merciful One teaches and exhorts to do mercy, and because he seeks to preserve those whom he has with great price redeemed shows how such as have become polluted after the grace of baptism may again be purged and made clean.[82]

This is sufficiently plain. Baptism takes away all previous sins; but it makes no provision for sins afterwards committed. For the removal of these, mere repentance and prayer are not enough. Fasting is not enough. There must be works of charity and mercy. These, by God's gracious appointment, have a real force to do away the stains thus contracted by the soul, and to recommend it anew to the Divine favor.

---

82. [Cyprian, *De Opere et Eleemosynis*, in *Tract.*, 225–26, Nevin's emphasis; *ANF* 5:476.]

The tract then goes on to exhort those to whom it is addressed, to make free and continual use of this heavenly indulgence. Quotations and examples are brought forward largely from the Bible. One is almost surprised to find them so full and apt. The use made of the case of Tabitha, in the Acts of the Apostles, (ix: 36–42), is striking. Alms had power here, it is said, to restore even from the first death. When Peter came into the room where her corpse lay, he found himself surrounded by widows weeping and showing the coats and garments which she had made while she was yet with them, "interceding for the deceased not so much with their voices as with her own works."[83] Peter felt that what was so asked could be obtained, and that Christ who had himself been clothed in his own poor would not be wanting now to their earnest supplications.

> After he had kneeled accordingly, and as a fit advocate of widows and the poor presented to the Lord the prayers committed to his charge, turning to the body, which was now washed and laid out upon the table, he said, "Tabitha, arise in the name of Jesus Christ." Nor did he fail to bring help at once, who had said in the Gospel that whatever was asked in his name should be granted. So death is suspended, the spirit returns, and to the admiration and astonishment of all the body is restored alive once more to the light of this world. So much could the merits of mercy accomplish; of such avail were righteous works! She who had ministered to distressed widows the means of living, was found worthy to be recalled to life by the prayer of widows.[84]

So throughout the tract, the giving of alms is enforced as something actually meritorious in the sight of God, by which men have it in their power to make satisfaction for their sins, and to lay up for themselves treasures in heaven. Such is the view of Cyprian everywhere, and such would seem to have been the doctrine of the universal church in the age to which he belonged.

[Martyrdom as a Good Work]

Another exemplification of the same general way of thinking is presented to us, in the vast amount which was made of confession and martyrdom. How far this went, we have had ample opportunity to see already. Martyrdom is regarded as a sort of sacrament. The baptism by water has its full parallel here, and in some respects more than this, in the baptism by blood. The second baptism in such form excels the first. "It is more ample in grace," according to Cyprian,

> more sublime in power, more costly in honor; a baptism, with which angels baptize; a baptism, in which God and his Christ exult; a baptism, after which there is no more sin; a baptism, which consummates the growth of our faith; a

---

83. [Cyprian, *De Opere et Eleemosynis*, in *Tract.*, 228; ANF 5:477.]
84. [Cyprian, *De Opere et Eleemosynis*, in *Tract.*, 228–29; ANF 5:477. See Acts 9:36–43.]

Document 3: Cyprian: Fourth and Last Article.

baptism, which as we leave the world unites us at once with God. In the baptism of water we obtain remission of sins; in the baptism of blood, the crown of virtue. It is a thing to be embraced, and desired, and sought with outmost importunate prayers, that we who are the servants of God may be also his friends *(De Exh. Martyrii*, 4).[85]

It is emphatically a good work, the sublimest act of faith, the most intense concentration of the whole meaning and power of the Christian life; and in the same proportion it carries in it the real merit of this life, power to please God, power to atone for sin, and a title to everlasting glory and renown in the world to come. For this way of looking at the subject, there was supposed to be full justification in those frequent passages of the Bible, in which the trials and sufferings of the pious for righteousness' sake are represented as being sure of a corresponding reward hereafter; such as "*Precious* in the sight of the Lord is the death of his saints."—"They that sow in tears shall reap in joy."—"Blessed are they which are persecuted for righteousness' sake; for theirs is the kingdom of heaven."—"Blessed are ye when men shall hate you, &c. Rejoice ye in that day, and leap for joy; for, behold, your reward is great in heaven."—"Whosoever will lose his life for my sake, the same shall save it."—"There is no man that hath left house, or parents, or brethren or wife, or children, for the kingdom of God's sake, who shall not receive manifold more in this present time, and in the world to come life everlasting."—"If we suffer, we shall also reign with him."[86] These, and many other texts besides of like strain, were taken, by the simplicity of the ancient church, in the most literal and strict sense. They were felt to mean precisely what they seem to say; and in view of them, there seemed to be no extravagance, in glorifying as was done on all sides the merit of confession, or in making it an object of ambition even, to win the laurels of martyrdom, and to wear its everlasting crown. To a generation, whose highest ideal of the perfection of man is a vision of rail-roads, electric telegraphs, natural science, material prosperity, and self-governing democracy, all this may appear sufficiently fanatical and not exactly according to evangelical rule. But the church in the beginning, it is hardly necessary to say, was no such generation. It had faith. Its ideal was in the world of things not seen and eternal.

[Virginity]

Another special and extraordinary form of merit was found in the state of virginity. In the third book of his *Testimonia*, Cyprian devotes a special head (c. 32) to this subject, made up altogether of such Scriptural passages as appear to him in point for establishing its claims. They are taken partly from the Old Testament, and partly from the New: Gen. iii: 16.—Math. xix: 11, 12.—Luke xx: 34–38.—I Cor. vii: 1–7, 32–34.— Ex.

---

85. [Cyprian, *De Exhortatione Martyrii*, in *Tract.*, 191; *ANF* 5:497.]

86. [In order, the scriptures quoted here are: Ps 166:15; Ps 126:5; Matt 5:10; Luke 6:22, 23; Luke 9:24; Luke 18:29–30; 2 Tim 2:13.]

xix: 15—I Sam. xxi: 5.—Rev. xiv: 4. It is not to be questioned but that these passages, rightly considered, are of real force in favor of the principle which is here involved. They go to show, in harmony with the natural religious sense of the whole world, that virginity and continence are not a matter of indifference in the service of God, but form in certain circumstances a special qualification or meetness for coming before him in an acceptable manner. Such was the view universally of the early church, back it would seem to the very time of the Apostles. Hence the great importance attached from the beginning to the celibacy of the clergy. Hence the account made of widows and virgins, devoted to God and consecrated to the service of the church. They form a standing class in the Christian congregation, as well known as any order of the clergy. Cyprian refers to them often, and speaks of their state always in terms of the highest respect. We have one tract from him, *De Habitu Virginum*, occupied wholly with this subject; which while it brings into view some faults and disorders belonging to the system as it then prevailed in Carthage, and aims severely at their correction, may be said notwithstanding to overflow with veneration throughout for the institute itself, as one that was felt to be of special ornament and worth for the Church.

The tract opens with a representation of the necessity of Christian discipline in general, for the purposes of salvation. All depends on knowing and firmly following the heavenly rules and precepts of the Gospel. Grace sets us free from our previous sins in baptism, makes us whole, and then says: "Sin no more, lest a worse thing come upon thee [John 5:14]." The command of innocence follows the gift of soundness, ("*dat innocentiae legem postquam contulit sanitatem*"); salutary discipline must complete what by Divine privilege is thus happily commenced and made possible.[87] So in the case of every age and state. But here he has to do with a state that is special, and as such bound to a special rule of sanctification.

> Our discourse is now to virgins, who in proportion as they stand higher in glory are also an object of greater concern. They are the flower of the ecclesiastical stock, the beauty and ornament of spiritual grace, a joyous progeny, a work of praise and honor whole and incorrupt, the image of God reflecting the sanctity of our Lord, the more illustrious portion of Christ's flock. Through these is made to rejoice, and in these largely flourishes, the glorious fecundity of the church as a mother; and the more the number of virgins is made to abound, so much the more does the joy of the mother increase. To these we now speak, these we exhort, with affection rather than authority; not as claiming, in our extreme littleness and insignificance, (of which we are fully conscious) any right of censure, but because the more concern quickens caution, the greater is our apprehension of the assaults of the Devil.[88]

---

87. [Cyprian, *De Habitu Virginum*, 104; *ANF* 5:430.]
88. [Cyprian, *De Habitu Virginum*, 105; *ANF* 5:431.]

Document 3: Cyprian: Fourth and Last Article.

And so the tract then goes on to enforce, on the part of those to whom it is addressed, a whole and entire consecration to Christ, outwardly as well as inwardly, in the spirit of their special vocation and engagement, that such high distinction in the church might not fail finally of its proper heavenly reward. Virgins must look upon themselves as more than others dead to the present world. They were to consider themselves married to the Lord. In their case especially all ornaments, all attention to dress, all vain company, were to be considered wholly out of place. They must not put themselves in any way of temptation; they are bound to avoid even the appearance of evil. Were any of them possessed of wealth? This could be no reason for laying it out in mere worldly show. Let it be devoted to charitable uses. Let it be put out to interest with God. Let it go to feed Christ in the persons of the poor. Those who had renounced the world, and embraced a state so high above it, should walk and live accordingly. The way to heaven is narrow and hard in any case; but the way of virginity, like that of martyrdom, as it looks towards a higher reward than that which awaits the common Christian life, lies also through greater difficulties and calls for greater diligence and care. Those who aspire to its celestial crown, cannot go too far in divorcing themselves from every worldly interest and expectation, and may well count every sacrifice cheap that serves in any way to help them forward in so noble a pursuit. There are different degrees of honor in heaven,[89] for different degrees of merit; as the seed which is sown in good ground is said to bring forth fruit, some an hundred-fold, some sixty-fold, some thirty-fold [Mark 4:20]. The first hundred-fold reward belongs to the martyrs. The second sixty-fold measure is reserved for virgins. Let them not shrink, with such prospect, from any self-denial requited by their state. Let them remain steadily true to their vows.

In the world to come, we are told, the children of the resurrection neither marry nor are given in marriage, but are equal to the angels [Luke 20:35–36]. "What others are to become thus hereafter," the address continues,

> ye have begun to be already. Ye possess the glory of the resurrection even now in this world; ye pass through the world without the world's contamination; by persevering in charity and virginity ye are equal to the angels of God. Only let the virginity remain complete and inviolate, and hold on steadily as it has bravely begun, seeking not outward ornaments of jewelry and apparel, but only those of the spirit. Let it regard God and heaven, and not bring down the eyes which have been raised on high to the desires of the flesh or world, nor fix them on things of the earth.[90]

The command to increase and multiply, it is said in conclusion, had regard to the wants of the world when it was yet void of population; it was for the use and service of nature. After it now comes, for such as can bear it, the rule of celibacy, in the service

---

89. [Perhaps implied in Matt 25:14–30; Luke 19:12–27; 1 Cor 3:12–15.]
90. [Cyprian, *De Habitu Virginum*, in *Tract.*, 115–16; *ANF* 5:436.]

of the world of grace. Not as a command however; but as a counsel only, submitted to free will and choice. Heaven is made up of many mansions; among which a superior place is reserved for such as accept this higher law. All who come to the laver of baptism are there purged from their old pollution by a new birth; but this bears a character of special sanctity in those, who break in full with the desires of nature and the flesh. They bear emphatically, even here in the body, the image of the heavenly Adam. Such is the high merit of virginity, when found true to the terms of its own institution.

> Let this be your affectionate industry and care, O excellent virgins, who set apart to God and to Christ are already gone before, in better and chief part, to the Lord to whom ye are consecrated. Let those advanced in years exercise authority over the younger; let the younger encourage their associates. Rouse one another with mutual exhortations, provoke one another by virtuous competition to glory. Hold out bravely, go forward with spirit, reach happily the end. Only see that ye then bear us in mind, when virginity shall have begun in you to wear its crown.[91]

Here we have very clearly the Catholic conception of *evangelical counsels*, as they are called, offering to such as have power to embrace them a higher form of righteousness than that which is necessary for all men as the condition simply of their salvation; and along with this, as a matter of course the conception also of a more than usual merit in the case of such eminent saints, as well as of a title to a larger measure of heavenly glory than is to be expected by others. In this way the door is thrown open at once for the whole ascetic system which fills so much space, and plays so important a part, in the theology and religious life of the ancient church.

It is the fashion with many in modern times, to dispose of all this side of Early Christianity in a very easy and summary way. They set it down at once for a wholesale corruption, brought into the church from the heathen world. The Oriental Philosophy abounded in ascetic maxims and practices. Gnosticism made a vast parade of similar delusions and dreams. Christianity resisted these errors; prevailed over them in fact in their foreign form; and then, strangely enough, made room for the vanquished foe in her own bosom. We have had occasion before to notice, how far this monstrous theory is carried by Isaac Taylor.[92] The old ascetic system of the church he finds to be a wretched compound simply of Buddhism and Brahminism[93] throughout, borrowed immediately from the conquered Gnostic sects. This is outrageously gross; and it is not easy to see certainly how it can be set in harmony with any sort of real faith whatever in the divine origin and true historical continuance of Christianity, as a revelation starting from Christ, and upheld by his Spirit. It represents however, as we all know, a

---

91. [Cyprian, *De Habitu Virginum*, in *Tract.*, 116–17; ANF 5:436.]

92. [Quoted at length above, in "Early Christianity: Third Article."]

93. [That is, Hinduism, specifically in its classical expression of rituals of the priests (*Brahmins*), the philosophy of the *Upanishads*, and meditative techniques.]

widely extended theological school, both in the Episcopal body and on the outside of it, which at times affects to glory notwithstanding, (precious inconsistency and contradiction!) in the purity and strength of the Primitive Church, as a legacy of praise which it fancies itself entitled in some kind of way to consider peculiarly its own. Neander of course is far more careful and just. And yet he too falls to some extent into the same view. The relation of Christianity to the world, he tells us, is a twofold one, it must first oppose its previous life as ruled by the principle of sin, and then take possession of it positively by filling the forms of nature with its own higher power. The negative side of this process, coming before the other in the beginning, had a tendency naturally to become extreme; and the false asceticism of the Pagan and Gnostic worlds falling in at the same time with this posture of things, forced its way gradually into the mind of the church, and made the error complete (K. G. 2nd ed. I. p. 473–478.).[94]

This is the exact counterpart of the supposed corruption of early Christianity, on another side, by the Jewish element. There the church having in the first place surmounted Judaism, is represented as afterwards allowing it to come to a resurrection again in her own bosom, and here the very same process is regarded as having place in the case of Paganism. In both cases, the conclusion is reached by adopting in the first place a hypothesis concerning the true nature of Christianity, which requires the facts exhibited in its actual history to be accounted for in this way. Give up the hypothesis, and the solution of itself at once falls to the ground. The great question is always, whether the hypothesis is to be regarded as true or false.

So far as the principle of the ascetic system is concerned, it would carry us quite too far to pretend to go into its examination here. We can only say, that the general spirit of the New Testament, in our opinion, together with the universal voice of natural religion in all ages of the world, and the religious instinct as it is felt by every unsophisticated mind, is full against the general position of Neander; and that the form in which the subject is placed by Isaac Taylor, and the school he represents, is nothing short of a low theory of naturalism, that will be found to be radically at war in the end with the universal conception of religion in any truly supernatural form.

[Conclusion: Implications for the "Historical Development" of Christianity]

We are now done with Cyprian and his theology. Our object has been to describe simply, rather than to explain or defend. We have wished however to make the picture properly coherent with itself, and to set one part of it in right relation always to another. So much was due, in a case of this sort, to simple historical verity. If the representation may have proved offensive to some, we are sorry for it; but we are not able to see well how it could be helped. What is the ground of dissatisfaction? That

---

94. [Neander, *Allgemeine Geschichte*, 473–78; *General History*, 1:275–78.]

the subject should have been brought into inquiry or review at all? Or, that it should not have been *forced* to present itself in quite another light? Are we to be silent where history is concerned, or must we bend it into a false and deceitful shape, to escape the glare of unpleasant truth—and this too to please those, who are forever wearying our ears with the stalest cant about intelligence, knowledge, free inquiry, coming to the light, and other such common places, and yet can bear no truth or fact, no inquiry or discussion whatever, that goes to disturb and unsettle in the least the profound sense they have of their own infallibility? Cyprian's system of religion, which was at the same time that of his age, we have found to be mainly Catholic, and not Protestant. All is conditioned by the old Catholic theory of the Church; all flows, from first to last, in the channel of the ancient Creed. The whole is in such view in perfect harmony with itself. There is nothing broken or fragmentary in the scheme; and no unprejudiced mind can fail to see, that it is in all material points, in its fundamental principles and leading elements, the same system that is presented to us in the Nicene period, and that is brought out still more fully afterwards in the Catholicism of the middle ages. It is not the Protestantism of the sixteenth century, and much less the Puritanism of the nineteenth. This then is the same result precisely that was reached in our articles on Early Christianity; only we have it here under a somewhat different view. The result may not be agreeable or pleasant. But what of that? The only question is, whether it is true. If it be so, we are bound to take it as it is, and to make of it afterwards what we can. Why should we not be willing to know the truth? Have we any interest in ignoring it, in shutting our eyes to it, in obstinately embracing instead of it a shadow or a lie. No sophistry can ever make early Christianity to be the same thing with Protestantism. Episcopalianism here too, with all its pretension and self-conceit, has just as little real historical bottom to stand upon as the cause of the Reformation under a different form. No part of the interest can ever be successfully vindicated, as being a repristination simply of what Christianity was in the beginning; and it is only a waste of strength, and a betrayal indeed of the whole cause, to pretend to make good its assumptions and claims in any such violently false way. Sooner or later history must revenge itself for the wrong it is thus made to bear. Any true defence of Protestantism, as all the waking part of the world is coming to see more and more, must be conducted in altogether different style. The fact now stated must be admitted, and boldly looked in the face. Early Christianity was in its constitutional elements, not Protestantism, but Catholicism. Then there are but two general ways of vindicating the Reformation.[95] We must either make all previous Christianity, back to the time of the Apostles, a Satanic apostasy and delusion, and say that the Church took a new start in the sixteenth century, as original as that of the day of Pentecost, and a good

---

95. [The reader should compare this schema for "vindicating the Reformation" with those given in Nevin, "The Anglican Crisis," MTSS 11:303–4 and above at the end of "Early Christianity," 160–61. The most thorough critical comparison of the schemata is Black, "A 'Vast Practical Embarrassment,'" 264–78; see also Payne, "Schaff and Nevin," 178, 181–82; Layman, "Revelation in the Praxis," 128–29.]

Document 3: Cyprian: Fourth and Last Article.

deal more safe and sure; which is to give up historical Christianity altogether, and so if we understand it the whole conception also of a supernatural holy and apostolic church. Or else we must resort to the theory of historical development, by which the Catholic form of the church, shall be regarded as the natural and legitimate course of its history onward to the time of the Reformation, and the state of things since be taken as a more advanced stage of that same previous life, struggling forward to a still higher and far more glorious consummation in time to come. To reject both of these solutions, and to quarrel only with the facts that imperiously require either one or the other as the only escape from the argument in favor of the Church of Rome, may well be pronounced *obscurantism* of the first order.

We of course reject in full the unhistorical theory; and one object we have had in view always, has been to expose its most insane and most perfectly untenable character. It is at last but a decent name for infidelity. Religion built on any such foundation as this, rests only on the sand or wind. We are shut up then of course, so far as we have any faith in Protestantism, to the theory of historical development, as the only possible way of setting it in living union with the Divine fact of early Christianity. But this theory may be carried out in various ways, as we have shown on a former occasion. The methods of Newman, Rothe, Schaff, Thiersch, are not just the same. Neander too has in some respects his own scheme. The whole later German theology, in its better form, moves in the bosom of this theory, is constructed upon it, or at least takes it for granted, though often in a vague and indefinite way. If it be asked now, what precise construction *we* propose to apply to the subject, we have only to say that we have none to offer whatever. That has been no part of our plan. If we even had a theory in our thoughts that might be perfectly satisfactory to our own mind, we would not choose to bring it forward in the present connection; lest it might seem that the subject was identified in some way, with any such scheme of explanation.[96] What we have wished, is to present the subject in its own separate and naked form, not entangled with any theory; that it may speak for itself; that it may provoke thought; that it may lead to some earnest and honest contemplation of the truth for its own sake. The importance

---

96. The "Obscurantism," with which we have to deal in this whole case, is ever ready to lay hold of the vague charge of *theory* and *speculation*, for the purpose of setting aside the force of facts, which it has no power to answer and no will to admit. It would fain have it that all turns here on some philosophical hobby of *historical development*, in the interest of which facts are forced to do service in a strained and violent way. We have however no such hobby to offer or defend. For development as such, in any shape, we care not a fig. We would prefer greatly indeed to have the riddle of church history satisfactorily solved, without recourse to any such help. Our trouble is altogether with *facts*. The theorization is all on the other side. All starts in a particular theory of Christianity, to which both the Bible and Church History are there required to bend throughout. Then follows a scheme of exegesis violent enough. Then again a method or plan of history, the most unnatural that can well be conceived, and as purely ideal as any construction of Hegel or Strauss. And this is to avoid speculation and "philosophy falsely so called!" [1 Tim 6:20, replacing "science" with "philosophy."] [The full import of what Nevin is saying here is a matter of controversy. Some recent scholarship claims that here Nevin begins a move away from *historical development* as a solution to the "church question." See the latter part of the volume's general introduction.]

of the subject, the nature of the facts in question, is not changed by any theory that may be brought forward for their right adjustment with the cause of Protestantism. This or that solution may be found unsatisfactory; but still the facts remain just what they were before. There they are, challenging our most solemn regard; and it is much if we can only be brought to see that they *are* there, and to look them steadily in the face. We have had no theory to assert or uphold. We offer no speculation. Our concern has been simply to give a true picture of facts. The difficulty of the whole subject is of course clearly before our mind. We feel it deeply, and not without anxiety and alarm. But we are not bound to solve it, and have no more interest in doing so than others. We have not made the difficulty in any way. We are not responsible for it, and we have no mind or care at present to charge ourselves with the burden of its explanation. There it stands before the whole world. It is of age too, we may say, full formed and full grown; let it speak then for itself.

J. W. N.

Epilogue: Nevin's "Dizziness" and His Relationship to Philip Schaff

David W. Layman, General Editor

"Rev. Mr. Stern says that for five years after his resignation from the theological seminary, Dr. Nevin lingered on the borders of Rome. Some polemist on the other side in the later liturgical controversy calls this period Dr. Nevin's 'five years of dizziness'."[1]

In his general introduction, Michael Stell has capably led us through the emergence and changes of "historical development" in Nevin's work, beginning with his earliest writings. He presents alternative readings to previous interpretations, including those of the general editor (David Layman). In this, he examines texts which have previously been uninterpreted, provides valuable correctives and advances the scholarly discussion. "Early Christianity" and "Cyprian" display Nevin's wrestling with the implications of this theory, and his efforts to make sense of the nature and significance of the church—what he and Schaff called "the church question"[2]—in light of the historical data. The conclusion of "Cyprian" gives us results which are ambiguous at best. Some might judge Nevin's investigations of the church fathers as an outright failure. If that is what it is, the evidence of this failure is manifested in the period of Nevin's life that Mercersburg historiography has come to call his "dizziness." Nichols used the word in the title of chapter 8 of his classic study *Romanticism in American Theology*, and thus gave it a solidity and significance it might not otherwise have had.[3] Past examinations of this episode simply took the phrase for granted rather than critically analyze its origins. It began with an anonymous critic and was promulgated by a hostile historian, James I. Good, who wrote the *History of the Reformed Church*

---

1. Good, *History*, 312.
2. See DeBie, *John Williamson Nevin*, 146–52.
3. 192–217.

in the U. S. in the Nineteenth Century from the perspective of the "Old Reformed or low-church ... party" of the German Reformed Church.[4]

"Dizziness"

The term "dizziness" had a history in the church's understanding of Nevin. On September 17, 1851, the *Weekly Messenger* of the German Reformed Church editorialized: Nevin's articles "have been rising in regular gradation high and still higher until our head is dizzy. We are at a dead halt.'"[5] Nevin had just started "Early Christianity" (September 1851). The inflection point seems to have been "The Anglican Crisis," Nevin's evaluation of the English secular authorities' attempt to regulate Anglican doctrine and practice. We know that after Nevin's death, Schaff thought that Mercersburg Theology "took a wrong & reactionary turn with Nevin's Anglican Crisis & articles on Cyprian, etc."[6] In "Anglican Crisis," Nevin criticized Protestants for defending secular control of the church (even while claiming to be defenders of religious freedom),[7] and described English Catholicism as being truer to the nature of the church. The church is a supernatural reality, with its power expressed in its sacramental life, and Nevin was convinced that Protestantism in its current state, in part or in whole, was not capable of bearing that reality. Nevin knew some readers would conclude that the only consistent response was conversion to Roman Catholicism. He countered with three additional options: evangelical sectarianism, a new divinely-authorized movement, or historical development.[8]

After that dialectical exercise in July 1851, the first essay of "Early Christianity" came along in September. Like many of Nevin's writings, this was instigated by his reading. Here the stimulus was two Protestant travel diaries in Catholic Europe. Nevin's excerpts from these travelogues make up approximately one-third of the first essay. As summarized in the editorial introduction to "Early Christianity" in this volume, one of the travelers, Daniel Wilson, was especially impressed by the piety of Charles Borromeo, sixteenth century Archbishop of Milan. He wistfully imagined that under the right circumstances he might have become the Luther of Italy. Nevin

---

4. Good, *History*, v. Good's interpretations of Nevin's development within the German Reformed Church have considerable value and insight, even if they were selective and biased. He liked Frederick Rauch (see 105)—the German university graduate who preceded Nevin at Mercersburg—and tried to separate Rauch's theology from the later emergence of "Mercersburg Theology" (106–7). But he ignored that it would have been very difficult for Nevin to move in a Hegelian direction without Rauch's preexisting influence at Mercersburg. He correctly interpreted Schaff as having brought about crucial changes in Nevin's thought (107–17), even if some of his details are debatable.

5 Quoted in Good, *History*, 278.

6. See full quotation of this letter below.

7. See the exposition in Layman, general introduction to *Born of Water*, MTSS 6:25.

8. Nevin, "Anglican Crisis," MTSS 11:303–6. See editorial introduction to "Early Christianity," above; Payne, "Schaff and Nevin," 178; Black, "A 'Vast Practical Embarrassment," 264–74.

made short work of Wilson's effort to separate Borromeo and other devout medieval and patristic leaders from their Catholic religious "system." They were not simply proto-Protestants, regrettably contaminated by a popular piety that had emerged in the millennium before the Reformation. Their devout commitment to Christian faith and practice was self-evident to any honest person.

In summary, first Nevin had attacked Protestant hypocrisy on the relation of church and state. Next, he had pointed out the contemporary weaknesses in Protestant ecclesiology. Then he showed Protestants had to recognize a real, positive Christian life active in the Roman Catholic Church. "Repristination" could not explain this similarity. The spiritual vitality of Roman Catholicism was precisely in the period Protestants would excise from the "true" church. This argument provides the "regular gradation" "rising higher and higher" that left the editor of the *Weekly Messenger* "dizzy." However, to project this dizziness on Nevin himself is more than the evidence at this moment in his life and work supports.

"Five Years"

The *terminus a quo*[9] for the ostensible five-year period was Nevin's resignation from the theological seminary at Mercersburg. The time-line that can be extracted from Nichols is as follows: overwhelmed by his work,[10] Nevin sent a letter to the seminary board "at the end of summer term of 1850, declaring his intention to cease instruction in theology at the end of the next term." "Next term" appears to have meant what we would call an academic year, since "in the spring of 1851, Nevin not only discontinued theological instruction . . . but also submitted his resignation outright."[11] The church did not act on the resignation until October, 1851.[12] The synod requested he withdraw the resignation, but if he would not do that, kept the chair open in the hope that Nevin could return. "Nevin was deeply moved by this demonstration," but apparently declined, since Schaff was the "sole member of the Mercersburg faculty in 1851–52."[13] So the *terminus a quo* appears to have been the *spring of 1851*.[14] The issue here was lack of adequate support for the seminary by the church, exacerbated by a chronic illness that Nevin had suffered from for most of his life.[15]

9. "Earliest limiting point," or beginning point.

10. E.g., Nevin was teaching algebra because the mathematics teacher had himself resigned in frustration.

11. Nichols, *Romanticism*, 194.

12. Nichols, *Romanticism*, 207.

13. Nichols, *Romanticism*, 207, 209.

14. This is separate from his resignation from Marshall College, which is dated at the beginning of 1853 (Appel, *Life*, 443).

15. Nevin complained of "dyspepsia," a chronic disease of the digestive tract. The probable nature of this illness is explained in detail in DeBie, *John Williamson Nevin*, 39. See also Hart, *John Williamson Nevin*, 45–47, 171–73.

What might have been the *terminus ad quem*[16] of the "dizziness?" "Five years" takes us into the liturgical controversy in the German Reformed Church. An effort at liturgical reform began in earnest in 1852. Nevin at first wanted to beg off, because he was convinced the church was not yet ready to make the sort of liturgy that was "theoretically correct." His long sabbatical had its desired effect: *by 1857 Nevin was showing renewed enthusiasm* for the work of the liturgical committee.[17] 1851 to 1856 gives us the five-year interval asserted by Nevin's critics.

"The Borders of Rome"

The above timeline shows that Nevin's resignation from the seminary was dictated by "burn-out" and chronic illness. The later attraction to Catholicism can be more specifically dated to mid-1852. "The Anglican Crisis" left him (and his readers) looking for some solution in Schaff's theory of "historical development." He picked up this possibility in the essays in this volume. "Early Christianity" (completed January 1852) provided the solution in *some* theory of historical development.[18] Then he began "Cyprian" in May 1852. In June of that year he admitted to James Alphonsus McMaster that "my sympathies have grown to be very strong towards Catholicism.... I would consider it now a great privilege, only to be *made inwardly sure* in any way that the Roman Catholic church is really what she claims to be."[19] In August, he told Orestes Brownson that although the first essay attempted to be "merely historical" (a claim he would make again and again), the second essay would show that "Cyprianic doctrine . . . goes back to the time of the Apostolic Fathers and underlies the whole structure of the Creed."[20] *The first sign of* theological *uncertainty was the summer of 1852.*[21] However, he was not ready to convert. The problem with making a "positive conversion to Catholicism" was that he would have to "set aside" a "whole habit of thought"; his objections were not found in "any distinct issue with Catholicism," but in the "inability to bring the question to any such issue."[22]

"Cyprian" was completed in November 1852. *At least three months later*—February 1853—Nevin had not moved off of this theological equipoise. Again, he wrote to McMaster. (The following quote stitches together excerpts from two secondary sources.)

---

16. "A final limiting point," or ending point.

17. Maxwell, *Worship and Reformed Theology*, 68, 71, 140–1, esp. 142–43 for the 1857 date. DeBie gives a history of the controversy in *John Williamson Nevin*, 292–312.

18. See above, 159–61, 164.

19. Quoted in Nichols, *Romanticism*, 211, emphasis original.

20. Quoted in Nichols, *Romanticism*, 212.

21. William Evans widens the window from 1851 to 1854 (*Companion*, 111).

22. Quoted in Nichols, *Romanticism*, 213. See longer quote there.

EPILOGUE: NEVIN'S "DIZZINESS" AND HIS RELATIONSHIP TO PHILIP SCHAFF

> I see well the necessity of something far beyond mere logic or natural evidence, to bring [?] the mind to a clear apprehension of the true mystery of the Christian Church, and a full and firm acquiescence in it for the purposes of salvation. Meditation [?] and prayer, rather than any dialectic process, must bring to a solution at last the great problem with which I feel myself confronted here now every day, and I may almost say every waking hour. The most powerful impressions of truth are those which come from flashes, sent out as it were from the invisible orb of the whole idea, rather than from this or that particular reflection or argument presented to the understanding in detail. Hence also the difficulties I feel are of a kind of [deletion?] which it is not easy to place in any well defined and fairly tangible shape. Controversy and debate in any ordinary form, have come to be for me in this way of very little interest or force.[23] I see so much of wholesale error and confusion in the world, that I never felt less disposition to be confidently dogmatic in any position that is not upheld by tradition in some form; and when it comes this, I find it more and more difficult, I confess, to make account of any opinion of judgment in such view, that ventures to place itself in contradiction to the authority of the Catholic Church.[24]

Protestantism or Catholicism? The question would not answered by logical debate but by an intuitive apprehension of the nature of "the whole." But both in this letter and one written a month prior (presumably to Marshall College trustee William Heyser), Nevin was clear that he was not ready to convert.

> My own daily prayer is, that God may enable me to *know* & to *obey* the truth, cost what it may. What are all time [?] interests in comparison with Eternal Life? Should it be made plain to me at any time here-after, that the Catholic Church is true mystery of godliness as it was in the beginning—however much [?] misunderstood [?] by the reigning spirit of the world—I trust that I shall have power through grace to stoop so far as may be required to enter into its bosom. For any such step however *I am not yet prepared, with all my strong Catholic sympathies or tendencies.*[25]

---

23. Nevin to J. A[lphonsus] McMasters, 26 February 1853, microfilm in the Lancastriana Collection, Lancaster Theological Seminary Library; original in the Brownson Archives, Notre Dame University Library; quoted in Layman, "Revelation in the Praxis," 124.

24. Brownson Archives, Notre Dame University, quoted in Nichols, *Romanticism*, 215.

25. J. W. Nevin letter dated 13 January 1853, in the William Heyser Diary, 1852–53, in the Lancastriana Collection, Lancaster Theological Seminary Library, emphasis added. Nichols, *Romanticism*, said this material is in "typescript" (215n42); however, at the time this writer consulted it, it was only available in its original hand script. Also contrary to the implication of that note, the letter was not itself bound in the diary, but had simply been placed within the bound volume. The quotation and commentary in this note are taken from Layman, "Revelation in the Praxis," 124–25 and n92.

Explaining the Data

Nevin's *theological* "dizziness" lasted approximately two years.[26] It began in the early summer of 1852, as he began to realize where his studies on Cyprian would be taking him. He held his dialectical balance throughout his composition of the essays. Doubtless after their completion, Nevin took a deep breath, so to speak, and perhaps even experienced a "nervous breakdown."[27] However, the seeming theological attraction of Rome did not break his resolve to be who he was until given good reasons to be otherwise.[28] He was balancing two mental extremes: the arsenal of objections to Roman Catholic culture and theology he had accumulated over the previous two years, *against* his disgust at "ultra-Protestant" anti-Romanism.[29] This balance was maintained until sometime in 1854. In November, he delivered the installation sermon for Dr. Bernard Wolff, who was replacing Nevin at the Mercersburg Seminary. Modern scholarship reads this as a sign that Nevin had decided to remain in the German Reformed Church.[30] However, in his own writings there is evidence that he was pivoting back towards Protestantism at the *beginning* of 1854.[31] In April, Nevin defended Calvin's formulation of the presence of Christ in the Eucharist. The "real presence" was in the "transaction" and not in the "elements,"[32] and Nevin insisted that if there was an authentically Protestant doctrine of the real presence, it would be found there.[33]

---

26. This claim and what follows expands an analysis first made in Layman, "Revelation in the Praxis," 131 and repeated in Nevin et al., *Born of Water*, MTSS 6:132n11. William Evans, *Companion*, 110–20 provides an alternative analysis, and extends the episode a little longer.

27. The view of DeBie, *John Williamson Nevin*, 290 and Gerrish, *Tradition and the Modern World*, 65–66. Gerrish thought the longer episode to be "more exactly, a depressive breakdown, induced partly by sheer exhaustion" (66). He tied it (correctly in this writer's judgment) to a general pattern of Nevin's life, who had a similar episode after college (203n55).

28. The letters quoted above suggest he was awaiting a "revelation," a mystical apprehension of the "whole" truth. It never came.

29. See Hart, *John Williamson Nevin*, 156–61 for this balancing act. Payne said "Schaff thought that Nevin should be prevented from making the leap by his own perception of the weaknesses of Roman Catholicism" ("Schaff and Nevin," 187)—as indeed it would appear he was.

30. Nichols, *Romanticism*, 234; Hart, *John Williamson Nevin*, 165–68. Good, *History*, 310–11 gave a collection of anecdotal information, intended to show that Nevin *was* considering conversion. The most intriguing items related that Nevin had decided *not* to convert, including an utterance by Wolff himself. Unfortunately, these items were not well dated. Nichols reasonably assumed Wolff's comment was in connection with the installation sermon. But we don't know *when* Wolff knew Nevin had agreed to give the sermon. Appel, *Life* says nothing about this sermon or its context. The text of the sermon is Nevin, "The Christian Ministry," MTSS 7:38–56.

31. Payne finds this in "The Dutch Crusade," published in January 1854 ("Schaff and Nevin," 187–88).

32. See Nevin, *Mystical Presence*, MTSS 1:51, 106.

33. Nevin, "Wilberforce on the Eucharist," MTSS 6:154–55; see the editorial commentary in that volume, 132–33; as well as DeBie, *John Williamson Nevin*, 290–91.

EPILOGUE: NEVIN'S "DIZZINESS" AND HIS RELATIONSHIP TO PHILIP SCHAFF

Either he had already decided to remain Protestant, or he was attempting to justify an emerging resolve to do so.[34]

If restricting the "dizziness" to two years is correct, Nevin's opponents extended the crisis at both ends by assuming that the stasis brought on by studying Cyprian was part of both his resignation from the seminary, and his reluctance to carry out the liturgical work. However, these three events in Nevin's life are chronologically distinct: lack of institutional support (1850 to spring 1851); "Cyprian" (the second half of 1852 into early 1853); and his desire not to expend energy on liturgical work for a church that was not ready for it (until mid-1856). Nevin's opponents conflated these three distinct crises.

Furthermore, based on the evidence in Good's *History*, it is probable the real dizziness was in the minds of Nevin's opponents and lay readers. This editor (Layman) is of the opinion that he kept his dialectical poise. He understood the spiritual and theological reasons to convert to Rome, but so long as he could be productive in the German Reformed Church, he saw no reason to do so. It was the difficulty of being productive in a church that did not provide sufficient resources for theological instruction that induced Nevin to step back from his role as theological teacher in the German Reformed Church.[35]

The heterogeneous character of his motivation is evident as late as March 30, 1853, in his letter declining the presidency of Franklin and Marshall College—soon after the letters quoted above, but a year before the "pivot" already observed. He explained that he had hoped that the college would have been formed earlier, in which case he would have been ready to serve "for a few years" before retiring. But the "delay" had pushed back the time for service to the time frame he had already projected for retirement.

> It would be impossible for me to throw myself into it with that sort of confidence and animation, that buoyancy of spirit and determination of zeal, which the success of the enterprise demands. Other claims and interests, partly of health, partly of taste and comfort, but most of all, I may say, in the form now of theological inquiry and religious conscience, stand powerfully in the way of my assuming responsibilities in this form, which reach with such uncertain distance into the future, and the bearing of which it is so impossible beforehand to calculate or foresee.[36]

---

34. See the interpretations in Hart, *John Williamson Nevin*, 164–68 and Black, "A 'Vast Practical Embarrassment,'" 282.

35. Nichols, *Romanticism*, 234, observed: "If this hypothesis [connecting Nevin's decision with the installation sermon] is sound, the inner crisis of Nevin's religious conscience was resolved in Carlisle at the same time Schaff returned to Mercersburg with new resources . . . and the . . . difficulties of the seminary and college were measurably overcome." Once the resources were available, the alleged dizziness quickly dissipated! Hart's interpretation implies something similar: "If the German Reformed Church could provide a [continued] platform upon which he might try to work out such an understanding of the Christian ministry [as stated in the sermon], Nevin was prepared to stay" (*John Williamson Nevin*, 167). It could and he did.

36. Quoted in Dubbs, *History*, 265–66. See quote by Nichols, *Romanticism*, 222.

Therefore, contrary to the public perception, his retirement was not a response to some sudden spiritual or theological crisis. (As the timeline described above shows, it took about sixteen months for Nevin to extricate himself from the seminary.) While "inquiry . . . and conscience" were *now* (spring 1853) a major factor, he was also motivated by "health" (his dyspepsia) and "taste and comfort." He wanted to be free to pursue his intellectual interests and be untrammeled in his spiritual journey, wherever it might lead. He doesn't seem "dizzy," but simply desirous of freedom of thought and action.

Nevin and Schaff

The 1889 Letter of Schaff

In a letter well-known to Mercersburg scholarship[37] written to Theodore Appel (Nevin's first biographer) after Nevin's death, Philip Schaff had this point of view on the course of events and Nevin's thought:

> It is a very delicate task for me to write on Dr. Nevin & my relations to Mercersburg theology. . . . We agreed in the development theory, but Dr. Nevin looked backward & became Romanizing. I look forward to new & higher developments. He was inclined to pessimism,[38] I am an optimist or at least an inveterate hoper. I believe that Christ rules supreme, & that his church is progressing, though in a zigzag line rather than in a straight course. Personally, I was always on the best of terms with Dr. Nevin; but I believe he cooled down towards me after I left for New York, or perhaps after his resignation [from the presidency of Marshall College] in 1853,[39] when I had to stem the current towards Romanism, and did it as gently & considerately as I could.
> . . . [Mercersburg Theology] really began with my "Principle of Protestantism," but took a wrong & reactionary turn with Nevin's Anglican Crisis & Articles on Cyprian, etc.[40]

There are reasons to question Schaff's criticisms.[41] At the time, Schaff seems to have agreed with Nevin's historiography.[42] Furthermore, we have the independent judgment of Emanuel Gerhart, who was criticizing Nevin in a series of letters. At the same

---

37. Payne, "Schaff and Nevin," 183–90; Graham, "Nevin and Schaff at Mercersburg," 77–80; Layman, general introduction to *Born of Water*, 24; DeBie, *John Williamson Nevin*, 313.

38. On Nevin's alleged pessimism, see the comment of DeBie, *John Williamson Nevin*, 307n74.

39. Layman favors the 1853 date as more significant, since that was when Nevin left Mercersburg and was therefore physically separated from Schaff: Layman, general introduction to *Born of Water*, 31.

40. Schaff to Theodore Appel, 13 February 1889 (Schaff Papers, Evangelical and Reformed Historical Society).

41. As do Layman, general introduction to *Born of Water*, MTSS 6:24–25; and Graham, "Nevin and Schaff at Mercersburg," 79.

42. Schaff, "German Theology and the Church Question," 140.

time, he thought that Schaff was "not far in the rear of Dr. N." Schaff *also* created "every imaginable difficulty against Protestantism" while he "magnifies all the advantages and claims of the R. Cath. Ch."[43]

Schaff's Influence on Nevin

A full discussion of the "dizziness" needs a re-analysis of the relationship of Nevin and Schaff. To whatever extent Nevin's historical studies *had* made him "dizzy," what had induced him to engage in those studies? Nichols followed Charles Hodge in suggesting that the preponderance of influence was from Nevin—16 years older—to Schaff.[44] The present writer (Layman) here proposes an alternative interpretation of the relationship. In January 1844 (the printing of the second edition of *Anxious Bench*), Nevin still shared a great deal with Princeton.[45] As shown in the general introduction to this volume, Nevin had assimilated idealism and a historical consciousness throughout the 1830s until 1844.[46] Then Schaff joined him at Mercersburg in the summer of 1844, delivered the *Principle of Protestantism*,[47] and convinced Nevin that historical change was "development, evolution, progress."[48] Judging from when they emerged in Nevin's thought, there were two other ideas that he owed to Schaff: the Reformation as organically arising out of medieval Christianity,[49] and the view that the movement of history was a manifestation of the mind of God (which probably originated with F. H. W. Schelling).[50]

---

43. Gerhart, unpublished letter to J. H. A. Bomberger, October 14, 1852 (Gerhart Papers, ERHS). At the time of the letter, Gerhart was president of a sister college, Heidelberg, in Tiffin, Ohio. In 1855 he returned east to become president of Franklin and Marshall College.

44. Nichols, *Romanticism*, 219. Layman previously gave reasons to doubt Hodge's evaluation: "Revelation in the Praxis," 132–38; see 135 on Hodge.

45. See esp. *Anxious Bench* MTSS 5:68n8: the editor of the *Weekly Messenger* appealed to Princeton in support of Nevin against the attacks of the Lutheran revivalist Benjamin Kurtz. Kurtz replied: of *course* Princeton would support Nevin, since that was where Nevin had learned his opinions about revivalism. DeBie, *John Williamson Nevin*, 206–8, explains the widening breach between Nevin and Princeton.

46. Other resources are DeBie, *John Williamson Nevin*, 93–98, 143–46; Hart, *John Williamson Nevin*, 72–77; Evans, *Companion*, 17, 20–21.

47. DeBie calls Schaff a *"wunderkind"* (*John Williamson Nevin*, 139), and describes the impact of his inaugural address, 138–140.

48. Nevin, translator's introduction to *Principle*, MTSS 3:49.

49. In "Catholic Unity," Nevin still believed that the Catholic Church was "Antichrist": MTSS 5:123. After becoming a colleague of Schaff, he transferred this title to "the sect system": editor's introduction to *Antichrist*, MTSS 5:161.

50. For the origins of Schaff's conviction, see Penzel, *German Education*, 117–18. Schaff gave a version of it in *Principle*, MTSS 3:167 and Nevin appears to have accepted it in *The Church*, MTSS 5:148. See Nevin et al., *Born of Water*, MTSS 6:23n128.

Interpreting Nevin's Disenchantment

This editor (Layman) believes that the impact of Schaff's *Principle* upon Nevin endured throughout the remainder of the 1840s, through the completion of "Cyprian." However, it seems that Nevin became increasingly uncomfortable with this formulation. William Evans interprets and extends Layman's earlier analysis: "It was one thing to affirm a dynamic view of church history (as Nevin did early on), but it was another to argue that the new stages dialectically preserve what is best about what precedes them."[51] In 1845, even before the major part of Nevin's corpus had been composed, Nevin thought the "prospect for the future [of the church] is dark and discouraging."[52] Then shortly after the aftermath of the "Cyprian" crisis, his disenchantment was expressed publicly in the baccalaureate address "Man's True Destiny." It was a passionate screed against the spiritual emptiness of the American gospel of freedom and prosperity.[53] From this point on, Nevin's assessment of America's religiosity would become increasingly negative, especially with respect to the belief that the humanity could be improved through science, technology, and social change.[54]

The above outline of Schaff's influence on Nevin suggests that *the greater part* of Nevin's intellectual framework from the middle of 1844 to 1852 or 1853 was dependent on Schaff. In Nevin's mind, important elements of the framework seem to have been intellectually compromised when it could not explain the data of "Cyprian." Something like that must be the explanation for Nevin's exasperation in the final footnote: "For [historical] development as such, in any shape, we care not a fig."[55] Furthermore, he could not easily see how American Christianity could prosper with a spirituality dominated by various forms of "rationalistic supernaturalism"[56] and humanitarianism. This analysis implies that *intellectually* it was Schaff who had the greater influence on Nevin. Schaff drew Nevin into a historical project that the latter's religious intuitions would not allow him to bring to fulfillment.[57] The project of liturgical reform

---

51. William Evans, *Companion*, 85. "Dialectically preserve" is shorthand for the Hegelian term *aufheben*: to contradict or cancel some historical reality and at the same time lift it up to a higher level.

52. Nevin to William Rollinson Whittingham, 2 August 1845, quoted in DeBie, *John Williamson Nevin*, 139.

53. Nevin, "Man's True Destiny," MTSS 11:336–44.

54. See also Payne, "Schaff and Nevin," 186.

55. See above, 313n96. In summary, there are three asseverations that support the claim that Nevin abandoned historical development: this quote; "Reply to 'An Anglican Catholic,'" 421, analyzed by Stell in the general introduction; and a second-hand quote from Orestes Brownson, restated in the final note of this epilogue.

56. The most complete comparison of several different expressions of this theological framework is found in Part 2 of Nevin, *Philosophy and the Contemporary World*, MTSS 11.

57. See the comment at Layman, general introduction to *Born of Water*, MTSS 6:33n179. Good, *History*, also said that Nevin was earlier a "speculative mystic," but later abandoned his "speculativeness and he rested in simple faith in God's Word" (599). However, he did not link this to Schaff. Black, "A 'Vast Practical Embarrassment,'" 283 gives another plausible analysis of the philosophical difference between Nevin and Schaff.

repeated this relational dynamic: initially, Schaff was more enthused about the project, but Nevin became energized as he became involved. When opposition emerged, it was Nevin who was given the task of writing a defense of the Revised Liturgy, and thus evoked the blame and antagonism for its putative theological flaws.[58] Schaff took the lead, and Nevin tried to follow; some of the consequences were negative for both Nevin and the church he loved.

Conclusion

However, Michael Stell, the editor of this volume, argues that Nevin did *not* reject "historical development." If that thesis is correct, then the narrative constructed by Layman (this general editor), and at least partially embraced by other scholars,[59] needs to be reevaluated. Stell's argument would seem to have three key elements. Firstly, when Nevin dismissed "development" as a "treacherous amphibological term" in 1874,[60] he was not repudiating "development" as such. His dialogue partner "Anglican Catholic" had criticized "development" as contrary to the nature of revelation; very well Nevin replied, let's just call it "historical movement." That still conveyed the essential point he wanted to preserve: "the life of man" necessarily "involv[es] the birth of new things continually out of the bosom of old things."[61] Furthermore (the second element), Nevin *immediately* reasserted that every Christian doctrine has had "its history, its rise, its movement, its progressive evolution."[62] Stell plausibly argues that such an expression shows that renouncing "development" was a purely rhetorical shift. In Stell's interpretation, Nevin still had the Germanic, rather than the English, understanding of historical development.[63] The third element comes from Nevin's interpretation of the "Old Catholic" movement and his lectures on the "philosophy or science of history," as preserved for us in Appel's *Life*.[64] These sources give abundant evidence that Nevin still understood history as a movement with a telos. This would appear to contradict Layman, the present editor,

---

58. Maxwell, *Worship and Reformed Theology*, 68, 71, 140–3. Schaff's attitudes are described in Good, *History*, 325–29, 339 (Schaff as "moving spirit"). This defense was Nevin, *Vindication of the Revised Liturgy*. For the antagonism it generated, see DeBie, *John Williamson Nevin*, 316–21.

59. Anticipated by DiPuccio, *Interior Sense*, 85; Layman's own argument is in the general introduction to *Born of Water*, 24, 31 and editor's introduction to Nevin, "Wilberforce on the Eucharist," MTSS 6:132; he was supported by William Evans, *Companion*, 84–85, 110–20; Evans, "Philosophical Idealism and the Reformed Theological Tradition," 411; and DeBie, *John Williamson Nevin*, 340.

60. Nevin, "Reply," 421.

61. Nevin, "Reply," 419, 421.

62. Nevin, "Reply," 422.

63. Payne, "Schaff and Nevin," 182: the English theory "posited a continuous and regular growth," while the Germanic version understood it as taking "into account opposing forces"—"in a zigzag line," as Schaff described it in his letter of 1889 (quoted above).

64. Appel, *Life*, 590–601.

that Nevin had come to think of history—as expressed by Michael Root in his foreword—as "one damned thing after another."

Whether or not the reader buys into an Hegelian dialectic, it remains the fact that historical scholarship proceeds by a process of competing narratives, contrasting emphases or foci, each of which point to core pieces of data to confirm key intuitions or insights. This process has already been evidenced in this Mercersburg Theology Study Series, where the editors have disputed with each other over the origins and timing of the ideas that gave rise to Mercersburg theology.[65] This editor (Layman) trusts that the present disagreement is a sign of the continuing vitality of Mercersburg scholarship. It is not the purpose of the series to end debate, but to spark, and support with detailed scholarship, new insights and understanding. Therefore, he declines to engage Stell's contribution with an extended critique,[66] but will permit each narrative to stand and present itself to the scholarly public.

---

65. See the debates in Nevin, *Mystical Presence*, MTSS 1:xxxiii notes 44 and 46 and Layman, general introduction to *Born of Water* MTSS 6:13n81. A recent tentative resolution of these debates is DeBie, *John Williamson Nevin*, 174–79.

66. He will confine himself to two comments: There are occasionally significant differences between Nevin's essays and his lectures. Just one dramatic example: Nevin objected to the Reformed dogma of the "threefold offices of Christ" (Nevin, "Bread of Life," MTSS 6:225 and n11). In contrast, in his theological lectures, the threefold offices organized his presentation in two different locations (Erb, *Dr. Nevin's Theology*, 123–26; 247–281; see Evans's exposition in *Companion*, 117–20). So we cannot assume *prima facie* that the philosophy of history lectures articulated a still-maintained philosophical viewpoint. After all, he was here in the role of a teacher, bringing forth a lifetime of reflection on his topic. It would have been odd to present lectures on the philosophy of history, and profess at the beginning that there *is no such* philosophy! Secondly, there is an obscure reference by Orestes Brownson. He claimed that "in a conversation" with Nevin, the latter "ridiculed" Schaff's theory of the continuity of the Reformation with the medieval church. Brownson further said "we presume" Nevin himself had "abandoned" it. "Union with the Church," 442. This essay was written in 1870. This was apparently said in a letter, so we cannot determine what Nevin actually said, nor conclude that Brownson's presumption was valid. Still, it is another datum supporting the claim of Layman et al. that Nevin had in some sense moved beyond Schaff. This editor acknowledges Black, "A 'Vast Practical Embarrassment,'" 281; the interested reader should consult Black for further evaluation.

Bibliography

"Account of the Bohon-Upas, or Poison-Tree, of the Island of Java. From the Travels of Mr. Foersech, A Dutch Surgeon." In *The Historical Magazine; or, Classical Library of Public Events . . .*, 34–37. London: D. Brewman, 1789–92. https://collections.library.yale.edu/catalog/2032619?child_oid=1120625.

Acta Proconsularia Sancti Cypriani. In *Patrologiæ Latina*, edited by J.-P. Migne, 3:1497–1506. Paris: Lutetiæ Parisiorum: J.-P. Migne, 1844.

Acts of St. Cyprian. In *The Acts of the Christian Martyrs*, texts and translations by Herbert Musurillo, 168–75. Oxford: Oxford University Press, 1972.

Allen, Michael, and Scott R. Swain. *Reformed Catholicity: The Promise of Retrieval for Theology and Biblical Interpretation*. Grand Rapids, MI: Baker Academic, 2015.

Allies, Thomas William. *The Church of England Cleared from the Charge of Schism, by the Decrees of the Seven Ecumenical Councils and the Traditions of the Fathers*. Oxford: John Henry Parker, 1848.

Ante-Nicene Christian Library. Vol. 17, *The Clementine Homilies and the Apostolical Constitutions*. Edited by Alexander Roberts and James Donaldson. Edinburgh: T. & T. Clark, 1870.

Ante-Nicene Christian Library. Vol. 20, *The Writings of Gregory Thaumaturgus, Dionysius of Alexandria, and Archelaus*. Edited by Alexander Roberts and James Donaldson. Edinburgh: T. & T. Clark, 1871.

Ante-Nicene Fathers. Vol. 1, *The Apostolic Fathers—Justin Martyr—Irenaeus*. Edited by Alexander Roberts and James Donaldson; revised by A. Cleveland Coxe. Buffalo, NY: Christian Literature Company, 1885.

Ante-Nicene Fathers. Vol. 2, *Fathers of the Second Century: Hermas, Tatian, Athenagoras, Theophilus, and Clement of Alexandria (Entire)*. Edited by Alexander Roberts and James Donaldson; revised by A. Cleveland Coxe. Buffalo, NY: Christian Literature Company, 1885.

Ante-Nicene Fathers. Vol. 3, *Latin Christianity: Its Founder, Tertullian*. Edited by Alexander Roberts and James Donaldson; revised by A. Cleveland Coxe. Buffalo, NY: Christian Literature Company, 1887.

Ante-Nicene Fathers. Vol. 5, *Fathers of the Third Century: Hippolytus, Cyprian, Caius, Novatian, Appendix*. Edited by Alexander Roberts and James Donaldson; revised by A. Cleveland Cox. Buffalo, NY: Christian Literature Company, 1886.

Appel, Theodore. *The Life and Work of John Williamson Nevin*. Philadelphia: Reformed Church, 1889. Reprint, New York: Arno, 1969.

BIBLIOGRAPHY

Appleyard, Ernest Silvanus. *Claims of the Church of Rome, Considered with a View to Unity*. London: James Darling, 1848.

Arnold, Brian. *Cyprian of Carthage: His Life & Impact*. Geanies House, Fearn, Ross-shire, Scotland: Christian Focus, 2017.

Athanasius [spurious]. *Quæstiones in Scripturam*. In *Patrologiæ Græca*, edited by J.-P. Migne, 28:711–74. Lutetiæ Parisiorum: J.-P. Migne, 1857.

Aubert, Annette G. *The German Roots of Nineteenth-Century American Theology*. Oxford: Oxford University Press, 2013.

Augustine, St. *Concerning the City of God Against the Pagans*. Translated by Henry Bettenson. New York: Penguin Putnam, 2003.

———. *The Confessions of St. Augustine of Hippo*. Translated by Maria Boulding. Edited by David Vincent Meconi. San Francisco: Ignatius, 1999.

Bains, David and Theodore Louis Trost. Editors' Introduction to *The Principle of Protestantism*. In *The Development of the Church: The Principle of Protestantism and Other Historical Writings of Philip Schaff*, by Philip Schaff, 27–34. Edited by David R. Bains and Theodore Louis Trost. MTSS 3. Eugene, OR: Wipf & Stock, 2016.

———. Editors' Introduction to *What is Church History? A Vindication of the Idea of Historical Development*. In *The Development of the Church: The Principle of Protestantism and Other Historical Writings of Philip Schaff*, by Philip Schaff, 225–31. Edited by David R. Bains and Theodore Louis Trost. MTSS 3. Eugene, OR: Wipf & Stock, 2016.

Barrett, Lee C. General Introduction to *The Heidelberg Catechism: The Mercersburg Understanding of the German Reformed Tradition*, by John Williamson Nevin and John Williams Proudfit, 1–48. Edited by Lee C. Barrett. MTSS 10. Eugene, OR: Wipf & Stock, 2021.

Barrow, Isaac. *The Pope's supremacy: To which are added a Sypopsis* [sic] *of the treatise; and two complete indexes*. New York: John C. Riker, 1845.

Barth, Karl. *Protestant Theology in the Nineteenth Century: Its Background & History*. Valley Forge, PA: Judson, 1973.

Billington, Ray Allen. *The Protestant Crusade, 1800–1860: A Study in the Origins of American Nativism*. New York: Macmillan, 1938; Chicago: Quadrangle, 1964.

Black, Andrew Donald. "A 'Vast Practical Embarrassment': John W. Nevin, The Mercersburg Theology, and the Church Question." PhD diss., University of Dayton, 2013.

Boettner, Loraine. *Roman Catholicism*. Phillipsburg, NJ: Presbyterian & Reformed, 1962.

Bokenkotter, Thomas. *A Concise History of the Catholic Church*. New York: Image, 2004.

Borneman, Adam S. General Introduction, Part 1 to *Philosophy and the Contemporary World: Mercersburg, Culture, and the Church*, by John Williamson Nevin, 3–17. Edited by Adam S. Borneman and Patrick Carey. MTSS 11. Eugene, OR: Wipf & Stock, 2023.

Brown, Peter. *The Cult of the Saints: Its Rise and Function in Latin Christianity*. Enlarged Edition. Chicago: University of Chicago Press, 1981, 2015.

Brownson, Orestes A. "Union with the Church." In *The Works of Orestes A. Brownson*, edited by Henry F. Brownson, 3:438–459. Detroit: Thorndike Nourse, 1883.

Butler, Alban. *The Lives of the Primitive Fathers, Martyrs, and other Principal Saints: compiled from original monuments, and other authentic records*. 3rd ed. 12 vols. Edinburgh: J. Moir, 1799.

Calvin, John. *Institutes of the Christian Religion*. Edited by John T. McNeill. Translated by Ford Lewis Battles. 2 vols. Philadelphia: Westminster, 1960.

Chalybäus, Heinrich Moritz. *Historical Development of Speculative Philosophy from Kant to Hegel*. Translated by Alfred Edersheim. Edinburgh: T. & T. Clark, 1854.

Clement of Rome, St. *Epistle to the Corinthians*. In *The Epistles of St. Clement of Rome and St. Ignatius of Antioch*, edited by Johannes Quasten and Joseph C. Plumpe, 9–49. ACW 1. Westminster, MD: Newman, 1946.

———. *Epistola ad Corinthios I* [trans. *First Epistle to the Corinthians*]. In *Patrum apostolicorum opera: textum ex editionibus praestantissimis repetitum recognovit, annotationibus illustravit, versionem Latinam emendatiorem, prolegomena et indices*, edited by Karl Joseph von Hefele, 54–137. 3rd ed. Tubingae: Henrici Laupp, 1847.

Collins, Roger. *Keepers of the Keys of Heaven: A History of the Papacy*. New York: Basic, 2009.

Crisp, Oliver D. *Deviant Calvinism: Broadening Reformed Theology*. Minneapolis: Fortress, 2014.

———. *Retrieving Doctrine: Essays in Reformed Theology*. Downers Grove, IL: IVP Academic, 2010.

Cyprian. *De Bono Patientiae*, in *Th. C. Cypriani Opera Genuina: Ad Optimorum Librorum Fidem Expressa Brevique Adnotatione Instructa*, Pars II: Tractatus, edited by David Johann Heinrich Goldhorn, 241–55. Bibliotheca patrum ecclesiasticorum Latinorum selecta 3. Lipsiae: Bernh. Tauchnitz, jun., 1839.

———. *On The Church: Select Treatises*. Popular Patristic Series, No. 32. Edited by John Behr. Translated by Allen Brent. Crestwood, NY: St. Vladimir's Seminary Press, 2006.

———. *Ad Demetrianum*, in *Th. C. Cypriani Opera Genuina: Ad Optimorum Librorum Fidem Expressa Brevique Adnotatione Instructa*, Pars II: Tractatus, edited by David Johann Heinrich Goldhorn, 210–25. Bibliotheca patrum ecclesiasticorum Latinorum selecta 3. Lipsiae: Bernh. Tauchnitz, jun., 1839.

———. *Ad Donatum De Gratia Dei*, in *Th. C. Cypriani Opera Genuina: Ad Optimorum Librorum Fidem Expressa Brevique Adnotatione Instructa*, Pars II: Tractatus, edited by David Johann Heinrich Goldhorn, 1–10. Bibliotheca patrum ecclesiasticorum Latinorum selecta 3. Lipsiae: Bernh. Tauchnitz, jun., 1839.

———. *De Exhortatione Martyrii* in *Th. C. Cypriani Opera Genuina: Ad Optimorum Librorum Fidem Expressa Brevique Adnotatione Instructa*, Pars II: Tractatus, edited by David Johann Heinrich Goldhorn, 189–210. Bibliotheca patrum ecclesiasticorum Latinorum selecta 3. Lipsiae: Bernh. Tauchnitz, jun., 1839.

———. *De Habitu Virginum*, in *Th. C. Cypriani Opera Genuina: Ad Optimorum Librorum Fidem Expressa Brevique Adnotatione Instructa*, Pars II: Tractatus, edited by David Johann Heinrich Goldhorn, 103–17. Bibliotheca patrum ecclesiasticorum Latinorum selecta 3. Lipsiae: Bernh. Tauchnitz, jun., 1839.

———. *De Haereticis Baptizandis*, in *Th. C. Cypriani Opera Genuina: Ad Optimorum Librorum Fidem Expressa Brevique Adnotatione Instructa*, Pars II: Tractatus, edited by David Johann Heinrich Goldhorn, 265–79. Bibliotheca patrum ecclesiasticorum Latinorum selecta 3. Lipsiae: Bernh. Tauchnitz, jun., 1839.

———. *De Idolorum Vanitate*, in *Th. C. Cypriani Opera Genuina: Ad Optimorum Librorum Fidem Expressa Brevique Adnotatione Instructa*, Pars II: Tractatus, edited by David Johann Heinrich Goldhorn, 10–16. Bibliotheca patrum ecclesiasticorum Latinorum selecta 3. Lipsiae: Bernh. Tauchnitz, jun., 1839.

———. *The Lapsed and the Unity of the Catholic Church*. Translated by Maurice Bevenot. ACW 25. Westminster, MD: The Newman Press, 1957.

———. *De Lapsis*, in *Th. C. Cypriani Opera Genuina: Ad Optimorum Librorum Fidem Expressa Brevique Adnotatione Instructa*, Pars II: Tractatus, edited by David Johann Heinrich Goldhorn, 134–55. Bibliotheca patrum ecclesiasticorum Latinorum selecta 3. Lipsiae: Bernh. Tauchnitz, jun., 1839.

———. *Letters of St. Cyprian of Carthage*. 4 vols. Trans. G.W. Clark. ACW 43, 44, 46, 47. Edited by Johannes Quasten et al. New York: Newman Press, 1984.

———. *De Mortalitate* in *Th. C. Cypriani Opera Genuina: Ad Optimorum Librorum Fidem Expressa Brevique Adnotatione Instructa*, edited by David Johann Heinrich Goldhorn, Pars II: Tractatus, 176–89. Bibliotheca patrum ecclesiasticorum Latinorum selecta 3. Lipsiae: Bernh. Tauchnitz, jun., 1839.

———. *De Opere et Eleemosynis*, in *Th. C. Cypriani Opera Genuina: Ad Optimorum Librorum Fidem Expressa Brevique Adnotatione Instructa*, Pars II: Tractatus, edited by David Johann Heinrich Goldhorn, 225–41. Bibliotheca patrum ecclesiasticorum Latinorum selecta 3. Lipsiae: Bernh. Tauchnitz, jun., 1839.

———. *De Oratione Dominica*, in *Th. C. Cypriani Opera Genuina: Ad Optimorum Librorum Fidem Expressa Brevique Adnotatione Instructa*, Pars II: Tractatus, edited by David Johann Heinrich Goldhorn, 155–76. Bibliotheca patrum ecclesiasticorum Latinorum selecta 3. Lipsiae: Bernh. Tauchnitz, jun., 1839.

———. *Testimonia Adversus Iudaeos*, in *Th. C. Cypriani Opera Genuina: Ad Optimorum Librorum Fidem Expressa Brevique Adnotatione Instructa*, Pars II: Tractatus, edited by David Johann Heinrich Goldhorn, 17–103. Bibliotheca patrum ecclesiasticorum Latinorum selecta 3. Lipsiae: Bernh. Tauchnitz, jun., 1839.

———. *Th. C. Cypriani Opera Genuina: Ad Optimorum Librorum Fidem Expressa Brevique Adnotatione Instructa*, Pars I: Epistolae. Edited by David Johann Heinrich Goldhorn. Bibliotheca patrum ecclesiasticorum Latinorum selecta 2. Lipsiae: Bernh. Tauchnitz, jun., 1838.

———. *De Unitate Ecclesiae*, in *Th. C. Cypriani Opera Genuina: Ad Optimorum Librorum Fidem Expressa Brevique Adnotatione Instructa*, Pars II: Tractatus, edited by David Johann Heinrich Goldhorn, 117–134. Bibliotheca patrum ecclesiasticorum Latinorum selecta 3. Lipsiae: Bernh. Tauchnitz, jun., 1839.

———. *De Zelo et Livore*, in *Th. C. Cypriani Opera Genuina: Ad Optimorum Librorum Fidem Expressa Brevique Adnotatione Instructa*, Pars II: Tractatus, edited by David Johann Heinrich Goldhorn, 255–65. Bibliotheca patrum ecclesiasticorum Latinorum selecta 3. Lipsiae: Bernh. Tauchnitz, jun., 1839.

Dabney, R. L. *Systematic Theology*. Carlisle: Banner of Truth, 1871. 2nd ed., 1985.

"Death of the Rev. Dr. Amasa Converse–9 December 1872." https://christianobserver.org/death-of-the-rev-dr-amasa-converse-9-december-1872/.

DeBie, Linden J. Editor's Introduction to *The Mystical Presence and the Doctrine of the Reformed Church on the Lord's Supper*, by John Williamson Nevin, xxiii–xliii. Edited by Linden J. DeBie. MTSS 1. Eugene, OR: Wipf & Stock, 2012.

———. "The Germ, Genesis and Contemporary Impact of Mercersburg Philosophy." *The New Mercersburg Review*, no. 40 (2009) 5–51. https://archive.lancasterseminary.edu/items/show/297.

———. *John Williamson Nevin: Evangelical Catholic*. Eugene, OR: Pickwick, 2023.

———. *Speculative Theology and Common Sense Religion: Mercersburg and the Conservative Roots of American Religion*. Eugene, OR: Pickwick, 2008.

Dennison, James T., ed. *Reformed Confessions of the 16th and 17th Centuries*. 4 vols. Grand Rapids: Reformation Heritage, 2008–14.

Denzinger, Heinrich. *Enchiridion Symbolorum: A Compendium of Creeds, Definitions and Declarations on Matters of Faith and Morals*. Edited by Peter Hünermann. 43rd ed. San Francisco: Ignatius, 2012.

Dictionary of the Christian Church. Edited by F. L. Cross and E. A. Livingstone. 3rd ed. Oxford: Oxford University Press, 1997.

Dictionary of Christianity in America. Edited by Daniel G. Reid. Downers Grove, IL: InterVarsity, 1990.

DiPuccio, William. *The Interior Sense of Scripture: The Sacred Hermeneutics of John W. Nevin*. Macon, GA: Mercer University Press, 1998.

Dowling, John. *The History of Romanism, from the Earliest Corruptions of Christianity to the Present Time*. A New Edition . . . From the Accession of Pope Pius IX. To the Present Time, AD 1853. New York: Edward Walker, 1853.

Dubbs, Joseph Henry. *History of Franklin and Marshall College*. Lancaster, PA: Franklin and Marshall College Alumni Association, 1903.

Dussinger, John A. "Middleton, Conyers (1683–1750)." In *Oxford Dictionary of National Biography, From the earliest times to the year 2000*, edited by H. C. G. Matthew and Brian Harrison, 38:51–56. Oxford: Oxford University Press, 2004.

Emerson, Matthew Y., et al. *Baptists and the Christian Tradition: Towards an Evangelical Baptist Catholicity*. Nashville, TN: B&H Academic, 2002.

Encyclopedia Britannica. December 27, 2017. "Argus." https://www.britannica.com/topic/Argus-Greek-mythology.

Eno, Robert B. *The Rise of the Papacy*. Wilmington: Michael Glazier, 1990.

Erb, William H., ed. *Dr. Nevin's Theology: Based on Manuscript Class-Room Lectures*. Reading, PA: I. M. Beaver, 1913.

Eusebius. *The History of the Church from Christ to Constantine*. Translated by G. A. Williamson. Harmondsworth, Middlesex, England: Penguin, 1965.

"Evangelical Religion in Lyons, France." *American and Foreign Christian Union* 2 (1851) 228–33, 264–66.

"Evans, Hugh Davey." *An Episcopal Dictionary of the Church*. https://www.episcopalchurch.org/glossary/evans-hugh-davey/.

Evans, Hugh Davey. "Sectarianism." *True Catholic* 6 (April 1849) 529–39.

Evans, William B. *A Companion to the Mercersburg Theology: Evangelical Catholicism in the Mid-Nineteenth Century*. Eugene, OR: Cascade Books, 2019.

———. General Introduction to *The Incarnate Word: Selected Writings on Christology*, by John Williamson Nevin et al., xv–xxxvi. Edited by William B. Evans. MTSS 4. Eugene, OR: Wipf & Stock, 2014.

———. *Imputation and Impartation: Union with Christ in American Reformed Theology*. Eugene, OR: Wipf & Stock, 2008.

———. "Philosophical Idealism and the Reformed Theological Tradition." In *The Routledge Handbook of Idealism and Immaterialism*, edited by Joshua Farris and Benedikt Paul Göcke, 402–18. Routledge Handbooks in Philosophy. Kindle Edition. New York: Routledge, 2022.

Fletcher, Richard. *The Barbarian Conversion: From Paganism to Christianity*. Berkeley: University of California Press, 1997.

Gäbler, Ulrich. *Huldrych Zwingli: His Life and Work*. Edinburgh: T & T Clark, 1986.

Garner, Bryan A. *A Dictionary of Modern Legal Usage*. 2nd ed. Oxford: Oxford University Press, 1995.

Gerhart, Emanuel Vogel. The Emanuel V. Gerhart Papers. Evangelical and Reformed Historical Society, Lancaster, PA.

Gerrish, B. A. *Tradition and the Modern World: Reformed Theology in the Nineteenth Century*. Chicago: University of Chicago Press, 1978.

Gibbon, Edward. *The History of the Decline and Fall of the Roman Empire*. Basil: J. J. Tourneisen, 1789.

Gibson, Jonathan and Mark Earngey, eds. *Reformation Worship: Liturgies from the Past for the Present*. Greensboro, North Carolina: New Growth, 2018.

Gieseler, John C. L. *A Compendium of Ecclesiastical History*. Translated by Samuel Davidson. 2 vols. New York: Harper & Brothers, 1849.

Giustiniani, Louis. *Intrigues of Jesuitism in the United States of America*. 7th ed. New York: R. Craighead, 1846.

———. *Papal Rome As It Is, by a Roman*. Baltimore: 7 S. Liberty Street, 1843.

González, Justo L. *A History of Christian Thought*. Vol. 1, *From the Beginnings to the Council of Chalcedon*. Revised ed. Nashville: Abingdon Press, 1970, 1987.

———. *The Story of Christianity*. 2 vols. New York: HarperCollins, 1984, 1985.

Good, James I. *History of the Reformed Church in the U.S. in the Nineteenth Century*. New York: Reformed Church in America, 1911.

Graham, Stephen. "Nevin and Schaff at Mercersburg." In *Reformed Confessionalism in Nineteenth-Century America: Essays on the Thought of John Williamson Nevin*, edited by Sam Hamstra Jr. and Arie J. Griffioen, 69–96. Lanham: Scarecrow, 1995.

Gutacker, Paul. "Joseph Milner and his Editors: Eighteenth- and Nineteenth-Century Evangelicals and the Christian Past." *Journal of Ecclesiastical History* 69, no. 1 (January 2018) 86–104.

Hamstra Jr., Sam. General Introduction to *One, Holy, Catholic, and Apostolic, Tome 1: Nevin's Writings on Ecclesiology (1844–1849)*, by John Williamson Nevin, 1–25. Edited by Sam Hamstra Jr. MTSS 5. Eugene, OR: Wipf & Stock, 2017.

Harrelson, Walter. "Shekinah." In *New Interpreter's Dictionary of the Bible*, 5:222. Nashville: Abingdon Press, 2009.

Hart, Darryl G. *John Williamson Nevin: High Church Calvinist*. Phillipsburg, NJ: Presbyterian and Reformed, 2005.

Hatch, Nathan O. *The Democratization of American Christianity*. New Haven: Yale University Press, 1991.

Hermas. *Hermae Pastor* [trans. *The Pastor of Hermas*]. In *Patrum apostolicorum opera: textum ex editionibus praestantissimis repetitum recognovit, annotationibus illustravit, versionem Latinam emendatiorem, prolegomena et indices*, edited by Karl Joseph von Hefele, 326–442. 3rd ed. Tubingae: Henrici Laupp, 1847.

Historiae ecclesiasticae scriptores: Eusebius Pamphilus, Socrates Scholasticus, Hermias Sozomenus, Theodoritus Episc. Cyri, Evagrius Scholasticus, Philostorgius, & Theodorus Lector. Vol 1. Trans. Henri de Valois. Augustae Taurinorum: Regia, 1746.

History of the Genesee Country. Edited by Lockwood R. Doty. Vol. 2. Chicago: S. J. Clarke, 1925.

Hodge, Charles. "The General Assembly." *Biblical Repertory and Princeton Review* 17, no. 3 (July 1845) 428–71.

———. "The Mystical Presence . . . by the Rev. John W. Nevin . . . ." *Biblical Repertory and Princeton Review* 20 (1848) 227–78.

———. *Systematic Theology*. 3 vols. New York: Charles Scribner, 1871–73. Reprint, Peabody, MA: Hendrickson, 1999.

Ignatius of Antioch, St. *Epistles*. In *The Epistles of St. Clement of Rome and St. Ignatius of Antioch*, edited by Johannes Quasten and Joseph C. Plumpe, 60–99. ACW 1. Westminster, MD: Newman, 1946.

Irenaeus of Lyons, St. *Adversus Haereses*. In *Patrologiæ Græca*, edited by J.-P. Migne, 7:433–1224. Lutetiæ Parisiorum: J.-P. Migne, 1857.

———. *Against the Heresies: Book 3*. Translated by Dominic J. Unger. ACW 64. New York: Newman, 2012.

Jerome, Saint. *On Illustrious Men*. Translated by Thomas P. Halton. The Fathers of the Church, 100. Washington, D.C.: Catholic University of America Press, 1999.

———. *Translatio Homiliarum Origenis in Ezechielem*. In *Patrologiæ Latina*, edited by J.-P. Migne, 25:691–786. Lutetiæ Parisiorum: J.-P. Migne, 1845.

Kasper, Walter. *The Catholic Church: Nature, Reality and Mission*. New York: Bloomsbury, 2015.

Kaye, John. *Some Account of the Writings and Opinions of Clement of Alexandria*. London: J. G. & F. Rivington, 1835.

Kelly, Joseph F. *The Ecumenical Councils of the Catholic Church: A History*. Collegeville, MN: Liturgical, 2009.

Kenrick, Francis Patrick. *The Primacy of the Apostolic See Vindicated*. Philadelphia: M. Fithian, 1845.

Layman, David W. General Editor's Introduction to *One, Holy, Catholic, and Apostolic, Tome 2: Nevin's Writings on Ecclesiology (1851–1858)*, by John Williamson Nevin, 1–6. Edited by Sam Hamstra Jr. MTSS 7. Eugene, OR: Wipf & Stock, 2017.

———. General Introduction to *Born of Water and the Spirit: Essays on the Sacraments and Christian Formation*, by John Williamson Nevin et al., 1–33. Edited by David W. Layman. MTSS 6. Eugene, OR: Wipf & Stock, 2016.

———. "Historicity and Unity in Nevin's Christology." *The New Mercersburg Review*, no. 8 (1990) 25–40.

———. "Nevin's Holistic Supernaturalism." In *Reformed Confessionalism in Nineteenth-Century America: Essays on the Thought of John Williamson Nevin*, edited by Sam Hamstra Jr. and Arie J. Griffioen, 193–208. Lanham: Scarecrow, 1995.

———. "Revelation in the Praxis of the Liturgical Community: A Jewish-Christian Dialogue, with Special Reference to the Work of John Williamson Nevin and Franz Rosenzweig." PhD diss., Temple University, 1994.

Littlejohn, W. Bradford. "Sectarianism and the Search for Visible Catholicity: Lessons from John Nevin and Richard Hooker." *Theology Today* 71 (2015) 404–415.

Locke, John. *Locke: The Political Writings*. Edited by David Wootton. Indianapolis: Hackett, 1993, 2003.

Machen, J. Gresham. *Christianity and Liberalism*. Grand Rapids: Wm. B. Eerdmans, 1923, 1992.

De Martyrio Sancti Polycarpi Epistola Circularis [trans. *Martyrdom of Polycarp*]. In *Patrum Apostolicorum Opera: Textum ex Editionibus Praestantissimis Repetitum Recognovit, Annotationibus Illustravit, Versionem Latinam Emendatiorem, Prolegomena et Indices*, edited by Karl Joseph von Hefele, 274–99. 3rd ed. Tubingae: Henrici Laupp, 1847.

BIBLIOGRAPHY

Maxwell, Jack Martin. *Worship and Reformed Theology: The Liturgical Lessons of Mercersburg.* Pittsburgh Theological Monograph Series, no. 10. Pittsburgh: Pickwick, 1976.

McGrath, Alister. *C.S. Lewis—A Life: Eccentric Genius, Reluctant Prophet.* Carol Stream, IL: Tyndale, 2013.

Miller, Samuel. *Letters Concerning the Constitution and Order of the Christian Ministry as Deduced from Scripture and Primitive Usage; Addressed to the Members of the United Presbyterian Churches in the City of New-York.* New York: Hopkins and Seymour, 1807.

Milner, John. *The End of Religious Controversy, in a Friendly Correspondence Between a Religious Society of Protestants and a Roman Catholic Divine.* Vol. 1, 2nd ed. London: Keating, Brown, 1819.

Milner, Joseph. *The History of the Church of Christ.* Vol. 1, Containing the Three First Centuries. York: G. Peacock, 1794.

Möhler, J. A. *Patrologie, oder christliche Literärgeschichte.* Vol. 1. Edited by F. X. Reithmayr. Regensburg: G. Joseph Manz, 1840.

Monk, Maria. *Awful Disclosures of Maria Monk or the Hidden Secrets of a Nun's Life in a Convent Exposed.* Philadelphia: T. B. Peterson, 1836.

Mosheim, Johann Lorenz von. *An Ecclesiastical History, from the Birth of Christ, to the Beginning of the Eighteenth Century . . . .* Translated by Archibald Maclaine. Vol. 1. London: Thomas Tegg, 1838.

Moss, C. B. *The Old Catholic Movement, Its Origins and History.* London: SPCK, 1948.

Mueller, Gustav E. "The Hegel Legend of 'Thesis-Antithesis-Synthesis.'" *Journal of the History of Ideas* 19, no. 3 (June 1958) 411–14.

Neander, Augustus. *Allgemeine Geschichte der christlichen Religion und Kirche.* Erste Band. Hamburg: Friedrich Perthes, 1842.

———. *General History of the Christian Religion and Church.* Translated by Joseph Torrey. Vol. 1. 2nd American ed. Boston: Crocker and Brewster, 1849.

Nevin, John Williamson. "Address on Behalf of the Faculty." In *Addresses Delivered on the Occasion of the Formal Opening of Franklin and Marshall College in the City of Lancaster, June 7, 1853*, 9–35. Lancaster: Board of Trustees, 1853.

———. "The Anglican Crisis." In *Philosophy and the Contemporary World: Mercersburg, Culture, and the Church*, edited by Adam Borneman and Patrick Carey, 269–306. MTSS 11. Eugene, OR: Wipf & Stock, 2023.

———. *Antichrist; or the Spirit of Sect and Schism.* In *One, Holy, Catholic, and Apostolic, Tome 1: Nevin's Writings on Ecclesiology (1844–1849)*, edited by Sam Hamstra Jr., 165–232. MTSS 5. Eugene, OR: Wipf & Stock, 2017.

———. "The Anti-Creed Heresy [John Williamson Nevin's Response to Proudfit]." In *The Early Creeds: The Mercersburg Theologians Appropriate the Creedal Heritage*, edited by Charles Yrigoyen Jr. and Lee C. Barrett, 196–209. By John Williamson Nevin et al. MTSS 8. Eugene, OR: Wipf & Stock, 2020.

———. *The Anxious Bench.* In *One, Holy, Catholic, and Apostolic, Tome 1: Nevin's Writings on Ecclesiology (1844–1849)*, edited by Sam Hamstra Jr., 27–103. MTSS 5. Eugene, OR: Wipf & Stock, 2017.

———. "Apollos: Or the Way to God." *MR* 21 (1874) 5–41.

———. "The Apostles' Creed." In *The Early Creeds: The Mercersburg Theologians Appropriate the Creedal Heritage*, edited by Charles Yrigoyen Jr. and Lee C. Barrett, 35–97. By John Williamson Nevin et al. MTSS 8. Eugene, OR: Wipf & Stock, 2020.

———. "Arianism." *MR* 14 (1867) 426–44.

———. "Athanasius." *MR* 14 (1867) 445–57.

———. "The Bread of Life: A Communion Sermon." In *Born of Water and the Spirit: Essays on the Sacraments and Christian Formation*, edited by David W. Layman, 214–44. By John Williamson Nevin et al. MTSS 6. Eugene, OR: Wipf & Stock, 2016.

———. Brownson Archives. Notre Dame University Library, Notre Dame, IN. Microfilm, Lancastriana Collection. Lancaster Theological Seminary, Lancaster, PA.

———. "Brownson's Quarterly Review." In *Philosophy and the Contemporary World: Mercersburg, Culture, and the Church*, edited by Adam Borneman and Patrick Carey, 198–243. MTSS 11. Eugene, OR: Wipf & Stock, 2023.

———. "Brownson's Review Again." In *Philosophy and the Contemporary World: Mercersburg, Culture, and the Church*, edited by Adam Borneman and Patrick Carey, 248–64. MTSS 11. Eugene, OR: Wipf & Stock, 2023.

———. "Catholicism." In *One, Holy, Catholic, and Apostolic, Tome 2: Nevin's Writings on Ecclesiology (1851–1858)*, edited by Sam Hamstra Jr., 11–32. MTSS 7. Eugene, OR: Wipf & Stock, 2017.

———. "Catholic Unity." In *One, Holy, Catholic, and Apostolic, Tome 1: John Nevin's Writings on Ecclesiology (1844–1849)*, edited by Sam Hamstra Jr., 112–32. MTSS 5. Eugene, OR: Wipf & Stock, 2017.

———. "The Christian Ministry." In *One, Holy, Catholic, and Apostolic, Tome 2: Nevin's Writings on Ecclesiology (1851–1858)*, edited by Sam Hamstra Jr., 35–56. MTSS 7. Eugene, OR: Wipf & Stock, 2017.

———. *The Church*. In *One, Holy, Catholic, and Apostolic, Tome 1: Nevin's Writings on Ecclesiology (1844–1849)*, edited by Sam Hamstra Jr., 138–58. MTSS 5. Eugene, OR: Wipf & Stock, 2017.

———. "Cyprian [First Article]." *MR* 4 (May 1852) 259–77.

———. "Cyprian: Fourth and Last Article." *MR* 4 (November 1852) 513–63.

———. "Cyprian: Second Article." *MR* 4 (July 1852) 335–87.

———. "Cyprian: Third Article." *MR* 4 (September 1852) 417–52.

———. "The Doctrine of the Reformed Church on the Lord's Supper." In *The Mystical Presence and the Doctrine of the Reformed Church on the Lord's Supper*, edited by Linden J. DeBie, 225–322. MTSS 1. Eugene, OR: Wipf & Stock, 2012.

———. "Early Christianity [First Article]." *MR* 3 (September 1851) 461–90.

———. "Early Christianity: Second Article." *MR* 3 (November 1851) 513–62.

———. "Early Christianity: Third Article." *MR* (January 1852) 1–54.

———. "Evangelical Radicalism." In *Philosophy and the Contemporary World: Mercersburg, Culture, and the Church*, edited by Adam Borneman and Patrick Carey, 310–14. MTSS 11. Eugene, OR: Wipf & Stock, 2023.

———. "The Heidelberg Catechism." *WM* 6, nos. 12–28; *WM* 7, nos. 32–49 (December 9, 1840–April 14, 1841; April 27–August 24, 1842).

———. "Historical Development." *MR* 1 (September 1849) 512–14.

———. "Hodge on the Ephesians." In *One, Holy, Catholic, and Apostolic, Tome 2: Nevin's Writings on Ecclesiology (1851–1858)*, edited by Sam Hamstra Jr., 62–125. MTSS 7. Eugene, OR: Wipf & Stock, 2017.

———. "Human Freedom." In *Philosophy and the Contemporary World: Mercersburg, Culture, and the Church*, edited by Adam Borneman and Patrick Carey, 54–74. MTSS 11. Eugene, OR: Wipf & Stock, 2023.

———. "Inspiration of the Bible, or the Internal Sense of the Holy Scripture." *Reformed Quarterly Review* 30 (January 1883) 5–39.

———. "Kirwan's Letters." *MR* 1 (May 1849) 229–63.

———. Lancastriana Collection. Lancaster Theological Seminary, Lancaster, PA.

———. "Man's True Destiny: A Baccalaureate Address to the First Graduating Class of Franklin and Marshall College, August 31, 1853." In *Philosophy and the Contemporary World: Mercersburg, Culture, and the Church*, 320–45, edited by Adam Borneman and Patrick Carey. MTSS 11. Eugene, OR: Wipf & Stock, 2023.

———. *My Own Life: The Earlier Years*. Papers of the Eastern Chapter, Historical Society of the Evangelical and Reformed Church, no. 1. Lancaster, PA: Eastern Chapter, Historical Society of the Evangelical and Reformed Church, 1964.

———. *The Mystical Presence and the Doctrine of the Reformed Church on the Lord's Supper*. Edited by Linden J. DeBie and W. Bradford Littlejohn. MTSS 1. Eugene, Oregon: Wipf & Stock, 2012.

———. "Natural and Supernatural." In *Philosophy and the Contemporary World: Mercersburg, Culture, and the Church*, edited by Adam Borneman and Patrick Carey, 350–76. MTSS 11. Eugene, OR: Wipf & Stock, 2023.

———. "Nature and Grace." *MR* 19 (October 1872) 485–509.

———. "Noel on Baptism." In *Born of Water and the Spirit: Essays on the Sacraments and Christian Formation*, edited by David W. Layman, 78–115. By John Williamson Nevin et al. MTSS 6. Eugene, OR: Wipf & Stock, 2016.

———. "The Old Catholic Movement." *MR* 20 (April 1873) 240–94.

———. "The Old Doctrine of Christian Baptism." In *Born of Water and the Spirit: Essays on the Sacraments and Christian Formation*, edited by David W. Layman, 196–213. By John Williamson Nevin et al. MTSS 6. Eugene, OR: Wipf & Stock, 2016.

———. "Once for All." *MR* 17 (1870) 100–24.

———. *One, Holy, Catholic, and Apostolic, Tome 1: Nevin's Writings on Ecclesiology (1844–1849)*. Edited by Sam Hamstra Jr. MTSS 5. Eugene, OR: Wipf & Stock, 2017.

———. *One, Holy, Catholic, and Apostolic, Tome 2: Nevin's Writings on Ecclesiology (1851–1858)*. Edited by Sam Hamstra Jr. MTSS 7. Eugene, OR: Wipf & Stock, 2017.

———. "Origin and Structure of the Apostles' Creed." In *The Early Creeds: The Mercersburg Theologians Appropriate the Creedal Heritage*, edited by Charles Yrigoyen Jr. and Lee C. Barrett, 255–261. By John Williamson Nevin et al. MTSS 8. Eugene, OR: Wipf & Stock, 2020.

———. *Philosophy and the Contemporary World: Mercersburg, Culture, and the Church*. Edited by Adam Borneman and Patrick Carey. MTSS 11. Eugene, OR: Wipf & Stock, 2023.

———. "A Plea for Philosophy." In *Philosophy and the Contemporary World: Mercersburg, Culture, and the Church*, edited by Adam Borneman and Patrick Carey, 75–94. MTSS 11. Eugene, OR: Wipf & Stock, 2023.

———. "Presbyterian Union Convention." *MR* 15 (1868) 73–109.

———. "Pseudo-Protestantism." *WM* 10, nos. 48–52 (August 13–27, 1845; September 3, 10, 1845).

———. "Puritanism and the Creed." *MR* (November 1849) 585–607. Reprinted in *The Early Creeds: The Mercersburg Theologians Appropriate the Creedal Heritage*, edited by Charles Yrigoyen Jr. and Lee C. Barrett, 103–21. By John Williamson Nevin et al. MTSS 8. Eugene, OR: Wipf & Stock, 2020.

———. "Religion A Life." *The New Mercersburg Review*, no. 17 (1995) 37–45. https://archive.lancasterseminary.edu/items/show/267.

———. "Reply to 'An Anglican Catholic.'" *MR* 21 (1874) 397–429.

———. "The Sect System." In *One, Holy, Catholic, and Apostolic, Tome 1: Nevin's Writings on Ecclesiology (1844–1849)*, edited by Sam Hamstra Jr., 238–71. MTSS 5. Eugene, OR: Wipf & Stock, 2017.

———. *A Summary of Biblical Antiquities: For the Use of Schools, Bible-Classes, and Families*. 2nd ed. Philadelphia: American Sunday-School Union, 1849. Reprint, Eugene, OR: Wipf & Stock, 2003.

———. "Thoughts on the Church." In *One, Holy, Catholic, and Apostolic, Tome 2: Nevin's Writings on Ecclesiology (1851–1858)*, edited by Sam Hamstra Jr., 131–171. MTSS 7. Eugene, OR: Wipf & Stock, 2017.

———. Translator's Introduction to *The Principle of Protestantism*, by Philip Schaff. In *The Development of the Church: "The Principle of Protestantism" and other Historical Writings of Philip Schaff*, edited by David R. Bains and Theodore Louis Trost, 35–54. MTSS 3. Eugene, OR: Wipf & Stock, 2016.

———. "The Unity of the Apostles' Creed." In *The Early Creeds: The Mercersburg Theologians Appropriate the Creedal Heritage*, edited by Charles Yrigoyen Jr. and Lee C. Barrett, 262–65. By John Williamson Nevin et al. MTSS 8. Eugene, OR: Wipf & Stock, 2020.

———. *Vindication of the Revised Liturgy, Historical and Theological*. In *Catholic and Reformed: Selected Theological Writings of John Williamson Nevin*, edited by Charles Yrigoyen Jr. and George H. Bricker, 313–403. Pittsburgh Original Texts and Translations 3. Pittsburgh: Pickwick, 1978.

———. "Wilberforce on the Eucharist." In *Born of Water and the Spirit: Essays on the Sacraments and Christian Formation*, edited by David W. Layman, 134–155. By John Williamson Nevin et al. MTSS 6. Eugene, OR: Wipf & Stock, 2016.

———. "The Year 1848." In *Philosophy and the Contemporary World: Mercersburg, Culture, and the Church*, edited by Adam Borneman and Patrick Carey, 22–48. MTSS 11. Eugene, OR: Wipf & Stock, 2023.

Nevin, John Williamson and Charles Hodge. *Coena Mystica: Debating Reformed Eucharistic Theology*. Edited by Linden J. DeBie. MTSS 2. Eugene, OR: Wipf & Stock, 2013.

Nevin, John Williamson, et al. *Born of Water and the Spirit: Essays on the Sacraments and Christian Formation*. Edited by David W. Layman. MTSS 6. Eugene, OR: Wipf & Stock, 2016.

———. *The Early Creeds: The Mercersburg Theologians Appropriate the Creedal Heritage*. Edited by Charles Yrigoyen Jr. and Lee C. Barrett. MTSS 8. Eugene, OR: Wipf & Stock, 2020.

Newman, John Henry. *Apologia Pro Vita Sua*. With Six Sermons. Edited by Frank M. Turner. New Haven: Yale University Press, 2008.

———. *An Essay on the Development of Christian Doctrine*. London: Basil Montagu Pickering, 1878. Reprinted Notre Dame: University of Notre Dame Press, 2012.

Nicene and Post-Nicene Fathers. Vol. 4, *Saint Augustin: The Writings Against the Manichæans, and Against the Donatists*. Edited by Philip Schaff. Buffalo: Christian Literature, 1887.

Nichols, James Hastings. *Romanticism in American Theology: Nevin and Schaff at Mercersburg*. University of Chicago Press, 1961. Reprint, Eugene, OR: Wipf & Stock, 2006.

OED Online. "Cormorant, n." September 2022. Oxford University Press. https://www-oed-com.ezproxy.ycp.edu:8443/view/Entry/41582.

———. "Principial, adj.." December 2022. Oxford University Press. https://www-oed-com.ezproxy.ycp.edu:8443/view/Entry/151452.

———. "Scout, v.2." June 2017. Oxford University Press. http://www.oed.com.ezproxy.ycp.edu:8000/view/Entry/173227.

Okun, Henry. "Ossian in Painting." *Journal of the Warburg and Courtauld Institutes* 30 (1967) 327–56.

Origen. *Commentariorum . . . ad Romanos*. In *Patrologiæ Græca*, edited by J.-P. Migne, 14:838–1292. Lutetiæ Parisiorum: J.-P. Migne, 1862.

———. *Commentary on the Epistle to the Romans, Books 6–10*. Translated by Thomas P. Scheck. The Fathers of the Church, 104. Washington: Catholic University of America Press, 2002.

The Oxford Companion to Philosophy. New Edition. Edited by Ted Honderich. Oxford: Oxford University Press, 2005.

Patrum Apostolicorum Opera: Textum ex Editionibus Praestantissimis Repetitum Recognovit, Annotationibus Illustravit, Versionem Latinam Emendatiorem, Prolegomena et Indices. Edited by Karl Joseph von Hefele. 3rd ed. Tubingae: Henrici Laupp, 1847.

Payne, John B. "John Williamson Nevin: The Early Years." *New Mercersburg Review* 36 (2005) 4–34. https://archive.lancasterseminary.edu/items/show/293.

———. "Schaff and Nevin, Colleagues at Mercersburg: The Church Question." *Church History* 61, no. 2 (June 1992) 169–90.

Penzel, Klaus. *The German Education of Christian Scholar Philip Schaff: The Formative Years, 1819–1844*. Toronto Studies in Theology, 95. Lewiston, NY: Edwin Mellen, 2004.

Pontius. *The Life of Cecil Cyprian*. In *Early Christian Biographies*, edited by Roy J. Deferrari, 5–24. Translated by Mary Magdeleine Müller and Roy J. Deferrari. The Fathers of the Church, 15. Washington, DC: Fathers of the Church, 1952.

The Puritan Recorder, no. 34, August 23, 1849. Quoted by John Williamson Nevin, "Puritanism and the Creed." *MR* (November 1849) 585–607. Reprinted in *The Early Creeds: The Mercersburg Theologians Appropriate the Creedal Heritage*, edited by Charles Yrigoyen Jr. and Lee C. Barrett, 103–21. By John Williamson Nevin et al. MTSS 8. Eugene, OR: Wipf & Stock, 2020.

Quoteresearch. "History is Just One Damn Thing after Another." https://quoteinvestigator.com/2015/09/16/history/#r+12001+1+5.

Reed, Rebecca. *Six Months in a Convent, or, The Narrative of Rebecca Theresa Reed, ...* Boston: Russell, Odiorne & Metcalf, 1835.

Robertson, O. Palmer. *The Christ of the Covenants*. Phillipsburg, NJ: P&R, 1980.

Rothe, Richard. *Die Anfänge der Christlichen Kirche und ihrer Verfassung*. Vol. 1. Wittenberg: Zimmermann'schen, 1837.

———. *Theologische Ethik*. Erster Band. Wittenberg: Zimmermann'sche, 1845.

Schaff, David Schley. "Thiersch, Heinrich Wilhelm Josias." In *The New Schaff-Herzog Encyclopedia of Religious Knowledge*, edited by Samuel Macauley Jackson, 11:415–16. New York: Funk and Wagnalls, 1911.

Schaff, Philip. *The Creeds of Christendom*. 3 vols. New York: Harper & Brothers, 1877.

———. *The Development of the Church: "The Principle of Protestantism" and other Historical Writings of Philip Schaff*. Edited by David R. Bains and Theodore Louis Trost. MTSS 3. Eugene, OR: Wipf & Stock, 2016.

———. "German Theology and the Church Question." *MR* 5 (1853) 124–44.

———. *History of the Christian Church*. Vol. 2, *Ante-Nicene Christianity A.D. 100–325*. New Edition. New York: Charles Scribner's Sons, 1884.

———. The Philip Schaff Papers. Evangelical and Reformed Historical Society, Lancaster, PA.

———. *The Principle of Protestantism as related to the Present State of the Church*. Chambersburg, PA: German Reformed Church, 1845. Reprinted in *The Development of the Church: "The Principle of Protestantism" and other Historical Writings of Philip Schaff*, edited by David R. Bains and Theodore Louis Trost, 35–205. Translated by John W. Nevin. Edited by. MTSS 3. Eugene, OR: Wipf & Stock, 2016.

———. *What is Church History? A Vindication of the Idea of Historical Development*. In *The Development of the Church: "The Principle of Protestantism" and other Historical Writings of Philip Schaff*, edited by David R. Bains and Theodore Louis Trost, 232–316. MTSS 3. Eugene, OR: Wipf & Stock, 2016.

Schatz, Klaus. *Papal Primacy from its Origins to the Present*. Collegeville, MN: Michael Glazier, 1996.

Schnorrenberg, Barbara Brandon. "Taylor, Isaac (1787–1865)." In *Oxford Dictionary of National Biography, From the earliest times to the year 2000*, edited by H. C. G. Matthew and Brian Harrison, 53:911–913. Oxford: Oxford University Press, 2004.

Schwaller, John Frederick. *History of the Catholic Church in Latin America: From Conquest to Revolution and Beyond*. New York: New York University Press, 2011.

Shields, Christopher. "Aristotle." *The Stanford Encyclopedia of Philosophy*. Spring 2022 Edition. https://plato.stanford.edu/archives/spr2022/entries/aristotle/.

Shriver, George H. "Philip Schaff: Heresy at Mercersburg." In *American Religious Heretics: Formal and Informal Trials*, edited by George H. Shiver, 18–55. Nashville: Abingdon, 1966.

Sieffert, Friedrich Anton Emil. "Rothe, Richard." In *The New Schaff-Herzog Encyclopedia of Religious Knowledge*, edited by Samuel Macauley Jackson, 10:100–103. New York: Funk and Wagnalls, 1911.

Simonetti, Manlio, ed. *Ancient Christian Commentary on Scripture: New Testament*. Vol. 1A, *Matthew 1–13*. Downers Grove, IL: InterVarsity, 2001.

"The Socialist's Creed." *New-York Observer* 29, no. 27 (July 3, 1851) n. p.

Stanley, Brian. *Christianity in the Twentieth Century: A World History*. Princeton, NJ: Princeton University Press, 2018. https://doi.org/10.2307/j.ctvc77716.

Stark, Rodney. *The Rise of Christianity: How the Obscure, Marginal Jesus Movement Became the Dominant Religious Force in the Western World in a Few Centuries*. New York: HarperCollins, 1997.

———. *The Triumph of Christianity: How the Jesus Movement Became the World's Largest Religion*. New York: HarperOne, 2011.

"Tampering with the Truth." *New-York Observer* 30, no. 31 (July 29, 1852) 2.

Taylor, Isaac. *Ancient Christianity: and the Doctrines of the Oxford Tracts for the Times*. 2 vols. 4th ed. London: Henry G. Bohn, 1844.

Tertullian, Q. Sept. Flor. *Liber De Præscriptionibus Adversus Hæreticos*. In *Patrologiæ Latina*, edited by J.-P. Migne, 2:9–886. Lutetiæ Parisiorum: J.-P. Migne, 1844.

Thiersch, Heinrich W. J. *Versuch zur Herstellung des historischen Standpuncts für die Kritik der neutestamentlichen Schriften*. Erlangen: Heyder, 1845.

———. *Vorlesungen über Katholicismus und Protestantismus*. 2 vol. Erlangen: Heyder, 1846.

Toynbee, Arnold J. *A Study of History*. Abridgement of Volumes VII–X by D. C. Somervell. New York: Oxford University Press, 1957.

Turretin, Francis. *Institutes of Elenctic Theology*. 3 vol. Translated by George M. Giger. Edited by James T. Dennison Jr. Phillipsburg: Presbyterian & Reformed, 1997.

De Vita et Passione Sancti Cæcilii Cypriani . . . per Pontium Diaconum. In *Patrologiæ Latina*, edited by J.-P. Migne, 3:1481–98. Lutetiæ Parisiorum: J.-P. Migne, 1844.

Vos, Geerhardus. *Biblical Theology: Old and New Testaments*. Carlisle: Banner of Truth Trust, 1975.

Webster, Noah. *An American Dictionary of the English Language*. Revised ed. New York: Harper & Brothers, 1846.

Wentz, Richard E. *John Williamson Nevin: American Theologian*. New York: Oxford University Press, 1997.

Wilson, Daniel. *Travels on the Continent of Europe through Parts of the Netherlands, Switzerland, Northern Italy, and France, in the Summer of 1823*. 4th London ed. In *The Christian Library: A Reprint of Popular Religious Works*, edited by Jonathan Going et al., 7:10–121. New York: Thomas George Jr., 1836.

Winebrenner, John, ed. *History of All the Religious Denominations in the United States: Containing Authentic Accounts of the Rise and Progress, Faith and Practice, Localities and Statistics, of the Different Persuasions: Written Expressly for the Work by Fifty-Three Eminent Authors, Belonging to the Respective Denominations*. 2nd ed. Harrisburg: John Winebrenner, 1848.

Witsius, Herman. *The Economy of the Covenants Between God and Man*. 2 vols. Grand Rapids: Reformation Heritage, 2010.

Index

African (churches), 42n3, 86, 127, 130, 199, 227, 244, 270, 282–84, 287, 291
Albigensians, 54, 80, 81, 116
Altar (sacrament/sacrifice of), 38, 68, 72, 98, 100, 104, 113, 144, 174, 178, 184, 197, 217, 229–31, 257, 284, 298
Ambrose, 37, 48–49, 54–55, 59, 63–67, 69–70, 115, 118–21, 124–28, 144–45, 260
American and Foreign Christian Union, 37, 42, 44
Anabaptists, 83
Ancient Christianity, and the Doctrines of the Oxford 'Tracts for the Times' (Taylor), 40, 64n58, 123–28, 131–33, 140–45
Die Anfänge der Christlichen Kirche (Rothe), 97n60, 100n65, 117n1, 153–4n59, 245, 261nn57–58
Angilbertus, 48
"The Anglican Crisis" (Nevin), 27n151, 36, 41n33, 167n4, 216n58, 312n95, 316, 318, 322
Anglicanism, 12, 32n5, 37, 40, 54, 63–65, 69–70, 74, 123, 129, 136, 137n32, 164, 167, 216, 235, 238, 240, 262, 316; *see also* "The Anglican Crisis;" Episcopalianism; Oxford (Movement); Puseyism; "Reply to 'An Anglican Catholic'"
Anicetus, 254
Anselm, 37, 55, 59
Anti-Catholicism (anti-Romanism), 54–61, 157–59, 164–65, 320
Antichrist, 201, 265, 271–73, 275, 277
    as papacy, 12n63, 15n82, 73–74, 76, 83, 90, 145, 161, 323n49
    as sectarianism, 12n63, 76n12, 162, 323n49
Antichrist: or the Spirit of Sect and Schism (Nevin), 21, 34n6, 35n11, 92n46
Antioch, 71n80, 80n20, 113, 225n89
Antoninus Pius, 47
Antony of the Desert, 128
Apostasy, 14, 34, 38–39, 220, 263–67, 312

Roman, 54, 63, 70, 73, 74, 76, 77, 81–89, 92, 101, 114–16, 121n5, 128–29, 137–38, 164, 181, 193
Apostles (apostolic), 27, 36, 38, 40n22, 43, 61, 63, 68, 72, 75–76, 82, 91, 95, 97–100, 106–9, 111, 114–15, 132–35, 138, 146, 147n47, 173, 178, 202, 209, 212–13, 216–19, 223–25, 238, 241, 243–45, 247–52, 254, 256, 259, 273, 278, 287, 308, 312
Apostles' Creed, 68, 84, 109, 111, 164, 207, 241, 246, 261–62, 267, 299
Apostolical Constitutions, 96, 134, 225, 253
Apostolic Fathers ("post-apostolic" or "immediately after the apostles"), 6, 39, 71n80, 76, 133–37, 146, 155, 164, 256, 260n56, 264, 267, 318
Apostolic succession, 99, 107, 212, 218, 221, 240, 265
Arianism (Arius), 86, 87, 121
"Arianism" (Nevin), 22n117
Aristotelian, 64n60, 302n79
Arnold of Brescia, 9
Asceticism, 128, 143, 310–11
Asia Minor, 42, 95n54, 113, 224, 282–83, 286–87
Athanasius, 68, 70n78, 119–21, 127, 129, 136, 251n26, 260, 262
"Athanasius" (Nevin), 22n117
Atonement, 4, 72, 229, 305
Augustine, 39, 48, 54, 60, 63, 64, 66, 69, 70, 91, 100, 108, 115, 118, 120–21, 124–25, 128–30, 260, 262, 269, 289
Aurelius (Antoninus), Marcus, 47
Austria, 130

Babylon, Mystical, *see* Antichrist
Bacon, Leonard, 37, 42–45, 61, 70–71, 92, 99, 113
Baptism, 37, 60, 68, 70n77, 72, 84, 93–94, 100–101, 121n5, 168, 202, 204, 217, 221–27, 231, 236, 239, 241, 246, 255, 263, 298, 300, 302, 305–8, 310

INDEX

Baptism (continued)
    Cyprian's baptism, 171
    Of heretics, 215, 218–19, 221, 226, 242, 282–89
    Infant Baptism, 84, 93, 227, 232, 300n76
    Martyrdom as baptism by blood, 306–7
Baptismal regeneration, 29, 36, 118, 170, 222, 225, 227, 236, 238n5, 241, 246, 255, 263, 265, 288
Baptists, 36, 72–74, 84, 94, 114, 120, 121, 233, 236n2, 240, 296–97
Barrett, Lee, xi–xii, 6n36
Barrow, Isaac, 65, 131
Basil the Great, 63, 68, 124–25, 127, 260
Baur, Ferdinand Christian, 71, 90–91, 156
Berg, Joseph F., 39n21, 122n5, 158n66
Bernard of Clairvaux, 55, 59, 70n78, 132
Bible, the, 5, 8, 32, 35, 37, 53, 62, 65, 67–68, 70–74, 76–79, 81, 87–88, 90, 91, 95, 96n56, 106–9, 118, 120, 122, 137n32, 138–40, 164, 212–13, 240, 246, 263–64, 299, 302, 306, 307, 313
    "Bible alone," 104–5, 142–43
    see also New Testament; Rule of faith
Bishop of Rome, 28, 118, 216, 274, 282–90
Bishops, 40, 66, 88–89, 99–101, 107, 127, 174, 178, 188–90, 196–201, 203, 210–18, 221, 224, 231n107, 235, 237, 243–44, 251n25, 257–59, 270, 274, 285–87, 291, 294–95;
    see also Episcopacy
Black, Andrew, 41n34, 156n62, 216n58, 312n95, 321n34, 324n57, 326n66
Blandina, 42, 46, 99n63, 112–13
Bohon Upas tree, 264
De Bono Patientiae (Cyprian), 290
Borromeo, Charles, 37, 48–49, 51–55, 58, 316–17
Brahminism, 310
Brownlee, William, 56–57n39
Brownson, Orestes, 148, 318, 326n66
Buddhism, 147n47, 310
Buffalo (NY), 57n39
Bullinger, Heinrich, 18, 20

Calvin, John, 1, 8–10, 15–20, 55, 60, 74, 83n24, 220n76, 320
    Institutes of, 38n19, 238n3, 246n13
Canon, formation of, 39, 88, 106
Carthage, 86n32, 166, 169, 171–72, 174–77, 179, 197–98, 217, 275, 280–83, 287, 290–91, 294–95, 308
Catholic Apostolic Church (Irvingism), 41n27
Catholicism, Roman, 1, 7, 12, 14, 18, 22–23, 36, 40–41, 51, 56, 58, 60n42, 65, 80, 83, 130–31, 135, 136n31, 148–51, 154n59, 156, 159–62, 168, 220n76, 312, 316–20; *see also* Anti-Catholicism; Rome (church); Papal Infallibility; Papal Primacy
"Catholic Unity" (Nevin), 7n40, 10–12, 14, 34n4, 323n49
Celibacy, 68, 114, 118–21, 125–26, 128, 132, 143, 171, 308–9
Cerinthus, 254
Cheverus, Jean-Louis Lefebvre de, 61n46
Christ, 1, 5–6, 10–12, 16, 26, 29, 35, 38, 41–44, 50–51, 54n36, 65, 67, 71n81, 74–79, 81, 86n33, 90, 95, 97–98, 101–2, 106, 108, 110–16, 120, 138–39, 145, 147n47, 157, 159, 161, 163n72, 164, 173–74, 177–85, 187–89, 192, 194, 196–97, 200–203, 205–15, 217, 219–22, 224–26, 228–30, 233, 238, 247–49, 251–52, 255, 257–59, 261, 264, 266, 271–73, 275, 277–78, 280–82, 287n48, 290, 292–94, 300–306, 308–10, 322, 326n66
    Body of, 10–11, 20, 32, 43, 103, 107, 203, 221, 241, 249, 251n25, 252, 282
    See also Eucharist, body and blood of Christ; Incarnation
Christian Church/Disciples of Christ (denominations), 236n2, 265n62
"The Christian Ministry" (Nevin), 211n47, 213n49, 219n71, 320n30
Christian Observer (Amasa Converse), 121–22n5
Christianity
    Ante-nicene Christianity, 148n49
    Development of, 34–35
    Early Christianity, 37–41, 61–62, 82n23, 93, 110, 114, 131, 134–35, 164, 255, 281, 310–13; *also see* Patristic
    In Middle Ages, 1, 14–15, 22, 38, 40n22, 54, 62, 65, 76, 80, 82, 89, 116, 123, 126, 138, 149, 152, 158, 220, 265, 312
    Nicene Christianity, 28, 40, 122n5, 123–30, 133–37, 144, 145n43, 158, 163, 267, 312
    Old Catholic Christianity, 89, 137n32, 149, 150, 152, 153, 160, 164, 227, 312
    Tridentine Christianity, 124, 148n49
    See also subheadings under Church
Chrysostom, St. John, 60, 63, 66, 68, 108, 113, 115, 120–21, 124–26, 129–30, 144n41, 255n41, 260
Church
    As catholic and apostolic, 34, 79, 243–63
    As constitution (supernatural/divine), 28, 36, 94, 95, 142, 158, 167, 188, 199, 207–24, 234–42, 246–47, 254–56, 259, 260, 262, 267–68, 282, 297, 303
    Cyprian's doctrine of, 236–239, 296–304

INDEX

Democratic idea of, 45, 72, 96–98, 99n63, 107, 211
In early Christianity, 39, 67–71, 241–63
As fact (supernatural/divine), 34, 35, 62n49, 97, 139, 145, 148, 155, 208, 213, 246, 262, 298, 313
Fathers of, 37, 39, 67, 70, 94–114, 120–21
History of, 2, 62–67, 119–138, 140, 148, 156–65, 267, 313, 324
Nevin's theology of, 10–15, 27–30
Primitive (church), 9n49, 43, 45, 64, 67, 72–75, 79–84, 94, 96, 99, 110, 115–16, 129, 131, 136–37, 155, 178, 236–37, 255, 264, 266, 311
Protestant doctrine of, 239–40
see also Christ, Body of; Ministry
Clement of Alexandria, 98, 252
Clement of Rome, 93, 97, 256–57
Cologne, 89
Common Sense (Realism), 70n79, 72, 85, 96n56, 98, 157n64
Communion of saints, 67, 114, 230, 242, 266, 299–300; *see also* saints (worship of/prayers to)
Confessors, 88, 126, 176–77, 179, 181–85, 187–92, 195–96, 206, 232, 274, 290; *see also* Martyrs
Congregationalism, 45, 62, 72–73, 84n27, 92, 94, 96, 99–100, 120, 122, 136, 210, 216n58; *see also* New England
Consensus Tigurinus, 18–20
Constance, bishop of, 8
Copernican system, 95, 118
Cornelius (in Acts), 304
Cornelius, bishop of Rome, 194n11, 198–200, 217, 270, 274
Curubis (Tunisia), 291
Cyprian, 27–28, 60, 64, 73, 84, 96, 100, 115, 124, 134, 136, 166–81, 185–86, 188–89, 193–95, 197–99, 202, 204, 206–8, 210–39, 246, 257, 260–62, 270–71, 273–74, 276–77, 280, 283–89
Martyrdom of, 166, 290–96
Religion of, 296–311
"Cyprian" (Nevin), 8, 27, 64n59, 97n59, 117n2, 156n62, 166–68, 315–16, 318, 320–21, 324
Cyril of Jerusalem, 68, 124

Dead, prayers for, 118–19, 128, 299
DeBie, Linden, 2n4, 3n16, 4n17, 10n53, 18n101, 26n146, 27n147, 320n27
Decian persecution, 174–88, 200, 269n3, 282n35
Decius (emperor), 177, 198n16, 269n3, 274

Deists, 297
Delphic Oracle, 126n12
Ad Demetrianum (Cyprian), 276, 279
Democracy (religious), 72, 85, 96–98, 107, 210, 307
Depravity, human, 72
Dionysius of Alexandria (the Great), 277n23
Dissenters (Great Britain), 12
Docetism, 101, 103
Donatism, 86
Donatus, bishop of Carthage, 170, 172
Dutch Reformed Church, 122n5, 158n66
Dwight, Timothy, 86

"Early Christianity" (Nevin), 8–9, 35n13, 36–37, 41, 122n5, 166, 168, 312, 315–18
England, 48, 51, 70, 74, 84n27, 89, 105, 125
England, John, 61n47
Enlightenment, vii, 112n90, 211
Ephesus, 244, 254
Ephesus, Council of, 43n6, 86
Ephraim Syrus, 69
Episcopacy, 27–28, 31, 34, 37, 62, 64–65, 67, 69, 72, 84, 94, 97, 100, 129, 163, 167, 212, 214, 234–39, 241, 243, 245, 256, 259, 262, 267
As "sacrament of unity" (*sacramentum unitatis*), 66, 98, 199, 202–3, 222
see also Bishop of Rome; Bishops
Episcopalianism, viii, 12n63, 33, 34, 56, 61–63, 65, 70, 84, 94, 120, 123, 136, 167, 215–16, 234, 237, 240, 245, 312; *see also* Anglicanism
Epochs, 13, 41, 150
Essay on the Development of Christian Doctrine (Newman), 1n1, 40n24, 70n78, 117n5, 147
Eucharist, 7–10, 15–20, 37, 54, 101–4, 190–92, 228–29, 231, 238n5, 241, 257, 263, 270, 298, 320
Body and blood of Christ, 16n88, 103, 181, 191–93, 228–29, 231, 263
Mystical presence in, 229, 298; *see also* *Mystical Presence* (Nevin)
See also Real Presence; Transubstantiation
Eusebius Pamphilus, 48, 277n23
Eutychianism, 43n6, 86n33
Evangelical (Protestantism/religion), 37, 54–55, 56n39, 58, 59, 61, 65, 67–70, 72–74, 85, 104, 108, 113–14, 118, 120, 128–29, 137, 138n35, 157–58, 167, 185, 210, 226, 236, 240, 251, 264, 265n63, 267, 296, 298, 303, 307, 316
In France, 42–45

343

INDEX

Evangelical Alliance, 27
Evangelical counsels, 310
"Evangelical Radicalism" (Nevin), 14n78, 37n8, 96n56, 296n72
Evans, Hugh Davey, 29n160, 31, 33, 35n9
Evans, William, xii, 2n4, 3n12, 9n53, 22n116, 26n146, 318n21, 320n26, 324, 325n59
De Exhortatione Martyrii (Cyprian), 272

Fabian, bishop of Rome, 177n17, 200
"Faith, obedience of," 204, 246, 252, 268, 303
Felicissimus (anti-Cyprian leader), 194–96, 198–99, 217, 241, 243
Fénélon, Francois, 50, 53, 55, 58
Firmilian (bishop), 218, 224, 287, 288–89
First Vatican Council, 22, 82n23
Ford, Henry, viii
Fortunatus (leader of anti-Cyprian faction), 172, 275
France, 37, 42–44, 50n32, 52, 54n36, 61n46, 80nn17–18, 296
Franklin and Marshall College, 13n71, 22, 24, 34n5, 321, 323n43
Frederick Barbarossa, 124n9
Freedom
　ethical, 23, 24, 35, 234
　political, 72, 163n72, 324; *see also* Democracy
The Friend (Nevin), 2n6

Galileo, 118
Gallus, Trebonianus (emperor), 198, 269, 282
Gelasius, Pope, 65n64
German Reformed Church, 6, 9, 11, 21, 122n5, 158n66, 316, 320–21
　liturgical work in, 21n112, 41n27, 318, 324–25
　The Weekly Messenger of, 7, 18n98, 316–17, 323n45
Germany, 52, 116, 154
　Culture of, 13
　Language of, 2
　Reformers of, 37, 53
　Theology and thought of, 3, 4, 8, 12–13, 111, 149
　Idea of historical development in, 24, 27–28, 39–40, 136n31, 150, 313, 325; *see also* Historical development
Gerrish, Brian, 20n108, 320n27
Gervasius and Protasius (supposed martyrs), 144
Gibbon, Edward, 80n20, 92, 112, 119, 255
Gieseler, Johann Karl Ludwig, 91–92, 119
Giustiniani, Louis, 56–57n39, 162n72

Gnosticism, 87, 92, 98, 101–2, 107, 112, 115, 143–44, 146, 164, 209, 234, 253n32, 254n39, 258, 268, 297, 299, 310–11
Good, James I., 21n115, 38n16, 39n21, 168n11, 315, 316n4, 320n30, 321, 324n57, 325n58
Good works (merit of), 57, 184, 207, 231, 303–5
Gorham Case, 36
Goths, 130, 269n3
De Gratia Dei (Cyprian), 170–71, 226
Gregory the Great (Pope), 66–67n66, 89
Gregory of Nazianzus, 63, 68, 126
Gregory of Nyssa, 63, 68, 124, 126

De Habitu Virginum (Cyprian), 275, 308
Hart, D. B., 2n4, 9–10n53, 320n29, 321nn34–35
Hegel, G. W. F., vii, 17n95, 25, 90n39, 91, 313n96
Hegelian dialectic, 17, 41, 71n81, 160, 326
　Nevin's use of, 8, 15, 18–19, 21, 23–24
Heidelberg Catechism, 6–10, 18, 22n117
"Heidelberg Catechism, The" (Nevin), 6–9, 82n23
Helffenstein, Jacob, 122n5
Hengstenberg, Ernst, 60n42
Henricians, 80
Heresy, 11, 51n32, 86–87, 99, 107, 161, 208, 213, 215, 219, 222, 239, 246, 248, 251–52, 254, 257–60, 299; *see also* schism
Hermas, 256–57
Heyser, William, 319
Hierarchy, church, 85, 98, 100, 125, 210–12, 240–41, 264
Hilary of Poitiers, 69
Historical development, viii, 3, 5, 7, 10–14, 15n82, 18, 21–36, 40, 41, 62–63, 71n81, 82n23, 90n39, 130n21, 136n31, 146–51, 156, 159, 161, 164, 168, 311–13, 315–16, 318, 322–25
　English versus German theory of, 40, 150–51, 325
　See also Germany, Idea of historical development in; Identity
History, vii, 8, 12, 24, 117n2
History of the Reformed Church in the U.S. (Good), 315–16, 39n21, 320n30, 324n57, 325n58
Hodge, Charles, 1, 8, 15, 17–21, 60n43, 323
Holy Spirit, 4, 49, 83n25, 95, 108, 115, 171, 183, 202, 209, 217, 221–2, 224–25, 226, 234, 247–49, 250, 252, 256, 262, 264, 270–71, 278, 281–83, 285, 288, 292, 296–298, 300, 301, 310
Hughes, John Joseph (archbishop), 59–60n42, 216
Hume, David, 3, 112

INDEX

Iconium (council), 224
Ideal and Actual, 10–11, 14, 145n45
Idealism, 3n16, 4, 7n40, 8, 12, 323
Identity (of church over time), viii, 6, 32, 65, 92, 95, 235, 237, 242–43, 250
De Idolorum Vanitate (Cyprian), 208
Ignatius, 71, 74, 92–103, 112–13, 115, 134, 142, 163, 245, 247, 256–60, 267
Ignatius Loyola, 70n78
Incarnation, 81, 87n35, 97–98, 101–2, 110, 207–8, 238, 246, 258, 262
Independents, *see* Congregationalism
India, 46n16, 86
Indulgence(s), 50, 53–54, 187–88, 194, 228, 231
Irenæus, 43, 46–48, 71, 74, 84, 93–113, 134, 136, 142, 163, 213, 243–56, 262
Irenée, St. (site), 46–47
Italy, 37, 49, 51, 53, 57n39, 80n17, 130, 211n45, 316

Jansenism, 50–51, 124
Jerome 63, 68n70, 69, 124, 169, 172, 260
Jews/Jewish/Judaism, 5, 14n81, 76, 78, 85, 90, 114, 133, 227, 231–34, 298, 311
John the Faster, 66n66
Jovinian, 68, 120
Jure divino, 27, 64, 96, 129, 211–12
Justification, 29, 55, 65, 70, 75, 90, 144, 301–3
Justin Martyr, 84, 94, 96, 141

Kant, Immanuel, 3
Kempis, Thomas à, 55
Kingdom of God, viii, 41, 68, 78, 98, 150, 210, 233, 257, 277, 282, 300, 307
Kinkel, Johann Gottfried, 211
"Kirwan" (Nicholas Murray), 158
Knox, John, 105
"Korah, Dathan, and Abiram," 206, 218, 223, 225, 253
Kossuth, Louis, 163n72, 211
Krauth, Charles Porterfield, viii
Kurtz, Benjamin, 122n5

Lapsed, the, 166–67, 174, 176, 177n17, 180–81, 187–92, 194–98, 206, 214, 231–32, 242, 272, 282n35
De Lapsis (Cyprian), 178, 181, 189, 193, 232
Layman, David, 3, 7n40, 10n53, 21, 26n145, 29, 168n10, 315, 320n26, 324–26
Leo (Pope), 67n66
Letters Concerning the Constitution and Order of the Christian Ministry (Samuel Miller), 122

Letters (Cyprian), 7 (183–84); 10 (182–83); 12 (184–85); 13 (185); 15 (192); 16 (176n15, 191); 17 (190–91); 27 (232); 33 (214); 42 (175n14); 43 (195–97); 48 (217); 51 (200); 52 (199); 54 (274–75); 55 (200, 214, 231); 57 (228–29, 270–72); 59 (217); 60 (275n18); 61 (275n18); 62 (280–81); 63 (229–30); 64[61] (227, 232); 66 (213–14); 68 (214–15); 69 (224); 70 (217, 283–84); 71 (284–85); 73 (217, 223, 285–86); 74 (221–22); 75 (224–25); 80 (294); 81 (295)
Liturgy, 21n112, 41n27, 72, 93, 230, 237, 318, 325
London, 129
Lucius (pope), 274
Lutheran (church/theology), viii, 7, 8, 15, 16, 110, 122n5, 137n32, 302, 323n45
Luther, Martin, 8, 18–20, 23n122, 37, 53, 55, 60, 74, 82, 141, 164, 302
Lyons, France, 42–48, 71, 74, 80n17, 93, 99, 101, 104, 112–13, 115, 134n29

Machen, J. Gresham, 162n71
Macpherson, James, 290n54
Manicheans, 87
"Man's True Destiny" (Nevin), 324
Marburg Colloquy, 19
Marshall College, 317n14, 319, 322; *see also* Franklin and Marshall College
Martyrs (martyrdom), 39, 42–43, 46–48, 59, 60n42, 68, 74, 76, 81, 88–89, 93, 98, 101, 104, 112–15, 126–27, 131–32, 138, 144, 166, 175–77, 179, 181–85, 187–88, 190–92, 194, 220, 229–30, 232, 242, 244, 267, 270–74, 277–78, 290, 292, 294, 303, 306–7, 309; *see also* Confessors; Cyprian, martyrdom of
Mather, Increase, 86
Mazzini, Giuseppe, 211
McMaster, James Alphonsus, 318
Mediating theology, 10n53, 15
Melchisedek, 229–30
Mercersburg, 6, 7, 9, 34n4, 322n39, 323
    Seminary, 6, 317, 320
    Mercersburg Review, 21
    Theology, 12, 15, 31, 33, 122n5, 316, 322
    Scholarship, 9–10n53, 322
Mercersburg Theology Study Series, 2, 30, 326
Methodists, 12n63, 34, 56, 69, 105, 120, 136, 255
Middleton, Conyers, 111–12
Milan, 37, 48–49, 51–55, 65, 67, 120n4, 127, 144n42
Milan, Edict of, 178n19
Milner, Joseph, 42, 46–48, 54, 69

345

INDEX

Ministry, 36n3, 39, 96–100, 106, 173, 209–14, 237–38, 246, 257, 259, 263, 265, 291, 298, 321n35
Miracles, 38–39, 41n33, 67–68, 75–76, 81, 88, 89, 111–12, 115, 118, 119, 121n5, 128, 133n27, 144, 206, 247
    Lack of in Protestantism, 38, 62–63, 83, 112, 149
Monasticism, 68n70, 86, 119, 143
Monk, Maria, 56–57n39
Monophysites, 86
De Mortalitate (Cyprian), 276–78
Mosheim, Johann Lorenz von, 7, 91–92, 119
"Mother of God," Mary as, 43, 126
Müntzer [Munzer], Thomas, 83
My Own Life (Nevin), 2–4, 9, 13n72
Mystical Presence, The (Nevin), 1, 4n16, 9, 15–17, 20, 37, 82n23

Neander, Johann August Wilhelm, 2–3, 14n81, 60n42, 87, 88, 119, 120, 148, 176, 177, 202n26, 218, 232–34, 241, 243, 311, 313
Neri, St. Philip, 58
Nestorianism (Nestorius), 43n6, 86, 92, 121
Nevin, John Williamson, 1–30, 31–32, 36–41, 158n66, 166–68, 315–26
    Dialectical method of, 15–21
    "Dizziness" of, 21–22, 315–22
    Debate with Hodge over *Mystical Presence*, 17–21
    Interpretation of historical development, 7, 10–30, 31–35, 40, 62–63, 130n21, 136n31, 130n21, 146–51, 156n62, 158–61, 164, 168, 311–13, 323–36
    Dyspepsia, 317, 322
    Lectures on philosophy of history, 22, 24–26, 29–30, 34n5, 150n51, 325, 326n66
    "Nervous breakdown," 320
New England, 39, 45, 59, 63, 70, 72, 74, 85, 92, 95, 96, 100–101, 104, 109, 113–14, 120, 129, 134n29, 266; *see also* Congregationalism
Newman, John Henry, 1, 30, 40, 70n78, 119, 135–36, 147–48, 150, 156, 313
New Testament, 9n49, 43, 45, 61, 63n54, 71n81, 73, 78, 80, 83, 87, 90, 92, 97, 99, 106–7, 114, 121n5, 130–31, 134–38, 146, 164, 212–13, 233, 236, 260, 300, 311
New York, 27, 57n39, 129, 216n57, 322
New York Observer, 59–60n42, 163n72, 263–65
Nicene Creed, 68n71, 69n72, 226n90
Nichols, James Hastings, 2n4, 3, 9n53, 21n115, 36, 122n5, 158n66, 315, 317, 319n25, 320n30, 321n35, 323

Nicole, Pierre, 50
Novatian(ism), 194, 195n12, 198–200, 214–16, 224, 241, 243, 275, 282n35
Numidia, 280–81

Obedience of faith, 204, 246, 252, 268, 303
"Old Catholic Movement, The" (Nevin), 12n63, 22–24, 27, 30, 62n52, 82n23, 325
De Opere et Eleemosynis (Cyprian), 304–7
De Oratione Dominica (Cyprian), 228, 304
Organicism, 6–7, 9n53, 10, 14–15, 20, 25, 27–30, 32, 34–35, 62n49, 90, 100–1, 106, 111, 116, 130, 137, 139, 143, 146, 151n53, 159, 237–38, 323
Oriental (philosophy/theosophy), 143, 147n47, 310
Origen, 220n76, 252–53
Original Sin (fall), 121, 299–301
Ossian, 290
Oxford (Movement), vii, 12, 40n22, 65, 69n76, 129, 132, 139, 142; *see also* Puseyism

Pagan(ism), 14n81, 43, 46–47, 49, 76, 85, 111n89, 133–34, 145n44, 169, 178, 233, 269, 276, 279, 311
Papacy, 12n63, 22, 37, 40, 54, 62n52, 65, 69, 72, 89, 101, 115–16, 122–23, 129, 137, 238n3, 246, 267
    As Antichrist, 76n12, 88n37, 264n61
    Infallibility of, 22–23, 62n52, 77, 82n23
    Primacy of, 27, 65–67, 69, 84, 202, 216, 218–19, 246, 284, 288; *see also* Stephen, Pope
    See also Peter, Chair or see of; Prelacy
Pascal, Blaise, 50, 58, 124
Paternus (proconsul), 291
Patristic (period), 21, 29, 40n22, 67, 110–11, 122, 126, 127n14, 134–35, 263–68, 303, 317
Paul (apostle), 5, 36, 51, 79, 99, 100n64, 173–74, 177, 202, 204–5, 210, 215, 219, 220, 232–34, 244, 256, 263, 272, 274, 280–81, 284–85, 301–3
Paul V, Pope, 50n29
Paul of Samosata, 80n20
Paulicians, 80, 81
Payne, John, 2n6, 9n53, 10, 40n26, 150n52, 168, 320n29, 320n31
Pelagius (Pelagianism), 121, 299–301
Penance, 118, 166–67, 189–92, 194, 196, 206, 228, 231–32, 241, 263, 270, 274, 298
Perpetua (martyr), 42
Peter (apostle), 36, 65–66, 78–79, 99, 100n64, 202, 213–19, 222–24, 235, 244, 246, 284, 288, 306

Chair or see of (*cathedra Petri*), 27–28, 66, 125, 200, 202, 217–19, 246
Peter, St. (basilica), 50n29, 89
Philadelphia, viii, 56–57n39, 122n5
Pius IV, 51n34
Pius IX, 22–23
Pittsburgh (Western Seminary), 9
Plague, 193, 269, 276–78
Pliny (the Elder), 142
Pliny (governor in Asia Minor), 95
Polycarp, 43n5, 47–48, 71, 74, 92, 96, 100, 113–15, 134, 163, 244, 254, 256, 267
Pontius (Cyprian's biographer), 169, 171, 174, 175n13, 176
Pothinus, 42–43, 46–48, 71, 99n63, 101, 113, 134n29
Poverty (voluntary), 68, 80, 86, 118, 171
Prayers for the dead, 68, 118–19, 128, 299
Prelacy (prelatical system), 49, 70, 72–73, 93, 119, 121, 123, 246
Presbyterianism, 1, 4–5, 7n36, 9n49, 34, 54, 56, 60, 62, 70, 72, 73, 84, 94, 99, 100, 105, 120–23, 136, 210
Prescription of Heretics (*Liber de Præscriptionibus Adversus Hæreticos*, Tertullian), 108, 243, 247, 252
Priesthood, 37, 68, 72, 97–98, 144, 173, 189, 195, 197, 206, 217–18, 221, 229, 264, 286, 297–98
  Universal priesthood of Christians, 211
Principle of Protestantism (Schaff), 10, 12, 149, 322–23
  Introduction to (Nevin), 10, 12–15
Private judgment, 12, 14, 68, 72, 105–6, 118, 223, 252, 253n33, 258, 275, 285
Protestantism, 1, 11–12, 14, 36–41, 44, 49, 56–57, 60–64, 67–70, 72–75, 77, 82, 90, 101, 108, 110–11, 116–18, 121n5, 128–30, 135–39, 141, 143, 146, 148–52, 154–64, 167–68, 220n76, 235, 237–40, 263–64, 266, 312–14, 316, 319–20, 323
  Development (growth) out of Catholicism, 38n16, 41, 62n49, 116, 159, 237
  see also Anti-Catholicism
Protestant Quarterly Review (Joseph F. Berg), 158
"Pseudo-Protestantism" (Nevin), 9n50, 15n85, 37
Purgatory, 49, 50, 68, 80, 118–19, 128, 239
Puritanism, 7n36, 8n44, 17, 32n4, 37–41, 63, 70, 74, 81, 83–84, 89, 100, 101, 104–6, 109–16, 119, 121–23, 129, 130n21, 131, 134, 137–39, 143, 154, 163, 167, 168n10, 227, 240, 255, 265n63, 266–67, 296, 299, 312
  In Catholic Europe, 42–54
  Ecclesiology of, 90–98
  Puritan theory of early Christianity, 37–39, 72–75, 79, 82n23, 83, 87, 91–92, 97, 137, 139
"Puritanism and the Creed" (Nevin), 109n86, 266n64
Puritan Recorder, 109–10n86, 154, 266
Puseyism, 69, 123, 129; *see also* Oxford (Movement)

Quakers, 84, 120, 233, 297
Quesuel, Pasquier, 50

Rauch, Frederick, 3n16, 316n4
Real Presence (Eucharist), 37, 68, 69n72, 72, 101, 104, 118, 296
  Reformed (Calvinian) doctrine of presence, 15–16, 320
  See also Transubstantiation
Reed, Rebecca, 56–57n39
Reformation, 6–7n36, 8–9, 11–12, 14–15, 24, 34, 38, 40, 55, 60, 62, 63n53, 64, 73–74, 80, 82–83, 90, 116, 125, 128n18, 135–37, 139, 146–50, 153–54, 158–59, 240, 312–13
  Growth out of medieval church, viii, 15, 40n25, 323, 326n66
Reformed (church/theology), 7, 12n63, 15–21, 38n16, 137n32, 316; *see also* German Reformed Church
Relics, 68, 113–14, 118–19, 121, 126, 128, 144, 295, 299
"Religion a Life" (Nevin), 2n6, 3, 5–6
"Reply to 'An Anglican Catholic'" (Nevin), 12n63, 22, 26–30, 167n4, 259n54, 324n55, 325
Repristinationism, 9n49, 32n4, 37, 40, 61–62, 99, 130n21, 136, 146, 164, 236n2, 312, 317
Resurrection, 79, 80n18, 102–104, 154–55, 262, 271, 300, 309
  Of Christ, 78, 97n59, 202, 209, 217, 223, 246, 282, 283, 301
Revelation, Christian, 26, 29, 31–33, 35, 41n28, 63, 75, 91, 105–6, 111, 120, 207–8, 212–13, 234, 247, 251, 261–62, 310
Righteousness, 150, 170, 206, 225–26, 255, 260, 278, 282, 301–4, 307, 310
Rochester (NY), 57n39
Romanism, *see* Catholicism, Roman; Apostasy, Roman; Papal Infallibility; Papal Primacy
Romanticism, vii

Romanticism in American Theology (Nichols), 2n4, 9n53, 158n66, 315, 319n25
Rome (church), 34, 36, 50, 55, 60, 62n52, 66, 73, 90, 99, 100n64, 107, 113, 116, 118, 120n4, 125, 128–29, 131, 137, 156, 159, 162–63, 167, 198–99, 215–19, 237, 244, 246, 254, 274, 282–90, 313
    And Nevin, 220n76, 315, 318–23
    see also Catholicism, Roman
Rome (city), 42, 43, 51–52, 71, 196, 275
Rome (empire), 145, 269, 294
Rongianism, 57n39
Root, Michael, vii–viii, 326
Rousseau, Jean-Jacques, 240
Rothe, Richard, 41, 97n60, 100n65, 152–56, 245, 260, 261n57, 313
Rule of faith (*regula fidei*), 39, 62, 68, 104–6, 110, 118, 213

Sabellians, 87
Sacraments, 17, 19, 36, 39, 54n36, 68, 71n79, 80, 85, 100–101, 110, 115, 119, 126–28, 130, 137n32, 144, 221, 225–33, 236, 240, 242, 246, 255, 263–64, 265, 267, 282–83, 296–98, 301, 303, 306, 316
Saints (worship of/prayers to), 54, 68, 69n73, 113, 119, 126–28, 131, 138, 144, 267, 275, 299, 300; see also communion of saints
Salvation, vii, 4, 65, 75, 77, 103, 108, 144, 155, 167, 170–71, 185, 188, 190, 192, 196, 201, 203–4, 206–8, 225–28, 231–32, 238–41, 243, 246, 248, 255–56, 258, 260, 265, 267, 278, 280, 282, 288, 292, 297–99, 301–5, 308, 310, 319
    Church ark of, 141, 166, 181, 203, 219, 220, 222, 262, 300
    "No salvation out of the Church" (*extra ecclesiam salus nulla*), 201, 219–20, 224
Salvian, 130, 145n43
Sanctification, 153, 227–28, 263, 282, 284, 297, 302–3, 305, 308
Sanctus (martyr), 112
Scandinavia, 127
Schaff, Philip, viii, 10, 12–13, 15n82, 17n95, 31, 32n4, 36–37, 38n16, 39n21, 40, 129n19, 135n30, 149, 151, 158n66, 160n68, 167n4, 168, 313, 315–18, 320n29, 321n35
    1889 Letter about Nevin, 322
    Influence on Nevin, 322–25
Schism, 7, 18, 66, 87, 88, 98–99, 107, 167, 195, 198–99, 201, 203–6, 208, 213, 216, 219–20, 239–41, 246, 248, 250–52, 257, 259, 275, 282–84, 288, 299–300, 303; *see also* Heresy; Novatianism
Scotland, 72, 96
Second Helvetic Confession, 18
Sectarianism ("sect system"), 11, 12, 31, 33, 54–67, 105–6, 111, 120, 129, 139, 146, 159, 240, 251–52, 260, 262, 264, 267, 275, 316
    As Antichrist, 76n12, 162n70, 323n49
"The Sect System" (Nevin), 21, 62n51, 68n68, 105n75
Severus, Septimus, 46–47
Sisters of Charity of St. Joseph's, 58, 59, 60n42
Sixtus II, Pope, 294
Sixtus V, Pope, 65n64
Smyrna, 48, 99, 113, 244, 256
Social Gospel, viii
Socialism, 59–60n42, 162n72
South America, 152
Spain, 80n17, 86, 130, 152
Spiritual Despotism (Taylor), 117n1, 123
Stark, Rodney, 133n27, 276n19, 277n23
Stell, Michael, viii, 1–2, 315, 324–26
Stephen, Bishop of Rome, 168, 214–15, 218–19, 221, 283–89, 291, 294
Storch [Storck], Nicholas, 83
Strauss, David Fredrich, 71, 90–91, 313n96
Summary of Biblical Antiquities (Nevin), 3n14, 4–5, 75n11, 82n23
Susannah (character in Apocrypha), 196
Synagogue of Satan, *see* Antichrist, as papacy
Synod of Dort, 7

Tabitha, 306
Tacitus, 142
Taylor, Isaac, 40, 64n58, 123–34, 138–45, 151n53, 310–11
Tertullian, 2, 60, 94, 96, 98, 106, 108, 111, 134, 142, 150–51n53, 172, 213, 242–43, 245, 247–48, 251–53, 256
Testimonia (Cyprian: "The Three Books of Testimony Against the Jews"), 212, 227, 307
Theological Ethics (*Theologische Ethik,* Thiersch), 153
Thiersch, H. W. J., 41, 110, 151–52, 156, 313
Tigris (river), 127
Toynbee, Arnold, vii note
Trajan, emperor, 47n18, 95, 113
Transubstantiation, 16, 50, 54, 85, 93, 101, 239
Trent, council of, 51, 55, 125
Trinity, 39, 50, 72, 80n20, 110, 203, 207–8
True Catholic, 31n1, 33
Tübingen school, 71n81, 91
Turretin, Francis, 18

INDEX

Ultramontanism, 22–23
Unitarians, 120
De Unitate Ecclesiae (*De catholicae ecclesiae unitate*, Cyprian), 28n153, 199, 201–7, 216, 285
United Brethren, 120
Utica (Tunisia), 294–95

Valerian persecution, 195n11, 290, 294
Vandals, 130
Vienne, France, 42–43, 47, 74, 93, 104, 115
Vigilantius, 68, 120
Virginity (virgins), 114, 127–28, 143, 180, 275n17, 293, 307–10
Virgin Mary, 43n6, 69n73, 127, 207
De Vita et Passione (Cyprian), 169
Voltaire (François-Maria Arouet), 112, 255
Volusianus (emperor), 269
Vorlesungen über Katholicismus und Protestantismus (Thiersch), 117n1, 151–52

Waldenses, 80, 164
Waldo, Peter, 80n17
Western Theological Seminary, 3n14, 5–6; *see also* Pittsburgh
What is Church History? (Schaff), 17n95, 32n4, 117n1, 150n52, 151
Wilson, Daniel, 37, 46, 55, 61, 65, 67, 69, 128, 316–17
Wiseman, Nicholas P. S. (cardinal), 216
Wolff, Bernard, 320
Works of mercy (charity), 304–6
Wycliffe [Wicliffe], John, 141

Zelo et Livore (Cyprian), 290n52
Zurich, 7–8, 20
Zwingli, Ulrich (Zwinglianism), 7–9, 15, 17–20, 37, 53, 55

www.ingramcontent.com/pod-product-compliance
Lightning Source LLC
Chambersburg PA
CBHW080726300426
44114CB00019B/2496